MOON HANDBOOKS®

BRITISH COLUMBIA

SEVENTH EDITION

ANDREW HEMPSTEAD

© ANDREW HEMPSTEAD

AVALON TRAVEL

CONTENTS

Discover British Columbia

Explore British Columbia

Downtown · Chinatown · False Creek · West End · Stanley Park · South of
Downtown · University of British Columbia · Richmond · Delta · Surrey · North
Shore · East from Downtown

Inner Harbour Sights · Old Town · South of the Inner Harbour · Rockland ·
Scenic Route to Oak Bay · The Gorge Waterway · West of Downtown · Saanich
Peninsula

Sooke · Highway 14 to Port Renfrew · The West Coast Trail · Duncan · Lake
Cowichan and Vicinity · North toward Nanaimo

Northern British Columbia 406

Know British Columbia

MAPS

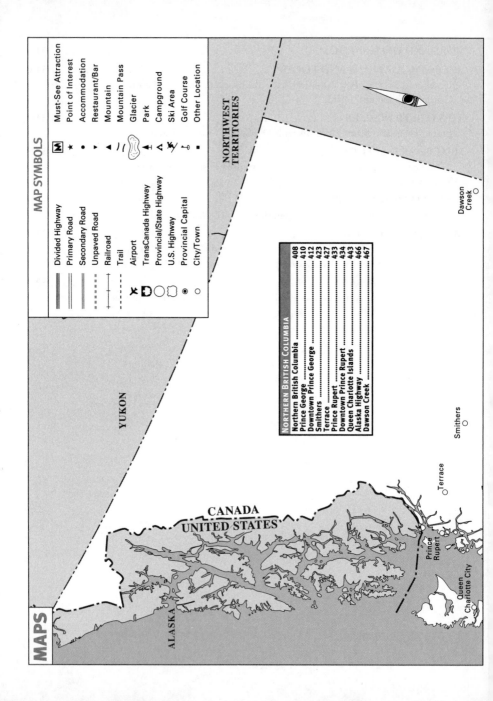

MAP SYMBOLS

Divided Highway		**M**	Must-See Attraction
Primary Road		★	Point of Interest
Secondary Road		•	Accommodation
Unpaved Road		▶	Restaurant/Bar
Railroad		◀	Mountain
Trail		)(	Mountain Pass
Airport	✈	◀	Glacier
TransCanada Highway		▲	Park
Provincial/State Highway		◢	Campground
U.S. Highway		⛷	Ski Area
Provincial Capital	◉	⛳	Golf Course
City/Town	○	■	Other Location

ALASKA

YUKON

NORTHWEST TERRITORIES

CANADA
UNITED STATES

Terrace

Smithers

Prince Rupert

Queen
Charlotte City

Dawson
Creek

© AVALON TRAVEL PUBLISHING, INC.

Discover British Columbia

British Columbia, the westernmost province of Canada, stretches from the Pacific Ocean to the towering heights of the Rocky Mountains. Sandwiched in between is some of this planet's most magnificent scenery—an enormous variety of terrain including spectacular mountain ranges, glaciers, rivers, lakes, rugged coastline, and hundreds of islands.

The province's largest city is Vancouver, a splendid conglomeration of old and new architectural marvels, parks and gardens, and sheltered beaches on the coast in the southwestern corner of the province. The provincial capital is old-world Victoria, perched at the southeastern tip of Vancouver Island, just across the Strait of Georgia from Vancouver. Victoria boasts an intriguing mixture of old English architecture, customs, and traditions, along with modern attractions, cosmopolitan restaurants, and an infectious joie de vivre.

But most of British Columbia lies away from the cities, in the surrounding vastness. The protected coastal waterways, the rugged west coast of Vancouver Island, the famous Canadian Rockies and many other mountain ranges, the remote northern wilderness, and the intriguing Queen Charlotte Islands provide experiences you'll never forget, along with enough ooh-and-aah scenery to keep even the most jaded jet-setter in awe. In these wild areas, you'll find endless opportunities for hiking or climbing, viewing the abundant wildlife, fishing in the hundreds of lakes and rivers, skiing and boarding any of the dozens of resorts, or immersing yourself in native culture.

Planning a trip can be overwhelming, but don't let it be. The first thing you should do is forget about any preconceived notions you have about travel to Canada—or more precisely British Columbia—and instead focus on the experience. Of course you'll want to visit the museums of Vancouver, take afternoon tea in Victoria, explore the region's six national parks, and maybe even try surfing off Long Beach, but try to think less about specific "sights" and open yourself to discovery.

Start by trying to identify the places you want to see, which parks you just can't miss, the towns that sound most appealing, and how much money you want to spend. Once you have put together an outline of your trip, book lodging—as far in advance as possible—especially if you're traveling in July or August.

It is possible to visit British Columbia without your own vehicle (or a rental), but you'll be confining yourself to the major cities and relying on public transportation and guided tours to get around. Driving is more practical, especially if you plan on visiting the parks and pursuing outdoor endeavors. Even though wilderness dominates the interior, central, and northern regions, British Columbia is dotted with towns and cities linked by well-traveled highways.

WHEN TO GO

Deciding when in the year you'll be visiting British Columbia usually depends on your own schedule, but the following thoughts may help you decide the best time to visit.

While British Columbia can be visited year-round, there are two major influxes of visitors—one in the warmer months and the other in winter. Summer revolves around activities such as hiking, biking, swimming, canoeing, fishing—just about anything you can do outdoors. In winter, the focus is on skiing and snowboarding.

The high season for travel to British Columbia is most definitely summer, or more precisely July and August. This is the time of year when parks come alive with campers, the lakes and streams with anglers, the mountains with hikers, the woods with wildlife, and the roadsides with stalls selling fresh produce. Summer daytime temperatures in Vancouver average a pleasant 23°C (73°F), while the provincial hot spot, the Okanagan Valley, experiences temperatures in the 30s (86–102°F) on many days.

Spring and fall are excellent times to visit British Columbia. While April–June is considered a shoulder season, in many ways the province is at its blooming best in spring. Crowds are at a minimum, the days are long, golfers hit the links in shirts and shorts, and lodging rates throughout the province are reduced. May in the Okanagan Valley is a delight, especially for travelers who enjoy wine festivals.

Fall (mid-Sept.–Nov.) can be tremendous, particularly September, with lingering warm temperatures and a noticeable decrease in crowds immediately after the long weekend (at the beginning of the month). While fall colors in general lack the intensity of those in the eastern provinces and New England, larch turn a brilliant yellow throughout high alpine areas in late September.

The two major cities, Vancouver and Victoria, can be visited year-round, with some outdoor activities—golfing, biking, hiking, and more—possible in the dead of winter on Vancouver Island. Alpine resorts throughout the province begin opening in December, and most have seasons extending through to April (or early June in the case of Whistler). The best snow conditions are January–February, although for winter enthusiasts looking for a combination of good snow and warmer weather, March is an excellent time of year to visit.

WHAT TO TAKE

You'll have little use for a suit and tie in British Columbia. Instead, pack for the outdoors. At the top of your must-bring list should be walking or hiking boots. If you buy shoes especially for the trip, make sure you wear them once or twice before leaving home—just to make sure they are comfortable. In summer, temperatures rarely drop below freezing anywhere in the province, so you don't need a down jacket or winter boots. But be geared up for a variety of weather conditions, especially at the change of seasons. Do this by preparing to dress in layers, including at least one pair of fleece pants and a heavy long-sleeved top. Bring sunglasses and a wide-brimmed hat to provide protection from the strong sunlight. Gloves and a wool hat are a good idea if you're camping. For dining out, casual dress is accepted at all but the most upscale restaurants in Vancouver and Victoria. Don't forget your swimming costume—for taking a dip in the warm waters off Vancouver Island or soaking in a hot tub up at a ski resort. Finally, bug spray is a summer necessity, but you can pick up the brands that are most effective once you arrive.

Winter temperatures vary greatly throughout the region. Golfers hitting the links on Vancouver Island in January will undoubtedly be warmly dressed, but they *will* be golfing. In the interior and through the northern half of the province, January brings extremely cold temperatures. For this climate, plan to dress in layers, starting with long thermal underwear. The best type of outer layer combines breathable, wind-resistant pants and a jacket. Warm boots with new liners, lined mittens, and a wool hat are a must. If you're traveling from warmer climes, purchasing all the winter necessities in Vancouver is a good idea.

Electrical appliances from the United States work in Canada, but those from other parts of the world will require a current converter (transformer) to bring the voltage down. Many travel-size shavers, hair dryers, and irons have built-in converters.

Choosing a suitcase or backpack is also important. Think about the type of traveling you'll be doing before making a final decision. A midsize suitcase with wheels is best for carting through airports and lugging around hotels. Fold-over bags are good for keeping formal clothing wrinkle-free, but unless you're in town on business or attending a snazzy function, you probably won't require much in the way of dressy clothing. Besides, this type of suitcase is a bother to pack and unpack.

Airlines allow at least one piece of carry-on luggage per person, which must be small enough to fit in the overhead compartments. (Most luggage stores have guidelines to help you choose the right size.) Pack your carry-on with valuables, medications, smaller breakable items, a sweater, bottled water, reading material, and vital documents (driver's license, credit card, passport, a printout of your reservations, etc.). Even if you're traveling by bus, train, or your own vehicle, it's a good idea to keep all these things in an easy-to-reach carry-on style bag. The most convenient carry-on bags are small backpacks, which can double as day packs for sightseeing or hiking.

VANCOUVER

Let your mind fill with images of dramatic, snowcapped mountains rising high above a city clinging to the coastline. A downtown core of century-old buildings and steel-and-glass skyscrapers overlooking the busy waterways. Manicured suburbs fringed by golden sandy beaches and rocky shorelines. Protected areas of magnificent old-growth forests and brilliant flower gardens overflowing with color. An out-doors-loving population, keen to take advantage of its magnificent surroundings. World-class accommodations and dynamic dining options. These are the magnificent images of Vancouver, British Columbia's largest city, with a population of two million.

VANCOUVER ISLAND

Victoria, the elegant capital of British Columbia on the southern tip of Vancouver Island, couldn't be more different from its neighbor, Vancouver. Victorians will be quick to tell you that the weather is nicer and the pace is slower than over on the mainland. And they are right on both accounts. But the city also projects an intriguing mixture of images, old and new. Well-preserved old buildings line inner-city streets; ancient totem poles sprout from shady parks; restored historic areas house trendy shops, offices, and exotic restaurants; dou-ble-decker buses and horse-drawn carriages compete for summer trade; and the residents keep alive the original traditions and atmosphere of Merry Olde England. Beyond city limits, the rest of Vancouver Island beckons, with an array of outdoor experiences that range from hiking the rugged West Coast Trail to surfing the waves of Long Beach.

SOUTHWESTERN BRITISH COLUMBIA

Exploring the southwest portion of mainland British Columbia is like taking three very different vacations, each leading to adventures farther afield. In the middle of the action is Vancouver, which is covered in another chapter. From this metropolis, the Sunshine Coast spreads out to the north. Reaching the Sunshine Coast is slightly complicated by ferry-only access, but this also contributes to the charm of its old-fashioned resort towns, which attract families, scuba divers, and sun-loving Canadians. North of Vancouver, the Sea to Sky Highway leads right into the heart of Whistler, a hip, outdoorsy resort town of epic proportions. Summer will keep you busy while winter will captivate you, especially if skiing and snowboarding are your thing. Traveling east from Vancouver, the road forks—head through the scenic Fraser Canyon to central British Columbia or follow the U.S. border along a winding mountain highway that passes through Manning Provincial Park before emerging at the Okanagan Valley.

OKANAGAN VALLEY

Tucked into the south-central portion of the province is the gorgeous Okanagan Valley. Around 180 kilometers (112 miles) from end to end, this super-fertile area is dotted with orchards and wineries, the latter a major attraction. But if the only thing you know about wine is that you like it, no worries—wine tasting in the Okanagan is a completely unsnobby affair. The entire valley positively brims with bustling tourist towns, world-class golf courses, marvelous resorts, and enough fun parks to keep the kids busy for an entire vacation. Cruise Highway 97, the valley's main thoroughfare, to hit all the hot spots—the major cities of Penticton, Kelowna, and Vernon; the most celebrated wineries; and the best beaches. You'll also encounter plenty of opportunities to explore places such as the fire-devastated Okanagan Mountain Provincial Park, landmarks such as Historic O'Keefe Ranch, and four-season playgrounds like Silver Star Mountain Resort.

THE KOOTENAYS

Named for the native people who were the original inhabitants of the southeastern corner of British Columbia, the Kootenay region is overwhelmingly beautiful—in a monotonous mountain-and-lakes kind of way. The main geographical feature is a series of brawny mountain ranges. Alpine snowfields feed mighty rivers and massive lakes, creating a recreational playground for anglers, canoeists, and kayakers. Dotted through the valleys are traditional towns of varying size. The largest of these is Nelson, a historically important mining center that absorbs a little earthiness from its counterculture vibe. Spend time exploring the ghost town of Sandon, step back in time at Fort Steele Heritage Town, and wrap up your Kootenay wanderings with a soak at Ainsworth Hot Springs. Throughout the mountains many parks merit special attention: White Grizzly Wilderness for the opportunity to view grizzly bears, Kokanee Creek to watch fish spawning along a shallow creekbed, and Akamina-Kishinena for its solitude.

CANADIAN ROCKIES

As you make your way east from the Kootenay region, the mountains become more dramatic—welcome to the Canadian Rockies. I leave the famous national parks you've heard about—Banff and Jasper—for another day, concentrating on the British Columbia side of the mountains, a vast area of wilderness where wildlife is abundant and hiking trails reach all the most scenic locales. The region—and in my opinion, Canada's wilderness—is at its most breathtaking at Lake O'Hara, in Yoho National Park. Adjacent Kootenay National Park offers up more magnificent Canadian wilds, along with hot springs, while Mt. Assiniboine's remoteness is a blessing for those looking for solitude. Within and beyond the national parks, creature comforts are still just a credit card away—book your accommodations at Emerald Lake Lodge or Lake O'Hara Lodge and you'll want for nothing.

CENTRAL BRITISH COLUMBIA

Cutting a swath across the province, the central region of British Columbia is extremely diverse. In the east is a series of glaciated mountain ranges where the highest peaks are protected by two national parks—Glacier (not to be confused with its namesake park in the United States) and Mount Revelstoke, where wilderness adventures are extremely accessible and the commercialism of the Canadian Rockies is nonexistent. The heart of central British Columbia is dominated by lakes, including Shuswap Lake. For westbound travelers, the scenery changes dramatically west of Salmon Arm, as mountains make way for sagebrush-covered hills. In the heart of this desert-like landscape is the city of Kamloops. From Kamloops, head northeast to wildlife-rich Wells Gray Provincial Park and the high peaks of Mount Robson Provincial Park, or west then north through the ranching country of the Cariboo.

NORTHERN BRITISH COLUMBIA

The northern half of British Columbia is for the adventurous. For starters, it's a long way from anywhere else. Secondly, you won't see any famous attractions or scenic wonders. Instead, you find lakes and forest and lots of both. For anglers, opportunities to catch a trophy-sized trout or steelhead are almost endless. The many towns provide excellent access to outdoor activities. The coastline of northern British Columbia is mostly inaccessible from land. But where highways do push down to the ocean, such as at Prince Rupert and Stewart, scenic rewards for driving to the end of the road abound. For a real adventure, jump aboard a ferry at Prince Rupert for the Queen Charlotte Islands, where totem pole villages abandoned by the fearless Haida are slowly being reclaimed by nature.

Trying to figure out the best way to see the highlights of British Columbia by looking at a map or flipping through this guidebook can be daunting. If all you have is one week, you must face reality—you're not going to see it all. This itinerary balances a little bit of everything—the major cities, mountains, and the ocean—without putting a ridiculous amount of mileage on your vehicle.

© ANDREW HEMPSTEAD

Pacific Rim National Park

DAY 1

Head north from Vancouver airport and loop around Point Grey to the Museum of Anthropology, a wonderful introduction to the history of the Pacific Northwest. Duck through the old-growth forest behind the museum to get a feel for the city's natural splendor. Check in to your hotel and take an evening stroll through Gastown.

DAY 2

Even if you hit Stanley Park as the sun first rises, you'll find that many locals have beaten you on their morning jog. Cross to the North Shore and take the Grouse Mountain Skyride. Drive the Sea to Sky Highway to Whistler. Spend the evening at your leisure exploring the resort village.

DAY 3

Catch the ferry from Horseshoe Bay to Nanaimo, on Vancouver Island. Drive across to Tofino, making a stop at Cathedral Grove.

DAY 4

Book a whale-watching tour for the morning, and then take a beach walk in Pacific Rim National Park before returning to Nanaimo for the night.

DAY 5

Detour from the Island Highway at Crofton Bay to catch a ferry to Salt Spring Island. Enjoy lunch at

© ANDREW HEMPSTEAD

Butchart Gardens

an outdoor Café in Ganges, then make the short ferry hop to Victoria.

DAY 6

Today is a walking day, so leave your vehicle at your accommodation and make your way to the Inner Harbour. The Royal British Columbia Museum is a must-see, Market Square and the surrounding streets are interesting to explore, and Barb's Place is perfect for lunch. Still hungry? Head to Oak Bay for afternoon tea.

DAY 7

Arrive at Butchart Gardens at opening time—before the bus tour crowd arrives—then return to Vancouver by ferry. You'll arrive in time for an afternoon flight home.

If you enjoy winter sports, you could spend an entire season exploring British Columbia. But you only have one week; hence this itinerary, which stops at the best-known resorts, detours to some lesser-known places, and finishes up with a round of golf, just because you can.

Blackcomb Mountain

DAY 1

You probably don't feel like doing much after arriving in Vancouver, but I urge you to suit up and head for Grouse Mountain, where the ski runs are lighted for night skiing and the views back down across British Columbia's largest city are breathtaking.

DAY 2

Head east, through the Fraser River Valley, to Kelowna. Spend the afternoon browsing through town or visiting a local winery. Spend the night at Big White Ski Resort.

DAY 3

Hit the slopes of Big White.

DAY 4

Families should spend an extra day in the Okanagan Valley, especially those with younger children who will gravitate to the Happy Valley Adventure Centre. Experienced skiers looking to indulge in British Columbia's legendary powder should drive to Rossland on Day 3 and spend today knee-deep in the deepest snow this side of a helicopter.

DAY 5

Regardless of your Day 4 itinerary, spend Day 5 enjoying the slopes of Silver Star before driving through Kamloops to Sun Peaks Resort.

DAY 6

Drive to Whistler via Vancouver. You'll have a few spare hours to visit a couple of Vancouver's better-known indoor attractions—like the Storyeum or Maritime Museum.

DAY 7

Skiers and boarders should rise early for a full day's skiing. Rather than trying to cover the entire resort, concentrate your efforts on either

Kelowna waterfront

© ANDREW HEMPSTEAD

Whistler or Blackcomb Mountain. Drive to Horseshoe Bay and make the short hop across Georgia Strait to Nanaimo.

DAY 8

Spend the day at Mt. Washington Alpine Resort, then choose a heritage home bed-and-breakfast in downtown Victoria for your final night in Canada.

DAY 9

Take advantage of Victoria's balmy winter weather by booking a morning tee time at a local links. Return to Vancouver by ferry—or take a floatplane for a treat.

Two weeks in British Columbia allows the opportunity to travel throughout the province, including to the northern region. Of course, you could also pad out the preceding itinerary with more time in Vancouver and Victoria—and that's what many travelers do—but I encourage you to get adventurous and travel farther afield. As with the other itineraries, I assume you have your own vehicle or will be renting one.

© ANDREW HEMPSTEAD

Seawall Promenade, Stanley Park

with a visit to Cathedral Grove and short walk along the driftwood-strewn beaches of Pacific Rim National Park, you will have time to enjoy a relaxing evening in Tofino.

DAY 1
Arrive in Vancouver for a two-night stay. Spend the rest of your first day exploring Gastown and the waterfront area. Rent a bike for an evening ride through Stanley Park.

DAY 2
Spend the day in Whistler, returning to Vancouver in time for dinner atop Grouse Mountain.

DAY 3
Catch a ferry to Victoria and visit capital sights such as the Royal British Columbia Museum and Butchart Gardens.

DAY 4
Make Tofino your final destination on Day 4. Even

DAY 5
Make your way north up the island to Telegraph Cove. Go whale-watching and continue north to Port Hardy.

DAY 6
The ferry from Port Hardy gets into Prince Rupert in the late afternoon, linking up with the ferry to the Queen Charlotte Islands

DAY 7
Even after 24 hours and two ferry trips, you'll be invigorated by the uniqueness of the Queen Charlotte Islands.

DAY 8
You have all day to visit Naikoon Provincial Park

Mount Robson (3,954 meters) is the highest peak in the Canadian Rockies.

and cross to Sandspit. Ferries depart the Queen Charlotte Islands for the mainland in the evening (book a cabin to get a good night's rest on board).

DAY 9
Arriving in Prince Rupert at dawn, take breakfast in Cow Bay while waiting for the Museum of Northern British Columbia to open. Head west, stopping at 'Ksan Historical Village. Aim for an overnight stay in Prince George, but don't push it (the more driving you get done today, the quicker you will reach the mountains the following day).

DAY 10
After the long haul across northern British Columbia, the first views of the Canadian Rockies are a relief. As Mount Robson comes into view, you will be wowed.

DAY 11
Drag yourself away from Mount Robson and head

south to Kamloops, then west along the Trans-Canada Highway to Revelstoke. Even if you're not a railway buff, Craigellachie (site of the last spike on the transcontinental railway) is a pleasant stop.

DAY 12
Drive the Meadows in the Sky Parkway and continue west to Yoho National Park. This may be the night for a splurge at the Emerald Lake Lodge.

DAY 13
Head south through the Columbia Valley. Stop at the Creston Valley Wildlife Management Area before continuing to Nelson.

DAY 14
It's a seven-hour drive to Vancouver from Nelson. En route, the wineries, golf courses, and abundance of water sports in the Okanagan Valley will tempt you to linger a day or two longer.

So you have just one week and want to concentrate your time on Vancouver Island? Not a problem. This itinerary mixes high tea with low tide to create a trip that has something for everyone. For many people, hiking the West Coast Trail is a major reason for traveling to the island, but because the route takes a minimum of four days to traverse, I leave it as an option that you could include in an extended tour of the island.

© ANDREW HEMPSTEAD

kayaking

WA

DAY 1

After catching a ferry across Georgia Strait from Vancouver, spend your first day exploring Victoria. Fans of flowers won't want to miss Butchart Gardens; history buffs should spend an hour or so in the Royal British Columbia Museum. Either way, head to Oak Bay for a traditional afternoon tea.

DAY 2

Drive north to Nanaimo. Walk along the harborfront, book an afternoon dive at one of the local wrecks, or go bungee jumping. Leave Nanaimo behind by late afternoon, heading for the west coast. Stop at Cathedral Grove to admire the old-growth forest. Stay in Tofino tonight.

DAY 3

Juggle your schedule to include both a whale-watching trip in Clayoquot Sound and a hike in Pacific Rim National Park. Spend another night in Tofino, or mix it up and move down the coast to Ucluelet.

DAY 4

Drive to Port Alberni and take a cruise aboard the MV *Lady Rose*. After returning to port, families may want to book a night at one of Parksville's many beach side resorts, while anglers could continue on to Campbell River.

DAY 5

Telegraph Cove will be a highlight of your time on Vancouver Island—even if you don't take a whale-watching trip.

Victoria Harbour Ferry

DAY 6

Head south to Crofton Bay and catch the ferry to Salt Spring Island. Spend the night on the largest of the Southern Gulf Islands, or continue to pretty Galiano Island.

DAY 7

Go kayaking, take a hike, or spend a relaxing morning soaking up island life—just read the timetable carefully to ensure the direct ferry back to Vancouver will arrive well before your flight home.

Truckers make the trip between Calgary and Vancouver in 12 or so hours. Many travelers heading to Vancouver from Alberta also drive the route nonstop, while others overnight along the way. But you're on vacation, so plan on expanding the drive to a weeklong sojourn that will—eventually—get you to Vancouver.

© ANDREW HEMPSTEAD

Okanagan Vineyard

DAY 1

Depart Calgary (Alberta) and try not to be tempted by the wonders of Banff National Park (leave them for another time) as you enter the mountains and head to Yoho National Park. Explore the Yoho Valley by road, then head to Emerald Lake for an afternoon walk. If you don't feel like splurging on a park accommodation, continue to Golden.

DAY 2

Ride the Kicking Horse Mountain Resort gondola, then hit the highway for Glacier National Park. Even from the highway, this park is spectacular, so unless you're a keen hiker or it's getting late in the day, continue to Revelstoke. Take in an outdoor evening concert in Grizzly Plaza.

DAY 3

Drive south from Revelstoke to Nelson. Break up the trip with a short detour to Sandon, British Columbia's only ghost town, and to watch spawning kokanee at Kokanee Creek Provincial Park. You'll find plenty of choices for dinner in Nelson.

DAY 4

Driving through the West Kootenays is a delight, although a roller-coaster highway means the trip takes longer than you might imagine. Stop for a swim in Christina Lake en route.

DAY 5

Spend the day at your leisure in the Okanagan Valley. Near Osoyoos, the Desert Centre is an interesting stop, unless it's a super-hot day—then stay close to the water or join a winery tour.

DAY 6

Head north from Vernon. Silver Star Mountain Resort will leave you with pleasant memories of the Okanagan. Cut across to Kamloops via Highway 97. Stop at Historic O'Keefe Ranch. Spend the night in Kamloops, taking in the Two River Junction dinner theater.

DAY 7

Give the direct Coquihalla Highway a miss and travel down the Fraser River Canyon to Hope. Suburban Vancouver is approaching, so if you feel like stalling the inevitable onslaught of city traffic, take a walk through the Othello-Quintette Tunnels.

© ANDREW HEMPSTEAD

the Othello-Quintette Tunnels

Explore
British Columbia

Vancouver

If you view this gleaming mountain- and sea-dominated city for the first time on a beautiful sunny day, you're bound to fall for it in a big way. See it on a dull, dreary day when the clouds are low and Vancouver's backyard mountains are hidden and you may come away with a slightly less enthusiastic picture—you'll have experienced the "permagray," as residents are quick to call it with a laugh.

But even gray skies can't dampen the city's vibrant, outdoorsy atmosphere. By day, the active visitor can enjoy boating right from downtown, or perhaps venture out to one of the nearby provincial parks for hiking in summer and skiing and snowboarding in winter. More urban-oriented visitors can savor the aromas of just-brewed coffee and freshly baked bread wafting from cosmopolitan sidewalk cafés, join in the bustle at seaside markets, bake on a local beach, or simply relax and do some people-watching in one of the city's tree-shaded squares. By night, Vancouver's myriad fine restaurants, hip nightclubs, and world-class performing-arts venues beckon visitors to continue enjoying themselves on into the wee hours.

PLANNING YOUR TIME

Deciding how best to spend your time in Vancouver is a personal thing—outdoorsy budget travelers will spend their days (and money) in a very different way than would a honeymooning

Must-Sees

Look for **M** to find the sights and activities you can't miss and **N** for the best dining and lodging.

VANCOUVER

Bowen Island

Grouse Mountain Skyride

Vancouver Maritime Museum

Stanley Park

Museum of Anthropology Canada Place

Granville Island

Storyeum

VanDusen Botanical Garden

Steveston

CANADA

UNITED STATES

Canada Place

M Vancouver Maritime Museum: The city's nautical past is on display at this museum, with attractions for all ages (page 40).

M VanDusen Botanical Garden: Garden lovers will be in their element at a formal garden in the heart of one of Vancouver's most upscale neighborhoods (page 41).

M Museum of Anthropology: Inspired by the longhouses of First Nations people, this museum houses a stunning collection of totem poles and related arts and crafts (page 42).

M Steveston: A restored cannery, heritage shipyards, and open parkland make the trip out to Steveston a pleasant detour from city sights (page 43).

M Grouse Mountain Skyride: Catch views extending across the city to Mount Baker in Washington State. Plentiful on-mountain activities make this a good half-day excursion (page 46).

M Bowen Island: From Vancouver, this is the most accessible of hundreds of islands dotting the Strait of Georgia, and seems a world away from the city (page 48).

M Canada Place: Its towering white sail-like architecture is a city landmark, taking pride of place along the Vancouver waterfront (page 32).

M Storyeum: Down the cobbled streets of Gastown, Vancouver's main tourist precinct, is this historic theater presentation of epic proportions (page 33).

M Granville Island: Interested in the arts? Want to learn about the history of fishing? Do you enjoy browsing through market stalls? You'll find all this and more on this bustling island (page 36).

M Stanley Park: This massive chunk of downtown has been protected in its forested, old-growth state for all time (page 38).

© ANDREW HEMPSTEAD

© AVALON TRAVEL PUBLISHING, INC.

couple looking to kick back and relax. But this is one of the true joys of visiting Vancouver—there really is something for everyone.

Regardless of whether you have a weekend or a full week scheduled for Vancouver, plan on rising early and heading out to Stanley Park for a walk or ride at least once. Visit the major museums—**Storyeum, Vancouver Museum, Vancouver Maritime Museum,** and the **Museum of Anthropology**—in the mornings. Leave the afternoons for outdoor pursuits that can be active (**kayaking** on False Creek), educational (**Capilano Salmon Hatchery),** or breathtaking (**Grouse Mountain Skyride).**

When it comes to dining out, choose a restaurant that specializes in wild salmon at least once; **Salmon House on the Hill** is my personal fave, but its North Shore location makes it difficult to reach without your own vehicle (A Kettle of Fish is a solid second choice).

HISTORY

The first Europeans to set eyes on the land encompassing today's city of Vancouver were gold-seeking Spanish traders who sailed through the Strait of Georgia in 1790. Although the forested wilderness they encountered seemed impenetrable, it had been inhabited by humans since becoming ice-free some 10,000 years earlier.

Not to be outdone, the Brits sent Captain George Vancouver to the area in 1792. Vancouver cruised through the Strait of Georgia in search of a northwest passage to the Orient, charting Burrard Inlet and claiming the land for Great Britain in the process. As stories of an abundance of fur-bearing mammals filtered east, the fur companies went into action. The North West Company sent fur trader/explorer Simon Fraser overland to establish a coastal trading post. In 1808 he reached the Pacific Ocean via the river that was later named for him, and he built a fur fort on the riverbank east of today's Vancouver. In 1827, the Hudson's Bay Company established its own fur fort on the Fraser River, 48 kilometers east of present-day Vancouver. Neither of these two outposts spawned a permanent settlement.

Vancouver Is Born

It wasn't until the discovery of gold up the Fraser River in the late 1850s that settlement really

looking across to Vancouver's West End from Kitsilano

took hold in the area. The town of New Westminster, just southeast of present-day Vancouver, was declared British Columbia's first capital in 1866.

The settlement of Vancouver began with the establishment of a brickworks ("Bricks? Why on earth make bricks when we've got all these trees?" said the Woodcutters' Union spokesman) on the south side of Burrard Inlet. Sawmills and related logging and lumber industries followed, and soon several boomtowns were carved out of the wilderness. The first was Granville (now downtown Vancouver), which the original settlers called Gastown after one of its earliest residents, notorious saloon owner "Gassy Jack" Deighton. In 1886 Granville, population 1,000, became the City of Vancouver. Not long thereafter, fire roared through the timber city. Just about everything burned to the ground, but with true pioneering spirit Vancouver was rebuilt at lightning speed.

A Growing City

In 1887, the struggling city got a boost with the arrival of the first transcontinental railroad. Selected as the western terminus for the Canadian Pacific Railway, Vancouver suddenly became Canada's transportation gateway to the Orient and an important player in the development of international commerce around the Pacific Rim. Additionally, the opening of the Panama Canal in 1915 created the perfect outlet for transporting the province's abundant renewable resources to North America's east coast and Europe, resulting in further development of the port facilities and a population boom. Granville Island and the far reaches of Burrard Inlet sprawled with industry, the West End developed as a residential area, the University of British Columbia grew in stature, and the opening of the Lions Gate Bridge encouraged settlement on the north side of Burrard Inlet.

Recent Times

From what began just 120 years ago as a cluster of ramshackle buildings centered around a saloon, Vancouver has blossomed into one of the world's greatest cities. While the city holds

2010 OLYMPIC WINTER GAMES

On July 2, 2003, Vancouver was named host city for XXI Olympic Winter Games. The dates are February 12–28, 2010, with the Paralympic Games following March 12–31. Venues are split between Vancouver and Whistler, 120 kilometers (75 miles) to the north. The opening ceremony will take place at the 55,000-seat, downtown B.C. Place Stadium. Vancouver will also host figure skating, speed skating, curling, hockey, freestyle skiing, and freestyle snowboarding. The latter two will take place at Cypress Mountain, on the North Shore. Alpine and Nordic skiing, ski jumping, bobsledding, luge, and skeleton will take place in and around the Whistler area. Both locations will host athletes in purpose-built villages. It is estimated that the games will attract 6,700 athletes and officials and 250,000 visitors. Although the event is still a long way off, preparations are well underway.

The **Vancouver 2010 Organizing Committee** (877/408-2010, www.vancouver2010.com) is the main body overseeing the planning, organizing, and staging of the games.

onto the largest port on North America's West Coast, boasting 20 specialized terminals that handle more tonnage than any other port in Canada, it is now a lot less reliant on its traditional economic heart for its growth. Even after the technology bust, the high-tech industry continues as the fastest-growing sector of Vancouver's economy. Worth $5 billion in 2004, this knowledge-based industry has both revitalized the local economy and created a major shift in government thinking. Tourism contributes over $5 billion annually to the local economy, with finance, real estate, insurance, and manufacturing also forming large slices of the local economic pie. Vancouver is also North America's second-largest moviemaking center. Worth $1 billion annually to the city, this exciting industry employs up to 50,000 people on as many as 30 simultaneous productions.

Vancouver

Sights

As British Columbia's largest city, Vancouver holds an abundance of world-class attractions, as well as many smaller gems that are easy to miss. Whether you're interested in visiting museums or exploring mountain peaks, you will find plenty to do in Vancouver—the hardest part will be working out how to best fit them into your itinerary. Luckily, many attractions are clustered around downtown, with others such as Granville Island and the city's three major museums farther out but easily reached by public transportation. Try to arrange your sightseeing schedule around the weather. If the forecast calls for a rainy day, concentrate on the museums, leaving the North Shore and Stanley Park for a sunny day.

GETTING ORIENTED

Vancouver isn't a particularly easy city to find your way around, although an excellent transit system helps immensely. **Downtown** lies on a spit of land bordered to the north and east by Burrard Inlet, to the west by English Bay, and to the south by False Creek, which almost cuts the city center off from the rest of the city. Due to the foresight of city founders, almost half of the downtown peninsula has been set aside as parkland.

The **City of Vancouver** officially extends south and west from downtown, between Burrard Inlet and the Fraser River, and encompasses the trendy beachside suburb of **Kitsilano** (known as "Kits" to the locals) and **Point Grey,** home of the University of British Columbia. To the east, the residential sprawl continues, through the suburbs of **Burnaby, New Westminster,** and **Coquitlam,** which have a combined population of well over 250,000.

Farther south, the low-lying Fraser River delta extends all the way south to the border. Between the north and south arms of the river is **Richmond,** home of Vancouver International Airport. South of the south arm is the mostly industrial area of **Delta,** as well as **Tsawwassen,** departure point for ferries to Vancouver Island.

Southeast of the Fraser River lies **Surrey,** another of those never-ending suburbs, this one with a population of 349,000. The sprawl continues east from Surrey. With Vancouver growing at an incredible rate, and as development to the south and north are restricted—by the international border and the Coast Mountains—there's nowhere to go but east. From Surrey, the Trans-Canada Highway passes through the Fraser River Valley and towns such as **Langley** (pop. 85,000), **Abbotsford** (pop. 110,000), and **Chilliwack** (pop. 65,000)—all now part of the city sprawl.

Across Burrard Inlet to the north of downtown, **North Vancouver** is a narrow developed strip backed up to the mountains and connected to the rest of the city by the Lions Gate Bridge. To its west are **Horseshoe Bay,** departure point for Sunshine Coast and Vancouver Island ferries, and **West Vancouver,** an upscale suburb.

DOWNTOWN

Granville Street was Vancouver's first commercial corridor, and if today you stand at its junction with West Georgia Street, you're as close to the "center" of the city as it's possible to be. From this busy intersection Granville Street extends north toward Burrard Inlet as a pedestrian mall, leading through the Central Business District (CBD) to Canada Place and the main tourist information center. Vancouver Art Gallery, all major banking institutions, shopping centers, and the city's best hotels are within a three-block radius of this intersection. To the south, between Dunsmuir and Robson Streets, is the **theater district** and Library Square. **Yaletown,** the hot spot for tech companies, is farther south, bordered by Homer, Drake, and Nelson Streets. East along the waterfront from Canada Place, and still within easy walking distance of the Granville and Georgia Streets intersection, is the oldest part of the city, **Gastown.** Beyond Gastown, North America's third-largest **Chinatown** is a hive of activity day and night. On the opposite side of the CBD is the **West End** and

VANCOUVER VIEWS

Whenever I visit a city for the first time, I like to start off by finding a viewpoint that lets me see the layout of the city. In Vancouver, the obvious option to get your bearings is to take a flightseeing trip in a helicopter or floatplane, but this also means paying out big bucks. Instead, consider one of the following less-expensive options.

Downtown

For immediate orientation from downtown, catch the high-speed, stomach-sinking glass elevator up the outside of 40-story **Harbour Centre Tower** (555 W. Hastings St., 604/689-0421; summer daily 8:30 A.M.–10:30 P.M., the rest of the year daily 9:30 A.M.–9 P.M.; adult $10, senior $9, student $7). The ride takes less than a minute and ends at **The Lookout!**, an enclosed room 167 meters above street level, from where views extend as far away as Mount Baker, 140 kilometers to the south. Walk around the circular room for 360-degree views and interpretive panels describing interesting facts about the panorama below and beyond. Keep your receipt and you can return any time during the same day (the top of the tower is a great place to watch the sun setting over the Strait of Georgia).

Down on the Waterfront

From Vancouver Visitor Info Centre, continue down Burrard Street to **Canada Place** and wander around the west side promenade for neck-straining views of the city close up, as well as North Vancouver and the rugged mountains beyond. For a look at the skyline and sparkling Canada Place from sea level, take the SeaBus from the adjacent Waterfront Station across Burrard Inlet to **Lonsdale Quay** ($3).

Stanley Park

Drive, walk, or cycle Stanley Park's 10-kilometer (6.2-mile) **Seawall Promenade** to appreciate the skyline to the east, the busy shipping lanes of First Narrows to the north, and the sandy beaches of English Bay to the west. Sunsets from **English Bay Beach,** in the West End, are delightful.

North Shore

The best views from the north side of Burrard

The view across the city from The Lookout! is spectacular.

Inlet are gained by taking the **Grouse Mountain Skyride** (Nancy Greene Way, 604/984-0661; adult $27, senior $25, child $15) up the slopes of Grouse Mountain. The panorama extends back across the inlet to downtown and beyond to Mount Baker, in Washington State, and west to Vancouver Island. In summer, the gondola departs the base station every 10 minutes 10 A.M.–10 P.M.

Head west along Highway 1 from the Grouse Mountain turnoff to Cypress Bowl Road. At the second switchback there's a particularly good city skyline view. Continue west to Horseshoe Bay, then return to the city along Marine Drive, which parallels Burrard Inlet, providing many glimpses of the city skyline. At **Lighthouse Park,** along this route, English Bay, Stanley Park, and Kitsilano Beach are laid out in all their glory from Point Atkinson.

Uptown

South of downtown, the **Kitsilano** foreshore provides that well-known view of the city skyline backed by the Coast Mountains. The south side of the city is relatively flat. The high point is 152-meter-high (500-foot-high) **Little Mountain,** in Queen Elizabeth Park, where the city skyline and abruptly rising mountains contrast starkly with the residential sprawl of Vancouver.

DOWNTOWN VANCOUVER SIGHTS

Lost Lagoon

STANLEY PARK

NATURE HOUSE ★

Coal Harbour

MV CONSTITUTION

STANLEY PARK BOAT RENTALS

Second Beach

LAGOON DRIVE

ROBSON ST

HARO ST

WEST GEORGIA

ALBERNI

PARK LANE

PENDER ST

BEACH

CHILCO AVE

GILFORD

COMOX

NELSON

BARCLAY

DENMAN PLACE DISCOUNT CINEMA ■

ROBSON PUBLIC MARKET ■

DENMAN ST

BIDWELL

Barclay Heritage Square ★

ROEDDE HOUSE MUSEUM

English Bay Beach

WEST END

PENRELL

DAVIE

CARDERO

Alexandra Park

BURNABY

NICOLA

BROUGHTON

English Bay

HARWOOD

Nelson Park

BEACH

JERVIS ST

BUTE ST

THURLOW ST

MOON

Sunset Beach Park

PACIFIC

ST PAUL'S HOSPITAL ■

0   300 yds

0   300 m

AVE

HOT WIRED COMPUTERS ■

DAVIE

HELMCKEN

Sunset Beach

BURRARD

DRAKE

HORNBY

HOWE

99

Kitsilano Point

VANCOUVER MARITIME MUSEUM ★

Vanier Park

VANCOUVER AQUATIC CENTRE ■

GRANVILLE

SEYMOUR

RICHARDS ST

99

MCNICHOL AVE

VANCOUVER MUSEUM/HR MACMILLAN SPACE CENTRE ★

Kitsilano Beach

WHYTE AVE

GORDON MACMILLAN SOUTHAM OBSERVATORY ★

BURRARD ST BRIDGE

ST

ST

GRANVILLE ISLAND BOAT RENTALS

GRANVILLE PUBLIC MARKET

99

Kitsilano Beach Park

CORNWALL

AVE

ECOMARINE OCEAN KAYAK CENTRE

GRANVILLE ST BRIDGE

ARTS CLUB/ BACKSTAGE LOUNGE

COOPER BOATING CENTER

ST

ARBUTUS

MAPLE

CYPRESS

BURRARD ST

ADVENTURE FITNESS/ ROWLAND'S REEF SCUBA SHOP

ST

GRANVILLE ISLAND MUSEUMS

GRANVILLE ISLAND

EMILY CARR INSTITUTE OF ART & DESIGN ★

W 1ST

AVE

ANDERSON

YEW

W 2ND

AVE

W 2ND

AVE

KIDS MARKET

W 3RD

AVE

GRANVILLE ISLAND INFORMATION CENTRE

KITSILANO

W 4TH

AVE

FAIRVIEW

Vancouver

Deadman's Island

Burrard Inlet

THE LANDING HILL'S NATIVE CRAFTS KITES ON CLOUDS
COMMISSIONER ST
Portside Park

STEAM CLOCK
WATER

VILLAGE GLOBAL COMMUNICATIONS
INUIT GALLERY OF VANCOUVER
GASTOWN
STORYEUM

W CANADA WILDERNESS COMMITTEE STORE
Maple Tree Square
HOTEL EUROPE

BYRNES BLOCK/ GAOLERS MEWS
STATUE OF GASSY JACK

BLOOD ALLEY
HASTINGS ST
CORDOVA

Victory Square
ABBOT

COAL HARBOUR SEAWALK
CORDOVA ST
HASTINGS ST

CANADA PLACE
SeaBus to Lonsdale Quay

SEAPLANE BASE

MELVILLE ST
VANCOUVER VISITOR INFO CENTRE
Sky Train
COMMISSIONER
HELIPORT

GEORGIA

HASTINGS
PENDER
Burrard
Waterfront
SINCLAIR CENTRE
SEE DETAIL
Portside Park

CHRIST CHURCH CATHEDRAL
GASTOWN
HARBOUR CENTRE TOWER
WATER
West Coast Express
ALEXANDER ST

CANADIAN CRAFT MUSEUM
CATHEDRAL PLACE

HONG KONG BANK BUILDING
E POWELL
GORE
DUNLEVY
Oppenheimer Park

VIRGIN MEGASTORE
PACIFIC CENTRE MALL
E CORDOVA

VANCOUVER ART GALLERY
Granville
THE BAY
Victory Square
E HASTINGS
VANCOUVER CENTENNIAL POLICE MUSEUM

Robson Square 99
ABBOTT
CARRALL
CHINATOWN
CARNEGIE READING ROOM

FORD CENTRE FOR THE PERFORMING ARTS
POST OFFICE
SHANGHAI ALLEY
E PENDER
CHINESE CULTURAL CENTRE

ORPHEUM THEATRE
QUEEN ELIZABETH THEATRE
Stadium
WORLD'S NARROWEST OFFICE BUILDING
KEEFER
TEN REN TEA & GINSENG CO

LEO'S CAMERAS
VANCOUVER PUBLIC LIBRARY
DR SUN YEN CLASSICAL CHINESE GARDEN
COLUMBIA
MAIN
JACKSON

Terry Fox Plaza
GM PLACE
UNION ST

BC SPORTS HALL OF FAME MUSEUM

YALETOWN
BC PLACE STADIUM
PLAZA OF NATIONS
Sky Train
Thornton Park
PACIFIC CENTRAL STATION

Main Street

SCIENCE WORLD
TERMINAL AVE

David Lam Park
CAMBIE BRIDGE
WESTERN
STATION
INDUSTRIAL AVE

False Creek

Charleston Park
1ST AVE
2ND
CAMBIE
COLUMBIA
MANITOBA
3RD
ONTARIO
QUEBEC
4TH
MAIN
2ND

© AVALON TRAVEL PUBLISHING, INC.

enormous **Stanley Park,** reached by walking along **Robson Street,** a two-kilometer-long strip of boutiques and restaurants.

ⓜ Canada Place

The stunning architectural curiosity with the billowing 27-meter-high Teflon-coated fiberglass "sails" on Burrard Inlet—the one that looks as if it might weigh anchor and cruise off into the sunset at any moment—is Canada Place, a city icon. Built as the Canada Pavilion for Expo86, this integrated waterfront complex is primarily a convention center and cruise-ship dock. The Vancouver Trade and Convention Centre, which makes up the bulk of the complex, is currently being expanded to triple its size at adjacent Burrard Landing, in a half-billion-dollar expansion project that will change the face of the downtown waterfront. The existing complex at the foot of Burrard Street also houses the luxurious 405-room Pan Pacific Hotel (the glass marvel with domed top), restaurants, shops, and an IMAX theater. Start your self-guided tour at the information booth near the main entrance; allow at least an hour to wander through the complex. Don't miss walking the exterior promenade—three and a half city blocks long—for splendid views of the harbor, the North Shore, the Coast Mountains, and docked Alaska-bound cruise ships.

Vancouver Art Gallery

Francis Rattenbury, architect of Victoria's Empress Hotel and many other masterpieces, designed Vancouver's imposing neoclassical-revival courthouse, which now houses Vancouver Art Gallery (750 Hornby St., 604/662-4700; daily 10 A.M.–5:30 P.M., until 9 P.M. on Thursday, closed Monday Oct.–May; adult $15, senior $11, child over 12 $10). Initially, the courthouse faced Georgia Street, and although the exterior retains its original 1911 design, the main entrance is now on Robson Street. The gallery houses a large collection of works by Canada's preeminent female artist, **Emily Carr,** who was born on Vancouver Island in 1871 and traveled the world honing her painting and drawing skills before settling in Vancouver in 1906. The Carr collection is on the third floor, along with the works of many other local artists. The gallery also holds pieces by contemporary artists from North America and Europe along with an impressive collection of historical art.

Guided tours are available. Kids will enjoy the children's gallery, while adults will appreciate the special-events program, including a lecture series, films, and concerts. The gift shop sells a wide selection of art books, jewelry, and gifts, and the gallery café is always crowded.

In the Vicinity

Diagonal from the art gallery and behind Cathedral Place is the **Canadian Craft & Design Museum** (639 Hornby St., 604/687-8266; Mon.–Sat. 10 A.M.–5 P.M., Thurs. until 9 P.M., Sun. noon–5 P.M.; adult $5, senior $3), which catalogs the history of arts and crafts throughout the ages. Media displayed include glass, wood, clay, metal, and fabric. The emphasis is on Canadian work, but a couple of other displays and touring exhibitions bring an international feel to the museum. As you'd expect, the gift shop offers an excellent choice of unique craft items; prices are reasonable. Entry is free Thursday evenings after 5 P.M. **Cathedral Place** is worth visiting for an intriguing sculpture, *Navigational Device,* in the lobby. The high-rise itself, built in 1991, replaced a classic art deco building. To placate opposition to the construction, architects incorporated the various art deco elements in its design, and even a copper-colored roof similar to that of the nearby Hotel Vancouver.

Next door to Cathedral Place is the **Hongkong Bank** building, which features a massive 27-meter-long aluminum pendulum in the lobby. Next door again, on the corner of West Georgia and Burrard Streets, is **Christ Church Cathedral.** When built in 1895, it was in the heart of a residential area. Over the ensuing century, it was engulfed by modern developments and is today Vancouver's oldest church, attracting more sightseers than believers. Across West Georgia Street from these buildings is the **Hotel Vancouver.** Built in 1887, the original hotel on this site featured 200 rooms, half of which had private bathrooms, unheard of in that day. It burnt to the ground in 1932 and was replaced by the hotel that stands today, which reflects the heritage of CPR-built hotels across the country with its distinctive château-style design topped by a copper roof.

Gastown

Just three blocks east of Canada Place, Gastown is a marvelous place to spend a few hours. It was the birthplace of Vancouver, officially named Granville in 1870 but always known as Gastown, for saloon owner "Gassy Jack" Deighton.

The Great Fire of 1886 destroyed almost all of Gastown's wooden buildings, but the district was rebuilt in stone and brick. By the 1960s, this historic district held nothing more than decrepit Victorian-era buildings and empty warehouses. A massive rejuvenation program commenced, and today historic Gastown is one of the city's most popular tourist attractions. Tree-lined cobblestone streets and old gas lamps front brightly painted, restored buildings housing galleries, restaurants, and an abundance of gift and souvenir shops.

Most of the action centers along **Water Street,** which branches east off Cordova Street and slopes gently toward the site of Gassy Jack's original saloon (now the Alhambra Hotel). As you first enter Water Street, you're greeted by **The Landing,** a seven-story heritage building that has had its exterior restored to its former glory and its interior transformed from a warehouse to an upmarket shopping arcade. It also holds eateries and the Steamworks Brewing Co., a pub/restaurant boasting harbor views. Continuing down the hill, on the corner of Water and Cambie Streets, is a **steam clock,** one of only two in the world (the other is a replica of this, the original one). Built by a local clock maker in the mid-1970s, it is powered by a steam system originally put in place to heat buildings along a 10-kilometer-long underground pipeline that snakes through downtown. Watch for the burst of steam every 15 minutes, which sets off steam whistles to the tune of Westminster chimes. Continue east along Water Street to the 1899 **Dominion Hotel,** then half a block south down Abbott Street to **Blood Alley,** the hangout of many infamous

late-19-century rogues. Most buildings still standing along Water Street were built immediately after the Great Fire of 1886, but the **Byrnes Block** (2 Water St.) is generally regarded as the oldest; it stands on the site of Deighton House, Gassy Jack's second and more permanent saloon.

Water Street ends at the cobbled **Maple Tree Square,** at the intersection of Water, Carrall, Powell, and Alexander Streets. A bronze **statue of Gassy Jack** watches over the square and the site of his original saloon from the top of a whiskey barrel. The **Alhambra Hotel,** which occupies the actual saloon site, was built in 1886 from bricks used as ballast in ships that sailed into Burrard Inlet.

⬛ Storyeum

Deep under the cobbled streets of Gastown is the Storyeum (142 Water St., 250/687-8142; daily 8:30 A.M.–7 P.M.; adult $22, senior $19, child $16), a living, learning, theatrical experience that transports visitors through the major events of British Columbia's history. The 72-minute "journey" begins with an elevator ride below street level. Capable of holding 200 people at once, the massive lift is a moving theater screen, with a 360-degree multimedia presentation of British Columbia's natural wonders shown as the slow descent is made. The stories that follow as you move through the attraction—a reenactment of life in a First Nations coastal village, the arrival of the first white explorers, the excitement of the Barkerville gold rush, Confederation, the first wave of immigrants, and more—are incredibly realistic, right down to the smell and sounds of a full-size train steaming into the city in 1885. The grand finale is a six-minute, 360-degree presentation of modern-day British Columbia, focusing on interesting individuals who call the province home. Back at street level is a recreation of Gastown 100 years ago, complete with stores and cafés.

CHINATOWN

The first Chinese came to the city in the 1880s to help the rail line construction. In total, the CPR employed 17,000 Chinese, and most settled around an area known as Shanghai Alley, at the west end of today's Chinatown. The heart of Chinatown has moved eastward over the years and is now centered on the block bordered by Main, East Pender, Gore, and Keefer Streets. With a population exceeding 30,000, it is the second-largest Chinese community in North America and one of the largest outside Asia.

Stroll through the neighborhood to admire the architecture—right down to the pagoda-roofed telephone booths—or to seek out one of the multitude of restaurants. You'll find markets and genuine Cantonese-style cuisine east of Main Street and tamer Chinese-Canadian dishes along Main Street and to the west. The district's intriguing stores sell a mind-boggling array of Chinese goods—wind chimes, soy sauce, teapots, dried mushrooms, delicate paper fans, and much, much more. Along Main Street shops sell ginseng, sold by the Chinese ounce (38 grams) for up to $400. In addition to selling the herb, the staff at **Ten Ren Tea and Ginseng Co.** (550 Main St., 604/684-1566) explains ginseng preparation methods to buyers and offers tea tasting as well.

To get to Chinatown from downtown catch bus no. 19 or 22 east along Pender Street. Try to avoid East Hastings Street at all times; it's Vancouver's skid row, inhabited by unsavory characters day and night.

Chinese Cultural Centre

This cultural center (50 E. Pender St., 604/687-0729) is the epicenter of community programs for the local Chinese population, but it holds interest for outsiders. Around the corner from the main entrance, the distinctive museum and archives building (555 Columbia St., 604/658-8880; Tues.–Sun. 11 A.M.–5 P.M.; adult $5, senior $3) catalogs the history of Chinese-Canadians in Vancouver. The center also sponsors activities ranging from bonsai displays to cooking classes; admission varies according to what's going on.

Dr. Sun Yat-Sen Classical Chinese Garden

Gardening enthusiasts won't want to miss this peaceful and harmoniously designed garden (578 Carrall St., 604/662-3207; daily 9:30 A.M.–7 P.M.; adult $8.25, senior and student $6.75) behind the Chinese Cultural Centre. Designed by artisans from Suzhou, China—a city famous for its green-thumbed residents—the garden features limestone rockeries, a waterfall and tranquil pools, and beautiful trees and plants hidden away behind tall walls. The garden is styled around Taoist traditions of balance and harmony, achieved through the use of buildings, rocks, plants, and water. The buildings and other manmade elements, including woodcarvings and sculptures, were shipped from China. This was the first authentic classical Chinese garden built outside China, and it remains to this day the largest. Well worthwhile are the tours (free with admission) conducted up to eight times daily. During summer, "Enchanted Evenings" held on the first Friday of each month give visitors a chance to tour the gardens and taste teas from around the world.

Adjacent to the gardens is **Dr. Sun Yat-Sen Park,** where admission is free.

World's Narrowest Office Building

Chinatown grew around the intersection of Pender and Carrall Streets, and although time has seen the heart of the neighborhood move eastward, it's worth wandering down the hill and around the original area. Opposite the entrance to Dr. Sun Yat-Sen Classical Chinese Garden is the **Sam Kee Building** (8 W. Pender St. at the corner of Carrall St.), best known as the world's narrowest office building. When city developers widened surrounding streets in 1912, the Chinese consortium that owned the lot decided to proceed with its planned building, just making it narrower than first intended. The result is a building 1.8 meters (six feet) wide, noted in the *Guinness Book of Records* as the "narrowest building in the world."

FALSE CREEK

False Creek, the narrow tidal inlet that almost cuts downtown off from the rest of the city, has undergone enormous changes over the last 25 years and is now a bona fide tourist attraction. Once Vancouver's main industrial area, False

Creek was transformed for Expo86 with the construction of the Plaza of Nations (which held the Expo's BC Pavilion) and Expo headquarters, now Science World.

B.C. Place Stadium

A Vancouver landmark, this 55,000-seat stadium (777 Pacific Blvd., 604/669-2300) will be the center of attention in 2010 for the opening ceremonies of the Olympic Winter Games. In the meantime, it comes alive for home games of the B.C. Lions, one of the Canadian Football League teams, and is the venue for major trade shows, concerts, and other big events. Stadium tours (604/661-7362; adult $6, senior $5, child $4) depart from Gate H every Friday mid-June through September at 11 A.M. and 1 P.M. and take in the playing field, locker rooms, media lounges, and corporate suites. At Gate A is the **B.C. Sports Hall of Fame and Museum** (604/687-5520; Tues.–Sun. 10 A.M.–5 P.M.; adult $6, senior and child $4). Displays in the Hall of Champions catalog the careers of British Columbia's greatest sports achievers, such as CART racer Greg Moore and skier Nancy Greene Raine. The most moving displays are dedicated to cancer victim Terry Fox and wheelchair-bound Rick Hanson, whose courage in the face of adversity opened the eyes of all Canadians in the late 1970s and early 1980s, respectively. Memorabilia, old photographs, and a few videos commemorate the greats, while the Participation Gallery allows you to run, jump, climb, row, and throw, testing yourself against professional athletes. The easiest way to get there is to take the SkyTrain to Stadium Station.

Science World

The impressive, 17-story-high, geodesic-shaped silver dome (it's best known locally as "the golf ball") stands above the waters of False Creek on the southeast side of city center (1455 Quebec St., 604/443-7440; daily 10 A.M.–5 P.M., until 6 P.M. weekends). Built as the Expo Preview Centre for Expo86, it later housed restaurants, shops, and an Omnimax theater. Today the Vancouver landmark is home to Science World, a museum providing exhibitions that "introduce the world of science to the young and the young at heart." The three main galleries explore the basics of physics, natural history, and music through hands-on displays, while a fourth gallery holds an ever-changing array of traveling exhibits. The

Science World is locally known as "the golf ball."

Science Theatre shows the feature *Over Canada,* a high-definition aerial tour over Canada accompanied by the sounds of Canadian musicians. The Omnimax theater, with one of the world's largest such screens (27 meters/89 feet wide), is still here, featuring science-oriented documentaries. Admission to Science World is adult $12.75, senior or child $8.50; in combination with a ticket to one Omnimax film admission it is $17.75 and $13.50.

The most enjoyable way to get to Science World is aboard a False Creek Ferry from Granville Island or the Vancouver Aquatic Centre. If you don't want to take the ferry, you can drive to the west end of Terminal Avenue—plenty of parking is available—or take the SkyTrain to Main Street Station then walk across the street.

Granville Island

Follow Granville Street southwest through downtown and cross False Creek by bridge or ferry to reach Granville Island. Regarded as one of North America's most successful inner-city, industrial-site redevelopments, the jazzed-up island is *the* place to go on a bright sunny day—allow at least several hours or an entire afternoon for this hive of activity.

You can spend the better part of a day just walking around the island looking at the marina, the many specialty businesses that reflect the island's maritime heritage, fresh food markets, gift shops, restaurants, and theaters. The highlight is colorful **Granville Island Public Market** (daily 9 A.M.–6 P.M.), a hub of activity from dawn to dusk and a lot more than a tourist attraction. Inside the market you'll find all kinds of things to eat—fresh fruit and vegetables, seafood from local waters, a wide variety of meats, specialty ingredients, and prepared ready-to-go meals—along with unique jewelry and crafts, potted plants, and cut flowers.

At the opposite end of the island is the **Emily Carr Institute of Art and Design** (1399 Johnston St., 604/844-3800; free). Named for one of Canada's best-known artists, the facility attracts students from across the country to study fine arts, applied arts, and media arts. Two gal-leries are open to the public. Near the island's vehicular access point, **Granville Island Museums** (1502 Duranleau St., 604/683-1939; Tues.–Sun. 10 A.M.–5:30 P.M.; adult $7.50, child $6) combines three museums under one roof—and one admission price for access to all three. If you're into fishing, the **Sport Fishing Museum** is worth a visit for the collection of historic rods, reels, flies, and gaffs; fishing-related artwork; and the photographic history of fishing in British Columbia. In keeping with the island's heritage, the **Model Ships Museum** displays models of vessels similar to those built on the island, such as tugs, steamers, and fishing boats. The signature exhibit is a four-meter-long replica of a warship. The **Model Trains Museum** claims to hold the world's largest collection of model trains on permanent public display, all running on operational layouts.

To get to the island by boat, jump aboard one of the small **False Creek Ferries.** The boats run regularly between the island, Vancouver Aquatic Centre at Sunset Beach ($2), and Vanier Park ($3.50). Parking on the island is almost impossible, especially on weekends when locals do their fresh-produce shopping. If you do find a spot, it'll have a three-hour maximum time limit. Take the first right upon entering the island to reach **Granville Island Information Centre** (1398 Cartwright St., 604/666-5784, www.granvilleisland.com; daily 9 A.M.–6 P.M.). If you're lucky you may snag one of the two five-minute parking spots out front.

WEST END

The West End (not to be confused with the West Side, south of downtown, or West Vancouver, on the north side of the harbor) lies west of the Central Business District, between Burrard Street and **English Bay Beach,** the gateway to Stanley Park. Wander down Robson or Denman Street and you'll soon see the appeal of the urban lifestyle afforded by life in the West End—the endless outdoor cafés, wide range of dining choices, fashionable boutiques, the sandy beaches of English Bay, and, of course, the proximity of Stanley Park.

Robson Street

What began as an enclave of European businesses has transformed itself into one of Vancouver's most fashionable shopping and dining precincts. If you like to shop in designer boutiques, sample European delicacies, and sip lattes at sidewalk cafés, then this is the place to do it.

The downtown end of this upmarket commercial corridor is glass-topped Robson Square (at Hornby Street). From this point, cross Robson Street to Vancouver's original courthouse—now the Vancouver Art Gallery—a grand stone edifice designed by Francis Rattenbury. Continue west one block to a cultural icon from a different era, the Virgin Megastore at Burrard Street, a massive music store owned by English entrepreneur Richard Branson. Heading east, the next few blocks hold the largest concentration of boutiques, cafés, and restaurants. If anywhere in the city could be called "coffee row," then this would be it. Local companies Blenz, Bagel Street Café, and the Bread Garden are well represented, and Seattle-based Starbucks has four outlets, including two kitty-corner to each other at Thurlow Street.

From the intersection with Jervis Street, Robson Street begins its gradual descent to the West End. The hustle and bustle is behind you, and the corridor is lined with hotels and motels that offer some of the best value to be found in Vancouver, a variety of restaurants, and apartment buildings from the 1960s and 1970s. **Robson Public Market** (1610 Robson St.) occupies an impressive atrium-topped building filled with meat, seafood, dairy products, fruits and vegetables, nuts, flowers, craft vendors, fresh juice and salad bars, and an international food fair.

Two blocks farther west you find yourself at Denman Street: turn left to make your way to English Bay Beach after passing through another restaurant-filled section of the West End; turn right to find bike-rental outlets catering to Stanley Park–bound cyclists.

Barclay Heritage Square

Most of the West End's turn-of-the-20th-century buildings are long gone, but a precinct of nine homes built between 1890 and 1908 has been saved and is preserved as Barclay Heritage Square, which looks much as it would have when the homes were first built, right down to the style of surrounding gardens.

© ANDEW HEMPSTEAD

sunset over English Bay

The only one of the nine open to the public is **Roedde House** (1415 Barclay St., 604/684-7040). Built in 1893, this Queen Anne Revival–style home is a classic example of Vancouver's early residential architecture. Francis Rattenbury, architect of Victoria's Fairmont Empress, designed the two-story residence for Gustav Roedde, Vancouver's first bookbinder. Typical of the era, it features a wide veranda, upstairs porch, and bay windows. It was restored using historical records to ensure accuracy—including the color of the walls and the interior furnishings. Tours of the house cost adult $4, senior and child $3 (June–Aug. Mon.–Sat. 10 A.M.–4 P.M., Sept.–May Wed.–Sat. 2–4 P.M.). The easiest way to get to the house is to take Broughton Street off Robson Street.

◪ STANLEY PARK

Beautiful Stanley Park, a lush 405-hectare (1,000-acre) tree- and garden-carpeted peninsula jutting out into Burrard Inlet, is a sight for sore eyes in any weather—an enormous peaceful oasis sandwiched between the city center's skyscrapers and the North Shore at the other end of Lions Gate Bridge. Unlike other famous parks, like New York's Central Park and London's Royal Park, Stanley Park is a permanent preserve of wilderness in the heart of the city, complete with dense coastal forests and abundant wildlife.

Walk or cycle the 10-kilometer (6.2-mile) **Seawall Promenade** or drive the perimeter via **Stanley Park Drive** to take in beautiful water and city views. Travel along both is one-way in a counterclockwise direction (those on foot can go either way, but if you travel clockwise you'll be going against the flow). For vehicle traffic, the main entrance to Stanley Park is at the beginning of Stanley Park Drive, which veers right from the end of Georgia Street; on foot, follow Denman Street to its north end to find a pathway leading around Coal Harbour into the park. Either way, you'll pass a small information booth where park maps are available. Just before the booth, take Pipeline Road to access **Malkin Bowl,** home to outdoor theater productions; a **rose garden;** and forest-encircled **Beaver Lake.**

Pipeline Road rejoins Stanley Park Drive near the Lions Gate Bridge, but by not returning to the park entrance you'll miss most of the following sights.

Vancouver Aquarium

In the forest behind the information booth is Canada's largest aquarium (604/631-2524; summer daily 9:30 A.M.–7 P.M., the rest of the year daily 10 A.M.–5:30 P.M.; adult $16.50, senior $12.50, child $9.50), the third largest in North America. Guarding the entrance is a five-meter-long killer whale sculpture by preeminent native artist Bill Reid. More than 8,000 aquatic animals and 600 species are on display, representing all corners of the planet, from the oceans of the Arctic to the rainforests of the Amazon. The Wild Coast exhibit features local marine mammals, including sea lions, dolphins, and seals. Other exhibits highlight regional marinelife, including Pacific Canada Pavilion, the first display inside the aquarium entrance. Pacific Canada is of particular interest as it contains a wide variety of sealife from the Gulf of Georgia, including the giant fish of the deep, halibut, and playful little sea otters who frolic in the kelp. At the far end of the aquarium, a large pool holding beluga whales—distinctive pure white marine mammals—and sea lions, which can be viewed from above or below ground, represents Arctic Canada. A part of the complex is also devoted to the rehabilitation of injured marine mammals, and there's a packed interpretive program of talks and tours.

Until the mid-1990s, Stanley Park was home to a zoo; what remains is the **Children's Farmyard** (daily 10 A.M. till dusk) where you can see all types of domesticated animals. It's linked to the aquarium by a short walking path.

Seawall Sights

The following sights are listed from the information booth, which overlooks Coal Harbour, in a counterclockwise direction. From this point, Stanley Park Drive and the Seawall Promenade pass the Royal Vancouver Yacht Club and **Deadman's Island.** Now a naval reserve, the island has a dark history, having witnessed many battles between native tribes, been the burial place of the last of the Coast Salish people, and been used as a quarantine station during an early smallpox epidemic. Off the island is a floating gas station, used by watercraft and floatplanes.

The first worthwhile stop at **Brockton Point** (which refers to the entire eastern tip of the park) is a collection of authentic totem poles from the Kwagiulth people, who lived along the coast north of present-day Vancouver. Before rounding the point itself, you pass the **Nine o'Clock Gun,** which is fired each evening at, you guessed it, 9 P.M. Its original purpose was to allow ship captains to set their chronometers to the exact time. Much of the Brockton Point peninsula is dedicated to sporting fields, and on any sunny afternoon young Vancouverites can be seen playing traditional British pursuits, such as rugby and cricket. Around the point, the road and the seawall continue to hug the shoreline, passing the famous *Girl in Wetsuit* bronze sculpture and a figurehead commemorating Vancouver's links to Japan. Then the two paths divide. The seawall passes directly under the **Lions Gate Bridge,** which opened up the North Shore for development after its 1938 opening. Meanwhile, the vehicular road loops back to a higher elevation to Prospect Point Lookout, a memorial to the SS *Beaver* (which was the first Hudson's Bay Company steamship to travel along this stretch of the coast), and a café (a stairway leads up from the seawall to the café).

The Lions Gate Bridge marks the halfway point of the seawall as well as a change in scenery. From this point to Second Beach the views are westward toward the Strait of Georgia and across English Bay to Central Vancouver. The next stretch of pleasant pathway, about two kilometers long, is sandwiched between the water and steep cliffs, with **Siwash Rock** being the only distinctive landmark. This volcanic outcrop sits just offshore, rising over 15 meters (50 feet) from the lapping waters of English Bay. If you're traveling along Stanley Park Drive, park at the **Hollow Tree** and walk back up the hill to a lookout high above the rock.

Continuing south, the seawall and Stanley Park Drive converge at the south end of **Third**

Beach, a popular swimming and sunbathing spot (and a great place to watch the setting sun). The beach's southern end is guarded by **Ferguson Point,** where a fountain marks the final resting spot of renowned native poet Pauline Johnson. One kilometer (.6 mile) farther back toward the city is **Second Beach,** where there's an outdoor swimming pool, a pitch-and-putt golf course, a putting green, tennis courts, and lawn bowling greens. On summer evenings an area behind the beach is set aside for local dance clubs to practice their skills. From Second Beach it's only a short distance to busy Denman Street and English Bay Beach, or you can cut across the park back to Coal Harbour.

Lost Lagoon

At the time of European settlement, Coal Harbour extended almost all the way across the peninsula to Second Beach. With the receding of the tides, the water would drain out from the head of the inlet, creating a massive tidal flat and inspiring native-born Pauline Johnson to pen the poem "Lost Lagoon," a name that holds to this day. A bridge across the harbor was replaced with a causeway in 1922, blocking the flow of the tide and creating a "real" lagoon. Over the years it has become home to large populations of waterfowl, including great blue herons, trumpeter swans, grebes, and a variety of ducks. A 1.6-kilometer (one-mile) walking trail encircles the lagoon, passing the **Nature House** (southeast corner, 604/257-8544), which holds natural history displays and general park information.

SOUTH OF DOWNTOWN

Officially divided into 18 municipalities, the City of Vancouver encompasses the entire peninsula, including the area south of downtown, a largely residential area that extends west to Point Grey and the University of British Columbia. Vancouver's three largest museums and a number of public gardens lie south of downtown.

Vancouver Museum

Regional history from Precambrian times to the present comes to life at Vancouver Museum (1100

KITSILANO

Named for a Squamish chief and known simply as "Kits" to locals, Kitsilano is a trendy beachside suburb southwest of downtown boasting a young, active population. Extending south to West 16th Avenue and west to Alma Street from Burrard Street, its main attractions are two not-to-be-missed museums in **Vanier Park.** This park extends from Burrard Street Bridge to Maple Street and is a popular spot for walkers, joggers, and cyclists. It's home to the famous Bard on the Beach summertime theater. Greenspace continues beyond Vanier Park to **Kitsilano Beach,** facing English Bay. Vancouver's most popular beach, this spot attracts hordes of bronzed (and not-so-bronzed) bodies to its long sandy beach, warm shallow waters, spectacular mountain views, the city's largest outdoor pool, beach volleyball, and surrounding cafés and restaurants.

Away from the Kitsilano waterfront are two main shopping and dining precincts: West 4th Avenue between Burrard and Balsam Streets and Broadway between Larch and Collingwood Streets.

Chestnut St., 604/736-4431; daily 10 A.M.–5 P.M., Thurs. until 9 P.M.; adult $10, senior $8, child $6) in Vanier Park. The West Coast Archaeology and Culture galleries hold ravishing masks, highly patterned woven blankets, and fine baskets. The Discovery and Settlement Gallery details European exploration of British Columbia—both by land and by sea. The Vancouver Stories gallery depicts various decades, including the 1950s, where a shiny 1955 Ford Fairlane is displayed and black-and-white TVs screen popular shows of the time. After browsing through the forestry and mill-town displays and the metropolis of Vancouver exhibit, you end up in the gallery of changing exhibitions, where you never know what you'll find. The complex also holds a gift shop and a self-serve restaurant overlooking Vanier Park. To reach the museum, catch bus no. 2 or 22 on Burrard Street and get off after Burrard Street Bridge at the Cornwall and Cypress Street stop, or catch a ferry to Vanier Park from Granville Island or

the Aquatic Centre at Sunset Beach. If you're driving, you'll find plenty of parking.

On the east side of the museum is the **City of Vancouver Archives** (1150 Chestnut St., 604/736-8561; Mon.–Fri. 9 A.M.–5 P.M.). This public facility holds around 500,000 photographs, 5,000 books, and a wealth of maps, documents, records, and reports that combine to tell the story of Vancouver's social, economic, and cultural history.

H.R. MacMillan Space Centre

Children especially will love the H.R. MacMillan Space Centre (604/738-7827; summer daily 10 A.M.–5 P.M., closed Monday the rest of the year; adult $13.50, senior $10.50, child $9.50), in the same building as the museum. The main features are displays related to planet Earth, the surrounding universe, and space exploration. Throughout the day, the Ground Station Canada Theater shows 20-minute audiovisual presentations that explore the universe. Other highlights are Virtual Voyages, a flight simulator that makes a five-minute virtual reality journey through space, and the Cosmic Courtyard, a fun learning center.

The Space Centre also presents a popular laser rock music show in the H.R. MacMillan Planetarium (Wed.–Sun. 9 P.M., additional shows Fri. and Sat. at 10:30 P.M.; $8.65).

Gordon MacMillan Southam Observatory

Adjacent to the museum complex is the Gordon MacMillan Southam Observatory (604/738-7827; donation), which is open for public stargazing Monday–Friday sunset to midnight when the skies are clear. You can also visit weekdays 1–3 P.M. to view the Cassgrain telescope.

Vancouver Maritime Museum

Just a five-minute stroll from Vancouver Museum is Vancouver Maritime Museum (1905 Ogden Ave., 604/257-8300; summer daily 10 A.M.–5 P.M., the rest of the year Tues.–Sat. 10 A.M.–5 P.M. and Sun. noon–5 P.M.; adult $8, senior and child $5.50), at the end of Cypress Avenue. Filled with nautical displays that showcase

British Columbia's seafaring legacy, exhibits chronicle everything from the province's first European explorers and their vessels to today's oceangoing adventurers, modern fishing boats, and fancy ships. Beyond the front desk is a historic RCMP vessel, the *St. Roch,* which fills the first main room. Now a National Historic Site, the *St. Roch* was the first patrol vessel to successfully negotiate the infamous Northwest Passage. Beyond the vessel and easy to miss are the large black-and-white images of local waterways from 100 years ago—a real eye-opener to how much and how quickly Vancouver has grown. Children tend to gravitate to the back of the museum to the Maritime Discovery Centre, where they can dress up as fishermen, try their hand at navigation, and crawl through a pirate's cave. To get there from downtown, take bus no. 22 south on Burrard Street or walk down Burrard Street to the Aquatic Centre and hop aboard a False Creek Ferry.

When you're done inside the museum, wander down to the water to view the small fleet of historic vessels docked in the manmade harbor.

VanDusen Botanical Garden

Formerly a golf course, this 22-hectare (54-acre) garden (5251 Oak St. at 37th Ave., 604/878-9274) is home to more 7,500 species from every continent except Antarctica. It's the place to feast your eyes on more than 1,000 varieties of rhododendrons, as well as roses, all kinds of botanical rarities, winter blossoms, an Elizabethan hedge maze, and a children's topiary garden featuring animal shapes. Look for the display board near the front entrance to see what's best for the time of year in which you're visiting. The complex also includes a shop selling cards, perfumes, soaps, potpourri, and all kinds of gifts with a floral theme. At popular **Shaughnessy Restaurant** (604/261-0011; daily 11:30 A.M.–3 P.M. and 5:30–9 P.M.), the light and airy decor, picture windows, and garden view bring the outside inside.

The garden is open in summer daily 10 A.M.–8 P.M., April and October daily 10 A.M.–6 P.M., and the rest of the year daily 10 A.M.–4 P.M. Admission April–September is adult $7.50, senior $5.70, child $3.90; the rest of the year it's adult $5.20, senior $3.60, child $2.10. Admission during special events held throughout the year is higher, including during the **VanDusen Flower and Garden Show,** held the second weekend of June, when entry is adult $13, senior, $12, child free. To get there by bus, take no. 17 south along Burrard Street. Oak Street runs parallel to Granville Street; access to the garden is on the corner of East 33rd Avenue.

Queen Elizabeth Park

Less than two kilometers (1.2 miles) from the VanDusen Botanical Garden, this 53-hectare (130-acre) park sits atop 152-meter-high (500-foot-high) **Little Mountain,** the city's highest point, with magnificent views of Vancouver and the Coast Mountains. Now operated by the Vancouver Board of Parks and Recreation, the land was sold to the city by the CPR in 1929 and quarried for rock to build roads. The land today is a paradise of sweeping lawns, trees, flowering shrubs, masses of rhododendrons—a vivid spectacle in May and June—formal flower gardens including a rose garden in the park's southwest corner, sunken gardens in the old quarry pits, and mature plantings of native trees from across Canada. Public facilities include tennis courts and a pitch-and-putt golf course.

The highlight of the park is the magnificent **Bloedel Floral Conservatory** (604/257-8570; summer Mon.–Fri. 9 A.M.–8 P.M. and Sat.–Sun. 10 A.M.–9 P.M., the rest of the year daily 10A.M.–5:30 P.M.; adult $4.10, senior $2.90, child $2), a glass-domed structure rising 40 meters (130 feet) and enclosing a temperature-controlled, humid tropical jungle. Inside you'll find a profusion of exotic flowering plants and a resident avian population including multihued parrots.

The park's main entrance is by the junction of 33rd Avenue West and Cambie Street; to get there from downtown take bus no. 15 south on Burrard Street.

UNIVERSITY OF BRITISH COLUMBIA

The UBC campus sprawls across **Point Grey,** the westernmost point of Vancouver and the southern extremity of Burrard Inlet. It enjoys a spectacular coastal location, surrounded by parkland laced with hiking trails. Many of the trails provide access to the beach. The campus encompasses over 400 hectares (990 acres) and serves up to 35,000 students at one time. If you're interested in learning more about the university, join one of the free student-led tours that leave the Student Union Building (near the main university bus interchange; May–Aug. Mon.–Fri. at 10 A.M. and 1 P.M.). Call 604/822-8687 for information.

Museum of Anthropology

Containing the world's largest collection of arts and crafts of the Pacific Northwest native peoples, this excellent on-campus museum should not be missed (6393 Northwest Marine Dr., 604/822-5087, summer daily 10 A.M.–5 P.M., the rest of the year Tues.–Sun. 11 A.M.–5 P.M.; adult $9, senior and child $7). Designed by innovative Canadian architect Arthur Erickson, the ultramodern concrete-and-glass building perches on a high cliff overlooking the Pacific Ocean and mimics the post-and-beam structures favored by the Coast Salish.

The entrance is flanked by panels in the shape of a Bent-box, which the Salish believed contained the meaning of life. Inside, a ramp lined with impressive sculptures by renowned modern-day carvers leads to the Great Hall, a cavernous room dominated by towering totem poles collected from along the coast and interspersed with other ancient works. A museum highlight is the collection of works by Haida artist Bill Reid, which includes *The Raven and the First Men.* It was carved from a four-ton chunk of yellow cedar, is drenched in natural light, and sits on sand from the Queen Charlotte Islands. The surrounding seats are a popular spot to sit and simply stare. Other displays include intricate carvings, baskets, ceremonial masks, fabulous jewelry, and European ceramics. The museum holds over 200,000 artifacts, most of which are stored in uniquely accessible research collections. Instead of being stored in musty boxes out back and available only to anthropologists, the collections are stored in the main museum—in row upon row of glass-enclosed cabinets and in drawers that visitors are encouraged to open. Details of each piece are noted in binders.

Outside, a deliciously scented woodland path on the left side of the museum leads to a reconstructed Haida village and contemporary totem poles with descriptive plaques.

If you have your own vehicle, make sure you have a fistful of change to park in the lot beside the museum ($1 for every 20 minutes). The museum is open until 9 P.M. on Tuesday, with admission free after 5 P.M.

University Gardens

Just south of the Museum of Anthropology is the serene **Nitobe Memorial Garden** (604/822-9666; summer daily 10 A.M.–6 P.M.; adult $3, senior $2, child $1.50), named for and dedicated to a prominent Japanese educator. Spread over one hectare (2.5 acres), this traditional Japanese garden of shrubs and miniatures has two distinct sections: the Stroll Garden, laid out in a form that symbolizes the journey through life, and the Tea Garden, the place to contemplate life from a ceremonial teahouse. The garden is surrounded by high walls (which almost block out the noise of traffic from busy Marine Drive), making it a peaceful retreat. Outside of summer, the garden is open limited hours (Mon.–Fri. 11 A.M.–2:30 P.M.), but admission is free.

Also on campus is the delightful **UBC Botanical Garden** (6804 Marine Dr., 604/822-4208; adult $5, senior $3, child $2). Set among coastal forest, the 44-hectare (110-acre) garden dates to the turn of the 20th century and features eight separate sections, which hold around 10,000 species of trees, shrubs, and flowers. The various gardens have themes of specific regions or environments. Highlights include Canada's largest collection of rhododendrons in the Asian Garden; a B.C. Native Garden alive with the plants, flowers, and shrubs found along the Pacific Northwest coast; a display of mountain plants from the world's continents in the Alpine Garden; medieval healing plants in the Physick Garden; and an interesting planting of fruit and vegetables in the Food Garden. Thriving in Vancouver's mild climate, the garden offers something of interest year-round, with the main season running mid-

March to mid-October when it's open 10 A.M.–6 P.M. (the rest of the year 10 A.M.–3 P.M.). From the Museum of Anthropology, follow Marine Drive south for 2.4 kilometers (1.5 miles) to 16th Avenue.

RICHMOND

The incorporated city of Richmond (pop. 170,000) sprawls across **Lulu Island** at the mouth of the Fraser River. Most visitors to Vancouver cross the island on their way north from the United States on Highway 99, or to and from the airport or Tsawwassen Ferry Terminal. Steveston is the main reason to visit Richmond, but on the way, consider escaping the suburban sprawl at **Richmond Nature Park** at the junction of Highways 91 and 99. This 85-hectare (210-acre) park has been left in its natural state; the only development comprises trails leading to ponds and fens. The park is open daily during daylight hours.

Steveston

On Lulu Island's southwestern extremity, the historic fishing village of Steveston is a lively spot worth a visit. In the 1880s it had over 50 canneries and was the world's largest fishing port. The harbor still holds Canada's largest fleet of commercial fishing boats.

One block south of Moncton Street and a short walk from the old cannery is redeveloped stretch of harborfront that bustles with activity in summer. Casual visitors and locals mingle at fishing-supply outlets, shops selling packaged seafood products, boutiques, and restaurants. Below the main wharf, fishing boats sell the day's catch—halibut, salmon, lingcod, rock cod, crab, and shrimp—to the general public at excellent prices. The fisherfolk are friendly enough, chatting happily about their catch and how best to cook it up. Naturally, seafood is the specialty at harborfront restaurants, all with outdoor tables. The most casual option is a take-out meal from **Sockeye City Diner** (604/275-6790); order at the window and spread out your feast on the wharf or dock. On a floating dock down toward the cannery is **Pa Jo's** (604/204-0767; daily

11 A.M.–7:30 P.M.), cooking up classic battered fish and chips with a wedge of lemon for around $9. Tables are set on the dock and on the wharf high above.

On the harborfront you'll find the **Gulf of Georgia Cannery National Historic Site** (12138 4th Ave., 604/664-9009; June–Sept. daily 10 A.M.–5 P.M., spring and fall Thurs.–Mon. 10 A.M.–5 P.M.; adult $6.50, senior $5, child $3.25), a cannery that operated 1894–1979. Much of the original cannery has been restored. In addition to canning line exhibits and demonstrations of the various machinery, an audiovisual presentation is offered in the Boiler House Theatre, and the Discovery area is set aside for children. Another historic site, the **Britannia Heritage Shipyard** (5180 Westwater Dr., 604/718-8050; May–Sept. Tues.–Sun. 10 A.M.–6 P.M., the rest of the year weekends noon–4 P.M.) is reached by following the signs east along Moncton Street. Dating to 1885, the actual Britannia Shipyard building is currently being restored, but it is surrounded by four already restored buildings from the same era, five others in various states of disrepair, and a variety of interesting wooden vessels.

Another interesting Steveston attraction is **Steveston Museum,** in the old Royal Bank building (3811 Moncton St., 604/271-6868; Mon.–Sat. 9:30 A.M.–5 P.M.; closed for lunch 1–1:30 P.M.). At the west end of Moncton Street is **Garry Point Park,** a windswept piece of land jutting into the Strait of Georgia, with views extending to the Southern Gulf Islands.

To get to Steveston, take Highway 99 to the Steveston Highway exit, then head west, passing by a magnificent Buddhist temple. Town center is south from the Steveston Highway along the No. 1 Road.

DELTA

Pass under the South Arm of the Fraser River via Highway 99 and the George Massey Tunnel and you'll emerge in the sprawling industrial and residential district of Delta (pop. 100,000). The first township in the Delta area was Ladner's Landing, which was developed as a port facility for local farmers. Take Highway 17 (Exit 28) south from Highway 99 and turn right on Ladner Trunk Road to access modern-day **Ladner Village.** In the heart of this riverside commercial center is **Delta Museum and Archives** (4858 Delta St., 403/946-9322; Tues.–Sat. 10 A.M.–3:30 P.M.; donation). This museum tells the story of the area's first inhabitants, the Salish, and the farming and fishing history of more recent times.

Entering Delta from the north, the George Massey Tunnel passes under 70-hectare (170-acre) **Deas Island,** where marshes, dunes, and a high density of birdlife are protected within the boundaries of a regional park. Deas is linked to the mainland by a causeway; take the same exit from Highway 99 as detailed above, but cross over the highway and head north beyond the Delta Town and Country Inn to McNeeleys Way, which crosses onto the island. East of the Deas Island access is **Burns Bog,** a natural waste-

land not suitable for development. In fact, it remains in its natural state, North America's largest urban wilderness and one of Canada's largest peat bogs.

In the opposite direction, River Road West provides access to Westham Island and George C. Reifel Bird Sanctuary. It passes through a typical suburban scene of modern houses and well-tended gardens but then enters a time warp of intriguing fishing shacks, maritime-related businesses, and floating houses.

George C. Reifel Bird Sanctuary

Two kilometers (1.2 miles) from Ladner Village along River Road West, cross Canoe Passage on the old wooden bridge to access this great wildlife sanctuary far enough from the city to be missed by most visitors (604/946-6980; gates open daily 9 A.M.–4 P.M.; adult $4, senior and child $2). The 350-hectare (800-acre) sanctuary protects the northern corner of low-lying Westham Island, a stopover for thousands of migratory birds in spring and fall. In the middle of a wide delta at the mouth of the Fraser River, the island is a world away from surrounding urban life.

The best time for a visit is during the spectacular snow goose migration, which runs from early November to mid-December. Otherwise, you'll see abundant migratory birdlife anytime between October and April. The island also serves as a permanent home for many bird species, including bald eagles, peregrine falcons, herons, swans, owls, and a parking lot filled with ducks.

The sanctuary, which provides free birdseed, encompasses many easy walking trails, an observation tower, and a couple of picnic areas.

SURREY

The City of Surrey is well within the Greater Vancouver Regional District (GVRD) but is officially its own incorporated city—with a population of 350,000, it's British Columbia's second largest. Surrey sprawls from the Fraser River in the north to White Rock and the international boundary in the south, and from Delta in the west to Langley in the east. Its first settlers were the Stewarts, who built a homestead beside the

© ANDREW HEMPSTEAD

Blue herons are one of many species at the Geroge C. Reifel Bird Sanctuary.

Nicomekl River in 1894. The original homestead is now the centerpiece of **Elgin Heritage Park** (13723 Crescent Rd., 250/543-3456; Mon.–Fri. 10 A.M.–4 P.M., Sat.–Sun. noon–4 P.M.). The farm's original workers' accommodations have been transformed into a weaving center, where textiles are created on antique looms and spinning wheels. Also on the property is a barn full of antique farm machinery and a covered display telling the story of the local crabbing industry. Behind the farmhouse picnic tables offer views north to the Coast Mountains. To get there, take the King George Highway exit off Highway 99, then turn onto Elgin Road, which becomes Crescent Road.

White Rock

Named for a 400-ton glacial erratic that sits by the shoreline, this incorporated city of 17,000 lies right on the international border and surrounds the **Douglas Border Crossing.** Take 8th Avenue west from the first interchange north of the border to reach downtown White Rock. Marine Drive hugs the coastline for five kilometers (3.1 miles), lined almost the entire way with outdoor cafés, restaurants, old beach houses, and

ocean-inspired condominiums. At around 149th Street is the main concentration of restaurants, an information center, and a long pier. Although the entire strip bustles with activity on summer weekends, this section is super-busy. The city's namesake lies above the high tide mark just south of the pier. It is now painted bright white and impossible to miss. The beach is no Caribbean gem, but at low tide, locals flock to the wide expanse of sand to bake in the sun, wade in shallow water, or play Frisbee.

NORTH SHORE

North of downtown lie the incorporated cities of **North Vancouver** (pop. 48,000) and **West Vancouver** (pop. 43,000), both of which are dramatically sandwiched between the North Shore Range of the Coast Mountains and Burrard Inlet. The North Shore is accessible from downtown via the **Lions Gate Bridge,** but the SeaBus, which runs from Waterfront Station to **Lonsdale Quay** (adults $3 each way), offers a more enjoyable alternative to getting caught in bridge traffic. At the lively quay, a small information center (to the right as you come out of

© ANDREW HEMPSTEAD

Crowds flock to White Rock beaches throughout the summer.

the SeaBus terminal) dispenses valuable information, and transit buses depart regularly for all the sights listed below.

Capilano Suspension Bridge

Admission at this major North Shore attraction (604/985-7474; summer daily 8 A.M.–dusk, the rest of the year daily 9 A.M.–5 P.M.) is a bit steep (adult $22, senior $16.50, child $11), but it's one of Vancouver's most popular sights. The first bridge across the Capilano River opened in 1899. That remarkable wood-and-hemp structure stretched 137 meters (450 feet) across the deep canyon. Today, several bridges later, a wood-and-wire suspension bridge spans the canyon some 70 fearsome meters (230 feet) above the Capilano River. Allow at least two hours to walk the bridge, step out onto the numerous cantilevered decks, take the Treetops Adventure suspended walkway, and wander along the forested nature trails. Back near the main entrance, native carvers display their skills in the Big House, and you'll find the requisite gift shop and eateries. To get there by car, cross Lions Gate Bridge, turn east onto Marine Drive then immediately north onto Capilano Road, continuing to 3735 Capilano, on your left. By bus, take no. 246 north on Georgia Street or hop aboard the SeaBus and take bus no. 236 from Lonsdale Quay.

If you don't want to spend the money, you can get much the same thrill by crossing the free bridge in Lynn Canyon Park.

Capilano Salmon Hatchery

This is my favorite North Shore attraction—and not only because it's free. If you've always wanted to know more about the miraculous life cycle of salmon, or want some facts to back up your fish stories, visit this hatchery on the Capilano River, just upstream from the suspension bridge (604/666-1790; summer daily 8 A.M.–8 P.M., until dusk the rest of the year). Beside the rushing Capilano River and ensconced in cool rainforest, salmon are diverted through a channel and into manmade spawning grounds. The channel is topped by a metal grate in one section and lined with glass windows in another. This allows up-close viewing of the salmon as they fight the cur-

rent through their July to October run. In addition to the life-cycle displays, an exhibit on fly-fishing holds some interesting old tackle.

Grouse Mountain Skyride

Continuing north, Capilano Road becomes Nancy Greene Way and ends at the base of the **Grouse Mountain Skyride** (604/980-9311; adult $27, senior $25, child $10), North America's largest aerial tramway. For an excellent view of downtown Vancouver, Stanley Park, the Pacific Ocean, and as far south as Mount Baker (Washington), take the almost-vertical eight-minute ride on the gondola to the upper slopes of 1,250-meter (4,100-foot) Grouse Mountain. The gondola runs year-round, departing every 15 minutes 10 A.M.–10 P.M. in summer.

The trip to the top is a lot more than a gondola ride—and it's easy to spend the best part of a day exploring the surrounding area and taking advantage of the attractions included in the price of the ride up. Of the many possible hikes, the one-kilometer (.6-mile) **Blue Grouse Interpretive Trail** is the easiest and most enjoyable, winding around a lake and through a rainforest. Another trail leads to a fenced area where wolves and bears are rehabilitated after being orphaned. The best-known hike is the **Grouse Grind,** from the base of the gondola to the top. It's so named for a reason—the trail gains over one kilometer (3,300 feet) of elevation in just 2.9 kilometers (1.8 miles). Thousands of locals make the trek daily as part of a self-imposed fitness program, with upwards of 100,000 completing the trail each summer season. Once at the top, it costs $5 for a one-way ticket back down. Other summit activities include a fun but touristy logging show, chairlift rides, a First Nations longhouse with dancing and storytelling, and wide-screen movie presentations of the outdoor wonders of British Columbia and local wildlife.

Mountaintop dining facilities are contained in a magnificent log day lodge decorated with stylish West Coast artwork. Options include a coffee bar; the casual **Altitudes Bistro,** where you can drink in some high-elevation sunshine from the expansive deck (daily 11 A.M.–10 P.M.); and the upscale **Observatory Restaurant,** which provides free Skyride tickets with dinner reservations (open daily from 5 P.M.).

In winter, skiers and snowboarders choose from beginner to moderately advanced runs on the slopes of Grouse Mountain, with the added magic of lighted runs after dark (see *Recreation*).

To get to the gondola, cross the Lions Gate Bridge from downtown; take the North Vancouver exit, then follow Capilano Road for five kilometers (3.1 miles) up the valley. By public transport, take the SeaBus to Lonsdale Quay, then take bus no. 236 to the gondola's lower terminal.

Lynn Canyon Park

On its way to Burrard Inlet, Lynn Creek flows through a deep canyon straddled by this 240-hectare (930-acre) park. Spanning the canyon is the "other" suspension bridge. The one here, built in 1912, is half as wide as its more famous counterpart over the Capilano River, but it's a few meters higher and, best of all, it's free. An ancient forest of Douglas fir surrounds the impressive canyon and harbors a number of hiking trails. Also visit **Lynn Canyon Ecology Centre** (604/981-3103; daily 10 A.M.–5 P.M.; free), where displays, models, and free slide shows and films explore plant and animal ecology.

Lynn Canyon Park is seven kilometers (4.3 miles) east of the Capilano River. To get there by car, take the Lynn Valley Road exit off Highway 1, east of the Lions Gate Bridge. By public transport, take the SeaBus to Lonsdale Quay, then bus no. 228 or 229.

Mount Seymour Provincial Park and Vicinity

Hikers and skiers flock to this 3,508-hectare (8,670-acre) park 20 kilometers (12.4 miles) northeast of downtown. The park lies off Mount Seymour Parkway, which splits east off the Trans-Canada Highway just north of Burrard Inlet. The long and winding access road to the park climbs steadily through an ancient forest of western hemlock, cedar, and Douglas fir to a small facility area at an elevation of 1,000 meters (3,300 feet). From the parking lot, trails lead to the summit of 1,453-meter (4,770-foot) Mount Sey-

mour; allow one hour for the two-kilometer (one-way) trek.

If you continue along Mount Seymour Parkway instead of turning north toward the park, you end up in the scenic little village of **Deep Cove** on the west shore of Indian Arm (off the northeast end of Burrard Inlet)—an excellent spot for a picnic. Take your sack lunch to the waterfront park and watch the fishing and pleasure boats coming and going in the bay. More adventurous visitors can swim, kayak, or scuba dive.

Cypress Provincial Park

This 3,012-hectare (7,440-acre) park northwest of downtown encompasses a high alpine area in the North Shore Mountains. To get to the park, take the TransCanada Highway 12 kilometers (7.5 miles) west of Lions Gate Bridge and turn north onto Cypress Bowl Road (Exit 8). Even the park access road up from the TransCanada Highway is worthwhile for the views. At the second switchback, the Highview Lookout provides a stunning panorama of the city, with interpretive panels describing the surrounding natural history. Just beyond the third switchback is another lookout, along with picnic tables. At the 12-kilometer (7.5-mile) mark, the road splits. Go straight ahead to reach Cypress Bowl ski area, where during summer over the next few years this will be a hive of activity as the area is redeveloped in preparation of hosting the freestyle skiing and snowboarding events of the 2010 Olympic Winter Games. Regardless of base area construction, there's plenty of hiking in the vicinity. From the main day lodge, well-marked hiking trails radiate out like spokes. One easy trail leads under the Black Chair (to the left as you stand in front of the day lodge) and passes a small alpine lake before ending after 1.3 kilometers (.8 mile) at a lookout; allow one hour for the round-trip. The 2.3-kilometer (1.4-mile) circuit to Yew Lake gains less elevation and is barrier free.

Lighthouse Park

On a headland jutting into Howe Sound, Lighthouse Park lies eight kilometers (five miles) west of the Lions Gate Bridge. Trails lead through the park to coastal cliffs and a lighthouse that guides shipping into narrow Burrard Inlet. Views from the lighthouse grounds are spectacular, extending west over the Strait of Georgia and east to Stanley Park and the Vancouver skyline.

Horseshoe Bay

The pretty little residential area of Horseshoe Bay offers plenty to see and do while you wait for the Vancouver Island or Sunshine Coast ferry. If you and your trusty vehicle are catching one of the ferries, buy your ticket at the car booth, move your automobile into the lineup, then explore the town. Several restaurants, a bakery, a supermarket, a pub, and a couple of good delis cater to the hungry and thirsty. A stroll along the beautiful waterfront marina is a good way to cool your heels and dawdle away some waiting time.

M Bowen Island

From Vancouver, this is the most accessible of hundreds of islands dotting the Strait of Georgia. The island is only a short ferry trip from Horseshoe Bay, but it seems a world away from the city. The first European settlers were loggers, but Bowen Island has also been home to a fishing and whaling industry. Vancouverites began holidaying on the island as early as 1900, and soon a hotel, complete with tennis courts, lawn bowling, and a grove of fruit trees, had opened. By the 1920s, the island was catering to tens of thousands of summer visitors annually, and grand plans were put in place to open North America's most luxurious resort. The development never eventuated, and today the island is home to a permanent population of 3,200, many of whom work in Vancouver, commuting daily across the water.

The ferry docks at the island's main settlement, aptly named **Snug Cove,** where you'll find all the services of a small town, including bed-and-breakfasts and cafés. There's good swimming at Mannion Bay, near Snug Cove, and **Bowen Island Sea Kayaking** (604/947-9266) rents kayaks (three hours, $30–40) and offers tours (three hours, $50 per person), but the rest of island is also good to explore. A two-kilometer

(1.2-mile) trail leads from Snug Cove to Killarney Lake, where birdlife is prolific and roads lead across to the island's west coast.

BC Ferries (604/669-1211) operates a 20-minute service between Horseshoe Bay and the island daily 6 A.M.–9:45 P.M. approximately once an hour. The fare is adult $6.25, child $3.25. The ferries also take vehicles ($19.75), but these aren't necessary as most visitors set out on foot. **Harbour Air** (604/274-1277) offers an interesting tour to Bowen Island, departing downtown at 7 P.M. April–September. For $175 you'll be whisked to the island by floatplane, enjoy dinner at an island restaurant, and return to your hotel by ferry and limousine.

Island information is available in the chamber of commerce office (Government St. and Grafton St., www.bowenisland.org) during regular business hours.

EAST FROM DOWNTOWN

When you leave Vancouver and head due east, you travel through the most built-up and heavily populated area of British Columbia, skirting modern commercial centers, residential suburbs, and zones of heavy industry. Greater Vancouver extends almost 100 kilometers (62 miles) along the Fraser Valley, through mostly residential areas. The main route east is the TransCanada Highway, which parallels the Fraser River to the south, passing through Burnaby, Langley, and Abbotsford. The original path taken by this highway crosses the Fraser River at New Westminster, the capital of British Columbia for a short period in the 1860s.

Burnaby

Immediately east of downtown, Burnaby was incorporated as a city in 1992 (its population of 200,000 makes it British Columbia's third largest city), but in reality it's part of Vancouver's suburban sprawl. It extends east from Boundary Road to Coquitlam, while Burrard Inlet lies to the north and riverside New Westminster to the southeast. The TransCanada Highway bisects Burnaby, but access is easiest via the SkyTrain, which makes four stops within the city. Among these stops is **Metrotown,** which is Vancouver's largest shopping mall.

Burnaby Village Museum is a four-hectare (10-acre) open-air museum (604/293-6500; May–early Sept. 11 A.M.–4:30 P.M.; adult $8, senior and child $5.70) in Deer Lake Park, on the south side of the TransCanada Highway; to get there take Exit 33 south, then turn left onto Canada Way and right onto Deer Lake Avenue, or take the SkyTrain to Metrotown Station and jump aboard bus no. 144. The village is a reconstruction of how a B.C. town would have looked in the first 20 years of the 1900s, complete with over 30 shops and houses, heritage-style gardens, a miniature railway, and costumed staff. But the highlight is a historic carousel with more than 30 restored wooden horses.

On the north side of the TransCanada Highway is **Burnaby Mountain Park,** which surrounds the campus of **Simon Fraser University,** the province's second-largest campus. Centennial Way (off Burnaby Mountain Parkway) leads to the park's high point, where views extend down Burrard Inlet to North Vancouver and its stunning mountain backdrop. Also at the summit is a collection of totem poles, some Japanese sculptures, a rose garden, and a restaurant. The university itself is worthy of inspection. Its unique design of "quadrants" linked by a massive fountain-filled courtyard is typical of architect Arthur Erickson, who was partly responsible for its design. The **Museum of Archaeology and Ethnology** (Academic Quadrangle 8602, 604/291-3325; Mon.–Fri. 10 A.M.–4 P.M.; donation) holds a collection of native artifacts gathered from along the Pacific Northwest coast.

Vicinity of Coquitlam

Coquitlam (pop. 115,000) is a residential area north and east of Burnaby. It lies at the head of Burrard Inlet, near Port Moody, which was once slated as the terminus of the transcontinental railway. There's nothing of real interest in Coquitlam itself, but Loco Road leads around Burrard Inlet to **Belcarra Regional Park,** which is lapped by the waters of Indian Arm.

North of Coquitlam is **Pinecone Burke Provincial Park,** which protects 38,000 hectares (94,000 acres) of the North Shore Range. It extends along the west shoreline of Pitt Lake (opposite Golden Ears Provincial Park) and as far west as the Boise Valley, scene of a short-lived gold rush in the late 1800s. Much of the park was logged over 100 years ago, but a few sections of old-growth forest remain, including a 1,000-year-old stand of cedar in the Cedar Spirit Grove. To get to the park from Highway 7, take Coast Meridian Road north to Harper Road, which leads to Munro and Dennett Lakes.

Golden Ears Provincial Park

Encompassing 62,540 hectares (154,540 acres) of the Coast Mountains east of downtown Vancouver, this park extends from the Alouette River, near the suburb of Maple Ridge, north to Garibaldi Provincial Park. To get to the main facility areas, follow Highway 7 east out of the city for 40 kilometers (25 miles) to Maple Ridge, then follow signs north. Much of the park was logged for railway ties in the 1920s, but today the second-growth montane forest—dominated by western hemlock—has almost erased the early human devastation.

The park access road follows the Alouette River into the park, ending at Alouette Lake. The river and lake provide fair fishing, but the park's most popular activity is hiking. **Lower Falls Trail** begins at the end of the road and leads 2.7 kilometers (1.7 miles) along Gold Creek to a 10-meter-high (33-foot-high) waterfall; allow one hour each way. Across Gold Creek, **West Canyon Trail** climbs 200 meters over 1.5 kilometers (.9 mile) to a viewpoint of Alouette Lake. This trail begins from the West Canyon parking lot, where you'll also find a 12-kilometer (7.5-mile) trail along the west bank of Gold Creek to Panorama Ridge and to the summit of the park's namesake, the **Golden Ears.** The name comes from the way the setting sun reflects off the twin peaks of Mount Blanchard. This trail gains 1,500 meters (4,920 feet) in elevation, making it an extremely strenuous hike, best undertaken as an overnight trip.

The turnoff to Golden Ears is in Maple Ridge, 34 kilometers (21 miles) west of Mission. From the west, it's a 40-kilometer (25-mile) drive from downtown, either along Highway 1, then Highway 7, or along the more scenic Highway 7A, a continuation of Hastings Street that follows the shoreline of Burrard Inlet through Coquitlam. Either way, from Highway 7, take 232nd Street north for five kilometers (3.1 miles), then 132nd Avenue east to access the park.

New Westminster

"New West," as it's best known, is a densely populated residential area 15 kilometers (9.3 mile) southeast of downtown. Its strategic location, where the Fraser River divides, caused it to become a hub of river transportation and a thriving economic center. It was declared the capital of the mainland colony in 1859, then the provincial capital 1866–1868. Only a few historic buildings remain, and the old port area has been totally overtaken by modern developments. The center of the action is **Westminster Quay Market,** along the riverfront and below the old main street. Although it's open for very un-market-like hours (not until 9:30 A.M. each day), it holds an interesting selection of fresh produce, takeout food stalls, and specialty shops. Out front is the **_Samson V,_** built in 1937 and the last remaining paddle wheeler left on the river when it was retired in 1980. It's now open for public inspection (June–Aug. daily noon–5 P.M.); call the local museum at 604/527-

4640 for details. Beside the market is the **Fraser River Discovery Centre** (788 Quayside Dr., 604/521-8401; Tues.–Sat. 10 A.M.–4 P.M., Sun. 1–4 P.M.), which describes the river and its importance to the development of New Westminster. Other interpretive boards are spread along the boardwalk in front of the market, as is the unlikely combination of a floating casino, a tugboat-themed playground, and the world's largest tin soldier.

An easy walk from the riverfront is **Irving House Historical Centre** (511 Royal Ave., 604/527-4640; summer Wed.–Sun. 9:30 A.M.–5 P.M.), once the home of riverboat captain William Irving and his family. Constructed in 1865, this Victorian-era mansion is one of Western Canada's oldest standing residential buildings. The adjacent **New Westminster Museum** (same hours) catalogs the history of the area.

The easiest way to reach New West from downtown is by SkyTrain. By vehicle, take the Kingsway out of the city. This stretch of road becomes 10th Avenue, winding around the north side of New West's downtown commercial district before crossing the Fraser River as McBride Boulevard. Turn right at the last intersection (Columbia Street) on the north side of the river to reach the riverfront and the heart of the action. Alternatively, take the SkyTrain from any downtown station.

Recreation

WALKING AND HIKING

Stanley Park

Vancouver is not a particularly good city to explore on foot, but it does have one redeeming factor for foot travelers—Stanley Park, an urban oasis crisscrossed with hiking trails and encircled by a 10-kilometer (6.2-mile) promenade that hugs the shoreline. The route passes many points of interest (see _Sights_), benches, and interpretive plaques pointing out historical events. Allow three hours for the entire circuit. The promenade can be walked in either direction, but those on bikes and skates must travel coun-

terclockwise. It is _always_ packed, especially in late afternoon and on weekends.

Away from the Seawall Promenade, you'll find most trails a lot less busy. A good alternative to exploring one long section of the promenade is to ascend the steps immediately north of Lions Gate Bridge to Prospect Point (and maybe stop for a snack at the café), then continue west along the Merilees Trail, which follows the top of the cliff band to Third Beach. Along the way, an old lookout point affords excellent views of Siwash Rock and the Strait of Georgia.

The isthmus of land linking the park to the rest of the downtown peninsula is less than one kilometer (.6 mile) wide, but it's mostly taken up by Lost Lagoon. A 1.5-kilometer (.9-mile) trail (30 minutes round-trip) encircles this bird-filled body of water. In the heart of the park is Beaver Lake, a small body of water, but still alive with birds throughout summer. Trails lead into this lake from all directions, and it can easily be circled in 20 minutes.

False Creek

From English Bay Beach, a promenade continues along English Bay to Sunset Beach and Vancouver Aquatic Centre. The small ferries that operate on False Creek, extending service as far west as the Aquatic Centre, open up a number of walking combinations around False Creek. Granville Island is a good starting point. No official trails go around the island, but if you walk east from the market, you pass a community of floating houses and go through a grassed area to Lookout Hill. Continue around the island and you'll come across a small footbridge leading to the mainland. From this point, it's seven kilometers (4.3 miles) around the head of False Creek, passing Science World and the Plaza of Nations, then closely following the water to the foot of Hornby Street for the short ferry trip back across to Granville Island; allow two hours without stopping.

Pacific Spirit Regional Park and Vicinity

This 762-hectare (1,880-acre) park on the Vancouver peninsula offers 35 kilometers (22 miles) of hiking trails through a forested environment similar to that which greeted the first European settlers more than 200 years ago. A good starting point is the **Park Centre** (16th Ave. W, west of Blanca St., 604/224-5739; Mon.–Fri. 8 A.M.– 4 P.M.), which has a supply of trail maps. The entire park is crisscrossed with trails, so although getting seriously lost is impossible, taking the wrong trail and ending up away from your intended destination is easy. One good trailhead is opposite a residential area in the east of the park, at the junction of Imperial Road and King Edward Avenue. From this point, the Imperial Trail heads west through a forest of red cedar and fir, crosses Salish Creek, then emerges on Southwest Marine Drive, across the road from a plaque that notes the many explorers who contributed to opening up Vancouver to European settlement. From this lofty viewpoint,

© ANDREW HEMPSTEAD

The Seawall Promenade around Stanley Park is the city's most popular walk.

STANLEY PARK

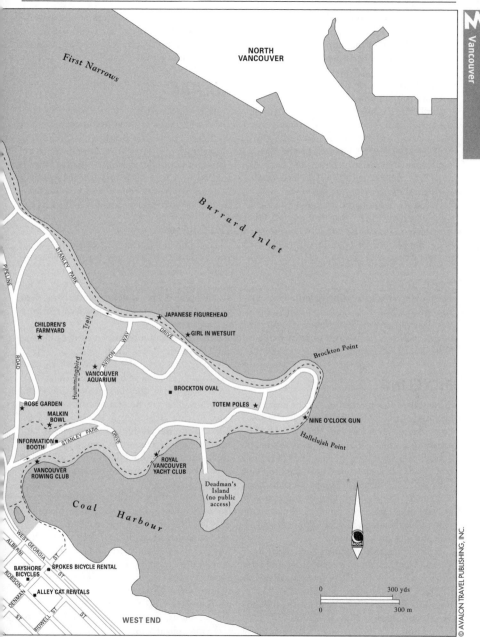

Vancouver

NORTH VANCOUVER

First Narrows

Burrard Inlet

Brockton Point

JAPANESE FIGUREHEAD
★ GIRL IN WETSUIT

CHILDREN'S
FARMYARD
★

STANLEY PARK

Hummingbird Trail

PIPELINE

ROAD

AVISON WAY

DRIVE

VANCOUVER
AQUARIUM
★

BROCKTON OVAL
■

ROSE GARDEN
★

TOTEM POLES ★

NINE O'CLOCK GUN
★

MALKIN
BOWL
★

Hallelujah Point

INFORMATION ■
BOOTH

STANLEY PARK DRIVE

VANCOUVER
ROWING CLUB
★

ROYAL
VANCOUVER
YACHT CLUB
★

Deadman's
Island
(no public
access)

Coal Harbour

WEST GEORGIA ST

ALBERNI

ROBSON
ST

BAYSHORE ■
BICYCLES

■ SPOKES BICYCLE RENTAL

DENMAN
ST

■ ALLEY CAT RENTALS

BIDWELL ST

ST

WEST END

0   300 yds

0   300 m

MOON

© AVALON TRAVEL PUBLISHING, INC.

the view extends across the Strait of Georgia. This trail is 2.8 kilometers (1.7 miles) one-way; allow two hours for the round-trip. In the same vicinity as the trailhead detailed above, at the west end of 19th Avenue, a short boardwalk trail leads to Camosun Bog, home to a great variety of plants and birds.

In the north of the park, north of Chancellor Boulevard, trails lead through deep ravines and across Marine Drive to Arcadia and Spanish Banks Beaches. Walk along these beaches then up any ravine, across Marine Drive, and along Admiral Trail, following the bluffs for a circuit that can be as short or as long as you wish.

For the more ambitious, it is possible to use the trails of Pacific Spirit Park and around Point Grey to circumnavigate the UBC campus; 14 kilometers (8.7 miles) round-trip (allow 4–5 hours).

North Shore

The provincial parks along the North Shore contain outstanding scenery and wildlife, crystal-clear lakes and rivers, and established trails that are generally well maintained and easy to follow. (These trails are covered in the *Sights* section.)

BICYCLING

Stanley Park is a mecca for cyclists; among its network of bike paths is the popular Seawall Promenade, which hugs the coast for 10 kilometers (6.2 miles). Bike travel is in a counter-clockwise direction. On the south side of English Bay, a cycle path runs from Vanier Park to Point Grey and the university, passing some of the city's best beaches on the way. On the north side of Burrard Inlet, hard-core mountain-bike enthusiasts tackle the rough trails of Cypress Provincial Park and Grouse Mountain.

Near the entrance to Stanley Park, where Robson and Denman Streets meet, there's a profusion of bike-rental shops. These include **Alley Cat Rentals** (1779 Robson St., 604/684-5117), **Bayshore Bicycles** (745 Denman St., 604/688-2453), and **Spokes Bicycle Rental** (1798 W. Georgia St., 604/688-5141). With this many outlets crowded around one block, competition

is fierce. Alley Cat Rentals offers the best deals: $6 per hour or $18 per day for a basic mountain bike and $12 per hour or $36 per day for a front suspension bike.

GOLFING

Golf in Vancouver has come a long way since 1892, when a few holes were laid out across the sand dunes of Jericho Beach. Today, the city is blessed with over 50 courses, most of which are open to the public. It is often quoted that in Vancouver it is possible to ski in the morning and golf in the afternoon, and because most courses are open year-round this really is true.

The Courses

There's a pitch-and-putt golf course in Stanley Park (604/681-8847; daily 8 A.M.–6:30 P.M.). With 18 holes under 100 yards each, the course makes a fun diversion. Greens fees are $9.75 for a round, plus $1 per club for rentals. For serious golfers, the following courses provide a truer test of the game.

One the best courses open to the public is the **University Golf Club** (5185 University Blvd., Point Grey, 604/224-1818). Contrary to its name, the course has no affiliation with a university, but it does have a strong teaching program. The course features fairways lined with mature trees and plays to 6,584 yards. The clubhouse exudes old-world charm and features an adjacent golf museum. Greens fees are $60 midweek and $70 on weekends. Those over 60 pay a discounted rate of $45 Monday–Thursday.

Vancouver Parks and Recreation operates three 18-hole courses on the south side of the city. **McCleery Golf Course** (7188 McDonald St., Southlands, 604/257-8191) has a flat, relatively easy layout with wide fairways. Rebuilt in the late 1990s, **Fraserview Golf Course** (7800 Vivian Dr., Fraserview, 604/257-6923) winds its way through a well-established forest. **Langara Golf Course** (6706 Alberta St. off Cambie St., South Cambie, 604/713-1816) is the most challenging of the three. Each course offers club rentals, carts, and lessons, and all but Langara have driving ranges. Greens fees at all three courses are $48–50 during the week and $50–53 on weekends. Monday–Thursday seniors play for a discounted rate of $35. Make bookings up to five days in advance by calling 604/280-1818, or call the courses directly on the day you want to play.

Water comes into play on 13 holes of the **Mayfair Lakes & Country Club** (5460 No. 7 Rd., Richmond, 604/276-0505), but its most unique feature is the salmon, which spawn in Mayfair's waterways. This course plays host to a stop on the Canadian Professional Tour each June but is open to the public the rest of the year, playing a challenging 6,641 yards from the back markers. Monday–Thursday green fees are $75, $85 Friday and weekends, with twilight and off-season rates discounted as low as $35.

Formerly a private club, **Gleneagles Golf Course** (6190 Marine Dr., West Vancouver, 604/921-7353), on the North Shore, has a sloping nine-hole layout with ocean views. Operating on a first-come, first-served basis, greens fees for nine holes are just $24.

Of the many golf courses spread out along the Fraser River Valley, **Meadow Gardens Golf Course** (19675 Meadow Gardens Way, off Hwy. 7, Pitt Meadows, 604/465-5474 or 800/667-6758), on the north side of the river, stands out. Water comes into play on 13 holes, including the signature 18th hole, a par 5 that comprises island-only landing areas for the drive and the second shot, and then the approach is played to an island green. Greens fees range $45–65 depending on the time of day and day of the week.

West Coast Golf Shuttle

The West Coast Golf Shuttle (604/730-1032 or 888/599-6800, www.golfshuttle.com) transports golfers to a "course of the day" and includes hotel pickups, a booked tee time, greens fees, club rentals, a power cart, and even umbrellas and sunscreen for a fee of $80–165 per person, depending on the course and day of the week. Club rentals are an additional $30. This company also organizes overnight Vancouver and Whistler golf packages

WATER SPORTS

Swimming and Sunbathing

All of Vancouver's best beaches are along the shoreline of English Bay; 10 have lifeguards on duty through the summer months 11:30 A.M.–8:45 P.M. Closest to downtown is **English Bay Beach,** at the end of Denman Street. Flanked by a narrow strip of parkland and a wide array of cafés and restaurants, this is *the* beach for people-watching. From English Bay Beach, the Seawall Promenade leads north to **Second** and **Third Beaches,** both short, secluded stretches of sand. To the south is **Sunset Beach,** most popular with families.

Swimmers take note: Even at the peak of summer, the water here only warms up to about 17°C (63°F), tops. If that doesn't sound very enticing, continue to the south end of Sunset Beach to **Vancouver Aquatic Centre** (1050 Beach Ave., 604/665-3424; adult $4.50, senior $3.20, child $2.30). Inside is a 50-meter heated pool, saunas, whirlpools, and a small weight room.

On the south side of English Bay, **Kitsilano Beach** offers spectacular views back across the bay to downtown and the mountains beyond. Take a dip in the adjacent public pool, which is 137 meters long and was built in 1931. The beach and pool are an easy walk from both Vanier Park and a False Creek Ferries dock.

The westernmost of the city's beaches is also the most infamous. **Wreck Beach** is a nudist hangout, where the unabashed prance around naked and nude dudes sell hot dogs and pop from driftwood concession stands. Swimming here isn't particularly good, but the beach still gets extremely busy. Access to the beach is down a steep trail from Northwest Marine Drive, near the end of University Boulevard (take Trail No. 4, 5, or 6).

Canoeing and Kayaking

Granville Island is the center of action for paddlers, and the calm waters of adjacent False Creek make the perfect place to practice your skills. For the widest choice of equipment, head to **Adventure Fitness** (1510 Duranleau St., 604/687-1528) or **Ecomarine Ocean Kayak Centre**

(1668 Duranleau St., 604/689-7575). Both rent single sea kayaks from $28 for two hours or $45 for 24 hours, and double sea kayaks and canoes cost from $35 for two hours, $50 for 24 hours. Both companies also teach kayaking.

The **Indian Arm** of Burrard Inlet allows for a real wilderness experience, right on the city's back doorstep. This 22-kilometer (13.7-mile) long fjord cuts deeply into the North Shore Range; the only development is at its southern end, where the suburb of Deep Cove provides a takeoff point for the waterway. **Deep Cove Canoe and Kayak Centre** (2156 Banbury Rd., Deep Cove, 604/929-2268; Apr.–Oct.) rents canoes and kayaks for $32 for two hours for a single kayak. If you'd prefer to take a tour, contact **Lotus Land Tours** (604/684-4922 or 800/528-3531), which charges $145 per person for a full-day tour, including downtown hotel pickups, a salmon barbecue on an uninhabited island, and instruction.

Boating and Yachting

The calm waters of False Creek and Burrard Inlet are perfect for boating and are always busy with pleasure craft. Beyond the natural harbors of Vancouver, and sheltered from the open ocean by Vancouver Island, the island-dotted Strait of Georgia is a boater's paradise. Along its length are forested coves, sandy beaches, beautiful marine parks, and facilities specifically designed for boaters—many accessible only by water.

For puttering around the inner-city waterways, rent a boat from **Stanley Park Boat Rentals** (1601 Bayshore St., 604/682-6257). This company will suggest a trip to suit your boating ability and time schedule, while also providing bait and tackle and directing you to the fishing hot spots.

Yachties and yachties-to-be should head for **Cooper Boating** (1620 Duranleau St., Granville Island, 604/687-4110 or 888/999-6419, www .cooperboating.com), which boasts Canada's largest sailing school and also holds the country's biggest fleet for charters. For those with experience, Cooper's rents yachts (from $370 per day for a Catalina 32) for a day's local sailing, or take to the waters of the Strait of Georgia on a bareboat charter (from $1,451 per week for a Catalina 27).

SKIING AND SNOWBOARDING

While Vancouver is the gateway to world-renowned Whistler/Blackcomb (see *Whistler* in the *Southwestern British Columbia* chapter), the city boasts three other alpine resorts on its back doorstep. They don't offer the terrain or facilities of Whistler, and their low elevations can create unreliable conditions, but a day's skiing or boarding at any one of the three sure beats being stuck in the hustle and bustle of the city on a cold winter's day.

Grouse Mountain

Towering above North Vancouver, the cut slopes of this resort (604/980-9311, www.grouse-mountain.com) can be seen from many parts of the city, but as you'd expect, on a clear day views from *up there* are much more spectacular. To get there, take Capilano Road north from the Trans-Canada, following it onto Nancy Greene Way, from which a gondola lifts you up 1,000 vertical meters (3,280 vertical feet) to the slopes. Four chairlifts and a couple of T-bars serve 24 runs and a vertical rise of 365 meters (1,200 feet). Advanced skiers and boarders shouldn't get too excited about a day on the slopes here—even the runs with names like Purgatory and Devil's Advocate are pretty tame. But schussing down the slopes of Grouse Mountain after dark is an experience you won't soon forget. Most runs are lighted and overlook the City of Vancouver, laid out in all its brilliance far below. Facilities at the resort include a snowboard park, a rental shop, a ski and snowboard school, and a couple of dining choices. Lift tickets are adult $42, youth $30, senior and child $18. Night skiing (after 4 P.M.) costs adult $32, youth $24, senior and child $15 until closing at 10 P.M.

Cypress Mountain

The eyes of the world will be on this small North Shore resort (604/926-5612, www.cypress-mountain.com) when it hosts the freestyle skiing and snowboarding events of the 2010 Olympic Winter Games. It currently offers about 25 runs across a vertical rise of 534 meters (1,750 feet). A quad chair and four doubles combine to open a wide variety of terrain on two mountain faces, most suited to beginners and intermediates. Spectacular views take in Howe Sound and Vancouver Island. Lift tickets are adult $42, senior and child $19.

Cypress also caters to cross-country skiers and snowshoers, with 16 kilometers (10 miles) of groomed and track-set trails, some of which are lighted for night skiing. A package of cross-country ski rentals, a lesson, and trail pass costs $60. Snowshoe rentals are $18 per day. If none of the above appeals, consider spending a few hours whizzing down the slopes of the Snow Tube Park; $13 per person includes all day use of the Tube Tow and a tube.

To get to the resort, take the TransCanada Highway 12 kilometers (7.5 miles) west from Lions Gate Bridge and turn north on Cypress Bowl Road. If you don't feel like driving up the mountain, catch the shuttle bus that departs hourly from Lonsdale Quay and Cypress Mountain Sports in Park Royal Mall, West Vancouver; $12 round-trip. For a snow report call 604/419-7669.

Mount Seymour

With the highest base elevation of Vancouver's three alpine resorts, Seymour's snow is somewhat reliable, but the area's relatively gentle terrain will be of interest only to beginning and intermediate skiers and boarders (604/986-2261, snow report 604/718-7771, www.mountseymour.com). Four chairlifts serve 20 runs and a vertical rise of 365 meters (1,200 feet). The emphasis is on learning at this hill, and a line of instructors always awaits your business. On-hill facilities include a snowboard park, toboggan run, and massive day lodge with rental shop. Daily lift passes are adult $34, senior $24, child $18. You can also rent snowshoes ($16) and tramp along the resort's trail system ($6 for a day pass), but the Friday-night guided snowshoe walk ($32) is a real treat—and not only because of the chocolate fondue at the end.

The resort is in Mount Seymour Provincial Park. To get there, head north off the TransCanada Highway 15 kilometers (9.3 miles) east of the Lions Gate Bridge, following the Mount Seymour Parkway to Mount Seymour Road. Call the resort for a shuttle schedule from the North Shore; $9 per person round-trip.

SPECTATOR SPORTS

Vancouverites love their sports—not just being involved themselves, but supporting local teams. With a long season and outside activities curtailed by the winter weather, ice hockey—known in Canada simply as "hockey"—draws the biggest crowds, but the city also boasts professional football, baseball, and soccer teams.

Hockey

In 1911 the world's second (and largest) artificial ice rink opened at the north end of Denman Street, complete with seating for 10,000 hockey fans. The local team, then known as the Vancouver Millionaires, played in a small professional league, and in 1915 Vancouver won its first and only **Stanley Cup,** the holy grail of professional ice hockey. Having joined the National Hockey League (NHL) in 1970, the **Vancouver Canucks** (604/899-7400, www.canucks.com) play out of General Motors Place (across from B.C. Place Stadium on Griffith Way), which was built for the now defunct Vancouver Grizzlies NBA franchise. The season runs October–April; ticket prices range $28–90.

Football

The **B.C. Lions** (604/589-7627, www.bclions .com) are Vancouver's Canadian Football League franchise. (American football fans might be surprised by some of the plays—the rules are slightly different than those of the NFL. And no, you're not imagining things—the playing fields are larger than those used in the game's American version.) CFL teams have been competing for the Grey Cup, named for Earl Grey, a former governor-general of Canada, since 1909. Vancouver joined the competition in 1954, first winning the Cup a decade later in 1964. In recent years, the Lions have struggled to gain a large support base, but they continue to perform well, last winning the Grey Cup in 2000 and before that in 1994. Home games are played at B.C.

Place Stadium, on the south side of downtown at the corner of Robson and Beatty Streets. The season runs June–November, with most games played in the evening; tickets range $20–60.

Soccer

Vancouver is a soccer stronghold and, with two professional teams and dozens of intracity leagues, is always well represented on the national team. Vancouver's professional men's soccer team, the **Whitecaps** (604/899-9283, www.whitecapsfc .com), plays in the A-League of the United Soccer League, competing against 20 other teams across North America through the summer months. Home games are played at Swangard Stadium, in Burnaby's Central Park. To get there, take the Kingsway out of the city to Boundary Road (Patterson SkyTrain station).

Local women players are represented in the W League and are also known as the Whitecaps (formerly the Vancouver Angels). This team also plays at Burnaby's Swangard Stadium. The season for both teams runs May–August and game-day tickets are in the $6–15 range.

Horse Racing

Talk in recent years has been of relocating Vancouver's main racing venue to the outlying suburbs, but for the time being, thoroughbred racing takes place in the Pacific National Exhibition grounds six kilometers (3.7 miles) east of downtown at **Hastings Park Racecourse** (corner of Renfrew St. and McGill St., 604/254-1631, www.hastingspark.com), as it has done for over 100 years. Full betting and a variety of dining facilities are offered. The season runs late April–November, with the first race starting at 1:03 P.M. The biggest races fall near the end of the season, including the BC Derby on the last Saturday in September. General admission is free, or pay $5 for entry to the clubhouse. Parking is $6.50.

Arts and Entertainment

There's never a dull moment in Vancouver when it comes to nightlife. The city's unofficial entertainment district extends southwest along Granville Street from Granville Street Mall, and south from this strip to False Creek. Cinemas line Granville Street Mall, while beyond the mall is a smattering of nightclubs, with the main concentration of these in Yaletown. Performing arts and concert venues are scattered throughout the city, but the three largest—Ford Centre for the Performing Arts, Queen Elizabeth Theatre, and B.C. Place Stadium—are south of Granville Street along Georgia Street.

For complete listings of all that's happening around the city, pick up the free *Georgia Straight* (www.straight.com). Friday and weekend editions of Vancouver's two daily newspapers, the *Province* and the *Vancouver Sun,* offer comprehensive entertainment listings. As in all other major cities across Canada, **Ticketmaster** (604/280-3311, www.ticketmaster.ca) has a monopoly on advance ticket sales to major entertainment events; have your credit card ready.

Tickets Tonight (200 Burrard St., 604/684-2787, www.ticketstonight.ca; Tues.–Sat. 10 A.M.–6 P.M.) sells half-price tickets the day of major performances. You must purchase them in person from the booth inside the downtown information center.

Depending on your point of view, Vancouver has the best and worst smoking regulations in Canada. The general rule is that smoking is prohibited in all indoor spaces, including restaurants, public transit, public buildings, museums, sporting venues, bars, and nightclubs. Many lodgings, including all bed-and-breakfasts, don't allow in-room smoking.

Bars

Ever since "Gassy Jack" Deighton set up the city's first liquor outlet (a barrel of whiskey atop a crude plank "bar") in the area that became known as Gastown, that part of the city has been a favorite drinking spot. The **Steamworks Brewing Co.** (375 Water St., Gastown, 604/689-2739; daily 11:30 A.M.–10 P.M.) is the perfect

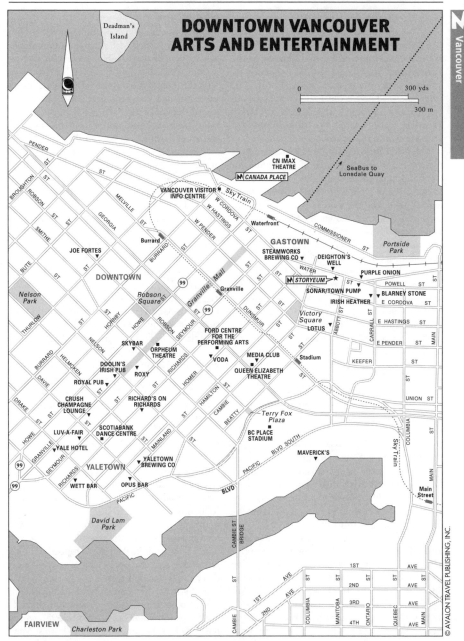

DOWNTOWN VANCOUVER ARTS AND ENTERTAINMENT

Deadman's Island

0   300 yds

0   300 m

Vancouver

PENDER ST

BROUGHTON ST

ROBSON ST

MELVILLE ST

GEORGIA ST

SMITHE ST

BUTE ST

THURLOW ST

BURRARD ST

HELMCKEN

DAVIE

NELSON

HORNBY ST

HOWE ST

SEYMOUR ST

ROBSON ST

RICHARDS ST

HOMER ST

HAMILTON ST

CAMBIE ST

BEATTY ST

MAINLAND ST

GRANVILLE

DRAKE ST

HOWE ST

SEYMOUR ST

RICHARDS ST

CN IMAX THEATRE

CANADA PLACE

VANCOUVER VISITOR INFO CENTRE

SeaBus to Lonsdale Quay

Sky Train

W CORDOVA
W HASTINGS
W PENDER

Waterfront

COMMISSIONER ST

Portside Park

GASTOWN

Burrard

STEAMWORKS BREWING CO

DEIGHTON'S WELL

WATER

PURPLE ONION

DOWNTOWN

Nelson Park

Robson Square

Granville

STORYEUM

SONAR/TOWN PUMP

POWELL ST

BLARNEY STONE

E CORDOVA ST

IRISH HEATHER

Victory Square

E HASTINGS ST

E PENDER ST

MAIN ST

LOTUS

FORD CENTRE FOR THE PERFORMING ARTS

SKYBAR

ORPHEUM THEATRE

VODA

MEDIA CLUB

Stadium

KEEFER ST

DOOLIN'S IRISH PUB

ROXY

QUEEN ELIZABETH THEATRE

ROYAL PUB

RICHARD'S ON RICHARDS

UNION ST

CRUSH CHAMPAGNE LOUNGE

Terry Fox Plaza

BC PLACE STADIUM

LUV-A-FAIR

SCOTIABANK DANCE CENTRE

PACIFIC BLVD SOUTH

MAVERICK'S

SKYTrain

COLUMBIA ST

YALE HOTEL

YALETOWN

YALETOWN BREWING CO

Main Street

WETT BAR

OPUS BAR

PACIFIC BLVD

JOE FORTES

David Lam Park

CAMBIE ST BRIDGE

FAIRVIEW

Charleston Park

1ST AVE

2ND AVE

COLUMBIA ST

MANITOBA ST

ONTARIO ST

QUEBEC ST

MAIN ST

1ST AVE

2ND AVE

3RD AVE

4TH AVE

© AVALON TRAVEL PUBLISHING, INC.

place to relax with a beer from the in-house brewery. The atmosphere is casual yet stylish, and you'll have great views across Burrard Inlet. At the far end of Gastown, the lively **Blarney Stone** (216 Carrall St., 604/687-4322) frequently resounds with rowdy Irish party bands. The evening crowd here is older and often single. In the same vein, across the road is the **Irish Heather** (217 Carrall St., 604/688-9779), renowned for its Guinness.

Yaletown Brewing Co. (1111 Mainland St., 604/681-2739) is the premier drinking hole for the hip population of inner-city Yaletown. The in-house brewery produces excellent beers, there's a great patio, and the food is of a high standard for a pub. Also in Yaletown, the **Opus Bar** (350 Davie St., 604/642-0557) serves up strong cocktails and imported beer in a sizzlingly hip setting off the lobby of the Opus Hotel. In the same vein, the upscale elegance of **Voda** (783 Homer St., 604/684-3003) makes it a favorite after-work and pre-clubbing hangout for Vancouver's young professionals. Through the earlier hours of the evening drinkers soak up the atmosphere over a martini, while top 40 and house music come on after 11 P.M. Toward the head of False Creek from Yaletown, **Maverick's** (770 Pacific Blvd. S, 604/683-4436) is the quintessential bar for young and restless drinkers. Always lively, the Maverick's patio (Vancouver's largest) overlooks the water and is perpetually crowded and noisy. Inside is a sports bar, restaurant, and nightclub. At the **Royal Pub** (1025 Granville St., 604/685-5335) join the throngs of young backpackers drinking up nightly specials before retiring to the upstairs hostel. **Doolin's Irish Pub** (654 Nelson St. at Granville St., 604/605-4351) dispenses mugs of Guinness and hearty food (such as ploughman's lunch for $8) daily from 11:30 A.M.

Toward the West End, **Joe Fortes Seafood and Chophouse** (777 Thurlow St., 604/669-1940) boasts a great bar, complete with a wide range of beers and a condensed menu from the adjacent restaurant. In the same part of town, **Checkers** (1755 Davie St., West End, 604/682-1831) is another popular bar, this one with a distinctive checkered decor and live rock on weekends.

Nightclubs

Nightclubs change names and reputations with regularity, so check with the free entertainment newspapers or www.clubvibes.com for the latest hot spots. Naturally, weekends are busiest, with the most popular clubs having cover charges up to $20 and long lines after 9 P.M. During the rest of the week, cover charges are reduced, and many places hold promotions with giveaways or discounted drinks.

Vancouver's unofficial entertainment district is at the southern end of downtown along and immediately south of Granville Street. Best known as Dick's on Dicks, **Richard's on Richards** (1036 Richards St., 604/687-6794) has been a staple of the Vancouver nightclub scene for over 20 years. It's most popular with the late-20s and over-30 crowds. The music is live through the week, with DJs spinning discs on weekends. The dance floor is always high energy. Best known as "the Fair," **Luv-A-Fair,** around the corner (1275 Seymour St., 604/685-3288), has been a part of Vancouver's after-dark scene for over a quarter of a century. It's as popular today as when it opened, especially on Thursday nights, which feature techno tunes. The Fair is a serious dance venue with a huge floor. Drinks here are relatively well priced. One of the hottest nightclubs in recent years has been **Wett Bar** (1320 Richards St., 604/662-7077), where a hanging light system produces incredible effects.

Up the hill from all of the above clubs, at **Crush Champagne Lounge** (1180 Granville St., 604/684-0355), the retro feel attracts an over-30 crowd. A house band plays through the week while weekends are the domain of name acts. Appealing to a similar age group is **Skybar** (670 Smithe St., 604/697-9199), a mega-trendy nightspot with drink prices to match. At street level is a martini bar, the second floor is mostly dance floor, and the complex is topped out by a retractable roof that opens up a palm tree–studded patio to the elements.

Away from the main entertainment district, Gastown holds a selection of nightclubs, including **Sonar** (66 Water St., 604/683-6695), which has grown to become one of the hottest Vancouver nightspots. Many DJs are imported from

London, and although most nights feature the latest techno, hip-hop, and house music from across the Atlantic, the club's appeal has broadened, and weeknights occasionally feature soul and jazz. The scene here appeals to serious dancers and those who want to be seen dancing. Sonar's cover is among the most expensive in the city. For serious dancing but a casual vibe and fun-loving staff, check out **Lotus,** between Gastown and Chinatown (455 Abbott St., 604/685-7777). Music includes house, techno, and trance. Escape the heat of the dance floor in the upstairs lounge or visit during the week, when themes such as Funky Tuesdays attract an older (late 20s) crowd.

Rock

The world's biggest rock, pop, and country acts usually include Vancouver on their world tours, and the city's thriving local music industry supports live bands at a variety of venues. Most big-name acts play B.C. Place Stadium, the Orpheum, or Queen Elizabeth Theatre. At the classic **Roxy** (932 Granville St., 604/331-7999), two house bands play rock 'n' roll music from all eras to a packed house during the week, with imported bands on weekends. The Roxy attracts a huge crowd every night of the week. The young, hip crowd, good music, and performance bartenders make this the city's most popular live music venue, so expect a line, especially after 9 P.M. weekends; cover charges range $5–10. The **Media Club** (695 Cambie St., 604/608-2871) books everything from soul to glam rock. The **Railway Club** (579 Dunsmuir St., 604/681-1625) is a private club where nonmembers are welcome (at a higher cover charge) to listen to acts that range from rock to country.

Jazz and Blues

The **Hot Jazz Society** (2120 Main St., 604/873-4131) presents live jazz on a regular basis; cover charge is $6–9. The **Coastal Jazz and Blues Society** (604/872-5200, www.jazzvancouver.com) maintains a listing of all the city's jazz and blues events.

Serious blues lovers should head to the historic **Yale Hotel** (1300 Granville St., 604/681-9253), which has hosted some of the greatest names in the business, including Junior Wells and Stevie Ray Vaughan. The hotel offers plenty of room for everyone, whether you want to get up

The Yale Hotel is a classic blues venue.

and dance or shoot pool in the back. Sunday is the only night without live performances, although a jam session starts up around 3 P.M. on Saturday and Sunday afternoons. Drinks are expensive and a $5–15 cover charge is collected Thursday–Saturday nights. The **Purple Onion** (15 Water St. in Gastown, 604/602-9442) features live jazz and blues some nights. Admission is free before 9 P.M. Also downtown, the **Wedgewood Hotel** (845 Hornby St., 604/689-7777) features a resident blues guitarist who performs nightly in the hotel's stylish lounge. No cover, but the drinks aren't cheap.

Comedy

Yuk Yuk's (Century Plaza Hotel, 1015 Burrard St., 604/696-9857) offers comedy nights Wednesday–Saturday. Admission costs $5 on Wednesday (amateur night), $8 on Thursday, $18 on Friday and Saturday. **Lafflines** (26 4th St., New Westminster, 604/525-2262) offers a similar program and attracts acts from throughout Canada. Wednesday–Sunday, the Arts Club (604/738-7013) hosts the **Vancouver Theatresports League** of improvised comedy on its New Revue Stage, Granville Island.

Theater

Vancouver has theaters all over the city—for professional plays, amateur plays, comedy, and "instant" theater. In total, the city boasts 30 professional theater companies and more than 20 regular venues.

The **Centre in Vancouver for Performing Arts** (777 Homer St., 604/602-0616, www.centreinvancouver.com) hosts the biggest of musical hits. The trilevel theater seats over 1,800 and boasts North America's largest stage. Matinees cost from $50, while evening shows range $55–90. One-hour tours of the complex depart from the lobby Mon.–Sat. at 10 A.M.; $4 per person. A similar facility is the **Chan Centre for the Performing Arts** (6265 Crescent Rd., 604/822-2697), comprising three stages including the 1,400-seat Chan Shun Concert Hall. It's on the UBC campus in Point Grey.

One of the great joys of summer in the city is sitting around Malkin Bowl in Stanley Park

watching **Theatre under the Stars** (604/687-0174, www.tuts.bc.ca; June–Aug. Mon.–Sat. at 7 P.M.). Since 1934 these shows have drawn around 1,000 theater-goers nightly, with performances usually musically oriented. The setting itself, an open amphitheater surrounded by towering Douglas fir trees, is as much of an attraction as the performance. Tickets (adult $29, senior $24, child $19) go on sale at noon daily from a booth beside the bowl. Another summer production is **Bard on the Beach** (604/739-0559, www.bardonthebeach.org), a celebration of the works of Shakespeare that takes place in huge, open-ended tents in Vanier Park. Tickets are well priced at just $17–27.

The **Arts Club Theatre** (604/687-1644, www.artsclub.com) always offers excellent theater productions at two Granville Island locations—the **New Revue Stage** and adjacent **Mainstage.** Productions range from drama to comedy to improv. Tickets run $21–35; book in advance and pick up your tickets at the door 30 minutes prior to showtime.

Since its inception in 1964, the **Playhouse Theatre Company** has grown to become the city's largest theater company. Seven productions are performed each year, ranging from classical to contemporary, with 8 P.M. start times and tickets ranging $31–42. Matinees (2 P.M.) cost around half the price of evening performances. The company is based at the **Playhouse Theatre** (160 W. 1st St., 604/873-3311).

For university productions, head out to **Frederic Wood Theatre,** on the UBC campus (604/822-2678). Performances run throughout the academic year; admission is generally around $8–12.

Music and Dance

The **Queen Elizabeth Theatre** (630 Hamilton St., 604/665-3050) is the home of **Vancouver Opera** (604/683-0222); tickets begin at $35 rising to $90 for the best seats. The theater also hosts music recitals and stage performances.

The historic **Orpheum Theatre,** on the corner of Smithe and Seymour Streets, dates to 1927 and houses its original Wurlitzer organ. Now fully restored, the theater provides excellent acoustics for the resident **Vancouver Symphony** (604/684-9100), as well as for concerts by the professional **Vancouver Chamber Choir** (604/738-6822), the amateur **Vancouver Bach Choir** (604/921-8012), and other musical groups. Renowned for its support of emerging musicians, the **Vancouver Recital Society** (604/602-0363) presents piano, cello, and violin players at the Vancouver Playhouse and Chan Centre for the Performing Arts through its October–April season.

Ballet British Columbia (604/732-5003) performs in the Queen Elizabeth Theatre (630 Hamilton St.) throughout its winter season. Tickets range $18–45. Vancouver's newest dance venue is the **Scotiabank Dance Centre** (677 Davie St., 604/606-6400). Designed by Arthur Erickson, this stunning seven-story, glass-enclosed building opened late in 2001, providing a home to around 30 professional and amateur dance companies. The center includes a small performance stage; call for a schedule.

Cinemas

Cinemas are in all the major shopping malls and elsewhere throughout the city. **Cineplex Odeon** (604/434-2463) operates 20 cinemas in Vancouver. Call or check the two daily papers for locations and screenings. Admission to first-run screenings is about $10.

If you're staying at a Robson Street or West End accommodation, head over to **Denman Place Discount Cinema** (corner of Denman St. and Comox St., 604/683-2201) for first- and second-run hits for $2.50–5. For foreign and Canadian indie films, check out **Pacific Cinematheque** (1131 Howe St., 604/688-8202).

At the far end of Canada Place, the **CN IMAX Theatre** (604/682-4629) provides spectacular movie entertainment and special effects on a five-story-high screen with wraparound surround sound. Films are generally on the world's natural wonders and last around 45 minutes, with two or three features showing each day, beginning around noon. Ticket prices range $9–13 per screening, or catch a double feature for a few bucks extra.

SHOPPING

Vancouver has shopping centers, malls, and specialty stores everywhere. Head to Gastown for native arts and crafts, Robson Street for boutique clothing, Granville Street Mall for department stores, Granville Island for everything from ships' chandlery to kids' clothing, Yaletown for the trendy clothes of local designers, the east side for army-surplus stores and pawnbrokers, Chinatown for Eastern foods, and the junction of Main Street and East 49th Avenue for Indian goods.

Gastown

Sandwiched between the many cafés, restaurants, and tacky souvenir stores along Water Street are other stores selling Vancouver's best selection of native arts and crafts. One of the largest outlets, **Hill's Native Crafts** (165 Water St., 604/685-4249) sells $10 T-shirts, towering $12,000 totem poles, and everything in between, including genuine Cowichan sweaters and carved ceremonial masks. **Images for a Canadian Heritage** (164 Water St., 604/685-7046) also features traditional native art. The **Inuit Gallery of Vancouver** (206 Cambie St., 604/688-7323) exhibits the work of Inuit and northwest coast native artists and sculptors. Among the highlights are many soapstone pieces by carvers from Cape Dorset, a remote Inuit village in Canada's new territory of Nunavut.

Down the street from Hill's Native Crafts, **Kites on Clouds** (131 Water St., 604/669-5677) sells hundreds of different kites, from the simplest designs to elaborate constructions priced at over $200. The **Western Canada Wilderness Committee Store** (227 Abbott St., 604/683-2567) features environmentally friendly souvenirs, including shirts, posters, and calendars. The **Sinclair Centre** itself is a local landmark; its four historic buildings now hold galleries, boutiques, and food outlets.

Granville Island

Arts and crafts galleries on Granville Island include **Wickaninnish Gallery** (1666 Johnston St., 604/681-1057), which sells stunning native art, jewelry, carvings, weavings, and original paintings; **Gallery of B.C. Ceramics** (1359 Cartwright St., 604/669-5645), showcasing the work of the province's leading potters and sculptors; and **Forge & Form** (1334 Cartwright St., 604/684-6298), which creates and sells gold and silver jewelry. Head to the **Umbrella Shop** (1550 Anderson St., 604/697-0919) if it looks like there's rain in the forecast.

Duranleau Street is home to many maritime-based businesses, adventure-tour operators, and charter operators. The **Quarterdeck** (1660 Duranleau St., 604/683-8232) stocks everything from marine charts to brass shipping bells. **The Ocean Floor** (1522 Duranleau St., 604/681-5014) sells a similar range of treasures, including seashells and model ships. To buy a sea kayak or canoe (from $1,100 secondhand), head to **Adventure Fitness** (1528 Duranleau St., 604/687-1528) or **Ecomarine Ocean Kayak Centre** (1668 Duranleau St., 604/689-7575). Both shops also carry related equipment, books, and nautical charts. The city's leading dive shop is **Rowand's Reef Scuba Shop** (1512 Duranleau St., 604/669-3483), with sales, repairs, rentals, and plenty of information on local dive spots.

Department Stores, Plazas, and Malls

Despite looking pretty dowdy these days, **Granville Street Mall** nevertheless forms the heart of the downtown shopping precinct; the two-block stretch of Granville Street is closed to private vehicles, though buses and taxis still pass through. Here you'll find the city's largest department store, **The Bay** (674 Granville St., 604/681-6211), a Canadian chain that evolved from the historic Hudson's Bay Company. Today the store emphasizes Canadian goods, from souvenirs to household appliances. Also on the mall, the **Pacific Centre** features 165 shops, a massive food court, and a three-story-high waterfall. In the center's southwest corner, **Oh Yes!, Vancouver** is a great place to shop for colorful city souvenirs.

Across Lions Gate Bridge in West Vancouver are a couple of shopping centers worth a mention. In a scenic location at Marine Drive and Taylor Way, **Park Royal Shopping Centre** holds almost 200 shops and three department stores. Also on the north side of Burrard Inlet is **Lonsdale Quay Market,** the terminus of the SeaBus from downtown. This bustling center features a great fresh-food market on the first floor and a range of boutiques and galleries on the second.

British Columbia's largest shopping complex, **Metrotown,** houses more than 200 shops. It's on the Kingsway in Burnaby; get there from downtown on the SkyTrain.

Outdoor and Camping Gear

A small stretch of West Broadway, between Main and Cambie Streets, holds Vancouver's largest concentration of outdoor equipment stores. The largest of these, and the largest in British Columbia, is **Mountain Equipment Co-op** (130 W. Broadway, 604/872-7858; Mon.–Wed. 10 A.M.–7 P.M., Thurs.–Fri. 10 A.M.–9 P.M., Sat. 9 A.M.–6 P.M.). Like the American R.E.I stores, it is a cooperative owned by its members; to make a purchase, you must be a member (a once-only charge of $5). The store holds a massive selection of clothing, climbing and mountaineering equipment, tents, backpacks, sleeping bags, books, and other accessories. To order a copy of the mail-order catalog, call 800/663-2667 or go online to www.mec.ca.

FESTIVALS AND EVENTS

Festivals of some description take place in Vancouver just about every month of the year. Whether it's a celebration of local or international culture, the arts, sporting events, or just a wacky long-time tradition, there's always a reason to party in Vancouver. Many of the most popular festivals are held during summer, the peak visitor season, but the rest of the year is the main season for performances by the city's dance, theater, and music companies, and not-to-be-missed events such as the Christmas Carol Ships Parade. For details and exact dates of the events listed contact the numbers or visit the websites given, or visit any local tourist information center.

Tickets for most major events can be booked through **Ticketmaster** (www.ticketmaster.ca);

for the arts, call 604/280-3311; for sporting events, call 604/280-4400.

Spring

The spring event schedule kicks off in a big way the third week of March with the **Vancouver Playhouse International Wine Festival** (604/872-6622, www.playhousewinefest.com). Hosted by various downtown venues, it is one of North America's largest, bringing together representatives from more than 150 wineries and 14 countries. Other public events include night-time gatherings, such as Bacchanalia, a gala dinner hosted by the Fairmont Vancouver.

The **Vancouver Sun Run** (604/689-9441, www.sunrun.com) is a 10-kilometer (6.2-mile) run (or walk) through the streets of downtown on the third Sunday in April. Attracting over 45,000 participants, it is Canada's largest (and the world's third largest) such run. For more serious runners, the **Vancouver International Marathon** (604/872-2928, www.vanmarathon.bc.ca) takes place two Sundays later.

The streets of New Westminster come alive in late May for **Hyack Festival** (604/522-6894, www.hyack.bc.ca), in celebration of spring and the history of British Columbia's one-time capital. Farther east, the country comes to the city for one of British Columbia's biggest rodeos, the **Cloverdale Rodeo and Exhibition** (604/576-9461, www.cloverdalerodeo.com) on the third weekend of May.

The third week of May is the **Vancouver International Children's Festival** (604/708-5655, www.childrensfestival.com), at Vanier Park; it's a kid's paradise, with face painting, costumes, plays, puppetry, mime, sing-alongs, storytelling, and fancy-hat competitions.

Summer

Two of summer's most popular cultural events take place from mid-June through to late in the season, meaning you can enjoy them at any time through the warmer months. **Bard on the Beach** (604/739-0559, www.bardonthebeach.org) comprises three favorite Shakespeare plays performed in open-ended tents in Vanier Park, allowing a spectacular backdrop of English Bay, the city skyline, and the mountains beyond. Tickets are well priced at just $17–24 for 1 P.M. and 4 P.M. matinees and from $27 for 7:30 P.M. evening performances. The other event, the **Kitsilano Showboat** (604/734-7332), takes place at nearby Kitsilano Beach. Amateur variety acts have been taking to this stage since 1935. Performances are Monday, Wednesday, and Friday nights over a 10-week summer season.

The **Alcan Dragon Boat Festival** (604/688-2382, www.adbf.com) comes to False Creek on the third weekend in June. In addition to the races, a blessing ceremony and other cultural activities take place in and around the Plaza of Nations.

The last week of June, Vancouver taps its feet to the beat of the annual **Vancouver International Jazz Festival** (604/872-5200, www.coastaljazz.ca), when more than 1,500 musicians from countries around the world gather to perform traditional and contemporary jazz at 40 venues around the city.

Canada Day is July 1. The main celebrations—music, dancing, and fireworks—are held at Canada Place, but if you head out to the **Steveston Salmon Festival** (604/277-6812) you'll come across a massive salmon barbecue and be granted free admission to the Gulf of Georgia Cannery.

The middle weekend of July, Jericho Beach Park draws lots of folks to the **Vancouver Folk Music Festival** (604/602-9798, www.thefestival.bc.ca). In addition to the wonderful music, the festival features storytelling, dance performances, live theater, and a food fair. Hosted at the Crofton House School (corner of Blenheim St. and W. 41st Ave., Kerrisdale), the **Chamber Music & Song Festival** (604/602-0363, www.vanrecital.com) presents six evenings of performances over two weeks by chamber musicians, such as piano, cello, and violin players. This is performing arts at its most casual—while the actual concerts are inside, the school's gardens come alive before each performance with hundreds of concert-goers enjoying catered dinners or a pre-ordered picnic basket.

Year after year, Vancouverites await with much anticipation the early August **Celebration of Light** (604/641-1193, www.celebration-of-light.com), the world's largest musical fireworks competition. Each year, three countries compete; each has a night to itself (the last Saturday in July, then the following Wednesday and Saturday), putting on a display that lasts up to an hour from 10:15 P.M.; then on the final night (second Wednesday in August), the three competing countries come together for a grand finale. The fireworks are let off from a barge moored in English Bay, allowing viewing from Stanley Park, Kitsilano, Jericho Beach, and as far away as West Vancouver. Music that accompanies the displays can be heard around the shoreline; if you're away from the action tune your radio to 101.1 FM for a simulcast.

Abbotsford International Airshow (604/852-8511, www.abbotsfordairshow.com), featuring Canada's famous Snowbirds, is held at Vancouver's "other" airport, east of the city in Abbotsford, on the second weekend of August.

On the last Sunday in August, the **Vancouver Pride Parade** (604/687-0955, www.vanpride.bc.ca) culminates a week of gay pride celebration. It runs along Denman Street, ending at Sunset Beach, where there's entertainment and partying.

Summer's busy event schedule winds up at the Pacific National Exhibition Grounds with **The Fair (Pacific National Exhibition)** (604/253-2311, www.pne.bc.ca) in late August. A highlight of this agricultural exposition is the twice-daily RCMP musical ride, a precision drill performed by Canada's famous Mounties.

Fall

Beginning the second week of September, **The Fringe Festival** (604/257-0350, www.vancouverfringe.com) schedules around 500 perfor-

mances by 100 artists from around the world at indoor and outdoor stages throughout Granville Island.

The **Vancouver International Film Festival** (604/685-0260, www.viff.org) is held late in September and features more than 300 of the very best movies from around 60 countries at theaters across downtown. One month later, literary types congregate on Granville Island for the **Vancouver International Writers Festival** (604/681-6330, www.writersfest.bc.ca).

Winter

Through the month of December, VanDusen Botanical Garden is transformed each evening by over 80,000 lights and seasonal displays such as a nativity scene during the **Festival of Lights** (604/878-9274). Another popular pre-Christmas event is the **Carol Ships Parade of Lights** (604/878-8999, www.carolships.org). For three weeks leading up to Christmas Eve, the waterways of Vancouver come alive with the sounds of the festive season as each night a flotilla of up to 80 boats, each decorated with colorful lights, sails around Burrard Inlet, Port Moody, Deep Cove, and around English Bay to False Creek, while onboard carolers sing the songs of Christmas through sound systems that can clearly be heard from along the shoreline.

While most normal folk spend New Year's Day recovering from the previous night's celebrations, up to 2,000 brave souls head down to English Bay Beach and go *swimming*. The information hotline for the **Polar Bear Swim** is 604/732-2304, but all you really need to know is that the water will be *very* cold. The stupidity starts at 2:30 P.M.

Accommodations

Whether you're looking for a luxurious room in a high-rise hotel or a dingy downtown dorm, Vancouver has accommodations to suit all budgets. Downtown hotel room rates fluctuate greatly depending on supply and demand, much more so than bed-and-breakfasts and motels in suburban locations. In Vancouver, demand is highest in summer and on weekdays, so if you're looking to save a few bucks plan on being in town in the cooler months (May and September are my favorite times to be in Vancouver), or stay at a business hotel as part of weekend package. One word of warning: If you plan to have a vehicle, prepare yourself for parking fees up to $25 per day in the downtown area; ask if weekend rates include free parking—they often do.

The following recommendations reflect my favorites in various price categories throughout the city. You won't find every downtown hotel mentioned here, and outside of downtown only convenient and good-value choices are included.

DOWNTOWN
Under $50
As you may imagine, the only downtown accommodations in this price range are backpacker lodges. For those on a budget, they are a great way to stay in the heart of the action and to mingle with like-minded travelers from around the world.

HI–Vancouver Downtown (1114 Burnaby St., 604/684-4565 or 888/203-4302, www.hihostels.ca) is typical of the new-look facilities operated by Hostelling International, the world's largest and longest-running network of backpacker accommodations. The complex offers a large kitchen, library, game room, public Internet access, a travel agency, bike rentals, bag storage, and a laundry. The dormitories hold a maximum of four beds but are small. For these beds members of Hostelling International pay $25.50, nonmembers $29.50; private rooms range $62.50–72 s or d. A daily shuttle runs between this hostel and the one out at Jericho Beach.

Housed in the old Royal Hotel, **HI–Vancouver Central** (1025 Granville St., 604/685-5335 or 888/203-8333, www.hihostels.ca) is closer to the nighttime action of the entertainment district and also has its own downstairs bar with nightly drink and food specials. Therefore, as you'd expect, it's more of a party atmosphere than the HI hostel on Burnaby Street and a *lot* more so than the hostel at Jericho Beach (see *Kitsilano, Shaughnessy, and Vicinity*). Amenities include lockers in every room, a smallish communal kitchen, a notice board in the lobby filled with things to do and see, and public Internet access. Members pay $25 for a dorm bed (nonmembers pay $29) or $59 s or d for a private room with an en suite bathroom (nonmembers $68).

Privately owned backpacker lodges in Vancouver come and go with predictable regularity. Many should be avoided. One exception is **Samesun Vancouver** (1018 Granville St., 604/682-8226 or 877/562-2783, www.samesun.com), which is excellent in all respects. Typical of inner-city hostels the world over, rooms in this old four-story building are small, but each has been tastefully decorated, and the communal lounge and kitchen areas serve guests well. Other facilities include a separate TV room, public Internet access, and a rooftop patio. Rates are $23.40 per person in a dormitory (maximum four beds) or $45–70 for a private room.

$50–100
Dating to the mid-1990s, the **YWCA** 733 Beatty St., 604/895-5830 or 800/663-1424, www.ywcahotel.com) is popular with female travelers, couples, and families who don't want to spend a fortune on accommodations but don't like the "backpacker scene" at regular hostels. It's a few blocks from Vancouver's business core, but the modern facilities and choice of nearby restaurants more than compensate for the walk. More than 150 rooms are spread over 11 stories. Each room has a telephone, and the private rooms have TVs. Communal facilities include two

Vancouver

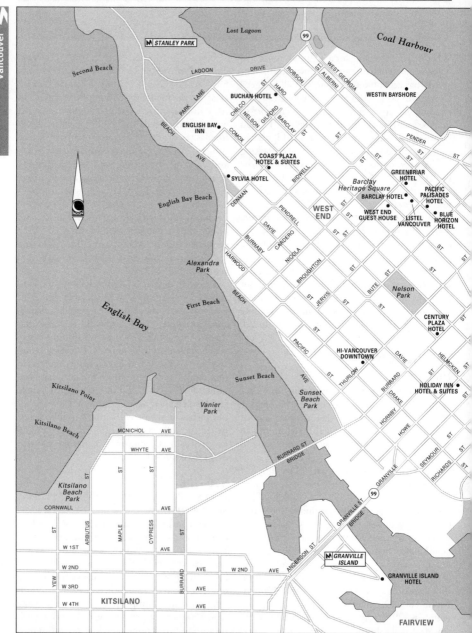

Lost Lagoon

99

Coal Harbour

M STANLEY PARK

LAGOON   DRIVE

Second Beach

WEST GEORGIA

WESTIN BAYSHORE

ROBSON ST

HARO

ALBERNI ST

PARK LANE

BUCHAN HOTEL

CHILCO   NELSON   GILFORD   BARCLAY

BEACH

ENGLISH BAY INN

PENDER ST

COMOX

ST

ST

AVE

COAST PLAZA HOTEL & SUITES

BIDWELL

GREENBRIAR HOTEL

SYLVIA HOTEL

Barclay Heritage Square

PACIFIC PALISADES HOTEL

English Bay Beach

DENMAN

PENDRELL

WEST END

BARCLAY HOTEL

WEST END GUEST HOUSE

LISTEL VANCOUVER

BLUE HORIZON HOTEL

DAVIE

CARDERO

BURNABY

NICOLA

Alexandra Park

HARWOOD

BROUGHTON

Nelson Park

First Beach

BEACH

JERVIS ST

BUTE ST

English Bay

ST

CENTURY PLAZA HOTEL

PACIFIC

Sunset Beach

AVE

THURLOW

HI-VANCOUVER DOWNTOWN

DAVIE

HELMCKEN

Kitsilano Point

Sunset Beach Park

BURRARD

HOLIDAY INN HOTEL & SUITES

DRAKE

Kitsilano Beach

Vanier Park

HORNBY

HOWE

MCNICHOL   AVE

SEYMOUR ST

WHYTE   AVE

BURRARD ST BRIDGE

RICHARDS ST

Kitsilano Beach Park

ST

ST

ST

GRANVILLE

CORNWALL

AVE

GRANVILLE ST BRIDGE

99

W 1ST

ARBUTUS

MAPLE

CYPRESS

ST

W 2ND

AVE

W 2ND

AVE

ANDERSON ST

M GRANVILLE ISLAND

YEW

W 3RD

BURRARD

AVE

GRANVILLE ISLAND HOTEL

W 4TH   KITSILANO

AVE

FAIRVIEW

Vancouver

DOWNTOWN VANCOUVER ACCOMMODATIONS

Deadman's Island

Burrard Inlet

CANADA PLACE

SeaBus to Lonsdale Quay

0   300 yds
0   300 m

COAL HARBOUR SEAWALK

VANCOUVER MARRIOTT PINNACLE

Sky Train

PAN PACIFIC HOTEL VANCOUVER

VANCOUVER VISITOR INFO CENTRE

FAIRMONT WATERFRONT

VANCOUVER-DAYS INN DOWNTOWN

Waterfront

W HASTINGS

W CORDOVA

COMMISSIONER

MELVILLE ST

GEORGIA

Burrard

BURRARD

W PENDER

GASTOWN

Portside Park

West Coast Express

ST

ALEXANDER

ST

FAIRMONT HOTEL VANCOUVER

CROWNE PLAZA HOTEL GEORGIA

FOUR SEASONS HOTEL

DELTA VANCOUVER SUITES

WATER ST

E POWELL

GORE

DUNLEVY

Oppen-heimer Park

ST

ST

Granville

RAMADA LIMITED DOWNTOWN

E CORDOVA

MAIN

Granville Mall

Robson Square

SUTTON PLACE HOTEL

99

VICTORIAN HOTEL

Victory Square

CHINATOWN

E HASTINGS

ABBOTT ST

ST

HOWE

HORNBY

ROBSON

SEYMOUR

RICHARDS

99

DUNSMUIR

E PENDER

CARRALL

TAYLOR ST

ST

SMITHE

KINGSTON HOTEL

Stadium

KEEFER

ST

JACKSON

BOSMAN'S HOTEL

HI-VANCOUVER CENTRAL

SAMESUN VANCOUVER

HAMILTON ST

CAMBIE ST

BEATTY ST

SANDMAN HOTEL DOWNTOWN VANCOUVER

YWCA HOTEL

BLVD NORTH

UNION

HOMER

NELSON ST

HOWARD JOHNSON HOTEL DOWNTOWN

Terry Fox

ST

MAINLAND ST

PACIFIC

BLVD SOUTH

COLUMBIA ST

Sky Train

YALETOWN

PACIFIC

OPUS HOTEL

PACIFIC BLVD

David Lam Park

CAMBIE ST

BRIDGE ST

Creek

MAIN ST

Thornton Park

Main Street

PACIFIC CENTRAL STATION

False

Creek

WESTERN ST

STATION ST

TERMINAL AVE

Charleston Park

CAMBIE ST

1ST AVE

2ND AVE

1ST ST

2ND ST

INDUSTRIAL AVE

2ND AVE

COLUMBIA ST

MANITOBA ST

2ND ST

ONTARIO ST

QUEBEC ST

3RD AVE

MAIN ST

4TH AVE

2N

© AVALON TRAVEL PUBLISHING, INC.

kitchens, three lounges, and two laundries. Guests also have use of the nearby YWCA Health and Wellness Centre, which houses a pool and gym. Single rooms share a bathroom and cost $59 (mid-Nov.–May $51); double rooms with shared bath are $70 (off-season $56) or pay $132 for an en suite double room (off-season $84).

In this price range, you also move into the domain of older hotels—some good, some bad. Of these, the **M Victorian Hotel** (514 Homer St., 604/681-6369 or 877/681-6369, www.victorianhotel.ca) is one of the best choices. Guest rooms have only basic amenities, but they are comfortably furnished and light on the wallet. The central location and complimentary breakfast make them even better value. The Victorian was built as a guesthouse in 1898, and the rooms are decorated in a regal color scheme, which complements the polished hardwood floors. Rooms that share bathrooms are $69–89 s or d, those with en suite bathrooms and lovely bay windows are $109–129. Rates drop by around 20 percent outside of summer.

Like the Victorian Hotel, the three-story **Kingston Hotel** (757 Richards St., 604/684-9024 or 888/713-3304, www.kingstonhotel-vancouver.com) is around 100 years old and has been extensively renovated. Most of the 55 rooms share bathrooms ($68 s, $78 d) but have a sink with running water, while en suite rooms are $98–135 s or d. Amenities include a sauna, laundry, TV rental, and TV lounge with a collection of old-time movies. The adjacent parkade is handy if you have a vehicle. Room rates include a continental breakfast. Weekly and off-season rates save a few bucks.

$100–150

Spending $100–150 a night will get you a room in one of the older downtown motels, most of which are southwest toward Granville Island, a 10-minute walk from the Central Business District. If you're looking for weekend or off-season lodgings, check the websites of the $200-plus recommendations below for rates that fall easily into this price range.

Best value of downtown accommodations advertising rack rates in this price range is **Bosman's**

Hotel (1060 Howe St., 604/682-3171 or 888/267-6267, www.bosmanshotel.com), offering 100 fairly standard midsize rooms and older facilities, including an outdoor pool and restaurant. Summer rates are $139 s or d with $10 discounts for seniors and auto club members.

A colorful paint job and bright fabrics can do a lot to reinvent an old hotel, and you won't find a better example than the centrally located **M Howard Johnson Hotel Downtown** (1176 Granville St., 604/688-8701 or 888/654-6336, www.hojovancouver.com). Rooms with double beds are $149 s or d, queen beds $159, and the junior suites are especially good value at $189. In wintertime rates are discounted to $79–149 and breakfast is included. Year-round, rates include a morning paper and passes to a nearby fitness facility. A downstairs restaurant and lounge complete what is all in all a very good deal. The only downsides are thin walls and the need to make advance reservations (it's usually the least expensive Vancouver property listed in travel agent databases, so it books up quickly in summer).

$150–200

With the exception of the first two recommendations, most accommodations in this price range are scattered between the Central Business District and Granville Island.

Least expensive of the CBD hotels is **Vancouver—Days Inn Downtown** (921 W. Pender St., 604/681-4335 or 877/681-4335, www.daysinnvancouver.com). The 85 rooms are small, and surrounding high-rises block any views. But each room is decorated in bright and breezy pastel colors, and tea- and coffeemakers are provided; in summer rooms start at $189 s or d, discounted to $125 in the low season.

While guest facilities at **Ramada Limited Downtown** (435 W. Pender St., 604/488-1088 or 888/389-5888, www.ramadalimited.org) are limited compared to other properties in this price category, like the Days Inn, the location is very central. As an old hotel, its 80 rooms are small, but they are well appointed and come with everything from hair dryers to Nintendo. The summer rack rate is $199 s or d, including a light breakfast, discounted to $159 on weekends and as low as $99 during winter. Look for the retro neon sign out front.

Sandman Hotels, Inns, and Suites is a western Canadian chain of 31 properties, including the flagship **Sandman Hotel Downtown Vancouver** (180 W. Georgia St., 604/681-2211 or 800/726-3626, www.sandmanhotels.com). This hotel features more than 300 rooms, including 87 self-contained suites in the Corporate Tower, an indoor pool, health club, lounge, and a 24-hour family restaurant. Summer rates are good value at $170 s or d. For older travelers, Sandman's 55 Plus Program is worth noting: sign up over the Internet (free) for a variety of benefits, including a 25 percent discount at all Sandman properties.

The best reason to stay at the **Century Plaza Hotel** (1015 Burrard St., 604/687-0575 or 800/663-1818, www.century-plaza.com) is the Absolute Spa, a favorite haunt of movie stars in Vancouver on location. Each of the 236 kitchen-equipped rooms is comfortable, but not as opulent as the spa facility. Other amenities include a café, steakhouse restaurant, and lounge. Studio rooms are $189–239 s or d; one-bedroom suites, each with a balcony, are $259; and the 30th-floor penthouse suites are a relatively reasonable $350. Weekly rates and spa packages are also available.

The seven-story, 245-room **Holiday Inn Hotel and Suites** (1110 Howe St., 604/684-2151 or 800/663-9151, www.vancouverholidayinn.com) features an indoor pool, health club, a kids' play room, a lounge, and two restaurants. Rooms come in a variety of configurations, but all are well equipped, and as at Holiday Inns the world over, children stay and eat free. Standard rooms are $199 s or d, while rooms with a kitchen are $299 s or d. Outside of summer, rooms are around half these prices and $200 will get you the hotel's best suite.

$200–250

Granville Island Hotel (1253 Johnston St., 604/683-7373 or 800/663-1840, www.granvilleislandhotel.com) enjoys a fabulous location on the island of the same name immediately south of downtown. The island is home to

attractions, theaters, art galleries, interesting shops, restaurants, bars, and Vancouver's best public market, but downtown is only a short bus or ferry ride away. The hotel itself is designed to attract a young, hip clientele. Contemporary and elegant, the rooms are very spacious and furnished with Persian rugs, marble-floored bathrooms, and modern necessities, such as high-speed Internet access. Most also have water views. Other facilities include a fitness center, rooftop Jacuzzi, sauna, and kayak rentals from the on-site marina. There's also an in-house brewery and excellent restaurant specializing in West Coast cuisine. Summer rates for standard rooms start at $220 s, $230 d, discounted to as low as $150 the rest of the year.

$250–300

Delta Hotels and Resorts, Canada's largest chain of upscale hotels, has two Vancouver properties, including **Delta Vancouver Suites,** in the heart of downtown (550 W. Hastings St., 604/689-8188 or 877/814-7706, www.deltahotels.com). None of the 226 "suites" is equipped with a kitchen, but each is spacious and has a separate bedroom and comfortable lounge area. In-room business facilities include a work desk stocked with supplies, two phone lines, high-speed Internet access, and personalized voicemail. Other guest facilities include a health club, indoor pool, saunas and a whirlpool, and a street level New York–style restaurant open for breakfast, lunch, and dinner. Rack rates are $299 s or d, but as this hotel is aimed primarily at business travelers, greatly reduced weekend and package rates are offered; check the Delta website for current deals. The top three floors are reserved for Signature Club guests, where for a $45 premium you'll enjoy the best views, upgraded room facilities, and use of a private lounge where a complimentary breakfast and afternoon snacks are served.

$300–400

Regarded as one of the world's hippest hotels, the **M Opus Hotel** (322 Davie St., Yaletown, 604/642-6787 or 866/642-6787, www.opushotel.com) fills a very distinct niche in the Vancouver scene—a mega-cool place to stay.

This means vibrant colors, striking decor, clean-line furnishings, 250-count linens, 27-inch TVs, CD players, luxurious bathrooms filled with top-notch bath products, valet-only parking, and upscale dining and drinking off the brightly minimalist lobby. Rooms are decorated in five color themes (chose your favorite when booking online) and come in a variety of configurations, including one daring layout with the bathroom on the floor-to-ceiling windowed outer wall. The biggest rooms are outfitted with wet bars and plasma screen TVs. Although rack rates are from $389 s or d, check the website for discounts and packages, such as bed-and-breakfast and back-to-bed (checkout is 3 P.M.) for $300 d. From the glass-bottled Norwegian mineral water you receive upon arrival to the front desk staff remembering your name, a stay at the Opus will be memorable.

Drawing a mix of upscale business travelers and international vacationers, the **Vancouver Marriott Pinnacle** (1128 W. Hastings St., 604/684-1128 or 800/2228-9290, www.marriott.com) is an excellent choice in the downtown core. Dating to 2000, this full-service property features 434 spacious rooms, each with stylish furniture, elegant bathrooms, a writing desk full of office supplies, two telephones (including a cordless) with voicemail and Internet access, a coffeemaker, ironing facilities, and also an umbrella for Vancouver's occasional rainy days. Guests enjoy complimentary use of the hotel's health club, which features a 17-meter indoor pool, a hot tub, a sauna, and a large outdoor patio area. Off the lobby is one of the city's premier restaurants, Show Case, along with an adjoining bar. Rack rates are $309 and $329 s or d for a queen and king bed respectively, discounted to $199 and $219 outside of summer. Weekend rates and special packages (check the Marriott website) are offered year-round.

Fairmont Hotels and Resorts, best known for landmark accommodations like the Fairmont Empress in Victoria and the Fairmont Banff Springs in Banff, operates two properties in the downtown area. The copper-roofed **Fairmont Hotel Vancouver** (900 W. Georgia St., 604/684-3131 or 866/540-4452, www.fairmont.com) is the company's Vancouver flagship and a downtown landmark—you can't help but notice the distinctive green copper roof, the gargoyles, and the classic, Gothic château-style architecture of this grand old hotel. The original Hotel Vancouver, which opened in 1887, was built by the Canadian Pacific Railway. Destroyed by fire in the early 1930s, it was rebuilt from the ground up and reopened amid much fanfare in 1939. The 1990s saw a $60-million refit—which included returning the exterior to its original color—an eight-year project. Today, with its former glory restored, the Hotel Vancouver is one of Canada's grandest accommodations, from the cavernous marble-lined lobby to the high ceilings and 556 elegantly furnished rooms. Facilities include restaurants, a comfortable lounge, an indoor pool, saunas, a weight room, health facilities, 24-hour room service, ample parking, and a large staff to attend to your every whim. The smallish standard rooms start at $350 s or d, but upgrading to a larger Fairmont Room is only a few dollars extra, and good-value packages are offered year-round, such as bed-and-breakfast for $259 high season, $199 low season.

You'll be knocked out by the views at the **Fairmont Waterfront** (900 Canada Place Way, 604/691-1991 or 866/540-4509, www.fairmont.com), sister property of the Hotel Vancouver but without the history. Rising 23 stories from beside Canada Place, the 489 rooms are all spacious, and over half of them enjoy stunning harbor views. Many of the artwork found throughout the hotel was specially commissioned for the property. Guest facilities include a third-floor health club and outdoor pool, and rooms are equipped with luxurious bathrobes, a work desk, and remote checkout. Standard, smallish rooms go for $359 s or d in summer, but if you're going to spend this much, consider upgrading to the larger Fairmont Deluxe room overlooking the harbor for an extra $40. Outside of summer, you'll get these same rooms for $229, *including* breakfast. Guests and nonguests alike can enjoy a grand Sunday brunch in the downstairs restaurant.

Memories of another era pervade at the **Crowne Plaza Hotel Georgia** (801 Georgia St., 604/682-5566 or 800/663-1111, www.hotel-georgia.bc.ca), across the road from the art gallery and kitty-corner to the Hotel Vancouver. Built in 1927 in a Georgian-revival style, this 313-room grande dame was restored to her former glory through the second half of the 1990s. Original oak furnishings, the oak-paneled lobby, and the brass elevator have been restored and all facilities upgraded, including a fitness center and various eating establishments. If this is your accommodation of choice, your name will join a guest list that has included Queen Elizabeth II, Katherine Hepburn, and the Beatles. The best views are from rooms facing the art gallery. In summer, rooms cost $369–399 s or d during the week, while on weekends breakfast and a late checkout are included in the rate of $319. Outside of summer, rooms start at $200, including breakfast on weekends.

Over $400

One block from the city end of Robson Street is the super-luxurious, European-style **Sutton Place Hotel** (845 Burrard St., 604/682-5511 or 800/961-7555, www.suttonplace.com; from $464 s or d), one of only a handful of properties in North America to get a precious five-diamond rating from the American AA. This, Vancouver's most elegant accommodation, features original European artwork in public areas and reproductions in the 397 rooms. Rooms are furnished with king-size beds, plush bathrobes, ice dispensers, and two phone lines, and guests enjoy a twice-daily maid service, complete with fresh flowers. Le Spa is an in-house spa, fitness, and health facility in the tradition of a luxurious European spa resort. Other facilities include a glass-enclosed pool, a business center, an English gentlemen's club-style lounge bar, and Fleuri, an upmarket restaurant. Discounted weekend and off-season rates are around $300.

Since the world's first Four Seasons Hotel opened in the Canadian city of Toronto in 1961

Pan Pacific Hotel provides breathtaking harbor views.

the company has expanded into 20 other countries, gaining a reputation for the very best in comfort and service. The Vancouver **Four Seasons Hotel** (791 W. Georgia St., 604/689-9333 or 800/268-6282, www.fourseasons.com) is no exception, getting a five-diamond rating from the American AA. The spacious rooms are luxuriously appointed, with guests enjoying fresh flowers, a wide range of in-room amenities, and twice-daily housekeeping. Other guest facilities include an indoor and outdoor pool complex, a business center, and various eating establishments, including casual dining in a plant-filled atrium and the grandly old-fashioned Chartwell Restaurant. Somewhat surprisingly, the Four Seasons is kid-friendly, with children supplied with teddy bears and mini bathrobes. Summer rates start at $425 s, $455 d, discounted well under $300 on the website.

For all the modern conveniences along with unbeatable city and harbor views, head for the sparkling **Pan Pacific Hotel Vancouver** (Canada Place, 604/662-8111 or 800/937-1515, www.panpacific.com). It garners a five-diamond rating from the American AA and is generally regarded as one of the world's top 100 hotels. It's part of the landmark Canada Place (the top eight floors of the 13-story complex are guest rooms), whose Teflon sails fly over busy, bustling sidewalks and a constant flow of cruise ships. The hotel lobby is up a massive escalator that begins at the city end of Canada Place. Each of the 504 spacious rooms boasts stunning views, contemporary furnishings, a luxurious marble bathroom, and in-room video checkout. Facilities include a pool, an extra-charge health club, Sails Restaurant, and Cascades Lounge. Rack rates for the least expensive city-view rooms are $490, but the hotel website regularly sells rooms with water views for around $400.

ROBSON STREET

Robson Street—with its sidewalk cafés, restaurants open till the wee hours, and fashionable boutiques—provides a great alternative to staying right downtown. And anyway, the accommodations along this strip are as central to the business district as many of those listed under *Downtown.* Although you'll generally get better value for your money and pay less for parking in this part of the city, the rates quoted below aren't discounted as much (if at all) on weekends, unlike the downtown business traveler–oriented hotels.

$100–150

Built in the 1920s, the European-style **Barclay Hotel** (1348 Robson St., 604/688-8850, www.barclayhotel.com; $95 s, $125 d) has 80 medium-size rooms, a small lounge, and an intimate restaurant. The rooms are stylish in a slightly old-fashioned way; each holds a comfortable bed, writing desk, couch, and older TV. Outside of summer, rates drop to a very reasonable $55–85. A buffet breakfast is included in all rates, making the Barclay a good deal at any time of the year.

The **Greenbrier Hotel** (1393 Robson St., 604/683-4558 or 888/355-5888, www.greenbrierhotel.com) looks a bit rough on the outside, but each of the 32 units were refurbished in the mid-1990s, and each has a large living area, full kitchen, and separate bedroom. Rates are $129–169 s or d, reduced to under $100 October–April.

One block farther toward Stanley Park, the **Riviera Hotel** (1431 Robson St., 604/685-1301 or 888/699-5222, www.rivieraonrobson.com; $108 s, $128 d) offers similar facilities, as well as harbor or city views from the upper floors. All rooms are large and comfortably furnished. One-bedroom suites are $188 s or d.

$150–200

A few blocks closer to downtown and a step up in quality is the 214-room **Blue Horizon Hotel** (1225 Robson St., 604/688-1411 or 800/663-1333, www.bluehorizonhotel.com). Facilities include an indoor lap pool, a fitness room, a sauna, and services for business travelers. The hotel is also home to popular Inlets Bistro and a sidewalk café. All 214 rooms are large, brightly lit, and have a work desk, coffee-making facilities, and in-room safe. One quirk of the layout is that every room is a corner room, complete with private balcony. To take advantage of this, request a room on a higher floor. Rooms on floors 15–30 cost $179–199 s or d. Also on the upper floors are one-bedroom, two-bathroom suites—good value at $259–299. Rates for rooms on the lower floors are $159–169 s or d.

$200–250

The ⚑ **Pacific Palisades Hotel** (1277 Robson St., 604/688-0461 or 800/663-1815, www.pacificpalisadeshotel.com) is touted as being a cross between "South Beach (Miami) and Stanley Park," a fairly apt description of this chic Robson Street accommodation. It was originally a luxury apartment building, and interior designers have given the entire hotel a "beachy," ultra-contemporary feel—each of the 233 spacious rooms is decorated with sleek furnishings and a dynamic color scheme. Many have views and all have a large work desk, super-comfortable beds, a coffeemaker, and high-speed Internet access. Amenities include a lounge and stylish restaurant, a fitness center, an 18-meter indoor lap pool, business services, and newspapers and coffee in the lobby each morning. Rack rates are a reasonable $200–225 s or d ($250 for a suite) in summer, discounted year-round on the website an up to 50 percent in winter. Parking is $24 per day.

Diagonally opposite Pacific Palisades, **Listel Vancouver** (1300 Robson St., 604/684-8461 or 800/663-5491, www.listel-vancouver.com) is independently owned but affiliated with the Sterling Hotels and Resorts chain. This elegant full-service lodging is best known for its innovative use of original and limited edition Northwest Coast artwork through 54 of the 130 rooms. Rooms themselves are well appointed, highlighted by contemporary furnishings, goose-down duvets, and luxurious bathrooms. Summer rates for a regular room are $240 s or d, while the rooms on the two Museum Floors, which in addition to artwork feature separate bedrooms and bay windows, are $300.

Over $250

The 510-room **Westin Bayshore** (1601 W. Georgia St., 604/682-3377 or 888/625-5144, www.westinbayshore.com) is unique within the downtown peninsula in that it offers a distinctive resort-style atmosphere—the perfect haunt for families. Lying right on Coal Harbour and linked to Stanley Park by a waterfront promenade, it has undergone massive renovations since the infamous recluse Howard Hughes spent four months in his Westin suite in 1971. The hotel now features a large outdoor pool surrounded by outdoor furniture settings and a poolside lounge, a health club, and a yacht charter operation down on the marina. Rooms in the main building feature floor-to-ceiling windows ($380–440 s or d), while those in the tower have private balconies ($500 s or d).

WEST END

The few accommodations at the west end of downtown are near some fine restaurants, close to Stanley Park and English Bay, and a 25-minute walk along bustling Robson Street from downtown proper.

$50–100

Overlooking English Bay and the closest beach to downtown, the old-style funky ⚑ **Sylvia Hotel** (1154 Gilford St., 604/681-9321, www.sylviahotel.com) is a local landmark sporting a brick and terra-cotta exterior covered with Virginia creeper. Built in 1912 as an apartment building and named after the owner's daughter, the eight-story Sylvia was the tallest building on this side of town until 1958. It went upscale in the 1960s, with the opening of Vancouver's first cocktail bar. Today, it's popular with budget travelers looking for something a little more than a hostel, with rates ranging $90–190 s or d (the less-expensive rooms are fairly small), with more expensive rooms featuring fantastic views and full kitchens. Rates outside of summer range $70–105 s or d. The Sylvia also has a restaurant and lounge.

A hostel for grownups, the three-story **Buchan Hotel** (1906 Haro St., 604/685-5354 or 800/668-6654, www.buchanhotel.com) is in a quiet residential area one block from Stanley Park. Built as an apartment hotel in 1926, the atmosphere today is friendly, especially in the evening when guests gather in the main lounge. On the downside, the rooms are small and sparsely decorated. Rates for rooms with shared bathroom facilities are $72 s, $78 d, and those with private bathrooms are $85 s, $95 d. The largest corner rooms are $125 s, $135 d.

$100–150

Built at the turn of the 20th century, the **West End Guest House** (1362 Haro St., 604/681-2889, www.westendguesthouse.com) has been lovingly refurbished in Victorian-era colors and furnished with stylish antiques to retain its original charm. Each of the eight guest rooms has a brass bed complete with cotton linen and a goose-down duvet, an en suite bathroom, a TV, and a telephone. Guests can relax either in the comfortable lounge or on the outdoor terrace and have the use of bikes. The smallest room costs $139 s, while the others range $169–255 s or d. After dishing up a full cooked breakfast (included in the rates), the friendly owners will set you up with a wealth of ideas for a day of sightseeing. Parking and use of bikes are free.

$150–200

One block from Stanley Park and nestled among towering apartment blocks is **English Bay Inn** (1968 Comox St., 604/683-8002), a quiet retreat from the pace of the city. The decor is stylish, in an old-fashioned way. Highlights include a lounge area with log fireplace and a small garden out the back. Rates start at $175 s or d, and the two-room suite goes for $295.

Over $200

Families especially will like **Aston Rosellen Suites** (2030 Barclay St., 604/689-4807 or 888/317-6648, www.rosellensuites.com), in a residential area right by Stanley Park. Each of the 30 extra-spacious units features modern furnishings, a separate living and dining area, a full kitchen, and modern conveniences such as stereos and voicemail. Rates are $209 for a one-bedroom unit, $239 for a two-bedroom unit, and $269–399 for larger units with fireplaces and private patios. Rates include access to a nearby fitness facility and indoor pool. Through summer,

a three-night minimum-stay policy is in effect. Check-in is daily 9 A.M.–5 P.M.

Coast Plaza Hotel & Suites (1763 Comox St., 604/688-7711 or 800/663-1144, www.coasthotels.com) is part of a 20-strong Pacific Northwest hotel chain renowned for providing good value and upmarket accommodations. A couple of blocks from English Bay and surrounded by good dining choices, this full-service hotel comes with 267 rooms on 35 levels. As a former apartment tower, its rooms are spacious; all have balconies, in-room coffee, and free local calls, and most feature kitchens. Amenities include a health club, an indoor pool, room service, a bistro (open daily at 6:30 A.M.), and a lounge. Regular rates are from $255 s or d, but as at other properties in the chain, a package is the way to go, even if it's just bed-and-breakfast; check the website for deals. (If you're traveling extensively in B.C., consider the Coast Hotels' frequent traveler program—it's free to join and offers a variety of discounts.)

NORTH SHORE

The best reason to stay on the North Shore is to enjoy the local hospitality at one of the many bed-and-breakfasts, but hotels and motels are also scattered through this part of the city.

$50–100

Perfect as a jumping-off point for the ferry trip to the Sunshine Coast or Vancouver Island is the **Horseshoe Bay Motel** (6588 Royal Ave., 604/921-7454), 12 kilometers (7.5 miles) west of the Lions Gate Bridge, tucked below the highway in Horseshoe Bay and right by the BC Ferries terminal. It's within easy walking distance of numerous cafés and restaurants, and the nearby Horseshoe Bay Marina is a pleasant place for an evening stroll. Rooms are clean and comfortable, but at $90 s or d you're paying for the location more than anything.

$100–150

Close to Grouse Mountain Gondola, **M Mountainside Manor** (5909 Nancy Greene Way, North Vancouver, 604/990-9772 or 877/990-9772, www.mountainsidemanor.com; May–Oct.) is a great place to unwind—especially in the outdoor hot tub. This modern home high above the city also features four comfortable rooms of different configurations, each with a en suite bathroom and a TV. The least expensive of the rooms is $110 s or d, while the best, the Mountain Room, offers spectacular views, a king-size bed, and a Jacuzzi tub, all for a reasonable $135 s or d (two-night minimum).

$150–200

If you're prepared to spend a bit more money (and to book well ahead), **Ⓜ Beachside B&B** (4208 Evergreen Ave., West Vancouver, 604/922-7773 or 800/563-3311, www.beach.bc.ca) is an excellent choice. Set on an absolute waterfront lot at Sandy Cove (access off Marine Drive), Beachside has its own private beach with views extending across Burrard Inlet to Stanley Park and the downtown skyline. The two larger suites have water views, semiprivate patios, and Jacuzzi tubs; $250 s or d. The smallest of the four rooms, which opens to a private patio, is $150 s or d. Each of the rooms has an en suite bathroom, TV and video, coffeemaker, and microwave. All rates include either a full, cooked breakfast in the dining room or an in-room continental breakfast.

Gracious **Thistledown House** (3910 Capilano Rd., North Vancouver, 604/986-7173 or 888/633-7173, www.thistle-down.com; $150–275) has been restored to resemble a country-style inn. Each of the five rooms has been tastefully decorated and has its own character, a private bathroom, a balcony, and many delightful touches, such as homemade soap. If you're going to splurge, request the Under the Apple Tree room, which features a king-size bed, split-level sitting room, and a large bathroom complete with a Jacuzzi tub. Rates include a gourmet breakfast served in the dining room and afternoon tea served in the cozy lounge or landscaped gardens, depending on the weather.

For old-fashioned charm, the pick of accommodations on the north side of Burrard Inlet is the **Park Royal Hotel** (540 Clyde Ave., West Vancouver, 604/926-5511 or 877/926-5511, www.parkroyalhotel.com). The Tudor-style accommodation sits on the banks of the Capilano River—you can fish for salmon and steelhead right on the property—and is surrounded by well-maintained gardens. The 30 rooms are small, but each has a brass bed. Rates start at $160 s or d, with rooms that have garden views ranging $190–230, depending on their size. To get there from downtown, take the Lions Gate Bridge over Burrard Inlet, turn left over the Capilano River, turn right onto Taylor Way, then take the next right, Clyde Avenue.

Yes, it's a chain motel, but at the **Holiday Inn Express Vancouver North Shore** (1800 Capilano Rd., 604/987-4461 or 800/663-4055, www.holiday-inn.com) you know exactly what you're paying for—a smartly decorated room with a light breakfast included in the rates of $189 s or d. Check the website for rooms discounted to around $140. An outdoor pool is a bonus.

Over $200

If you don't have transportation but don't want to stay downtown, the **Lonsdale Quay Hotel** (123 Carrie Cates Court, North Vancouver, 604/986-6111 or 800/836-6111, www.lonsdalequayhotel.com) is a good choice. It enjoys an absolute waterfront location above lively Lonsdale Quay Market and the SeaBus Terminal, making it just 12 minutes to downtown by water. Each of the 70 rooms is equipped with modern furnishings and amenities that normally only come with a more expensive downtown room, such as Internet access, a daily newspaper, and a water cooler. Hotel guests are also provided with a fitness center, a sauna and whirlpool, covered parking, and a complimentary North Shore shuttle. The hotel has a restaurant, but downstairs, spread through the market, is a wider choice of waterfront cafés, restaurants, and lounges. One- and two-bedroom suites start at $205 and $265 respectively, but for the best rooms, with a stunning view across Burrard Inlet to the panorama of downtown, you'll pay from $300. Outside of summer, these same $300 rooms are discounted to $200.

KITSILANO, SHAUGHNESSY, AND VICINITY

Hip Kitsilano and old-money Shaughnessy are two of Vancouver's most upscale residential neighborhoods. Accommodations in this part of the city are nearly all bed-and-breakfasts, and the following are my favorites.

Under $50

If you're on a budget and don't need to stay right downtown, **HI–Vancouver Jericho Beach** (1515 Discovery St., Point Grey, 604/224-3208 or 888/203-4303, www.hihostels.ca; May–Sept.) is a good alternative choice. The location is fantastic—in scenic and safe parkland behind Jericho Beach, across English Bay from downtown and linked to extensive biking and walking trails. Inside the huge white building are separate dorms for men and women, rooms for couples and families, a living area with TV, and a kitchen. Additional amenities include a large café open for breakfast and dinner through summer (good food, reasonable prices), a handy information board, public Internet access, lockers, left-luggage service ($5 a bag per week), free parking (limited), and a shuttle to the downtown hostel and rail/bus station. Members pay $19 per night, nonmembers $23 for a dorm bed, or $60 and $69 respectively for a double room. To get there, take Northwest Marine Drive off 4th Avenue West and turn right down Discovery Street at the arts center.

$50–100

Tucked away near the south end of Pacific Spirit Regional Park (off Dundar Street) is **Pacific Spirit Guest House** (4080 West 35th Ave., 604/261-6837 or 866/768-6837, www.vanbb.com; $80 s, $90 d), a budget-priced bed-and-breakfast. Choose between the guest room with a king-size bed or one with garden views. All guests are welcome to relax in the lounge and help themselves to tea and coffee, or take advantage of the large collection of books and music in the library. In the morning, a huge, multicourse breakfast will set you up for a day of sightseeing.

$100–150

On the southern edge of Shaughnessy, **Beautiful B&B** (428 W. 40th Ave., just off Cambie St., 604/327-1102, www.beautifulbandb.bc.ca) is a colonial-style two-story home on a high point of land where views extend across the city to the North Shore Range. Both Queen Elizabeth Park and VanDusen Botanical Garden are within walking distance. The house is decorated with antiques and fresh flowers from the surrounding garden. Two rooms share a bathroom ($135–175 s or d), while the Honeymoon Suite features a fireplace, panoramic views, and a huge en suite bathroom complete with soaker tub ($245 s or d).

M Arbutus Garden House (4470 Maple Cres., Shaughnessy, 604/738-6432 or 866/824-8911, www.arbutushouse.com; mid-June–Oct.) is a magnificent 1922 three-story home surrounded by similar grandiose homes that make up one of Vancouver's most prestigious suburbs. The house itself features a distinct heritage character and elegant touches, such as oak flooring, leaded windows, and stylish antiques, throughout. The four guest rooms are spacious, and each features fresh flowers picked daily, a small writing desk, robes, slippers, and tea- and coffee-making facilities. Guests also enjoy use of separate TV and sitting rooms, decks, and the surrounding gardens and outdoor furniture. Each morning, a gourmet breakfast is served in an elegant dining room, with an oak table as its centerpiece. Summer rates range $135–165 s or d, with the largest room featuring a gas fireplace, bar fridge, and a luxurious bathroom complete with a heated floor.

Farther west, in the suburb of Kitsilano, is **Penny Farthing Inn** (2855 W. 6th Ave., 604/739-9002, www.pennyfarthinginn.com), another heritage house, this one with four antique-filled rooms, hardwood floors, and stained-glass windows. The least expensive room is $105 s, $115 d, while the suite, complete with mountain views, a brass bed, and separate lounge area with a TV, small fridge, and CD player, is $170 s or d. It's a five-block walk, downhill all the way, to the water, then a similar distance east to famous Kitsilano Beach—the perfect place to watch the last rays of sun hit downtown.

KINGSWAY

The Kingsway is a main thoroughfare linking downtown to Burnaby. It is lined with a smattering of inexpensive motels—perfect if you want to save a few dollars and like the convenience of being a short bus ride from downtown. Another advantage is that you won't need to worry about parking (or paying for parking). Nearby is a cluster of inexpensive restaurants, the perfect place for a budget-conscious traveler to end the day with a good meal (see *West Broadway* under *Food*).

$50–100

The least-expensive lodging choices in this part of the city are old motels along the Kingsway, the main route between downtown and New Westminster. At the bottom of the price spectrum is the **2400 Motel** (2400 Kingsway 604/434-2464 or 888/833-2400), an old roadside-style place with basic rooms, cable TV, and coffee and newspapers offered in the office each morning. Rates start at $75 s or d, with kitchenettes for $105 and two-bedroom units from $110 for four adults. It's near Nanaimo Street and within walking distance of the 29th Avenue SkyTrain station.

$100–150

Pillow Suites (2859 Manitoba St., Mt. Pleasant, 604/879-8977, www.pillow.net) is a unique lodging three blocks west of the Kingsway and a few hundred meters east of City Hall. The six suites are spread through three adjacent, colorfully painted heritage houses. Each unit is fully self-contained with a kitchen, en suite bathroom, telephone, cable TV, fireplace, and private entrance. Rates range from $115 for the Country Store, formerly a corner store and now filled with brightly painted appliances, to $255 for a complete three-bedroom house that sleeps six comfortably.

Within walking distance of a SkyTrain station is **Days Inn—Vancouver Metro** (2075 Kingsway, 604/876-5531 or 800/546-4792, www.daysinn.com). It was built in the 1960s as the Kingsway Lodge, and although it still holds its original configuration of 66 rooms, it is a pleas-

ant place to stay, with rooms opening to a private and quiet courtyard. The renovated rooms are typical of other Days Inn properties with a simple, contemporary feel, and each has amenities, such as hair dryers and coffeemakers. Summer rates are $109–129 s or d, dropping as low as $79 the rest of the year.

$150–200

Holiday Inn Vancouver Centre (711 W. Broadway, 604/879-0511 or 800/465-4329, www.hivancouver.com; $179–199 d) lies on the south side of False Creek. As well as enjoying city views, it's just 200 meters downhill to waterfront Charleson Park and then less than one kilometer west along False Creek to Granville Island. The hotel itself features 193 rooms spread over 16 floors, an indoor pool complex that opens to an outdoor deck with great views, a lounge, and a restaurant (or eat at nearby Tojo's). The moderately sized rooms each have a work desk, comfortable beds, and a coffeemaker. Rates are discounted year-round on weekends.

RICHMOND

The following Richmond accommodations are good choices for those visitors who arrive late at or have an early departure from the international airport. Also, if you arrive in Vancouver and want to head straight over to Vancouver Island, staying in this vicinity saves an unnecessary trip into downtown. All accommodations detailed in this section offer complimentary airport shuttles.

$100–150

The **Coast Vancouver Airport Hotel** (1041 Southwest Marine Dr., 604/263-1555 or 800/716-6199, www.coasthotels.com) lies farther from the airport (toward the city) than the rest of the lodgings detailed in this section, but with free airport transfers, free long-term parking, and in-house dining, it is still aimed directly at airport travelers. No surprises with the rooms here—each has modern decor, a work desk, ironing facility, coffeemaker, and free local calls. Other amenities include a fitness center, sports bar, and family restaurant. Instead of paying the rack rate ($129 s or d), inquire about the Coast's many packages suited to arriving and departing air passengers, such as $99 s or d for breakfast and seven days' parking.

Three kilometers (1.9 miles) from the airport, the **Holiday Inn Express Vancouver Airport** (9351 Bridgeport Rd., 604/273-8080 or 888/831-3388, www.holiday-inn.com) is a typical modern, multistory airport hotel, with large and comfortably furnished rooms. The rates of $149 s or d ($129 outside of summer) include a large breakfast bar, which offers everything from toast and jam to fresh fruit and yogurt.

$150–200

Don't be put off by the name of the **Vancouver Airport Conference Resort** (10251 St. Edwards Dr., 604/278-9611 or 866/482-8444, www.vacr.bc.ca); it's a wonderful place for families or for those who want to pretend they're not in a city at all. Set on 5.7 hectares (14 acres) of landscaped grounds, fun facilities include a fitness center, large water slide, one indoor and two outdoor pools, tennis and squash courts, and bike rentals. Children can take advantage of a giant indoor water slide, a Creative Centre, and their own swim club, while parents enjoy inexpensive child care. The pick of many eateries includes one restaurant specializing in West Coast cuisine and another with poolside patio-style seating. Rack rates start at $159 s or d, but it's worth the extra $30 to stay in the rooms overlooking the pool area. As well as an airport shuttle, buses to the local shopping mall are provided. It is also a pickup point for Quick Shuttle to Seattle.

Centrally located three kilometers (1.9 miles) from the main airport terminals, the **Radisson President Hotel and Suites** (8181 Cambie Rd., 604/276-8181 or 800/333-3333, www.radissonvancouver.com) is a sprawling complex of 184 guest rooms, a fitness center, indoor pool, and several restaurants. The rooms are spacious and well appointed, making the rates of $179 s or d, including breakfast, reasonable. Travelers 55 and older get a better deal—they pay from $129 s or d.

Right at the international airport, the **Fairmont Vancouver Airport** (3111 Grant Mc-

Conachie Way, 604/207-5200 or 888/540-4441, www.fairmont.com) was one of the world's most technologically advanced hotels when it opened in 1999. Tightened security has put an end to some of the innovations (such as checking in for flights from the rooms), but it's still impressive—the 398 rooms are equipped with remote-controlled everything, right down to the drapes, fog-free bathroom mirrors, and floor-to-ceiling soundproofed windows. Other more traditional hotel conveniences include a huge work center, a health club (where swimmers take to the self-adjusted current of a lap pool), and the Spa at the Fairmont massage and treatment facility. Standard rooms are $189 s or d, but a wide variety of packages are offered, such as accommodation and a week's parking for $169. Rooms on the Entrée Gold Floor—where rates include breakfast, use of a private lounge, and extras such as touch-screen phones—start at $289 s or d, but, again with these rooms, a package is the way to go.

DELTA

Separated from Richmond by the South Arm of the Fraser River, Delta is a continuation of Vancouver's sprawl. It's an ideal place to stay if you're planning to get an early morning jump on the crowds for the ferry trip over to Vancouver Island, or if you're arriving from the United States and don't feel like tackling city traffic after a long day's drive.

$50–100

The **Delta Town and Country Inn** (6005 Hwy. 17, 604/946-4404 or 888/777-1266, www.deltainn.com) is ideally situated and an excellent value. It's at the junction of Highway 99 and Highway 17, halfway between the airport and the ferry terminal, but the setting is parklike and quiet, with most of the 50 rooms enjoying views over extensive gardens and a landscaped pool area. In addition to the large pool, facilities include tennis courts, a restaurant, and a sports bar. Each of the spacious rooms features comfortable beds, a work desk, a high-quality TV, and a coffeemaker. Rates through summer are

$99 s or d, including breakfast, and drop to $79 the rest of the year.

$100–150

The closest accommodation to the southern departure point for ferries to Vancouver Island is the **Coast Tsawwassen Inn** (1665 56th St., 604/943-8221 or 800/943-8221, www.coasthotels.com), four kilometers (2.5 miles) northeast of the ferry terminal back toward the city along Highway 17. The hotel comprises two separate sections, one containing 50 newly decorated guest rooms, an indoor and outdoor pool, a fitness center, two restaurants, and a lounge. The other part of the complex holds 89 much larger suites, each with a kitchen and private patio. Regular rooms are $119 s or d and the suites are $149; both these rates include a shuttle service that runs to the ferry and airport terminals and to a local shopping mall.

BURNABY

Under $50

Although it's about 20 kilometers (12 miles) east of downtown Vancouver, **Simon Fraser University** (Housing and Conference Services, Room 212, McTaggart-Cowan Hall, 604/291-4503) offers inexpensive dorm rooms to summer travelers. The hilltop campus is known for its modern architecture and excellent city views. Single or twin, fully furnished townhouse units with shared bathrooms are available May–August; from $26 s, $45 twin. Each room has a desk and fridge; kitchen facilities, TV lounges, and laundry are shared. The university is between Highways 7 and 7A in Burnaby. To get there by public transport, take the SkyTrain to the Production Way station and transfer to one of the regularly scheduled University buses.

$50–100

The least-expensive motel in this sprawling suburban area immediately east of downtown is the **401 Motor Inn** (2950 Boundary Rd., 604/438-3451 or 877/438-3451; $75 s, $80 d). From the TransCanada Highway eastbound, take Exit 28A south onto Boundary Road or westbound Exit 28B onto the Grandview Highway and take Boundary Road to the south; either way it's less than 200 meters (220 yards) from the highway and on the left. It's also possible to reach the 401 by taking Boundary Road north from the Kingsway. The motel itself is an older, two-story property set around a small outdoor pool. Rooms are moderately sized, and a light breakfast is included in the rates.

Falling in the same price range, the **Happy Day Inn** (7330 6th St., 604/524-8501 or 800/665-9733, www.happydayinn.com) is farther east (almost in New Westminster). Rooms are brightly decorated and each is air-conditioned. Amenities include a small fitness facility and a sauna. Standard rooms are $76 s, $82 d; kitchenettes $79 s, $83 d; twin rooms that sleep up to four $94. These rates are discounted 10 percent outside of summer, or book through the Internet to save a few bucks. To get there, take Edmonds Street east from the Kingsway to 6th Street.

$100–150

Coming into the city on the TransCanada Highway, there's a cluster of motels just west of where the highway crosses the Fraser River, including **Best Western Chelsea Inn** (725 Brunette Ave., 604/525-7777 or 800/528-1234, www.bestwestern.com). This motel features 61 well-appointed rooms, each with a lounge and coffee-making facilities. One room caters to the needs of travelers with disabilities. Other amenities include a heated outdoor pool, Jacuzzi, and laundry. Breakfast at the hotel restaurant is included in the rates, but this eatery also offers lunch and dinner choices of healthy West Coast fare. Rates range $122–150 s or d, and as at all Best Westerns, travelers 55 and older are offered discounted rooms (and a late checkout).

$150–200

Holiday Inn Metrotown (4405 Central Blvd., 604/438-1881 or 877/323-1177, www.holiday-inn.com) is part of Vancouver's biggest shopping complex and is connected to downtown by the SkyTrain. The 100 rooms are spread over six stories in this contemporary hotel. Each is spacious and well appointed, and guests enjoy an evening turndown service. Other facilities include a wide range of recreational amenities, including an outdoor swimming pool, a tennis court, and a fitness center. Rack rates are $179 s, $189 d, but Holiday Inn Great Rates ($129 s or d) apply year-round, and weekend rates ($139) include a breakfast voucher.

ABBOTSFORD
$100–150

If you are using Vancouver's second airport, at Abbotsford, **Holiday Inn Express** (2073 Clearbrook Rd., Clearbrook, 604/859-6211 or 800/665-7252, www.holiday-inn.com) is a convenient accommodation. It features large rooms and an indoor pool. Summer rates are $129 s or d, discounted to well under $100 in winter. Like all Holiday Inn Express hotels, this one includes a light breakfast in the rates, but there's also an adjacent family-style restaurant.

CHILLIWACK

Just over 100 kilometers (62 miles) from downtown, Chilliwack forms the eastern extent of Vancouver's sprawl. If you're heading into the city after a long day on the road or want an early start for an eastbound road trip, the following two accommodations are excellent choices.

$50–100

Take Exit 119B eastbound or Exit 119A westbound to access **Rainbow Motor Inn** (45620 Yale Rd., 604/792-6412 or 800/834-5547, www.rainbowmotorinn.com). Extensively renovated inside and out, this motel provides comfortable, no-frills accommodations for $79 s, $89 d, or pay $5 extra for a room with a kitchenette. Each of the 40 rooms is air-conditioned and has a small refrigerator. Rates include discounted dining at two adjacent restaurants.

$100–150

The **Best Western Rainbow Country Inn** (43971 Industrial Way, 604/795-3828 or 800/665-1030, www.rainbowcountryinn.com)

is reached by taking Exit 116 (Lickman Road). The 74 rooms are set around a huge atrium, complete with dense tropical shrubbery, a waterfall, and a swimming pool. This is also the setting for the hotel's restaurant, open throughout the day but also popular with the locals for Sunday brunch. Rates for the moderately sized standard rooms are $115 s or d, or pay $130 for room with a king-size bed and jetted tub.

CAMPGROUNDS

You won't find any campgrounds in the city center area, but a limited number dot the suburbs along the major approach routes. Before trekking out to any of them, ring ahead to check for vacancies. Commercial and provincial park campgrounds are listed in the invaluable *Accommodations* guide, a free publication produced by Tourism British Columbia (250/387-1642 or 800/435-5622, www.hellobc.com).

Unless otherwise noted, the campgrounds below are open year-round.

North

The closest campground to downtown is **Capilano RV Park** (295 Tomahawk Ave., North Vancouver, 604/987-4722, www.capilanorvpark.com). To get there from downtown, cross Lions Gate Bridge, turn right on Marine Drive, right on Capilano Road, and right again on Welch Street. From Highway 1/99 in West Vancouver, exit south on Taylor Way toward the shopping center and turn left over the Capilano River. It's about an hour walk to downtown from the campground, over Lions Gate Bridge and through Stanley Park. Amenities include a 13-meter pool, a big hot tub, a TV and games room, and a laundry. Sites are equipped with 15- and 30-amp power as well as sewer, water, cable, and telephone hookups. These sites range $35–48 per night. It gets crowded in summer; even though there are more than 200 sites, you'll need to book well ahead to be assured of a site through summer. The park is really intended for vehicle camping and RVs, but limited spots are available for tents ($30). No bookings are taken for the tenting area, so call ahead and ask if they have any grassy areas left.

South

Large **Richmond RV Park,** 15 kilometers/9.3 miles south of downtown (6200 River Rd., 604/270-7878 or 800/755-4905, www.richmondrvpark.com; Apr.–Oct.), is just off the final flight path for Vancouver International Airport. Aside from noise from the airport, the location is excellent. Across the road from the campground entrance is the Fraser River, and along the top of the dike separating the river from the road a footpath leads in both directions along the river. The path is extremely popular with local walkers, joggers, dog exercisers, cyclists, and even seaplane and jet enthusiasts—the seaplane terminal is within sight. Grassy banks and strategic benches along the path encourage quiet reflection on a bright sunny day. Facilities include free showers, a coin-op laundry, and a game room. Tent sites are $19, while serviced sites range $26–29. To get there, take Exit 36 from Highway 99, head west along Westminster Highway, then take No. 2 Road north to River Road and turn right. Buses to downtown leave from Richmond Centre Mall, a 10-minute walk away.

Parkcanada (604/943-5811, www.parkcanada.com) is very convenient to the BC Ferries terminal at Tsawwassen, a 30-minute drive south of city center. The campground has a small outdoor pool, but next door is a much larger water park—perfect for the kids. Other amenities include a store with groceries and some RV supplies, a laundry, a lounge, and free showers. Unserviced sites, suitable for tents, are $18; serviced sites range $21–34 depending on the size of the RV or trailer and the amp required. To get there, follow the ferry signs from Highway 99 and turn right off Highway 17 at 52nd Street. Take the first left, and you're there.

Farther south along Highway 99 is **Peace Arch RV Park** (14601 40th Ave., 604/594-7009, www.peacearchrvpark.com), which sprawls over four hectares (10 acres) between White Rock and Delta, 10 kilometers (6.2 miles) from the Douglas Border Crossing (take Exit 10—King George Highway—north from Highway 99,

then the first right, 40th Avenue). The well-tended facilities include a heated pool, playground and mini-golf, game room, coin-operated showers, and a laundry. Sites in the tent area are $18.50, while hookups go for $27.50.

East

Adjacent to Burnaby Lake Regional Park, **Burnaby Cariboo RV Park** (8765 Cariboo Place, Burnaby, 604/420-1722 or 800/667-9901, www.bcrvpark.com) offers luxurious facilities, including a large indoor heated pool, fitness room, Jacuzzi, sundeck, playground, lounge, barbecue area, grocery store, and laundry facility. The campground offers 217 paved sites, each with full hookups, including 30-amp power, cable TV, telephone, and Internet access; $38–44 per night. Sites in the private, walk-in tenting area cost $25 per night. The park is 17 kilometers (10.6 miles) east of downtown. To get there, take Exit 37 (Gaglardi) from the TransCanada Highway, turn right at the first traffic light, then take the first left, then the first right into Cariboo Place. The Production Way SkyTrain station is an eight-minute walk from this campground.

Farther east, **Dogwood Campground & RV Park** (15151 112th Ave., Surrey, 604/583-5585) is 35 kilometers (22 miles) from downtown. It's right beside the TransCanada Highway; to get there from downtown, take Exit 48 and cross back over the highway, turning left onto 154th Street. Eastbound travelers (heading toward the city) should take Exit 50, turn north over the highway and follow 160th Street north to 112th Avenue. Turn left and follow this street to the end. Facilities are adequate and modern, but basic, and include a pool and laundry. Tent sites are $21, hookups $30.

Anmore Camp & RV Park (3230 Sunnyside Rd., Anmore, 604/469-2311) is tucked away on Buntzen Lake, near the head of Burrard Inlet, north of Coquitlam and the TransCanada Highway. To get there, head north along Highway 7 from Exit 44 of the TransCanada Highway; take Highway 7A west, back toward the city, then Loco Road north, and follow the signs. It's the forested setting that makes this campground worth the drive, but other highlights include a

Vancouver

small heated pool, canoe and bike rentals, a barbecue area, a laundry, and a small general store. Tent sites are $24 per night, hookups $28–30.

Provincial Parks

Most provincial parks that surround Vancouver offer camping, but none offer hookups and all are seasonal. They also fill up very fast, especially on weekends. Reserve a spot by calling BC Parks' Discover Camping (604/689-9025 or 800/689-9025) or book online (www.discovercamping.ca). Reservations are taken between March 15 and September 15, for dates up to three months in advance. The reservation fee is $6.42 per night, to a maximum of $19.26, and is in addition to applicable camping fees.

Of the provincial parks immediately north of the city, the only one with a campground is **Golden Ears,** 40 kilometers (25 miles) northeast from downtown, near the suburb of Maple Ridge. To get there, take Highway 7 from downtown through Coquitlam and Pitt Meadows to Maple Ridge and follow the signs north on 232nd Street. The park holds almost 400 sites in two campgrounds near Alouette Lake. The campgrounds are linked by hiking trails. Facilities include hot showers, flush toilets, and a picnic table and fire ring at each site; $22 per night. Traveling north on Highway 99 toward Whistler, **Porteau Cove Provincial Park,** 20 kilometers (12 miles) north of Horseshoe Bay, offers 60 sites in a pleasant wooded setting with mountain views. Through summer, sites are $22, discounted to $17 the rest of the year.

If you're traveling the TransCanada Highway, the closest provincial park campground is at **Cultus Lake,** 100 kilometers (62 miles) east of downtown and seven kilometers (4.3 miles) south of downtown Chilliwack (Exit 119). This park has four campgrounds, each with showers and access to a long sandy beach. All sites are $22, which includes the use of hot showers.

Food

Vancouver is the shining jewel in Canada's otherwise tarnished culinary crown, overcoming the country's bland reputation as a gastronomical backwater. With almost 3,000 restaurants, cafés, and coffeehouses, and as home to almost 100 cultures, this ethnic crossroads is a gourmet feast.

The local specialty is West Coast or "fusion" cuisine, which combines fresh Canadian produce, such as local seafood and seasonal game, with Asian flavors and ingredients, usually in a healthy, low-fat way. Although this style of cooking only came to prominence in the early to mid-1990s, local food critics are already labeling it passé. Sure, the term has been overused, but the many restaurants that continue to thrive on its basic principles are testament to its popularity with locals and visitors alike.

Vancouver has no tourist-oriented, San Francisco–style Fisherman's Wharf, but however and wherever it's prepared, seafood will always dominate local menus. Pacific salmon, halibut, snapper, shrimp, oysters, clams, crab, and squid are all harvested locally, while mussels, lobster, tiger prawns, and Atlantic salmon are imported from Canada's Atlantic provinces or from farther afield. Restaurants throughout the city specialize in seafood; for the freshest, straight from the trawlers, along with a lively atmosphere, head to Steveston on the city's southern outskirts. Granville Island and Chinatown are also good bets to find fresh seafood.

Most downtown restaurants are open for lunch and dinner throughout the week and Saturday night only on weekends. In touristy areas such as Gastown and along Robson Street, restaurants open daily for lunch and dinner, and along late-night haunts such as Davie Street, many places stay open 24 hours a day. Smoking is banned in all Vancouver restaurants and bars.

DOWNTOWN DINING

Downtown Vancouver has so many good dining options that it is a shame to eat in a food court, but as in cities around the Western world, they are a good place for a fast, reliable, and inexpensive meal. The southwest corner of the Pacific Centre (at Howe and Georgia Streets, diagonally opposite the art gallery) holds a glass-domed food court with many inexpensive food bars and seating indoors and out.

Family Dining

Of course, if you have a family, you're welcome at most restaurants. These are simply recommendations that specialize in keeping all ages happy—without breaking the bank.

Although this book purposely ignores the fast-food chains, **White Spot** is worthy of inclusion. The first White Spot restaurant—a drive-in—opened in Vancouver at the corner of Granville Street and 67th Avenue, South Granville, in 1928, dishing up hamburgers and milk shakes. Today, 50 White Spots across

DOWNTOWN DINING CLASSICS

While the best known of Vancouver's restaurants are judged by their food, the service, the decor, and the crowd they attract, none of that matters to the following places. At the places listed here, though, you can expect hearty portions, inexpensive prices, and, at all except the infamous Elbow Room, friendly service.

The **Elbow Room,** one block south of Granville Street (560 Davie St., 604/685-3628, Mon.–Fri. 7:30 A.M.–3:30 P.M., Sat.–Sun. 8:30 A.M.–4 P.M.), is a Vancouver institution where portions are huge and the prices reasonable ($8 for the Lumberjack breakfast), but it's the service that you'll remember long after the meal. Feel like coffee? Get it yourself. A glass of water, maybe? "Get off your ass and get it yourself," a sign declares. The waiters take no nonsense, and the constant banter from the open kitchen, if not memorable, is at the least unique. But it's all in good fun, and if you get abused you'll join a long list of celebrities whose photos adorn the walls. If you don't finish your meal, you must make a donation to a local charity; if it's a pancake you can't finish, you're advised to "just rub it on your thighs, because that's where it's going anyway!" Sunday morning is when the kitchen and wait staff are at their wittiest.

"Quality Food, Snappy Service" is the catch-cry at **The Templeton** (1087 Granville St., 604/685-4612; daily 9 A.M.–11 P.M.), which has been serving downtown locals since 1934. Eat at the low counter or in the vinyl booths, each with a small jukebox, and enjoy traditional diner fare as well as more exotic creations, such as grilled ahi tuna with a dab of pineapple salsa on top and a side of organic greens ($13). Wash it down with a banana split ($7). Two blocks from Granville Street, the **Korner Restaurant** (1099 Richards St., 604/682-8678; Mon.–Sat. 10:30 A.M.–2:30 P.M. and 5:30P.M.–2:30 A.M.) is an old-style diner where the daily soup and sandwich special is a bargain at $4.

In the same vicinity, Davie Street north of Granville holds a couple of classic diners, including **Hamburger Mary's** (1202 Davie St., 604/687-1293), complete with chrome chairs, mirrored walls, and an old jukebox. Delicious hamburgers attract the crowds to Mary's; starting at $5.50, they aren't particularly cheap, but they come with fries, and extras such as salad are just $1. Breakfast ($5 for eggs, bacon, hash browns, and toast) begins daily at 7 A.M., and the last burgers are flipped in the early hours of the morning. Wash down your meal with one of Mary's famous milkshakes.

Vancouver's oldest restaurant, the **Only Cafe,** between downtown and Chinatown (20 E. Hastings St., 604/681-6546; daily 11 A.M.–8 P.M.), has been serving bargain-basement seafood for over 80 years. The decor is very 1950s, with two U-shaped counters, two duct-taped booths, and no bathrooms, but the food is always fresh and cooked to perfection. Up the hill from the Only Cafe, beyond Main Street, is the **Ovaltine Café** (251 E. Hastings St., 604/685-7021; daily 6 A.M.–midnight), easily spotted by the classic neon sign hanging out front. This classic diner has been serving up cheap chow for over 50 years.

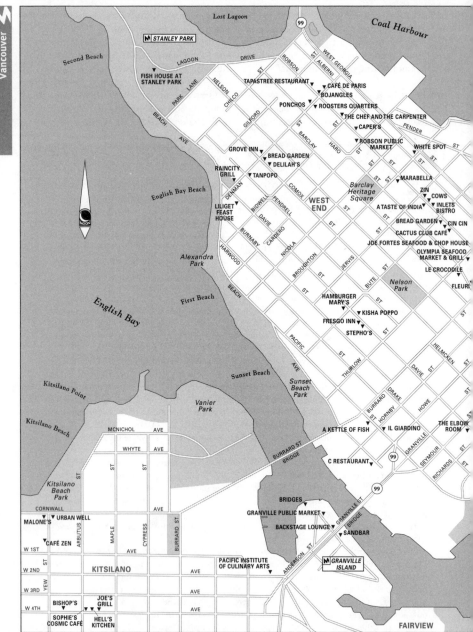

Lost Lagoon

Coal Harbour

STANLEY PARK

99

Second Beach

LAGOON

DRIVE

WEST GEORGIA

ROBSON

ST

ALBERNI

Park Lane

NELSON

FISH HOUSE AT
STANLEY PARK

CHILCO

ST

TAPASTREE RESTAURANT

CAFÉ DE PARIS
BOJANGLES

GILFORD

ST

PONCHOS

ROOSTERS QUARTERS

BEACH

ST

THE CHEF AND THE CARPENTER

AVE

BARCLAY

HARO

ST

CAPER'S

PENDER

ROBSON PUBLIC
MARKET

GROVE INN

WHITE SPOT

ST

ST

ST

BREAD GARDEN

ST

RAINCITY
GRILL

DELILAH'S

TANPOPO

COMOX

ST

ST

MARABELLA

English Bay Beach

DENMAN

PENDRELL

WEST
END

Barclay
Heritage
Square

ZIN

COWS

BIDWELL

A TASTE OF INDIA

INLETS
BISTRO

LILIGET
FEAST
HOUSE

DAVIE

ST

BREAD GARDEN

CIN CIN

BURNABY

CARDERO

NICOLA

CACTUS CLUB CAFÉ

JOE FORTES SEAFOOD & CHOP HOUSE

HARWOOD

OLYMPIA SEAFOOD
MARKET & GRILL

Alexandra
Park

BROUGHTON

ST

JERVIS

LE CROCODILE

BEACH

BUTE

Nelson
Park

FLEURI

First Beach

ST

English Bay

HAMBURGER
MARY'S

KISHA POPPO

ST

FRESGO INN

PACIFIC

STEPHO'S

ST

HELMCKEN

Sunset Beach

AVE

DAVIE

ST

Sunset
Beach
Park

THURLOW

ST

Kitsilano Point

DRAKE

BURRARD

HOWE

Vanier
Park

HORNBY

Kitsilano Beach

MCNICHOL

AVE

A KETTLE OF FISH

IL GIARDINO

THE ELBOW
ROOM

WHYTE

AVE

ST

GRANVILLE

ST

SEYMOUR

ST

Kitsilano
Beach
Park

BURRARD ST
BRIDGE

C RESTAURANT

99

RICHARDS

ST

CORNWALL

AVE

99

MALONE'S

URBAN WELL

ARBUTUS

MAPLE

CYPRESS

BURRARD ST

BRIDGES

GRANVILLE PUBLIC MARKET

GRANVILLE ST
BRIDGE

CAFÉ ZEN

BACKSTAGE LOUNGE

W 1ST

AVE

SANDBAR

W 2ND

YEW

ST

KITSILANO

AVE

PACIFIC INSTITUTE
OF CULINARY ARTS

ANDERSON

ST

GRANVILLE
ISLAND

W 3RD

AVE

W 4TH

BISHOP'S

JOE'S
GRILL

AVE

SOPHIE'S
COSMIC CAFÉ

HELL'S
KITCHEN

FAIRVIEW

DOWNTOWN VANCOUVER FOOD

Vancouver

Deadman's Island

Burrard Inlet

SeaBus to
Lonsdale Quay

0   300 yds
0   300 m

FIVE SAILS
MISAKI
CANADA PLACE

SHOW CASE

VANCOUVER VISITOR
INFO CENTRE

AQUA RIVA

Waterfront

MELVILLE ST

W CORDOVA
W HASTINGS

W PENDER

Burrard

GEORGIA

BURRARD ST

KITANOYA
GUU

GASTOWN

COMMISSIONER ST

Portside
Park

West Coast Express

ALEXANDER ST

WATER ST
CAFÉ

OLD SPAGHETTI
FACTORY

WATER ST

BROTHERS RESTAURANT

900 WEST

DOWNTOWN

Robson
Square

99

Granville Mall

Granville

POWELL ST

E CORDOVA ST

GORE

DUNLEVY

Oppen-
heimer
Park

PISTOL &
BURNES

BACCHUS RESTAURANT

GOTHAM
STEAKHOUSE

DUNSMUIR ST

Victory
Square

ABBOTT ST

CARRALL ST

MAIN ST

OVALTINE
CAFÉ

E HASTINGS ST

HORNBY

HOWE

ROBSON

99

RICHARDS ST

THE ONLY CAFÉ

SMITHE

ST

KISHU

TAYLOR ST

E PENDER ST

SEYMOUR

Stadium

BOSS BAKERY & RESTAURANT

FU WAH

CHINATOWN

KEEFER ST

THE TEMPLETON

VILLA DEL LUPO

HAMILTON ST

GAIN WAH RESTAURANT

HON'S WUN TUN HOUSE

JACKSON ST

KENT'S
KITCHEN

UNION ST

HOMER

NELSON ST

CAMBIE ST

BEATTY ST

BLVD NORTH

STEAMROLLERS

MAINLAND ST

PACIFIC

BLVD SOUTH

COLUMBIA ST

DON'T SHOW THE ELEPHANT

COAST
ELIXIR

PACIFIC

PACIFIC BLVD

SkyTrain

Main
Street

Thornton
Park

MAIN ST

YALETOWN

David Lam
Park

CAMBIE ST
BRIDGE

Creek

False

TERMINAL
AVE

WESTERN ST

STATION ST

INDUSTRIAL AVE

Charleston
Park

1ST AVE

2ND AVE

1ST
AVE

2ND
AVE

CAMBIE ST

COLUMBIA ST

MANITOBA ST

3RD AVE

4TH AVE

ONTARIO ST

QUEBEC ST

MAIN ST

2ND

© AVALON TRAVEL PUBLISHING, INC.

Canada still offer burgers—including the famous Triple O—as well as everything from pastas to stir-fried vegetables. For a sample, visit White Spot's downtown location (1616 W. Georgia St., 604/681-8034).

At the bottom end of Gastown, the unique decor at **Brothers Restaurant** (1 Water St., 604/683-9124; daily for lunch and dinner) features monastery-like surroundings of wood, brick, stained glass, chandeliers, and monkish murals. Enjoy delicious soups (try the Boston clam chowder), salads, sandwiches, and entrées (from $15)—all served by waiters appropriately dressed in monk attire—accompanied by congregational sing-alongs and laser light shows. The daily lunch specials are good value, as are the early dinner deals available Monday–Thursday before 6 P.M.

The **Old Spaghetti Factory** (53 Water St., 604/684-1288; daily for lunch and dinner) is a family-friendly favorite offering lunch entrées from $6 and dinner entrées from $10, including salad, bread, dessert, and coffee. This place is worth a visit for the eclectic array of furnishings, from old lamps to a 1904 trolley car.

West Coast

With its prime waterfront location between Canada Place and Gastown, **⚲ Aqua Riva** (200 Granville St., 604/683-5599) features stunning views across Burrard Inlet to the North Shore Range through floor-to-ceiling windows. It's less touristy than you may imagine (Vancouver's two daily newspapers are in the same building, so it fills with media types through the lunch hour), and well priced for the high standard of food offered. The restaurant itself is cavernous with a variety of seating arrangements, dominated by a huge mural. The least expensive way to enjoy the dramatic view is with a pizza baked in a wood-fired oven ($14–18). Other mains, mostly seafood and including a delicious alderwood-grilled wild salmon, are all under $30 (pastas average $20). Lunch mains, including gourmet sandwiches, range $9–20. Whether it's lunch or dinner, finish up with a slice of caramelized banana cream pie ($7.50). A massive curved bar runs through

the middle of Aqua Riva. Vancouver's licensing regulations require that alcohol served in a restaurant can't be consumed without food, so although it's okay to stop here and soak up the views over a locally brewed beer or one of the many martinis on the drink list, you'll probably be offered a menu.

Typifying the new wave in Vancouver's hotel dining scene is **Show Case,** at street level of the Vancouver Marriott Pinnacle (1128 W. Hastings St., 604/639-4040). Floor-to-ceiling windows, contemporary styling, a split-level restaurant/bar layout, and a six-meter-long canvas hanging from the ceiling create a bright, eye-pleasing environment very different from the elegant old-world feel of Vancouver's other top-end hotel restaurants. Breakfast comprises all the usual traditional North American choices ($14.50 for a full, cooked breakfast including coffee), but it's lunch and dinner that shine, with exotic dishes prepared using local seafood and game, simply and stylishly presented. The tasting menu gives diners the opportunity to experience a variety of dishes, each accompanied by matching wines. The bar menu is tapas in name only—servings of battered halibut, gourmet sandwiches, and the like for $8–14. Combining an à la carte entrée and four serving stations, Sunday brunch is among the best in the city; in addition to the usual hot choices, offerings include a wide variety of fresh seafood, cheeses, and rich desserts for $32 per person.

At Gastown's busiest intersection, opposite the crowd-drawing steam clock, is **⚲ Water Street Cafe** (300 Water St., 604/689-2832; daily 11:30 A.M.–9:30 P.M.), in the 1906 Edward Hotel. Unlike when you're dining at most other Gastown eateries, here you won't feel like you're in the touristy quarter of Vancouver. White linens, dark blue carpets, and lots of polished woodwork ooze style, while service is professional. Most importantly, the food is well priced and delicious. The wild salmon topped with hazelnuts and a maple butter sauce ($20) is a good choice, or go for something lighter, such as the prawn and papaya salad ($15). A good selection of pasta ($14–17) provides a break from seafood.

Seafood

At Canada Place is **Five Sails,** in the Pan Pacific Vancouver Hotel (604/891-2892; daily 6–10 P.M.). The fabulous setting and harbor views are reflected in the prices. The menu features dishes originating in the chef's French homeland but steers away from using "fusion" techniques that are prevalent through many of Vancouver's better restaurants. At Five Sails you'll enjoy modern cooking, mostly seafood-oriented, with highlights of locally harvested crab, salmon, sea bass, mussels, and scallops. For an appetizer, the cod chowder ($10) is an easy choice, while main dishes, such as seared scallops and mushrooms in a rosemary butter sauce, range $30–45.

Steak

Steak lovers who feel like a splurge should consider **Gotham Steakhouse** (615 Seymour St., 604/605-8282; daily from 5 P.M.). The cavernous room holding this restaurant is divided into a restaurant and a bar, meeting in the middle under a 13-meter-high arched ceiling. With furnishings of thick leather seats, dark-colored hardwood tables, and plush velvet carpet, both sections exude the atmosphere of a private gentlemen's club. All appetizers rely on seafood as a base, but it's the main-course steak dishes that people talk about at Gotham. If the steak here isn't the best in Vancouver, servings are certainly the most generous, especially the signature dish, a $48.95 porterhouse. Other mains range $26–47, earning Gotham awards from city magazines as the "Best Restaurant when Someone Else is Paying."

French

For Vancouver's finest French cuisine, go to the small, intimate **Le Crocodile** (909 Burrard St., 604/669-4298; lunch Mon.–Fri., dinner Mon.–Sat.), which has won innumerable awards over its two decades as one of Vancouver's premier restaurants. Named after a restaurant in the owner's hometown, Le Crocodile is elegant, but not as intimidating as its reputation. The smallish menu relies heavily on traditional French techniques, which shine through in appetizers (or entrées as they are properly called at Le Crocodile), such as wild mushroom soup with truffle oil ($7) or frog legs sautéed in a chive butter sauce ($12.50), and mains like grilled beef tenderloin with peppercorn sauce ($36).

⚑ Fleuri, in the Sutton Place Hotel (845 Burrard St., 604/642-2900), is one of Vancouver's best hotel restaurants, and you needn't spend a fortune to enjoy dining in what is generally regarded as one of the world's best hotels. Every afternoon, high tea—complete with scones and cream, finger foods, and nonalcoholic beverages—costs $21. The restaurant is also open for breakfast, lunch, and dinner; the dinner menu is French influenced (mains $25–34), with a magnificent seafood buffet offered on Friday and Saturday nights. Fleuri is also regarded as having one of the city's best Sunday brunch spreads. Adjacent to the restaurant is the Gerald Lounge, the perfect spot for a pre-dinner drink.

Italian

Of Vancouver's many Italian restaurants, one of the most popular is **Il Giardino** (1382 Hornby St., 604/669-2422; Mon.–Fri. noon–2:30 P.M. and daily 5:30–11 P.M.), operated by Umberto Menghi, a legendary Vancouver restaurateur with other restaurants in Whistler and a cooking school in Tuscany. Il Giardino is on the south side of downtown in a distinctive yellow Italian-style villa. The light, bright furnishings and enclosed terrace provide the perfect ambience for indulging in the featured Tuscan cuisine. Expect to pay $12–16 for lunch entrées, $16–33 for dinner entrées.

Of a similar high standard, **Villa del Lupo** (869 Hamilton St., 604/688-7436; daily 5:30–11:30 P.M.) was voted Vancouver's best Italian restaurant through most of the 1990s. It's still extremely popular, especially with theatergoers as it's in the heart of the entertainment district. The breads and pastas ($19–24) are prepared daily, and Fraser River Valley produce is used whenever possible (free-range chickens, for example). The drink menu features Italian and Italian-style Californian wines and favorite Italian coffees. Look for the profusion of shrubbery out front.

Other European

After massive renovations to the grand old Hotel Vancouver, the Timber Club, famous as a meeting place of the city's social set, reopened as **900 West** (900 W. Georgia St., 604/669-9378; lunch Mon.–Sat., dinner daily), with the same elegant surrounds as a luxurious cruise ship dining room of days gone by. The Continental menu is varied, offering everything from grilled halibut to a rack of lamb. Mains start at $26, or relax with a snack in the wine bar. Can't decide on dessert? Live entertainment accompanies evening diners.

The Wedgewood Hotel's signature dining room, the **Bacchus Restaurant** (845 Hornby St., 604/608-5319), has the feeling of a romantic European bistro with its dark cherry wood paneling, stone fireplace, and elegant table settings over white linen. The emphasis is on classical European presentations of local game and produce, with a menu that changes with the seasons. The continental buffet breakfast is $19, lunch is around $15, and dinner mains range $18–35. It's open throughout the day, and afternoon tea ($21, or add a glass of Moet Champagne and pay $36) is served daily 2–4 P.M.

Japanese

Many inexpensive Japanese restaurants are scattered between Granville Street and Gastown, a reflection of the many English-language schools concentrated in the area. They are busiest at lunchtime, when the local student population hits the streets looking for a quick and inexpensive meal, and many excellent deals can be found. **Kishu** (418 W. Georgia St., 604/688-0939; Mon.–Fri. 10 A.M.–10 P.M., Sat. noon–10 P.M., Sun. noon–8 P.M.) is a notch above the rest in terms of decor but is typical price-wise. Lunch specials are all around $7, or try an 18-piece sushi plate and a bowl of miso soup for just $12.

Kitanoya Guu (375 Water St., 604/685-8682; daily 11:30 A.M.–10:30 P.M.) is a groovy Japanese restaurant with an energetic chef who oversees the needs of mostly young, always loud, patrons. Known in Japan as izakaya-style dining, the atmosphere is informal, with a menu that encourages sharing. It's similar to a North American neighborhood pub, but instead of wings and nachos, choices include *harumaki* (spring rolls), *shiso-age* (chicken and plum sauce wrapped in thin bread), and *maguro* (tuna with avocado and mango sauce).

At the opposite end of the Japanese dining experience spectrum, **Misaki** (in Canada Place, 604/891-2893) offers the peace and tranquility of an upmarket Tokyo restaurant. The cuisine combines traditional Japanese and contemporary fusion cooking, with most dishes making use of produce available locally. It's not particularly cheap (expect to pay $80 for two), but Misaki is among the best in the city and is half the price you would expect to pay in Tokyo.

YALETOWN AND VICINITY

The Elbow Room (see sidebar, *Downtown Dining Classics*) is on the edge of Yaletown, but it probably doesn't want to be associated with this hip neighborhood. On the other hand, continue down Davie from the Elbow Room and you'll find the quintessential Yaletown hangout in **Don't Show the Elephant** (1027 Hamilton St., 604/331-1018; daily except Tues. 2 P.M.–midnight), named for the exact English translation of a Japanese phrase that means "a person who doesn't boast." This small café is minimalist design at its simplest, with the only splash of color coming from the back wall, which is lined with hundreds of Norwegian CDs. You can order freshly squeezed juices, iced coffee, iced black tea mocha, or a large pot of specialty tea, then choose an accompanying cake or pastry from the glass cabinet. The name, the decor, the blown-glass coffee machine, and the prices will all catch your attention, but nothing more so than the bathroom. Or the bathroom door to be precise—it's completely transparent, until you lock the door and it goes opaque.

In the vicinity is **Steamrollers** (437 Davie St., 604/608-0852; Mon.–Sat. 10 A.M.–10 P.M., Sun. 10 A.M.–8 P.M.), at street level of a residential high-rise. What at first looks like just another trendy little big-city café is in fact one of Vancouver's best-value eateries. The name "Steamrollers" is derived from the process of steaming tortillas before they are rolled up as burritos around a wide variety of steamed fillings and wrapped in tinfoil. The finished product is absolutely massive (one burrito can easily feed two people) and goes for $5–7 (the Chicken Deluxe, chock-full of chicken breast, rice, pinto beans, cheese, lettuce, salsa, and yogurt, is my fave). You can add a side of soup or salad ($2), or order mini steamrollers for the kids ($3.50).

Seafood

Slick and chic, **Coast** (1257 Hamilton St., 604/685-5010; daily from 5:30 P.M.) is a cavernous dining room that bristles with energy. Formerly it was a warehouse, but the industrial feel has been softened with a light color scheme and modern furnishings. Or you can sit outside, but the view isn't very pleasant. The menu of fresh seafood is a knockout from beginning to end. Start with a seafood nectar, such as lobster essence ($7), which comes with chunks of sourdough bread for dipping. Then move on to entrées such as tempura-battered halibut with aromatic duqqa fries ($22) or one of seasonal grill choices ($27) that may include swordfish or salmon.

One of Vancouver's finest seafood restaurants is **M A Kettle of Fish** (900 Pacific St., 604/682-6853; lunch Mon.–Fri., dinner daily), near the Burrard Street Bridge. The casual decor features café-style seating and abundant greenery, while the menu swims with schools of piscatory pleasures. New England clam chowder ($7) is one of more than 20 appetizers, while traditionally prepared entrées, such as grilled sea bass with a honey glaze ($24) and Dungeness crab ($36), make up the main menu. The extensive wine list is especially strong on white wines—the perfect accompaniment for a feast of seafood.

A throwback to the overindulgence of the 1980s, **C** (1600 Howe St., 604/681-1164; Mon.–Fri. 11:30 A.M.–2:30 P.M. and 5:30 A.M.–11 P.M. and for Sun. brunch 11 A.M.–2 P.M.) employs one of Canada's brightest young chefs to deliver immaculately presented seafood in a chic-industrial setting. Encompassed within shiny white walls, tables are spread out, with patio settings soaking up the water views and a few upstairs in a more intimate environment.

For lunch or dinner, the Russian caviar or the shucked oysters provide ideal (but expensive) starter dishes to share. The taster box of salmon, squid, and abalone is also easy to recommend. Main meals offered change with the seasons, with halibut, salmon, and Alaskan crab regular staples. Lunch mains range $17–32, dinner mains $28–50.

French Contemporary

Elixir, in the Opus Hotel (322 Davie St., 604/642-6787; Sun.–Wed. 6:30 A.M.–11 P.M., Thurs.–Sat. 6:30 A.M.–11 P.M.), is a stylish, energetic bistro at street level of Vancouver's hippest hotel. The contemporary French menu blends easily with the young, money-to-burn crowd—and prices are not as outrageous as you might imagine. The three-course Express Dinner ($30) changes nightly, while a plat du jour choice (such as sable fish poached in red wine; $19) is offered on a weeklong rotation.

DAVIE STREET

The downtown end of Davie Street, between Burrard and Bute Streets, holds many coffeehouses and inexpensive dining options. It is a popular after-hours haunt, with many places open 24 hours to cater to the nightclub crowd. Whether it's a slice of pizza for a buck, seafood, or sushi, you'll find it along Davie Street.

The **Fresgo Inn** (1138 Davie St., 604/689-1332) is a cavernous self-serve cafeteria where breakfast is bargain priced (eggs, bacon, and pancakes is just $4.50) and hamburgers cost from $3.50. A longtime favorite, once open 24 hours, it now closes at 3 A.M. Monday–Saturday and at midnight on Sunday.

Restaurants

Expect to wait for a table at **Stepho's** (1124 Davie St., 604/683-2555, daily noon–11:30 P.M.), one of Vancouver's best-value restaurants. Locals line up here to enjoy the atmosphere of a typical Greek taverna—complete with terra-cotta floors, white stucco walls, arched doorways, blue and white tablecloths, travel posters, and lots of colorful flowering plants. All the favorite Greek dishes are offered, such as souvlakis or a steak and Greek salad combination for under $10, and portions are generous. Start with freshly prepared *tzatziki* ($3.50) and finish off with a delicious baklava, which costs just $3, and coffee for a buck.

Kisha Poppo (1143 Davie St., 604/681-0488; daily 11:30 A.M.–3 P.M. and 5–11:30 P.M.) serves up westernized Japanese food in a sterile diner-style atmosphere. But the price is right. All-you-can-eat soup, starters, sushi, hot mains such as teriyaki, and dessert is offered through lunch ($9 per person) and dinner ($13). The regular menu is also well priced, with, for example, a sushi/teriyaki combo dinner for $15.95.

CHINATOWN

Vancouver is home to an estimated 300 Chinese restaurants, as many as any city across North America. Besides the sheer number of restaurants, the quality is generally excellent and the cost reasonable, mostly due to the accessibility of fresh produce and seafood. Within the city itself, you can't go wrong in Chinatown, a few blocks east of the city center. Chinatown encompasses six blocks, but restaurants and fresh-produce stalls are concentrated within the two blocks bordered by Main, Keefer, Gore, and East Hastings Streets. Within this area, look for stalls selling fish, fruit, vegetables, and other exotic goodies up Pender Street and one block on either side of Pender along Gore Street. These markets are especially busy early in the morning when local restaurateurs are stocking up for the day's trade.

Dining in Chinatown offers two distinct options—traditional eateries, where you'll find the locals, and the larger, westernized restaurants that attract non-Chinese and a younger Chinese crowd. A perfect combination of the two is **Kent's Kitchen** (232 Keefer St., 604/669-2237), a modern café-style restaurant where the service is fast and efficient, the food freshly prepared, and the prices incredibly low. Two specialty dishes, rice, and a can of pop make a meal that costs just $5, with more unusual dishes such as pig's feet for $3.75 including rice. The most expensive combination is a large

portion of shrimp and sweet and sour pork, which along with rice and pop is $8.50 (and could easily feed two people).

Next door to Kent's, **Hon's Wun Tun House** (230 Keefer St., 604/688-0871) is a large, bright, and modern restaurant that attracts a younger Chinese crowd for mostly westernized Chinese food. The menu lists more than 300 dishes, all under $10, and all prepared within sight of diners. Across the parkade entrance from the main restaurant is another Hon's, this one a takeout.

Tiny **Gain Wah Restaurant** (218 Keefer St., 604/684-1740) is typical of the many hundreds of noodle houses found in Hong Kong. In Asia, noodle houses cater to the poorer end of the population, and although this is a westernized version of those across the Pacific, dining here is still extremely inexpensive. The restaurant is best noted for congee, a simple soup of water extracted from boiling rice. A bowl of congee costs $1.50, with flavorings an additional $.25–2. On the main menu, no dish, except those containing seafood, is over $10. The friendly staff is willing to describe the more unfamiliar dishes.

Around the corner from Keefer Street, Gore Street is less westernized; beyond the large fish market you'll find **Fu Wah** (555 Gore St., 604/688-8722), which has a ridiculously inexpensive lunchtime dim sum menu.

A couple of other recommendations are the **Boss Bakery and Restaurant** (532 Main St., 604/683-3860), always crowded and offering a great selection of Chinese- and Western-style pastries, and the **Buddhist Vegetarian Restaurant** (137 E. Pender St., 604/683-8816), which serves up inexpensive vegetarian food in bland surroundings.

ROBSON STREET

Linking downtown to the West End, Robson Street holds the city's largest concentration of eateries, ranging from Joe Fortes, one of Vancouver's finest seafood restaurants, to the city's Hooters franchise. In addition to a number of fine-dining restaurants, dozens of cafés sprinkle the sidewalks with outdoor tables—perfect for people-watching.

Cafés and Coffeehouses

It's been said that Vancouver is addicted to coffee, and walking along Robson Street, it would be hard to disagree. The street harbors multiple outlets of the main coffeehouse chains, including six **Starbucks** stores (of 100 citywide) and four of the city's 20 **Blenz** outlets.

One of the best spots in all of Vancouver for coffee and a light snack is at one of the 20-odd **Bread Garden** cafés scattered throughout the metropolitan area. In this part of the city, the Bread Garden is half a block off busy Robson Street (812 Bute St., 604/688-3213). It's open 24 hours a day and is always busy—so much so that patrons often need to take a number and wait for service. The coffee is great, as are the freshly baked muffins and pastries. Salads and healthy sandwiches are also available.

At the west end of Robson Street, **Caper's** (1675 Robson St., 604/687-5288) is a cavernous store selling groceries and pre-made meals for the health-conscious. Caper's also has an in-house bakery, deli, and juice bar.

Seafood

Half a block off Robson, **M Joe Fortes Seafood and Chophouse** (777 Thurlow St., 604/669-1940; daily 11:30 A.M.–10:30 P.M.) is named after one of Vancouver's best-loved heroes, a Caribbean-born swimming coach and lifeguard at English Bay. This restaurant is a city institution and is always busy with the young and beautiful set. The comfortable interior offers elegant furnishings, bleached-linen tablecloths, a rooftop patio, and an oyster bar where you can relax while waiting for your table. At lunch, the specialty grilled fish goes for $15–20. The dinner menu is slightly more expensive, although midweek "blue plate" specials, such as jambalaya, are well priced. Of the grilled fish ($22–32) on offer, try something different, like the delicately textured black cod or arctic char, caught in Canada's northern waters. Joe's is one of the few Vancouver restaurants with a dedicated area for smokers.

While the oysters at Joe's are hard to beat, those at the **Olympia Seafood Market and Grill** (820 Thurlow, 604/685-0716; daily 11 A.M.–7 P.M.), one block away, come pretty close. What was

originally a fish market—and still looks like one—now sells cooked fish and chips (boxed, with a slice of lemon, for $7–10), either to take out or to enjoy at the short counter. You can still get fresh and packaged seafood to go—everything from marlin to caviar is on the menu.

North American

The menu at the **Cactus Club Cafe** (1136 Robson St., 604/687-3278; daily 11 A.M.–midnight or later) features mostly Southwestern dishes (and a great Caesar salad), but the decor of this busy restaurant is, well, different. It's covered with cow kitsch, from gold-framed paintings to papier-mâché cows hanging from the ceiling.

Global

At street level of the trendy Pacific Palisades Hotel, the decor at **Zin!** (1277 Robson St., 604/408-1700; Tues.–Sun. for lunch and dinner) was revamped in 2004, toning down the clashing color schemes and club-like ambience to create a subtler space. The menu remains notable; it steers away from fusion cooking, instead offering cuisine from around the world that sticks to its country of origin in all respects. The variety of choice is reflected in the restaurant's name, which comes from zinfandel, a California grape, which produces a versatile wine that can be enjoyed with most food types. The origin of dishes is truly global—from southern-style fried chicken accompanied by macaroni and cheese to goat cheese fondue. Dinner mains range $17–28, or choose the three-course tasting menu ($25), which highlights a different region of the world each week. The drinks menu is equally diverse; all major wine-producing countries are represented, and martinis are popular, but the local favorite is the unusual combination of Chai tea infused with a shot of sambuca.

European

The Chef and the Carpenter (1745 Robson St., 604/687-2700) serves up great country-French cuisine in an intimate yet relaxed atmosphere. Portions are large, but save room for the delicious desserts. Main meals range $18–22.

Open weekdays for lunch and daily for dinner (reservations required).

Named for a traditional Italian toast, **CinCin** (1154 Robson St., 604/688-7338; lunch Mon.–Fri., dinner daily from 5 P.M.) is a Mediterranean-style restaurant with a loyal local following. The centerpiece of the dining room is a large open kitchen, with a wood-fired oven and a rotisserie in view of diners. The heated terrace fills up quickly, but it's the place to watch the Robson Street action from above. The specialty is fancy pizza (from $14), but the oven is also used to cook dishes like a rack of lamb broiled in a rosemary marinade ($32) and ahi tuna ($35). Grilled dishes are similarly priced, while pastas range $14–24. CinCin also does a wicked antipasti ($22 per person). This restaurant has been honored by dozens of awards, including for its wine list, featuring more than 300 well-priced choices.

East Indian

A Taste of India (1282 Robson St., 604/682-3894; daily 11 A.M.–midnight) stands out along this strip of fashionable boutiques and trendy cafés. The decor—complete with plastic flowers—is nothing to write home about, but this restaurant is worth visiting for its wide selection of traditional East Indian dishes at reasonable prices. Lunches are all under $10, while the most expensive dinner entrée is a prawn curry served with rice for $16. Also on the menu are kebabs, more than a dozen vegetarian specialties (such as a spicy potato and cauliflower dish), and dishes from the Tandoori oven.

WEST END

Denman Street is the center of the dining action in this trendy part of downtown. Toward the English Bay end of Denman Street there is a definite seaside atmosphere, with many cafés and restaurants offering water views and attracting droves of beach-lovers in their summer wear.

Cafés and Cheap Eats

For a quick bite to eat before heading back to the beach, search out your favorite flavors from the strip of sidewalk eateries along the south end of Denman Street. The **Bread Garden** (1040 Denman St., 604/685-2996) is a busy café open 24 hours. Raised a few steps from street level, the long row of outdoor tables is great for people-watching.

Away from the beach, near the crest of Denman Street, a couple of older-style places have survived, offering old-fashioned service and good value. The best of these for breakfast is the **Grove Inn** (1047 Denman St., 604/687-0557), where the breakfast special is $5 before 10 A.M.

For chicken cooked to perfection, head over the hill to **Rooster's Quarters** (836 Denman St., 604/689-8023), a casual eatery chock-full of chicken memorabilia. A full chicken with accompanying vegetables and fries (for two) is a reasonable $17.

At the street's north end is **Bojangles** (785 Denman St., 604/687-3622), a small café on a busy intersection. Its few sidewalk tables and inside counters are perfect places for watching in-line skaters practice their newfound skills (or lack thereof) as they leave surrounding rental shops.

First Nations Cuisine

Head for the West End to find the city's finest traditional First Nations cuisine at the native-owned and -operated **M Liliget Feast House** (1724 Davie St., 604/681-7044; daily 5–10 P.M.). From street level, a narrow stairway leads down to the restaurant, a cavernous room styled on a traditional longhouse. Peeled cedar columns rise from the hardwood floor, native artwork adorns the walls, and traditional music plays softly in the background. Menu items include smoked *oolichan,* stir-fried herring roe, bannock bread, seaweed and wild rice, watercress salad, a traditional salmon soup, seafood or caribou barbecued over an alderwood fire, and steamed fern shoots. The food is cooked using traditional techniques and recipes. Dining here isn't particularly cheap; most people opt for the Liliget Feast Platter, which lets you sample a variety of game and seafood delicacies ($50 for two). It's an experience you won't forget in a hurry.

West Coast Contemporary

You'll find contemporary West Coast cuisine at

DINING IN STANLEY PARK

The simplest way to enjoy a meal in Stanley Park is by having a picnic—smoked salmon, a selection of cheeses, a loaf of sourdough bread—you know the drill. But for something a little more formal, three restaurants are all excellent alternatives, for lunch or dinner.

The least expensive place to eat in Stanley Park is **Prospect Point Café,** near the south end of Lions Gate Bridge (604/669-2737; summer daily 11 A.M.–8 P.M., shorter hours the rest of the year), with a large deck that allows sweeping views across to the North Shore. Grilled salmon (around $20) is the specialty, but you can also order dishes such as a Bavarian smokie ($8) and a smoked salmon Caesar salad ($13). Get there by driving along the Stanley Park loop road or by walking up the steps from the sea level promenade.

Between Second and Third Beaches is the **Sequoia Grill** (Ferguson Point, 604/669-3281; daily 11:30 A.M.–2:30 P.M. and 5–9:30 P.M.), an intimate restaurant of connected rooms with bright, elegant surroundings set among towering trees. Healthy, contemporary cooking is the order of the day. Look for starters such as carrot and ginger soup ($7) and mains that range from a half serving of pea risotto ($9) to herb-crusted rack of lamb ($34). Vegetable sides are extra (be careful with the oven-roasted cherry tomatoes—they can be very hot). Reservations aren't generally necessary through the day, but reserve a table on the deck to enjoy watching the evening sunset.

The **Fish House at Stanley Park** (8901 Stanley Park Dr., 604/681-7275; daily 11 A.M.–9 P.M.) lies in the southwest corner of the park, away from the crowded promenade and surrounded by a bowling green and tennis courts. The atmosphere is as refined as at the Sequoia Grill, but a less-adventurous menu attracts a slightly older crowd. Seating is in one of three rooms or out on a deck. The service is efficient and the food well prepared. All the usual seafood dishes are offered, as well as a few unique choices. A meal could go something like this: clams steamed open in a creamy bacon broth to start, maple-glazed salmon as a main, and pavlova (meringue topped with whipped cream and fruit) for dessert. Expect to pay around $35 for this or a similar combination. Afternoon tea ($22) is served daily 2–4 P.M.

Delilah's (1789 Comox St., 604/687-3424; daily from 5:30 P.M.). One of Vancouver's favorite restaurants, Delilah's features well-prepared dishes that take advantage of seasonal produce and locally harvested seafood served in an elegant European-style setting. The fixed-price two-course dinner costs from $26.50, depending on the season; a four-course feast ($38) is also offered. Start your evening meal with one of Delilah's delicious martinis.

The innovative menu and extensive by-the-glass wine list at nearby **Raincity Grill** (1193 Denman St., 604/685-7337; daily 11:30 A.M.–2:30 P.M. and 5–10:30 P.M.) have gained this restaurant numerous awards. The interior is stylish and the table settings are more than adequate, but it's the views across English Bay through high windows that are most impressive (on the downside, inside can get crowded and noisy).

Or take advantage of a sprawling outdoor patio in warmer weather. The menu changes with the season but always includes seafood and carefully selected local game, such as free-range chicken from Fraser River Valley farms. Lunch entrées (the salad of smoked steelhead is a particular treat) are $10–17, dinner (such as roasted loin of lamb with potato puree, green beans, and mint jus) ranges $21–33. Sweet treats include a tasty rhubarb crumble ($8.50). Dinner reservations are essential.

Mexican

Ponchos (827 Denman St., 604/683-7236; daily 5–11 P.M.) is a friendly, family-run Mexican restaurant where the walls are decorated with colorful ponchos, you eat from tiled tables, and a guitar-playing singer serenades diners between courses. The menu is extremely well priced, with authentic Mexican food costing from $5 and combination meals for around $14.

European

The atmosphere at **Tapastree Restaurant** (1829 Robson St., 604/606-4680; daily for dinner) is inviting and cozy, and the service is faultless. But it's the food that really shines; the tapas-only menu features choices such as vegetarian antipasto and seared tuna with Chinese mustard, which are mostly under $10. It's one block along Robson from Denman.

Around the corner, **Café de Paris** (751 Denman St., 604/687-1418; Mon.–Fri. 11:30 A.M.–2 P.M., daily 5:30–10 P.M.) is an intimate yet casual city-style French bistro. Classic French main courses (don't dare call them entrées at this very French restaurant) range $18–26, but the daily three-course table d'hôte is the best value at around $35. Wines offered are almost exclusively French.

Japanese

The contemporary **Tanpopo** (upstairs at 1122 Denman St., 604/681-7777; daily 11:30 A.M.–10 P.M.) features a wide range of Japanese dishes, including a sushi boat ($28 for two) packed with westernized favorites. More popular are the buffets (lunch $13, dinner $22), which include miso soup, sushi, tempura, teriyaki, noodles, and dessert.

GRANVILLE ISLAND AND VICINITY

Granville Island Market

This market, on Johnston Street, bustles with locals and tourists alike throughout the day. In the tradition of similar European markets, shopping here is an unpretentious and practical affair, with lots of talking, poking, and inquiring at stalls selling fresh meats, seafood, fruit and vegetables, and cheeses and at specialty stalls stocked with prepackaged goodies to go. At the Burrard Inlet end of the market you'll find a variety of takeout stalls, and while there's a large expanse of indoor tables, most people head outside to enjoy their meal among the sights and sounds of False Creek. It is difficult to go past the **Stock Market** (604/687-2433) when recommending a stall to grab lunch. Starting at $3.50, the soups are absolutely mouthwatering, but it's worth the extra

If the sun is shining, head to Bridges, on Granville Island, for food served with a view.

money for a huge serving of red snapper chowder for $6 (or go for the small serving for $4.50). Around the corner from the Stock Market a stall sells good fish and chips. While the market is officially open daily 9 A.M.–6 P.M., some food stalls open earlier and others later.

Island Restaurants

The distinctive yellow building on Granville Island's northern tip is **Bridges** (1696 Duranleau St., 604/687-4400). With stunning water views, the restaurant's outside, absolute-waterfront eating area is very popular. Diners also have the choice of three other dining areas (each with its own menu). The outside menu features typical wide-ranging bistro-style fare of hamburgers, salads, and pastas, as well as basic seafood dishes such as a platter to share for $38. The food is nothing special, but the views are unbeatable and the service professional. Inside, the bistro offers a similar menu, or eat in the pub and save a few bucks on the same dishes while listening to yachties talking too loud on their cell phones. The upstairs dining room is more formal and is open nightly for a seafood-oriented menu.

Under the Granville Street Bridge, **Sandbar** (1535 Johnston St., 604/669-9030; daily 11:30 A.M.–11 P.M.) is hidden from the main road that loops around the island, but well worth searching out. Downstairs features an open kitchen and water views, a world away from the hustle and bustle of the nearby marketplace. The upstairs room features a private deck complete with its own elevated waterfront bar. The menu comprises mostly seafood, cooked with a distinct Asian feel. Highly recommended is the Wok of Seafood ($15), a Chinese-style combination of "whatever's available at the market." Other mains range $12–23.50. Unlike at most other city restaurants, lunch and dinner are similarly priced.

Pacific Institute of Culinary Arts

Students from around the world are attracted to the M Pacific Institute of Culinary Arts (1505 W. 2nd Ave., 604/734-4488; lunch weekdays 11:30 A.M.–2 P.M., dinner Mon.–Sat. 6–9 P.M.) for its state-of-the-art facilities and world-class

teachers led by chef Walter Messiah. Cuisine prepared by these budding chefs is served up to the public in the institute's 50-seat dining room. While the quality of the food is impossible to fault, its presentation is also impeccable. The three-course set menus are a bargain at $22 (lunch) and $34 (dinner); dinner Saturday is $36. The Saturday brunch buffet is $25. Desserts and pastries produced by the institute's bakery classes are also tempting (offered Mon.–Sat. 8 A.M.–7 P.M. at the café-style bakery).

The Pacific Institute is right by the entrance to Granville Island. If the culinary courses interest you, contact the institute (604/734-4488 or 800/416-4040, www.picularts.bc.ca). In addition to the three- to 12-month intensive courses, casual cooking and wine instruction classes are offered.

KITSILANO

The main concentration of restaurants on the south side of False Creek is in Kitsilano, along West 4th Avenue between Burrard and Vine Streets. This part of the city was the heart of hippiedom 30 years ago, and while most restaurants from that era are long gone, a few remain, and other, newer additions to the local dining scene reflect that period of the city's history.

Cool and Casual

Retro-hip **Sophie's Cosmic Café** (2095 W. 4th Ave., at Arbutus St., 604/732-6810; daily 8 A.M.–9:30 P.M.) typifies the scene, with a definite "cosmic" look, but also provides good value and fast, efficient service. Standard bacon and eggs is $7 and omelets are around $10. The rest of the day, check the blackboard above the food service window for dishes such as a nut and herb burger ($8). Expect to wait for a table on Sunday morning.

For pizza with attitude, choose to dine in or take out from **Hell's Kitchen** (2041 W. 4th Ave., 604/736-4355; daily 10 A.M. until late). Some of the fancy names were beyond me (the Daisy Duke is a smoked chicken pizza?), but they taste good and the price is right ($11 for a 11-inch personal pizza). Huge take-out slices are $3.50 each.

Joe's Grill (2061 W. 4th Ave., 604/736-6588; daily 7 A.M.–10 P.M.), one block east from Sophie's, has survived from the 1960s serving up typical greasy spoon fare at good prices. A breakfast of eggs, bacon, and hash browns is $5; the daily soup-and-sandwich special is just $6; the milk shakes are to die for; and coffee refills are free. In diner tradition, seating is at tables or booths.

Beachside

Biceps and butts are the order of the day along trendy Kitsilano Beach, and when the beautiful people have finished sunning themselves, they head across the road to drink and dine at a small concentration of eateries spread around the foot of Yew Street. A good choice for breakfast is **Café Zen** (1631 Yew St., 604/731-4018), with a solid choice of favorites under $8. When the sun is shining, the most popular gathering spot is **Malone's Bar and Grill** (2202 Cornwall Ave., 604/737-7777). Pub grub is the order of the day, with all the usual burgers and salads for $8–12, but the real reason to stop by is to soak up the beachside atmosphere and take in the view.

On the same corner, the **Urban Well** (1516 Yew St., 604/737-7770) has a few outdoor tables with a healthy menu of wraps, salads, and vegetarian burgers. It's open in summer daily noon–2 A.M.; in winter it's closed for lunch during the week, opening at 5 P.M. Why the late hours at what seems like just another café, you may ask? Coming by a bar license in Vancouver is next to impossible, but restaurant licenses are handed out much more freely. So, like other "restaurants" with dance floors and DJs, the Urban Well serves up food as required by law but is primarily in business for the after-dark crowd.

West Coast

At the **Livingroom Bistro** (2958 W. 4th Ave., 604/737-7529; daily from 5:30 P.M.), the menu may reflect modern tastes, but as a throwback to days gone by in Kitsilano, the atmosphere is typically bohemian. The owners have cleverly created a classy restaurant using retro-style furnishings, right down to mismatched plates.

The starters are perfect for sharing, including delicious smoked salmon and cream cheese rolls ($9). For mains, the vegetarian dishes—think portobello mushrooms stuffed with corn and couscous ($12)—shine, and things only get better with hearty choices like a palate-pleasing roasted rack of lamb for a very reasonable $20.

Vegetarian

A throwback to the hippie era of the 1960s is **⋈ Naam** (2724 W. 4th Ave. at Stephens St., 604/738-7151), a particularly good natural-food restaurant in a renovated two-story private residence. Boasting large servings, excellent service, and an easy-going atmosphere that has become legendary, it's open 24 hours a day, every day of the week. Veggie burgers start at $5, full meals range $8–11.

European

Well-regarded by both locals and cuisine-savvy travelers, the much-lauded **Bishop's** (2183 W. 4th Ave., 604/738-2025; daily 5:30–10 P.M.) is very French in all aspects. Owner and longtime Vancouver restaurateur John Bishop makes all diners feel special, personally greeting them at the door, escorting them to their table, and then describing the menu and wine list as required. Elegant surroundings, parched-white linen, and soft jazz background music complete the picture. The menu features French classics but changes as seasonal items become available, such as salmon and halibut, Fraser River Valley vegetables, and fruits from the Okanagan Valley. Expect to pay around $100 for three courses for two, sans drinks. Reservations are required.

African

One of Vancouver's few African eateries, **Nyala Ethiopian Restaurant** (2930 W. 4th Ave. at McDonald St., 604/731-7899; daily 5–11 P.M.), provides the opportunity to try some unique dishes without spending a fortune. *Pakora,* an appetizer of battered vegetables, is an Ethiopian staple, and it can be combined with a variety of stir-fries to create a main meal for around $18.

Vegetarians are well catered to with meat-free dishes under $10. On Sunday, Monday, Wednesday, and Thursday a vegetarian buffet is offered for $13.

WEST BROADWAY

Broadway runs parallel to 4th Avenue, which is five blocks farther south. The restaurants listed here are farther east than those along West 4th Avenue and are generally less "trendy," appealing to those looking for value. This area of town also holds many outdoor clothing and equipment shops, so if you have any money left from a shopping spree, the following are perfect choices for lunch. The easiest way to get here by public transportation from downtown is to catch the Sky-Train to Broadway, then jump aboard a westbound bus. If you're after a *really* cheap meal, get off the bus at Kingsway (two blocks east of Main Street, the beginning of West Broadway) and cross the road to **Reno's** (151 E. Broadway, 604/876-1119), an old-style restaurant where diners order at the cash register, sit at the counter or booths, and enjoy free newspapers and bottomless coffee. Cooked breakfasts are $5 and a burger and fries is just $3.50.

Wonderful to Weenies

One of only three Canadian restaurants with the Relais Gourmand designation, **Lumière** (2551 W. Broadway, 604/739-8185; daily for dinner) is one of Vancouver's finest eateries. In the minimalist room, you'll enjoy superb French cooking amid a young, smartly dressed crowd. Most diners gravitate to classic dishes such as duck breast poached in olive oil with pan-seared foie gras on the side. Expect to pay $23–35 per main.

Feenie's (2563 W. Broadway, 604/739-7115; daily for lunch and dinner) is owned by one of Canada's top young chefs, Robert Feenie, who also oversees the kitchen at adjacent Lumière. The casual dining room buzzes with energy, with hip locals sipping martinis at the big red bar or tucking into dishes such as a Feenie's Weenie ($8) or a slab of shepherd's pie filled with duck confit ($14) at comfortable booths.

Asian

Nakornthai (401 W. Broadway, at Yukon St., 604/874-8923; daily for lunch and dinner) specializes in the cuisine of Thailand, where many dishes are based on thick, milk-based sauces. Pork is a staple in Thai cooking, prepared here in many different ways. The restaurant itself is small but clean, well decorated, and bright and airy. It's also very inexpensive, with hearty lunch specials from just $5.

In the small mall at the intersection of Broadway and Oak Street (behind 7-Eleven), **Sami's** (986 W. Broadway, 604/736-8330; daily for lunch and dinner) offers westernized East Indian cooking, including a mouthwatering lamb vindaloo. Considering its unpretentious location and low prices (all mains $9–14), the food here is remarkably good. Wine by the glass or bottle is also among the cheapest in the city.

One block north of West Broadway at Granville Street is **Vij's** (1480 11th Ave., 604/736-6664; daily from 5:30 P.M.), one of Vancouver's most acclaimed Asian restaurants. Vikram Vij, the East Indian owner, is a master at combining the intense flavors of his homeland with the tastes of his Vancouver customers, thereby creating a unique menu that appeals to everyone. Presentation and service are of the highest standard, but the food really makes this restaurant stand out. Appetizers are all under $10, and mains, such as a selection of local shellfish in a coconut saffron curry, range $18–28. No reservations are taken, and getting a table often involves a wait, which in itself says something about a place in a nondescript building within one block of a kilometer-long strip of other restaurants.

Russian

Vancouver's only Russian restaurant is **Rasputin's** (457 W. Broadway, near Cambie St., 604/879-6675), with a welcoming atmosphere and waitpersons who understand that most diners aren't going to be familiar with many items on the menu. Borscht, a hearty beet-based soup, is the best-known Russian dish, and Rasputin's does it well. A big steaming bowl, almost a meal in itself, is $5, but the best way to sample everything

Vancouver

(including a shot of vodka) is with The Feast, which is $29 per person.

NORTH SHORE

If you've crossed Burrard Inlet on the SeaBus, visit **Lonsdale Market** for local produce, including a couple of market stalls selling seafood fresh from the trawlers. Between the market and the SeaBus terminal (near the bus interchange) is the **Lonsdale Café** (147 Chadwick Court, 604/988-2761), with a few outdoor tables. Service is fast, and the daily lunch soup-and-sandwich special is just $5.

The pick of spots for breakfast or lunch in suburban Ambleside, west of Lonsdale Quay and the Lions Gate Bridge, is **Savary Island Pie Company** (125 E. 2nd St., 604/985-9192; daily 6 A.M.–7 P.M.). Join the line at this super-popular café and order a slice of foccacia pizza ($4) or a generous slab of shepherd's pie ($8.50), saving room for an oatmeal cookie or brownie.

Seafood

On the north side of Burrard Inlet, 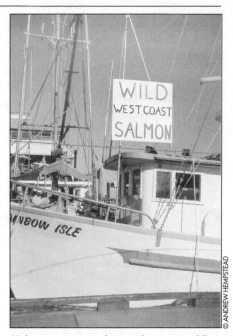 **Salmon House on the Hill** (2229 Folkstone Way, West Vancouver, 604/926-3212; daily 11:30 A.M.–2:30 P.M. and 5–10 P.M.) offers a relaxed atmosphere while providing panoramic views across Burrard Inlet to Stanley Park and the city center from its elevated mountainside location. The cavernous interior is full of northwest coast native arts and crafts—including a dugout canoe suspended over the main dining area. For an appetizer, the seafood chowder ($7.50) is my recommendation. It's not a huge serving, but it is thick and delicious. Another good starter is the sample platter of salmon prepared in various ways ($15). The house spe-

© ANDREW HEMPSTEAD

Make sure you try salmon at least once while in Vancouver—whether fresh off a trawler or at a specialty dining room like Salmon House on the Hill.

cialty of salmon barbecued over an open-flame, alderwood-fired grill is also hard to go past. And the price for this signature dish is right at just $25. Lunch ranges a reasonable $10–15 for dishes such as a smoked salmon sandwich with a dab of coleslaw on the side. The wine list features plenty of local B.C. choices. To get there, take the 21st Street exit off Upper Levels Highway to Folkstone Way; turn left on Ski Lift Road.

Information

Before leaving home contact **Tourism Vancouver** (Suite 210, 200 Burrard St., Vancouver, BC V6C 3L6, 604/682-2222, www.tourismvancouver.com). The website should have everything you need, but you can also request an information package that will come by regular post. The next best website is www.foundlocally.com/vancouver, which has been around since the beginning of the Internet phenomenon; extra at this site include a distance calculator, a search engine, and local-oriented information such as TV listings.

Vancouver falls within the Vancouver, Coast, and Mountains Tourism Region (604/739-9011 or 800/667-3306, www.vcmbc.com), one of six such regions throughout the province ("Coast" means the Sunshine Coast and "Mountains" means Whistler and vicinity).

INFORMATION CENTERS
Downtown

The city's main information center is **Vancouver Visitor Info Centre,** right downtown in the heart of the waterfront district one block from Canada Place (200 Burrard St., 604/683-2000; May–Sept. daily 8:30 A.M.–6 P.M., the rest of the year Mon.–Sat. 8:30 A.M.–5:30 P.M.). Brochures line the lower level while on the upper level specially trained staff provide free maps, brochures, and public transportation schedules; book sightseeing tours; and make accommodations reservations. Look for public transportation information and timetables to the right as you enter the center.

On Granville Island, **Granville Island Information Centre** (1398 Cartwright St., 604/666-5784, www.granvilleisland.com) is open year-round, daily 9 A.M.–6 P.M.

South

If you approach Vancouver from the south on Highway 5 (Highway 99 in Canada), the first official information center you'll come to is the **Peace Arch Provincial Visitor Centre** (summer 8 A.M.–8 P.M., the rest of the year 9 A.M.–5 P.M.) immediately north of the border and right beside the highway. A currency exchange is on-site.

Those heading into the city may want to continue to the **Delta Visitor Info Centre** (6201 60th Ave., 604/946-4232, www.deltachamber.com; daily in summer, weekdays only during the rest of the year), which is well signposted from the main highway into the city.

Farther north along Highway 99, **Richmond Visitor Info Centre** is right by the highway, to the right as you emerge on the north side of the George Massey Tunnel under the Fraser River. Operated by Tourism Richmond (604/271-8280 or 877/247-0777, www.tourismrichmond.com), it's open March–June daily 9:30 A.M.–5 P.M., July–August daily 9 A.M.–7 P.M., September daily 9:30 A.M.–5 P.M., and October Monday–Saturday 10 A.M.–4 P.M.

Vancouver International Airport has information booths on the arrivals levels of the international and domestic terminals; both are open every day of the year 8 A.M.–11:30 P.M.

North

A handy source of information north of the harbor is the small information center in the historic building beside Lonsdale Quay, which is open in summer daily 9 A.M.–6 P.M.

East

If you're approaching the city from the east along Highway 1, **Chilliwack Visitor Info Centre** (44150 Luckakuck Way, 604/858-8121 or 800/567-9535, www.tourismchilliwack.com) is a good place to stop, stretch your legs, and gather some brochures.

A further 40 kilometers (25 miles) west toward the city, take Exit 92 to reach the **Abbotsford Visitor Info Centre** (in the local chamber of commerce building, 2462 McCallum Rd., 604/859-9651, www.abbotsfordchamber.com).

Continuing west, take Highway 10 south from Exit 66 and follow Glover Road into downtown Langley for the **Langley Visitor**

Vancouver

Info Centre (5761 Glover Rd., 604/530-6656, www.langleychamber.com). Glover Road also leads north of the TransCanada Highway (take Exit 66 and head north along 232nd Street) to Fort Langley, a delightful riverside community, and the **Fort Langley Visitor Info Centre,** on the west side of the main street just before the river (23325 Mavis Ave., 604/513-8787, www.fortlangley.com).

At Exit 50 of the TransCanada Highway, cross back over the highway and continue west along 104th Avenue to the **Surrey Visitor Info Centre** (13450 102nd Ave., 604/581-1415 or 877/581-1415, www.surreytourism.ca), which is closed weekends outside of the busy summer season.

Across the Fraser River from Surrey, Tourism New Westminster (604/526-1905, www.tourism-newwestminster.org) operates **New Westminster Visitor Info Centre,** in the riverfront market (810 Quayside Dr.). This location is out of the way for highway travelers, but if you do make the detour, take Brunette Avenue south from Exit 40 off the TransCanada Highway.

For travelers approaching Vancouver from the east along Highway 7, **Mission Visitor Info Centre** (34033 Lougheed Hwy., 604/826-6914, www.missionchamber.bc.ca), in the town of the same name, has a wealth of Vancouver information.

Operated by the local chamber of commerce, **Coquitlam Visitor Info Centre** (1207 Pinetree Way, 604/464-2716, www.tricitieschamber.com) is also by Highway 7, at the north side of its intersection of Highway 7A. As well as Coquitlam and Port Coquitlam, the center represents Port Moody and the wilderness areas to the north.

BOOKS AND BOOKSTORES

Vancouver Public Library

In November 1995, after two years of construction and $100 million, Vancouver Public Library opened its doors to the public (350 W. Georgia St., 604/331-3600; year-round Mon.–Thurs. 10 A.M.–9 P.M., Fri.–Sat. 10 A.M.–6 P.M., and Sun. 1–5 P.M.). The magnificent nine-story facility is a far cry from the city's first library, which opened with a grant of £250 back

in 1887. Its elliptical facade contains a glass-walled promenade rising six stories above a row of stylish indoor shops and cafés. Once inside, you'll soon discover that the city also found enough money to stock the shelves; the library holds more than one million books. To help you find that one book you're searching for, use the self-guided tour brochure available at the information desk.

More than 20 other affiliated libraries are spread across the city. Call 604/331-3600 or go to www.vpl.vancouver.bc.ca for addresses and opening hours. One branch library of particular interest is the **Carnegie Reading Room** (corner of E. Hastings St. and Main St., 604/665-3010; daily 10 A.M.–10 P.M.). It is named for its benefactor, U.S. philanthropist Andrew Carnegie, whose $50,000 donation went a long way toward its 1902 completion as Vancouver's first permanent library.

General Bookstores

Per capita, residents of Vancouver buy more books than the residents of any other North American city. And they buy them from a huge number of bookstores scattered throughout the city. The Canadian bookstore giant **Chapters/Indigo** (www.chapters.indigo.ca) has multiple Vancouver stores, each stocking more than 100,000 titles. All have public-accessible computers to help search out particular subjects, authors, or titles; a large collection of local and Canadian fiction and nonfiction; an extensive newsstand; discounted books; and an in-house Starbucks coffeehouse. Chapters locations include: downtown (788 Robson St. at Howe St., 604/682-4066), south of False Creek (2505 Granville St. at Broadway, 604/731-7822), and in major shopping centers such as Burnaby's Metrotown. Independent booksellers have been disappearing at an alarming rate across North America, and Vancouver is no exception. As recently as the late 1990s, local **Duthie Books** boasted nine stores across the city, including in a prime Granville Street Mall location; they've been reduced to one store (2339 W. 4th Ave., Kitsilano, 604/732-5344, www.duthiebooks.com; open Mon.–Fri. 9 A.M.–9 P.M., Sat. 9 A.M.–6 P.M., Sun. 10 A.M.–6 P.M.). Other independents include **Granville Book Company** (850 Granville St., 604/687-2213) and, on Granville Island, **Blackberry Books** (1663 Duranleau St., 604/685-6188). Both stock touristy-type coffee-table books and a wide range of western Canadiana.

To save a few bucks on current titles or pick up new books at bargain prices, search out the **Book Warehouse** in the heart of the CBD (550 Granville St., 604/683-5711) and southwest of downtown (1181 Davie St., 604/685-5711).

UBC Bookstore

Until Chapters began opening its megastores across the city, the bookstore on the campus of the UBC (6200 University Blvd. at Westbrook Mall, 604/822-2665) held Vancouver's largest stock of books. Still, with almost 100,000 titles, it is an impressive place to browse. Books on just about every subject imaginable are stocked, and the staff can lay their hands on requested titles very quickly. Closed Sunday.

Travel Bookstores

Vancouver has three excellent bookstores specializing in travel-related literature; all are in close proximity to each other in the area between Granville Island and Point Grey. **Wanderlust** (west of Cypress St. at 1929 W. 4th Ave., Kitsilano, 604/739-2182; Mon.–Fri. 10 A.M.–7 P.M.,

Sat. 10 A.M.–5 P.M., Sun. noon–5 P.M.) stocks general travel guides, maps, atlases, and travel accessories. Farther west is **The Travel Bug** (3065 W. Broadway, 604/737-1122, www.travelbug-books.ca; Mon.–Sat. 10 A.M.–6 P.M., Sun. noon–5 P.M.), with an equally impressive collection of travel guides and more regional titles than you ever imagined existed. The owners at both these bookstores are very knowledgeable about the pros and cons of the various guidebook series, so they are a good source of information as to which books are best suited to your needs and interests. Back toward the city, **International Travel Maps and Books** (530 W. Broadway, 604/879-3621, www.itmb.com; Mon.–Fri. 9 A.M.–6 P.M., Sat. 10 A.M.–5 P.M., Sun. noon–5 P.M.) is part bookstore, part distributor, part publisher, with a particularly good selection of maps.

Secondhand and Antique Bookstores

Vancouver has some fantastic secondhand bookstores, including a few specializing entirely in nonfiction. The largest concentration lies along West Pender Street between Richards and Hamilton Streets. **Macleod's Books** (455 W. Pender St., 604/681-7654) stocks a wide range of antique titles, including many of the earliest works on Western Canada. Across the road, **Criterion Books** (434 W. Pender St., 604/685-2224) stocks newer titles, but the Western Canada section is just as good. On the corner of West Hastings and Hamilton Streets is **Stephen C. Lunsford Books** (604/681-6830), with plenty of old Canadian nonfiction titles. The **ABC Book Empo-**rium (1234 Granville St., 604/682-3019) offers an excellent section of fiction (downstairs) and nonfiction (upstairs), all of which is organized by author or subject.

NEWSPAPERS AND PERIODICALS

Vancouver's two newspapers are the *Province* (www.vancouverprovince.com), published daily except Saturday, and the *Vancouver Sun* (www.vancouversun.com), published daily except Sunday. Both are published by the same company, CanWest Global Communications (www.canada.com), with the *Province* more tabloid-driven than the *Sun*. Both are available at newsstands and vending machines throughout the city for under a buck. Canada's two national dailies, the *Globe and Mail* (www.globeand-mail.com) and the *National Post,* are both based in Toronto but are readily available in Vancouver.

Many free publications are distributed throughout the city. The weekly *Georgia Straight* (www.straight.com) features articles on local issues, as well as a full entertainment rundown for the city. The *Westender,* also a weekly, spotlights downtown issues and has good restaurant reviews. The weekly *Terminal City* (terminalcity.ca) and, for the hip set, *Loop* both have offbeat articles and music and entertainment diaries. *Coast* is a lifestyle magazine focusing on outdoor recreation in the region, while the monthly *Common Ground* (www.commonground.ca) is dedicated to health and personal development.

Services

EMERGENCY SERVICES

For emergencies call 911. For medical emergencies contact the downtown **St. Paul's Hospital** (1081 Burrard St., 604/682-2344), which has an emergency ward open 24 hours a day, seven days a week. Other major hospitals are: **Vancouver General Hospital** (899 W. 12th Ave., 604/875-4111) and **Lions Gate Hospital** (231 E. 15th St., 604/988-3131). **Seymour Medical Clinic** (1530 W. 7th Ave., 604/738-2151) is open 24 hours. For emergency dental help, call the **AARM Dental Group** (1128 Hornby St., 604/681-8530). For the **RCMP** call 911 or 604/264-3111.

ACCESS FOR DISABLED TRAVELERS

For those with special needs, a section under *Tips for Travelers* in the *Know British Columbia* chapter is dedicated to you. The good news about Vancouver specifically is that all of the city's top sights and a small percentage of rooms in most major hotels are wheelchair accessible. Theaters and performing arts venues are also usually wheelchair accessible. Vancouver's public transit system, Translink, has HandyDART buses that provide door-to-door wheelchair-accessible service for about the same price you'd pay on regular buses (call 604/453-4634 for bookings), and the SkyTrain and SeaBus are wheelchair accessible. **Vancouver Taxi** (604/871-1111) has wheelchair-accommodating cabs.

COMMUNICATIONS

Telephone Services

The **area code** for Vancouver is **604.** (The rest of British Columbia 250. Dial these prefixes for all long-distance calls.)

Village Global Communications (470 W. Cordova St., 604/687-2040; daily 9 A.M.–7 P.M.) is designed especially for visitors. From its private booths you can call anywhere in North America for $.50 a minute or anywhere in the world at posted, discounted rates; pay by cash or credit card. The center can also be used for sending and receiving faxes, and as you'll read below, also has Internet access.

Postal Services

Vancouver's **main post office** (349 W. Georgia St., 604/662-5722) is open Monday–Saturday. **Postal Station A** (757 W. Hastings St.) and the branch at **Bentall Centre** (595 Burrard St.) are also open on Saturday.

Visitors can have their mail sent to them c/o General Delivery, Postal Station A, Vancouver, BC V3S 4P2, Canada. The West Hastings Street post office will hold the mail for two weeks, then return it to the sender.

Public Internet Access

Most of Vancouver's major hotels have in-room Internet access, but for those not traveling with a laptop, **Village Global Communications** (470 W. Cordova St., 604/687-2040; daily 9 A.M.–7 P.M.) in Gastown is an option. Another downtown Internet café is **Hot Wired Computers** (1072 Davie St., 604/682-5272; Mon.–Fri. 9 A.M.–midnight, weekends 10 A.M.–midnight). If you have a vehicle, kill two birds with one stone at **Cold Coin Laundry** (3496 West Broadway, 604/737-9642; daily 7 A.M.–10 P.M.), which has laundry facilities, public Internet access ($4 per hour), and better coffee than you might imagine.

CURRENCY EXCHANGE

Head to any bank for the best exchange rate, or change money with one of the following operators: **Custom House,** with booths in The Landing (375 Water St., Gastown, 604/482-6000) in Canada Place, and at the Tsawwassen ferry terminal, or with **Calforex** (1146 Robson St., 800/769-2025).

PHOTOGRAPHY

One-hour film processing is offered by dozens of outlets throughout Vancouver. Two of the most reliable are **London Drugs,** with branches throughout Greater Vancouver (call 604/872-8114 for the location nearest to you), and **Lens and Shutter** (2912 W. Broadway, 604/736-3461, and another outlet in the lower level of the Pacific Centre). **Leo's Cameras** (1055 Granville St., 604/685-5331; Mon.–Fri.

9 A.M.–5 P.M., Sat. 10 A.M.–4 P.M.) has an excellent selection of new and used camera equipment, with knowledgeable staff on hand to answer any questions. Prices are competitive, especially for film and accessories.

If you've arrived in Vancouver with a video camera or in fact any electrical appliance from another country, you should be able to find parts, plugs, and adapters at **Foreign Electronics** (111 W. Broadway, 604/879-1189).

Getting There

AIR

Vancouver International Airport

Vancouver International Airport (YVR; www.yvr.ca) is on Sea Island, 15 kilometers (9.3 miles) south of Vancouver city center and linked to the mainland by bridge. It is Canada's second busiest airport, handling more than 16 million passengers and 300,000 tons of cargo annually. For airline contact information, go to the *Know British Columbia* section of this book. From the airport, connections can easily be made throughout the city by shuttle bus, regular public transportation, or taxi.

In the **International Terminal,** Level 2 is for arrivals, Level 3 for departures (the check-in area for U.S.-bound flights is Concourse E). Each level holds an information booth (open daily 8 A.M.–11:30 P.M.), currency exchange facilities, a business center, play areas for children, ATMs, duty-free shops, gift shops, newsstands, a post office, cafés, and restaurants. Car-rental and shuttle services all have outlets on the arrivals level. Scattered around the new terminal are many pieces of stunning art: a five-meter-high cedar carving of a Salish couple extending a traditional native welcome greets arriving passengers, while on Level 3 is a large bronze sculpture of a canoe by Haida artist Bill Reid.

Linked to the International Terminal by a concourse is the **Domestic Terminal.** Level 2 handles all arrivals and holds an information booth, car-

rental agencies, ATMs, shops, and restaurants. Level 3 is for departures.

The **South Terminal** is used by intraprovincial airlines such as Pacific Coastal. It is only a small terminal, which means you don't have to walk for miles, and crowds are generally nonexistent. Services include a café, gift shop, car rentals, and shuttles to the other two main terminals.

Airport Transportation

The **Vancouver Airporter** (604/946-8866 or 800/668-3141, www.yvrairporter.com) leaves the arrivals level of both terminals every 15–30 minutes 6:30 A.M.–11:30 P.M. daily, shuttling passengers along three routes between the airport and more than 40 downtown accommodations and Pacific Central Station. The one-way fare is adult $12, senior $9, child $5, with a slight discount offered for a round-trip purchase. Buy tickets from the driver or from the ticket offices on the arrivals levels of both terminals.

To get to downtown by public transport, jump aboard bus no. 100 (Midway Connector) on Level 3 (basic fare $3) and get off at 70th Street and Granville, then take bus no. 20 (Vancouver) to downtown.

A cab from the airport to downtown takes from 25 minutes and runs around $30. Cabs line up curbside on the arrivals level of both the international and domestic terminals 24 hours daily. All cabs that pick up from the airport must be accredited by the innovative YVR Taxi Program. Administered by the Vancouver Airport

Authority, the program gives incoming visitors the peace of mind that their driver will speak English, know the way around the city, load all baggage, accept credit cards, and accept U.S. dollars at an acceptable rate.

Airport Car Rental
If you've booked a rental car, you'll find check-in desks for **Alamo, Avis, Budget, Hertz, National,** and **Thrifty** on the ground level of the parkade. **Discount, Dollar,** and **Enterprise** operate beyond the main parkade entrance toward the Economy Parking Lot. For detailed information on renting a vehicle, see *Driving* under *Getting Around.*

Airport Parking
A covered concourse links the domestic and international terminals to a multistory, short-term parking lot. Closest to the terminals, short-term parking is $2.75 for every 30 minutes for a maximum of four hours. Beyond this section of the parkade is the Economy Parking Lot, where leaving your vehicle for 30 minutes costs $2.25 to a maximum of $11 per day, $66 per week, and $170 per month. The airport authority also manages a long-term parking lot ($8.55 per day, $55.58 per week, $162.45 per month) and provides shuttles to the terminals. For general airport parking information, call 604/276-6104. Many other companies offer long-term parking, but off Sea Island and away from the airport. One of these, **Park'N Fly** (6380 Miller Rd., 604/270-9476, www.parknfly.ca) charges $70 per week, complete with a complimentary shuttle to either terminal and an on-site, full-service Air Canada check-in. Check the Park'N Fly website for a discount coupon.

RAIL

Vancouver is served by **VIA Rail** (416/366-8411 or 888/842-7245, www.viarail.ca) passenger trains from across the country and is the terminus for the **Rocky Mountaineer Vacations** (604/606-7245 or 800/665-7245,

© ANDREW HEMPSTEAD

Pacific Central Station is the Vancouver terminus of all long-distance rail and bus services.

www.rockymountaineer.com). For details on both these services, including schedules and pricing, go to the *Know British Columbia* chapter of this book.

The Vancouver terminus of all VIA Rail services is **Pacific Central Station** (1150 Station St.), two kilometers (1.2 miles) southeast of downtown, a $7 cab ride or just a few minutes on the SkyTrain from any of the four downtown stations. Inside the station you'll find a currency exchange, cash machines, lockers, a newsstand, information boards, and a McDonald's restaurant. Pacific Central Station is also the long-distance bus depot. The Rocky Mountaineer terminates behind Pacific Central Station off Terminal Avenue (1755 Cottrell St.).

BUS

All long-distance bus services terminate at **Pacific Central Station** (1150 Station St.), two kilometers (1.2 miles) southeast of downtown. **Greyhound** (604/482-8747 or 800/661-8747, www.greyhound.ca) has services from throughout Canada to Vancouver.

For travel between Seattle and Vancouver, **Quick Shuttle** (604/940-4428 or 800/665-2122, www.quickcoach.com) is the best option. Fares of US$34 from Seattle and US$44 from SeaTac include drop-offs at major downtown Vancouver hotels.

Getting Around

TRANSLINK

Translink (604/953-3333, www.translink.bc.ca) operates an extensive network of buses, trains, and ferries that can get you just about anywhere you want to go within Vancouver. The free brochure *Discover Vancouver on Transit* is available from all city information centers and is an invaluable source of information. The brochure includes details of many attractions and how to reach them by public transportation.

Buses run to all corners of the city between 5 A.M. and 2 A.M. every day of the year. Transfers are valid for 90 minutes of travel in one direction.

SkyTrain is a computer-operated (no drivers) light-rail transit system that runs along 28 kilometers (17.3 miles) of elevated track from downtown Vancouver through New Westminster and over the Fraser River to King George Highway in Surrey. It stops at 20 stations along its 39-minute route. The four city-center stations are underground but are clearly marked at each street entrance.

The double-ended, 400-passenger **SeaBus** scoots across Burrard Inlet every 15–30 minutes, linking downtown Vancouver to North Vancouver in just 12 minutes. The downtown terminus is Waterfront Station, beside Canada Place and a five-minute walk from the Vancouver Visitor Info Centre. The terminal in North Vancouver is at Lonsdale Quay, where you can catch Translink buses to most North Shore sights.

On weekdays between 5:30 A.M. and 6:30 P.M. the city is divided into three zones, and fares vary adult $2–4, senior $1.50–3, for each sector (Zone 1 encompasses downtown and Greater Vancouver; Zone 2 covers all the North Shore, Burnaby, New Westminster, and Richmond; and Zone 3 extends to the limits of the Translink system). At other times (including all weekend), travel anywhere in the city costs $2 one-way. Pay the driver (exact change only) for bus travel or purchase tickets from machines at any SkyTrain station or SeaBus terminal. Request a free transfer from the driver if required. A **DayPass** costs adult $8, senior $6 and allows unlimited travel for one day anywhere on the Translink system. They are available at all SeaBus and SkyTrain stations and FareDealers (convenience stores such as 7-Eleven and Mac's) throughout the city.

West Coast Express

Primarily a commuter service for residents living along the Fraser Valley, this relatively new rail service is extremely comfortable, with passengers enjoying the use of work desks, power outlets for computers, and speeds of up to 120 kph (75 mph). Terminating at Waterfront Station, this service originates at Mission (adult $9, senior and child $6.25 to downtown). Other stops are made at Port Moody, Coquitlam, Port Coquitlam, Pitt Meadows, and Maple Ridge. For further information contact Translink (604/953-3333).

Disabled Passengers

Translink's small **HandyDART** buses (604/430-2692) provide door-to-door wheelchair-accessible service for about the same price you'd pay on regular buses. Many other city buses are equipped with wheelchair lifts, and all SkyTrain stations as well as the SeaBus and West Coast Express are fully wheelchair accessible. The best source of further information is the *Rider's Guide to Accessible Transit,* available by calling Translink (604/953-3333).

DRIVING

An excellent public transit system makes up for the fact that Vancouver isn't the world's most driver-friendly city, especially downtown, where congestion is a major problem, particularly during rush hour. West Georgia Street is a particular trouble spot, with traffic from all directions funneling onto Lions Gate Bridge to cross to the North Shore. Many downtown streets are one-way and lack left-turn lanes, adding to the congestion. On a larger scale, Vancouver lacks any real expressways, meaning a tortuous trip through downtown to get anywhere on the North Shore.

Downtown Parking

Downtown metered parking costs $1 per 30 minutes but is often difficult to find during business hours. Most shopping centers have underground parking, and a few multistory parking lots are scattered throughout the city core (including between Water and Cordova Streets, Gastown; access from either side). These cost from $5 per hour and from $20 per day, with discounts for full-day parking for early arrivals. One place you'll be assured of finding parking is under the downtown hotels, which generally charge $5–8 per hour for nonguests.

Guests at these same hotels pay up to $30 per 24-hour period for parking; often, weekend hotel rates include free parking. Throughout the residential areas of downtown, parking in many streets is designated for permit-holding residents only—look for the signs or expect to be towed.

Car Rental

All major car-rental companies are represented in Vancouver, and while in many cases the vehicles are stored away from downtown, delivery to your accommodation is complimentary. Most companies also have check-in desks at the airport (Alamo, Avis, Budget, Discount, Dollar, Enterprise, Hertz, National, and Thrifty). Book through the company's websites or toll-free numbers (see *Getting Around* in the *Know British Columbia* chapter) but use these numbers to speak with local operators: **Alamo** (604/684-1401), **Avis** (604/606-2869), **Budget** (604/668-7000), **Discount** (604/310-2277), **Dollar** (604/637-1680), **Enterprise** (604/688-5500), **Hertz** (604/606-4711), **National** (604/609-7150), **Rent-a-wreck** (604/688-0001), and **Thrifty** (604/606-1666).

TAXI, BOAT, AND BIKE

Taxi

Cabs are easiest to catch outside major hotels or transportation hubs. Fares in Vancouver are a uniform $2.30 flag charge plus $1.25 per kilometer (plus $.30 per minute when stopped). Trips within downtown usually run under $10. The trip between the airport and downtown is $30. A 10–15 percent tip to the driver is expected. Major companies include: **Black Top** (604/683-4567 or 800/494-1111), **Vancouver Taxi** (877/871-1111), and **Yellow Cab** (604/681-1111 or 800/898-8294).

A number of wheelchair-accommodating taxicabs are available from Vancouver Taxi. The fares are the same as regular taxis.

Boat

Apart from the SeaBus (see *Translink*), the only other scheduled ferry services within the city are on False Creek. Two private companies, **Granville Island Ferries** (604/684-7781) and **Aquabus** (604/689-5858), operate on this narrow waterway. From the main hub of Granville Island, 12- to 20-passenger ferries run every 15 minutes daily 7 A.M.–10 P.M. to the foot of Hornby Street, and under the Burrard Street Bridge to the Aquatic Centre (at the south end of Thurlow Street) and Vanier Park (Vancouver Museum). Every 30–60 minutes both companies also run down the head of False Creek to Stamps Landing, the Plaza of Nations, and Science World. Fares range $2.50–5 each way, with discounts for seniors and kids; schedules are posted at all docking points.

Bicycle

Downtown Vancouver is not particularly bicycle friendly, but nearby areas such as Stanley Park and the coastline west of Kitsilano are perfect places for pedal power. The main concentration of rental shops surrounds the corner of Robson and Denman Streets, two blocks from Stanley Park. Expect to pay from $5 per hour or $15 per day for the most basic mountain bike and $12 per hour or $36 per day for a suspension mountain bike. Most of the shops also rent in-line skates and tandem bikes. **Alley Cat Rentals** (1779 Robson St., 604/684-5117) is by far the least expensive place to rent, but you can also try **Bayshore Bicycles** (745 Denman St., 604/688-2453) or **Spokes Bicycle Rental** (1798 W. Georgia St., 604/688-5141).

TOURS

If you don't have a lot of time to explore Vancouver on your own, or just want an introduction to the city, consider one of the many tours available—they'll maximize your time and get you to the highlights with minimum stress.

Bus Tours

Gray Line (604/879-3363 or 800/667-0882, www.grayline.ca) offers a large variety of tours. The 3.5-hour Deluxe Grand City Tour, which includes Stanley Park, Chinatown, Gastown, Robson Street, and English Bay, costs adult $49,

senior $47, child $32. Another option with Gray Line is a downtown loop tour aboard an old English double-decker bus (mid-Apr.–October). You can get on and off as you please at any of the 21 stops made on the two-hour loop. Tickets cost adult $28, senior $27, child $16. Gray Line also has tours to Grouse Mountain (late Mar.–Oct.; adult $79, senior $74, child $55), Bowen Island (late May–Sept.; adult $65, senior $60, child $45), Steveston Village (May–Sept.; adult $47, senior $45, child $37), as well as a nature-oriented Coastal Rainforest Adventure (Apr.–Oct.; adult $70, senior $66, child $60) led by respected guides from Rockwood Adventures. All ticket prices include pickups at major downtown hotels.

Vancouver Trolley Company

From the main pickup point, a trolley-shaped booth at the top end of Water Street, this company (604/801-5515 or 888/451-5581) operates an old-fashioned trolley through the streets of downtown Vancouver. The two-hour loop stops at 23 tourist attractions, from Stanley Park in the north to Science World in the south. Trolleys run April–October daily 9 A.M.–4 P.M., coming by each stop every half hour. Tickets are adult $24, child $12. In July and August an extra loop is made, starting at 7 P.M. in Gastown, with hotel pickups until 7:40 P.M., then it's off on a two-hour tour through downtown, to Stanley Park, and as far away as Queen Elizabeth Gardens; adult $28, child $14. Reservations aren't necessary,

Harbor Cruises

June–September, **Harbour Cruises** (604/688-7246 or 800/663-1500) offers a 75-minute tour of bustling Burrard Inlet on the paddle wheeler MV *Constitution*. Tours depart from the north foot of Denman Street, up to three times daily April–October; adult $19, senior and student $16, child $7. In the evening (June–Sept. at 7 P.M.), the paddle wheeler heads out onto the harbor for a three-hour Sunset Dinner Cruise. The cruise costs $65, which includes dinner and, if booked through Gray Line (604/879-3363), hotel transfers.

While puttering around False Creek on a small ferry is an inexpensive way to see this part of the city from water level, **Granville Island Ferries** (604/684-7781) also offers a 30-minute guided tour of the historic waterway for just $8 per person. Departures are daily 10 A.M.–5 P.M. from below Bridges Restaurant on Granville Island.

Flightseeing

Flightseeing tours of the city are offered by **Harbour Air** (604/688-1277, www.harbour-air.com) from its seaplane base on the west side of Canada Place. Options range from a 20-minute flight over downtown ($95 per person) to a full-day trip to Victoria including time at Butchart Gardens ($240 per person).

Vancouver

Vancouver Island

Vancouver Island, the largest isle in North America's Pacific, stretches for more than 450 superb kilometers off the west coast of mainland British Columbia. A magnificent chain of rugged snow-capped mountains, sprinkled with lakes and rivers and pierced by deep inlets, effectively divides the island into two distinct sides: dense, rain-drenched forest and remote surf- and wind-battered shores on the west, and well-populated, sheltered, beach-fringed lowlands on the east. Much of the lush, green island is covered with dense forests of Douglas fir, western red cedar, and hemlock. The climate, stabilized by the Pacific Ocean and warmed by the Japanese current, never really gets too hot or too cold, but be prepared for cloudbursts, especially in winter.

Victoria, the provincial capital, lies at the southern tip of the island and is connected to the much larger city of Vancouver by regular ferry services. Its deeply entrenched British traditions make Victoria unique among North American cities. The rest of the island draws scenery buffs, outdoor adventurers, wildlife watchers, and students of northwest Native American art and culture.

Backpackers head west from Victoria to Port Renfrew, the starting point of the **West Coast Trail.** Island-hoppers take Highway 17 north up the Saanich Peninsula to Swartz Bay, jump

© ANDREW HEMPSTEAD

Must-Sees

Look for **M** to find the sights and activities you
can't miss and **M** for the best dining and lodging.

M Fairmont Empress: You don't need to be a guest
at this historic hotel to admire its grandeur. Plan on
eating a meal here for the full effect (page 122).

M Royal British Columbia Museum: If you visit
only one museum in Victoria, make it this one,
where you can come face-to-face with an Ice Age
woolly mammoth (page 122).

M Goldstream Provincial Park: Laced with hiking trails, Goldstream Provincial Park is a great escape from the city. If you're visiting in late fall, a trip
to the park is worthwhile to view the spectacle of
spawning salmon (page 129).

M Butchart Gardens: Even if you have only one
day in Victoria, make time to visit one of the world's
most delightful gardens (page 130).

M Galiano Island: Each of the Southern Gulf
Islands has its own charms, but a personal favorite
for kayaking is Galiano Island (page 164).

M Pacific Rim National Park: Canada isn't
renowned for its beaches, but this park protects
some magnificent stretches of sand (page 181).

M Telegraph Cove: It's worth the drive to Telegraph Cove on northern Vancouver Island just to

Fairmont Empress

wander around the postcard-perfect boardwalk village, but you'll also want to take a tour boat in
search of orca whales (page 205).

M Alert Bay: On Cormorant Island, Alert Bay is
a hotbed of native history. A cultural center and
some of the world's tallest totem poles are highlights (page 207).

Vancouver Island

To Prince Rupert

Cape Scott

Queen Charlotte Strait

Cape Scott
Provincial Park

Port Hardy

Holberg

Coal
Harbour

19 Sointula

Malcolm
Island

Knight Inlet

M ALERT BAY

Port
McNeill

M TELEGRAPH
COVE

Johnstone Strait

Sayward

Port Alice

19

Kyuquot

Kyuquot Sound

Zeballos

Tahsis

28

Gold River

Golden

Strathcona
Provincial
Park

PACIFIC

Nootka Sound

Clayoquot

Arm

Provincial

OCEAN

Park

Clayoquot Sound

Tofino

MOON

M PACIFIC RIM NATIONAL PARK

Long Beach

0   30 mi

0   30 km

VANCOUVER ISLAND

Gold Bridge

D'Arcy

Mt Currie

Pemberton

99

Whistler

Garibaldi

Provincial Park

Quadra Island

Cortes Island

99

Campbell River

28

Brackendale

19

Powell River

Saltery Bay

101

Egmont

Squamish

Buttle Lake

Courtenay

Comox

Forbidden

Denman Island

Texada Island

Cumberland

Hornby Island

Sechelt

Lasqueti Island

Qualicum Beach

Gibsons

Horseshoe Bay

Parksville

Strait of Georgia

4

Coombs

Port Alberni

VANCOUVER

Nanaimo

Gabriola Island

Alberni Inlet

Tsawwassen

Ucluelet

Thetis Island

GALIANO ISLAND

Barkley Sound

Cowichan Lake

Ladysmith

Chemainus

Mayne Island
North Pender Island

Bamfield

Duncan

Salt Spring Island

Saturna Island

Broken Group Islands

Carmanah Walbran Provincial Park

Lake Cowichan

Cowichan River Provincial Park

West Coast Trail

Sidney

PACIFIC RIM NATIONAL PARK

17

Port Renfrew

CANADA
UNITED STATES

14

Jordan River

VICTORIA

Sooke

14

San Juan Islands

Juan de Fuca Strait

Olympic Peninsula

on a ferry, and cruise the scenic **Southern Gulf Islands.** Other explorers head north up the Island Highway, Highway 1/19, which follows the Strait of Georgia all the way to the island's northern tip. The old highway has mostly been replaced by the Inland Island Highway, but to take in the best the island has to offer, stick to the old route. Along the way you'll pass sandy beaches, resorts, and old logging, mining, and fishing towns that now base their existence to a large degree on tourism.

At Parksville, Highway 4 turns off west and leads through "oooh" and "aaah" mountain scenery to the relatively untamed west coast. There you'll find picture-perfect fishing villages, driftwood-littered sand for as far as you can see, and **Pacific Rim National Park,** the only national park on the island. Also on the west coast is **Tofino,** a base for sea kayaking and whale-watching on Clayoquot Sound. Farther north up Highway 19, at Campbell River, Highway 28 cuts west to Gold River, passing through enormous **Strathcona Provincial Park.**

North of Campbell River lies a surprisingly large area mostly untouched by civilization—in fact, today you can still find maps of the island that fizzle out above Campbell River. Unique **Telegraph Cove,** a boardwalk village known for its fishing and whale-watching activities, and intriguing **Alert Bay** on Cormorant Island are highlights north of Campbell River. Finally, the road ends at **Port Hardy,** the largest community north of Campbell River and the terminus for ferries to Prince Rupert.

PLANNING YOUR TIME

Many visitors to **Victoria** spend a few nights in the city as part of a longer vacation that includes the rest of Vancouver Island. At an absolute minimum, plan on spending two full days in the capital, preferably overnighting at a character-filled bed-and-breakfast. Regardless of how long you'll be in the city, much of your time will be spent in and around the **Inner Harbour,** a busy waterway surrounded by the city's top sights and

best restaurants. At the top of the must-see list is the **Royal British Columbia Museum,** which will impress even the biggest museophobes. Victoria's most-visited attraction is **Butchart Gardens,** an absolutely stunning collection of plants that deserves at least half a day of your time. **Goldstream Provincial Park** and the scenic waterfront drive between downtown and Oak Bay are two outdoor destinations you should figure into your schedule.

Exploring Vancouver Island beyond Victoria requires some advance planning and an idea of where you want to end up. If you have just a day to spare, you can take the oceanside drive west from Victoria to **Port Renfrew** or travel north as far as **Nanaimo,** but to explore the island farther you should schedule at least two days and preferably more. The **Southern Gulf Islands,** linked to Victoria by ferry and floatplane, make a good overnight trip from the capital. Plan on at least two nights out from Victoria to do the west coast town of **Tofino** and the adjacent **Pacific Rim National Park** justice. Incorporating other parts of the province into an itinerary that includes Vancouver Island is easy. The most obvious and useful option is to do your thing on Vancouver Island and then catch a ferry from Comox to Powell River (covered in the *Southwestern British Columbia* chapter), and then drive down the Sunshine Coast to Vancouver. A more ambitious loop is to catch the ferry from the northern tip of Vancouver Island to Prince Rupert (see *Northern British Columbia*), then return to Vancouver through the central portion of the province.

While Victoria is busy year-round, the travel seasons on the rest of Vancouver Island are more defined. July and August are very busy, especially along east coast resort towns and around Tofino. Travel in May, June, or September and you'll miss the crowds while saving money on accommodations. Winters are relatively mild, and although you wouldn't want to plan a kayaking trip through the Southern Gulf Islands, this is an excellent time of year to head to Pacific Rim National Park to watch storms batter the west coast.

Victoria

Many people view the city for the first time from the Inner Harbour, coming in by boat the way people have for almost 150 years; on rounding Laurel Point, Victoria sparkles into view. Ferries, fishing boats, and seaplanes bob in the harbor, with a backdrop of manicured lawns and flower gardens, quiet residential suburbs, and striking inner-city architecture. Despite the pressures that go with city life, easygoing Victorians still find time for a stroll along the waterfront, a round of golf, or a night out at a fine restaurant.

Victoria doesn't have as many official sights as Vancouver, but this isn't a bad thing. Once you've visited "must-sees" like the Royal British Columbia Museum and Butchart Gardens you can devote your time to outdoor pursuits such as whale-watching, a bike ride through Oak Bay, or something as simple as enjoying a stroll along the beach. You will be confronted with oodles of ways to trim bulging wallets in Victoria. Some commercial attractions are worth every cent, others are routine at best, although the latter may be crowd pleasers with children, which makes them worth considering. Discovering Victoria's roots has been a long-time favorite with visitors, but some locals find the "more English than England" reputation tiring. Yes, there's a tacky side to some traditions, but high tea, double-decker bus tours, and exploring formal gardens remain true joys in Victoria.

HISTORY

In 1792, Captain George Vancouver sailed through the Strait of Georgia, noting and naming Vancouver Island. But this had little effect on the many indigenous communities living along the shoreline. Europeans didn't see and exploit the island's potential for another 50 years, when the Hudson's Bay Company established control over the entire island and the mainland territory of "Columbia."

Fort Victoria

Needing to firmly establish British presence on the continent's northwest coast, the Hudson's Bay Company built Fort Victoria—named after Queen Victoria—on the southern tip of Vancouver Island in 1843. Three years later, the Oregon Treaty fixed the U.S.–Canada boundary at the 49th parallel, with the proviso that the section of Vancouver Island lying south of that line would be retained by Canada. To forestall any claims that the U.S. may have had on the area, the British government went about settling the island. In 1849, the island was gazetted as a Crown colony and leased back to the Hudson's Bay Company. Gradually land around Fort Victoria was opened up by groups of British settlers brought to the island by the company's subsidiary, Puget Sound Agricultural Company. Several large company farms were developed, and Esquimalt Harbour became a major port for British ships.

The Growth of Victoria

In the late 1850s gold strikes on the mainland's Thompson and Fraser Rivers brought thousands of gold miners into Victoria, the region's only port and source of supplies. Overnight, Victoria became a classic boomtown, but with a distinctly British flavor; most of the company men, early settlers, and military personnel firmly maintained their homeland traditions and celebrations. Even after the gold rush ended, Victoria remained an energetic bastion of military, economic, and political activity, and was officially incorporated as a city in 1862. In 1868, two years after the colonies of Vancouver Island and British Columbia were united, Victoria was made capital. Through the two world wars, Victoria continued to grow. The commencement of ferry service between Tsawwassen and Sidney in 1903 created a small population boom, but Victoria has always lagged well behind Vancouver in the population stakes.

INNER HARBOUR SIGHTS

The epicenter of downtown Victoria is the foreshore of the Inner Harbour, which is flanked by the parliament buildings, the city's main museum,

Vancouver Island

Vancouver Island

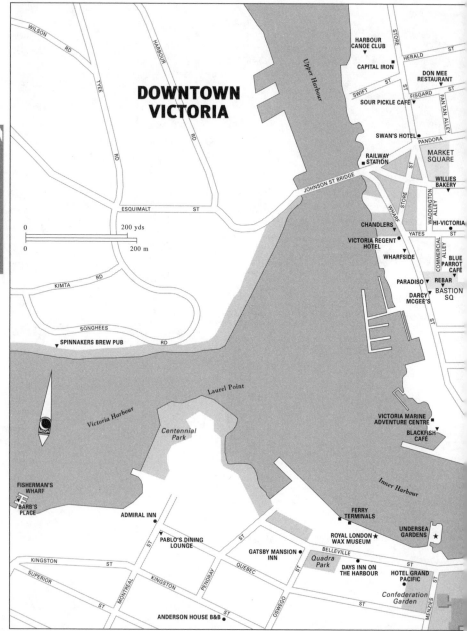

Vancouver Island

WILSON RD
HARBOUR RD
TYEE RD
RD

DOWNTOWN VICTORIA

Upper Harbour

STORE
HARBOUR CANOE CLUB ▼
CAPITAL IRON ■
HERALD ST
DON MEE RESTAURANT
SWIFT ST
FISGARD ST
SOUR PICKLE CAFÉ ▼
FAN TAN ALLEY

SWAN'S HOTEL ●
PANDORA
RAILWAY STATION ■
MARKET SQUARE
STORE ST

JOHNSON ST BRIDGE

ESQUIMALT ST

WILLIES BAKERY
WADDINGTON ALLEY
HI-VICTORIA

0   200 yds
0   200 m

WHARF
CHANDLERS ●
VICTORIA REGENT HOTEL ●
WHARFSIDE ▼
STORE
YATES ST
COMMERCIAL ALLEY
BLUE PARROT CAFÉ

PARADISO ▼
DARCY MCGEE'S ▼
REBAR ▼
BASTION SQ

KIMTA RD

SONGHEES RD

SPINNAKERS BREW PUB ▼

Laurel Point

Victoria Harbour

Centennial Park

VICTORIA MARINE ADVENTURE CENTRE ▼
BLACKFISH CAFÉ ▼

Inner Harbour

FISHERMAN'S WHARF
BARB'S PLACE ▼

ADMIRAL INN ▼

PABLO'S DINING LOUNGE ▼

KINGSTON ST
SUPERIOR ST
MONTREAL ST
KINGSTON ST
PENDRAY ST
QUEBEC ST
OSWEGO ST

ST
GATSBY MANSION INN ●
Quadra Park
BELLEVILLE
DAYS INN ON THE HARBOUR

FERRY TERMINALS

ROYAL LONDON WAX MUSEUM ★
UNDERSEA GARDENS ★

HOTEL GRAND PACIFIC
Confederation Garden
MENZIES ST

ANDERSON HOUSE B&B ●

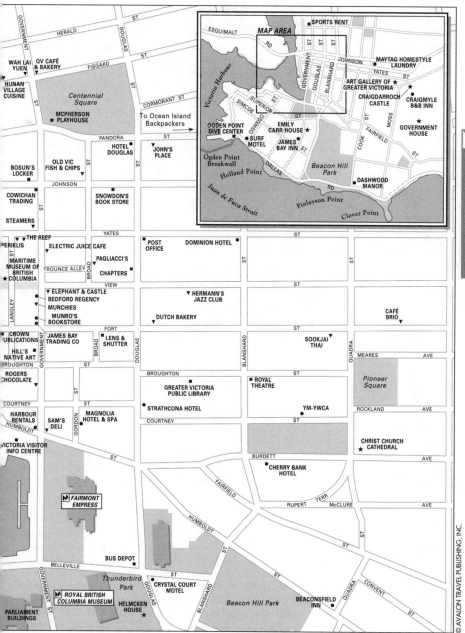

Vancouver Island

TOURING VICTORIA

The classic way to see Victoria is from the comfort of a horse-drawn carriage. Throughout the day and into the evening **Victoria Carriage Tours** (250/383-2207 or 877/663-2207) has horse carriages lined up along Menzies Street at Belleville Street awaiting passengers. A 30-minute tour costs $80 per carriage (seating up to six people), a 45-minute tour costs $120, or take a 60-minute Royal Tour for $160. Tours run 9 A.M.–midnight and bookings aren't necessary, although there's often a line.

Big red double-decker buses are as much a part of the Victoria tour scene as horse-drawn carriages. These are operated by **Gray Line** (250/388-6539 or 800/663-8390) from beside the Inner Harbour. There are many tours to choose from, but to get yourself oriented while

also learning some city history, take the 90-minute Grand City Drive Tour. It departs from the harborfront every half hour 9:30 A.M.–4 P.M.; adult $18, child $9. The most popular of Gray Line's other tours is the one to Butchart Gardens ($42.50, including admission price).

On the Water

Victoria Harbour Ferry (250/708-0201) offers boat tours of the harbor and Gorge Waterway. The company's funny-looking boats each seat around 20 passengers and depart regularly 9 A.M.–8:15 P.M. from below the Empress Hotel. The 45-minute loop tour allows passengers the chance to get on and off at will; adult $14, senior $12, child $7, or travel just pieces of the entire loop for $3 per sector.

and the landmark Fairmont Empress Hotel. Government Street leads uphill from the waterfront through a concentration of touristy shops and restaurants, while Douglas Street, parallel to the west, is the core street of a smallish Central Business District.

Above the northeast corner of the harbor is the **Victoria Visitor Info Centre** (812 Wharf St., 250/953-2033, www.tourismvictoria.com), the perfect place to start your city exploration. Be sure to return to the Inner Harbour after dark, when the parliament buildings are outlined in lights and the Empress Hotel is floodlit.

M Fairmont Empress

Overlooking the Inner Harbour, the pompous, ivy-covered 1908 Fairmont Empress is Victoria's most recognizable landmark. Its architect was the well-known Francis Rattenbury, who also designed the parliament buildings, the CPR steamship terminal (now housing the wax museum), and Crystal Garden. It's worthwhile walking through the hotel lobby to gaze—head back, mouth agape—at the interior razzle-dazzle, and to watch people-watching people partake in traditional afternoon tea (see sidebar, *Treating Yourself to Afternoon Tea*). Browse through the

conservatory and gift shops, drool over the menus of the various restaurants, see what tours are available, and exchange currency if you're desperate (banks give a better exchange rate). Get a feeling for the hotel's history by joining a tour.

Behind the Empress Hotel is **Miniature World** (649 Humboldt St., 250/385-9731; adult $9.50, child $6.50), a longtime favorite among Victoria's many commercial attractions. The 80 settings range from the historic Canadian Pacific Railway to a futuristic space.

M Royal British Columbia Museum

Canada's most-visited museum and easily one of North America's best, the Royal British Columbia Museum (675 Belleville St., 250/356-7226, summer daily 9 A.M.–6:30 P.M., the rest of the year daily 9 A.M.–5 P.M.) is a must-see attraction for even the most jaded museum-goer. Its fine Natural History Gallery displays are extraordinarily true to life, complete with appropriate sounds and smells. Come face-to-face with an ice-age woolly mammoth, stroll through a coastal forest full of deer and tweeting birds, meander along a seashore or tidal marsh, then descend into the Open Ocean Exhibit via submarine—a very real trip not recommended for claustro-

© ANDREW HEMPSTEAD

Thunderbird Park

phobes. The First Peoples Gallery holds a fine collection of artifacts from the island's first human inhabitants, the Nuu-chah-nulth (Nootka). Many of the pieces were collected by Charles Newcombe, who paid the Nuu-chah-nulth for them on collection sorties in the early 1900s. More modern human history is also explored here in creative ways. Take a tour through time via the time capsules; walk along a turn-of-the-20th-century street; and experience hands-on exhibits on industrialization, the gold rush, and the exploration of B.C. by land and sea in the Modern History and 20th Century Galleries.

The main gift shop stocks an excellent collection of books on Canadiana, wildlife, history, and native Indian art and culture, along with postcards and tourist paraphernalia, while the Out of the Mist gift shop sells native arts and crafts. Next door, the tearoom is always crowded. A new addition to the museum is the **National Geographic Theatre,** showing nature-oriented IMAX films daily 9 A.M.–8 P.M. (additional charge).

Admission outside of summer is a very worthwhile adult $11, senior and youth $7.70. In summer, admission jumps to around $23 for adults, which includes access to a traveling exhibit.

Surrounding the Museum

In front of the museum, the 27-meter-high **Netherlands Centennial Carillon** was a gift to the city from British Columbia's Dutch community. The tower's 62 bells range in weight 8–1,500 kilograms (18–3,300 pounds) and toll at 15-minute intervals daily 7 A.M.–10 P.M.

On the museum's eastern corner, at Belleville and Douglas Streets, lies **Thunderbird Park,** a small green spot chockablock with authentic totem poles intricately carved by Northwest Coast native peoples. Best of all, it's absolutely free.

Beside Thunderbird Park is **Helmcken House** (10 Elliot St., 250/361-0021; summer daily 10 A.M.–5 P.M., the rest of the year daily noon–4 P.M.; adult $5, senior $4, child $3), the oldest house in the province still standing on its original site. It was built by Dr. J. S. Helmcken, pioneer surgeon and legislator, who arrived in Victoria in 1850 and aided in negotiating the union of British Columbia with Canada in 1870. Inside this 1852 residence restored rooms have been decorated with Victorian period furniture, and on display is a collection of the good doctor's gruesome surgical equipment (which will help you appreciate modern medical technology).

Parliament Buildings

Satisfy your lust for governmental, historic, and architectural knowledge all in one go by taking a free tour of the harborside Provincial Legislative Buildings, a.k.a. the parliament buildings. These prominent buildings were designed by Francis Rattenbury and completed in 1897. The exterior is British Columbia Haddington Island stone, and if you walk around the buildings you'll no doubt spot many a stern or gruesome face staring down from the stonework.

On either side of the main entrance stand statues of Sir James Douglas, who chose the location of Victoria, and Sir Matthew Baillie Begbie, who was in charge of law and order during the gold-rush period. Atop the copper-covered dome stands a gilded statue of Captain George Vancouver, the first mariner to circumnavigate Vancouver Island. Walk through the main entrance and into the memorial rotunda, look skyward for a dramatic view of the central dome, then continue upstairs to peer into the legislative chamber, the home of the democratic government of British Columbia. Free guided tours are offered every 20 minutes 9 A.M.–noon and 1–5 P.M. in summer, less frequently (Mon.–Fri. only) in winter. Tour times differ according to the goings-on inside; for current times, call the tour office at 250/387-3046.

Laurel Point

For an enjoyable short walk from downtown, continue along Belleville Street from the parliament buildings, passing a conglomeration of modern hotels, ferry terminals, and some intriguing architecture dating back to the late 19th century. A path leads down through a shady park to Laurel Point, hugging the waterfront and providing good views of Inner Harbour en route. If you're feeling really energetic, continue to **Fisherman's Wharf,** where an eclectic array of floating homes are tied up to floating wharves.

Commercial Attractions

Along the waterfront on Belleville Street, across the road from the parliament buildings, is the former CPR steamship terminal, now the **Royal London Wax Museum** (470 Belleville St., 250/388-4461; daily 9 A.M.–5 P.M., until 7:30 P.M. in summer). As you enter the grandly ornate building, pay the admission (adult $9, senior $8, child $5) to the cashier on the right. Inside the attraction proper is a series of galleries filled with around 300 wax figures—British royalty, famous folks such as Mother Teresa and Albert Einstein, Canadian heroes like courageous cancer victim Terry Fox, and Arctic explorers. About halfway through, choose between Storybook Land and the Chamber of Horrors. If you have children (or even if you don't), you may want to bypass the latter. The hideous story of Madame Tussaud and her work that led to the famous London wax museum is interesting, but

other displays are gruesome at best. By the time I'd watched the workings of the Algerian Hook and emerged at the gallery of movie stars, even Goldie Hawn was looking creepy.

A visit to the **Pacific Undersea Gardens** (490 Belleville St., 250/382-5717; summer daily 9 A.M.–6 P.M., the rest of the year daily 9 A.M.–5 P.M.; adult $9, senior $8, child $5), on the water beside the wax museum, is of dubious value. Local species on display include tasty snapper, enormous sturgeon, schools of salmon, and scary wolf eels. Scuba divers miked for sound make regular appearances at the far end.

OLD TOWN

The oldest section of Victoria lies immediately north of the Inner Harbour between Wharf and Government Streets. Start by walking north from the Inner Harbour along historic Wharf Street, where Hudson's Bay Company furs were loaded onto ships bound for England, gold seekers arrived in search of fortune, and shopkeepers first established businesses. Cross the road to cobblestoned **Bastion Square,** lined with old gas lamps and decorative architecture dating from the 1860s to 1890s. This was the original site chosen by James Douglas in 1843 for Fort Victoria, the Hudson's Bay Company trading post. At one time the square held a courthouse, jail, and gallows. Today, restored buildings house trendy restaurants, cafés, nightclubs, and fashionable offices.

Maritime Museum of British Columbia

At the top (east) end of Bastion Square, the Maritime Museum of British Columbia (250/385-4222; daily 9:30 A.M.–4:30 P.M., until 6 P.M. in summer; adult $8, senior $5, child $3) is housed in the old provincial courthouse building. It traces the history of seafaring exploration, adventure, commercial ventures, and passenger travel through displays of dugout canoes, model ships, Royal Navy charts, figureheads, photographs, naval uniforms, and bells. One room is devoted to exhibits chronicling the circumnavigation of the world, and another holds a theater. The museum also has a nautically oriented gift shop.

Other Old Town Sights

Centennial Square, bounded by Government Street, Douglas Street, Pandora Avenue, and Fisgard Street, is lined with many buildings dating from the 1880s and '90s, refurbished in recent times for all to appreciate. Don't miss the 1878 **City Hall** (fronting Douglas Street) and the imposing Greek-style building of the Hudson's Bay Company. Continue down Fisgard Street into colorful **Chinatown,** one of Canada's oldest Chinese enclaves. It's a delicious place to breathe in the aroma of authentic Asian food wafting from the many restaurants. Chinese prospectors and laborers first brought exotic spices, plants, and a love of intricate architecture and bright colors to Victoria in the 19th century. Poke through the dark little shops along Fisgard Street, where you can find everything from fragile paper lanterns and embroidered silks to gingerroot and exotic canned fruits and veggies, then cruise Fan Tan Alley, the center of the opium trade in the 1800s. Walk south along Store Street and Wharf Street back to Bastion Square.

SOUTH OF THE INNER HARBOUR

Emily Carr House

In 1871 artist Emily Carr was born in this typical upper-class 1864 Victorian-era home (207 Government St., 250/383-5843; mid-May–mid-Oct. daily 10 A.M.–5 P.M.; adult $5.50, senior and student $4.50, child $3.25). Carr moved to the mainland at an early age, escaping the confines of the capital to draw and write about the British Columbian native peoples and the wilderness in which she lived. She is best remembered today for her painting, a medium she took up in later years.

Beacon Hill Park

This large, hilly city park—a lush, sea-edged oasis of grass and flowers—extends from the back of the museum along Douglas Street out to cliffs that offer spectacular views of Juan de Fuca Strait and, on a clear day, the distant Olympic Mountains. Add a handful of rocky points to scramble on and many protected pebble-and-sand beaches and you've found yourself a perfect spot to indulge your senses. Catch a sea breeze and gaze at all the strolling, cycling, dog-walking, and pram-pushing Victorians passing by. On a bright sunny day you'll swear that most of Victoria is here, too. The park is within easy walking distance from downtown and can also be reached by bus no. 5. For a tidbit of history, walk through the park to rocky Finlayson Point, once the site of an ancient fortified native village. Between 1878 and 1892 two enormous guns protected the point against an expected but unrealized Russian invasion.

ROCKLAND

This historic part of downtown lies behind the Inner Harbour, east of Douglas Street, and is easily accessible on foot.

Christ Church Cathedral

On the corner of Quadra and Courtney Streets, Christ Church Cathedral (250/383-2714) is the seat of the Bishop of the Diocese of British Columbia. Built in 1896, in 13th-century Gothic style, it's one of Canada's largest churches. Self-guided tours are possible Monday–Friday 8:30 A.M.–5 P.M. and Sunday 7:30 A.M.–8:30 P.M. In summer, the cathedral sponsors free choral recitals each Saturday at 4 P.M. The park next to the cathedral is a shady haven to rest weary feet, and the gravestones make fascinating reading.

Art Gallery of Greater Victoria

From Christ Church Cathedral, walk up Rockland Avenue through the historic Rockland district, passing stately mansions and colorful gardens on tree-lined streets. Turn left on Moss Street and you'll come to the 1889 Spencer Mansion and its modern wing, which together make up the Art Gallery of Greater Victoria (1040 Moss St., 250/384-4101; daily 10 A.M.–5 P.M., Thurs. 10 A.M.–9 P.M.; adult $6, senior and child $4). The gallery contains Canada's finest collection of Japanese art, contemporary art, Emily Carr pieces, traveling exhibits, and a

© ANDREW HEMPSTEAD

Craigdarroch Castle, one of Victoria's grandest residences, is open to the public for inspection.

Japanese garden with a Shinto shrine. The Gallery Shop sells art books, reproductions, and handcrafted jewelry, pottery, and glass.

Government House

Continue up Rockland Avenue from the art gallery to reach Government House, the official residence of the lieutenant governor, the queen's representative in British Columbia. The surrounding gardens, including an English-style garden, rose garden, and rhododendron garden, along with green velvet lawns and picture-perfect flower beds, are open to the public throughout the year. On the front side of the property, vegetation has been left in a more natural state, with gravel paths leading to benches that invite pausing to take in the city panorama.

Craigdarroch Castle

A short walk up (east) from the art gallery along Rockland Avenue and left on Joan Crescent brings you to the baronial four-story mansion known as Craigdarroch Castle (1050 Joan Cres., 250/592-5323; summer daily 9 A.M.–7 P.M., the rest of the year daily 10 A.M.–4:30 P.M.; adult $10, child $6). From downtown take bus no. 11 (Uplands) or no. 14 (University) to Joan Crescent, then walk 100 meters (110 yards) up the hill. The architectural masterpiece was built in 1890 for Robert Dunsmuir, a wealthy industrialist and politician who died just before the building was completed. For all the nitty-gritties, tour the mansion with volunteer guides who really know their Dunsmuir, then admire at your leisure all the polished wood, stained-glass windows, Victorian era furnishings, and the great city views from upstairs.

SCENIC ROUTE TO OAK BAY

This route starts south of the Inner Harbour and follows the coastline all the way to the University of Victoria. If you have your own transportation, this is a "must-do" in Victoria; if you don't, most city tours take in the sights. You can take Douglas Street south alongside Beacon Hill Park to access the coast, but it's possible to continue east along the Inner Harbour to the mouth of Victoria Harbour proper, passing the Canadian Coast Guard Base and the **Ogden Point Breakwall,** the official start of the Scenic Drive (marked by blue signs). The breakwall is only three meters (10 feet) wide, but it extends for 800 meters (half a mile) into the bay. It's a super-popular stroll, especially in the early morning.

For the first few kilometers beyond the breakwall, the Olympic Mountains in Washington State are clearly visible across the Strait of Georgia, and many lookouts allow you to stop and take in the panorama, including **Clover Point.** A few hundred meters beyond Clover Point, **Ross Bay Cemetery** is the final resting place of many of early Victoria's most prominent residents. Volunteer hosts are on hand through summer to point out the graves of Emily Carr; British Columbia's first governor, Sir James Douglas; members of the coal-baron Dunsmuir family; and Billy Barker, of gold-rush fame. The gates are open weekdays through daylight hours.

Continuing east, Dallas Road takes you through quiet residential areas, past small pebble beaches covered in driftwood, and into the ritzy mansion district east of downtown, where the residents have grand houses, manicured gardens, and stunning water views.

Continue through the well-manicured fairways of Victoria Golf Club on Gonzales Point to Tudor-style **Oak Bay Beach Hotel,** a rambling old building with an English pub serving up hearty fare in an old-fashioned dining room or out on a patio with water views. From the nearby marina, the coastal road continues north to Cadboro Bay, home to the **Royal Victoria Yacht Club.** The **University of Victoria** lies on a ridge above Cadboro Bay; from here head southwest along Cadboro Bay Road then Yates Street to get back downtown, or to go north take Sinclair Road then Mackenzie Avenue to reach Highway 17, the main route north up the Saanich Peninsula toward famous Butchart Gardens.

THE GORGE WATERWAY

This natural canal leads north from the Inner Harbour to Portage Inlet, a small saltwater lake beside Highway 1. The best way to see the Gorge is from sea level, aboard a **Victoria Harbour Ferry** (250/708-0201). This company runs funky little 12-passenger vessels to a turnaround point at Gorge Park by the Tillicum Road Bridge. The round-trip is $16 per person.

Point Ellice House and Garden

Built in 1861, this restored mansion (250/380-6506, May–mid-Sept. daily 10 A.M.–4 P.M.) sits amid beautiful gardens along the Gorge on Point Ellice, less than two kilometers (1.2 miles) from the Inner Harbour. The house's second owner, Peter O'Reilly, a successful entrepreneur and politician, bought it in 1868 and entertained many distinguished guests there. Original Victorian-era artifacts clutter every nook and cranny of the interior. Admission is adult $5, senior $4, child $3, but the best reason to visit is to enjoy a traditional English afternoon tea served 11 A.M.–3 P.M. ($16.95 includes admission). To get there from the Inner Harbour, jump aboard a Victoria Harbour Ferry (10 minutes and $3 each way), or by road take Government or Douglas Street north from downtown, turn left on Bay Street, and turn left again on Pleasant Street.

Craigflower Manor

Completed in 1856 using local lumber, this stately home on the Gorge Waterway was built for Kenneth MacKenzie, who employed colonists to farm the surrounding land. It was one of the island's first farms, aiding in the transition of the area from a fur-trading camp to a permanent settlement. Surrounded by commercial and residential sprawl, the scene today is far cry from the 1800s when the grand home was a social hub for Victorian socialites and naval officers from nearby Esquimalt. You can wander through the grounds and ask questions of volunteers who tend to gardens filled with the same vegetables and herbs that the original owners planted; ask to peek inside the main residence. Directly across the Gorge Waterway is Craigflower Schoolhouse, dating from a similar era as the manor and built from lumber cut from a steam-powered sawmill operated by the Mackenzie family. It served children from the adjacent farm while the second floor provided living quarters for the teacher's family. To reach Craigflower, take Gorge Road (Highway 1A) north from downtown to the Craigflower Bridge (around four kilometers/2.5 miles). The schoolhouse is on the left, the manor is across the bridge on the right.

WEST OF DOWNTOWN

CFB Esquimalt Naval & Military Museum

This small museum (250/363-4312; Mon.–Fri. 10 A.M.–3:30 P.M.; adult $2, senior and child $1) lies within the confines of **CFB Esquimalt,** on Esquimalt Harbour west of downtown A couple of buildings have been opened to the public, displaying naval, military, and general maritime memorabilia. To get there from downtown, take the Johnson Street Bridge and follow Esquimalt Road to Admirals Road; turn north, then take Naden Way and you're on the base; follow the museum signs.

Fort Rodd Hill National Historic Site

Clinging to a headland across the harbor entrance from CFB Esquimalt, this picturesque site (603 Fort Rodd Hill Rd., Colwood, 250/478-5849; Mar.–Oct. daily 10 A.M.– 5:30 P.M., Nov.–Feb. daily 9 A.M.–4:30 P.M.; adult $4, senior $3, child $2) comprises **Fort Rodd,** built in 1898 to protect the fleets of ships in the harbor, and **Fisgard Lighthouse,** which dates to 1873. It's an interesting place to explore; audio stations bring the sounds of the past alive, workrooms are furnished as they were in the late 19th century, and the lighthouse has been fully restored and is open to visitors. To get there from downtown, take the Old Island Highway (Gorge Road) and turn left on Belmont Road, then left onto Ocean Boulevard. By bus, take no. 50 from downtown, then transfer to no. 52.

While you're in the vicinity, continue down the forested road beyond the historic site turnoff to **Esquimalt Lagoon,** a haven for a great variety of birdlife. The lagoon is separated from the open water by a narrow 1.5-kilometer-long causeway. An unpaved road leads along its length, providing access to a driftwood-strewn beach that is a popular swimming and sunbathing spot in summer.

© ANDREW HEMPSTEAD

Photogenic Goldstream Falls is a natural highlight in Goldstream Provincial Park.

Goldstream Provincial Park

Lying 20 kilometers (12 miles) from the heart of Victoria, this 390-hectare (960-acre) park straddles Highway 1 northwest of downtown. The park's main natural feature is the Goldstream River, which flows north into the Finlayson Arm of Saanich Inlet. Forests of ancient Douglas fir and western red cedar flank the river; orchids flourish in forested glades; and at higher elevations forests of lodgepole pine, western hemlock, and maple thrive.

The park's highlight event occurs late October through December, when chum, coho, and chinook salmon fight their way upriver to spawn themselves out on the same shallow gravel bars where they were born four years previously. Bald eagles begin arriving in December, feeding off the spawned-out salmon until February. From the picnic area parking lot, two kilometers (1.2 miles) north of the campground turnoff, a trail leads 400 meters (440 yards) along the Goldstream River to **Freeman King Visitor Centre** (250/478-9414; daily 9 A.M.–5 P.M.), where the life cycle of salmon is described.

Even if the salmon aren't spawning, Goldstream is a great place to visit at any time of year, with a hike for you no matter what your fitness level. Starting from the visitor center, the 200-meter (220-yard) **Marsh Trail** will reward you with panoramic water views from the mouth of the Goldstream River. Another popular destination is **Goldstream Falls,** in the south end of the park. This trail leaves from the back of the park campground and descends to the picturesque falls in around 300 meters (200 yards). Noncampers should park at the campground entrance, from where it's 1.2 kilometers (.7 mile) to the falls. One of the park's longer hikes is the **Goldmine Trail,** which begins from a parking lot on the west side of Highway 1 halfway between the campground and picnic area. This trail winds two kilometers (1.2 miles) each way through a mixed forest of lodgepole pine, maple, and western hemlock, passing the site of a short-lived gold rush and coming to **Niagara Falls,** a poor relation of its eastern namesake but still a picturesque flow of water. Of a similar length but more strenuous is the trail to the summit of 419-meter (1,370-foot) **Mount Finlayson,** which takes around one hour each way and rewards successful summiteers with views back across the city and north along Saanich Inlet. The trail is accessed from Finlayson Arm Road. (For details about camping in Goldstream Provincial Park, see *Campgrounds.*)

SAANICH PENINSULA

The Saanich Peninsula is the finger of land that extends north from downtown. It holds Victoria's most famous attraction, Butchart Gardens, as well as Victoria International Airport and the main arrival point for ferries from Tsawwassen. If you've caught the ferry over to Vancouver Island from Tsawwassen, you'll have arrived at **Swartz Bay,** on the northern tip of the Saanich Peninsula; from here it's a clear run down Highway 17 to downtown Victoria. If you've been in Goldstream Provincial Park or are traveling down the island

Butchart Gardens is one Victoria attraction you won't want to miss.

© ANDREW HEMPSTEAD

Vancouver Island

from Nanaimo on Highway 1, head north and south, respectively, to **Mill Bay,** where a ferry departs regularly for **Brentwood Bay** on the Saanich Peninsula. (Brentwood Bay is home to Butchart Gardens.) Ferries run in both directions nine times daily 7:30 A.M.–6 P.M. Peak one-way fares for the 25-minute-long crossing are adult $5, child $2.75, vehicle $13.50. For exact times contact **BC Ferries** (250/386-3431, www.bcferries.com).

Butchart Gardens

Carved from an abandoned quarry, these delightful gardens are Victoria's best-known attraction. They're approximately 20 kilometers north of downtown (800 Benvenuto Dr., Brentwood Bay, 250/652-4422, www.butchartgardens.com). The gardens are open every day of the year from 9 A.M., closing in summer at 10 P.M. and in winter at 4 P.M., with varying closing hours in other seasons. Admission in summer is adult $21, child $10.50; it's much lower in winter.

A Canadian cement pioneer, R. P. Butchart, built a mansion near his quarries. He and his wife, Jennie, traveled extensively, collecting rare and exotic shrubs, trees, and plants from around the world. By 1904, the quarries had been abandoned, and the couple began to beautify them by transplanting their collection into a number of formal gardens interspersed with concrete footpaths, small bridges, waterfalls, ponds, and fountains. The gardens now contain more than 5,000 varieties of flowers, and the extensive nurseries test-grow some 35,000 new bulbs and more than 100 new roses every year. Go there in spring, summer, or early autumn to treat your eyes and nose to a marvelous sensual experience (many a gardener would give both hands to be able to work in these gardens). Highlights include the Sunken Garden (the original quarry site) with its water features and annuals; the formal Rose Garden, set around a central lawn; and the Japanese Garden, from where views extend to Saanich Inlet. In winter, when little is blooming and the entire landscape is green, the basic design of the gardens can best be appreciated. Summer visitors are in for a special treat on Saturday nights

(July and August only), when a spectacular fireworks display lights up the garden.

As you may imagine, the attraction is super busy throughout spring and summer. For this reason, try to arrive as early as possible, before the tour buses come. Once through the tollgate and in the sprawling parking lot, make a note where you park your vehicle. Once on the grounds, pick up a flower guide and follow the suggested route. Once you've done the rounds (allow at least two hours) you can choose from a variety of eateries. A gift shop specializes in—you guessed it—floral items, and another store sells seeds.

To get there from downtown, take Highway 17 north to the Brentwood–Butchart Gardens turnoff, turn left on Keating Crossroad, and follow the signs. **Island Coachlines** (250/388-6534) runs a regular shuttle out to the gardens from its downtown depot (700 Douglas St.) for $4 each way, or join one of the many guided tours of Victoria that include this famous attraction. Buses no. 74 and 75 from downtown go to Brentwood Bay.

Victoria Butterfly Gardens

In the same vicinity as Butchart Gardens, Victoria Butterfly Gardens (corner of Benvenuto Rd. and W. Saanich Rd., 250/652-3822; summer daily 9 A.M.–5 P.M., Mar.–mid-May and Oct. daily 9:30 A.M.–4:30 P.M.; adult $8.75, senior $7.75, child $5) offers you the opportunity to view and photograph some of the world's most spectacular butterflies at close range. Thousands of these beautiful creatures—species from around the world—live here, flying freely around the enclosed gardens and feeding on the nectar provided by colorful tropical plants. You'll also be able to get up close and personal with exotic birds such as parrots and cockatoos.

Sidney

The small town of Sidney lies on the east side of the Saanich Peninsula, overlooking the Strait of Georgia. As well as being the departure point for ferries to the San Juan Islands (Washington), the waterfront area is a pleasant spot to spend a sunny day exploring bustling Port Sidney Marina and the many outdoor cafés. From the marina, the **Sidney Harbour Cruise** (250/655-5211) runs four tours daily around the harbor and to a couple of the inner Gulf Islands; $15 per person. The only official attraction is **Sidney Museum** (9801 Seaport Place, at the end of Beacon Ave., 250/656-2140; daily 10 A.M.–4 P.M.; donation). The highlight is a display pertaining to whales, which includes skeletons.

RECREATION

All of Vancouver Island is a recreational paradise, but Victorians find plenty to do around their own city. Walking and biking are especially popular, and from the Inner Harbour, it's possible to travel on foot or by pedal power all the way along the waterfront to Oak Bay. The best place to get information on a wide variety of operators is the **Inner Harbour Centre,** based on a floating dock just around the corner from the information center (Wharf St., 250/995-2211 or 800/575-6700, www.marine-adventures.com).

Hiking

If you're feeling energetic—or even if you're not—plan on walking or biking at least a small section of the Scenic Marine Drive, which follows the shoreline of Juan de Fuca Strait from Ogden Point all the way to Oak Bay. The section immediately south of downtown, between Holland Point Park and Ross Bay Cemetery, is extremely popular with early-rising locals, who start streaming onto the pedestrian pathway before the sun rises. Out of town, **Goldstream Provincial Park,** beside Highway 1, and **East Sooke Regional Park,** off Highway 14 west of downtown, offer the best hiking opportunities.

The **Galloping Goose Regional Trail** follows a rail line that once linked Victoria and Sooke. For 55 kilometers (34 miles) it parallels residential back streets, follows waterways, and passes through forested parkland. The rail bed has been graded the entire way, making it suitable for both walkers and cyclists. The official starting points are the disused railway station at the top end of downtown (where Wharf and Johnson Streets merge) and the end of the trail in Sooke. Bus

© ANDREW HEMPSTEAD

Vancouver Island

The very British pastime of lawn bowling is a popular activity throughout the city.

no. 1 will bring you back to the city. Obviously, you can't walk the entire trail in a day, but traversing even a couple of short sections during your stay is worthwhile for the variety of landscapes en route.

Biking

For those keen on getting around by bike, it doesn't get much better than the bike path following the coastline of the peninsula on which Victoria lies. From downtown, ride down Government Street to Dallas Road, where you'll pick up the separate bike path running east along the coast to the charming seaside suburb of Oak Bay. From there, Oak Bay Road will take you back into the heart of the city for a round-trip of 20 kilometers. You can rent bikes at **Sports Rent,** just north of downtown (1950 Government St., 250/385-7368); from $6–8 per hour, $25–35 per day. As well as renting bikes, **Harbour Rentals** (directly opposite the information center at 811

Wharf St., 250/995-1661) rents strollers, scooters, and watercraft.

Kayaking

Daily through summer, **Ocean River Sports** (Market Square, 1824 Store St., 250/381-4233 or 800/909-4233, www.oceanriver.com) organizes guided three-hour paddles in the Inner Harbour ($60 per person). Ocean River also offers kayaking courses, sells and rents kayaks and other equipment, and runs overnight tours as far away as the Queen Charlotte Islands. **Sports Rent** (1950 Government St., 250/385-7368) rents canoes, kayaks, and other outdoor equipment. Expect to pay about $35 per day and from $145 per week for a canoe or single kayak.

Whale-Watching

Heading out from Victoria in search of whales is something that can be enjoyed by everyone. Both resident and transient whales are sighted, along with sea lions, porpoises, and seals. Trips last 2–3 hours, are generally made in sturdy inflatable boats with an onboard naturalist, and cost $75–100 per person. Recommended operators departing from the Inner Harbour include **Cuda Marine** (250/995-2832 or 866/995-2832), **Great Pacific Adventures** (250/386-2277 or 877/733-6722), **Orca Spirit Adventures** (250/383-8411 or 888/672-6722), and **Prince of Whales** (250/383-4884 or 888/383-4884). **Sea Quest Adventures** (250/655-4256 or 888/656-7599) is based in Sidney, on the Saanich Peninsula, and offers whale-watching cruises on the Strait of Georgia. The waters here are calmer than those experienced from trips departing the Inner Harbour. The local whale-watching season runs from mid-April to October.

Scuba Diving

Close to downtown Victoria lie a number of good dive sites, notably the Ogden Point breakwall. At the breakwall, **Ogden Point Dive Center** (199 Dallas Rd., 250/380-9119, www.divevictoria.com) offers rentals, instruction, and a daily (10 A.M.) guided dive. Other amenities include lockers and showers. Another recom-

mended Victoria dive shop for sales, service, and rentals is **Ocean Sports** (800 Cloverdale Ave., 250/475-2202).

To access the great diving in the Straits of Georgia and Juan de Fuca, you'll need to charter a boat. One particularly interesting site lies in the shallow waters off Sidney, just north of Victoria, where a 110-meter destroyer escort was scuttled especially for divers.

Swimming and Sunbathing

The best beaches are east of downtown. At **Willows Beach,** Oak Bay, most of the summer crowds spend the day sunbathing, although a few hardy individuals brave a swim; water temperature here tops out at around 17°C (63°F). Closer to downtown, at the foot of Douglas Street, the foreshore is mostly rocky, but you can find a couple of short, sandy stretches here and there. **Elk Lake,** toward the Saanich Peninsula, and **Thetis Lake,** west of downtown along Highway 1, are also popular swimming and sunbathing spots. Within walking distance of downtown, **Crystal Pool** (2275 Quadra St., 250/361-0732) has an Olympic-size pool, diving facilities, a kids' pool, sauna, and whirlpool.

ARTS AND ENTERTAINMENT

Victoria has a vibrant performing arts community, with unique events designed especially for the summer crowds. The city lacks the wild nightlife scene of neighboring Vancouver, but a large influx of summer workers keeps the bars crowded and a few nightclubs jumping during the busy season. The city does have more than its fair share of British-style pubs, and you can usually get a good meal along with a pint of lager. The magazine *Monday* (www.mondaymag.com) offers a comprehensive arts and entertainment section.

Theater

Dating to 1914 and originally called the Pantages Theatre, the grand old **McPherson Playhouse** (known lovingly as the "Mac" by local theater goers) went through hard times during the 1990s but has seen a recent revival of fortunes and now hosts performing arts. It's in Centennial Square, at the corner of Pandora Avenue and Government Street. The Mac's sister theater, the **Royal Theatre** (across downtown at 805 Broughton St.), began life as a roadhouse and was used as a movie theater for many years. Today it hosts stage productions and musical recitals. For schedule information and tickets at both theaters call the Royal & McPherson Theatres Society (250/386-6121 or 888/717-6121, www.rmts.bc.ca).

Performing arts on a smaller scale can be appreciated at the **Belfry Theatre,** in a historic church (1291 Gladstone St., 250/385-6815), which offers live theater October–April; tickets cost $26–33 per person.

Music and Dance

Pacific Opera Victoria (250/385-0222, www.pov.bc.ca) performs three productions each year (usually Oct.–Apr.) in the McPherson Playhouse. Tickets run $20–65. The **Victoria Operatic Society** (250/381-1021) presents opera year-round; call for the current schedule.

At the **Symphony Splash** on the first Sunday of August, the **Victoria Symphony** performs on a barge moored at the Inner Harbour. This kicks off the performing-arts season, with regular performances through May at the Royal Theatre and other city venues. Tickets range $16–32. For details call 250/385-9771 or the box office at 888/717-6121.

Drinking and Dancing

The **Strathcona Hotel** (919 Douglas St., 250/383-7137) is Victoria's largest entertainment venue, featuring four bars, including one serving a magnificent rooftop patio and the Sticky Wicket, an English bar complete with mahogany paneling.

Closer to the Inner Harbour and converted from an old grain warehouse is **Swans Hotel** (506 Pandora St., 250/361-3310; daily from 11 A.M.), which brews its own beer. Unlike many other smaller brewing operations, this one uses traditional ingredients and methods, such as allowing the brew to settle naturally rather than be filtered. The beer is available at the hotel's bar, in its restaurants, and in the attached liquor store. The main bar is a popular hangout for local businesspeople and gets busy weeknights 5–8 P.M.

A few blocks farther north and right on the water is the **Harbour Canoe Club** (450 Swift St., 250/361-1940), housed in an 1894 redbrick building that was at one time home to generators that powered Victoria's street lights. This place is popular with the downtown crowd and has a great deck.

Also offering magnificent water views is **Spinnakers Brew Pub,** across the Inner Harbour from downtown (308 Catherine St., 250/384-6613; daily 11 A.M.–2 P.M.). Having opened in 1984 as Canada's first brewpub, Spinnakers continues to produce its own European-style ales, including the popular Spinnakers Ale. The original downstairs brewpub is now a restaurant while upstairs is now the bar. Most importantly, both levels have outdoor tables with water views. The classic Spinnakers combo is a pint of India Pale Ale ($5.50) and a half dozen local oysters ($8).

Victoria's many English-style pubs usually feature a wide variety of beers, congenial atmosphere, and inexpensive meals. The closest of these to downtown is the **James Bay Inn** (270 Government St., 250/384-7151). Farther out, **Six Mile House** (494 Island Hwy., 250/478-3121) is a classic Tudor-style English pub that was extensively restored in 1980. To get there, head west out of the city along Highway 1 and take the Colwood exit.

Most of Victoria's nightclubs double as live music venues. **Legends,** in the Strathcona Hotel (919 Douglas St., 250/383-7137), has been a city hot spot for over 30 years. It comes alive with live rock 'n' roll some nights and a DJ spinning the latest dance discs on other nights. In the same hotel, **Big Bad John's** is the city's main country music venue. Known locally as the "Ingy," the **Ingraham Hotel,** north of downtown (2915 Douglas St., 250/385-6731), has cover bands playing Wednesday–Saturday and a country jam on Sunday afternoon. At the bottom of Bastion Square, **D'Arcy McGee's** (1127 Wharf St., 250/380-1322) offers live music—

Celtic sounds draw the biggest crowds—Friday and Saturday night.

Victoria boasts several good jazz venues. The best of these is **Hermann's Jazz Club** (753 View St., 250/388-9166). **Steamers** (570 Yates St., 250/381-4340) draws diverse acts but generally features jazz and blues on Tuesday and Wednesday nights. Check the Victoria Jazz Info Line (250/388-4423, www.vicjazz.bc.ca) for a schedule of local jazz performances

SHOPPING

Victoria is a shopper's delight. Most shops and all major department stores are generally open Monday–Saturday 9:30 A.M.–5:30 P.M. and stay open for late-night shopping Thursday and Friday nights until 9 P.M. The touristy shops around the Inner Harbour and along Government Street are all open Sunday. Government Street is the main strip of tourist and gift shops. The bottom end, behind the Empress Hotel, is where you'll pick up all those tacky T-shirts and such. Farther up the street are more stylish shops, such as **James Bay Trading Co.** (1102 Government St., 250/388-5477), which specializes in native arts from coastal communities; **Hill's Native Art** (1008 Government St., 250/385-3911), selling a wide range of authentic native souvenirs; and **Cowichan Trading** (1328 Government St., 250/383-0321), featuring Cowichan sweaters. Traditions continue at **Rogers Chocolates** (913 Government St., 250/384-7021), which is set up like a candy store of the early 1900s, when Charles Rogers first began selling his homemade chocolates to the local kids.

Old Town

In Old Town, the colorful, two-story **Market Square** courtyard complex was once the haunt of sailors, sealers, and whalers, who came ashore looking for booze and brothels. It's been jazzed up, and today shops here specialize in everything from kayaks to condoms. Walk out of Market Square on Johnson Street to find camping-supply stores and the interesting **Bosun's Locker** (580 Johnson St., 250/386-1308), filled to the brim with nautical knickknacks. Follow Store Street north from Market Square to find a concentration of arts and crafts shops along Herald Street. In the vicinity, **Capital Iron** is the real thing. Housed in a building that dates to 1863, this business began in the 1930s by offering the public goods salvaged from ships. In the years since, it's evolved into a department store stocking an eclectic variety of hardware and homeware products.

FESTIVALS AND EVENTS

Spring

Officially, of course, February is still winter, but Victorians love the fact that spring arrives early on the west coast—which is the premise behind the **Flower Count,** over the last week in February. While for other Canadians summer is a long way off, locals count the number of blossoms in their own yards, in parks, and along the streets. Totals are tabulated and gleefully reported across Canada.

The birthday of Queen Victoria (May 24) has been celebrated in Canada since 1834 and is especially relevant to those who call her namesake city home. The Inner Harbour is alive with weekend festivities that culminate in a downtown **Victoria Day Parade** on the holiday Monday. (Although Queen Victoria's birthday was May 24, the event is celebrated with a public holiday on the Monday preceding May 25.)

While most visitors associate Victoria with afternoon tea at the Empress, cowboys know Victoria for the **Luxton Pro Rodeo** (250/478-4250, www.rodeocanada.com), on the third weekend in May. Sanctioned by the Canadian Professional Rodeo Association, the event features all traditional events as well as mutton-busting for the kids. Access to the Luxton Rodeo Grounds, west of the city toward Sooke, is free, with admission to the rodeo itself costing $12.

The weekend following the rodeo, Victoria hosts the **Swiftsure International Yacht Race** (250/592-9098, www.swiftsure.org). With more than 60 years of history behind it, this yacht race attracts thousands of spectators to the shoreline of the Inner Harbour to watch vessels cross the finish line in six different classes, including the popular pre-1970 Classics division.

More than 200 musicians from around the world descend on the capital for **Jazzfest International** (250/388-4423, www.vicjazz.bc.ca), a weeklong celebration at various city venues the last week of June.

Summer

FolkFest (250/388-4728, www.icafolkfest.com), for 10 days from the last Sunday in June, features contemporary and traditional, professional and amateur jazz centered on the Wharf Street waterfront, in addition to an arts and crafts market, a harborfront beer garden, and an International Food Village. The best part is that entry to most performances is free.

On the first Sunday in August, the **Symphony Splash** (250/385-9771, www.symphonysplash.ca) is a treat for the eyes and ears. The local symphony orchestra performs from a barge moored in the Inner Harbour to masses crowded around the shore in this unique musical event that attracts upwards of 40,000 spectators, who line the shore or watch from kayaks.

Running 10 days in late August at venues scattered across the city, the **Victoria Fringe Festival** (250/383-2663, www.victoriafringe.com) includes more than 350 acts performing at six venues throughout the city, including outside along the harbor foreshore and inside at the Conservatory of Music on Pandora Street. All tickets are under $10.

DOWNTOWN ACCOMMODATIONS

Victoria accommodations come in all shapes and sizes. A couple of downtown hostels cater to travelers on a budget while there is also a surprising number of convenient roadside motels with rooms for under $100, including one right off the Inner Harbour. Bed-and-breakfasts are where Victoria really shines, with over 300 at last count. You'll be able to find bed-and-breakfast rooms under $100, but to fully immerse yourself in the historic charm of the city, expect to pay more. In the same price range are boutique hotels such as

the Bedford Regency—older hotels that have been restored and come with top-notch amenities and full service. Finally, if you have wads of cash to spare or are looking for a splurge, the surrounding area is blessed with two lodges (Sooke Harbour House and The Aerie) that regularly garner top rankings in all the glossy travel magazine polls, and a third (Brentwood Bay Lodge & Spa) of equal quality opened in 2004.

In the off-season (Oct.–May), nightly rates quoted below are discounted up to 50 percent, but again, occupancy rates are high as Canadians flock to the country's winter hot spot. No matter what time of year you plan to visit, arriving in Victoria without a reservation is unwise, but especially so in the summer months, when gaggles of tourists compete for a relative paucity of rooms. As a last resort, staff at the **Victoria Tourist Info Centre** (Wharf St., 250/953-2022 or 800/663-3883, www.victoriatourism.com) can offer help finding a room.

Regardless of your budget, you can't go wrong staying at one of the personally selected places below.

Under $50

Budget travelers are well catered to in Victoria, and while the accommodation choices in the capital are more varied than in Vancouver, there is no one backpacker lodge that stands out above the rest.

In the heart of downtown Victoria's oldest section is **Hostelling International Victoria** (516 Yates St., 250/385-4511 or 888/883-0099, www.hihostels.ca). The totally renovated hostel enjoys a great location only a stone's throw from the harbor. Separate dorms and bathroom facilities for men and women are complemented by two fully equipped kitchens, a large meeting room, lounge, library, game room, travel services, public Internet terminals, and an informative bulletin board. Members of Hostelling International pay $20 per night, nonmembers $24; private rooms range $48–60 s or d.

Housed in the upper stories of an old commercial building, **Ocean Island Backpackers Inn** (791 Pandora Ave., 250/385-1788 or 888/ 888-4180, www.oceanisland.com) lies just a couple of blocks from downtown. This a real party place—exactly what some young travelers are looking for, but annoying enough for some to generate letters to harried travel writers. On the plus side, the lodging is clean, modern, and welcoming throughout. Guests have use of kitchen facilities, a laundry, and a computer for Internet access. There's also plenty of space to relax, such as a reading room, music room (guitars supplied), TV room, and street level bar open until midnight. Dorm beds are $21–24 per person while private rooms are $52 s or d. Parking is an additional $5 per day, or the owners will make pickups from the bus depot.

If you have your own transportation, **Selkirk Guest House** (934 Selkirk Ave., 250/389-1213 or 800/974-6638, www.selkirkguesthouse.com) is a good choice. This family-run accommodation is in an attractive historic home on the south side of the Gorge Waterway just under three kilometers (1.9 miles) from downtown (cross the Johnson Street Bridge from downtown and take Craigflower Road). It has all the usual facilities, plus a private dock, waterfront hot tub, and pleasant gardens. Dorm beds are $22 and breakfast is an additional $5.

$50–100

The centrally located **Hotel Douglas** (1450 Douglas St., 250/383-4157 or 800/332-9981, www.hoteldouglas.com) is one of Victoria's many old hotels, this one dating to 1911 and five stories high. Guests have use of a coin laundry, and downstairs is a 24-hour café and an old-fashioned lounge with food service. The rooms are basic and small but comfortable. One drawback is that half the rooms share bathrooms ($55 s, $65 d). Larger en suite rooms are $80 s, $90 d.

In a quiet residential area immediately east of downtown, **Craigmyle B&B Inn** (1037 Craigdarroch Rd., Rockland, 250/595-5411 or 888/595-5411; $65–175 s or d) has been converted from part of the original Craigdarroch Estate (it stands directly in front of the famous castle). This rambling 1913 home is full of character, comfortable furnishings, and lots of original stained-glass windows. Rooms include singles, doubles, and family suites; some share

bathrooms while others have en suite facilities. An inviting living room with a TV, a bright sunny dining area, and friendly longtime owners make this a real home-away-from-home. Check-in is 2–6 P.M.

Another excellent choice at the lower end of the price spectrum is **Selkirk Guest House** (934 Selkirk Ave., Esquimalt, 250/389-1213 or 800/974-6638, www.selkirkguesthouse.com), on the Gorge Waterway three kilometers (1.9 miles) from the Inner Harbour. While the house has been extensively renovated and offers comfortable accommodations, it's the location that sets this place apart from similarly priced choices. The only thing separating the house from the water is the manicured garden, complete with a hot tub that sits under an old willow tree. Three of the guest rooms share bathrooms and a kitchen ($80–90 s or d), while the more spacious Rose Room has an en suite bathroom, a fireplace, its own kitchen, and a veranda overlooking the garden ($95 s or d). Breakfast is an additional $5 per person. Younger travelers will love the trampoline and treehouse.

Just one block from the Inner Harbour and kitty-corner to the bus depot is the old **Crystal Court Motel** (701 Belleville St., 250/384-0551), with 56 park-at-the-door-style motel rooms, half with kitchenettes. As you'd expect with any accommodation falling into this price category in such a prime position, the rooms are fairly basic; $98 s, $104 d, $114 for a kitchenette. Ask for a nonsmoking room when making your reservation.

Farther from the harbor, but still within walking distance, is the 1897 **Cherry Bank Hotel,** across Douglas Street in a quiet location (825 Burdett Ave., 250/385-5380 or 800/998-6688; $79–99 s or d). Be sure to request a room in the original wing, otherwise you'll pay the same for a motel-like room lacking character. The rooms have no TV or phone. Downstairs is a lounge and a restaurant known for excellent ribs. Rates include a full breakfast served in a wonderfully old-fashioned dining room.

$100–150

Value wise, you'll get the biggest bang for your

buck with the first two choices in this price range. On the downside, you'll be a little way from the waterfront.

Heritage House (3808 Heritage Lane, 250/479-0892 or 877/326-9242, www.heritage-housevictoria.com), a beautiful 1910 mansion surrounded by trees and gardens, sits in a quiet residential area near Portage Inlet, five kilometers (3.1 miles) northwest of city center. Friendly owners Larry and Sandra Gray have lovingly restored the house to its former glory. Guests choose from several outstanding rooms, one with a view of Portage Inlet from a private veranda. Enjoy the large communal living room and a cooked breakfast in the elegant dining room. It's very busy in summer but quieter November–April. Reservations are necessary year-round. Rooms vary in size and furnishings; from $135 s or d. Heritage Lane is not shown on any Victoria maps; from city center, take Douglas Street north to Burnside Road East (bear left off of Douglas). Just across the TransCanada Highway, Burnside makes a hard left (if you continue straight instead you'll be on Interurban Road). Make the left turn and continue down Burnside to just past Grange Road. The next road on the right is Heritage Lane.

East of downtown in the suburb of Oak Bay, the Tudor-style **Oak Bay Guest House,** one block from the waterfront (1052 Newport Ave., 250/598-3812 or 800/575-3812, www.beds-breakfasts.com; $135–180 s or d), has been taking in guests since 1922. It offers 11 smallish antique-filled rooms, each with a private balcony and a bathroom. The Sun Lounge holds a small library and tea- and coffee-making facilities while the Foyer Lounge features plush chairs set around an open fireplace. Rates include a delicious four-course breakfast.

Dating to 1911 and once home to artist Emily Carr, **James Bay Inn** (270 Government St., 250/384-7151 or 800/836-2649, www.james-bayinn.com) is five blocks from the harbor and within easy walking distance of all city sights and Beacon Hill Park. From the outside, the hotel has a clunky, uninspiring look, but a bright and breezy decor and new beds in the simply furnished rooms make it a pleasant place to rest

your head. Summer rates range $120–179 s or d, discounted as low as $60 in winter. All guests enjoy discounted food and drink at the downstairs restaurant and pub.

Away from the water, but still just one block from Douglas Street, is the 1876 **Dominion Hotel** (759 Yates St., 250/384-4136 or 800/663-6101, www.dominion-hotel.com), Victoria's oldest hotel. Millions of dollars have been spent restoring the property with stylish wooden beams, brass trim and lamps, ceiling fans, and marble floors reliving the Victorian era. The restored Boutique Rooms ($149–249 s or d) are absolutely charming with large beds and lovely bathrooms. Some rooms at the Dominion haven't been renovated in years; sold as Standard Rooms (you won't find pictures on the Dominion website), they are a little overpriced at $89–119 s, $99–139 d. Tea with toast is included in all these rates. The Dominion offers some attractive off-season, meal-inclusive deals—just make sure you know which class of room you'll be in.

$150–200

If you're looking for a modern feel, centrally located **Swans Suite Hotel** (506 Pandora Ave., 250/361-3310 or 800/668-7926, www.swans-hotel.com) is an excellent choice. Located above a restaurant/pub complex that was built in the 1880s as a grain storehouse, each of the 30 split-level suites holds a loft, full kitchen, dining area, and bedroom. The furnishings are casual yet elegantly rustic, with West Coast artwork adorning the walls and fresh flowers in every room. The rates of $159 for a studio, $189 for a one-bedroom suite, and $259 for a two-bedroom suite are great value. In the off-season all rooms are discounted up to 50 percent.

A few blocks back from the Inner Harbour is **Andersen House Bed and Breakfast** (301 Kingston St., 250/388-4565 or 877/264-9988, www.andersenhouse.com). Built late in the 19th century for a retired sea captain, the house features large high-ceilinged rooms all overlooking gardens that supply the kitchen with berries and herbs. Each has an en suite bathroom, private entrance, and CD player (complete with CDs). In the traditions of its original owner, the house is decorated with furnishings from around the world, including contemporary paintings. My fave of the four guest rooms is the Garden Studio, an oversized space with stained-glass windows, a jetted tub, and doors that open to a private corner of the garden. Summer rates range $195–275 s or d, while in the cooler months these same rooms are offered for $95–175.

Separated from downtown by Beacon Hill Park, **Dashwood Manor** (1 Cook St., 250/385-5517 or 800/667-5517, www.dashwoodmanor .com), a 1912 Tudor-style heritage house on a bluff overlooking Juan de Fuca Strait, enjoys a panoramic view of the entire Olympic mountain range. The 14 rooms are elegantly furnished, and hosts Dave and Sharon Layzell will happily recount the historic details of each room. Rates range from $155 s or d up to $295 for the Oxford Grand, which holds a chandelier, stone fireplace, and antiques. Off-season rates range $75–145.

Yes, it's a chain hotel, but **Days Inn on the Harbour** (427 Belleville St., 250/386-3451 or 800/665-3024, www.daysinnvictoria.com) has a prime waterfront location that will make you feel like you're paying more than you really are. Befitting the location, rooms have a subtle nautical feel and, like all Days Inns, practical yet comfortable furnishings. Standard rooms start at $169 s or d, but it's well worth the extra $10 for a harbor view. In winter, you'll pay just $100 for a suite with a view. Year-round bonuses include free parking, in-room coffeemakers, and complimentary newspapers and bottled water.

In the oldest section of downtown, surrounded by the city's best dining and shopping opportunities, is the **Bedford Regency** (1140 Government St., 250/384-6835 or 800/665-6500), featuring 40 guest rooms of varying configurations. Stylish, uncluttered art deco furnishings and high ceilings make the standard rooms ($165 s or d) seem larger than they really are. A better deal are the deluxe rooms and suites, which provide more space and better amenities for only slightly more money (from $180 s or d). The downstairs Belingo Lounge is the perfect place to relax with a glass of Pacific Northwest wine.

© ANDREW HEMPSTEAD

Gatsby Mansion Inn

$200–250

Right on the Inner Harbour, **Gatsby Mansion Inn** (309 Belleville St., 250/388-9191 or 800/563-9656, www.bellevillepark.com) has a very central position across from the water. Dating to 1897, this magnificent 20-room property has been elegantly restored, with stained-glass windows, a magnificent fireplace, lots of exposed wood, crystal chandeliers under a gabled roof, and antiques decorating every corner. Afternoon tea is served in a comfortable lounge area off the lobby, and the restaurant has a nice veranda. Through summer, rooms start at $235 s; $245 d; the biggest and best of these, with a king bed and harbor view, is $309 s, $319 d. Packages offered make staying at the Gatsby Mansion more reasonable, or visit in winter for as little as $129 s, $139 d.

Just four blocks from the Inner Harbour, the 1905 **Beaconsfield Inn** (988 Humboldt St., 250/384-4044 or 888/884-4044, www.beaconsfieldinn.com; $219–359 s or d) is exactly what you may imagine a Victorian bed-and-breakfast should be. Original mahogany floors, high ceilings, classical molding, imported antiques, and fresh flowers from the garden create an upscale historic charm throughout. Each of the nine guest rooms is individually decorated in a style matching the Edwardian era. I stayed in the Emily Carr Room. Named for the renowned artist who spent her early years in the city, this room has a rich burgundy and green color scheme, Emily Carr prints on the walls, a regal mahogany bed topped by a goose-down comforter, an oversized bathroom and double-jetted tub, and a separate sitting area with a fireplace. After checking in, you'll be invited to join other guests for tea in the library, then encouraged to return for a glass of sherry before heading out for dinner. Breakfast—served in a formal dining room or the more casual conservatory—is a grand affair, with multiple courses of hearty fare delivered to your table by your impeccably presented host.

Around the southern end of the Inner Harbour, the **Admiral Inn** (257 Belleville St., 250/388-6267 or 888/823-6472, www.admiral.bc.ca) has been creeping up in price, but it's still an excellent place to stay away from the downtown crowd but still within walking distance of the main attractions and best restaurants. Spacious rooms come with a balcony or patio while extras include free parking, a light breakfast, kitchens in many rooms, and discount coupons for local attractions. Throw in friendly owner-operators and you have good value at $219–249 s or d ($129–159 in winter).

Enjoying an absolute waterfront location right downtown is the **Victoria Regent Hotel** (1234 Wharf St., 250/386-2211 or 800/663-7472, www.victoriaregent.com). The exterior of this renovated building is nothing special, but inside, the rooms are spacious and comfortable. The best value rooms at the Regent are the suites, which include a full kitchen, a balcony, and a daily newspaper; $269 s or d, or $299 with a water view. Regular rooms are $200 s or d.

$250–300

The **M Magnolia Hotel & Spa** (623 Courtney St., 250/381-0999 or 877/624-6654, www.magnoliahotel.com) is a European-style boutique hotel just up the hill from the harbor. It features an elegant interior with mahogany-paneled walls, Persian rugs, chandeliers, a gold-leafed ceiling, and fresh flowers throughout public areas. The rooms themselves are each elegantly furnished and feature floor-to-ceiling windows, heritage-style furniture in a contemporary room layout, richly colored fabrics, down duvets, a work desk with cordless phone, and coffee-making facilities. Many also feature a gas fireplace. The bathrooms are huge, with each having marble trim, a soaker tub, and separate shower stall. The Magnolia is also home to an Aveda Lifestyle Spa, two restaurants, and a small in-house brewery. Rates of a reasonable $269 s or d include a light breakfast, daily newspaper, passes to a nearby fitness facility, and, unlike most other downtown hotels, free parking. Off-season rates range $169–209 s or d.

Holding a prime waterfront position next to the Parliament Buildings is the **Hotel Grand Pacific** (463 Belleville St., 250/386-0450 or 800/228-5151, www.hotelgrandpacific.com). First opened in 1989, the Grand Pacific has been an ongoing construction project, with extra wings added through the ensuing years. Aside from more than 300 rooms, this property is also home to Spa at the Grand, a health club, restaurants and lounges, and a currency exchange. Standard rooms, with king or twin beds, cost $259 s or d (check the Internet for these same rooms sold for under $200), or pay $329 for water views. All rooms are well appointed, spacious, and have small private balconies.

Over $300

The grand old **Fairmont Empress** (721 Government St., 250/384-8111 or 800/257-7544, www.fairmont.com) is Victoria's best-loved accommodation. Covered in ivy and with only magnificent gardens separating it from the Inner Harbour, it's also in the city's best location. Designed by Francis Rattenbury in 1908, the Empress is one of the original Canadian Pacific Railway hotels. Rooms are offered in 90 different configurations—as in other hotels of the era, most are small, but each is filled with Victorian period furnishings and antiques.

Vancouver Island

The least expensive Fairmont Rooms start at $299, but if you really want to stay in this Canadian landmark, consider upgrading to an Entrée Gold room. Although not necessarily larger, these rooms have views, a private check-in, nightly turndown service, and a private lounge where hors d'oeuvres are served in the evening; $429–499 includes a light breakfast. If you can't afford to stay at the Empress, plan on visiting one of the restaurants or the regal Bengal Lounge.

SAANICH PENINSULA ACCOMMODATIONS

With the exception of the sparkling new Brentwood Bay Lodge & Spa, the accommodations detailed here are along Highway 17, the main route between downtown Victoria and the BC Ferries terminal at Swartz Bay. These properties are best suited to travelers arriving at or departing from the airport or ferry terminal, but they are also handy to Butchart Gardens.

$50–100

Right beside the highway, **Western 66 Motel** (2401 Mt. Newton Cross Rd., 250/652-4464 or 800/463-4464, www.western66travel.com) has a large variety of affordable rooms, English-style gardens, complimentary coffee in the lobby each morning, and an inexpensive restaurant on the premises. Rooms start at $90 s or d, but traveling families will want to upgrade to the super-spacious family rooms that sleep up to six people.

$100–150

Just off the main highway between the ferry terminal and downtown, on the road into downtown Sidney, is **M Cedarwood Inn & Suites** (9522 Lochside Dr., 250/656-5551 or 877/656-5551, www.cedarwoodinnandsuites.com), highlighted by a colorful garden with outdoor seating overlooking the Strait of Georgia. Regular motel rooms go for $109 s or d, but the individually furnished cottages are a better deal; some have full kitchens (from $139 s or d).

At the same intersection as the Western 66 is **Quality Inn Waddling Dog** (2476 Mt. Newton

Cross Rd., 250/652-1146 or 800/567-8466, www.qualityinnvictoria.com; $120–130 s or d), styled as an old English guesthouse complete with an English pub. The Waddling Dog offers well-priced packages that include admission to Butchart Gardens.

Over $300

You'll feel like you're a million miles from the city at **Brentwood Bay Lodge & Spa** (849 Verdier Ave., Brentwood Bay, 250/544-2079 or 888/544-2079, www.brentwoodbaylodge.com), an upscale retreat overlooking Saanich Inlet. One of only three Canadian properties with the Small Luxury Hotels of the World designation, Brentwood ensures you will want for nothing. You can learn to scuba dive, take a water taxi to Butchart Gardens, enjoy the latest spa treatments, or join a kayak tour. The 33 rooms take understated elegance to new heights. Filling with natural light, they feature contemporary West Coast styling (lots of polished wood and natural colors), the finest Italian sheets on king-size beds, and private balconies. Modern conveniences like DVD entertainment systems, high-speed Internet access, and free calls within North America are a given. Dining options include a wood-fired grill, an upscale restaurant, a coffee bar, and a deli serving up picnic lunches. Summer rates are $495 s or d, with rates discounted to $300 between mid-October and April.

MALAHAT ACCOMMODATIONS

This small community is strung out along the main route up the island 25 kilometers (15.5 miles) from downtown Victoria, making it a good place to spend the night for those who want to get an early start on northward travel.

$50–100

If you just need somewhere to spend the night, it's hard to go past the eight-room **Malahat Oceanview Motel** (Hwy. 1, 250/478-9231 or 877/478-8181; $65–105 s or d). No surprises here—expect fairly basic motel rooms with distant water views from private and semiprivate balconies.

Over $250

For a splurge, consider **The Aerie** (600 Ebedora Lane, 250/743-7115 or 800/518-1933, www .aerie.bc.ca), a sprawling complex of Mediterranean-style villas high above the waters of Saanich Inlet and surrounded by well-manicured gardens. No expense has been spared fitting out the 23 units. Each features a king-size bed, private balcony, lounge with fireplace, and luxurious bathroom complete with soaker tub. Upon arrival guests receive fresh flowers and gourmet chocolates. The resort also has an indoor pool, outdoor hot tub, hiking trails leading through the forested hillside, tennis courts, and a restaurant considered one of the province's best. Rates start at $295 s or d, which includes a small hamper of breakfast treats delivered to the room followed by a full breakfast in the dining room. The resort is home to two restaurants: Bonelli, a casual Mediterranean-style dining room that sprawls onto a huge terrace, and an extravagant dining room decorated with a gold-leafed ceiling, faux marble columns, crystal chandeliers, and elegant table settings with high-backed chairs. The cuisine is traditional French and is accompanied by a French-influenced wine list. To get there take the Spectacle Lake Provincial Park turnoff from Highway 1, then take the first right and follow the winding road up to the resort.

CAMPGROUNDS

West

Closest camping to downtown is at **Westbay Marine Village** (453 Head St., Esquimalt, 250/385-1831, www.westbay.bc.ca), across Victoria Harbour from downtown. Facilities at this RV-only campground include full hookups and a laundry. It is part of a marina complex comprising floating residences and commercial businesses, such as fishing charter operators and restaurants. Water taxis connect the "village" to downtown. Rates range $25–40 per night, depending on the view (the $40 sites have unobstructed views across to the Inner Harbour).

Fort Victoria RV Park (340 Island Hwy., 250/479-8112, www.fortvicrv.com) is six kilometers (3.7 miles) northwest of city center on Highway 1A. This campground provides hookups, free showers, laundry facilities, and opportunities to join charter salmon-fishing trips. Tenting sites are $24, hookups are $28–30.

Continuing west along Highway 1, take Exit 10, stay in the Colwood Lane, and then take Six Mile Road back under the highway to reach **Thetis Lake Campground** (West Park Lane, 250/478-3845), which features pleasant shaded sites, coin-operated showers, and laundry facilities. It adjoins Thetis Lake Park, which is crisscrossed by hiking trails and holds one of the city's favorite swimming and sunbathing spots. Unserviced sites are $22, hookups $25–30.

North Along Highway 1

Farther west, Highway 1 curves north through **Goldstream Provincial Park** (19 kilometers/11 miles from downtown) and begins its up-island journey north. The southern end of the park holds 161 well-spaced campsites scattered through an old-growth forest—it's one of the most beautiful settings you could imagine close to a capital city. The campground offers free hot showers but no hookups. Sites are $22 per night. Although the park's interpretive center is farther north along the highway, many trails lead off from the campground, including a five-minute walk to photogenic Goldstream Falls. The campground is also within walking distance of a grocery store.

In Malahat, seven kilometers (4.3 miles) farther north along Highway 1, is **Victoria West KOA** (250/478-3332 or 800/562-1732, www.victoriakoa.com; May–Sept.). Facilities include free showers, an outdoor pool, laundry, store, and game room. Unserviced sites are $30, hookups $32–38, and Kamping Kabins start at $66.

Saanich Peninsula

If you're coming from or heading for the ferry terminal, consider staying at **McDonald Provincial Park,** near the tip of the Saanich Peninsula 31 kilometers (19 miles) north of the city center. Facilities are limited (no showers or hookups); campsites are $14 per night.

Also on the peninsula, halfway between downtown Victoria and Sidney, is **Island View Beach**

RV Park (Homathko Dr., 250/652-0548), right on the beach three kilometers (1.9 miles) east of Highway 17. Sites are $22–27 and you'll need quarters for the showers.

FOOD

While Victoria doesn't have a reputation as a culinary hot spot, for the past decade things have improved greatly with the opening of numerous restaurants serving top-notch cuisine with influences from around the world. Local chefs are big on produce organically grown and sourced from island farms. Seafood—halibut, shrimp, mussels, crab, and salmon—also features prominently on many menus.

Because of the thriving tourist trade centered on the Inner Harbour, chances are you will find something to suit your tastes and budget close at hand—Italian, Mexican, Californian, and even vegan cuisine. Mixed in with a few tourist traps (which advertise everywhere) are numerous excellent harborfront choices that are as popular with the locals as with visitors. Unlike in many cities and aside from a small Chinatown, ethnic restaurants are not confined to particular streets. On the other hand, Fort Street east of Douglas has a proliferation of restaurants that are as trendy as it gets on the island.

You still find great interest in traditional English fare, including afternoon tea, which is served everywhere from motherly corner cafés to the grand Fairmont Empress. English cooking in general is much maligned, but worth trying. For the full experience, choose kippers and poached eggs for breakfast, a ploughman's lunch (crusty bread, a chunk of cheese, pickled onions), and then roast beef with Yorkshire pudding (a crispy pastry made with drippings and doused with gravy) in the evening.

Cheap Eats and Treats

Murchies (1110 Government St., 250/381-5451) began as an importer of fine teas but has branched into the coffee business, with a popular café adjacent to a shop selling teas and coffees sourced from around the world.

At the foot of Bastion Square, a cobbled pedestrian mall, quiet **Paradiso** (10 Bastion Square, 250/920-7266; Mon.–Fri. 7 A.M.–6 P.M., Sat. 8 A.M.–6 P.M., Sun. 9 A.M.–6 P.M.) serves coffees, pastries, and muffins. The Paradiso's outdoor tables are reason enough to stop by. Tucked into a Bastion Square alley, **Blue Carrot Café** (18 Bastion Square, 250/381-8722) is a quieter spot with similar hours.

In Old Town, **Willies Bakery** (537 Johnson St., 250/381-8414) is an old-style café offering cakes, pastries, and sodas, with a quiet cobbled courtyard in which to enjoy them. Ignore the dated furnishings at the **Dutch Bakery** (718 Fort St., 250/383-9725; closed Sunday) and tuck into freshly baked goodies and handmade chocolates.

Diner Dining

While tourists flock to the cafés and restaurants of the Inner Harbour and Government Street, Douglas Street remains the haunt of lunching locals. Reminiscent of days gone by, **John's Place** (723 Pandora Ave., 250/389-0711; Mon.–Fri. 7 A.M.–9 P.M., Sat.–Sun. 8 A.M.–10 P.M.), just off Douglas Street, serves up excellent value for those in the know. The walls are decorated with movie posters, old advertisements, and photos of sports stars, but this place is a lot more than just another greasy-spoon restaurant. The food is good, the atmosphere casual, and the waitresses actually seem to enjoy working here. It's breakfast, burgers, salads, and sandwiches through the week, but weekend brunch is busiest, when there's nearly always a line spilling onto the street.

Family-Style Restaurants

Right across from the information center, and drawing tourists like a magnet, is **Sam's Deli** (805 Government St., 250/382-8424; daily 7:30 A.M.–10 P.M.). Many places nearby have better food, but Sam's boasts a superb location and a casual, cheerful atmosphere that makes it perfect for families. The ploughman's lunch, a staple of English pub dining, costs $8.50, while sandwiches (shrimp and avocado is in-house feature) range $5.50–9 and salads are around $6–9. Wondering how the weather is in Victoria? Check out the Sam Cam at www.samsdeli.com—and then, when you're in town, try to spot it high above the sidewalk tables.

Touristy **Wharfside Eatery** (1208 Wharf St., 250/360-1808) is a bustling waterfront complex with a maritime theme and family atmosphere. Behind a small café section and a bar is the main dining room and a two-story deck, where almost every table has a stunning water view. The lunch menu covers all bases, with dishes in the $10–19 range. Seafood starters to share include a tasting plate of salmon and mussels steamed in a creamy tomato broth. The lunchtime appetizer menu runs through to the evening menu (same prices), which also includes wood-fired pizza ($18–20 for two people), standard seafood dishes under $30, and a delicious smoked chicken and wild mushroom penne ($20). The cheesecake is heavenly.

Seafood

Victoria's many seafood restaurants come in all

TREATING YOURSELF TO AFTERNOON TEA

Afternoon tea, that terribly English tradition that started in the 1840s as a mid-meal snack, is one ritual you should definitely partake in while visiting Victoria. Many North Americans don't realize that there is a difference between afternoon tea and high tea, and even in Victoria the names are sometimes used in place of one another. Afternoon tea is the lighter version, featuring fine teas (no tea bags) accompanied by delicate crust-less sandwiches, scones with clotted cream and preserves, and a selection of other small treats. High tea (traditionally taken later in the day, around 6 P.M.) is more substantial—more like dinner in North America.

The best place to immerse yourself in the ritual is at one of the smaller tea rooms scattered around the outskirts of downtown. You can order tea and scones at the **James Bay Tea Room** (332 Menzies St., 250/382-8282), but apart from the faux-Tudor exterior, it's not particularly English inside. Instead, continue on to Oak Bay to the **Blethering Place Tearoom** (2250 Oak Bay Ave., 250/598-1413; daily 11 A.M.–6 P.M.), which looks exactly like a tearoom should, right down to the regulars blethering (chatting) away with the friendly staff in white aprons. Tea and scones is $6, a full afternoon tea is $15, or pay $17 and end the procession of food with a slab of trifle. **Windsor House Tea Room** (2540 Windsor Rd., Oak Bay, 250/595-3135; Mon.–Sat. noon–5 P.M.) has an authentic feeling, right down to a picture of the Queen Mother hanging from the wall. As well as afternoon tea favorites, you can order meals such as quiche and meat pies. **White Heather Tea Room** (1885 Oak Bay Ave., 250/595-8020; Tues.–Sat. 9:30 A.M.–5 P.M., Sun. 10 A.M.–5 P.M.) is a smaller, more homely setting, with a great deal of attention given to all aspects of afternoon tea—right down to the handmade tea cozies.

If the sun is shining, a pleasant place to enjoy afternoon tea is **Point Ellice House,** a historic waterfront property along the Gorge Waterway (250/380-6506; May–mid-Sept. daily 11 A.M.–3 P.M.). The price of $16.95 includes a tour of the property. As you'd expect, it's a touristy affair at **Butchart Gardens** (800 Benvenuto Dr., Brentwood Bay, 250/652-4422, www.butchartgardens.com); afternoon tea is $20 and high tea (with Cornish pastries, quiche, and more) is $27.

The **Fairmont Empress** (721 Government St., 250/389-2727) offers the grandest of grand afternoon teas, but you pay for it—$50 per person. Still, it's so popular you must book at least a week in advance through summer and reserve a table at one of seven sitting times between noon and 5 P.M.

Finally, **Murchies** (1110 Government St., 250/381-5451), in the heart of the tourist precinct, sells teas from around the world as well as tea paraphernalia such as teapots, gift sets, and collector tins. The adjacent café pours teas from around the world in a North American–style coffeehouse.

forms. Fish and chips is a British tradition and is sold as such at **Old Vic Fish & Chips** (1316 Broad St., 250/383-4536; open Mon.–Thurs. 11 A.M.–7 P.M., Fri.–Sat. 11 A.M.–8 P.M.).

Occupying a prime location on a floating dock amid whale-watching boats, seaplanes, and shiny white leisure craft, the **Ⓜ Blackfish Cafe** (Wharf St., 250/385-9996) is just steps from the main tourist trail, but it's far enough removed to make it a popular haunt with locals wanting a quiet, casual, waterfront meal. The setting alone makes the Blackfish a winner, but the menu is a knockout. Choose pan-fried oysters ($9) or grilled chili-lime marinated prawns to share, then move on to mains like seafood risotto ($23). The Blackfish opens Monday–Saturday at 6:30 A.M. and on weekends at 7:30 A.M., closing between 7 and 9 P.M. depending on the season. To get there, walk north along the harbor from the information center.

Chandlers (1250 Wharf St., 250/385-3474; daily 11:30 A.M.–10 P.M. for lunch and dinner) is on the main strip of tourist-catching restaurants along the waterfront, but it's generally regarded as Victoria's finest seafood restaurant. The stately setting is a lot quieter than the nearby Wharfside, and the dishes are a little more inventive. Salmon, a menu staple, comes in variety of ways including poached with a maple glaze ($23). Lunches such as smoked salmon pasta range $7–13.

Away from the tourist-clogged streets of the Inner Harbour is **Ⓜ Barb's Place** (Fisherman's Wharf, at the foot of St. Lawrence St., 250/384-6515; daily from 8 A.M.), a sea-level eatery on a floating dock. It's not a restaurant as such, but a shack surrounded by outdoor table settings, some protected from the elements by a canvas tent. The food is as fresh as it gets. Choose cod and chips ($7), halibut and chips ($9.50), clam chowder ($6), or splash out on a steamed crab ($16). Adding to the charm are surrounding floating houses and seals that hang out waiting for handouts. An enjoyable way to reach Barb's is by ferry ($3 from the Inner Harbour).

Pub Meals

Right in the heart of downtown is the **Elephant and Castle** (corner of Government St. and View St., 250/383-5858). This English-style pub features exposed beams, oak paneling, and traditional pub decor. A few umbrella-shaded tables line the sidewalk out front. All the favorites, such as steak and kidney pie and fish and chips, range $8–14.50. Open daily for lunch and dinner.

Swan's Hotel (506 Pandora St., 250/361-3310; daily 7 A.M.–1 A.M.) is home to an English-style pub with matching food, such as bangers and mash (sausages and mashed potatoes) and shepherd's pie, all around $10–12. In addition to the typical pub pews, the hotel has covered a section of the sidewalk with a glass-enclosed atrium.

While many city pubs exude the English traditions for which Victoria is famous, **Spinnakers Brew Pub** (308 Catherine St., Esquimalt, 250/386-2739; daily from 11 A.M.) is in a class by itself. It was Canada's first in-house brewpub, and it's as popular today as when it opened in 1985. The crowds come not only for the beer, but also for great food served up in a casual, modern atmosphere. British-style pub fare, such as a ploughman's lunch, is served in the bar while West Coast and seafood dishes like sea bass basted in an ale sauce are offered in the downstairs restaurant.

Italian

The energetic atmosphere at **Ⓜ Café Brio** (944 Fort St., 250/383-0009; daily from 5:30 P.M.) is contagious, and the food is as good as anywhere in Victoria. The Mediterranean-inspired dining room is adorned with lively artwork and built around a U-shaped bar, while out front is a handful of tables on an alfresco terrace. A creative menu combines local, seasonal produce with Italian expertise and flair. The crab salad is always a good choice to begin with, followed by wild salmon prepared however your server suggests. Order the chocolate cake smothered in chocolate espresso sauce, even if you're full. Mains range $9–28, with side dishes such as grilled asparagus and mushroom fricassee extra.

One of the most popular restaurants in town is **Pagliacci's** (1011 Broad St., 250/386-1662; daily 11:30 A.M.–midnight), known for hearty Italian food, homemade bread, great desserts, and loads of atmosphere. Small and always busy, the restaurant attracts a lively local crowd, many with children; you'll inevitably have to wait for a table during the busiest times (no reservations taken). Pastas ranging $10–14 include a prawn fettuccine topped with mint chutney. A jazz combo plays Wednesday–Sunday nights.

Other European Restaurants

A good place to go for a menu of well-rounded Greek favorites is **Periklis** (531 Yates St., 250/386-3313). Main courses range $14–25, and almost anything might be happening on the floor—from exotic belly dancers to crazy Greek dancing.

Beyond the west end of Belleville Street is **Pablo's Dining Lounge** (225 Quebec St., 250/388-4255; daily from 5 P.M.), a long-time Victorian favorite serving a variety of European cuisines. Atmosphere in the Edwardian house is relaxed yet intimate, and the dishes are all well prepared and well presented. Everything is good, but the beef tenderloin topped with crabmeat and béarnaise sauce ($34) is simply the best.

Vegetarian

Green Cuisine, at the courtyard level of Market Square (560 Johnson St., 250/385-1809; daily 10 A.M.–8 P.M.) takes the vegetarian theme to the fullest, with a vegan menu that uses no oils, sugars, or refined flours. A small buffet is offered, but the regular menu provides many choices, from chili to fruit juices.

M **Rebar** (50 Bastion Square, 250/361-9223; Mon.–Sat. 8:30 A.M.–9 P.M., Sun. 8:30 A.M.–3:30 P.M.) is a 1970s-style vegetarian restaurant with a loyal local following. Dishes such as the almond burger ($7.50) at lunch and Thai tiger prawn curry ($16) at dinner are full of flavor and made with only the freshest ingredients. Still hungry? Try the nutty carrot cake ($5.50). Children are catered to with fun choices such as banana and peanut butter on sunflower seed bread ($4). It's worth stopping by just for juice; vegetable and fruit juices, power tonics, and wheatgrass infusions are made to order for under $5.

Chinese

Victoria's small Chinatown surrounds a short, colorful strip of Fisgard Street between Store and Government Streets. The restaurants

© ANDREW HEMPSTEAD

Victoria's Chinatown is small, but it holds a variety of inexpensive restaurants.

welcome everyone, and generally the menus are filled with all the familiar westernized Chinese choices. Near the top (east) end of Fisgard is **QV Cafe and Bakery** (1701 Government St., 250/384-8831), offering inexpensive western-style breakfasts in the morning and Chinese delicacies the rest of the day. One of the least expensive places in the area is **Wah Lai Yuen** (560 Fisgard St., 250/381-5355; daily 10 A.M.–9 P.M.), a large, simply decorated, well-lighted restaurant with fast and efficient service. The wonton soups (from $3) are particularly good, or try the hearty chicken hot pot ($8.50) or scallops and broccoli ($14.50).

Named for the Chinese province renowned for hot and spicy food, **Hunan Village Cuisine** (546 Fisgard St., 250/382-0661; Mon.–Sat. for lunch and daily for dinner) offers entrées ranging $8–15. Down the hill a little is **Don Mee Restaurant** (538 Fisgard St., 250/383-1032; Mon.–Fri. for lunch, daily for dinner), specializing in the cuisine of Guangzhou. Entrées run about $7 each, while four-course dinners for two or more diners are a good deal at under $15 per person.

Other Asian

Step into the world of British colonialism at the **Bengal Lounge,** in the Fairmont Empress (721 Government St., 250/389-2727). The curry lunch buffet (daily 11:30 A.M.–3 P.M.; $23) and curry dinner buffet (Sun.–Thurs. 6–9 P.M.; $28) come with the three condiments I love to have with curry—shaved coconut, mango chutney, and mixed nuts. Friday and Saturday evenings an à la carte East Indian menu is offered, with live background jazz; prices range from $6.50 for soup to a reasonable $14–23 for main courses. Because this is a lounge bar, children 19 and under are not permitted. If you're traveling as a family and want to dine at the Empress, consider a meal at **Kipling's,** which serves up buffets for breakfast ($23), lunch ($21), and dinner ($29) in a casual atmosphere.

If you've never tried Thai cuisine, you're in for a treat at **Sookjai Thai** (893 Fort St., 250/383-9945; Mon.–Fri. 11:30 A.M.–2:30 P.M., Mon.–Sat. 5–9 P.M.). The tranquil setting is the

perfect place to sample traditional delights such as *tom yum goong,* a prawn and mushroom soup with a hint of tangy citrus ($9), and baked red snapper sprinkled with spices sourced from Thailand ($16). The snapper is the most expensive main, with a number of inspiring vegetarian choices all under $10.

INFORMATION CENTERS

Tourism Victoria (250/953-2033 or 800/663-3883, www.tourismvictoria.com) runs the bright, modern **Victoria Visitor Info Centre** (812 Wharf St.), which overlooks the Inner Harbour from. The friendly staff can answer most of your questions. They also book accommodations, tours and charters, restaurants, entertainment, and transportation, all at no extra cost; sell local bus passes and map books with detailed area-by-area maps; and stock an enormous selection of tourist brochures. Also collect the free *Accommodations* publication and the free local news and entertainment papers—the best way to find out what's happening in Victoria while you're in town. The center is open year-round daily 9 A.M.–5 P.M.

Saanich Peninsula

Coming off the ferry from Vancouver, stop in at **Saanich Peninsula Visitor Info Centre,** three kilometers (1.9 miles) south of the terminal (daily 9 A.M.–5 P.M.). It is operated by the local chamber of commerce (250/656-3616, www.spcoc.org).

BOOKS AND BOOKSTORES

Library

Greater Victoria Public Library (735 Broughton St., at the corner of Courtney St., 250/382-7241, www.gvpl.ca) is open Monday–Friday 9 A.M.–6 P.M., Saturday 9 A.M.–1 P.M.

Bookstores

Don't be put off by the touristy location of **Munro's Bookstore** (1108 Government St., 250/382-2464 or 888/243-2464), in a magnificent neoclassical building that originally opened as the Royal Bank in 1909. It holds a comprehensive collection of fiction and nonfiction titles related to Victoria, the island, and Canada in general. Munro's may be the grandest bookstore in town, but it's not the largest. That distinction goes to **Chapters** (1212 Douglas St., 250/380-9009; Mon.–Sat. 8 A.M.–11 P.M., Sun. 9 A.M.–11 P.M.). **Crown Publications** (521 Fort St., 250/386-4636) is a specialty bookstore with a great selection of western Canadiana and maps. In seaside Oak Bay, **Ivy's Bookshop** (2188 Oak Bay Ave., 250/598-2713) is a friendly little spot with a wide-ranging selection that spans local literature to current bestsellers.

For secondhand and rare West Coast and nautical titles, search out **Wells Books** (824 Fort St., 250/360-2929). Also, **Snowdon's Book Store** (619 Johnson St., 250/383-8131) holds a good selection of secondhand titles.

EMERGENCY SERVICES

In a medical emergency call 911 or contact **Victoria General Hospital** (1 Hospital Way, 250/727-4212). For non-urgent cases, a handy facility is **James Bay Medical Treatment Centre** (230 Menzies St., 250/388-9934). For dental problems, try **Cresta Dental Centre** (3170 Tillicum Rd., at Burnside St., 250/384-7711). **Shopper's Drug Mart** (1222 Douglas St., 250/381-4321) is open daily 7 A.M.–7 P.M.

ACCESS FOR DISABLED TRAVELERS

Victoria has fewer amenities than Vancouver for disabled travelers, although things have improved greatly in the last few years. Many main route transit buses have wheelchair lifts, while Handy-DART (250/727-7811) vans provide door-to-door wheelchair-accessible service beyond the bus system. For general information see *Tips for Travelers* in the *Know British Columbia* section of this book.

COMMUNICATIONS
Telephone and Internet Services
The **area code** for Victoria is **250,** the same as all

of British Columbia except Vancouver and the Lower Mainland. The cost for local calls at pay phones is $.35 and from $2.50 per minute for long-distance calls.

Most of Victoria's downtown accommodations have in-room Internet access. Those that don't, like the hostel, have inexpensive Internet booths near the lobby. A good option for travelers on the run is the small café on the lower level of the Hotel Grand Pacific (463 Belleville St.; daily 7 A.M.–7 P.M.), where public Internet access is free with a purchase.

Postal Services
The main **post office** is on the corner of Yates and Douglas Streets.

CURRENCY EXCHANGE

A currency exchange booth is opposite the baggage carousels at Victoria International Airport, but to ensure the best rates head downtown to one of the major banks, such as the **Bank of Montreal** (1225 Douglas St., 250/405-2090). Private downtown exchange shops include **Custom House Currency Exchange** (818 Wharf St., 250/389-6007 or 800/345-0007) and **FX Connectors Currency Exchange** (1208 Wharf St., 250/380-7888).

PHOTOGRAPHY

Lens & Shutter (615 Fort St., 250/383-7443) is the best downtown photo shop, with a wide selection of film and digital accessories as well as a reliable developing service. One block away, the **One Hour Photo Express** (705 Fort St., 250/389-1984) is exactly that. On the road out of town, **Japan Camera** (Mayfair Mall, 3147 Douglas St., 250/382-4435) is no cheaper for film and processing, but it is the only such shop open on Sunday. A reliable, centrally located repair shop is **Victoria Camera Service** (665 Queens Ave., 250/383-4311). If you're not a photographer, don't worry—the number of coffee-table books, postcards, and calendars sold along Government Street will astound you.

GETTING THERE

Getting to Victoria is easy; it's a short hop by ferry from the San Juan Islands, and once you've arrived getting around the compact city is even easier.

By Air

Vancouver Island's main airport is on the Saanich Peninsula, 20 kilometers (12.4 miles) north of Victoria's city center. The facility has undergone a complete revamp in recent years, with the new departure terminal completed in late 2004. Once you've collected your baggage from the carousels, it's impossible to miss the rental-car outlets (Avis, Budget, Hertz, and National) across the room, where you'll also find a currency exchange and information booth. Outside is a taxi stand and ticket booth for the AKAL Airporter. The modern terminal also houses a lounge and various eateries. Parking out front is $2 per two hours.

The **AKAL Airporter** (250/386-2525 or 877/386-2525, www.victoriaairporter.com) operates buses between the airport and major downtown hotels every 30 minutes; $13 per person one-way, $20 round-trip. The first departure from downtown to the airport is 4:30 A.M. A taxi costs approximately $45 to downtown.

Scheduled flights link the international airports of Vancouver and Victoria, but it's such a short flight (25 minutes from terminal to terminal) that unless you are on a connecting flight, the alternatives are more practical. **Air Canada** (888/247-2262, www.aircanada.ca), its connector airlines, and **WestJet** (800/538-5696, www.westjet.com) fly the route multiple times daily. Both airlines also fly to Victoria from most western Canadian cities. **Pacific Coastal** (604/273-8666 or 800/663-2872, www.pacific-coastal.com) and **Sonicblue Airways** (604/278-1608 or 800/228-6608, www.sonicblueair.com) fly into Victoria from the South Terminal at Vancouver International Airport.

Smaller airlines, including those with floatplanes, provide a handy direct link between Victoria and Vancouver, departing from the downtown Vancouver waterfront and landing on the Inner Harbour. These include **Harbour Air** (250/384-2215 or 800/665-0212, www.harbour-air.com) and **West Coast Air** (250/388-4521 or 800/347-2222, www.westcoastair.com). Both Victoria terminals are on Wharf Street.

By Bus

The main Victoria **bus depot** is behind the Empress Hotel (710 Douglas St.). **Pacific Coach Lines** (604/662-7575 or 800/661-1725, www.pacificcoach.com) operates bus service between Vancouver's Pacific Central Station and downtown Victoria, via the Tsawwassen–Swartz Bay ferry. In summer the coaches run hourly 6 A.M.–9 P.M.; $32.25 one-way, $62.50 round-trip, which includes the ferry fare. The trip takes 3.5 hours. This same company also runs buses to the Victoria depot from downtown Vancouver hotels ($36.25 one-way, $70.50 round-trip) and from Vancouver International Airport ($37.75 one-way, $73.50 round-trip).

By Ferry

From Tsawwassen (Vancouver): Ferries run regularly across the Strait of Georgia from Tsawwassen, 30 kilometers (19 miles) south of Vancouver, to the **Swartz Bay Ferry Terminal,** 32 kilometers (20 miles) north of Victoria. Through summer, ferries run hourly 7 A.M.–10 P.M., the rest of the year slightly less frequently. The crossing takes 90 minutes. You can expect a wait in summer; limited vehicle reservations (604/444-2890 or 888/724-5223, www.bcferries.com) are accepted for $15 per booking. Peak fares are adult $10.25, child 5–11 $5.25, vehicle $35.75, motorcycle $18. For information, contact **BC Ferries** (250/386-3431 or 888/223-3779, www.bcferries.com).

From Seattle: Clipper Navigation (800/888-2535, www.clippervacations.com) offers a fleet of foot-passengers-only ferries connecting Seattle's Pier 69 with Victoria's Inner Harbour. Its turbojet catamaran, the *Victoria Clipper IV,* is North America's fastest passenger ferry, traveling at speeds of up to 45 knots (over 80 kph/50 mph). This speedy vessel makes the crossing in two hours. The cost is adult US$81 one-way, US$133 round-trip. The company's other vessels make the trip in 2.5 hours and cost adult US$70 one-way, US$114 round-trip. The service runs year-round. In summer, up to five sailings a day are offered, with some stopping off at Friday Harbor in the San Juan Islands. All vessels feature spacious seating arrangements, writing tables, complimentary tea and coffee, and light snacks. Discounts apply outside of the busy summer months and on tickets purchased 14 or more days in advance. Seniors also get a break, and children travel for half price.

Clipper Navigation also offers a plethora of reasonably priced accommodations and tour packages in Victoria (from US$165 including transportation from Seattle; high season). For schedules and tour information drop by one of its offices: Pier 69, Seattle (206/448-5000), or at the Inner Harbour terminal (Belleville St., 250/382-8100).

From Anacortes: Washington State Ferries (206/464-6400, 250/381-1551, or 888/808-7977, www.wsdof.wa.gov/ferries) runs a regular ferry schedule between Anacortes and the San Juan Islands, with the 7:50 A.M. sailing continuing to Sidney, on the Saanich Peninsula 32 kilometers (20 miles) north of Victoria. The return sailing departs Sidney at 11:45 A.M. The one-way fare is adult US$13.80, senior US$6.90, vehicle and driver US$47. Reservations must be made at least 24 hours in advance.

From Port Angeles: Black Ball Transport (250/386-2202 in Victoria, or 360/457-4491 in Port Angeles, www.cohoferry.com) operates the **MV Coho** across Juan de Fuca Strait between Port Angeles and Victoria's Inner Harbour. It makes four crossings daily in each direction from mid-May to mid-October, two crossings daily the rest of the year. Advance reservations are not accepted—phone a day or so

HEADING UP THE ISLAND FROM VICTORIA

O nce you've finished exploring the delights of Victoria, there's only one way to go, and that's north. Vancouver Island is blessed with an excellent public transport system, including buses that travel to all corners and a rail service that closely follows the Strait of Georgia as far north as Courtenay. If you're driving, the road ends at Port Hardy, from where BC Ferries provides service to Prince Rupert, the gateway to northern British Columbia and a stop on the long route north to Alaska.

By Road

From downtown Victoria, take Douglas Street north for three kilometers (1.9 miles) to Highway 1, which jogs westward through Victoria's residential suburbs before turning north and running up the east side of the island to Nanaimo (113 km/71 miles), Courtenay (220 km/137 miles), Campbell River (260 km/162 miles), and Port Hardy (495 km/309 miles).

Island Coachlines (250/385-4411 or 800/318-0818, www.victoriatours.com) serves all of Vancouver Island, including Tofino, from the main bus depot centrally located in downtown Victoria (710 Douglas St., corner of Belleville Street). No bookings are taken, so just roll up, pay the fare, and jump aboard.

By Rail

VIA Rail (250/383-4324 or 800/561-8630, www.viarail.ca) operates the Malahat passenger train on a schedule that departs Victoria for Courtenay Monday–Saturday at 8:15 A.M. and Sunday at noon, and departs Courtenay for Victoria Monday–Saturday at 1:15 P.M. and Sunday at 5:15 P.M. This route is so scenic that many make the train trip a one-day excursion, going as far as Nanaimo and spending a few hours in the city before returning; it's a cheap day out at under $50 for the round-trip.

before your planned departure for estimated waiting times. The one-way fare is adult US$7.75, child US$3.90, vehicle US$29.75. The Port Angeles terminal is on Railroad Avenue, where nearby parking is US$10 per day. The other option from Port Angeles is the passenger-only **Victoria Express** (250/361-9144 or 800/663-1589, www.victoriaexpress.com). This company operates 2–4 sailings daily in each direction between June and September; US$10 each way.

GETTING AROUND

The best way to get to know this compact city is on foot. All the downtown attractions are within a short walk of one another, and the more remote sights are easily reached by road or public transit. In summer, various tours are offered, giving you the choice of seeing Victoria by horse-drawn carriage, bus, boat, bicycle, limo—you name it. But if you still feel the need to have a car readily available, you'll be pleased to know that parking is plentiful just a few blocks from the Inner Harbour.

Victoria Regional Transit System

Most of the inner-city attractions can be reached on foot. However, the local bus network is excellent, and it's easy to jump on and off and get everywhere you want to go. Pick up an *Explore Victoria* brochure at the information center for details of all the major sights, parks, beaches, and shopping areas, and the buses needed to reach them. Bus fare for travel within Zone 1, which covers most of the city, is adult $2, senior or child $1.25. Zone 2 covers outlying areas such as the airport and Swartz Bay ferry terminal; adult $3, senior or child $2. Transfers are good for travel in one direction within 90 minutes of purchase. A DayPass, valid for one day's unlimited bus travel, costs adult $6, senior or child $4. For general bus information call

250/385-2551 or surf the Internet to www.transitbc.com.

Ferry

The most enjoyable way to get around the city is aboard a **Victoria Harbour Ferry** (250/708-0201). The company's distinctive 12-passenger ferries ply two routes departing from the Inner Harbour. One takes in harborside docks including Fisherman's Wharf, Ocean Pointe Resort, and Westbay Marine Village, while the other heads up the Gorge Waterway; $3 per sector, or make the round-trip as a tour for $14–16.

Taxi

Taxis operate on a meter system, charging $2.75 at the initial flag drop plus around $2 per kilometer. Call **Blue Bird Cabs** (250/382-4235 or 800/665-7055), **Empress Taxi** (250/381-2222), or **Victoria Taxi** (250/383-7111).

Car Rental

It's best to call around and compare prices for rental cars—some lesser-known agencies advertise cheaper daily rates than others, but their cars are often used, old, large, and less economical, and usually must be returned to Victoria. Renting by the week is the best deal, with unlimited kilometers thrown in as a bonus. If you don't want to return the car to Victoria, you'll probably have to pay a drop charge; the farther up the island you go, the higher the fee. For a used car in the low season, rates start around $30 a day, plus $.15 per kilometer, plus gas. As with accommodations and many attractions, prices are higher in peak tourist periods. One recommended local company is **Island Rent-A-Car** (250/384-4881, www.islandcar.ca). Local contacts for the majors are: **Avis** (250/386-8468), **Budget** (250/953-5300), **Discount** (250/310-2277), **Enterprise** (250/475-6900), **Hertz** (250/952-3765), **National** (250/386-1213), and **Thrifty** (250/383-3659).

Vicinity of Victoria

Two highways lead out of Victoria: Highway 14 heads west and Highway 1 heads north. Highway 14 is a spectacular coastal route that ends in **Port Renfrew,** 104 kilometers (65 miles) from Victoria. Along this ocean-hugging stretch of road are provincial parks, delightful oceanfront lodgings, and a panorama that extends across Juan de Fuca Strait to the snowcapped peaks of the Olympic Mountains in Washington State. Port Renfrew is the southern terminus of the rugged and remote 77-kilometer (48-mile) **West Coast Trail,** which challenges hikers from around the world each summer. Highway 1 leads north from Victoria to **Duncan, Chemainus,** and **Ladysmith,** each with its own particular charm. West of Duncan is massive **Cowichan Lake,** an inland paradise for anglers and boaters, and **Carmanah Walbran Provincial Park,** protecting a remote watershed full of ancient Sitka spruce that miraculously escaped logging.

SOOKE

About 34 kilometers (21 miles) from Victoria, Sooke (with a silent "e") is a forestry, fishing, and farming center serving a surrounding population of 11,000. The town is best known for a lodge that combines luxurious accommodations with one of Canada's most renowned restaurants, but there are a couple of other diversions worth investigating.

The town spreads for many miles along the shore of Canada's southernmost harbor. The safe haven for boats is created by **Whiffen Spit,** a naturally occurring sandbar that extends for over one kilometer. Take Whiffen Spit Road (through town to the west) to reach the spit. It's a 20-minute walk to the end and along the way you may spot seals and otters along the shoreline.

Sooke Regional Museum (corner of Sooke and Phillips Roads, 250/642-6351; daily 9 A.M.–6 P.M.) lies just beyond Sooke River Bridge. When you've finished admiring the historic artifacts, relax on the grassy area in front or wander around the back to count all 478 growth rings on the cross-section of a giant spruce tree. The museum is also home to **Sooke Visitor Info Centre.**

Across the harbor is **East Sooke Regional Park,** protecting 1,422 hectares (3,512 acres) of coastal forest and rocky shoreline. It holds around 50 kilometers (31 miles) of trails leading along sea cliffs, to the open meadows of an abandoned apple orchard, and to lofty lookouts. Pick up a map from the visitor center to help find your way to around the park. The main access is Gillespie Road, which branches south off Highway 14 on the east side of Sooke. One kilometer (.6 mile) down Gillespie Road is a pullout on the left. Park here to access the Galloping Goose Trail. Linking downtown Victoria and Sooke, this stretch is a pleasant walk or bike through old-growth forest, with a spur to the left leading to a lookout above Roche Cove.

Accommodations

Sooke River Estuary Bed & Breakfast (2056 Glenidle Rd., 250/642-4655 or 888/681-4677, www.sookeriver.com; $159–169 s or d) takes full advantage of its waterfront location at the mouth of the Sooke River. The two suites and one cottage are comfortable and come with niceties such as robes, fireplaces, and roomy bathrooms with top-notch amenities. The Harbourside Cottage is a real treat—jetted tub with water views, laundry facilities, basic cooking facilities, and a private deck. The rates include a generous, multicourse breakfast delivered to your room. This is a professionally run bed-and-breakfast with hosts that will fill you with ideas for local sightseeing and dining.

M Sooke Harbour House (1528 Whiffen Spit Rd., 250/642-3421 or 800/889-9688, www.sookeharbourhouse.com) combines the elegance of an upscale country-style inn with the atmosphere of an exclusive oceanfront resort. The restaurant attracts discerning diners from throughout the world, but the accommodations offered are equally impressive. The sprawling waterfront property sits on a bluff, with 28 guest

Vancouver Island

rooms spread through immaculately manicured gardens. Each of the rooms reflects a different aspect of life on the West Coast, and all have stunning views, a wood-burning fireplace, and deck or patio. Rates range $375–575 s or d, which includes breakfast and a picnic lunch; off-season, these rates are reduced up to 40 percent.

Food

For a simple, old-fashioned diner-style meal, head to **Mom's Café** (2036 Shields Rd., 250/642-3314), where breakfasts are all under $10 and halibut with fries is $9. Turn right onto Shields Road one block west of the Petro Canada gas station.

17 Mile House (5126 Sooke Rd., 250/642-5942; daily 11 A.M.–10 A.M.) is a charming relic from the past. It dates from an era when travelers heading to Sooke would stop for a meal 17 miles from Victoria's City Hall. The walls are decorated with a century's worth of memorabilia, and there's still a hitching post out back. The rotating nightly specials haven't changed for years, but no one seems to mind, especially on Saturday when a prime rib dinner is served up for $18. One thing that definitely wasn't on the menu 100 years ago is a delicious sesame teriyaki grilled salmon dish ($16).

One of Canada's finest dining experiences can be had at **M Sooke Harbour House** (34 kilometers/21 miles west of downtown at 1528 Whiffen Spit Rd., Sooke, 250/642-3421 or 800/889-9688; daily from 5 P.M.). The decor is country-style simple, not that anything could possibly take away from the food and views. The menu changes daily, but most dishes feature local seafood, prepared to perfection with vegetables and herbs picked straight from the surrounding garden. Many diners disregard the cost and choose the eight-course Gastronomical Tasting Menu ($100 per person), which represents a wide variety of seafood, including wild sea asparagus harvested from tidal pools below the restaurant. Otherwise, dinner entrées range $28–40, with vegetarians offered at least one choice. The cellar is almost as renowned as the food—it holds upward of 10,000 bottles.

HIGHWAY 14 TO PORT RENFREW

The road west from Sooke takes you past gray pebbly beaches scattered with shells and driftwood, past **Gordon's Beach** to **French Beach Provincial Park** (about 20 kilometers/12 miles from Sooke). Here you can wander down through a lush forest of Douglas fir and Sitka spruce to watch Pacific breakers crashing up on the beach—and keep an eye open for whales and eagles. It's a great place for a windswept walk, a picnic, or camping ($12 per night, pit toilets provided). An information board at the park entrance posts fairly detailed maps and articles on area beaches, points of interest, plants, and wildlife.

Continuing west, the highway winds up and down forested hills for another 12 kilometers (7.5 miles) or so, passing evidence of regular logging and signposted forest trails to sandy beaches. Along this stretch of coast are two great accommodations. The first, three kilometers (1.9 miles) beyond French Beach, is **Point No Point Resort** (250/646-2020, www.pointnopointresort.com), which features 25 cabins, each with ocean views, a full kitchen, and fireplace. Explore the shore out front, relax on the nearby beach, or scan the horizon for migrating whales, with the Olympic Mountains as a backdrop. Rates range $160–240 s or d, with the least expensive cabins older and smaller (you're really paying for the position). Afternoon tea ($15) and full meals (mains $25–30) are available in the lodge restaurant. Two kilometers (1.2 miles) farther west, high upon oceanfront cliffs, **Fossil Bay Resort** (250/646-2073, www.fossilbay.com) offers six modern cottages, each with a hot tub, private balcony, fireplace, king-size bed, and full kitchen; $220 s or d, discounted for more than two nights. These two places are understandably popular, so make reservations well in advance, especially for weekends.

Jordan River

When you emerge at the small logging town of Jordan River, take time to take in the smells of the ocean and the surrounding windswept landscape. The town comprises only a few houses, a local logging operation, and a small recreation area. The recreation area lies on a point at the mouth of the Jordan River. It's not the best camping spot you'll ever come across, but no signs prohibit overnight stays; surfers often spend the night here, waiting for the swells to rise and the long right-handed waves known as Jordans to crank up. Note: **Sports Rent** (1950 Government St., Victoria, 250/385-7368) rents surfboards and wetsuits.

Across the road from the ocean is **Shakies,** a popular burger stand, and a little farther along is **Breakers,** a small café with great ocean views.

China Beach

Three kilometers west of Jordan River, a 700-meter (.4-mile) one-way trail leads through Sitka spruce to pebbly China Beach, which is strewn with driftwood and backed by a couple of protected picnic sites. Camping (back up by the highway) is $14 per night. The beach and campground have recently been incorporated within 1,277-hectare (3,156-acre) **Juan de Fuca Provincial Park,** which protects a narrow coastal strip between Jordan River and Botanical Beach near Port Renfrew. China Beach is also the beginning of the 47-kilometer (29-mile) **Juan de Fuca Trail,** a coastal hiking route that ends at Port Renfrew.

Port Renfrew

This small seaside community clings to the rugged shoreline of Port San Juan, 104 kilometers (65 miles) from Victoria. An eclectic array of houses leads down the hill to the waterfront. Follow the signs to **Botanical Beach,** a fascinating intertidal pool area where low tide exposes hundreds of species of marine creatures at the foot of scoured-out sandstone cliffs. The three-kilometer (1.9-mile) road to the beach is rough and can be impassable in winter.

Accommodations are available at the **Trailhead Resort,** in the heart of town (250/647-5468, www.trailhead-resort.com). Its motel rooms are relatively new, basic but practical, with a balcony out front ($85 s or d), or choose to stay in a fully self-contained two-bedroom cabin

($160–200). On site a store sells camping and fishing gear. Right on the water, **Arbutus Beach Lodge** (5 Queesto Dr., 250/647-5458 or 866/772-8887) offers basic cabin or lodge room accommodations and a great communal lounge and deck area overlooking the ocean. Rates of $70–125 s or d include a light breakfast. Beyond town, at the mouth of the San Juan River, **Port Renfrew Marina and RV Park** (250/647-0002, www.portrenfrewmarina.com; Apr.–Oct.) has unserviced campsites ($18) but no showers. This place is primarily a marina complex, with boat charters and fishing gear for sale.

San Juan Valley

If you don't want to return to Victoria along Highway 14, and you're eventually heading north up the island, consider traveling through the **San Juan Valley** to Lake Cowichan. The valley is forested with massive Douglas fir, up to 800 years old. Be aware that the valley is a maze of unpaved logging roads, so pack a good map. The road's usually in good condition, but find out from locals the present conditions and whether logging is active in the area—logging trucks don't give way, *you* do. Make sure you have enough gas, and drive with your headlights on so the trucks see you from a good distance. You'll find rustic campgrounds (no services or hookups) at **Fairy Lake,** six kilometers (3.7 miles) from Port Renfrew, and **Lizard Lake,** 12 kilometers (7.5 miles) farther along the road.

THE WEST COAST TRAIL

The magnificent West Coast Trail meanders 77 kilometers (48 miles) along Vancouver Island's untamed western shoreline, through the West Coast Trail unit of **Pacific Rim National Park.** It's one of the world's great hikes, exhilaratingly challenging, incredibly beautiful, and very satisfying—many hikers come back to do it again. The very quickest hikers can complete the trail in four days, but by allowing six, seven, or eight days you'll have time to fully enjoy the adventure. The trail extends from the mouth of the Gordon River near Port Renfrew to Pachena Bay, near the remote fishing village of Bamfield on

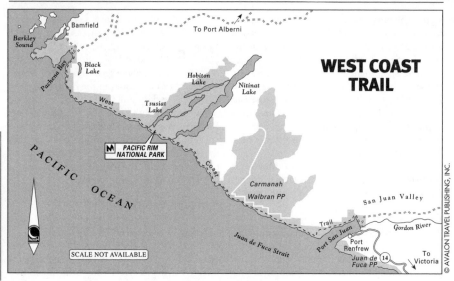

WEST COAST TRAIL

© AVALON TRAVEL PUBLISHING, INC.

Barkley Sound. Along the way you'll wander along beaches, steep clifftops, and slippery banks; ford rivers by rope, suspension bridge, or ferry; climb down sandstone cliffs by ladder; cross slippery boardwalks, muddy slopes, bogs, and deep gullies; and balance on fallen logs. But for all your efforts you're rewarded with panoramic views of sand and sea, dense lush rainforest, waterfalls cascading into deep pools, all kinds of wildlife—gray whales, eagles, sea lions, seals, and seabirds—and the constant roar and hiss of the Pacific surf pummeling the sand.

History

This stretch of the coast, the southernmost section of Pacific Rim National Park, was nicknamed "Graveyard of the Pacific" due to the great number of shipwrecks that occurred along here. After the SS *Valencia* ran aground in 1906 and most of the passengers and crew drowned or died from exposure, the Canadian government constructed a lifesaving trail to help future survivors penetrate the dense coastal forest. The trail followed a rugged telegraph route toward Victoria that connected lighthouses and towns and was kept open by telegraph linesmen and lighthouse keepers. Since the trail was incorporated

into Pacific Rim National Park in the mid-1960s, it has gained enormous popularity. A quota system is now in use to prevent degradation of the fragile coastal environment.

Hiking Conditions

The trail can be hiked in either direction, so take your choice. The first two days out from Gordon River traverse difficult terrain, meaning more enjoyable hiking for the remaining days. The first two days out from Pachena Bay are relatively easy, meaning a lighter pack for the more-difficult section.

Hikers must be totally self-sufficient, as no facilities exist along the route. Go with at least two other people, and travel as light as possible. Wear comfortable hiking boots, and take a stove, at least 15 meters (50 feet) of strong light rope, head-to-toe waterproof gear (keep your spare clothes and sleeping bag in a plastic bag), a small amount of fire starter for an emergency, suntan lotion, insect repellent, a first-aid kit (for cuts, burns, sprains, and blisters), and waterproof matches. Rainfall is least likely in the summer; July is generally the driest month, but be prepared for rain, strong winds, thick fog, and muddy trail conditions even then.

Along the trail two river crossings are made via ferry. One is at Gordon River outside of Port Renfrew. The other, midway along the trail, crosses Nitinat Narrows, the treacherous mouth of tidal Nitinat Lake. Ferries run April 15–September 30 daily 9 A.M.–5 P.M. The ferry fees ($14 each) are collected on behalf of private operators in conjunction with the trail permit. When there is no ferry service (Oct. 1–Apr. 14), the West Coast Trail is closed.

Permits
A quota system is in effect on the trail to reduce the environmental impact caused by overuse. In peak season only 52 hikers a day are issued permits to start down the trail (26 from each end). Reservations for 42 of the 52 slots are accepted starting March 1 for the following season; call Tourism BC (250/387-1642 or 800/435-5622 7 A.M.–6 P.M.). The nonrefundable reservation fee is $25 per person, which includes a waterproof trail map. The remaining 10 spots a day are allocated on a first-come, first-served basis (five from each end; no reservation fee), but expect a wait of up to three days in summer. For the first and last months of the hiking season, there is no quota. Once at Port Renfrew or Bamfield, all hikers must head for the registration office to obtain a trail-use permit ($90 per person), pay for the ferry crossings ($28), and attend a 90-minute orientation session.

Transportation
Unless you plan on turning around and returning to the beginning of the trail on foot, you'll want to make some transportation arrangements. Getting to and from either end of the trail is made easier by **West Coast Trail Express** (250/477-8700 or 888/999-2288, www.trailbus.com), which departs Victoria daily in the morning to both ends of the trail. The fare between Victoria and Port Renfrew is $35 one-way, while between Victoria and Pachena Bay it's $55. Pickups are made along the way, including from Nanaimo and Port Alberni. Travel between the trailheads costs $50. (If you leave your vehicle at the Port Renfrew end of the trail and return by bus, you won't have to shuttle a vehicle out to remote

Bamfield). Pachena Bay lies 11 kilometers from Bamfield, and taxis operate between the two points. West Coast Trail Express also rents camping and hiking gear.

Information
The first step in planning to hike the West Coast Trail is to do some research at the Parks Canada website (www.pc.gc.ca). The invaluable information covers everything you need to know, including an overview of what to expect, instructions on trail user fees, a list of equipment you should take, a list of relevant literature, tide tables, and advertisements for companies offering trailhead transportation.

Seasonal park information/registration centers are in Port Renfrew (250/647-5434) and Pachena Bay (250/728-3234). The recommended topographic map *West Coast Trail, Pacific Rim National Park—Port Renfrew to Bamfield* is available at most specialty map stores, as well as at the information centers (registration offices) at each end of the trail. The cost of a trail-use permit includes this map.

DUNCAN
Duncan, self-proclaimed "City of Totems," lies at the junction of Highways 1 and 18, about 60 kilometers (37 miles) north of Victoria. The small city of 5,500 serves the surrounding farming and forestry communities of the Cowichan Valley. Native carvers, many from the local Cowichan band, have created some 80 intricate and colorful totem poles here. Look for the poles along the main highway near the information center, beside the railway station in the old section of town, by City Hall, and inside local businesses.

Sights
Follow the signs off the main highway to the city center for a quick wander around the renovated **Old Town.** (Free two-hour parking is available by the old railway station on Canada Avenue.) Start your totem-pole hunt here or just wander down the streets opposite the railway station to appreciate some of the pleasing older

architecture, such as City Hall on the corner of Kenneth and Craig Streets. Two distinctly different native carvings stand side by side behind City Hall—a Native American carving and a New Zealand Maori carving donated by Duncan's sister city, Kaikohe.

Apart from the famous totem poles, Duncan's main attraction is the excellent **Quw'utsun' Cultural Centre,** on the south side of downtown (200 Cowichan Way, 250/746-8119; May–Sept. daily 9 A.M.–6 P.M., Oct.–Apr. daily 10 A.M.–5 P.M.; adult $10, senior $8, child $6). Representing the arts, crafts, legends, and traditions of a 3,500-strong Quw'utsun' population spread through the Cowichan Valley, this facility features a long house, a carving shed, dance performances, a café with native cuisine (and summertime salmon barbecues), and a gift shop selling Cowichan sweaters.

Another local attraction is the 40-hectare **BC Forest Discovery Centre** (one kilometer/.6 mile north of town, 250/715-1113; early April to mid-Oct. daily 10 A.M.–4 P.M., July–Aug. until 6 P.M.; adult $9, senior $8, child $5). You can catch a ride on an old steam train and puff back in time, through the forest and past a farmstead, a logging camp, and Somenos Lake. Then check out the working sawmill, restored planer mill, blacksmith's shop, and forestry and lumber displays. The main museum building holds modern displays pertaining to the industry, including hands-on and interactive computer displays and an interesting audiovisual. The grounds are a pleasant place to wander—through shady glades of trees (most identified) or over to the pond where you'll find a gaggle of friendly geese awaiting a tasty morsel.

Practicalities
N Sahtlam Lodge and Cabins (5720 Riverbottom Rd. W, 250/748-7738 or 877/748-7738, www.sahtlamlodge.com) is beside the Cowichan River west of town. Three cabins are spread across the property, and each is equipped with an old-style fireplace, woodstove, and full kitchen. Rates are $165–180 s or d, with multiple-night stays discounted 30 percent. A breakfast basket delivered daily to your cabin is included. Overlooking

the river, the original 1920s lodge now houses an intimate restaurant open Wednesday, Friday, and Saturday for a $30 fixed-price dinner. Because it has just three tables, you'll need to reserve. On the south side of the river is the turnoff to **Duncan RV Park and Campground** (2950 Boys Rd., 250/748-8511), which is one block west of the highway, right beside the river. Sites are $16–20; full hookups available.

Always crowded with locals, **Arbutus Cafe** (corner of Kenneth St. and Jubilee St., 250/746-5443) concocts a great shrimp salad for $7, sandwiches and hamburgers for $5–9, and specialty pies from $4.

Stop at **Duncan Visitor Info Centre** (250/746-4636 or 888/303-3337, www.duncancc .bc.ca; Mon.–Sat. 9 A.M.–5 P.M.), on the west side of the highway in Overwaitea Plaza, for the complete rundown on the area. The center staff provides information on local hiking and fishing, and on traveling the logging roads beyond Lake Cowichan. They also offer a map showing the location of all Duncan's totem poles.

LAKE COWICHAN AND VICINITY
Cowichan River
This famous salmon and steelhead fishing river has its source at Lake Cowichan, draining into the Strait of Georgia beyond Duncan. Much of its length is protected by **Cowichan River Provincial Park,** which extends over 750 hectares (1,850 acres) and 20 kilometers (12 miles). There are three access points to the park, including Skutz Falls, where salmon spawn each fall. Trails are well signposted and link into the TransCanada Trail, which follows the river west to Lake Cowichan.

Lake Cowichan
Don a good pair of walking shoes, grab your swimsuit, sleeping bag, fishing pole, and frying pan, and head west from Duncan to Lake Cowichan, Vancouver Island's second-largest lake. The massive, 32-kilometer-long (20-mile-long) inland waterway, called Kaatza ("Land Warmed by Sun") by local Coast Salish, is a pop-

ular spot for canoeing, water-skiing, swimming, and especially fishing—the lake and river are well stocked with kokanee and trout (steelhead, rainbow, brown, and cutthroat). Boat-launching facilities and excellent campsites are found at regular intervals along the lakeshore. Numerous logging roads, some paved, encircle the lake (75 kilometers/47 miles round-trip) and provide hikers access into the adjacent wilderness, which includes the legendary **Carmanah Valley** (see *Carmanah Walbran Provincial Park*).

The sleepy lakeside village of **Lake Cowichan** (pop. 3,200) lies on the eastern arm of Cowichan Lake, 30 kilometers (18.6 miles) from Duncan. Campers have the choice of staying at the local municipal campground, **Lakeview Park** (three km/1.9 miles west of Lake Cowichan, 250/749-6244; $20 per night) or **Gordon Bay Provincial Park,** on the south side of the lake 23 kilometers (14.3 miles) farther west ($22). Both campgrounds have hot showers. **Rail's End Pub** (109 Southshore Rd., 250/749-4001; daily from 11 A.M.) has a good family-style restaurant overlooking the outlet of Cowichan Lake.

On the waterfront is **Cowichan Lake Visitor Info Centre** (125 Southshore Rd., 250/749-3244, www.cowichanlakecc.ca; in summer daily Mon.–Sat. 9 A.M.–4 P.M., Sun. 1–4 P.M.). The center is a good source of information on fishing conditions and on the logging roads leading to the Carmanah Valley and Port Renfrew. Next door is the **Kaatza Station Museum,** at the end of a rail line that once linked the lake to the main line up Vancouver Island's east coast.

Carmanah Walbran Provincial Park

Eyed by logging companies for many years, the remote **Carmanah Valley** was first protected with provincial park status in 1990. The Upper Carmanah Valley and adjacent Walbran Valley were added in 1995, providing complete protection of the 16,450-hectare (40,650-acre) watershed. For environmentalists, creation of the park was a major victory—this mist-shrouded valley extending all the way to the rugged west coast holds an old-growth forest of absolute wonder. Man's impact in the valley has been almost nonexistent. Many 800-year-old Sitka spruce

and 1,000-year-old cedar trees—some of the world's oldest—rise up to 95 meters (300 feet) off the damp valley floor here. Others lie where they've fallen, their slowly decaying moss- and fern-cloaked hulks providing homes for thousands of small mammals and insects.

It's possible to reach the park via logging roads from Port Renfrew in the south and Port Alberni in the north, but the easiest access is gained by following the south shore of Cowichan Lake to Nitinat Main, a logging road that leads south to Nitinat Junction (no services). There the road is joined by a logging road from Port Alberni. From this point Nitinat Main continues south to a bridge across the Caycuse River. Take the first right after crossing the river. This is Rosander Main, a rough road that dead-ends at the park boundary. The park is signposted from Nitinat Junction, but the signs are small and easy to miss.

From the road's-end parking lot, a rough 1.3-kilometer (.8-mile) hiking trail (30 minutes each way) descends to the valley floor and Carmanah Creek. From the creek, trails lead upstream to the Three Sisters (2.5 kilometers/1.5 miles; 40 minutes), through Grunt's Grove to August Creek (7.5 kilometers/4.6 miles; two hours), and downstream through a grove of Sitka spruce named for Randy Stoltmann, a legendary environmentalist who first brought the valley's giants to the world's attention (2.4 kilometers/1.5 miles; 40 minutes).

Facilities in the park are limited to a primitive camping area at the end of the access road ($5 per person per night). For park information, stop by the visitor center in Lake Cowichan.

NORTH TOWARD NANAIMO

Nanaimo is just 45 kilometers (28 miles) north of Duncan—less than 30 minutes along the divided highway—but a number of small towns invite short detours along the way.

Chemainus

The town of Chemainus (pop. 600) bills itself as "The Little Town that Did." Did what, you ask? Well, Chemainus has always been a sleepy little mill town; its first sawmill dates back to 1862. In 1982, MacMillan Bloedel shut down the town's antiquated mill, which employed 400 people, replacing it a year later with a modern mill employing only 155 people. Chemainiacs did not want their town to die. Needing tourists, they hired local artists to cover many of the town's plain walls with larger-than-life murals depicting the town's history and culture. The result was outstanding. In 1983, the town received a first place award at a downtown revitalization competition held in New York.

Follow the signs to Chemainus from Highway 1 and park at **Chemainus Visitor Info Centre** (9758 Chemainus Rd., 250/246-3944; May–Sept. daily 9 A.M.–5 P.M.), where you'll see the first enormous mural—a street scene. From there you can explore the rest of Chemainus on foot, following the yellow footprints into town. Walk down to shady, waterfront **Heritage Park,** passing a mural information booth (where there's a small replica of the waterwheel that powered the original 1862 sawmill) and a detailed map of the town.

The **Chemainus Theatre Festival** (9737 Chemainus Rd., 250/246-9820 or 800/565-7738) is a year-round production of international musical hits. It runs Wednesday–Saturday with tickets ranging $25–30 ($42–52 with dinner). **Chemainus Tours** (250/246-5055) operates horse-drawn carriage rides around town, passing all the murals along the route. The rides depart from Waterwheel Park every half hour; adult $7, child $3.

Ladysmith

The trim little waterfront village of Ladysmith has a couple of claims to fame. The first is its location straddling the 49th parallel, the invisible line separating Canada from the United States. After much bargaining for the 1846 Oregon Treaty, Canada got to keep all of Vancouver Island despite the 49th parallel chopping the island in two. The second claim is a little less historically important—Ladysmith was the birthplace of TV starlet Pamela Anderson.

Southern Gulf Islands

Spread through the Strait of Georgia between mainland British Columbia and Vancouver Island, this group of islands is within Canadian territory but linked geologically to the San Juan Islands, immediately to the south. Six of the islands—Salt Spring, North Pender, South Pender, Galiano, Mayne, and Saturna—are populated, and each is linked to the outside world by scheduled ferry service.

The mild, almost Mediterranean climate, beautiful scenery, driftwood-strewn beaches, quaint towns, and wide-ranging choice of accommodations combine to make the islands very popular in summer, when laid-back locals share their home with flocks of visitors. Still, there's plenty of room to get away from the hustle, with mile after mile of remote coastline and easily reached peaks beckoning to be explored. After kayaking, biking, or hiking, the best way to end the day is at one of the many island restaurants, feasting on salmon and crab brought ashore that morning.

The Land

The islands have been partly cleared for agriculture, but where old-growth forests survive, you'll find stands of magnificent Douglas fir and western red cedar, with gnarled arbutus (Pacific madrone) dominating the shoreline. Closer to ground level, lots of daisies, native roses, bluebells, and orchids flower through summer. In late summer, gooseberries, huckleberries, and blackberries are ripe for the picking. The surrounding waterways host an incredibly diverse number of marine mammals, including sea lions, seals, sea otters, and orcas. If you spent a full year on the islands counting bird species, you'd come up with over 300, including bald eagles, blue herons, cormorants, hummingbirds, robins, wrens, finches, and swallows. Fall is the best time to watch for migrating shorebirds, who stop to rest and feed throughout the archipelago. Children will love exploring tidal pools, where colorful anemones and starfish are among the many critters that make a

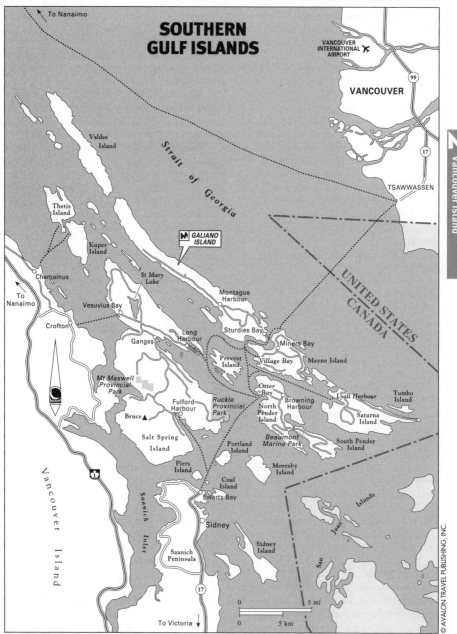

SOUTHERN GULF ISLANDS

To Nanaimo

VANCOUVER INTERNATIONAL AIRPORT

VANCOUVER

99

TSAWWASSEN

17

Vancouver Island

Valdes Island

Strait of Georgia

Thetis Island

Kuper Island

Chemainus

To Nanaimo

Crofton

Vesuvius Bay

St Mary Lake

GALIANO ISLAND

Montague Harbour

UNITED STATES
CANADA

Long Harbour

Ganges

Sturdies Bay

Miners Bay

Prevost Island

Village Bay

Mayne Island

Mt Maxwell Provincial Park

MOON

Fulford Harbour

Ruckle Provincial Park

Otter Bay

Browning Harbour

Lyall Harbour

Tumbo Island

North Pender Island

Saturna Island

Bruce ▲

Salt Spring Island

Portland Island

Beaumont Marine Park

South Pender Island

Piers Island

Vancouver Island

Saanich Inlet

Coal Island

Swartz Bay

Moresby Island

San Juan Islands

Sidney

Sidney Island

Saanich Peninsula

17

0   5 mi

0   5 km

To Victoria ↓

© AVALON TRAVEL PUBLISHING, INC.

home. **Gulf Islands National Park** protects pockets of land on Mayne and Saturna Islands, the Penders, and 14 uninhabited islands.

Traveling to and Around the Islands

The main transportation provider is **BC Ferries** (250/386-3431 or 888/223-3779, www.bcferries.com), which operates scheduled year-round services between the Southern Gulf Islands and out to the islands from both Vancouver Island and Vancouver. The main departure points are Swartz Bay, 32 kilometers (20 miles) north of Victoria, and Tsawwassen, on the south side of Vancouver. All ferries take vehicles (including RVs), motorcycles, bicycles, canoes, and kayaks. It's important to check the timetables (online or posted at each terminal) because some ferries are nonstop and others make up to three stops before reaching the more remote islands. Also try to avoid peak periods, such as Friday and Sunday afternoons. Aside from that, simply roll up and pay your fare.

Regardless of the final destination, the round-trip fare from Swartz Bay (Victoria) to any of the Southern Gulf Islands is a very reasonable adult $6.50, child $3.25, vehicle $21. Interisland travel is charged on a one-way basis: adult $3.50, child $1.75, vehicle $7.50. The fare system is designed to be flexible; for example, if you plan to travel to Galiano Island from Swartz Bay, with a stop on Salt Spring Island on the way out, you would pay the interisland fare departing Salt Spring then use the return portion of the main ticket from Galiano, for a total of $10 per person.

From the mainland Tsawwassen terminal (south of downtown Vancouver), the fare is the same regardless of which island you travel to: one-way adult $10.25, child $5.25, vehicle $38. This is the only route where reservations are accepted; make your booking online at www.bcferries.com.

Island Practicalities

Many visitors own island getaways or rent cottages by the week, but there are still plenty of options for shorter stays. Choices range from primitive tent sites to world-class lodges, with bed-and-breakfasts—there are hundreds—falling somewhere in the middle price-wise. Whatever your preference, make reservations for summer as far in advance as possible, especially for weekends. Be aware many bed-and-breakfasts close through winter, and some don't take credit or debit cards.

You will find cafés and restaurants on each island, but not a single McDonald's or similar fast-food chain. Groceries and gas are available in most villages; banks and ATMs are less common.

Before you head for the islands, get the latest rundown from the Victoria Visitor Info Centre downtown, from the Saanich Peninsula Visitor Info Centre on Highway 17 near the Swartz Bay Ferry Terminal, or from Tourism Vancouver Island (250/754-3500, www.islands.bc.ca). *Island Tides* is a free bimonthly publication; look for the most recent edition online at www.islandtides.com. The website www.gulfislands.net is loaded with tourist information, or pick up the free hard-copy version once you're en route by ferry.

SALT SPRING ISLAND

Largest of the Southern Gulf Islands, 180-square-kilometer (70-square-mile) Salt Spring (pop. 10,000) lies close to Vancouver Island, immediately north of Saanich Inlet. Ferries link the south and north ends of the island to Vancouver Island, and myriad roads converge on the service town of **Ganges.** The island is home to a large number of artisans, along with hobby farmers, retirees, and wealthy Vancouverites who spend their summers at private getaways.

Ganges

Ask any longtime local and he or she will tell you that the island's main town, Ganges, is over commercialized. But it's still quaint, and well worth visiting—at the very least to stock up with supplies. Set around a protected bay, the original waterfront buildings have undergone a colorful transformation, and where once you would have found boat-builders you can now browse through art galleries, shop for antiques, or dine on innovative cuisine. One of the most eye-catching shops is the boardwalk gallery featuring the

© ANDREW HEMPSTEAD

The Ganges waterfront is lined with cafés and restaurants.

whimsical painting of Jill Louise Campbell. On a smaller scale, **Mahon Hall** (114 Rainbow Rd., 250/537-0899; mid-May–mid-Sept. daily 10 A.M.–5 P.M.) is filled with arty booths, while the Saturday market in Centennial Park showcases the work of local artists. Head to **Salt Spring Books** (104 McPhillips Ave., 250/537-2812) to pick up some holiday reading or check your email on the public-access computers. Within walking distance of the waterfront, at the end of Seaspring Drive, is **Mouat Park,** a quiet reprieve from the bustle.

Exploring the Rest of the Island

Even if you've never kayaked, plan on joining a tour with Ganges-based **Sea Otter Kayaks** (250/537-5678 or 877/537-5678). Get a feel for paddling on the two-hour tour ($35), enjoy the calm evening water on the Sunset Paddle ($40), or spend a full day ($105) exploring the coastline, with a break for picnic lunch on a remote beach.

Landlubbers have plenty to see on Salt Spring. From the Fulford Harbour ferry terminal, take Beaver Point Road east to 486-hectare (1,200-acre) **Ruckle Provincial Park.** The access road ends at the rocky headland of Beaver Point, from where trails lead north along the coastline, providing great views across to North Pender Island. The land now protected as a park was donated to the province by the Ruckle family; the Ruckles' 1876 farmhouse still stands.

Along the road north to Ganges, small **Mount Maxwell Provincial Park** protects the slopes of its namesake mountain. A rough unsealed road off Musgrave Road leads to the 588-meter (1,930-foot) summit, from where views extend south across the island to Vancouver Island and east to the other Gulf Islands. South of Mount Maxwell is 704-meter (2,300-foot) **Mount Bruce,** the island's highest peak.

Accommodations and Camping

The island's least expensive accommodation is **HI–Salt Spring Island** (640 Cusheon Lake Rd., 250/537-4149, www.hihostels.ca; mid-Mar.–mid-Oct.), on the east side of the island. You can choose to stay in a regular dorm, but the most popular room is a treehouse accessed via a ladder and hatch. The interior features a tree through the middle, a skylight over the bed, and wicker furniture. There's also a caravan and a tepee spread around the four-hectare (10-acre) property. Rates start at $17 for members of Hostelling International ($21 for nonmembers).

Maple Ridge Cottages (301 Tripp Rd., 250/537-5977, www.mapleridgecottages.com; $129–169 s or d) is on the banks of St. Mary Lake, a largish body of freshwater that holds a hungry population of bass and trout that can be caught right from the shoreline. For me, the allure of the wooden cottages is the location, but their rustic charm brings back families year after year. Relax on the deck while your catch of the day cooks on the barbecue for the full effect. Free use of canoes and kayaks is a popular bonus.

One of the island's premier accommodations is **Hundred Hills House** (104 Arnell Way, 250/537-1898, www.hundredhillshouse.com; $200 s or d), a five-minute drive from Ganges.

Vancouver Island

The styling is simple and elegant, with big windows to take in the water views. Most importantly for many, the two guest units have private entrances and bathrooms en suite. Both also have a private deck, a fireplace, and high-tone extras such as fine linens, a four-piece bathroom, and in-room entertainment centers. Breakfasts are elaborate.

Salt Springs Spa Resort (1460 North Beach Rd., 250/537-4111 or 800/665-0039, www .saltysprings.com) commands lots of attention for its spa services, but the accommodations are also noteworthy. Each spacious unit features lots of polished wood topping out in a vaulted ceiling, a modern kitchen, a fireplace, and a two-person spa tub filled with mineral water. Guests have use of rowboats, mountain bikes, a game room, and a barbecue area. Summer rates are $200 during the week and $250 on weekends, discounted as low as $120 in winter.

The campground in **Ruckle Provincial Park** conceals 78 sites in a forest of Douglas fir overlooking Swanson Channel. The camping area is a short walk from the parking lot, making this place unsuitable for RVs; $14 per night. On the north side of the island on St. Mary Lake, **Lakeside Gardens Resort** (250/537-5773; Apr.–Nov.) offers campsites with full hookups for $25, rustic cabins that share bathrooms for $65, and self-contained cottages for $125.

Food

Head to Ganges and wander around the waterfront for the island's widest choice of dining options. In the heart of the action is the ⚏ **Tree House Café** (106 Purvis Lane, 250/537-5379; daily 8 A.M.–10 P.M.). The "tree" is a plum tree and the "house" is the kitchen. Most people dine outside in the shade of the tree, choosing freshly made dishes such as salmon frittata ($10) for breakfast, tuna melt on sourdough ($8) at lunch, or Thai chicken curry ($12) in the evening.

Around the corner from the Tree House is **La Cucina e Terrazza** (Mouat's Landing, 250/537-5747; 11 A.M.–9 P.M.), where the atmosphere is refined casual. The winsome menu ranges from Italian favorites like Gorgonzola linguine ($14) to locally inspired dishes such as a duo of grilled salmon and halibut ($21). Sit inside for the wonderful smells wafting from the kitchen or outside to soak up the harbor views.

Information

Salt Spring Island Visitor Info Centre (121 Lower Ganges Rd., 250/537-4223 or 866/216-2936, www.saltspringtoday.com; summer daily 8 A.M.–6 P.M., the rest of the year Mon.–Fri. 8:30 A.M.–4:30 P.M.) is in downtown Ganges, on the main road above the marina.

Transportation

Salt Spring has two ferry terminals with year-round service to two points on Vancouver Island. If you're traveling up from Victoria, the Swartz Bay terminal is the most convenient departure point, with 10–12 departures daily for **Fulford Harbour,** a 20-minute drive south of Ganges. Sailings are even more frequent on the 20-minute run between Crofton, near the Vancouver Island town of Duncan, and **Vesuvius Bay,** at the island's north end. Interisland ferries depart from a third terminal, at **Long Harbour, east of Ganges.**

From the mainland, sailings depart the Tsawwassen terminal (south of downtown Vancouver) bound for Long Harbour. Direct sailings take 80 minutes, while those that make stops at other Gulf Islands take up to three hours—so check a timetable before boarding.

THE PENDERS

It's just a short hop by ferry from Salt Spring Island to **Otter Bay** on North Pender Island. Originally North and South Pender Islands were joined, but around 100 years ago a canal was dredged between the two as a shipping channel. Today, a rickety wooden bridge forms the link. Between them, the two islands are home to 2,000 people, most of whom live on North Pender. The island has dozens of little beaches to explore, with public roads providing ocean access at over 20 points. One of the nicest spots is **Hamilton Beach** on Browning Harbour.

Accommodations and Camping

The least expensive way to enjoy an overnight stay on North Pender Island is to camp at **Prior Centennial Campground** (mid-May–mid-Oct.; $14), a unit of Gulf Islands National Park. Sites are primitive, with no showers or hookups, but the treed location is excellent. The facility is six kilometers (3.7 miles) south of the ferry terminal.

The island's premier accommodation is the **Oceanside Inn** (Armadale Rd., five km/3.1 miles from the ferry terminal, 250/629-6691, www.penderisland.com). Each room is elegantly furnished, and a wide balcony takes advantage of the waterfront location. Off-season rates start at $149 s or d, rising to $169–239 in summer. Rates include breakfast, use of a fitness room, and small luxuries such as fluffy bathrobes.

Other Practicalities

The commercial hub of the Penders is the **Driftwood Centre,** a city-like shopping mall overlooking cleared pasture land south of the ferry terminal. It holds gas, groceries, booze, a bank, and eateries, including a super-busy bakery. For something a little more substantial, move along the mall to the **Pistou Grill** (250/629-3131; Tues.–Sat. 11:30 A.M.–2:30 P.M. and 5:30–8:30 P.M.) for surprisingly innovative cooking that includes seared halibut drizzled with a Chardonnay sauce ($19). Also in the mall is **Talisman Books** (250/629-6944; Mon.–Sat. 10 A.M.–5 P.M., Sun. 11 A.M.–4 P.M.), stocking an excellent range of local literature and best sellers.

Pender Island Visitor Info Centre (250/629-6541; summer daily 9 A.M.–6 P.M.) is a small booth up the hill from the ferry terminal.

MAYNE ISLAND

Separated from Galiano Island by a narrow channel, Mayne Island is just 21 square kilometers (eight square miles) in area. Its year-round population of fewer than 1,000 triples in summer, but the island never really seems crowded. Ferries dock at village-less **Village Bay;** all commercial facilities are at nearby **Miners Bay,** which got its name during the Cariboo gold rush when miners used the island as a stopping point. From the ferry terminal, narrow roads meander to all corners of the island, including to **Georgina Point Lighthouse,** which was manned 1885–1997. Island beaches are limited to those at **Oyster Bay,** but visitors can enjoy interesting shoreline walks or take the road to the low summit of Mount Park for panoramic views. For something a little different, wander through **Dinner Bay Park,** where a small Japanese garden takes pride of place.

The best island kayaking originates from the sandy beach in Bennett Bay, which is within Gulf Islands National Park. From its base in Miners Bay, **Mayne Kayaking** (250/539-5599) provides rentals and kayak drop-offs.

Accommodations

The least expensive island accommodation is **Springwater Lodge** (250/539-5521, www.springwaterlodge.com), an old hotel overlooking Active Pass from the west side of Village Bay. Rooms are basic at best and bathrooms are shared, but at $40 s or d you know what you're getting. Beside the hotel are four well-equipped cabins that go for $95 per night. The inn also has a restaurant open daily for all three meals.

Overlooking Miners Bay, two kilometers (1.2 miles) east of the ferry terminal, is **Tinkerers' Garden Retreat** (417 Sunset Pl., 250/539-2280; May–Oct.). This delightful old house sits right on the bay, a great base for exploring the area on foot or bike (bike rentals available). Rooms are smallish and simply furnished, but guests have use of a communal lounge and the relaxing gardens. Rates of $95–115 s or d include a full breakfast to set you up for a day of island exploration.

Set on four hectares (10 acres) overlooking a protected waterway, less than two kilometers (1.2 miles) south of the ferry terminal, is **Ñ Oceanwood Country Inn** (630 Dinner Bay Rd., 250/539-5074, www.oceanwood.com). Paths lead through the very private property, past herb and rose gardens and down to the water's edge. Within the lodge itself are four communal areas, including a well-stocked library, a comfortable lounge, and a restaurant (see *Food*). Each of the 12 rooms has its own character; some have a private balcony, others a deck or hot tub, and the largest features a split-level living area, luxurious bathroom, and private deck with hot tub. Rates start at $179 s or d; rooms with ocean views range $240–349. A cooked breakfast and tea and coffee throughout the day are included.

Camping at **Mayne Island Eco Camping** (359 Maple Dr., Miners Bay, 250/539-2667, www.mayneisle.com) is pleasant but primitive. Spread around the back of a short beach, some sites are right on the water while others are spread through the forest. Facilities include outhouses, a (hot) water-fed "tree" shower, and kayak rentals. Part of the same property is **Seal Beach B&B** (same contact information), where West Coast–themed guest rooms rent for $115 s or d per night.

Food

No-frills, short order grills are the order of the day at the old **Springwater Lodge** (Village Bay, 250/539-5521). Head to the **Sunny Mayne Bakery Café** (Miners Bay, 250/539-2323; daily 7 A.M.–6 P.M., until 7 P.M. on weekends) for freshly baked breads, sumptuous cakes and pastries, healthy sandwiches, and the island's best coffee concoctions.

The bright and breezy dining room at the **Oceanwood Country Inn** (630 Dinner Bay Rd., 250/539-5074) is primarily the domain of registered guests, but each evening at 6 P.M. the doors open to all for a four-course table d'hôte dinner ($50 per person) that includes a choice from two entrées that focus on creative presentations of local produce and seafood.

Information and Books

The website www.mayneislandchamber.ca is loaded with useful information, including links to current weather conditions, accommodations, services, and, for those who fall in love with island living, real estate agents.

Stock up on reading material at **Miners Bay Books** (478 Village Bay Rd., 250/539-2667).

GALIANO ISLAND

Named for a Spanish explorer who sailed through the Strait of Georgia over 200 years ago, this long, narrow island, 27 kilometers (17 miles)

The beaches of Galiano Island are among the finest in the Southern Gulf Islands.

from north to south but only a few kilometers wide, has some delightful beaches and good kayaking. Most of the population (1,000) lives in the south, within a five-minute drive of the ferry terminal at **Sturdies Bay.**

Montague Harbour Provincial Park

Climbing out of Sturdies Bay, roads tempt exploration in all directions. Take Porlier Pass Road to reach Montague Harbour Provincial Park, which protects an 89-hectare (210-acre) chunk of coastal forest and a beach of bleached-white broken seashells. You can walk out along the beach and return via a forested trail in around 20 minutes. At the end of the beach are *middens,* manmade piles of empty shells that accumulated over centuries of native feasting. The island is dotted with many less-obvious access points, many of which aren't even signposted. The beach below Active Pass Road is typical; look for the power pole numbered 1038 and make your way down the steep trail to a protected cove. Ask at the information center or your accommodation for a full listing of similar spots.

Other Recreation

The best way to explore local waterways is with **Galiano Island Kayaking,** based at the marina in Montague Harbour (250/539-2442). Three-hour guided tours, either early in the morning or at sunset, are $45. Another tour takes in the local marinelife on a six-hour paddle for $75. Those with previous experience can rent a kayak; $48 per day for a single or $70 for a double.

Galiano Golf Club (Linklater Rd., 250/539-5533) is typical of the many courses on the Southern Gulf Islands, with nine holes, inexpensive greens fees ($18), a relaxed atmosphere, and a clubhouse offering rentals and meals.

Accommodations and Camping

Many of the travelers you'll meet on the ferry trip to Galiano will be staying for a week or more in an island cottage. If this style of vacation sounds ideal, check www.galianoisland.com for a choice of rentals, but do so well before planning your visit as the best ones fill fast. **Paradise Rock Ocean Front Cottage** (310 Ganner Dr.,

250/539-3404; $150 per night) is typical in all respects—water views from a private setting, self-contained, and with a deck holding a propane barbecue—except that it can be rented for as little as two nights.

Set on Sturdies Bay waterfront is the **Bellhouse Inn** (29 Farmhouse Rd., 250/539-5667 or 800/970-7464, www.bellhouseinn.com; $135–195), an 1890s farmhouse that has been taking in travelers since the 1920s. Each of the three guest rooms has water views, and the most expensive features a hot tub, private balcony, and fireplace. Rates include a full breakfast and personal touches such as tea or coffee delivered to the room before breakfast.

You'll see the magnificent gardens of the **M Galiano Inn** (134 Madrona Dr., 250/539-3388 or 877/530-3939, www.galianoinn.com), at the head of Sturdies Bay, before the ferry docks. The elegant guest rooms infused with European charm come in two sizes (queen $249, king $299), and all have views extending down the bay to Mayne Island. Other highlights include private balconies, super-comfortable beds, plush robes, luxury bathrooms with soaker tubs, and extras such as CD players and coffeemakers. The inn is also home to the **Madrona del Mar Spa,** the place to get pampered with a soothing hot stone massage or kick back in the seaside hot tub. Guests can also book tours aboard the inn's own motor cruiser, including wine-tasting on nearby Saturna Island.

The campground in **Montague Harbour Provincial Park,** 10 kilometers (6.2 miles) from the ferry, is one of the best in the Southern Gulf Islands. Sites are below a towering forest of old-growth cedar and fir trees and open to a white shingle beach that is aligned perfectly to watch the setting sun. As with all provincial park campgrounds, facilities are limited to picnic tables, pit toilets, and drinking water; $14 per night and no reservations taken. The gates are open mid-April to mid-October.

Food

To immerse yourself in island life, plan on dining at the **Grand Central Emporium** (2470 Sturdies Bay Rd., 250/539-9885; Mon.–Fri.

6:30 A.M.–3:30 P.M., Sat.–Sun. 7:30 A.M.–3:30 P.M. and for dinner Tues.–Sun.), which is decorated in lumberjack artifacts and has seating ripped from old buses. Free-range eggs are the prime ingredient in the omelets, which are huge (ham and Swiss cheese for $9). Sandwiches and burgers dominate the lunch menu. In the evening, the blackboard dinner menu (mains under $20) reflects whatever is in season; often live music plays in the background. While you're waiting for a ferry—or even if you're not—line up at the **Max & Moritz** food wagon, in front of the parking lot at the ferry terminal, for a combination of German and Indonesian dishes, such as *nasi goring* ($5).

The stellar food is reason enough to dine at **Atrevida** (Galiano Inn, 134 Madrona Dr., 250/539-3388), but the unobstructed water views cost no extra. Although the upscale dining room has a touch of old-world elegance the cooking is healthy and modern, with a seasonal menu that makes use of fresh island produce and local seafood. Professional service and an impressive wine list round out what many regard as the finest restaurant on the Southern Gulf Islands. In summer, a sunken patio buzzes with activity as locals and visitors from outlying islands enjoy lunchtime barbecues in a cultured garden setting.

Information and Books

Right at the ferry terminal is **Galiano Island Visitor Info Centre** (250/539-2233, www.galianoisland.com; July–Aug. daily 9 A.M.–5 P.M.). The Southern Gulf Islands have a surprising number of bookstores, and none are better than **Galiano Island Books** (Madrona Dr., 250/539-3340; daily 10 A.M.–5 P.M.), down the first left after exiting the terminal area. Stop by for works by island writers as well as Canadiana, children's titles, and some great cooking books that use local ingredients.

SATURNA ISLAND

Most remote of the populated Southern Gulf Islands, Saturna protrudes into the heart of Georgia Strait and features a long, rugged northern coastline and over half its land area within Gulf Islands National Park. It offers a range of accommodations, but other services are limited (no banks or bank machines) and ferries only stop by a couple of times a day.

From the ferry dock at **Lyall Harbour,** the island's main road loops east then south along the coastline for 14 kilometers (8.7 miles), ending at **East Point Regional Park.** Go swimming or simply admire the sweeping views across the border to the San Juans. Before the park, **Winter Cove** is another picturesque diversion. On Canada Day (July 1), everyone gathers on this beach for a lamb barbecue.

Accommodations and Food

Most accommodations on Saturna Island are in private home bed-and-breakfasts. A short walk from where the ferry docks is **Lyall Harbour B&B** (121 E. Point Rd., 250/539-5577 or 877/473-9343; $85 s, $95 d). Each of the three guest rooms is spacious and features modern furnishings, a fireplace, and a deck with ocean views; Breakfast is served in a sun-drenched solarium.

Overlooking Boot Cove and also within walking distance of the dock is **Saturna Lodge** (130 Payne Rd., 250/539-2254 or 888/539-8800, www.saturna-island.bc.ca; May–Oct.). Right on the water, this modern accommodation offers seven guest rooms, a hot tub, a lounge with fireplace, and extensive gardens. Rates range $135–195 including breakfast. Within the lodge a small restaurant has a big reputation for seafood and local game and produce. The owners are involved in various projects around the island, including **Saturna Island Vineyards** (Harris Rd., 250/539-5139; May–Oct. daily 11:30 A.M.–4:30 P.M.), which sources Pinot Noir, Merlot, and Chardonnay grapes from four island vineyards. Stop by the barn-shaped cellar door for tastings and a tour.

Expect simple home-style cooking, a casual ambience, and friendly service at **Saturna's Café** (Narvaez Bay Rd., off East Point Rd., 250/539-2936; daily except Tues. 9:30 A.M.–2 P.M. and Wed.–Mon. for dinner from 6 P.M.).

Nanaimo and Vicinity

Nanaimo (pronounced na-NYE-mo) sprawls lazily up and down the hilly coastal terrain between sparkling Nanaimo Harbour and Mount Benson, on the east coast of Vancouver Island. With a population of 75,000, it's the island's second-largest city and one of the 10 largest cities in British Columbia. It's also a vibrant city enjoying a rich history, mild climate, wide range of visitor services, and a direct ferry link to both of Vancouver's ferry terminals.

The **Nanaimo Parkway** bypasses the city to the west along a 21-kilometer (13-mile) route that branches off the original highway five kilometers (3.1 miles) south of downtown, rejoining it 18 kilometers (11 miles) north of downtown.

History

Five native bands lived here (the name Nanaimo is a derivative from the Salish word Sney-Ny-Mous, or "Meeting Place"), and it was they who innocently showed dull, black rocks to Hudson's Bay Company employees in 1851. For most of the next century, mines in the area exported huge quantities of coal. Eventually, oil-fueled ships replaced the coal burners, and by 1949 most of the mines had closed. Surprisingly, no visible traces of the mining boom remain in Nanaimo, aside from a museum (built on top of the most productive mine) accurately depicting those times and a sturdy fort (now a museum) built in 1853 in case of a native attack.

Nanaimo was officially incorporated in 1874, which makes it the province's third-oldest town. When the coal mines closed, forestry and fishing became mainstays of the city. Today Nanaimo is also a major deep-sea shipping port.

SIGHTS

Downtown Nanaimo lies in a wide bowl sloping down to the waterfront, where forward thinking by early town planners has left wide expanses of parkland. Down near the water, the Civic Arena building is a good place to park your car and go exploring on foot. Right in front of the Civic Arena is **Swy-A-Lana Lagoon,** a man-made tidal lagoon full of interesting marinelife. A promenade leads south from the lagoon to a bustling downtown marina filled with commercial fishing boats and leisure craft. Beside the marina is a distinctive mast-like sculpture that provides foot access to a tiered development with various viewpoints. Up in downtown proper, many historic buildings still stand, most around the corner of Front and Church Streets and along Commercial Street. Look for hotels dating to the 19th century, the Francis Rattenbury–designed courthouse, and various old commercial buildings. Up Fitzwilliam Street are the 1893 St. Andrew's Church and the 1883 railway station.

The Bastion

Overlooking the harbor at the junction of Bastion and Front Streets stands the Bastion, a

© ANDREW HEMPSTEAD

the Bastion, a fort built in 1853

Vancouver Island

To Piper's Lagoon Park

To Horseshoe Bay (Vancouver)

DEPARTURE BAY RD

HAMMOND BAY RD

To Long
Lake and
Parksville

Departure
Bay Beach

Departure
Bay

To Tsawwassen
(Vancouver)

ISLAND HWY

Beban
Park

NORTHFIELD RD

VISITOR INFO
CENTRE

To Bailey
Theatre

NANAIMO REGIONAL
GENERAL HOSPITAL

BRECHIN RD

OCEAN
EXPLORERS
DIVING

Newcastle

Island

Gabriola

BUCCANEER INN

BLUEBIRD MOTEL

COLONIAL MOTEL

MOBY DICK
OCEANFRONT LODGE

Protection
Island

Island

TOWNSITE RD

BOWEN RD

STEWART
AVE

WESTWOOD RD

Millstone River

JINGLE POT RD

To Westwood Lake
RV Camping
and Cabins

Westwood
Lake

WAKESIAH AVE

2ND ST

3RD ST

4TH ST

CAMPBELL ST

WENTWORTH ST

FITZWILLIAM ST

TERMINAL AVE

ALBERT ST

SEE "DOWNTOWN
NANAIMO" MAP

VICTORIA RD

NANAIMO INTERNATIONAL
HOSTEL

Duke
Point

NANAIMO LAKES RD

6TH ST

7TH ST

Nanaimo

Harbour

Northumberland Channel

MOON

Nanaimo River

NANAIMO PKWY

10TH ST

Petroglyph PP

LIVING FOREST
OCEANSIDE
CAMPGROUND

DUKE POINT HWY

SCALE NOT AVAILABLE

To Bungy Zone and Victoria

well-protected fort built in 1853 by the Hudson's Bay Company to protect employees and their families against an attack by natives. Originally used as a company office, arsenal, and supply house, today the fort houses the **Bastion Museum** (June–Aug. daily 10 A.M.–5 P.M.; $1). For the benefit of tourists, local university students dressed in appropriate gunnery uniforms and led by a piper parade down Bastion Street daily at noon in summer. The parade ends at the Bastion, where the three cannons are fired out over the water. It's the only ceremo-nial cannon firing west of Ontario. For a good vantage point, be there early.

Nanaimo District Museum

In Piper Park, just across Front Street from the Bastion and up the stairs, is Nanaimo Museum (100 Cameron St., 250/753-1821; summer daily 10 A.M.–5 P.M., the rest of the year Tues.–Sat. 10 A.M.–5 P.M.; adult $2, senior $1.75, child $.75). Walk around the outside to appreciate harbor, city, and mountain views, as well as replica petroglyphs of animals, humans, and spiritual

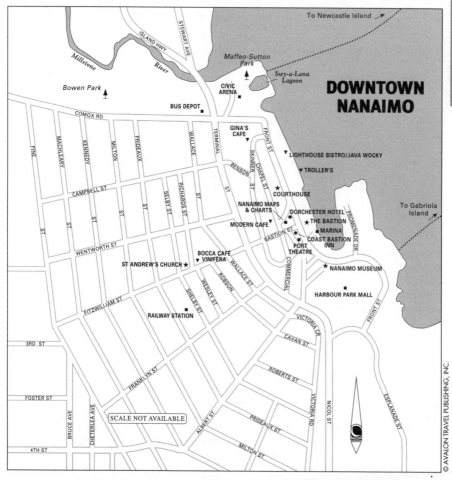

NANAIMO'S WORLD CHAMPIONSHIP BATHTUB RACE

O n the last Sunday of every July the waters off Nanaimo come alive for the World Championship Bathtub Race, the grand finale of the annual Nanaimo Marine Festival. The idea for the race was conceived back in 1967, when the chairman of the city's Canada Centennial Committee, Frank Ney, was asked to come up with a special event for the occasion. Bathtub racing was born over a cup of coffee, and Ney went on to be elected mayor of Nanaimo.

Originally, competitors raced across the Strait of Georgia between Nanaimo and Kitsilano Beach, Vancouver. Today, they leave from downtown, racing around Entrance and Winchelsea Islands to the finish line at Departure Bay in a modified bathtub fitted with a 7.5-horse-power outboard motor. The racers are escorted by hundreds of boats of the more regular variety, loaded with people just waiting for the competitors to sink! Every bathtubber wins a prize—a golden plug for entering, a small trophy for making it to the other side of the strait, and a silver plunger for the first tub to sink! These days, the sport and the festivities around it have grown enormously, attracting tens of thousands of visitors to Nanaimo. And "tubbing," as the locals call it, has spread to other provincial communities, where preliminary races qualify entrants for the big one.

creatures. Then allow at least an hour for wandering through the two floors of displays inside, which focus on life in early Nanaimo and include topics such as local geology, native peoples, and pioneers. An exhibit on the coal-mining days features a realistic coal mine from the 1850s. Don't miss the impressive native carvings by James Dick. Displays are changed regularly, so something's always new, and the summer interpretive program includes walks, talks, and shows.

Newcastle Island Provincial Marine Park

Newcastle Island is a magnificent chunk of wilderness separated from downtown Nanaimo by a narrow channel. It's mostly forested, ringed by sandstone cliffs and a few short stretches of pebbly beach. Wildlife inhabitants include deer, raccoons, beavers, and more than 50 species of birds.

When Europeans arrived and began mining coal, they displaced natives who had lived on the island for centuries. Coal was mined until 1883, and sandstone—featured on many of Nanaimo's historic buildings—was quarried here until 1932. The pavilion and facilities near the ferry dock date to the 1940s. Back then, the island was a popular holiday spot, at one point even boasting a floating hotel.

A 7.5-kilometer (4.7-mile) trail (allow 2–3 hours) encircles the island, leading to picturesque Kanaka Bay, Mallard Lake, and a lookout offering views east to the snowcapped Coast Mountains.

Camping on the island costs $14, and meals are available in the **Pavilion Restaurant** (summer daily 9 A.M.–7:15 P.M., until 9:15 P.M. Fri.–Sat. nights). Ferries (250/754-7893) depart for the island from Maffeo-Sutton Park in summer daily 10 A.M.–7 P.M. on the hour, with extra sailings at 8 P.M. and 9 P.M. on Friday and Saturday. The round-trip fare is adult $7, senior or child $6, bicycle $2.50.

Other Parks

Along the Millstone River and linked by a trail to the waterfront promenade, 36-hectare (89-acre) **Bowen Park** remains mostly in its natural state, with stands of Douglas fir, hemlock, cedar, and maple. It's home to beavers and birds, and even deer are occasionally sighted within its boundaries. Street access is from Bowen Road.

On the road into downtown Nanaimo from the south, two kilometers (1.2 miles) north of the Nanaimo Parkway intersection, **Petroglyph Provincial Park** features a short trail leading to ancient petroglyphs (rock carvings). Petroglyphs, found throughout the province and common along the coastal waterways, were made with stone tools, and they recorded important ceremonies and events. The designs at this park were carved thousands of years ago and are believed to represent human beings, animals (real and supernatural), bottom fish, and the rarely depicted sea wolf, a mythical creature part wolf and part killer whale.

West of downtown (take Wentworth Street then Jingle Pot Road across the Nanaimo Parkway), 106-hectare (262-acre) **Westwood Lake Park** surrounds the crystal-clear waters of its namesake lake. Resident flocks of Canada geese and ducks, tame enough to snatch food from your fingers, inhabit the park. The lake's healthy population of cutthroat trout attracts anglers year-round.

Along Hammond Bay Road, north of downtown and beyond Departure Bay, is **Piper's Lagoon Park,** encompassing an isthmus and a rocky headland that shelter a shallow lagoon. A trail from the parking lot leads to the headland, with views of the mainland across the Strait of Georgia. Continuing north, more trails lead through **Neck Point Park** to rocky beaches and oceanside picnic areas.

RECREATION
On and Under the Water
The obvious way to appreciate the harbor aspect of Nanaimo is by boat. To arrange a cruise, wander down to the marina below the Bastion and inquire among the fishing and sightseeing charter boats, or stop by the Nanaimo Visitor Info Centre and ask for a list of local guides and charters, plus current prices. One vessel, the *Bastion City* (250/753-2852), takes passengers on 2.5-hour narrated cruises of the harbor and adjacent islands. During the cruise, you might spot sea lions—who come into the harbor in March and early April to feed on abundant schools of herring—seals, orcas, bald eagles, blue herons, and cormorants. Cruises cost adult $30, senior $25, child $16.

Various dives can be accessed from Nanaimo, including a number of vessels that have been sunk especially for diving enthusiasts, including the HMAS *Cape Breton* and HMAS *Saskatchewan,* both 120-meter-long navy destroyer escorts. The much smaller *Rivtow Lion,* a rescue tug, was scuttled in the shallow waters of Departure Bay, making it a popular spot for novice divers. Marinelife is also varied, with divers mixing with harbor seals, anemones, sponges, salmon, and "tame" wolf eels. Near the Departure Bay ferry terminal, **Ocean Explorers Diving** (1690 Stewart Ave., 250/753-2055 or 800/233-4145) is a well-respected island operation, offering equipment rentals, charters, guided tours (from $60 per dive including air), and lessons.

Bungee Jumping
Nanaimo is home to **Bungy Zone** (250/753-5867), North America's only bridge-based commercial bungee jump. People flock here from afar to have their ankles tied and connected to "Bungee Bridge" by a long elastic rope. Next they dive head first 42 meters (138 feet) down almost to the surface of Nanaimo River, rebounding until momentum dissipates. To receive this thrill of a lifetime you have to part with $100, and if you have any cash left over, you'll find must-have T-shirts, hats, posters, videos, stickers, and other souvenirs to prove to the world that you really did it. At the same facility, other adrenaline rushes can be had by taking the Ultimate Swing ($60 per person) or the Flying Fox ($60). All of the above are thoroughly entertaining to watch, with good viewing areas and plenty of parking provided. The site is 13 kilometers south of downtown.

Arts and Entertainment
Lovers of the arts will find Nanaimo to be quite the cultural center, especially since the opening of the **Port Theatre** (125 Front St., 250/754-8550) in 1998. This magnificent 800-seat theater in an architecturally pleasing circular concrete-and-glass building opposite the harbor showcases theater productions, musicals, and music performances by a wide range of artists. The **Nanaimo Theatre Group** (250/758-7246) presents live performances at the Port Theatre and in the Bailey Theatre (2373 Rosstown Road).

The best place in Nanaimo for a quiet drink in a relaxing atmosphere is upstairs in the **Lighthouse Pub** (50 Anchor Way, 250/754-3212), built out over the water in front of downtown. This casual pub gets very busy in summer, with nightly drink specials, a pool table, and a good selection of pub food. For nautical atmosphere, head over to the **Dinghy Dock Marine Pub,** moored at Protection Island (250/753-2373); ferries depart regularly from Nanaimo Boat Basin. Bands play nightly at the **Queens Hotel** (34 Victoria St., 250/754-6751).

The **Nanaimo Art Gallery** (150 Commercial St., 250/754-1750; Tues.–Sat. 11 A.M.–5 P.M.) displays and sells works by a diverse range of island artists.

Events

The year kicks off in early April with the **Sea Lion Festival,** which coincides with the end of the December–April herring run through the Strait of Georgia. Attracted by the fish, hundreds of sea lions congregate on log booms for a quick and easy feed. Festivities include boat trips out on the water, onshore entertainment, and educational displays. The **Heritage Days** festival in late June celebrates the city's past with concerts and historical displays. **Canada Day** celebrations center on Maffeo-Sutton Park and end with an evening concert in nearby Bowen Park. July's **Nanaimo Marine Festival** is best known for the World Championship Bathtub Race (see sidebar), but also includes a silly boat race on Swy-A-Lana Lagoon, a parade of boats on wheels, a street fair, and fireworks.

ACCOMMODATIONS AND CAMPING

Under $50

A few of Nanaimo's older motels offer rooms under $50 outside of summer, but only **Nanaimo International Hostel** (65 Nicol St., 250/753-1188, www.nanaimohostel.com) falls into this price range year-round. In a converted house, this accommodation enjoys a convenient location three blocks from the train station and seven blocks from the bus depot. The hostel operates year-round, providing dormitory-style accommodations as well as campsites, a kitchen, laundry, TV room, and bicycle rentals. Guests can get discounts at many local restaurants and attractions. All beds are $19; register after 4 P.M.

$50–100

On an island of overpriced accommodations, two places, both on the same street in Nanaimo, stand out as being excellent value. The first of these, across from the waterfront and within easy walking distance of downtown and the Departure Bay ferry terminal, is the two-story **N Buccaneer Inn** (1577 Stewart Ave., 250/753-1246 or 877/282-6337, website www.buccaneerinn.com). Bedecked by a nautical-themed mural and colorful baskets of flowers, the motel is surrounded by well-maintained grounds, a sundeck, picnic tables, and a barbecue facility. The rooms themselves are spacious and brightly decorated, and each has a desk, coffee-making facilities, a small fridge, and Internet connections. The smallest rooms are $65 s, $70 d, while kitchen suites, some with gas fireplaces, start at $100 s, $110 d. The Fireplace Suite, complete with a wood-burning fire, soaker tub, and separate bedroom, is $160 s, $170 d. Off-season rates range $55–100. Friendly owner/operators provide a wealth of information on the local area (as does the motel website).

A few blocks toward downtown from the Buccaneer is the **Moby Dick Oceanfront Lodge** (1000 Stewart St., 250/753-7111 or 800/663-2116, www.mobydicklodge.com). This four-story waterfront motel faces Newcastle Island, offering water views from every room. The rooms are extra large, and each has a kitchen and private balcony, making the rates of $75 s, $85 d extremely good value.

A bunch of other motels fall into the lower end of the $50–100 price range, most along a short stretch of the old Highway 19 (Terminal Avenue) three kilometers north of downtown. These include the **Bluebird Motel** (995 Terminal Ave., 250/753-4151 or 877/764-3832, www.theblue birdmotel.com), which charges $49 s, $59 d, and the nine-room **Colonial Motel** (950 Terminal Ave., 250/754-4415, www.colonialmotel.ca), where rooms are $49 s, $59 d. Outside of summer, the best way to snag a cheap room is to cruise this strip looking for discounted rates posted out front.

$100–150
As you'd expect, accommodations right downtown are more expensive than those farther out. A bit nicer than you'd expect from the bland exterior, the **Best Western Dorchester Hotel** (70 Church St., 250/754-6835 or 800/661-2449, www.dorchesternanaimo.com) offers water views and a rooftop terrace from a very central location. Rooms in this historic building won't win any design awards, but they're relatively modern and many have water views. Rack rates are $120–160, but online specials usually have rooms at $100, even in summer.

Also right downtown, the **Coast Bastion Inn** (11 Bastion St., 250/753-6601 or 800/663-1144, www.coasthotels.com) is a full-service 179-room hotel with an exercise room, café and restaurant, lounge, and water views from every room. Advertised rates are from $149 s or d, but as with other properties in this chain, search the website for packages that offer decent discounts, even in summer.

$150–200
Seven kilometers (4.3 miles) north of downtown, the three-story **Ramada Resort on Long Lake** (4700 Island Hwy. N, 250/758-1144 or 800/565-1144, www.ramadananaimo.com) is an excellent choice for families. The inn boasts a short stretch of private beach along the lakeshore; canoe rentals are available. Other amenities include an exercise room, sauna, spa, and a delightful waterfront café. Rooms are modern, and many have water views and kitchens; rates range 159–219 s or d including a light breakfast.

Camping
Two commercial campgrounds lie within 10 kilometers (6.2 miles) of city center, but the nicest surroundings are in the provincial park out on **Newcastle Island** (250/391-2300; see *Sights*), connected to downtown by regular ferry service. The island isn't suitable for RVers, but

it's ideal for those with a lightweight tent. Facilities include picnic tables and a barbecue shelter. If you don't want to cook, eat at the restaurant on the island. Sites are $14.

The closest of the commercial campgrounds to downtown is **Westwood Lake RV Camping and Cabins** (380 Westwood Rd., 250/753-3922), on the edge of beautiful Westwood Lake. Amenities include canoe rentals, a barbecue area, game room, laundry, and hot showers. Unserviced sites are $18, hookups $23, and basic rooms in a panabode (prefab log) building go for $60 s or d ($70 with linen).

Living Forest Oceanside Campground (6 Maki Rd., 250/755-1755, www.campingbc.com) is on 20 hectares (49 acres) of coastal forest at the braided mouth of the Nanaimo River south of downtown. The location is delightful and facilities modern, including a laundry, general store, game room, and coin showers. Tent sites are $20, serviced sites $23–30, with the best of these enjoying water views.

FOOD
First things first. This is the place to try a delicious chocolate-topped **Nanaimo Bar,** a layered delicacy that originated in this city. I visit **Nanaimo Bakery** (2025 Bowen Rd.) for my annual Nanaimo Bar fix.

If you're wandering along the harbor and looking for a spot to relax with a hot drink, you won't do better than **Javawocky** (90 Front St., 250/753-1688; Mon.–Fri. from 6:15 A.M., Sat.–Sun. from 7 A.M.), overlooking the harbor. It offers all the usual coffee drinks, great milk shakes, inexpensive cakes and pastries, and light lunchtime snacks.

In the heart of downtown, the **Modern Café** (221 Commercial St., 250/754-5022; daily 11 A.M.–11 P.M.), which isn't, has hearty, no-frills cooking.

Seafood
Head down to the marina at the foot of Wharf Street for seafood straight from the fishing boats. You can buy salmon, halibut, cod, snapper, shrimp, crabs, mussels, or whatever the day's

catch might be at very reasonable prices—perfect if you're camping or have a motel room with a kitchen (many local accommodations also have outdoor barbecue facilities). Also at the marina is **Troller's** (250/741-7994), with tables and chairs set up around a small takeout counter on one of the arms of the floating dock. Expect to pay $6–8 for fish and chips.

Other Restaurants

Dinghy Dock Marine Pub (250/753-2373; daily 11 A.M.–11 P.M., later on weekends) offers a unique dining experience; the floating restaurant is moored at nearby Protection Island. Well known for great food and plenty of seagoing atmosphere, the pub also hosts live entertainment on Friday and Saturday nights from May to September. To get to the restaurant, take a ferry from Nanaimo Boat Basin. Ferries depart hourly 9:10 A.M.–11:10 P.M.; for information call 250/753-8244.

In the seaplane terminal on the waterfront (below the Bastion), the **Lighthouse Bistro** (50 Anchor Way, 250/754-3212; daily 11 A.M.–11 P.M.) is built over the water and has a large heated outdoor deck. The salmon chowder is excellent, served with delicious bread. Also on the menu are tasty appetizers, salads, burgers, sandwiches, croissants, pasta dishes, and good daily specials. Expect to pay $7–10 for a lunch entrée, $14–22 at dinner. Upstairs is the **Lighthouse Pub,** with a similar menu and specials such as $.25 wings daily 4–8 P.M.

Up Fitzwilliam Street from the center of town, in the Old Quarter, are a couple of noteworthy restaurants, including **Boca Cafe Vinifera** (4270 Fitzwilliam St., 250/753-1797; Mon.–Sat. 8 A.M.–8 P.M., Sun. 8 A.M.–6 P.M.), an inviting little space that is a favorite with locals looking for a little style. From the freshly made sandwiches at lunch to the perfectly cooked pastas ($12–16) in the evening, everything is delightful. Boca also offers one of the city's best wine lists.

For some of the best Mexican food on the island, head for **Gina's Cafe,** behind the courthouse (47 Skinner St., 250/753-5411; daily for lunch and dinner). The building, a converted residence, is hard to miss—the exterior is painted shades of purple and decorated with a fusion of Mexican and maritime memorabilia.

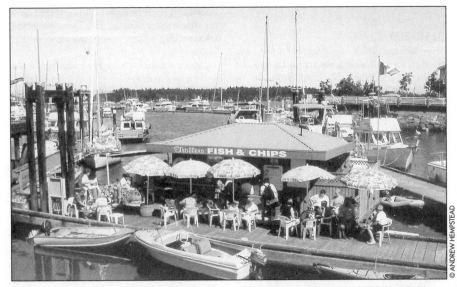

Troller's, down on the marina, provides the perfect setting for enjoying a meal of fish and chips.

INFORMATION AND SERVICES

Nanaimo is promoted to the world by **Tourism Nanaimo** (250/756-0106 or 800/663-7337, www.tourismnanaimo.com). The main **Nanaimo Visitor Info Centre** (2290 Bowen Rd., Mon.–Fri. 9 A.M.–5 P.M., Sat.–Sun. 10 A.M.–4 P.M.) is north of downtown and off the main highway in the grounds of Beban Park.

For maps, nautical charts, and books about Vancouver Island, visit **Nanaimo Maps and Charts** (8 Church St., 250/754-2513). Numerous used bookstores can be found along Commercial Street.

The main **post office** is on Front Street in the Harbour Park Mall. For emergencies, head to **Nanaimo Regional General Hospital** (1200 Dufferin Cres., 250/754-2141). If you need a pharmacy, go to the centrally located **Pharmasave** (530 5th St., 250/753-8234).

TRANSPORTATION

Getting There

It's possible to get to Nanaimo by airplane, train, or bus, but most people arrive by vehicle up Highway 1 from Victoria or by ferry from the mainland. **BC Ferries** (250/386-3431 or 888/223-3779, www.bcferries.com) operates regular services between Vancouver and Nanaimo along two different routes. Ferries leave Vancouver's Tsawwassen terminal up to eight times a day for the two-hour trip to Nanaimo's **Duke Point** terminal, 20 minutes south of downtown and with direct access to the highway that bypasses the city. The terminal itself is worthy of mention. Built at a cost of $50 million, it sits on a 10-hectare (25-acre) peninsula of land where lookouts, walking paths, and a cultural center keep Vancouver-bound passengers occupied while awaiting ferries. Through downtown, at the north end of Stewart Avenue, is the **Departure Bay** terminal. This facility contains a large lounge area with a café and large-screen TVs. Ferries from Vancouver's Horseshoe Bay terminal leave up to 11 times a day for Departure Bay. Fares on both routes are the same: peak one-way travel costs adult $10.25, child $5.25, vehicle $35.75. Limited reservations are taken via the website ($15 plus ferry fare). The **Nanaimo Seaporter** (250/753-2118) meets ferries at both terminals, transporting passengers to downtown accommodations and the bus depot.

Baxter Aviation (250/754-1066 or 800/661-5599) and **Harbour Air** (250/714-0900) fly daily between Vancouver and the seaplane base in downtown Nanaimo; $75 one-way.

The **Island Coach Lines** bus depot is at the rear of the Howard Johnson hotel (corner of Terminal Ave. and Comox Rd., 800/753-4371). Buses depart regularly for points north and south of Nanaimo and west to Port Alberni and Tofino.

A great way to travel up the island is aboard the **Malahat,** a scheduled train service that departs Victoria Monday–Saturday at 8:15 A.M. and on Sunday at noon, running as far north as Courtenay. Get off at Nanaimo (2.5 hours from Victoria), spend a couple of hours exploring the city or Newcastle Island, then jump aboard the return service to Victoria that same afternoon. The one-way fare is $23; a same-day round-trip ticket costs $40. The station is on Selby Street, up the hill from downtown (250/383-4324, www.viarail.ca).

Getting Around

Nanaimo Regional Transit System (250/390-4531) buses run daily. The main routes radiate from the Harbour Park Mall (at the south end of downtown) north to Departure Bay, west to Westwood Lake, and south as far as Cedar. An all-day pass is $4.

Rental-car agencies in Nanaimo include: **Avis** (250/245-4166), **Budget** (250/754-7368), **Discount** (250/758-5171), **National** (250/758-3509), and **Rent-a-wreck** (250/753-6461).

GABRIOLA ISLAND

Like the Southern Gulf Islands, Gabriola (pop. 3,500) is partly residential but also holds large expanses of forest, abundant wildlife, and long stretches of unspoiled coastline. The ferry from Nanaimo docks at Descanso Bay, on the west side of the island.

Take Taylor Bay Road north from the ferry terminal to access the island's best beaches, including those within tiny **Gabriola Sands Provincial Park**. Walk out to the park's southern headland to view sandstone cliffs eroded into interesting shapes by eons of wave action. The North and South Roads encircle the island, combining for a 30-kilometer (18.6-mile) loop perfect for a leisurely bike ride. Many scenic spots invite you to pull off—at petroglyphs, secluded bays, and lookouts. **Drumbeg Provincial Park** protects the island's southeast corner, where a short trail through dense forest leads to a secluded bay.

Practicalities

A rambling island-style property known as the Grande Hotel sat empty for a number of years before being transformed into the **Ⅿ Inn at Dragon's Keep** (2950 Dragon's Lane, 250/247-7407 or 877/273-2785) with 10 classy rooms, most with water views and two with private balconies ($90–150 s or d). Also in the main lodge is a restaurant dishing up innovative food that takes advantage of local produce. You can also camp ($25 per site) or rent a sleeping cabin with no water or power ($45).

For a romantic bed-and-breakfast accommodation, **Marina's Hideaway** (943 Canso Dr., 250/247-8854 or 888/208-9850; $135 s or d), overlooking Northumberland Channel, is an excellent choice. Each of the three spacious guest rooms in this magnificent waterfront home has a king-size bed, gas fireplace, private entrance, and balcony.

Basic services are available a little over one kilometer (.6 mile) from the ferry terminal on North Road. There you'll find a café, grocery store, and **Gabriola Island Visitor Info Centre** (250/247-9332 or 888/284-9332, www.gabriolaisland.org; mid-May–mid-Sept. daily 9 A.M.–6 P.M.).

BC Ferries (250/386-3431) schedules 15 sailings daily between the terminal off Front Street in Nanaimo (downtown, across from Harbour Park Mall) and Gabriola Island. The trip takes 20 minutes each way. The peak round-trip fare is adult $5.75, child $3.25, vehicle $15.50. For a taxi, call **Gabriola Island Cabs** (250/247-0049).

Highway 4 to the West Coast

From Nanaimo, it's 35 kilometers (21.7 miles) northwest up Highway 19 to one of Vancouver Island's main highway junctions, where Highway 4 spurs west to Port Alberni and the island's west coast. Follow Highway 4 to its end to reach **Pacific Rim National Park,** a long, narrow park protecting the wild coastal strip and some magnificent sandy beaches, and **Tofino,** a picturesque little town that makes the perfect base for sea kayaking, whale-watching, or fishing excursions.

HIGHWAY 4 TOWARD PORT ALBERNI

Englishman River Provincial Park

After turning off Highway 19, make your first stop here, where Englishman River—full of steelhead, cutthroat, and rainbow trout—cascades down from high Beaufort Range snowfields in a series of beautiful waterfalls. Within the park you'll find a picnic area, easy hiking trails to both the upper and lower falls, crystal-clear swimming holes, and plenty of campsites among tall cedars and lush ferns ($17 per night; no showers).

To get there, turn off Highway 4 on Errington Road, three kilometers (1.9 miles) west of the highway junction, and continue another nine kilometers (5.6 miles), following signs.

Coombs

What started just over 30 years ago as a simple produce stand has grown into the **Old Country Market** (250/248-6272; daily 8 A.M.–9 P.M.), the lifeblood of Coombs, along Highway 4A west of Nanaimo. Before moving inside the market building, stand out front and look upward, to where several goats can be seen contentedly grazing along the roof line, seemingly oblivious to the amused, camera-clicking visitors. Inside is a selection of goodies of epic proportions—a bakery, a deli, an ice-cream stand, and a wealth of healthy island produce. Behind the main building and in an adjacent property are rows of arty shops selling everything from pottery to jewelry to kites.

Little Qualicum Falls Provincial Park

This 440-hectare (1.090-acre) park lies along the north side of the highway, 10 kilometers west of Coombs. The park's main hiking trail leads alongside the Little Qualicum River to a series of plummeting waterfalls. Take your fishing pole along the riverside trail and catch a trout, stop for an exhilarating dip in one of the icy emerald pools, and stay the night in a sheltered riverside campsite ($17 per night; no showers). The source of the Little Qualicum River is **Cameron Lake,** a large, deep-green, trout-filled body of water just outside the western park boundary.

Cathedral Grove

At the west end of Cameron Lake, Highway 4 dives into one of the last remaining easily accessible stands of old-growth forest remaining in British Columbia. The tallest trees are protected by **MacMillan Provincial Park.** The road through the park is very narrow, so take extra care pulling into the main parking lot. From this point, a 500-meter (.3-mile) trail leads through a majestic stand of 200- to 800-year-old Douglas firs that rise a neck-straining 70 meters (230 feet) from the forest floor.

PORT ALBERNI AND VICINITY

If you hit Port Alberni on a cloudy day, you won't know what you're missing—until the sky lifts! Then beautiful tree-mantled mountains suddenly appear, and Alberni Inlet and the Somass River turn a stunning deep blue. Situated at the head of the island's longest inlet, Port Alberni is an industrial town of 19,500 centered around the forestry industry. The town's three mills—lumber, specialty lumber, and pulp and paper—are its main sources of income. The town is also a port for pulp and lumber freighters, deep-sea vessels, and commercial fishing boats.

Alberni Harbour Quay is the colorful epicenter of the Port Alberni waterfront.

Despite all the industry, Port Alberni has much to offer, including interesting museums, nearby provincial parks, and a modern marina filled with both charter fishing boats and tour boats, including the famous MV *Lady Rose.*

Sights

Follow the signs from Highway 4 to brightly decorated **Alberni Harbour Quay** at the end of Argyle Street. For a great view of the quay, harbor, marina, inlet, and surrounding mountains, climb the clock tower. Also on the quay is the **Forestry Visitor Centre,** operated by the logging giant Weyerhaeuser (250/720-2108; summer daily 9:30 A.M.–5:30 P.M., the rest of the year Fri.–Sun. 11 A.M.–4 P.M.), where you can view interpretive displays on logging, milling, and replanting, and arrange tours through local industry. Off Argyle Street is Industrial Road, which leads to the **Maritime Discovery Centre** (250/723-6164; mid-June–early

Sept. daily 10 A.M.–5 P.M.; free), ensconced in a red-and-white lighthouse. Children will love the hands-on displays that explore the importance of the ocean to the town's history.

Alberni Harbour Quay is also the starting point for the **Alberni Pacific Railway,** which runs twice a day Thursday through Monday to **McLean Mill National Historic Site** (250/723-1376; July–Aug. daily 10 A.M.–5 P.M.). The mill has Canada's only steam-powered sawmill, and it still works, so you can watch workers milling lumber through the clunky contraption. Admission to the site is adult $6.50, child $4.50, or pay adult $22, child $16 for a ticket that includes the train ride. To get to the mill under your own steam, take Highway 4 west through town and turn north on Beaver Creek Road.

Find out more about the origins of the famous West Coast Trail, see a collection of Nuu-chah-nulth artwork, or tinker with a variety of operating motorized machines from the forestry industry at the **Alberni Valley Museum** (corner of 10th Ave. and Wallace St., 250/723-2181; Mon.–Sat. 10 A.M.–5 P.M.; donation).

MV Lady Rose

The *Lady Rose* (250/723-8313 or 800/663-7192, www.ladyrosemarine.com), a vintage Scottish coaster, has been serving the remote communities of Alberni Inlet and Barkley Sound since 1949 as a supply and passenger service. But because of the spectacular scenery along the route, the cruise is also one of the island's biggest tourist attractions. Depending on the time of year, orcas and gray whales, seals, sea lions, porpoises, river otters, bald eagles, and all sorts of seabirds join you on your trip through magnificent Barkley Sound. The vessel is also a great way to reach the remote fishing village of Bamfield and the only way to reach the Broken Group Islands (see sidebar, *The Broken Group Islands*).

Year-round, the MV *Lady Rose* departs Alberni Harbour Quay Tuesday, Thursday, and Saturday at 8 A.M., reaching Kildonan at 10 A.M. and Bamfield at 12:30 P.M., then departing Bamfield at 1:30 P.M. and docking back in Port Alberni at 5:30 P.M. In summer, sailings are also made to Bamfield on Sunday, with a special stop

for kayakers in the Broken Group Islands. If you want to stay longer in Bamfield, accommodations are available. June–September an extra route is added to the schedule, with the vessel departing Monday, Wednesday, and Friday at 8 A.M. for the Broken Group Islands, arriving at Ucluelet at 1 P.M. for a 90-minute layover before returning to Port Alberni around 7 P.M. One-way fares from Port Alberni are: Kildonan $16, Bamfield $24, Broken Group Islands (Sechart) $24, Ucluelet $27. Children under 16 travel for half price. In summer the *Lady Rose* does a roaring business—book as far ahead as possible.

Fishing

Along with at least one other Vancouver Island town, Port Alberni claims to be the "Salmon Capital of the World." The fishing in Alberni Inlet is certainly world-class, but probably no better than a handful of other places on the island. The main salmon runs occur in fall, when hundreds of thousands of salmon migrate up Alberni Inlet to their spawning grounds.

To get the rundown on fishing charters head down to the full-service **Port Alberni Marina** (5104 River Rd., 250/723-8022; daily in summer dawn–dusk, winter 9 A.M.–5 P.M.). The owners, local fishing guides, have put together all kinds of printed information on local fishing. They know all the best spots and know how to catch the lunkers. Expect to pay $300 for two people, $330 for three for a six-hour guided morning charter; $200 for two, $220 for three, for a four-hour guided afternoon charter. The marina also rents boats (from $15 per hour or $90 per day, plus gas) and fishing rods ($12 per day), sells bait and tackle, and provides information about sportfishing/accommodations packages in the region.

The annual **Port Alberni Salmon Festival** (250/723-8165) fishing derby each Labour Day weekend (first weekend in September) draws up to 3,000 anglers chasing $60,000 in prize money. Crowds of fishing enthusiasts gather to watch thousands of pounds of salmon being weighed in at Clutesi Haven Marina, and multitudes of salmon-eaters throng to a three-day salmon barbecue.

Della Falls

In the remote southern section of **Strathcona Provincial Park** (see *Northern Vancouver Island*), difficult-to-reach Della Falls is accessible only from Port Alberni. The 440-meter (1,440-foot) waterfall northwest of town is one of the highest in North America, and getting to it requires a lot of effort: first by boat or canoe along Great Central Lake, then by a rough 16-kilometer (10-mile) hike (eight hours each way) up the Drinkwater Creek watershed.

Accommodations and Camping

Whether you're in search of a tent site with water views, a cozy bed-and-breakfast, or a luxurious motel room, Port Alberni has something to suit, although Port Alberni motels are generally more expensive than those on other parts of the island.

Within walking distance of the quay is **Blue-bird Motel** (3755 3rd Ave., 250/723-1153 or 888/591-3888, www.bluebirdmotel.net), which charges $69 s, $79 d for reliable but unsurprising rooms. Right downtown, the **Coast Hospitality Inn** (3835 Redford St., 250/723-8111 or 800/663-1144; $130 s, $135 d) is part of the upscale Coast Hotels and Resorts chain (www.coasthotels.com). Each of the large rooms is air-conditioned and features a comfortable bed and a writing desk

The best camping is out of town, at **Underwood Cove Marina** right on Alberni Inlet (250/723-9812). Choose between open and wooded full-facility sites ($16–28 per site) in a relatively remote setting with sweeping views of the inlet from a sandy log-strewn beach. To get there take 3rd Avenue south to Ship Creek Road and follow it for 14 kilometers (8.7 miles). **Stamp River Provincial Park,** northwest of Port Alberni, enjoys a beautiful location on the river of the same name; $17 per site. To get there follow Highway 4 west, and immediately after crossing Kitsuksus Creek take Beaver Creek Road north for 14 kilometers (8.7 miles).

Food

At any time of day, the best place to find something to eat is down at Alberni Harbour Quay,

which holds small cafés offering outdoor seating. **McMuggin's** (5440 Argyle St., 250/723-1166) features huge sandwiches (around $6) made to order on bread baked daily on the premises—when my wife tried the milk shake ($3.50) accompanying my sandwich she wished she had one, too. At the entrance to the quay is **Blue Door Cafe** (5415 Argyle St., 250/723-8811; daily from 5 A.M.), a small old-style place that's a real locals' hangout. Breakfasts are huge; an omelet with all the trimmings goes for $6–7.50, and bottomless self-serve coffee is an extra buck. Through downtown to the west, the **Westwind Pub** (4940 Cherry Creek Rd., 250/724-1324) is a nautical-themed bar with a good selection of reasonably priced meals.

Information

On the rise above town to the east is **Port Alberni Visitor Info Centre** (2533 Redford St., 250/724-6535 or 866/576-3662; summer daily 8 A.M.–6 P.M., the rest of the year Mon.–Fri. 9 A.M.–5 P.M.). This excellent facility is a great source of information on Pacific Rim National Park, transportation options to Bamfield, and all west coast attractions. The best source of pre-trip planning is the Alberni Valley Chamber of Commerce website (www.avcoc.com).

BAMFIELD

One of the island's most remote communities, this tiny fishing village lies along both sides of a narrow inlet on Barkley Sound. Most people arrive here aboard the **MV *Lady Rose*** from Port Alberni, but the town is also linked to Port Alberni by a rough 100-kilometer (62-mile) logging road. It's well worth the trip out to go fishing, explore the seashore, or just soak up the atmosphere of this picturesque boardwalk village. Bamfield is also the northern terminus of the **West Coast Trail** (see *Vicinity of Victoria*).

Practicalities

On the boardwalk, but across the channel from the road side of the village, **Bamfield Lodge** (250/728-3419, www.bamfieldlodge.com) comprises self-contained cabins set among trees and overlooking the water. The cabins are $100 per night, which includes boat transfers from across the channel. The lodge owners also operate a restaurant and a charter boat for fishing and wilderness trips.

WEST FROM PORT ALBERNI

Highway 4 west from Port Alberni meanders through unspoiled mountain wilderness, and you won't find a gas station or store for at least a couple of hours. The highway skirts the north shore of large Sproat Lake, whose clear waters draw keen trout and salmon anglers. Along the highway, camping at **Sproat Lake Provincial Park** is $17 per night. Provided they're not out squelching a fire, you can also see the world's largest water bombers—Martin Mars Flying Tankers—tied up here. Originally designed as troop carriers for World War II, only five were ever built and only two remain, both here at Sproat Lake. Used to fight wildfires, these massive flying beasts—36 meters (118 feet) long and with a wingspan over 60 meters (200 feet)— skim across the lake, each filling its tank with 27 tons of water.

Ninety-one kilometers (56.5 miles) from Port Alberni, Highway 4 splits, leading eight kilometers (five miles) south to Ucluelet or 34 kilometers (21 miles) north through Pacific Rim National Park to Tofino.

UCLUELET

A small town of 1,800 on the northern edge of Barkley Sound, Ucluelet (yoo-CLOO-let) has a wonderfully scenic location between the ocean and a protected bay. Like nearby Tofino the remote town grew as a logging and fishing center, but unlike its neighbor, tourism has been slower to catch on. You can enjoy all the same pursuits as in Tofino—beachcombing, whale-watching, kayaking, and fishing—but in a more low-key manner.

The Nuu-chal-nulth people lived around the bay where Ucluelet now sits for centuries before the arrival of Europeans (in their language, the town's name means "People with a Safe Land-

ing Place"). During the last century or so, Ucluelet has also been a fur sealers' trading post and a logging and sawmill center. But fishing remains the steady mainstay, as evidenced by the town's resident fishing fleet and several fish-processing plants.

Sights and Recreation

Drive through town to reach **He-tin-kis Park,** where a short trail leads through a littoral rainforest to a small stretch of rocky beach. The park and beach are part of the **Wild Pacific Trail,** an ambitious project that will eventually wander along the coastline all the way to Pacific Rim National Park. You can take the trail or continue southward by vehicle to reach the end of the road. The lighthouse here is not the world's most photogenic, but it gets the job done—keeping ships from running ashore along this stretch of particularly treacherous coastline.

Many visitors who choose to stay in Ucluelet do so for the fishing, particularly for chinook salmon (Feb.–Sept.) and halibut (May–July). The fall runs of chinook can yield fish up to 20 kilograms (44 pounds), and the town's busy charter fleet offers deep-sea fishing excursions as well as whale-watching trips.

Accommodations and Camping

If you're looking at sharing inexpensive accommodations with an outdoorsy crowd, reserve a bed at **Surfs Inn** (1874 Peninsula Rd., 250/726-4426, www.surfsinn.ca), within a restored home along the main road into town. Communal facilities include a lounge with wood-burning fireplace, a modern kitchen, and plenty of space to store bikes and surfboards. The guest rooms have dorm beds ($20 per person), one double bed ($30), or one double bed and an en suite bathroom ($40).

Terrace Beach Resort (1002 Peninsula Rd., 250/726-2901 or 866/726-2901, www.terrace-beachresort.ca) is the first in what will surely be a wave of Tofino-style accommodations in Ucluelet. The weathered "eco-industrial" exterior is a little deceiving, as the guest rooms feature West Coast contemporary styling throughout very livable units that range from one-bedroom motel rooms to multistory oceanfront cabins, linked by elevated boardwalks and all enclosed in an old-growth forest. Rates for the smallest start at $99 s or d, but if it's off-season, consider upgrading to one of the cabins for $199 s or d ($349 in summer). Don't be surprised to see actor Jason Priestly wandering through the forest—he and his family own the lodge.

At unique **Canadian Princess Resort** (Peninsula Rd., 250/726-7771 or 800/663-7090, www.obmg.com), you can spend the night aboard the 75-meter (240-foot) steamship *Canadian Princess,* which is permanently anchored in Ucluelet Harbour. The least expensive rooms aboard this historic gem are small and share bathroom facilities, but they're still decent value at $75 s, $85 d. The resort also offers modern, more-expensive onshore rooms and has a large fleet of boats for fishing charters. Most people staying here do so on a multinight fishing package.

Island West Fishing Resort (160 Hemlock St., 250/726-7515, www.islandwest resort.com) has its own marina right on the inlet and serves as the base of operations for a wide range of charter boats. The resort also has a good restaurant and pub. In the height of summer, rooms—each with full kitchen—run from a reasonable $99 s or d. Waterfront RV parking (not suitable for tents) costs $25. Tent campers should backtrack to **Ucluelet Campground** (260 Seaplane Base Rd., 250/726-4355; Apr.–Oct.; $25–30 per site), along the way into town.

Food
Get your morning caffeine fix along with a chocolate-cluster muffin at **Cynamoka Coffee House** (1536 Peninsula Rd., 250/726-3407; daily 7 A.M.–6 P.M.). It's through town, up a steep driveway to the right. Anglers head to the pub or restaurant at **Island West Fishing Resort** (250/726-7515). Locals congregate at **Smiley's** (1922 Peninsula Rd., 250/726-4213) for breakfast, lunch, and dinner, and for its bowling lanes. If you're camping or have access to a barbecue, stop at **Oyster Jim's** (2480 Pacific Rim Hwy., 250/726-7350) to pick up fresh oysters that open naturally over hot coals.

PACIFIC RIM NATIONAL PARK

Named for its location on the edge of the Pacific Ocean, this park encompasses a long, narrow strip of coast that has been battered by the sea for eons. The park comprises three "units," each very different in nature and each accessed in different ways. The section at the end of Highway 4 is the **Long Beach Unit,** named for an 11-kilometer (6.8-mile) stretch of beach that dominates the landscape. Accessible by vehicle, this is the most popular part of the park and is particularly busy in July and August. To the south, in Barkley Sound, the **Broken Group Islands Unit** (see sidebar, *The Broken Group Islands*) encompasses an archipelago of 100 islands, accessible by the MV *Lady Rose* from Port Alberni. Farther south still is the **West Coast Trail Unit,** named for the famous 77-kilometer (48-mile) hiking

© ANDREW HEMPSTEAD

one of the many hiking trails through the lush rainforest of Pacific Rim National Park

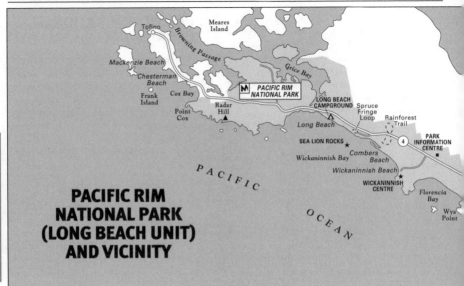

PACIFIC RIM NATIONAL PARK (LONG BEACH UNIT) AND VICINITY

Vancouver Island

trail between Port Renfrew and Bamfield (see *Vicinity of Victoria*).

Flora and Fauna

Like the entire west coast of Vancouver Island, Pacific Rim National Park is dominated by littoral (coastal) rainforest. Closest to the ocean, clinging to the rocky shore, a narrow windswept strip of Sitka spruce is covered by salty water year-round. These forests of spruce are compact and low-growing, forming a natural windbreak for the old-growth forests of western hemlock and western red cedar farther inland. The old-growth forests are strewn with fallen trees and lushly carpeted with mosses, shrubs, and ferns.

The ocean off western Canada reputedly holds more species of marinelife than any other temperate coast. Gray whales migrate up the coast each spring; seals and porpoises inhabit the park's waters year-round; sea lions overwinter on rocky offshore outcrops; and salmon spawn in the larger creeks through late fall. The tidal zone is the best place to search out smaller sea creatures—anemones, shellfish, and starfish are all colorful residents of the rocky shoreline.

The park's largest land mammal is the black bear, some of which occasionally wander down to the beach in search of food. Also present are blacktail deer, raccoons, otters, and mink. Bald eagles are year-round residents, but it's the migratory birds that arrive in the largest numbers—in spring and fall, thousands of Canada geese, pintails, mallards, and black brants converge on the vast tidal mudflats of **Grice Bay,** in the north of the park beyond the golf course.

Climate

Pacific Rim National Park receives heavy rainfall (3,000 millimeters/120 inches annually), and the weather here can only be described as extremely changeable. It can be windy and wet in the morning, yet warm and dry in the afternoon—always carry extra clothes and raingear while exploring the park. In summer the average temperature is 15°C (59°F), and dense morning fog usually clears in the afternoon. In winter the park experiences a good proportion of its annual rainfall, and the average temperature is 6°C (43°F). In spring you can expect 10°C (50°F) days, 6°C days in autumn.

Kennedy Lake

To Port Alberni

4

MOON

Ucluelet Inlet

Port Albion

Ucluelet

0   2.5 mi
0   2.5 km

© AVALON TRAVEL PUBLISHING, INC.

Vancouver Island

Long Beach

Ensconced between rocky headlands is more than 11 kilometers (6.8 miles) of hard-packed white sand, covered in twisted driftwood, shells, and the occasional Japanese glass fishing float. Dense rainforest and the high snowcapped peaks of the Mackenzie Range form a beautiful backdrop, while offshore lie craggy surf-battered isles home to myriad marinelife. You can access the beach at many places, but first stop at the **Wickaninnish Centre** (250/726-4212; mid-Mar.–mid-June daily 10:30 A.M.–6 P.M., mid-June–Aug. 8 A.M.–8 P.M., Sept.–mid-Oct. 10 A.M.–6 P.M.), which overlooks the entire beach from a protected southern cove. This is the place to learn about the natural and human history of both the park and the ocean through exhibits and spectacular hand-painted murals.

Through summer Long Beach attracts hordes of visitors. Most just wander along the beach soaking up the smells and sounds of the sea, but some brave the cool waters for swimming or surfing. The waves here are reputed to be Canada's best; rent boards and wetsuits in Ucluelet and Tofino. In winter, hikers dress for the harsh elements and walk the surf-pounded beach in search of treasures, admiring the ocean's fury during the many ferocious storms.

Hiking

The most obvious place for a walk is Long Beach, but other options are worth consideration. From the Wickaninnish Centre, an 800-meter (.5-mile) trail (15 minutes each way) leads south around a windswept headland, passing small coves and Lismer Beach, then descending a boardwalk to pebbly **South Beach.** Back up the hill, the **Wickaninnish Trail** leads 2.5 kilometers (1.6 miles) over to Florencia Bay; allow 50 minutes each way. The beach along the bay can also be accessed by road off the Wickaninnish Centre access road. Continuing northwest toward Tofino, the **Rainforest Trail** traverses an old-growth littoral rainforest in two one-kilometer (.6-mile) loops (allow 20 minutes for each). Farther north, at the back of the Combers Beach parking lot, is the trailhead for the 1.6-kilometer (one mile) **Spruce Fringe Loop.** This trail leads along the beach past piles of driftwood and through a forest of Sitka spruce.

Camping

The park's one official campground fills up *very* fast every day through summer. But it's in a marvelous location behind **Green Point,** a beautiful bluff above the beach. Facilities include drive-in sites, washrooms, picnic tables, an evening interpretive program, and plenty of firewood, but no showers or hookups. Mid-March to mid-October, walk-in sites are $14 per night, semi-serviced $20; the rest of the year they're $12 and $18. Some sites can be reserved through the Parks Canada Campground Reservation Service (877/737-3783, www.pccamping.ca) for a small additional fee. (The walk-in campground at Schooner Cove, still marked on some maps, has been closed for a number of years.) The closest commercial campgrounds are in Ucluelet and Tofino.

Services and Information

There are no stores or gas stations in the park, but

THE BROKEN GROUP ISLANDS

These 100 or so forested islands in the mouth of Barkley Sound, south of Ucluelet, once held native villages and some of the first trading posts on the coast. Now they're inhabited only by wildlife and visited primarily by campers paddling through the archipelago in canoes and kayaks. The islands offer few beaches, so paddlers come ashore in the many sheltered bays.

Marinelife abounds in the cool and clear waters; seals, porpoises, and gray whales are present year-round. Birdlife is also prolific. Bald eagles, blue herons, and cormorants are permanent residents, and large numbers of loons and Canada geese stop by on their spring and fall migration routes.

The archipelago extends almost 15 kilometers (9.3 miles) out to sea from Sechart, the starting point for kayakers. The protected islands of **Hand, Gibraltar, Dodo,** and **Willis** all hold campsites and are good destinations for novice paddlers. Farther out, the varying sea conditions make a higher level of skill necessary. Predictably, a westerly wind blows up early each afternoon through summer, making paddling more difficult.

The best way to reach the Broken Group Islands is aboard the **MV _Lady Rose_** (250/723-8313 or 800/663-7192, www.ladyrosemarine.com) from Port Alberni or Ucluelet. Based in Port Alberni, this historic vessel departs Alberni Harbour Quay June–September Monday, Wednesday, and Friday at 8 A.M., dropping kayakers at **Sechart,** the site of a whaling station and now home to **Sechart Lodge** (book in conjunction with the tour boat; $100 s, $155 d including meals). Originally an office building for a local forestry company, the lodge was barged to the site and converted to basic but comfortable guest rooms and a restaurant. The _Lady Rose_ then continues to Ucluelet, departing that village at 2 P.M. and making another stop at Sechart before returning to Port Alberni. In July and August, an additional Sunday sailing departs Port Alberni at 8 A.M., stopping at Sechart and returning directly to Port Alberni. The one-way fare between Port Alberni and Sechart is $24; between Ucluelet and Sechart it's $15.

The company that operates the boat also rents kayaks ($35–50 per day), which are left at Sechart so you don't have to pay a transportation charge. If you bring your own kayak, the transportation charge is $15–20 each way. The trip out on this boat is worthwhile just for the scenery, with the Ucluelet sailing passing right through the heart of the archipelago.

supplies and gas are available in Ucluelet and Tofino. The **Wickaninnish Restaurant** in the Wickaninnish Centre (250/726-7706; mid-Mar.–mid-Oct. daily 10:30 A.M.–6 P.M.) overlooks the wide sweeping bay for which it's named. It's not particularly cheap (lunch entrées $12–21), but the views are magnificent, and even if you don't indulge in a full meal, it's a great place to sip a coffee while watching the ocean. Sunday brunch is particularly popular.

The **Park Information Centre** is in the ocean-front Wickaninnish Centre (250/726-4212; mid-Mar.–mid-June daily 10:30 A.M.–6 P.M., mid-June–Aug. 8 A.M.–8 P.M., Sept.–mid-Oct. 10 A.M.–6 P.M.).

Park Fee

You're not charged a fee just to travel straight through the park to Tofino, but if you stop anywhere en route a strictly enforced charge applies. A two-hour permit is $5 per vehicle, a one-day permit is $13, and a season pass is $45.

Tofino

The bustling fishing village of Tofino sits at the very end of a long narrow peninsula, with the only road access to the outside world being winding Highway 4. The closest town of any size is Port Alberni, 130 kilometers (81 miles) to the east (allow at least 2.5 hours); Victoria is 340 kilometers (211 miles) distant.

Originally the site of a native Clayoquot village, Tofino was one of the first points in Canada to be visited by Captain Cook. It was named in 1792 for Don de Vincent Tofino, a hydrographer with a Spanish expedition. Aside from contact with fur traders and whalers, the entire district remained basically unchanged for almost 100 years.

Fishing has always been the mainstay of the local economy, but Tofino is also a supply center for the several hundred hermits living along the secluded shores of the sound and for the hordes of visitors that come in summer to visit Pacific Rim National Park, just to the south. In winter it's a quiet, friendly community with a population of fewer than 1,500. In summer the population swells to several times that size and the village springs to life—fishing boats pick up supplies and deposit salmon, cod, prawns, crabs, halibut, and other delicacies of the sea, and cruising, whale-watching, and fishing boats, along with seaplanes, do a roaring business introducing visitors to the natural wonders of the west coast.

The town lies on the southern edge of sheltered **Clayoquot Sound,** known worldwide for an ongoing fight by environmentalists to save the world's largest remaining coastal temperate forest. Around 200,000 hectares (494,000 acres) of this old-growth forest remain; a number of parks, including **Clayoquot Arm Provincial Park, Clayoquot Plateau Provincial Park, Hesquiat Peninsula Provincial Park, Flores Island Provincial Park,** and **Maquinna Marine Provincial Park** have resulted from the Clayoquot Sound Land Use Decision. An influx of environmentally conscious residents over the last two decades has added flavor to one of the west

coast's most picturesque and relaxing towns. And due to a large number of aware residents who like Tofino exactly the way it is, it's unlikely that high-rise hotels or fast-food chains will ever spoil this peaceful coastal paradise.

SIGHTS AND RECREATION

Tofino is best known for whale-watching, kayaking, and the long sandy beaches south of town, but there are a couple of interesting diversions well worth a stop. The first is **Tofino Botanical Gardens** (1084 Pacific Rim Hwy., 250/725-1220; daily 8 A.M.–dusk; adult $10, child $6), just before town. Developed by knowledgeable locals, it showcases local flora with the emphasis on a fun, educational experience. One garden is devoted to native species you would find in the adjacent national park, another to plants you can eat (but aren't allowed to). This is the only botanical garden I've visited where a colorfully painted camper van from the '70s is incorporated into a display. Another botanical point of interest is the massive cedar tree, estimated to be over 800 years old, on the right-hand side of the road as you enter town. Wire stays are the only things that stop it from toppling over.

Sun, Sand, and Surf

If you fancy a long walk along a fabulous shell-strewn stretch of white sand, like to sit on craggy rocks watching the waves disintegrate into white spray, or just want a piece of sun all your own to lie in and work on your tan, head for **Chesterman Beach,** just south of Tofino. From that beach, at low tide you can walk all the way out to **Frank Island** to watch the surf pound the exposed side while the tide creeps in and cuts you off from civilization for a few hours. The turnoff (not marked) to Chesterman Beach is Lynn Road, on the right just past the Dolphin Motel as you leave Tofino. Follow the road and park at one of three small parking lots; the parking lot at the corner of Lynn and Chesterman Beach Roads is closest to Frank Island.

SEE DETAIL

CAMPBELL ST

GIBSON ST

BLUE HERON
RESTAURANT

ARNET ST

TOFINO
SWELL
LODGE

4

TOFINO

Tofino Inlet

TOFINO BOTANICAL ★
GARDENS

MIDDLE
BEACH LODGE

MacKenzie Beach

MACKENZIE
BEACH RD

△ BELLA
PACIFICA

■ LIVE TO SURF

△ CRYSTAL COVE
BEACH RESORT

DOLPHIN
MOTEL

WICKANINNISH INN

Chesterman Beach

LYNN RD

PACIFIC

OCEAN

CHESTERMAN
BEACH RD

4

Frank Island

PACIFIC RIM HWY

Cox
Bay

WHALERS ON
THE POINT
GUESTHOUSE

HIMWITSA
LODGE

INN AT
TOUGH CITY

TOFINO SEA
KAYAKING
COMPANY

MAIN ST

EAGLE AERIE
GALLERY

2ND ST

CABLE COVE INN

POST OFFICE ■

CAMPBELL ST

SCHOONER
RESTAURANT

3RD ST

FIBRE
OPTIONS

COMMON LOAF
BAKE SHOP

NEILL ST

4TH ST

HOSPITAL

Tofino

SHELTER
RESTAURANT ▼

1ST ST

GIBSON ST

PACIFIC SANDS
BEACH RESORT

TOFINO VISITOR
INFO CENTRE

M PACIFIC RIM
NATIONAL PARK

0   0.25 mi

0   0.25 km

© ANDREW HEMPSTEAD

Vancouver Island

sunset at Chesterman Beach

Surfers wanting to hit the water should head south of town to **Live To Surf** (1180 Pacific Rim Hwy., 250/725-4464). The shop rents surfboards for $25 per day and wetsuits for $20, and offers lessons for $75 for two people. The staff will also tell you where the best surf can be found, and if there's no surf, they'll tell you how good it was last week. Check www.livetosurf.com for west coast surf reports. Next door is **Surf Sister** (250/725-4456 or 877/724-7873), Canada's only all-women surf school.

Whale-Watching

Each spring around 20,000 Pacific gray whales migrate between Baja and Alaska, passing through the waters off Tofino between March and May. Most of them continue north, but some stay in local waters through summer. Their feeding grounds are north of Tofino within **Maquinna Marine Park.** During the spring migration and some feeding periods, gray whales are also frequently sighted in the calm inland waters around **Meares Island,** just off Tofino.

Whale-watching is one of the most popular activities in town, and companies search out whales to watch them cruise up the coast, diving, surfacing, and spouting. On the whale-watching trips, you'll likely spy other marinelife as well; look for sea lions and puffins sunning themselves on offshore rocks, dolphins and harbor seals frolicking in the bays and inlets, and majestic bald eagles gracefully swooping around in the sky or perching in the treetops. Trips depart mid-February to October and generally last 2–3 hours. Expect to pay about $80 per person. (See *Local Charter Operators* for contact numbers.)

Hot Springs

Pamper yourself and take a boat or floatplane to **Hotsprings Cove,** Vancouver Island's only hot spring. Water bubbles out of the ground at a temperature of 87°C (189°F), tumbles over a cliff, then drops down through a series of pools—each large enough for two or three people—and into the sea. Lobsterize yourself silly in the first pool, or go for the ultimate in hot/cold torture by immersing yourself in the last pool, where at high tide you'll be slapped by breathtakingly refreshing ocean waves.

Several companies offer excursions out to the hot springs (see *Local Chart Operators*), and although prices vary slightly, expect to pay around $80–90 for a six- to seven-hour trip departing around 10 A.M., with about three hours ashore at the hot springs and the chance to see whales en route. **Tofino Air,** based at the 1st Street dock (250/725-4454), offers a scenic 15-minute flight to the hot springs by floatplane; from $100 per person round-trip, minimum three persons.

Local Charter Operators

The streets of downtown Tofino hold a profusion of charter operators offering a wide variety of trips. All of those listed below go whale-watching and head out to Hotsprings Cove. Other options include a tour of Meares Island and fishing charters. For details, head to any of the following: **Adventures Pacific** (120 4th St., 250/725-2811 or 888/486-3466), **Jamie's** (606 Campbell St., 250/725-3919 or 800/667-9913), **Remote Passages** (71 Wharf St., 250/725-3330 or 800/666-9833), **Sea Trek** (441 Campbell St., 250/725-4412 or 800/811-9155), **Seaside Adventures** (300 Main St., 250/725-2292 or 888/332-4252), or the **Whale Centre** (411 Campbell St., 250/725-2132 or 888/474-2288), where a gray whale skeleton is on display. Even with all these operators, business is brisk, so book ahead if possible.

Sea Kayaking

Exploring the waters around Tofino by sea kayak has become increasingly popular in recent years. **Tofino Sea Kayaking Company** (320 Main St., 250/725-4222, www.tofino-kayaking.com) has designed tours to meet the demand and suit all levels of experience. Excursions range from a 2.5-hour harbor paddle ($44 per person) to an overnight trip to a remote lodge on Vargas Island ($360 per person). The company's experienced staff will also help adventurous, independent paddlers plan an itinerary—many camping areas lie within a one-day paddle of Tofino. Single kayak rentals are $48 for one day or $40 per day for two or more days. Double kayaks are $84 and $74, respectively. Rental prices include all the accessories. At the company base, right on the harbor, is a shop selling provisions, accessories (such as marine charts), and a wide range of local literature. There's also a coffee shop, bookstore, and a few rooms renting for $50 s, $60 d per room per night.

Eagle Aerie Gallery

This art gallery (350 Campbell St., 250/725-3235; summer daily 9 A.M.–8 P.M., the rest of the year daily 9:30 A.M.–5:30 P.M.) features the eye-catching paintings, prints, and sculptures of Roy Henry Vickers, a well-known and highly respected Tsimshian artist. You can watch a video about the artist, then browse among the artworks—primarily native Canadian designs and outdoor scenes with clean lines and brilliant colors. If you fall for one of the most popular paintings but can't afford it, you can buy it in card or poster form. The gallery itself is built on the theme of a west coast native longhouse, with a carved and painted exterior and interior totem poles.

Pacific Rim Whale Festival

Tofino and Ucluelet join together each spring to put on the annual Pacific Rim Whale Festival, which features educational shows and special events in the adjacent national park, a native song and dance festival, a parade, crab races, plays at the local theater, dances, concerts, a golf tournament, and a multitude of events and activities in celebration of the gray whale spring migration. The festival takes place the last two weeks of March. To receive a Pacific Rim Whale Festival package, including a calendar of events, whale-watching information, and accommodations brochures, call 250/725-3414.

ACCOMMODATIONS AND CAMPING

Tofino boasts plenty of accommodations, both in town and south along the beach-fringed coastline. But getting a room or campsite in summer can be difficult if you just turn up, so book as far ahead as possible. As elsewhere in the province, high-season rates apply late June to early September. A month either side of this time and you'll enjoy big discounts when the weather is still warm enough to take advantage of Tofino's outdoor attractions. Winter in Tofino is known as the "storm-watching" season—when rates are reduced up to 50 percent (although no one can guarantee the big storms).

Under $50

Tofino's least expensive accommodation is **Whalers on the Point Guesthouse** (81 West St., 250/725-3443, www.tofinohostel.com). Affiliated with Hostelling International, it is a world away from hostels of old, appealing to all travelers. The building is a stylish log structure, with a stunning waterfront location, of which the communal lounge area takes full advantage. Other facilities include a modern kitchen, laundry, large deck with a barbecue, game room, and bike rentals. Dorm beds are $24 for members ($26 for nonmembers). Private rooms with shared bathrooms cost $70 s or d ($75 for nonmembers). Check-in is between 7 A.M. and noon and 5–11 P.M.

$50–100

Of Tofino's regular motels, least expensive is **Dolphin Motel,** on the highway into town, (250/725-3377, www.dolphinmotel.ca), which charges $85–109 s or d.

Continuing into town, **Tofino Swell Lodge** (341 Olsen Rd., 250/725-3274; $90 s, $105 d) is above a busy marina. This seven-room motel offers well-decorated rooms, shared use of a fully equipped kitchen and living room (complete with stereo, TV, and telescope), and pleasant gardens with incredible views of Tofino Inlet, tree-covered Meares Island, and distant snowcapped mountains.

$100–150

Out of town to the south are a number of ocean-front resorts. Of these, **Ⲙ Middle Beach Lodge** (250/725-2900 or 866/725-2900, www.middle-beach.com) does the best job of combining a unique west coast experience with reasonable prices. It comprises two distinct complexes: At the Beach, more intimate, with its own private beach, and the other, At the Headland, with luxurious self-contained chalets built along the top of a rugged headland. A short trail links the two, and

© ANDREW HEMPSTEAD

The Inn at Tough City

guests are welcome to wander between them. Outdoor settings are scattered throughout the property. Rates "At the Beach" start at $120, ocean views from $160, and all rates include a gourmet continental breakfast served in a magnificent common room. Rates "At the Headlands" start at $165 rising to over $400. This part of the complex has a restaurant with a table d'hôte menu offered nightly.

Overlooking the water right downtown is **The Inn at Tough City** (350 Main St., 250/725-2021, www.toughcity.com), a newer lodging constructed with materials sourced from throughout the region. The bricks, all 30,000 of them, were salvaged from a 100-year-old building in Vancouver's historic Gastown, while stained-glass windows, hardwood used in the flooring, and many of the furnishings are of historical value. The rooms are decorated in a stylish heritage color scheme, and beds are covered in plush down duvets. Summer rates are $140–175 s or d, discounted as low as $75 in winter.

$150–200

The **Cable Cove Inn** (201 Main St., 250/725-4236 or 800/663-6449, www.cablecoveinn.com) has a Main Street address, but you'd never know it sitting on the private deck of your ocean-facing room. It's tucked away in a quiet location overlooking a small cove, yet it's only a two-minute walk from the center of town. Well-furnished in a casual yet elegant style, each of the six rooms features a private deck and a fireplace. The least expensive room is $160 s or d, while the others, ranging $185–205, each have a hot tub. Outside of summer, rooms range $110–175. A continental breakfast is included in these rates.

In the best location in town, right beside the main dock, is **Himwitsa Lodge** (300 Main St., 250/725-3319 or 800/899-1947, www.himwitsa.com). No expense has been spared in the four contemporary upstairs suites, each with hot tub, comfortable lounge and writing area, TV and videocassette player, fully equipped kitchen, and private balcony with spectacular ocean views. Summer rates are $180–245 s or d with a two-day minimum; from $120 the rest of the year.

Over $200

You'll find cheaper places to stay in Tofino, but you'll won't find a lodge like **M Pacific Sands Beach Resort** (Cox Bay, 250/725-3322 or 800/565-2322, www.pacificsands.com), which is perfect for families and outdoorsy types who want to kick back for a few days. Set right on a popular surfing beach eight kilometers (five miles) south of town, guest units come in a variety of configurations, starting with one-bedroom, kitchen-equipped suites that rent from $210 per night in summer ($140 in winter). Some of these hold a prime beachfront location—ask when booking. The best units are the newest—two-level timber-frame villas equipped with everything from surfboard racks to stainless steel kitchen appliances ($285–450). The heated floors and gas fireplaces are a plus during the winter "storm-watching" season. Pacific Sands is a family-run operation, which translates to friendly service and repeat guests that have been visiting since childhood (and still bring their surfboards).

If you subscribe to one of those glossy travel mags, you've probably read about the **M Wickaninnish Inn** (Osprey Lane, Chesterman Beach, 250/725-3100, www.wickinn.com; from $440 s or d), which is regarded as one of the world's great resorts-and regularly features at the top of "Top Ten" lists. Just for good measure, the in-house Pointe Restaurant is lauded in a similar manner. Everything you've read is true—if you want to surrender to the lap of luxury in a wilderness setting, this is the place to do it. Designed to complement the rainforest setting, the exterior post-and-beam construction is big and bold, while the interior oozes West Coast elegance. Public areas such as the restaurant, an upscale lounge, a relaxing library, and a downstairs TV room (plasma, of course) make the resort feel like a world unto itself, but it's the guest rooms that will wow you. Spread through two wings, the 76 rooms overflow with amenities, including fireplaces, oversized soaker tubs, super-comfortable beds, and furniture made from recycled old-growth woods. The ocean views through floor-to-ceiling windows will captivate you the most. The menu of spa treatments is phenomenal—think hot stone massage for two in a hut overlooking the ocean, a full body exfoliation, or a sacred sea hydrotherapy treatment. The Wickaninnish is a five-minute drive south of Tofino, but who cares? You won't want to leave.

Camping

All Tofino's campgrounds are on the beaches south of town, but enjoying the great outdoors comes at a price in this part of the world, with some campsites costing over $50 a night. Best of the bunch is **Bella Pacifica Campground** (250/725-3400, www.bellapacifica.com; $29–41), which is right on MacKenzie Beach and offers protected tent sites, full hookups, coin-operated showers, and a laundry. Along the same stretch of sand, **Crystal Cove Beach Resort** (250/725-4213, www.crystalcovebeachresort.com) is one of the province's finest campgrounds. Facilities are modern, with personal touches such as complimentary coffee each morning and a book exchange. Many of the sites are in a private heavily wooded area (unserviced $37, hookups $49) while others are right along the beach ($55).

OTHER PRACTICALITIES

Food

Tofino has grocery stores, fish and seafood stores, bakeries, and a variety of cafés and restaurants, many of them serving locally caught seafood. The **Common Loaf Bake Shop** (180 1st St., 250/725-3915; daily 8 A.M.–6 P.M.) is a long-time favorite with locals (delicious cinnamon rolls for $1.80); sit outside or upstairs, where you'll have a magnificent view down Tofino's main street and across the sound.

The **Schooner Restaurant** (331 Campbell St., 250/725-3444; daily 9 A.M.–3 P.M. and 5–9:30 P.M.) has been dishing up well-priced seafood for 50 years. Over time the menu has gotten more creative (soya marinated salmon baked on a cedar plank), but old favorites (grilled halibut) still appear. Expect to pay $7–12 for starters and $20–28 for a main. Also of note is the service, which is remarkably good for a tourist town.

In Weigh West Marine Resort's **Blue Heron Restaurant** (634 Campbell St., 250/725-3277)

you can savor delicious clam chowder with garlic toast for $6.50, and seafood or steak dinners for $13–19. In the same complex is a pub with inexpensive meals and water views.

In an unassuming building near the entrance to town, the **Shelter Restaurant** (601 Campbell St., 250/725-3353; daily from 5:30 P.M.) brings some big-city pizzazz to tiny Tofino. Inside, an open dining room serves imaginative treats such as crab fritters ($13) and prosciutto-wrapped halibut ($28).

South of Tofino, the ⛰ **Pointe Restaurant** (Wickaninnish Inn, Osprey Lane, Chesterman Beach, 250/725-3100; daily from 7:30 A.M.) is quite simply superb in every respect. The sweeping ocean views from anywhere within the circular dining room, which is built on a rocky headland, are as good as from any restaurant in Canada (ask for a window table when reserving). At breakfast, mimosas encourage a holiday spirit, or get serious by ordering eggs Benedict with smoked salmon ($14). The lunch and dinner menus highlight seafood and island produce. Lunch includes seafood chowder ($11) and a wild salon BLT ($16). A good way to start dinner is with seared scallops ($13) or roasted oysters ($3 each) before moving on to the steamed halibut ($29) or smoked black cod ($32). Rounding out a world-class dining experience is the impeccable service and a wine list dominated by Pacific Northwest bottles.

Information and Services

Tofino Visitor Info Centre (250/725-3414, www.tofinobc.org; summer Sun.–Thurs. 10 A.M.–4 P.M., Fri.–Sat. 10 A.M.–6 P.M.) is along the Pacific Rim Highway, eight kilometers (five miles) before town.

Wildside Booksellers (320 Main St., 250/725-4222) stocks an excellent selection of natural history titles, while the bookstore in the **Tofino Sea Kayaking Company** (320 Main St., 250/725-4222) building specializes in recreation guides.

The **post office,** a **laundry,** and **Tofino General Hospital** (250/725-3212) are all on Neill Street.

Transportation

Tofino Bus (546 Campbell St., 250/725-2871 or 866/986-3466, www.tofinobus.com) runs one bus daily between Victoria and Tofino, making pickups at both Nanaimo ferry terminals. The fare from Victoria is $50. Three times daily, this company runs a bus between Tofino and Ucluelet ($15 round-trip), with stops made at lodges and hiking trails along the way.

North Vancouver Air (604/278-1608 or 800/228-6608, www.northvanair.com) flies from its base near Vancouver's South Terminal to Tofino. Though it doesn't offer any scheduled flights, **Tofino Air** (based at the foot of 1st St., 250/725-4454) provides scenic floatplane flight-seeing and charters.

Getting around town is easiest on foot. You can rent bikes from **Fiber Options** (corner 4th St. and Campbell St., 250/725-2192) for $25 per day (blend in with the locals by adding a surf-board rack for $7).

North from Nanaimo

Back on the east side of the island, the Inland Island Highway north of the Highway 4 junction bypasses a stretch of coast that has developed as a popular holiday area, with many beaches, resorts, and waterfront campgrounds. Just over halfway between Nanaimo and Campbell River is the **Comox Valley,** a popular year-round destination where you'll find more great beaches and fishing, and great downhill skiing and boarding on the back doorstep during the colder months. Again, this area is bypassed by Highway 19, so grab a good map and stick to the coastal route wherever possible.

PARKSVILLE

Golden sand fringes the coastline between Parksville (pop. 10,000) and Qualicum Beach. Parksville Beach claims "the warmest water in the whole of Canada." When the tide goes out along this stretch of the coast, it leaves a strip of sand up to a kilometer wide exposed to the sun. When the water returns, voilà—sand-heated water.

Rathtrevor Beach Provincial Park, a 347-hectare (860-acre) chunk of coastline just south of Parksville, features a fine two-kilometer-long (1.2 mile-long) sandy beach, a wooded upland area, nature trails, and bird-watching action that's particularly good in early spring, when seabirds swoop in for an annual herring feast. The children will probably want to make a stop at **Riptide Lagoon** (250/248-8290; daily 10 A.M.–8 P.M.), near the park entrance. This over-the-top mini-golf complex costs $6.50 per game for adults, $4.50 for children.

Practicalities

Parksville's many accommodations have been developed for vacationing families—with weekly rentals of self-contained units within walking distance of the water. Overlooking Craig Bay on the southeast side of town, **Gray Crest Seaside Resort** (1115 Island Hwy. E, 250/248-6513 or 800/663-2636, www.graycrest.com) is typical. Guests swim in the water out front or in the heated pool while children make the most of a huge playground. The most basic units ($125 s or d) have balconies with water views but are slightly dated. More desirable are the Deluxe Suites (from $188), for their beachfront setting and full kitchens.

Right off Parksville's waterfront downtown strip is **Surfside RV Resort** (200 Corfield St., 250/248-9713, www.surfside.bc.ca), packed with families throughout summer. It has all the usual facilities in a prime oceanfront locale (although no surf as the name suggests). Sites range $38–48, with the more expensive ones lining the beachfront. At **Rathtrevor Beach Provincial Park,** south of downtown off Highway 19A (take Exit 46 from the south), campers choose the natural setting over modern facilities (no hookups). Walk-in tent sites are $14, pull-throughs $22.

Traveling north from Nanaimo, take Exit 46 from Highway 19 and follow Highway 19A for just under one kilometer (.6 mile) to reach **Parksville Visitor Info Centre** (1275 Island Hwy. E, 250/248-3613; July–Aug. daily 8 A.M.–8 P.M., the rest of the year Mon.–Sat. 9 A.M.–5 P.M.) Adjacent to the information center is the outdoor **Craig Heritage Museum** (250/248-6966; free), comprising historic buildings such as a post office and church.

QUALICUM BEACH

This beach community (pop. 7,000) is generally quieter than Parksville, but it shares the same golden sands of Georgia Strait and attracts the same droves of beach-goers, sun worshippers, anglers, and golfers on summer vacation. You can stay on Highway 19 and take the Memorial Avenue exit to reach the heart of the town, but a more scenic option is to continue along the old coastal highway through Parksville. This route is lined with motels, resorts, and RV parks. The attractive downtown area, locally known as "the Village," is away from the beach area up Memorial Avenue. If you appreciate high-quality arts and crafts, detour off the main drag at this point and head for the **Old Schoolhouse Gallery and Art Centre** (122 Fern Rd. W, 250/752-6133). The gallery occupies a beautifully restored 1912 building, while working artist studios below allow you a chance to see woodcarving, printmaking, pottery, weaving, painting, and fabric art in progress. Don't miss a stop at the gallery shop, where all kinds of original handcrafted treasures are likely to lure a couple of dollars out of your wallet. Through town to the west, take Bayswater Road inland a short way to reach **Big Qualicum River Fish Hatchery,** where a wooded trail leads to holding tanks and an artificial spawning channel.

Practicalities

Like the rest of the world, you probably never saw the 1977 Brian Dennehy movie *Ants!,* about a colony of evil ants that terrorized guests at a seaside resort. Of course, I'm mentioning the movie for a reason—it was filmed at the Tudor-style **Qualicum Heritage Inn** (427 College Rd., 250/752-9262, www.qualicumher-

itageinn.com). Originally a boarding school, this 1935 building now houses 70 guest rooms in four different wings. The rooms ooze historic charm, helped along by dark woods and understated floral fabrics. Rates range $109–139 s or d. **Old Dutch Inn** (2690 West Island Hwy., 250/752-6914 or 800/661-0199, www.old-dutchinn.com) is across the road from the ocean and within walking distance of Qualicum Beach Golf Club. Amenities include an indoor pool, sauna and whirlpool, and a restaurant with lots of outdoor seating. The rooms could be nicer, but the location can't be beat; $89–119 midweek, $99–129 weekends.

Give the central campgrounds a miss and continue 16 kilometers (10 miles) northwest from Qualicum Beach to **Qualicum Bay Resort** (5970 West Island Hwy., 250/757-2003 or 800/663-6899, www.resortbc.com). Separated from the water by a road, facilities at this family-oriented resort include a manmade swimming lake, a playground, a game room, an ice cream stand, and a restaurant. Tent sites are $15, hookups $26–30, camping cabins (no linen, share bathrooms) $35, and basic motel rooms $85–140 s or d.

One of the few remaining houses set right on the waterfront has been converted to the **M Beach House Café** (2775 West Island Hwy., 250/752-9626; daily 11 A.M.–2 P.M. and 5–9:30 P.M.). Plan to eat outside on the glassed-in patio, then order grilled salmon cakes ($12), spicy goulash ($18.50), or curried shrimp ($18).

For the complete rundown on this stretch of the coast, stop in at **Qualicum Beach Visitor Info Centre** (250/752-9532, www.qualicum .bc.ca), on the promenade as you enter town from the southeast.

QUALICUM BEACH TO THE COMOX VALLEY

Horne Lake Caves Provincial Park

If you can drag yourself away from the beach, consider a half-day detour inland to one of Vancouver Island's most intriguing natural attractions, the Horne Lake Caves. To get there, continue along the old coastal highway for 11 kilometers (6.8 miles) beyond Qualicum Beach and turn off at the Horne Lake Store, following the road for 16 kilometers (10 miles) west to Horne Lake. Two caves are open for exploration without a guide. There's no charge for entering these caves, but you'll need a helmet and light source, which can be rented for $5. Several different guided tours of the more interesting caves are offered. The 90-minute tour of Riverbend Cave includes a short walk, underground exploration, and explanation (adult $17, child $15). All caves are open mid-June to September daily 10 A.M.–4 P.M. A private contractor (250/757-8687, www.hornelake.com) runs the tours using qualified guides. The company also operates the campground ($15–20 per night), has canoes for rent, and organizes educational programs such as rock climbing and guided nature walks.

Denman Island

Buckley Bay, 35 kilometers (22 miles) northwest of Qualicum Beach, is the departure point for ferries across Bayne Sound to Denman Island. Like all ferries through the Strait of Georgia, they are operated by **BC Ferries** (250/335-0323) and require no reservations. The service runs hourly 7 A.M.–11 P.M. and costs adult $5.75, child $2.70, vehicle $12.75. Ten minutes after leaving Buckley Bay you'll be driving off the ferry and onto this rural oasis, similar to the Southern Gulf Islands in appearance, sans the crowds. Fishing, hiking, biking, bird-watching, and scuba diving are prime draws here, and you'll also find good beaches, parks, and an artisan community along narrow winding roads.

Within walking distance of the ferry is Denman Village, boasting a number of early-20th-century heritage buildings. Across the island, 23-hectare (57-acre) **Fillongley Provincial Park** features forested trails, long stretches of beach, and 10 campsites for $14. At **Boyle Point Provincial Park** in the south, an 800-meter (.5-mile) loop trail (15 minutes round-trip) leads to a lookout with views across to Chrome Island, where a lighthouse stands.

Hornby Island

Every hour 8 A.M.–6 P.M., a small ferry departs the southern end of Denman Island for Hornby Island, a short, 10-minute run across Lambert Channel. The fares are adult $5.75, child $2.70, vehicle $12.75. This small, seldom-visited island has great beaches, especially along crescent-shaped Tribune Bay, where the longest stretch of sand is protected by 95-hectare (235-acre) **Tribune Bay Provincial Park.** Continue beyond that park and take St. John's Point Road to 287-hectare (710-acre) **Helliwell Provincial Park,** on a rugged, forested headland where trails lead through an old-growth forest of Douglas fir and western red cedar to high bluffs. Allow 90 minutes for the full five-kilometer (3.1-mile) loop.

Neither of the island's provincial parks has a campground. Instead, stay at the beautifully located **Tribune Bay Campsite** (250/335-2359, www.tribunebay.com), where tent camping is $25 and powered sites are $28. Right by the ferry dock, **Hornby Island Resort** (4305 Shingle Spit Rd., 250/335-0136) offers boat rentals, tennis courts, a restaurant and pub, and a laundry. The motel rooms ($90) have water views but need renovating; the cabins are perfect for families who need to spread out (July–Aug. $850 per week, the rest of the year $125 per night), and a few RV sites ($30 per night) are off to one side.

COMOX VALLEY

The three communities of **Courtenay, Cumberland,** and **Comox** lie in the beautiful Comox Valley, nestled between Georgia Strait and high snowcapped mountains to the west. The valley lies almost halfway up the island, 220 kilometers (137 miles) from Victoria, but direct flights to the mainland have created a mini-boom in recent years, especially since WestJet starting offering inexpensive flights between Calgary and Comox. The three towns merge into one, but each has its own personality—Courtenay the staid town with a compact downtown core and all the visitor services you need; Cumberland, away from the water but historically charming nonetheless; and Comox, a sprawl of retiree housing developments and golf courses extending across a wide peninsula to the ocean.

© ANDREW HEMPSTEAD

The white cliffs at Kye Bay are off the main tourist path, but worth visiting for their distinctive geological origins.

Courtenay Sights

The valley's largest town and a commercial center for local farming, logging, fishing, and retirement communities, Courtenay (pop. 22,000) extends around the head of Comox Harbour. It's not particularly scenic but has a few interesting sights and plenty of highway accommodations. It was named for Captain George Courtenay, who led the original surveying expedition of the area in 1848.

As you enter Courtenay from the south, you pass all sorts of restaurants, the information center, and motel after motel. Continue into the heart of town and the pleasing downtown area with its cobbled streets, old-fashioned lamps, brick planters full of flowers, and numerous shops. The main attraction downtown is **Courtenay and District Museum** (207 4th St., 250/334-0686; May–Aug. Tues.–Sat. 10 A.M.– 5 P.M., Sunday noon–5 P.M., the rest of the year

Tues.–Sat. 10 A.M.–4:30 P.M.). The highlight is a full-size replica of an *elasmosaur*. The original— 12 meters (39 feet) long and 80 million years old—was found at the nearby Puntledge River. Daily in July and August and weekends April–June and September, the museum leads tours out to the site, on which you have the chance to dig for your very own fossil (adult $20, child $12.50). Other museum exhibits include realistic dioramas and a replica of a bighouse containing many native artifacts and items, some formerly belonging to prominent chiefs. Finish up in the gift shop, which is well stocked with local arts and crafts.

From downtown, cross the bridge to the totem pole–flanked entrance to **Lewis Park,** at the confluence of the Puntledge and Tsolum Rivers. The two rivers join here to form the very short Courtenay River.

Cumberland Sights

Coal was first discovered in the Comox Valley in 1869, and by the mid-1880s extraction of the most productive seam was going ahead, near present-day Cumberland. The mine was operated by the Union Colliery Co., which brought in thousands of Chinese workers. Cumberland's Chinatown was once home to 3,000 people, second in size only to San Francisco's Chinatown. **Cumberland Museum** (2680 Dunsmuir St., 250/336-2445; daily 9 A.M.–5 P.M., closed Sun. outside summer; $3) is a small but excellent facility, with interesting historic photos. Before leaving pick up a heritage walking tour brochure and ask directions to the overgrown remains of the Chinese settlement, which lies around 1.6 kilometers (one mile) west of the museum.

Comox Sights

The population of Comox is quoted at 12,000, and there's certainly enough room for everyone, but you'd never know it, driving along forested roads that lead to golf courses, retirement communities, and a magnificent stretch of coastline. To reach Comox's small downtown area, take Comox Road eastward after crossing the Courtenay River along Highway 19A.

Through downtown is a highlight of the valley,

Vancouver Island

FORBIDDEN PLATEAU

This high plateau west of the Comox Valley was "forbidden" according to ancient legend. The village of Comox was threatened by Cowichan warriors many moons ago, so the Comox men sent their women and children up the mountain to be out of harm's way. When the danger was over, the men went up to collect their families, but they had disappeared without a trace—and were never seen again. Not knowing how or why the party disappeared off the face of the planet, the plateau became for the Comox a fearful and forbidden place. But judging by the number of hikers who explore Forbidden Plateau and return to tell the tale, the legend has been put to rest.

Filberg Heritage Lodge and Park (Comox Ave. at Filberg Rd., 250/339-2715). A high hedge hides the property from the outside world, but the grounds are open daily dawn to dusk and no admission is charged to wander through the beautifully landscaped grounds that stretch down to Comox Harbour. At the bottom of the garden is the main house, built by a logging magnate 1929. Filled with period antiques and quirky architecture, it's open for inspection in summer daily 11 A.M.–5 P.M. (admission $3). In early August, **Filberg Festival** features gourmet food, free entertainment, and unique arts and crafts from the best of B.C.'s artisans.

From the lodge, take Pritchard Road north and you'll eventually reach the Canadian Forces Base, which doubles as the local airport for commercial flights. Cross Knight Road to reach **Comox Air Force Museum and Airpark,** at the entrance to Comox Air Force Base (Ryan Rd., 250/339-8162; year-round daily 10 A.M.–4 P.M.; donation). The museum isn't huge, but it's chock-full of air force memorabilia. Once you've gone through the indoor displays, wander down to the airpark (May–Sept. daily 10 A.M.–4 P.M.), a five-minute walk south, where around a dozen planes from various eras are parked.

On the other side of the runway is **Kye Bay,** a wide strip of sand perfect for families. To the east, beyond the headland, are intriguing **white cliffs.** At the end of an ancient ice age, as the sheet of ice that covered this region retreated, it stalled, leaving behind a massive mound of finely ground glacial silt. Wind and water action in the ensuing years have uncovered the silt, forming white cliffs that stand in stark contrast to the surrounding bedrock. To reach Kye Bay from the airport, head east on Knight Road (past the entrance to the main terminal) and take Kye Bay Road around the south end of the runway.

Another interesting spot is **Seal Bay Nature Park,** north of downtown along Anderton Road then Waveland Road. The park protects one of the region's few undeveloped stretches of coastline. Trails lead through a lush forest of Douglas fir and ferns to a pleasant rocky beach where bald eagles and seals are often sighted.

Kayaking

Comox Valley Kayaks (2020 Cliffe Ave., 250/334-2628 or 888/545-5595) offers a sunset paddle for $35, three-hour sea-kayaking lessons for $40 per person, and full-day guided trips from $75. Or rent a kayak for some exploration by yourself, around the local waterways or out on nearby Denman and Hornby Islands; $35–63 for 24 hours. The company also rents canoes—great for nearby Comox Lake—for $28 per day.

Mt. Washington Alpine Resort

Vancouver Island is not usually associated with snow sports by outsiders, but locals know they don't need to leave their island home to enjoy world-class skiing and boarding at **Mt. Washington Alpine Resort** (250/338-1386 or 888/231-1499, mountwashington.ca), 35 kilometers (22 miles) northwest of Courtenay. The scope and popularity of the resort is remarkable—it ranks fourth in British Columbia for the number of "skier days" and has a modern base village with more than 3,500 beds—but not surprising, considering it receives an annual snowfall of nine meters (30 feet) and temperatures that remain relatively warm compared to the interior of British Columbia. Seven chairlifts serve 370 hectares (915 acres) with the vertical rise a respectable 500 meters (1,640 feet) and the longest run just under two kilometers (1.2 miles). Other facilities include a terrain park and a half pipe. Lift tickets are adult $47, senior $39, and child $25. A cross-country pass to the groomed trails of Paradise Meadows is $18.

Between July and mid-October, the resort welcomes outdoor enthusiasts who come to hike through alpine meadows, ride the chairlift (adult $11, senior or child $9), mountain bike down the slopes, or go trail riding through the forest. A wealth of other activities are on offer—from mini-golf to a bungee trampoline—making it a good place to escape the beachy crowd for a day or two. Inexpensive summer packages (see the website) encourage overnight stays.

Accommodations and Camping

The valley's least-expensive motels are strung out along the highway (Cliffe Avenue) as you enter Courtenay from the south. The **Anco Motel** (1885 Cliffe Ave., 250/334-2451; $50 s, $60 d) is typical, with an outdoor pool as a bonus.

If you're looking for something more than simply somewhere to rest your head, consider staying at **Ⅺ Mt. Washington Guest House** (1203 Fosters Pl., 250/898-8141, www.mtwashingtonguesthouse.com), in the base village of Mt. Washington Alpine Resort, 35 kilometers (22 miles) northwest of Courtenay. This modern alpine chalet has a limited number of dorm beds ($24 per person) and two private guest rooms ($65 s or d), along with a clean, well-equipped kitchen, a big deck from where the views extend forever, a hot tub, and Internet access. You'll spend most of your time away from your room, pursuing the many activities offered at the resort. Winter is high season, and rates rise accordingly (dorm $30–35, private room $75–100) but are still excellent value.

Overlooking Gartley Bay south of Courtenay is **Kingfisher Oceanside Resort** (4330 South Island Hwy., 250/338-1323 or 800/663-7929, www.kingfisherspa.com), set around well-manicured gardens and a large heated pool right on the water. The resort also holds a spa facility, yoga lounge, a bar with outdoor seating, and a restaurant renowned for its West Coast cuisine (and a

great Sunday brunch buffet). Accommodation choices are in regular rooms, each with a private balcony ($155 s or d), or newer beachfront suites, each with a fireplace, hot tub, and kitchen (from $190–425 s or d).

An excellent choice for campers looking for a vacation vibe is **Seaview Tent and Trailer Park** (Lazo Rd., Comox, 250/339-3946), within walking distance of the beach. Unserviced sites are $20–24, hookups $28–34. To get there from the highway, take Comox Road through downtown Comox and turn right onto Balmoral Avenue (which leads into Lazo Road).

Food

In downtown Courtenay, **Leung Grocery** (456 5th St., 250/334-3824) is a local favorite serving food at a well-worn Formica counter. Across the road in more salubrious surroundings is **Union Street Grill** (477 5th St., 250/897-0081; Mon.–Fri. 11 A.M.–9 P.M., Sat.–Sun. 11:30 A.M.–9 P.M.). Come here for well-priced global choices that include a delicious jambalaya ($15.50) and expertly prepared fish from local waters ($14–19). Save room for a slice of chocolate mocha fudge cake ($6). Also in downtown Courtenay is the **Rose Tea Room** (180 5th St., 250/897-1007; Mon.–Sat. 10 A.M.–5 P.M.), a friendly little place where older locals catch up over simple sandwiches, scones and tea, and decadent rocky road brownies.

Occupying one of Courtenay's original residences, the **Old House Restaurant** (1760 Riverside Lane, 250/338-5406) sits among landscaped gardens right on the river. Downstairs is a casual restaurant/pub with a large outdoor deck, while upstairs is a more formal eatery with the ambience of an elegant country lodge. Both are open daily for lunch and dinner, with the Sunday brunch buffet (10 A.M.–2 P.M.; $17) filling the restaurant with hungry patrons.

Within the waterfront grounds of **Filberg Heritage Lodge** is a small café (Comox Ave. at Filberg Rd., 250/339-2715; Mon.–Fri. 11 A.M.–3 P.M., Sat.–Sun. 11 A.M.–5 P.M.), with picnic tables spread out under mature trees. A delightful setting more than makes up for the uninspiring café fare.

Information

Comox Valley Visitor Info Centre (2040 Cliffe Ave., 250/334-3234, www.comoxvalleychamber.com; summer daily 8:30 A.M.–6 P.M., the rest of the year Mon.–Fri. 9 A.M.–6 P.M.) is on the main highway leading into Courtenay—look for the totem pole out front. Information is also available at **Cumberland Visitor Info Centre** (2755 Dunsmuir Ave., 250/336-8313).

Transportation

Getting to Courtenay by public transportation is easy. The most scenic way to arrive from Victoria is aboard VIA Rail's **Malahat** train (250/383-4324, www.viarail.ca). This service terminates in Courtenay, departing Victoria Monday–Saturday at 8:15 A.M., Sunday at noon. Similarly priced, **Island Coach Lines** (250/334-2475 or 800/318-0818) runs buses 3–5 times daily between Victoria and Courtenay, continuing north to Campbell River and Port Hardy.

BC Ferries (250/386-3431, www.bcferries.com) sails four times daily between Comox and Powell River, allowing mainlanders easy access to midisland beaches and snow slopes and saving visitors to northern Vancouver Island from having to backtrack down to Nanaimo or Victoria. To get to the terminal stay on Highway 19 through Courtenay, then take Ryan Road east to Anderton Road. Turn left and follow the signs down Ellenor Road to the terminal. The regular one-way fare for this 75-minute sailing is adult $8, child $4, vehicle $27. Round-trip travelers can save 15 percent by buying the **Circlepac** ticket, good for round-trip travel from mainland British Columbia and ferry connections along the Sunshine Coast.

NORTH TOWARD CAMPBELL RIVER

An enjoyable place to pitch a tent, **Miracle Beach Provincial Park** is about three kilometers (1.9 miles) off the main highway, 23 kilometers (14.3 miles) north of Courtenay. Highlights include a wooded campground, sandy beach, good swimming and fishing, and nature trails. Look for porpoises and seals at the mouth of Black Creek, orcas in the Strait of Georgia, black-tailed deer, black bear, and raccoons in the park, and seabirds and crabs along the shoreline. In summer you can take a nature walk with a park naturalist, participate in a clambake or barbecue, or watch demonstrations and films at the Miracle Beach Nature House. Campsites cost $22 per night.

A few kilometers north of Miracle Beach and 18 kilometers (11.2 miles) south of Campbell River is **Salmon Point Resort** (2176 Salmon Point Rd., 250/923-6605 or 866/246-6605, www.salmonpoint.com), also offering great views of the Strait of Georgia and the snowcapped peaks of the Coast Mountains. Facilities are excellent, including a restaurant overlooking the water, a couple of recreation rooms (one for adults only), fishing guide service and tackle, boat rentals ($70 per day), a heated pool, heated bathrooms, and a laundry. All campsites sit among small stands of pines; tents $20, hookups $27–33. Cottages range $75–150 per night.

Northern Vancouver Island

The northern section of Vancouver Island is mountainous, heavily treed, dotted with lakes, riddled with rivers and waterfalls, and almost completely unsettled. Just one main highway serves the region, though hundreds of kilometers of logging roads penetrate the dense forests. The gateway to the north is **Campbell River,** another small city that proudly calls itself the "Salmon Capital of the World." From this point north, the Island Highway follows a winding route over mountains and through valleys, first hitting the coast near **Telegraph Cove,** one of Canada's most photogenic communities and the departure point for orca-watching trips to the nutrient-rich waters of Johnstone Strait and Robson Bight. The island's northernmost town is **Port Hardy,** terminus for ferries heading north to Prince Rupert and the gateway to the wild west coast and **Cape Scott Provincial Park.**

CAMPBELL RIVER

A gateway to the wilderness of northern Vancouver Island, this city of 30,000 stretches along Discovery Passage 260 kilometers (162 miles) north of Victoria and 235 kilometers (146 miles) southeast of Port Hardy. Views from town—of tree-covered Quadra Island and the magnificent white-topped mountains of mainland British Columbia—are superb, but most visitors come for the salmon fishing. The underwater topography creates the prime angling conditions; Georgia Strait ends just south of Campbell River, and Discovery Passage begins. The waterway suddenly narrows to a width of only two kilometers (1.2 miles) between Vancouver and Quadra Islands, causing some of the strongest tides on the coast, attracting bait fish, and forcing thousands of migrating salmon to concentrate off Campbell River, much to every angler's delight.

Sights
The best place to absorb some of the local atmosphere is **Discovery Pier.** The 180-meter-long (590-foot-long) pier is fun to walk on

whether you're into fishing or not. Its benches and protected shelters allow proper appreciation of the marina, strait, mainland mountains, and fishing action, even on wet and windy days.

The **Museum at Campbell River** (corner of Island Hwy. and 5th Ave., 250/287-3103; May–Sept. Mon.–Tues. 9 A.M.–5 P.M., Sun. noon–4 P.M., the rest of the year Tues.–Sun. noon–4 P.M.; $4) sits on four hectares (10 acres) overlooking Discovery Passage. First check out the photos and interesting written snippets that provide a look at Campbell River's early beginnings. Then feast your eyes on mystical artifacts, a huge collection of masks, exciting artwork, baskets, woven articles, carved-wood boxes, colorful button blankets, petroglyphs, and totem poles. Worth watching in the museum's theater is *Devil Beneath the Sea,* a documentary cataloging the destruction of nearby Ripple Rock by the world's largest nonnuclear explosion. Finish up in the gift shop, where you can buy stunning native prints, masks, postcards, and other paraphernalia.

Soak up native culture at the **Gildas Theatre** (Discovery Harbour Centre, 1370 Island Hwy., 250/287-7310). Through song, dance, and storytelling, performers tell the story of a young Laichwiltach man who learns about the world of spirits by traveling beyond the confines of his village. Performances run mid-June to mid-September Tuesday–Saturday at 4 P.M., with an extra show at 1 P.M. on Saturday. Admission is adult $15, child $7.50.

Fishing
A major attraction about Campbell River is that the fishing can be enjoyed by all ages and on all budgets—a father and son can fish off the pier while Bill Gates may be jetting in over the top to a private island. May through October is peak season for salmon fishing, but fishing is also good for steelhead (peak season is Jan.–April) and cutthroat trout (Mar.–May).

Regardless of whether you're a first-timer or an old timer, **Discovery Pier,** right downtown, is a

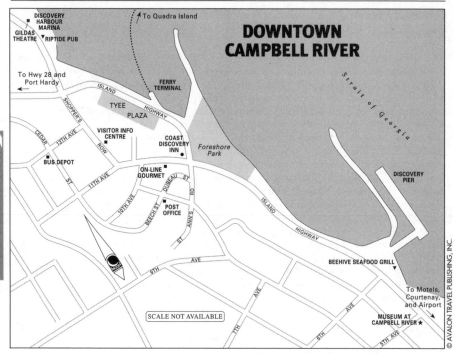

fantastic place to fish for salmon. The pier sports built-in rod holders, fish-cleaning stations, glassed-in shelters for non-anglers, and colorful signs describing the fish you're likely to catch. Anglers cast for salmon, bottomfish, and the occasional steelhead, hauling them up in nets on long ropes. When the salmon are running, the pier gets extremely busy, and for a reason—chinook salmon over 14 kilograms (30 pounds) are not uncommon. Rod rentals are available on the pier ($3.50 per hour, $9 per half day, $17 per day). Don't forget; you also need a license.

If you're fishing between July 15 and September 15, you may want to try qualifying for **Tyee Club** membership (www.tyeeclub.org). This club (its name is a native word meaning "chief"), famous among anglers around the world, has been dedicated to upholding the traditional methods of sportfishing since 1924. Several rules must be followed in order to become a member: You have to preregister your intent to fish under club rules; troll from a rowboat in the mouth of the Camp-

bell River without using a motor; use a rod 1.8–2.7 meters (6–9 feet) long, an artificial lure, and a line not more than 9 kilograms (20 pounds) pretested breaking weight; then catch a trophy-size tyee (a chinook weighing over 14 kilograms/30 pounds).

The local information center will help out with basic fishing and boat charter information, or head to the experts at the **River Sportsman** (2115 Island Hwy., 250/286-1017) for licenses, tackle, and maybe a few tips.

Accommodations

As Campbell River is a resort, every kind of accommodation you could possibly want is here, from campgrounds and RV parks to luxury hotels and exclusive fishing lodges.

Along the highway south of town only the road separates several motels from Discovery Channel. If you want to save your money for a fishing charter, no worries—book a room at the **Big Rock Motel** (1020 Island Hwy.,

250/923-4211 or 877/923-4211; $58 s, $68 d), your average two-story, cinder-block motel. Continuing north you'll come to the **Best Western Austrian Chalet** (462 Island Hwy., 250/923-4231 or 800/667-7207), with a wide range of facilities including an indoor pool, a sauna, a restaurant and pub, and even a putting green. Rates start at $99 s, $109 d ($10 extra for an ocean view). Through Campbell River to the north is **Friendship Inn Motel** (3900 Island Hwy., 250/287-9591; $58 s, $64 d), another reasonable cheapie. RV sites here are $28. Right downtown, **Coast Discovery Inn** (975 Shopper's Row, 250/287-7155 or 800/663-1144, www.coasthotels.com; $135 s, $145 d) is a full-service hotel with a fitness room, restaurant, and pub.

Bed-and-breakfast accommodations are provided by **Pier House** (670 Island Hwy., 250/287-2943; $60–80 s, $80–100 d), across the road from Discovery Pier. The old antique-filled house has a library and three guest rooms with shared or private bathrooms. Rates include a cooked breakfast.

N Painters Lodge (1625 MacDonald Rd., 250/286-1102 or 800/663-7090, www.painterslodge.com; Mar.–Oct.) is one of the better-value fishing lodges. It's a grandly presented property that wouldn't look out of place in the English countryside, except that it's not. It's built right on Discovery Passage, with a private marina and every facility a serious angler could ask for. There's also a pool, a restaurant, and free boat shuttles to a sister resort on nearby Quadra Island. Most guests stay as part of a package (for example, $600 for three days, inclusive of flights from Vancouver, accommodation, and fishing trips), but you can also book a room for $189 per night ($229 with a water view).

Camping

Many campgrounds line the highway south of town, but although they're close to the water, the surroundings are generally nothing special. One of the better choices is **Campbell River Fishing Village and RV Park** (260 Island Hwy., 250/287-3630, www.fishingvillage.bc.ca), two kilometers (1.2 miles) south of downtown. As the name suggests, it's set up for anglers, with boat rentals, guided charters, rentals (everything from rods to depth sounders), a tackle shop, and fish-freezing facilities. Other amenities include a playground, laundry, and communal fire pit. Sites are $20–25 per night. On the north side of the city, RVers can park their rigs beside the **Friendship Inn Motel** (3900 Island Hwy., 250/287-9591) for $28 per night. Less-commercial options with limited facilities include **Elk Falls Provincial Park,** six kilometers (3.7 miles) west of town on Highway 28, and **Loveland Bay Provincial Park,** on the shore of Campbell Lake 20 kilometers (12 miles) west of town; $14 and $11, respectively.

Food

One of the best places to go for a meal is the two-story **Beehive Seafood Grill** (921 Island Hwy., 250/286-6812; daily 11 A.M.–10 P.M.), overlooking Discovery Pier and the marina from an absolute waterfront location. The house specialty is, of course, seafood, including clam chowder for $5.50, fish and chips for around $11, and salmon, cooked however you prefer, for $19. Farther north along the harborfront is **Riptide Pub** (1340 Island Hwy., 250/830-0044; daily for lunch and dinner), which is a good place for a full meal, although it doesn't take full advantage of its waterfront location (unless you score a table on the glassed-in patio). The sleek interior is a little nicer than you may imagine while the food is exactly what you'd expect—fresh scallops, oysters, mussels, halibut and salmon (mains $12–20). Save room for a slice of cheesecake.

Information and Services

Park in the large parking lot of **Tyee Plaza** and you're within easy walking distance of the information center and all services. At the front of the parking lot is **Campbell River Visitor Info Centre** (1235 Shopper's Row, 250/287-4636; summer daily 8 A.M.–8 P.M., the rest of the year Mon.–Fri. 9 A.M.–5 P.M.). Aside from tons of brochures, free tourist papers, and information on both the local area and Vancouver Island in general, the knowledgeable staff can answer just about any question on the area you could think

Vancouver Island

up. For other information contact **Campbell River Tourism** (250/286-1616, www.campbellrivertourism.com).

Other plaza tenants include banks, a big box grocery store, a laundry, and various family-style eateries. Across from the plaza is the **post office** (Beech St.) and **On-Line Gourmet** (970 Shoppers Row, 250/286-6521; closed Sun.), where you can check your email for a small charge. The **hospital** is at 375 2nd Avenue (250/287-7111).

Transportation

Campbell River Airport, off Erickson Road 20 kilometers (12 miles) south of downtown, is served by **Pacific Coastal** (800/663-2872) from Vancouver. For transportation between the airport and accommodations, call the **Campbell River Airporter** (250/286-3000). From Victoria, **Island Coach Lines** (250/287-7151) operates 3–5 buses daily to Campbell River, with at least one continuing north to Port Hardy timed to link with the ferry departing for Prince Rupert. The bus depot is on Cedar Street behind the Royal Bank.

Get around town by **Campbell River Transit System** (250/287-7433; $2 per sector) departing from Tyee Plaza via Shopper's Row. Rental-car agencies in Campbell River include: **Budget** (250/923-4283), **National** (250/923-1234), and **Rent-a-wreck** (250/287-8353).

QUADRA ISLAND

A 10-minute ferry ride across Discovery Passage from downtown Campbell River takes you to Quadra Island (pop. 2,500), which blends beautiful scenery, native culture, and upscale fishing lodges to create a unique and worthwhile detour from your up-island travels. The ferry docks in the south of the island, where most of the population resides. This narrow peninsula widens in the north to an unpopulated area where provincial and marine parks protect a wealth of wildlife. Marinelife around the entire shoreline is widespread; orcas cruise Discovery Passage, and seals and sea lions are commonly spied in surrounding waters.

Captain Vancouver may have been the first European to step onto the island when he made landfall at **Cape Mudge** in 1792, but the island had been inhabited by native people for many centuries before. Learn about the island's long and rich native history at the **Kwagiulth Museum** (Cape Mudge Village, 250/285-3733; summer Mon.–Sat. 10 A.M.–4:30 P.M. and Sun. noon–4:30 P.M., the rest of the year Tues.–Sat. 10 A.M.–4:30 P.M.; adult $4, senior and child $3). This excellent facility displays a wide variety of ceremonial dresses used in potlatches, as well as masks and other native artifacts. Native petroglyphs found at the island's southern end have been moved to the museum grounds and can be viewed at any time.

At the island's southern tip, **Cape Mudge Lighthouse** was built in 1898 to prevent shipwrecks in the wild surging waters around the point. On the east coast is **Heriot Bay,** the name of both a cove and the island's largest community. Narrow Rebecca Spit, site of **Rebecca Spit Marine Park,** protects a beach-lined bay from the elements. Roads lead north from Heriot Bay to the island's wild northern reaches, where you can go hiking to the low summit of **Chinese Mountain** (three kilometers/1.9 miles; allow one hour each way); around **Morte Lake** (five kilometers/3.1 miles; allow 90 minutes for the loop), and in the far north to **Newton Lake** from Granite Bay (four kilometers/2.4 miles; 75 minutes each way).

Practicalities

Adjacent to Cape Mudge Lighthouse is **M Tsa-Kwa-Luten Lodge** (250/285-2042 or 800/665-7745, www.capemudgeresort.com). Built by the local Kwagiulth people, the centerpiece of this magnificent waterfront lodge is the foyer, built in the style of a bighouse (a traditional meeting place) using locally milled woods. Each of the 35 spacious rooms is decorated in northwest native theme, and each has a private balcony with water views. Rates start at a reasonable $125 s or d, with meal packages available. The lodge coordinates fishing charters and cultural activities, and its restaurant specializes in native foods.

Another option is **Heriot Bay Inn** (Heriot Bay Rd., 250/285-3322, www.heriotbayinn .com), a historic lodging with a full-service marina, a restaurant, a pub with a great ocean side deck, and kayak and mountain-bike rentals. Rooms are $84 s or d (as low as $50 in winter), including breakfast, and cottages cost $129 per night. The inn also offers a campground; $15 for tents, $20–22 with full hookups. Another option for campers is the charming **We Wai Kai Campground** (250/285-3111, www.wwkamp-site.com), along a pleasant beach at the head of Heriot Bay. Regular sites are $19, or pay $2 extra for water views.

BC Ferries (250/286-1412) offers services from Campbell River to the island, every hour on the hour 6 A.M.–11 P.M.; round-trip fare is adult $5.25, child $2.75, vehicle $13. For a cab, call **Quadra Taxi** (250/285-3598).

CORTES ISLAND

Accessible by ferry from Quadra Island, Cortes Island (pronounced cor-TEZ—it was named by an early Spanish explorer) is a relatively remote place, closer to the mainland than to Vancouver Island. Few visitors venture out here, but those who do are rarely disappointed. Aside from three small villages, the island remains in its natural state. **Manson's Landing Provincial Park** is a beautiful little spot sandwiched between a large tidal lagoon and the forested shoreline of **Hague Lake.** In the south of the island is **Smelt Bay Provincial Park,** another great spot for swimming, beachcombing, and taking in the unique island environment.

Practicalities

Accommodations on the island are limited, so unless you plan to camp, make reservations before coming over. **Smelt Bay Provincial Park,** 25 kilometers (15.5 miles) from the ferry terminal, offers campsites for $14 per site. Closer to the terminal, **Gorge Harbour Marina Resort** (Hunt Rd., Gorge Harbour, 250/935-6433) offers tent sites ($15) and full hookups ($21) beside the island's main marina, as well as four rooms ($70 s or d for bed and breakfast), bike and boat rentals,

fishing charters, and a restaurant. **Mansons Landing Community Hall** (weekdays only) is home to a small café and the post office.

The island has no official visitor center. You can get an idea of island life by checking out the online version of the local newspaper (www.corte-sisland.com), which has everything you'll need to know for a visit, as well as things you probably don't want to know, such as where to purchase the annual calendar of naked residents.

The ferry trip between Heriot Bay on Quadra Island and Cortes Island takes 40 minutes. **BC Ferries** (250/286-1412) operates scheduled service between the two islands six times daily, with the first departing Quadra Island at 9 A.M. and the last departing Cortes Island at 5:50 P.M. Peak round-trip fare is adult $6.25, child $3.50, vehicle $15.75.

HIGHWAY 28

Running from the east coast to the west coast through the northern section of magnificent **Strathcona Provincial Park,** Highway 28 is another island road worth traveling for the scenery alone. The first place to stop is 1,087-hectare (2,690-acre) **Elk Falls Provincial Park,** six kilometers (3.7 miles) west of Campbell River. Here you can follow beautiful forest trails to waterfalls, go swimming and fishing, and stay the night (Apr.–Oct.) in a wooded campsite; $14 per night, no showers. Not far beyond the park, the highway parallels Upper Campbell Lake for 20 kilometers (12 miles) before splitting, with the main highway continuing west to Gold River and a side road following the east shore of Buttle Lake into Strathcona Provincial Park.

Strathcona Provincial Park

British Columbia's oldest and Vancouver Island's largest park, Strathcona preserves a vast 250,000-hectare (617,800-acre) wilderness in the northern center of Vancouver Island. Vancouver Island's highest peak, 2,220-meter (7,280-foot) **Golden Hinde,** is within the park. The peak was named for Sir Francis Drake's ship, in which he circumnavigated the world in the 1570s (some believe he would have sighted the peak from his ship). The

Vancouver Island

park's other superlative natural features include 440-meter-high (1,440-foot-high) **Della Falls,** one of North America's highest waterfalls (see *Port Alberni and Vicinity*) and a 1,000-year-old, 93-meter-high (300-foot-high) Douglas fir, British Columbia's tallest known tree. Douglas fir and western red cedar carpet the valley, and wild-flowers—lupine, Indian paintbrush, moss campion, and kinnikinnick—cover the high slopes. Resident mammals include black bears, wolves, wolverines, cougars, marmots, deer, and the island's only herd of elk. Cutthroat trout, rainbow trout, and Dolly Varden fill the park's lakes. And all kinds of birds soar the skies , including the provincial bird, the Steller's jay.

You'll get a taste of Strathcona's beauty along Highway 28, but to get into the park proper turn south off Highway 28 halfway between Campbell River and Gold River. This access road hugs the eastern shore of **Buttle Lake,** passing many well-marked nature walks and hiking trails. One of the first is the short walk (10 minutes each way) to **Lupin Falls,** which are more impressive than the small creek across from the parking lot would suggest. Continuing south along the lakeshore past driftwood-strewn beaches, you'll come to the **Karst Creek Trail** (two-kilometer/1.2-mile loop; allow 40 minutes), which passes through a karst landscape of sinkholes and disappearing streams. At the lake's southern end, where the road crosses Thelwood Creek, a six-kilometer (3.7-mile) trail (2.5 hours each way) climbs a steep valley to **Bedwell Lake** and surrounding alpine meadows.

As the road continues around the lakeshore, look for **Myra Falls** across the water. After passing through the Westmin Resources mining operation, the road ends on the edge of an old-growth forest. From this point, explore on foot by taking the **Upper Myra Falls Trail** (three kilometers/1.9 miles; one hour each way) to a lookout point above the falls.

Apart from numerous picnic areas along the shore of Buttle Lake, the only facilities within the park are two campgrounds. **Buttle Lake Campground** is beside Buttle Lake, just west of the junction of Highway 28 and the park access road. **Ralph River Campground** is farther south, on the shore of Buttle Lake. Both have pit toilets, picnic tables, and fire rings, and both charge $14 per night.

Gold River

Those looking for a glimpse of Vancouver Island away from the touristy east coast will find the 90-kilometer (56-mile) drive west from Campbell River to Gold River (pop. 1,400) both enjoyable and interesting. Boat tours into Nootka Sound make the trip even more worthwhile.

Beyond the west boundary of Strathcona Provincial Park, Highway 28 descends along the Heber River to its confluence with the Gold River, where the town lies. Built in 1965 to house employees of a pulp mill, it was the first all-electric town in Canada. The orderly streets seem a little out of place amid the surrounding wilderness, which is why most residents and visitors alike are drawn to the area. The natural highlight of Gold River is **Upana Caves,** but unless you're a spelunker, chances are you've never heard of them. The caves, accessed 16 kilometers (10 miles) west of town from Head Bay Forest Road, are the largest cave system north of Mexico and include a river that flows underground for 150 meters (500 feet) through eroded limestone bedrock. Meanwhile, anglers and kayakers head out to Muchalat Inlet while golfers walk the fairways of the town's nine-hole course simply because it's there.

Rooms at the **Ridgeview Motor Inn** (395 Donner Court, 250/283-2277 or 800/989-3393; $95–130 s or d) were a lot nicer than I expected, and each comes with a fridge, TV, and phone. A light breakfast is included in the rates. The adjacent pub/restaurant serves up decent food. The **Lions Campground,** on the edge of town, has unserviced sites.

At the entrance to town, make a stop at the **Gold River Visitor Info Centre** (Muchalat Dr., 250/283-2418, www.goldriver.ca; mid-May–Aug. daily 9 A.M.–4:30 P.M.).

Nootka Sound and Beyond

Unless you're into caving, the best reason to travel west from Campbell River is to take a cruise along Muchalat Inlet to Nootka Sound. The

MV *Uchuck III* (250/283-2325, www.mvuchuck. com), a converted World War II minesweeper, departs year-round from the dock at the end of Highway 28 (14 kilometers/8.7 miles west from Gold River). Its primary purpose is dropping supplies at remote west coast communities and logging camps, but interested visitors are more than welcome and are made to feel comfortable by the hardworking crew. The main sailing departs year-round every Monday at 9 A.M. for **Tahsis** and **Zeballos,** with an overnight stop in the latter included in the rate of $185 s, $295 d ($65 for children). The one-way fare to Zeballos is $40 (but you'll need to make lodging arrangements because the return trip departs the following morning. A second sailing departs year-round Thursday at 7 A.M., heading out to the open ocean and up the coast to **Kyuquot.** This is also an overnight trip, with meals and accommodations included in the price of $245 s, $385 d ($95 for children). A third sailing departs mid-June to mid-September every Wednesday at 10 A.M., visiting two points of historical interest: the spot where in 1778 Captain James Cook and his men became the first Europeans to land on the west coast, and **Friendly Cove,** where in 1792 Captain George Vancouver and Don Juan Francisco de la Bodega y Quadra negotiated possession of Nootka Sound territory. Fare for this six-hour tour is adult $40, senior $37, child $20.

Tahsis is also accessible by road from Gold River (70 kilometers/43.5 miles one-way), from where another logging road continues north to **Zeballos.** Gold was discovered in the region in the late 1700s, but it was over a century later, in 1924, that mining began on the Zeballos River. The mining took place inland, but the township grew on the ocean, where supplies were dropped off and the ore shipped out. Mining continued until 1948, but a road linking Zeballos to the outside world wasn't completed until 1970. Today, Zeballos is a quiet backwater, a base for commercial and recreational fishing boats, and home to a couple of small lodges. Contact the local information center (250/761-4070, www.zeballos.com) for information.

NORTH TO PORT McNEILL

Highway 19, covering the 235 kilometers (146 miles) between Campbell River and Port Hardy, is a good, fast road with plenty of straight stretches and not much traffic. Passing through kilometer after kilometer of relatively untouched wilderness, with only logged hillsides to remind you of the ugliness humanity can produce with such ease, it's almost as though you've entered another world, or at least another island. Stop at all the frequent rest areas for the very best views of deep blue mountains, white peaks, sparkling rivers and lakes, and cascading waterfalls.

The last town before Highway 19 jogs inland is **Sayward,** a small logging town (pop. 1,000) on Johnstone Strait. Down on the waterfront, the main attraction is the **log sort,** where cut logs from active logging areas are brought to be sorted for transportation south.

After taking a convoluted inland route for 130 kilometers (81 miles), Highway 19 returns to the coastline at **Port McNeill,** another logging town. Larger than Sayward, it's the regional headquarters for three logging companies and home of "the world's largest burl," on the main highway two kilometers (1.2 miles) north of town at the entrance to a logging company office—you can't miss it. The center of town comprises a shopping plaza and industrial waterfront development. Port McNeill is also the jumping-off point for ferry trips to Alert Bay and Malcolm Island.

TELEGRAPH COVE

Most visitors come to Telegraph Cove to go whale-watching on Johnstone Strait (see sidebar), but the village itself is well worth the eight-kilometer (five-mile) detour from the highway just east of Port McNeill. Built around a deep sheltered harbor, it's one of the last existing "boardwalk" communities on the island. Many of the buildings stand on stilts and pilings over the water, linked by a boardwalk.

Fewer than five people live here year-round, but the population swells enormously during late

Vancouver Island

WHALE-WATCHING IN JOHNSTONE STRAIT

More than 50 whale-watching operations have sprung up around Vancouver Island in recent years, but the opportunity to view orcas (killer whales) close up in Johnstone Strait is unparalleled. These magnificent, intelligent mammals spend the summer in the waters around Telegraph Cove and are most concentrated in **Robson Bight,** where they rub on the gravel beaches near the mouth of the Tsitka River, an area that has been established as a sanctuary for the whales.

Stubbs Island Whale Watching (250/928-3185 or 800/665-3066, www.stubbs-island .com) was the province's first whale-watching company, and continues to lead the way in responsible whale watching. The company's two boats, *Lukwa* and *Gikumi,* depart daily from Telegraph Cove on 3–4-hour cruises from late May to early October. The experienced crew takes you out to view the whales in their natural

© JIM BORROWMAN

habitat and to hear their mysterious and beautiful sounds through a hydrophone (underwater microphone). Both boats are comfortable, with covered areas and bathrooms.

The cost of the cruise is adult $75, senior or child 1–12 $65. Reservations are required and you should call ahead as far as possible to ensure a spot. Dress warmly and don't forget your camera for this experience of a lifetime.

spring and summer when whale-watching, diving, and fishing charters do a roaring trade, canoeists and kayakers arrive to paddle along Johnstone Strait, and the campground opens for the season. Walk along the boardwalk, passing cabins, kayak rentals, an interpretive center, the **Killer Whale Café and Old Saltry Pub,** and a store selling groceries and fishing tackle.

A two-hour boat ride across Johnstone Strait from Telegraph Cove is **Knight Inlet,** home to a large population of grizzly bears. **Tide Rip Grizzly Tours** (250/928-3090 or 888/643-9319, www.tiderip.com) has bear-watching tours departing Telegraph Cove daily mid-May to mid-October. For the first two months, when the bears come down to waterline to feed, the boat doesn't dock, but from mid-August onward, when bears are feeding on salmon, the tour includes two hours spent in a specially built bear

viewing platform. The tour cost is $325 per person ($229 early in the season).

Accommodations and Lodging

Many of the buildings on the boardwalk have been converted to guest accommodations and can be rented by the night (reserve well in advance). The quarters range from extremely basic cabins ($90 s or d) to three-bedroom self-contained apartments ($250). About the only thing they have in common is the incredible setting. Overlooking the cove, **Wastell Manor** has been restored, with the four well-furnished guest rooms ranging $145–175. A short walk from the village is a campground with wooded sites, showers, a laundry, boat launch, and store. Sites are $20–25. For reservations in Telegraph Cove, contact **Telegraph Cove Resorts** (250/928-3131, www .telegraphcoveresort.com).

MALCOLM ISLAND

This largish island, immediately offshore from Port McNeill, is home to around 800, most of whom live in the village of **Sointula.** The first European settlers were of Finnish descent. They arrived around 1900, after migrating across Canada in search of a remote, peaceful place to call their own. Meaning "harmony" in Finnish, Sointula evolved as a socialist community where everyone shared everything. To some extent, these utopian ideals continue to this day, with descendants of the original settlers operating a fleet of fishing boats and the general store as cooperatives. In town, wander along the residential streets and admire the trim homes and well-tended gardens, then walk the three-kilometer (1.9-mile) Mateoja Trail from the end of 3rd Street to a popular bird-watching spot, Big Lake.

Practicalities

One of the many upscale fishing lodges scattered through this part of the world is **M Sund's Lodge** (250/973-6381, www.sundslodge.com; mid-June–early Sept.), on a beautiful waterfront property east of Sointula. It is everything a luxurious fishing lodge should be, but is a completely unpretentious family-run operation. Inside the spacious guest cabins you'll find super-comfortable beds, log furniture, top-notch bathrooms, and original art. Guests stay as part of all-inclusive packages, which include memorable meals and as much guided fishing as you can handle. Drive across the island to **Bere Point** to reach the island's only official campground.

The easiest way to reach Malcolm Island is with **BC Ferries** (250/956-4533), which makes the short run across Broughton Strait around eight times daily. The round-trip fare is adult $6.25, child $3.25, vehicle $15.75.

M ALERT BAY (CORMORANT ISLAND)

This fascinating village is the only settlement on crescent-shaped Cormorant Island, which lies in Broughton Strait 45 minutes by ferry from Port McNeill. The island's population of 600 is evenly split between natives and nonnatives.

Alert Bay holds plenty of history. Captain Vancouver landed there in the late 1700s, and it's been a supply stop for fur traders and gold miners on their way to Alaska, a place for ships to stock up on water, and home base to an entire fishing fleet. Today the village is one of the region's major fishing and marine service centers, and it holds two fish-processing and -packing plants. Half the island is owned by the Kwakiutl, whose powerful art draws visitors to Alert Bay.

Sights

All the island's numerous attractions can be reached on foot or by bicycle. Start by wandering through the village to appreciate the early-20th-century waterfront buildings and the colorful totems decorating **Nimpkish Burial Ground.**

For an outstanding introduction to the fascinating culture and heritage of the Kwakiutl, don't miss the **U'Mista Cultural Centre** (Front St., 250/974-5403; Mon.–Fri. 9 A.M.–5 P.M., Sat. noon–5 P.M.; adult $7, senior $6, child $3). Built to house a ceremonial potlatch collection confiscated by the federal government after a 1921 ban on potlatches, the center contains masks and other Kwakiutl art and artifacts. Take a guided tour through the center, then wander at leisure past the photos and colorful displays to watch two award-winning films produced by the center—one explains the origin and meaning of the potlatch. The center also teaches local children the native language, culture, song, and dance.

Also on the north end of the island you'll find the **Indian Bighouse,** the world's second tallest totem pole (it's 53 meters/174 feet high—the highest is in Victoria), and the historic century-old **Anglican Church.** Take a boardwalk stroll through the intriguing ecological area called **Gator Gardens** to see moss-draped forests, ghostly black-water swamps, and lots of ravens, bald eagles, and other birds.

Practicalities

The island's least expensive accommodation is **Alert Bay Camping** (250/974-5213; 12–18 per night), overlooking Broughton Strait, with a cookhouse and barbecues. The **Nimpkish Hotel** (318 Fir St., 250/974-2324 or 800/888/646-7547, www.nimpkishhotel.com) has four small, simple rooms ($60 s or d) and downstairs restaurant with tables that sprawl outside to a wide waterfront deck.

BC Ferries (250/956-4533) runs to the island from Port McNeill many times daily, with most sailings stopping en route at Malcolm Island. The peak round-trip fare is adult $6.25, child $3.25. You can take a vehicle over for

$15.75 round-trip, but there's no real point because everything on the island is reachable on foot.

Across from the waterfront is **Alert Bay Visitor Info Centre** (116 Fir St., 250/974-5024; summer daily 9 A.M.–6 P.M., the rest of the year Mon.–Fri. 9 A.M.–5 P.M.).

PORT HARDY

Port Hardy (pop. 4,600) lies along sheltered Hardy Bay, 235 kilometers (146 miles) north of

Campbell River and 495 kilometers (308 miles) north of Victoria. It's the largest community north of Campbell River and the terminus for ferries sailing the Inside Passage to and from Prince Rupert. The ferry is the main reason most people drive this far north, but Port Hardy is also a good base from which to explore the wild and untamed northern tip of the island or fish for salmon in the sheltered waters of "King Coho Country."

Sights and Recreation

As you enter the Port Hardy area, take the scenic route to town via Hardy Bay Road. You'll pass several original chainsaw woodcarvings and skirt the edge of peaceful Hardy Bay before entering downtown via Market Street.

One of the most enjoyable things to do in town is to stroll along the **seawalk** to **Tsulquate Park,** where you can appreciate native carvings and do some beachcombing if the tide is out. Many bald eagles reside around the bay, and if you're lucky you'll see them swooping about in the neighborhood. Also along the seawalk, you'll pass **Watchman's Bay,** where another chainsaw woodcarving holds representations of the fishing, logging, and mining industries that support the town, and **Carrot Park,** with its unusual "Mile Zero Trans Carrot" sculpture. For years the residents of northern Vancouver Island pleaded for a link with the populated south. Throughout the years various governments made promises and "dangled the carrot" but never came through with the money required to complete the task. Eventually north islanders launched a massive Carrot Campaign, using every means possible to spread the word of their plight. When the campaign became an item on national radio and television, the government relented, kicking in "the rest of the carrot."

Another interesting place to spend a little time is the small **Port Hardy Museum** (7110 Market St., 250/949-8143; Tues.–Sat. noon–4:30 P.M.). Browse through artifacts and an old photograph collection, finishing up in the gift shop, where you can buy books, postcards, T-shirts with native designs, and crafts by local artists.

© ANDREW HEMPSTEAD

Vancouver Island

heading north with BC Ferries

At **Quatse River Hatchery** (Byng Rd., 250/949-9022; Mon.–Fri. 8 A.M.–4:30 P.M.), on the scenic Quatse River, you can observe incubation and rearing facilities for pink, chum, and coho salmon, as well as steelhead. Good fishing on the river attracts droves of anglers year-round, but the Quatse is by no means the only fishing game in town. With so much water—both salt and fresh—surrounding Port Hardy, visiting fisherfolk probably won't know where to start. Ask at the local sporting-goods store on Market Street for the best fishing spots, or take a fishing charter (inquire at the information center for current guides and skippers).

Accommodations and Camping

Accommodations in Port Hardy are limited and often fill up, especially on the night prior to ferry departures. Book ahead.

In a town of boring, overpriced motel rooms, ◾ **Bear Cove Cottages** (6715 Bear Cove Hwy., 250/949-7939 or 877/949-7939, www.bearcovecottages.ca) stands out—but there are only eight of them, so you'll need to reserve well in advance. Located right near the ferry terminal, 10 kilometers (6.2 miles) out of town, they sit in a neat row high above the ocean but with stunning water views. Each modern unit comes with a compact but well-designed kitchen, fireplace, bathroom with jetted tub, and private deck. Between May and September the rates are $125 s or d, while the rest of the year the price drops to $75.

South of downtown, two hotels overlook Port Hardy's busy harbor from the marina. The **Quarterdeck Inn** (6555 Hardy Bay Rd., 250/902-0455 or 877/902-0459, www.quarterdeckresort .net) offers harbor views from each of its 40 small-ish rooms. Facilities include a fitness room, sauna, and a laundry. At $100–120 s or d (including a light breakfast) and relative to the other town motels, this place is good value. The adjacent **Glen Lyon Inn** (6435 Hardy Bay Rd., 250/949-7115 or 877/949-7115, www.glenlyoninn.com) has rooms in an original wing for $90 s, $95 d and larger, newer, and much nicer rooms in a 2000 addition for $115 s, $125 d.

Both Port Hardy's commercial campgrounds are south of town, halfway around Hardy Bay to the ferry terminal. The pick of the two is **Quatse River Campground** (Byng Rd., 250/949-2395 or 866/949-2395), operated in conjunction with the adjacent salmon hatchery. Sites are shaded by a lush old-growth forest and you can fish in the river right off the camping area—then move over to the communal fire pit and recall stories of the one that got away. Unserviced sites are $16, or pay $20 for a site with power and water. In the vicinity is **Sunny Sanctuary Campground** (8080 Goodspeed Rd., 250/949-8111 or 866/251-4556), also on the Quatse River. Facilities include a barbecue shelter, modern bathrooms, firewood and fire rings, and a small store. The open and treed sites are $16–21.

Food

Port Hardy doesn't offer a large variety of dining options. Wander around town and you'll soon see what there is. At **Captain Hardy's** (Market St., 250/949-7133) the advertised breakfast specials are small and come on plastic plates, but cost only about $4. The rest of the day, this place offers good fish and chips from $6.

Dine at the **Oceanside Restaurant,** south of downtown in the Glen Lyon Inn (Hardy Bay Rd., 250/949-3050), for the opportunity to see bald eagles feeding right outside the window. The menu is fairly standard but well-priced, with many seafood choices. It's open daily for breakfast, lunch, and dinner.

Information

The energetic staff at the downtown **Port Hardy Visitor Info Centre** (7250 Market St., 250/949-7622; summer Mon.–Fri. 8:30 A.M.–6 P.M. and Sat.–Sun. 9 A.M.–5 P.M., the rest of the year Mon.–Fri. 8:30 A.M.–5 P.M.) will happily fill you in on everything there is to see and do in Port Hardy and beyond.

Getting There

Port Hardy Airport, 12 kilometers (7.5 miles) south of town, is served by **Pacific Coastal** (604/273-8666 or 800/663-2872) from Vancouver. It's a spectacular flight, with stunning views of the Coast Mountains for passengers seated on the plane's right side.

Airport facilities include parking ($3 per day), Budget and National rental-car outlets, and a small café. **North Island Transportation** (250/949-6300) offers twice-daily shuttle service between the airport and downtown.

Island Coach Lines (250/949-7532) operates once-daily bus service up the length of the island, scheduled to correspond with ferry departures. The departure of the southbound bus links with ferry arrivals. The journey between Victoria and Port Hardy takes a painful nine hours and costs around $100 one-way. The depot is the North Island Transportation Ltd. ticket office (7210 Market St.).

Getting Around

The local **bus depot** (7210 Market St., 250/949-6300) is the base for **North Island Transportation Ltd.** Head here for all your transportation needs; the company arranges transportation to the ferry terminal or airport, runs a taxi service, and also acts as ticket agent for Island Coach Lines.

Continuing North by Ferry

Most people arriving in Port Hardy do so with

the intention of continuing north with **BC Ferries** (250/386-3431 or 888/223-3779, www.bc-ferries.com) to Prince Rupert and beyond. The ferry terminal is at Bear Cove, 10 kilometers (6.2 miles) from downtown Port Hardy. The *Queen of the North* departs Port Hardy at 7:30 A.M. every second day, arriving in Prince Rupert the same evening at 10:30 P.M. The service runs year-round, but departures are less frequent outside of summer. Peak one-way fare is adult $106, child 5–11 $53, vehicle $240. (These peak-season fares are discounted up to 40 percent outside of summer.) A three-meal buffet package is offered for $45, and cabins cost $50–60 for the day. Make reservations as far in advance as possible in summer.

Prince Rupert is the northern terminus of the BC Ferries network. From there, you can head east along the Yellowhead Highway and explore northern British Columbia or jump aboard an Alaska Marine Highway ferry and continue north up the Inside Passage. (See *Prince Rupert* in the *Northern British Columbia* chapter).

Another option is the route dubbed the Discovery Coast Passage. BC Ferries sails two routes through this area, both departing Port Hardy. The main one is via Shearwater, then east up Dean Channel to Ocean Falls and Bella Coola. Sailings depart in either direction around every three days in summer. One-way fares between Port Hardy and Bella Coola are adult $110, child 5–11 $55, vehicle $215.

CAPE SCOTT PROVINCIAL PARK

Cape Scott Provincial Park encompasses 22,566 hectares (55,760 acres) of rugged coastal wilderness at the northernmost tip of Vancouver Is-

land. It's the place to go if you really want to get away from everything and everyone. Rugged trails, suitable for experienced hikers and outdoorspersons, lead through dense forests of cedar, pine, hemlock, and fir to 23 kilometers (14.3 miles) of beautiful sandy beaches and rocky promontories and headlands.

To get to the park boundary, you have to follow 67 kilometers (42 miles) of logging roads (remember that logging trucks always have the right of way), then hike in. Near the end of the road is a small Forest Service campground ($8 per night). The hiking trail to **Cape Scott Lighthouse** (23 kilometers/14.3 miles; about eight hours each way) is relatively level, but you'll need stout footwear. A cove east of the cape was once the site of an ill-fated Danish settlement. Around 100 Danes moved to the area in 1896, cutting themselves off from the rest of the world and forcing themselves to be totally self-sufficient. By 1930, the settlement was deserted, with many of the residents relocating to nearby Holberg.

A shorter alternative to the long trek out to the cape is the trail to beautiful **San Josef Bay** at the southern boundary of the park (2.5 kilometers/1.6 miles; 45 minutes each way).

Before setting off for the park, go by the Port Hardy Visitor Info Centre and pick up the park brochure and detailed logging-road maps for the area. Be well equipped for unpredictable weather, even in midsummer.

South of the park is rugged and remote **Raft Cove.** To get there turn off seven kilometers (4.3 miles) before the park, following a rough 12-kilometer (7.5-mile) logging road to a slight rise where the road ends. From this point, a narrow and rough trail leads 1.5 kilometers (.9 mile) to the cove.

Southwestern British Columbia

Once you've reluctantly decided to drag yourself away from Vancouver, you'll be confronted by a variety of things to see and do within a day's drive of the city.

Although British Columbia is best known for its mountains, a stretch of coastline northwest of Vancouver is a watery playground perfect for swimming, sunbathing on sandy beaches, canoeing and kayaking, beachcombing, scuba diving, boating, and fishing. Known as the **Sunshine Coast,** the region is reached by taking a ferry from Horseshoe Bay (west of North Vancouver) then continuing up Highway 101. The highway winds along the Strait of Georgia, passing seaside villages, provincial parks, and marine parks, and ending near **Powell River,** a large tourist town and service center. Powell River is the gateway to the paddler's paradise at **Desolation Sound** and on the **Powell Forest Canoe Route.**

Spectacular Highway 99, the aptly named **Sea to Sky Highway,** leads you northeast out of Vancouver along the edge of island-dotted **Howe Sound.** You pass numerous provincial parks before coming to the resort town of **Whistler.** This year-round outdoor-sports mecca offers outstanding opportunities for hiking, biking, golfing, fishing, and other warm-weather pursuits. But it's best known for its alpine resort: Whistler/Blackcomb, boasting North America's highest lift-served vertical rise.

Must-Sees

Look for ⓜ to find the sights and activities you can't miss and Ⓝ for the best dining and lodging.

ⓜ **Gibsons:** The Sunshine Coast is dotted with picturesque villages, none more scenic than Gibsons, where cafés and interesting shops line the rocky foreshore (page 216).

ⓜ **Savary Island:** The only sandy island in the Strait of Georgia, Savary Island stands out among the hundreds of Gulf Islands for its great beaches (page 224).

ⓜ **Whistler Gondola:** Whistler is worth visiting regardless of the season or your interests. One thing everyone should do is ride the gondola for the views alone (page 231).

ⓜ **Othello-Quintette Tunnels:** At a glance, Hope doesn't have much to offer the visitor, but tucked in the mountains behind town are the Othello-Quintette Tunnels, which wind through a rugged canyon (page 247).

ⓜ **Hell's Gate:** Even if you don't ride the tramway, Hell's Gate is an interesting and scenic stop along the Fraser Canyon (page 250).

ⓜ **Manning Provincial Park:** This spectacular park in the Cascade Mountains stretches down to the Canada–U.S. border, and has abundant

© BONNY MAKAREWCZ

Take a summer gondola ride to access alpine hiking areas in Whistler.

wildlife, including black bear, moose, elk, coyote, and beaver (page 252).

ⓜ **Grist Mill:** At Keremeos is a delightful spot to step back in time and learn about the lifestyle of early pioneers (page 256).

Southwestern B.C.

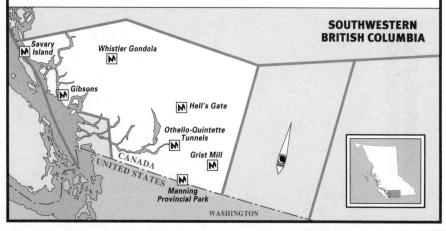

SOUTHWESTERN BRITISH COLUMBIA

Savary Island ⓜ

Whistler Gondola ⓜ

Gibsons ⓜ

ⓜ Hell's Gate

Othello-Quintette Tunnels ⓜ

Grist Mill ⓜ

CANADA
UNITED STATES

ⓜ Manning Provincial Park

WASHINGTON

SOUTHWESTERN
BRITISH COLUMBIA

Southwestern B.C.

© AVALON TRAVEL PUBLISHING, INC.

From Vancouver two routes head east—you can zip along the TransCanada Highway on the south side of the wide **Fraser River** or meander along slower Highway 7 on the north side of the river. Both highways take you through the lush, fertile, and obviously agricultural Fraser Valley, converging at **Hope.** After exploring Hope's spectacular canyon formations, you have another choice of routes: north along the Fraser River Canyon, northeast to Kamloops along the Coquihalla Highway, or east along Highway 3 to the picturesque lakes and alpine meadows of **Manning Provincial Park.**

PLANNING YOUR TIME

After exploring Vancouver, you're faced with a decision—where to next? This chapter covers three of the options, while a fourth, Vancouver Island, is covered in the previous chapter. Your choice of direction is dependent on two main elements: the time of year and your interests. The first option is to jump aboard a ferry for the **Sunshine Coast.** Rather than backtracking, plan on catching a ferry from Powell River across to Vancouver Island (make the detour to delightful **Lund** before you do). Of course, you can make this loop by traveling in the opposite direction—from Vancouver Island to Powell River and down to Vancouver. One important thing to remember is that travel along this strip of coastline takes a lot

longer than you may imagine from looking at a map, mostly due to two unavoidable ferry rides.

Regardless of the season, include **Whistler** in your British Columbia travels. The resort is close enough to Vancouver for a day trip, but it's easy to spend at least a full day exploring the main mountain by gondola, which means if you want to bike, hike, or golf, you'll need at least two days. Winter is high season in Whistler; in return for skiing or boarding some of the world's best-known slopes, you'll be paying big bucks for accommodations. The vast majority of Whistler visitors return to Vancouver, but the **Gold Nugget Route** continues north through Lillooet to central British Columbia, eliminating the need to backtrack.

Most travelers heading east from Vancouver do so on their way to the Okanagan, Kamloops, or beyond. But there are many reasons to stop, including **Harrison Hot Springs,** so plan your time accordingly. Once at Hope, the highway divides, and you're faced with three more options. Heading north is the zippy Coquihalla Highway or the more scenic Highway 1 through the Fraser River Canyon, which passes natural highlights such as **Hell's Gate.** Also from Hope, Highway 3 veers east along the U.S. border to mountainous **Manning Provincial Park** and a string of delightful towns such as **Keremeos,** where a historic grist mill continues to grind wheat for delicious breads.

The Sunshine Coast

The 150-kilometer-long (93-mile-long) Sunshine Coast lies along the northeast shore of the Strait of Georgia between Howe Sound in the south and Desolation Sound in the north. This rare bit of sun-drenched Canadian coastline is bordered by countless bays and inlets, broad sandy beaches, quiet lagoons, rugged headlands, provincial parks, and lush fir forests backed by the snowcapped Coast Mountains. It's well worth visiting, whether on a day-trip from Vancouver, on the "circle route" to Vancouver Island and back, or on a relaxing extended vacation.

The route from Vancouver is punctuated by two ferry rides and offers delightful glimpses of wilderness islands in the Strait of Georgia. Settlement began here in the late 19th century, and as you work your way up this stretch of the coastline note the odd assortment of place-names left by Coast Salish natives and Spanish and British navigators.

Today the area is a recreation paradise. Boasting Canada's mildest climate, the Sunshine Coast enjoys moderately warm summers and mild winters, with only 940 millimeters (37 inches) of rain annually and 2,400 hours of sunlight—a

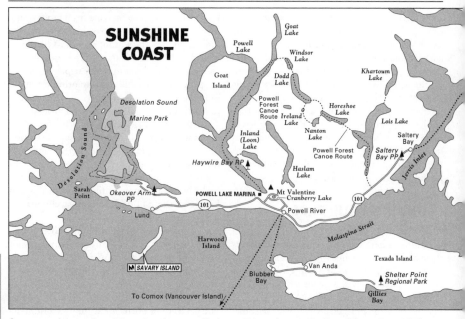

few more hours than Victoria, the so-called provincial hot spot. Boaters and kayakers can cruise into beautiful marine parks providing sheltered anchorage and campsites amid some of the most magnificent scenery along the west coast, or anchor at sheltered fishing villages with marinas and all the modern conveniences.

Traveling along the Coast

Although the Sunshine Coast is part of the mainland, a trip north entails two trips with **BC Ferries** (604/669-1211 or 888/223-3779, www .bcferries.com). From **Horseshoe Bay,** at the west end of Vancouver's North Shore, ferries regularly cross Howe Sound to **Langdale,** the gateway to the Sunshine Coast. From there, Highway 101 runs up the coast 81 kilometers (50.3 miles) to **Earls Cove,** where another ferry crosses Jervis Inlet to **Saltery Bay.** These trips take 40 and 50 minutes respectively and run approximately every two hours between 6:30 A.M. and 11:30 P.M. The ferry charge is adult $8.75, child $4.25, vehicle $30, which includes one-way travel on both ferries or round-trip travel on just one ferry.

From the terminal at Saltery Bay, Highway 101 continues 35 kilometers (22 miles) to Powell River. From here you can return along the same route or loop back on Vancouver Island via the **Powell River–Comox ferry** (adult $8, child $4, vehicle $27).

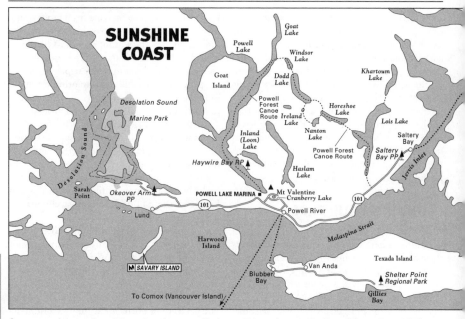 Gibsons

A delightful hillside community of 4,000 at the mouth of Howe Sound, Gibsons offers recreation galore. The town has two sections: the original 100-year-old fishing village around the harbor and a commercial corridor along the highway. Around the harbor, Gower Point Road is a charming strip of seafaring businesses, antique dealers, arty shops, and cafés (this was the setting for the popular 1970s TV series *The Beachcombers*). Down on the harbor itself is a marina and the pleasant Gibsons Seawalk, a 10-minute, scenic meander (lighted at night).

Elphinstone Pioneer & Maritime Museum (716 Winn Rd., 604/886-8232; summer daily 9 A.M.–5 P.M.) features intriguing pioneer and Coast Salish native displays and holds what must

© AVALON TRAVEL PUBLISHING, INC.

be one of the largest seashell collections on the planet (some 25,000). In summer locals participate in a couple of salmon derbies and revel at the annual **Sea Cavalcade,** which features a swimming race from nearby Keats Island to Gibsons, a parade, and fireworks.

On the main road, **Cedars Inn** (895 Gibsons Way, 604/886-3008 or 888/774-7044, www.thecedarsinn.com; $88 s, $94 d) features a heated outdoor pool, sauna, small exercise room, and restaurant.

Gibsons has a surprisingly good selection of eateries, most in the original part of town on a hill above the marina. For homestyle cooking at reasonable prices, try **Molly's Reach** (647 School Rd., 604/886-9710; breakfast, lunch, and dinner). Food is also offered at the **Waterfront Restaurant** (442 Marine Dr., 604/886-2831; daily 8 A.M.–8 P.M.) overlooking the marina.

At the east entrance to town, **Gibsons Visitor Info Centre** (900 Gibsons Way, 604/886-2325 or 866/222-3806, www.gibsonslandingbc.com; daily 9 A.M.–5 P.M.) is a good first stop for Sunshine Coast information.

Roberts Creek

About nine kilometers (5.6 miles) northwest of Gibsons is the small artistic community of Roberts Creek (take the lower road off Highway 101), where arts-and-crafts appreciators can often snatch up a bargain. In an old-growth forest, **Roberts Creek Provincial Park,** 14 kilometers (8.7 miles) northwest of Gibsons, holds hiking trails, waterfalls, a picnic ground, and a pebbly beach. Campsites are $14 per night.

The relaxed atmosphere at **Up the Creek Backpacker's B&B** (1261 Roberts Creek Rd., 604/885-0384 or 877/885-8100, www.upthecreek.ca) is reason enough to rest your head here overnight. Throw in well-priced beds, modern amenities such as a full kitchen and Internet access, and friendly owners, and you'll want to stay longer. Accommodations are in bright dorms ($20 per person) or private rooms ($65 s or d), with a self-serve breakfast an extra $3 per person.

Sechelt and Vicinity

The native cultural center and regional service center of Sechelt (pop. 7,800) perches on the

© JIM BORROWMAN

Pacific whiteside dolphin

isthmus of the Sechelt Peninsula between the head of Sechelt Inlet and the Strait of Georgia. Logging, fishing, and summer tourism support the town.

One of the area's nicest spots is **Porpoise Bay Provincial Park,** four kilometers (2.5 miles) north of Sechelt via East Porpoise Bay Road. The park offers open grassy areas among forests of fir and cedar, along with a broad sheltered sandy beach along the eastern shore of Sechelt Inlet. Hiking trails connect the beach with a day-use area and campground, and a woodland trail meanders along the bank of Angus Creek, where chum and coho salmon spawn in fall. The park is a handy base for kayakers and canoeists exploring Sechelt Inlets Provincial Marine Recreation Area. Porpoise Bay and the nearby rivers are also noted for good sportfishing, and oysters and clams are found along the inlet northwest of the park. The 84-site campground ($19) has hot showers. Also on Sechelt Inlet is **Porpoise Bay Charters** (604/885-5950), a well-established company with kayak rentals and tours, diving charters, and a few waterfront cabins ($105 s or d).

Back in Sechelt, the **Driftwood Inn** (5454 Trail Ave., 604/885-5811) features large but unexceptional rooms from $129 s, $139 d. At the inn, Pebbles Restaurant has water views. Out of town to the west, **Lord Jim's Resort** (604/885-7038 or 877/296-4593, www.lordjims.com) is an absolute waterfront complex overlooking Halfmoon Bay. It has a wonderful restaurant (for the food and view), rooms from $115 s, $145 d, and cabins for $120–190 s or d.

Sechelt Visitor Info Centre (604/885-0662; summer 9 A.M.–6 P.M., the rest of the year Mon.–Fri. 9 A.M.–5 P.M.) is in the large Trail Bay Mall shopping complex along Highway 101.

Pender Harbour

Along the shores of Pender Harbour lie the villages of Madeira Park, Garden Bay, and Irvines Landing. Boating and ocean fishing are popular activities on this stretch of coast, and Ruby and Sakinaw Lakes—between Madeira Park and Earls Cove—are a trout fisher's delight in season. Canoeists head for the chain of eight lakes between Garden Bay and Egmont, where those casting a line will find good fishing for cutthroat trout May–October.

Pender Harbour is also orca habitat. These highly intelligent gentle giants, also known as killer whales, travel in pods of up to 100. Feeding on salmon found year-round in these waters, they grow up to nine meters long, weighing as much as eight tons. Keep your eyes on the water and your camera ready to capture their triangular dorsal fins slicing through the water.

Skookumchuck Narrows Provincial Park

Just before Earls Cove, take the road north to Egmont, then the four-kilometer (2.5-mile) hiking trail (one hour each way) along Sechelt Inlet to a tidal oddity protected as a park. Meaning "Turbulent Water" in Chinook, Skookumchuck protects Narrows and Roland Points and the 400-meter-wide (1,300-foot-wide) rock-strewn waterway between them. The tides of three inlets roar through this narrow passage four times a day. The resulting rapids and eddies boisterously boil and bubble to create fierce-looking whirlpools—fascinating to see when your feet are firmly planted on terra firma, but very dangerous for inexperienced boaters unfamiliar with the tides. It's a particularly amazing spectacle one hour after the ebb of extra low spring tides, when the rapids may reach as high as five meters (16 feet) and the water whooshes past at 20 kph (12 mph). At any low tide, you'll also see abundant marine creatures in tidal pools—it's a fascinating spot. Take a picnic lunch, pull up a rock, and enjoy the view.

Earls Cove

Earls Cove marks the end of this section of Highway 101. From here, BC Ferries offers regular service across Jervis Inlet to Saltery Bay. The 16-kilometer (10-mile) crossing takes 50 minutes.

Saltery Bay and Vicinity

Less than two kilometers (1.2 miles) from the Saltery Bay ferry terminal is 140-hectare (346-acre) **Saltery Bay Provincial Park,** one of the Sunshine Coast's diving hot spots. All the best dive spots are accessible as shore dives, including a bronze mermaid. The park is broken into two sections. The southernmost is where the diving

CIRCLEPAC

A special fare known as Circlepac has been designed expressly for those who want to explore both the Sunshine Coast and Vancouver Island on a loop trip. The fare includes passage on the ferry from Vancouver to Vancouver Island, on the ferry from Comox to Powell River, and on the two ferries along the Sunshine Coast, all at a savings of 15 percent off the individual one-way fares. The only catch is that travel is only allowed outside of peak hours. Request the Circlepac fare when you purchase the first sector.

takes place, and it also holds a campground ($17 per night). Less than one kilometer (.6 mile) farther up the road is the park's day use area, with picnic tables and a grassed area fronting the rocky foreshore.

Bookended by the park's two sections is **Kent's Beach Resort** (604/487-9386, www.kentsbeach.com; Mar.–Oct.), one of the coast's many old-fashioned, family-friendly oceanfront resorts. In July and August, the eight self-contained cabins are rented by the week ($300–400). The rest of the operating season, you can snag your waterfront getaway for just $70–90 per night. Either way, furnishings are sparse (bring your own bedding), but the setting is unbeatable. Camping is $18–25 per night, with the more expensive sites right on the waterfront.

From Saltery Bay, it's 30 kilometers (19 miles) of winding road to Powell River. Along the way you'll cross Lois River, the outlet for large Lois Lake, and pass a string of coastal communities clinging to the rocky shoreline of Malaspina Strait.

POWELL RIVER

Situated between Jervis Inlet and Desolation Sound along the edge of Malaspina Strait, Powell River (pop. 16,500) is almost surrounded by water. The town is actually a municipality made up of four communities. **Townsite,** the original "Powell River," is occupied by an ugly waterfront pulp mill and a number of boarded-up

Southwestern B.C.

buildings. A few kilometers south is **Westview,** Powell River's main service center, home to the ferry terminal and information center as well as accommodations and restaurants. The other two official communities are **Wildwood,** north of Townsite, and **Cranberry,** east of Townsite.

Powell River was named in 1885 after Dr. Israel Powell, Superintendent of Indian Affairs for B.C., who led the movement that brought B.C. into confederation with Canada in 1871. During the early years of the 20th century, logging of the tall and slender local trees began in the forests around Lois, Horseshoe, and Nanton Lakes, producing exceptionally fine flagpoles that were exported to the rest of the world. In 1912, Powell River became the first town in western Canada to manufacture newsprint.

Today Powell River holds one of the world's largest pulp and paper mill complexes and is a thriving center for the region's abundant outdoor-recreation opportunities, including salmon fishing (good year-round), trout fishing, scuba diving, sailing, canoeing, kayaking, and hiking.

Sights

Start your exploration with by visiting the excellent **Powell River Historical Museum** across the road from Willingdon Beach (Marine Ave.,

604/485-2222; summer daily 10 A.M.–5 P.M., the rest of the year Mon.–Fri. only), which is like wandering back in time. Peruse the vast collection of photographs (the province's third-largest archives) and other displays to find out about this seashore community and to see what the area was like before the town was established. Also see well-preserved artifacts, native carvings and baskets, the shanty home of a hermit who once lived along Powell Lake, and even sand from around the world.

North through the main built up area is the original townsite, built around a bay that still holds a working pulp and paper mill complex. The *Heritage Walk* brochure (available at the information center) will guide you around the interesting array of buildings that date from 1910 to the 1930s. Many—such as the grand Hotel Rodmay and the imposing Federal Building—have been boarded up for decades. Drive along Sycamore Street and you'll see many Craftsman-style homes in varying states of disrepair. **Norske Canada** operates the mill, and tours are available June–September Monday–Friday four times a day. Book through the information center (604/485-4701).

Hiking

While most visitors to Powell River spend their time enjoying water-oriented sports, the hiking around town is also good—and chances are you'll have the trails to yourself.

From Powell River's municipal campground, the 1.2-kilometer (.7-mile) **Willingdon Beach Trail** spurs north past interpretive boards describing natural features and the uses of old logging machinery scattered along the trail. The trail ends at a viewpoint overlooking historic Townsite and the pulp operations. One of the most popular short local trails is the one-kilometer (.6-mile) hike up **Mount Valentine,** north of Cranberry. The trail leads to a stunning panoramic view of Malaspina Strait and the Strait of Georgia. Access is from the end of Crown Avenue: take Manson Avenue east to Cranberry Street, turn left, then turn right on Crown.

Another trail loops around **Inland Lake,** north of Powell River between Powell and Haslam

Lakes. The wheelchair-accessible trail is 13 kilometers (eight miles) round-trip, has bridges and boardwalks over swampy areas, and offers picnic sites at regular intervals. Minimal elevation gain is made; allow 3–4 hours. An interesting addition to this hike is a two-kilometer (1.2-mile) spur leading to **Lost Lake;** follow the main trail clockwise from the parking lot 800 meters (.5 mile) to the spur junction. To get to the trailhead from Westview, take Manson Avenue north for five kilometers (3.1 miles), turn right on Cranberry Street, then left on Haslam Street, from where a signposted logging road leads north to the lake and a primitive campground.

Canoeing and Kayaking

The sheltered Sunshine Coast provides plenty of opportunities for good lake and ocean canoeing or kayaking. The most popular canoe trip is the **Powell Forest Canoe Route** (see sidebar), while kayakers find solitude in **Desolation Sound** (see *Lund and Vicinity*).

Mitchell Canoe & Kayak (Myrtle Point Rd., 604/487-1699, www.canoeingbc.com) rents canoes for the Powell Forest Canoe Route. Prices range $26–33 for one day, or $23–26 per day for five or more days. The company also rents all the necessary accessories and fishing gear, provides free parking, and runs a shuttle service to and from the put-in ($60). Basic paddling courses start at $40, and fully guided overnight tours are available.

Although **Powell River Sea Kayak** (Malaspina Rd., 604/483-2160 or 866/617-4444, www.bcseakayak.com) outfits for the Powell Forest Canoe Route, kayaks are its specialty. Single and double kayaks for use around local waterways rent for $35–55 for one day, $60–90 for two days, additional days $20–35. Guided two-hour tours are $39, overnight sea-kayaking trips start at $200, and three-hour basic kayaking classes run from $40.

Scuba Diving

Known as the "Diving Capital of Canada," the Strait of Georgia provides divers with exceptionally clear, relatively warm water and more than 100 exciting dives mapped by local experts.

Southwestern B.C.

POWELL FOREST CANOE ROUTE

This four- to eight-day backcountry canoe route is a great way to get away from it all, surrounding yourself with tree-covered lowlands and rugged mountain peaks while slipping through fjordlike lakes. Take side trips and you can extend the water distance from 67 kilometers (41.6 miles) to more than 150 kilometers (93 miles), or just do one or two sections of the trail—all the major lakes can be reached by road.

To reach the put-in at **Lois Lake,** take Highway 101 east of Powell River 20 kilometers (12.4 miles) to a logging road that branches north off the highway. Follow that road for one kilometer (.6 mile), then turn right on the Branch 41 logging road and follow it seven kilometers (4.3 miles) to a primitive lakeside campground. The route includes paddling along part of Lois Lake, then the lengths of **Horseshoe, Dodd, Windsor,** and **Goat Lakes** to **Powell Lake.** Powell Lake Marina is the most popular pull-out point. In total, the route requires 57 kilometers (35.4 miles) of paddling and 10 kilometers (6.2 miles) of portaging. The longest single paddle is 28.5 kilometers (17.7 miles), and the longest portage is 2.5 kilometers (1.6 miles). Carry a tent, stove, and supplies, and stay at one of the 20 Forest Service recreation sites and camping areas along the route. Don't forget your fishing rod and tackle—all the lakes are stocked with cutthroat trout, and some hold rainbow trout and kokanee.

The route's major outfitter is **Mitchell Canoe & Kayak** (Myrtle Point Rd., 604/487-1699, www.canoeingbc.com). Canoe rentals range $26–33 for one day, $115–130 for five days. The company provides all accessories and free car parking, and shuttles paddlers to and from the route. A three-day guided paddle is $299 per person.

For a map and brochure describing the route in detail and to find out present water levels and campfire regulations contact the **Powell River Visitor Info Centre** (4690 Marine Ave., Westview, 604/485-4701).

Conditions are particularly excellent in winter, when visibility reaches 30 meters. Expect to see underwater cliffs and abundant marinelife, including sponges, giant octopuses, wolf eels, perch, lingcod, tubeworms, sea anemones, nudibranchs (including intriguing hooded nudibranchs), sea stars, crabs, and tunicates. Seals can be seen year-round, sea lions November–April.

The highlight for wreck divers on the Sunshine Coast is the HMCS *Chaudiere,* sunk in 1993 to form an artificial reef. The hull provides a home for colorful marinelife, and giant holes have been cut through it to enable adventurous divers to do some inside exploration.

Diving gear and a list of charter operators are available at **Alpha Dive Services** (7013 Thunder Bay St., 604/485-6939), on the south side of town.

Fishing

With ocean to the west and lakes to the east, Powell River is a fishing fantasy come true. Salt-water fishing for chinook salmon is good year-round but particularly good in autumn and mid-winter. Coho salmon usually arrive around April or May. Sport anglers also pursue red snapper, perch, flatfish, lingcod, and rockfish. Bring your own boat (launching ramps are free) or charter one with or without a guide and equipment. Dangle a line from the wharf, docks, or break-waters, or hurl it out from the shore; a saltwater fishing license is required.

Cutthroat trout inhabit more than a dozen local lakes, most of which are accessible by logging road. Many of the lakes are stocked with rainbow trout and kokanee, and in a couple you can also catch Dolly Varden. Note that you need separate fishing licenses for freshwater and salt-water fishing. Head to **Taw's Cycle and Sport** (4597 Marine Ave., 604/485-2555) for all your tackle needs.

Accommodations

Powell River doesn't have a great number of motel

rooms, so try to reserve a room in advance or plan to camp or head north to Lund (where you'll also need reservations). A solid cheapie is **Westview Centre Motel** (4534 Marine Ave., 604/485-4023 or 877/485-4023), where basic rooms sell for $58 s, $68 d per night.

One of the most attractive and relaxing lodgings in Powell River is **Beacon Bed and Breakfast** (3750 Marine Dr. 604/485-5563 or 800/485-5563, www.beaconbb.com), which overlooks Malaspina Strait and the peaks of Vancouver Island two kilometers (1.2 miles) south of the ferry terminal. Within the two-story home are three guest rooms, each with ocean views. Facilities include a lounge area overlooking the water, an outdoor hot tub, Internet access, and in-room luxuries like fluffy robes. Rates are $90–125 s, $100–135 d, which includes a big breakfast that will set you up for a day of outdoor activities.

The ordinary rooms at **Beach Gardens Resort** (five km/3.1 miles south of the ferry terminal, 7074 Westminster Ave., 604/485-6267 or 800/663-7070, www.beachgardens.com; $105–165 s or d) are more than made up for by amenities like an indoor swimming pool, sauna, tennis courts, a fitness room, and a marina with boat rentals and divers' air (it's a great place to meet fellow scuba enthusiasts). The resort's restaurant offers lunchtime buffets and a pub.

Camping

Willingdon Beach Municipal Campground (Marine Ave., 604/485-2242) enjoys a great waterfront location one kilometer (.6 mile) north of the ferry terminal. You'll find sheltered and very popular campsites along the beach, as well as a laundry and washrooms with free hot showers. Basic tent sites are $16, hookups $18–22.

Canoeists find **Haywire Bay Regional Park** handy. It's seven kilometers north of town on Powell Lake, at one end of the Powell Forest Canoe Route. The park's campground offers hot showers, a sandy beach, and a boat launch. Sites are $14. It's accessible by boat or canoe from Powell Lake Marina, and also by road; from the ferry terminal drive up Duncan Street, turn left on Manson Avenue and follow it for five kilometers (3.1 miles), then turn right on Cranberry

Street and left on Haslam Street, from where a signposted logging road (on the left) leads north four kilometers (2.5 miles) to Haywire Bay.

Food

Head to **Rocky Mountain Pizza and Bakery Co.** (4471 Marine Ave., 604/485-9111, Mon.–Sat. from 6:30 A.M., Sun. from 8 A.M.). for great bakery items, coffee as strong (or as weak) as you like it, and daily newspapers. The rest of the day it's pizza, pizza, and more pizza until 6 or 7 P.M., depending on the season. Taste teas from around the world at the **Little Tea Pot** (4582 Willingdon Ave., 604/485-5955; Apr.–Oct. daily 10 A.M.–8 P.M., Nov.–Mar. daily 10 A.M.–5 P.M.), which has a few outside tables with water views. Tea-tasting traditions—such as a timer that lets you know when your tea is steeped—add to the charm. At the entrance to Willingdon Beach, the **Beach Hut** is busy throughout summer serving battered fish and chips, hamburgers, and the Sunshine Coast's best ice cream.

Whooters (4680 Marine Dr., 604/485-0970; daily for lunch and dinner) is a small-town restaurant that tries hard. Sit out on the deck or inside surrounded by owl memorabilia. Most lunches are under $10, including a tangy seafood Caesar. I made my way through the long dinner menu and settled on baked snapper topped by a dollop of cilantro salsa ($18), and wasn't disappointed.

At the marina overlooking Powell Lake, north of town, the **Shinglemill** (604/483-2001) is part pub, part restaurant, with the former spilling out on to a wide deck. The pub menu is wide-ranging; a good choice is the seafood chowder served in a sourdough bread bowl ($6.25). In the restaurant, mains like salmon baked in a soy-ginger glaze range $13–23.50. The restaurant is open daily for dinner while the pub is open daily 11 A.M.–11 P.M. Whichever room you choose, you'll be pleasantly surprised by the well-priced wine list. Another popular place for seafood is the **Beach Gardens Resort** (7074 Westminster Ave., 604/485-6267), south of town, where the outdoor tables overlook Malaspina Strait. Sample the lunch buffet, salad bar, or bistro, or go for the formal sit-down dinner.

Southwestern B.C.

Southwestern B.C.

Information and Services

Powell River Visitor Info Centre (4690 Marine Ave., 604/485-4701, www.discoverpowellriver.com; summer Mon.–Sat. 9 A.M.–9 P.M. and Sun. 9 A.M.–5 P.M., the rest of the year weekdays only) is along the main strip of shops. Coming off the ferry from Vancouver Island, drive up the hill to Marine Avenue and turn left; it's three blocks down on the right. **Powell River Public Library** (4411 Michigan Ave., 604/485-4796; Mon.–Sat. 10 A.M.–5 P.M.) is a good place to hang out on a rainy day.

Head to **River City Coffee** (4801 Joyce Ave., 604/485-0011; daily from 8 A.M.) to check your email.

Transportation

Powell River Municipal Airport is east of town, off Duncan Street. **Pacific Coastal** (604/483-2107 or 800/663-2872) flies at least three times daily between Powell River and its hub at the South Terminal of Vancouver International Airport.

The **bus depot,** on the corner of Joyce Avenue and Glacier Street, is served by **Malaspina Coach Lines** (604/885-4511 or 877/227-8287). Malaspina runs twice daily in both directions between Powell River and Vancouver's Pacific Central Station.

The ferry terminal in Powell River is at the foot of Duncan Street, right downtown. **BC Ferries** (604/485-2943) has regular sailings between Powell River and Comox on Vancouver Island. One-way fares for the 75-minute sailing are adult $8, child $4, vehicle $27. You can't make reservations—just roll up and join the queue.

Sunshine Coast Transit System (604/885-3234) operates local bus service between Sunshine Coast communities; $2 per sector (no Sunday service).

TEXADA ISLAND

A 35-minute ferry trip from the Powell River ferry terminal, Texada is one of the largest of the Gulf Islands (50 kilometers/31 miles from north to south and up to 10 kilometers/6.2 miles wide), but the permanent population is only 1,400 and

services are limited. Originally home to a whaling station, the island has also housed a couple of mining operations and a distillery that supplied illegal liquor to the United States during Prohibition.

From the ferry terminal at Blubber Bay, the island's main road winds south for eight kilometers (five miles) to **Van Anda,** a historic village that once boasted saloons, an opera house, and a hospital. Take a walk along Van Anda's Erickson Beach to appreciate the island's natural beauty. Continuing south, the road leads to Gillies Bay and beyond to **Shelter Point Regional Park,** which has some short but enjoyable hiking trails and a sandy spit that leads to a private high-tide island. At low tide, look for colorful starfish along the shoreline, or maybe try your hand digging for clams. Campsites overlooking the water are $17.

Getting to Texada

The short hop over to the island from Powell River with **BC Ferries** (604/485-2943) costs adult $5.75, child $3, vehicle $14.50 round-trip. Ferries depart about every two hours 8 A.M.–11 P.M.; no reservations taken.

LUND AND VICINITY

Twenty-eight kilometers (17 miles) north of Powell River, Highway 101 dead-ends on the old wooden wharf of Lund, a tiny fishing village founded in 1889 and named after the Swedish hometown of the first settlers. Lund lies on a secluded harbor backed by the magnificent peaks of the Coast Mountains. Although best known as the gateway to Desolation Sound, it's worth the trip out just for the relaxed atmosphere and surrounding beauty. Wander around the bustling marina, cruise over to the white-sand beaches of Savary Island, or relax with a cold drink on the deck of the Lund Hotel. At the back of the Lund Hotel, **Rockfish Kayak** (604/414-9355) rents kayaks for $30–55 per day; transport the kayaks to Okeover Arm and you're on your way.

▶ Savary Island

A geological quirk created Savary Island, the only sandy island in the Strait of Georgia. While the hundreds of other Gulf Islands are rocky in origin, Savary is composed of glacial till that was left behind after the last ice age. Over time, the island has become forested, but it is still ringed by telltale sandy beaches. A few hundred lucky souls have summer homes on Savary, but most visitors arrive just for the day, traveling by water taxi (604/483-9749), which departs 4–5 times daily for $8 round-trip. By the island dock is a café and bike rental outlet.

Okeover Arm

The shallow, sheltered waters of Okeover Arm— a southern arm of Desolation Sound—provide the perfect environment for all kinds of prolific marinelife; try to time your visit with the receding tide. Access is via Malaspina Road, off Highway 101 south of Lund. Forested four-hectare (10-acre) **Okeover Arm Provincial Park** lies on the water; it's a small, rustic park with just a few undeveloped campsites ($14), a pit toilet, and a kayak- and boat-launching ramp, but it's a great spot to camp if you're into canoeing or kayaking.

Lund Hotel

Desolation Sound Marine Park

Desolation Sound was named by Captain Vancouver after his visit in 1792—he was obviously unimpressed, as the name implies. Today, 8,256 hectares (20,400 acres) of the sound are protected in the largest of British Columbia's 50 marine parks. The park also preserves over 60 kilometers (37 miles) of shoreline, a number of offshore islands, the Gifford Peninsula, and a section of mainland that includes Unwin Lake. A wilderness-seeker's paradise, the park is totally undeveloped and without road access. The sound is a popular yachtie hangout and a haven for sea kayakers, who need to be totally self-sufficient here.

Accommodations

The only accommodation right in town is the **Lund Hotel** (604/414-0474 or 877/569-3999, www.lundhotel.com), which sits right on the harbor. This 100-year-old property has undergone massive renovations, and unfortunately the historic charm of the original guest rooms has

been replaced by contemporary styling and hand-painted murals. Still, rates of $115 s, $125 d are reasonable. The hotel complex holds a pub, restaurant, kayak rental shop, laundry, post office, art gallery, and grocery store.

If you're looking for something a little different, choose to stay at the **M Magical Dome** (off Baggi Rd., 604/483-9160, www.magical-dome.com), a five-minute drive from Lund. As far as I know, it's the only place in Canada where you can stay in a geodesic dome—a quirky architectural style that employs dozens of triangular panels to form a rigid spherical structure that creates the most space with the least amount of materials. Inside is a bedroom, loft with second bed, well-equipped kitchen, lounge area, and wood-burning fireplace. Adjacent is a modern bathhouse, complete with sauna. Rates for the entire dome are $110 per night, discounted to $75 between October and April.

Set on three hectares (7.4 acres) overlooking Okeover Arm, **M Desolation Resort** (2694

© ANDREW HEMPSTEAD

Southwestern B.C.

Dawson Rd., 604/483-3592 or 800/399-3592, www.desolationresort.com) offers a wonderful escape at reasonable prices. Accommodation is in freestanding wood chalets set high above the lake edge on stilts. All feature rich-colored wood furnishings, and even the smallest (the bottom half of one unit) has a king-size bed, large deck, kitchen, separate living and dining areas, and a barbecue. Rates range from just $120 for the unit detailed above to $270 for four guests sharing a two-bedroom, two-bathroom chalet. Fishing, canoeing, and kayaking are practically right out your door at the private marina.

Food
In addition a fine choice of accommodations, Lund is home to a couple of the Sunshine Coast's premier restaurants. The food at **Lund Hotel** (604/414-0474) is overshadowed by the views, es-pecially if you talk your way to an outside table. Crab cakes topped with crab salad are a good starter, followed by seafood fettuccine as a main and a slab of mud cake for dessert. Choose this combo and you'll pay around $30—about the same as a main meal in Vancouver.

The upscale **M Laughing Oyster** (Vander-maeden Rd., 604/483-9775; daily noon–8:30 P.M.) is a hidden gem. Overlooking the water from an elevated setting, diners are seated outside on a deck or inside on tiers that allow everyone to enjoy the view. Starters include oysters prepared in a variety of ways (you can see the restaurant's oyster farm from the deck) and a healthy blue cheese salad. Mains range $18–25 and include a perfectly presented baked halibut dish. Even if you're full, try a slice of melt-in-your-mouth pecan pie for desert. The Laughing Oyster is a well-signposted, five-minute drive from Lund.

Sea to Sky Highway

The spectacular, aptly named Sea to Sky Highway (Highway 99) runs 105 kilometers (65 miles) between Horseshoe Bay and Whistler. With the almost-vertical tree-covered **Coast Mountains** to the east and island-dotted **Howe Sound** to the west, this cliff-hugging highway winds precariously through a dramatic glacier-carved landscape.

The weather certainly affects what you see and how you feel about this part of British Columbia. On sunny days everything seems to be bright blue, emerald green, and sparkling clean; only water trickling down the roadside cliffs gives you the clue that it rains a bit around here. On the other hand, after a string of dull drizzly days, impressive waterfalls, one after another, plummet down those same cliffs right beside you to abruptly disappear underneath the highway, and the scenery merges into a magnificent blue-and-gray blur.

Along the road expect some tight corners, narrow stretches, and enough traffic to keep your concentration at an optimum. Be aware of potential hazards in bad weather (washouts can occur), and if you want to go slowly to absorb everything, use the slow-lane pullouts.

HORSESHOE BAY TOWARD SQUAMISH
Porteau Cove Provincial Park
On the east shore of Howe Sound, Porteau Cove is best known among the diving fraternity for its artificial reef of four sunken wrecks but also offers good swimming and fishing. In addition, the area's strong winds and lack of waves make for perfect windsurfing conditions. The park holds boat-launching and scuba-diving facilities, an ecology information center, picnic tables, and a waterfront campground for tents and RVs. A day pass is $5 per vehicle and camping is $22 per night March–October (free the rest of the year).

Furry Creek Golf and Country Club
North up Howe Sound beyond Porteau Cove is Furry Creek Golf and Country Club (604/896-2224 or 888/922-9461; mid-March to mid-

Oct.), generally regarded as one of British Columbia's most scenic courses. Immaculately manicured, the course is bordered on one side by the driftwood-strewn beaches of Howe Sound and on the other by towering mountains. It is relatively short, at just over 6,000 yards, but water comes into play on many holes, including one where the green juts into the sound and is almost an island. In summer, greens fees are $109, with the price of a round decreasing to $89 later in the afternoon and to as low as $69 the rest of the year. All rates include valet parking, a locker, power cart, tees, and a towel.

Britannia Beach

Small Britannia Beach is worth a stop to visit the **B.C. Museum of Mining** (800/896-4044 or 604/688-8735; mid-May–early Oct. daily 9 A.M.–4:30 P.M.; adult $13, senior and student $11), overlooking Howe Sound,. In the early 1930s the Britannia Beach Mine was the British Empire's largest producer of copper, producing more than 600,000 tons. Today it's not a working mine but a working museum. Ever wondered what it's like to slave away underground? Here's your chance to don a hard hat and raincoat, hop on an electric train, and travel under a mountain, without even getting your hands dirty. See fully functional mining equipment, along with demonstrations and displays on the techniques of mining. Then take a step into the past in the museum, where hundreds of photos and artifacts tell the story of the mine. Outside of the main mid-May to early October season, the site is open Monday–Friday 9 A.M.–4:30 P.M., but no tours are offered. In return, admission is reduced to $5 per person.

Continuing North

Straddling the highway, tiny **Murrin Provincial Park** provides good boating, fishing, swimming, and walking trails, as well as steep cliffs that attract novice and intermediate rock climbers. The park has picnic tables but no campsites ($3 per day admission). Farther up the highway, stop at **Shannon Falls Provincial Park** to view the spectacular 335-meter-high (1,100-foot-high) namesake falls from a platform at the base. You can picnic here or hike a few trails. No campsites are available, but just across the road is **Klahanie Campground and RV Park** (604/892-3435). This pleasant campground has sites for $18–24 and an adjacent restaurant with spectacular views (daily 6:30 A.M.–9 P.M.).

SQUAMISH

Squamish (pop. 15,500), 67 kilometers (42 miles) north of Vancouver and 53 kilometers (33 miles) south of Whistler, enjoys a stunning location at the head of Howe Sound, surrounded by snowcapped mountains. The name Squamish is a native Coast Salish word meaning "Mother of the Wind"—the town gets stiff breezes year-round, delighting today's sailors and windsurfers.

The first white settlers made their home in the valley in 1888, logging the local giant cedar and fir trees for a living. Squamish quickly became a logging town, then a railroad town; at one time it was the southern terminus for the Pacific Great Eastern rail line. Today lumber is still the lifeblood of the area—the town holds four sawmills, and along **Mamquam Blind Channel** on the east side of town you can see logs being boomed in preparation for towing to other mills.

Town Sights

See around 65 vintage rail cars and engines in a mock working railyard, complete with a station garden, replica workers' home, and a restored station at the **West Coast Railway Heritage Park** (Industrial Way, one km from Hwy. 99, 604/898-9336; May–Oct. daily 10 A.M.–5 P.M.; adult $10, child $8.50). Also in town is the **Squamish Valley Museum,** in a heritage house on 2nd Avenue (Wed.–Sun.). Farther along 2nd Avenue, at Victoria Street, a colorful mural covers the exterior of the Ocean Pub, depicting the natural and human elements of life along the west coast.

Rock Climbing

Although Squamish has a reputation as an industrial town, it is also the center of a growing

THE EAGLES OF BRACKENDALE

Squamish itself doesn't have a ton of sights, but if you're in the area during winter, **Brackendale,** just to the north along Highway 99, is definitely worth a stop. Through the colder months of the year, the riverflats behind this sleepy little town are home to a larger concentration of bald eagles than anywhere else on the face of the earth. Over 3,000 of these magnificent creatures descend on a stretch of the Squamish River between the Cheakamus and Mam-quam tributaries to feed on spawned out salmon that litter the banks. The dead fish are the result of a late-fall run of an estimated 100,000 chum salmon. The birds begin arriving in late October, but numbers reach their peak around Christmastime, and by early February the birds are gone. The best viewing spot is from the dike that runs along the back of Brackendale.

The best place to learn more about these creatures is the **Brackendale Art Gallery** (604/898-3333; Jan. daily noon– 5 P.M., weekends only the rest of the year), which has an adjacent bird-watching tower that rises some 11 meters (36 feet) above the surrounding trees. Through January, the gallery is "Eagle Count Headquarters," with slide presentations, talks, and other eagle-related activities. Guided walks to the site cost $35 per person. To get to the gallery, follow the main Brackendale access road over the railway tracks, take the first right, and look for the gallery nestled in the trees on the right.

recreation-based economy. Leading the way is rock climbing on the 762-meter-high (2,500-foot-high) **Stawamus Chief,** clearly visible across the highway from downtown. The "Chief," as it's best known, is one of the world's largest granite monoliths. It formed around 100 million years ago as massive forces deep inside the earth forced molten magma through the crust—as it cooled, it hardened and fractured, creating a perfect environment for today's climbers. The face offers a great variety of free and aided climbing on almost 1,000 routes, which take in dikes, cracks, slabs, chasms, and ridges.

The Chief gained status as a provincial park in 1995, but facilities are still limited. Climbers camp at the base for $11 per night but head into town to the aquatic center to shower and soak in a hot tub ($3 per visit). If you've never climbed or are inexperienced, consider using the services of **Squamish Rock Guides** (604/815-1750, www.squamishrockguides.com) for a variety of courses with equipment supplied; expect to pay around $175 per person for a full day's instruction. **Vertical Reality Sports Store** (3785 2nd Ave., 604/892-8248) offers a full range of climbing equipment and sells local climbing guides.

Other Recreation and Events

At first it may be difficult to see past the industrial scars along Squamish's waterways, but on the west side of downtown a large section of the delta where the Squamish River flows into Howe Sound has escaped development. It comprises tidal flats, forested areas, marshes, and open meadows—and over 200 species of birds call the area home. Hiking trails lace the area, and there are three main access points: Industrial Road, the end of Winnipeg Street, and the end of Vancouver Street, all of which branch off Cleveland Avenue. Nearby Garibaldi Provincial Park offers many opportunities for more experienced hikers. For a bird's-eye view of the area, take to the air from Squamish Municipal Airport with **Glacier Air** (604/898-9016 or 800/265-0088).

Squamish celebrates two very different lifestyles at its major annual events. The last week of June is the **Squamish Adventure Festival,** a semi-social gathering of adventure-loving folk who come for the mountain biking, windsurfing, whitewater kayaking, rock climbing, and even kiteflying. Then, early in August, Squamish is mobbed by loggers from around the world who congregate for the annual **Squamish Days Logger Sports** (604/898-3500). Don't be too surprised to see people competing at racing up trees, rolling logs, and throwing axes. The show also includes an RV rally, Truck Loggers Rodeo, dances, pageants, and parades.

Accommodations

The best place to stay around Squamish is **𝕸 Dryden Creek Resorts,** six kilometers (3.7 miles) north of town at Depot Road (604/898-9726 or 877/237-9336, www.drydrencreek.com). It's on six hectares (14 acres) of landscaped parkland with Garibaldi Provincial Park as a backdrop. Each of the six suite-style studios has a cedar ceiling, large skylights, and a fully equipped kitchen with hand-crafted cabinets. Rates of $79–89 s or d include complimentary coffee and chocolates. The resort's campground offers a choice of forested or creekside sites; unserviced sites $18, hookups $20–26.

Rooms at the **Garibaldi Budget Inn** (38012 3rd Ave., 604/892-5204 or 888/313-9299) go for just $49 s, $69 d, but if you're planning a big night out across the road at Squamish's infamous Ocean's Pub you probably don't care that they are ordinary at best. Also right downtown, **Howe Sound Inn** (37801 Cleveland Ave., 604/892-2603 or 800/919-2537, www.howesound.com) is a stylish place with 20 modern rooms from $105 s or d. In keeping with the local scene, the inn has a climbing wall, along with underground parking, in-room Internet access, a restaurant, and an in-house brewery.

Information

For detailed information on Squamish, local provincial parks, and Whistler, follow the signs from the highway downtown to **Squamish Visitor Info Centre** (37950 Cleveland Ave., 604/892-9244 or 866/333-2010, www.squamishchamber.bc.ca; summer daily 9 A.M.–5 P.M., the rest of the year Mon.–Fri. 9 A.M.–4 P.M.). **Squamish Public Library** (37907 2nd Ave., 604/892-3110) is open daily except Friday.

NORTH TOWARD WHISTLER

Garibaldi Provincial Park

This beautiful park encompasses 195,000 hectares (481,850 acres) of pristine alpine wilder-

ness east of Highway 99. Dominated by the snowcapped and glaciated Coast Mountains, the park reaches a high point at 2,678-meter (8,790-foot) **Mount Garibaldi,** named in 1860 after Italian soldier and statesman Giuseppe Garibaldi. Other park features include 2,315-meter (7,600-foot) **Black Tusk,** the **Gargoyles** (eroded rock formations reached by a trail from the park's southern entrance), and a 1.6-kilometer-long (one-mile-long) lava flow above the west side of **Garibaldi Lake.**

Garibaldi is a true wilderness park, with road access only up to the park boundary. From late July through early September, the hiking is fabulous—through forests of fir, red cedar, hemlock, and balsam, across high meadows crowded with spectacular wildflowers, and past bright blue lakes, huge glaciers, and jagged volcanic peaks and lava flows. If you're in the right spot at the right time, you may see black and grizzly bears, mountain goats, and deer. And you'll certainly spy lots of marmots, chipmunks, squirrels, and birds. In winter and spring the park is thickly blanketed in snow, luring experienced cross-country skiers. Snow can linger well into July, and the higher peaks are permanently mantled.

Between Squamish and Pemberton, five clearly marked entrance roads lead off Highway 99 to trailheads providing access into the five most popular areas of the park: **Diamond Head, Black Tusk/Garibaldi Lake, Cheakamus Lake, Singing Pass,** and **Wedgemount Lake.** Aside from these five areas, the rest of the park is untouched wilderness, explored only by mountaineers and experienced cross-country skiers. All major trails have backcountry tent sites.

Alice Lake Provincial Park

Alice Lake, surrounded by a 400-hectare (1,000-acre) park of open grassy areas, dense forests, and impressive snowcapped peaks, is particularly good for canoeing, swimming, and fishing for small rainbow and cutthroat trout. A 1.4-kilometer (.9-mile) trail encircles the lake while others lead to three smaller bodies of water; allow 20 minutes for the loop. A campground with showers and picnic tables is open year-round; walk-in sites are $17 while other sites are $22 per night

March–October, free the rest of the time. It costs $5 per vehicle for a day pass. The park entrance is 13 kilometers (eight miles) north of Squamish and the lake just under two kilometers (1.2 miles) from the highway.

Brandywine Falls Provincial Park

If you like waterfalls, stop at this small park 45 kilometers (28 miles) north of Squamish and follow the 300-meter (.2-mile), five-minute trail from the parking lot. It's the kind of trail that excites all your senses—magnificent frosty peaks high above, dense lush forest on either side, a fast, deep river roaring along on one side, the pungent aroma and cushiness of crushed pine needles beneath your feet.

The trail takes you to a viewing platform to see 66-meter-high (220-foot-high) **Brandywine Falls,** where the waters plummet down a vertical lava cliff into a massive swirling plunge pool, then roar down a forest-edged river into a lake. It's most magnificent early in summer. The falls were named in the early part of the 20th century by two railroad surveyors who made a wager on guessing the falls' height, the winner to receive bottles of, you guessed it, brandywine. From the trail to the falls you can also branch off on another trail that leads either to **Swim Lake** (400 meters/.25 miles; 10 minutes) or along the **Calcheak Trail** (four kilometers/2.5 miles; 70 minutes). Aside from hiking, the park is also a good spot for swimming and fishing. A campground near Highway 99 provides gravel campsites; $14 per night May–October, no charge the rest of the year.

Whistler

Magnificent snowcapped peaks, dense green forests, transparent lakes, sparkling rivers, and an upmarket, cosmopolitan village right in the middle of it all: welcome to Whistler (pop. 10,000), one of the world's great resort towns, just 120 kilometers north (75 miles) of Vancouver along Highway 99. The Whistler Valley has seen incredible development in recent years and is now British Columbia's third-most popular tourist destination (behind Vancouver and Victoria), attracting around two million visitors annually. Things will be even busier in February 2010 when Whistler hosts the downhill, Nordic, and sliding events of the Olympic Winter Games. The crowds and the costs might not be for everyone, but there *is* a great variety of things to in Whistler, and the village takes full advantage of magnificent natural surroundings, making a trip north from Vancouver well worthwhile at any time of year.

Best-known among skiers and boarders, the town is built around the base of one of North America's finest resorts, **Whistler/Blackcomb,** which comprises almost 3,000 hectares (7,400 acres) on two mountains accessed by an ultra-modern lift system. A season stretching from November to early June doesn't leave much time for summer recreation, but in recent years, the "off-season" has become almost equally busy. Among the abundant summertime recreation opportunities: lift-served hiking and glacier skiing and boarding; biking through the valley and mountains; water activities on five lakes; horseback riding; golfing on some of the world's best resort courses; and fishing, rafting, and jet-boating on the rivers. The more sedentary summer visitor can simply stay in bustling **Whistler Village** and enjoy a plethora of outdoor cafés and restaurants.

History

Although natives took advantage of the abundant natural resources of the Whistler Valley for thousands of years, and gold seekers passed through on their way to the Cariboo goldfields, the history of Whistler as a resort town doesn't *really* begin until the 1960s and is associated almost entirely with the development of the ski area. At this time the only development was a bunch of ramshackle summer holiday houses around Alta Lake (which was also the name of the "town"), population 300.

In 1964 the rough and treacherous road linking the valley to Vancouver was finally paved, and in 1965 the Garibaldi Lift Co. began constructing the first lifts on the west side of what was then called **London Mountain.** The lift system of that first season consisted of just one gondola and two T-bars. Still, skiers were impressed, and so were investors, who began plans for major base area facilities. The idea of a European-style ski-in, ski-out village was promoted throughout the 1970s, but it wasn't until 1980 that Whistler Village officially opened. The lift system on what became known as Whistler Mountain (after the shrill call of marmots that lived around its summit) had by this time expanded greatly, but the capacity of the resort doubled for the 1980–81 season with the opening of a resort on adjacent Blackcomb Mountain. In 1986 Intrawest bought Blackcomb from the original developer, Aspen Skiing Corporation, and it was evident to everyone that the future for the valley was bright. Each year onward saw one or both of the mountains construct more lifts, including 1986, when the first lift was opened above the tree line, and 1994, when the $12 million Excalibur gondola began operation.

Throughout the last two decades of the 20th century, on-mountain construction was overshadowed by developments in the valley below: Intrawest spent $25 million on base facilities at Blackcomb, some of the best-known names in the golf world were brought in to design championship-standard golf courses, in 1995 Whistler Village Centre opened, and the population increased 10-fold in 20 years.

In 1997 the inevitable happened, and the two mountains came under the control of one company, Intrawest, which bought Whistler Mountain to create the megaresort of **Whistler/Blackcomb.** The company has continued to upgrade the lifts and skier facilities, but the basic integration of the two ski areas was in place well before the takeover.

Overdevelopment is an ongoing concern throughout the valley. The latest community plan has recommended capping the number of "beds" at 52,500, up from the current number of 42,000. The main reason for a cap on development is a lack of available land, but poor road access from Vancouver is also a contributing factor.

SUMMER SKIING

Just because the calendar, thermometer, and sun's angle say it's summer doesn't mean skiing is months away. Whistler/Blackcomb is one of just two North American resorts offering lift-served summer skiing. Between late June and early August (but very weather dependent), a T-bar on Blackcomb Mountain's **Horstman Glacier** opens up a small 45-hectare (110-acre) area with a vertical rise of 209 meters (520 feet). The lift opens daily noon–3 P.M.; $45 per person includes lift transportation from the valley floor. The slopes can get crowded, with local and national ski teams in training and with visitors enjoying the novelty of summer skiing. But if it gets too bad, just go back to the valley floor for golf or water sports.

But the demand for both motel rooms and residential lots is seemingly never-ending, pushing up the costs of living and staying in the village (empty lots rarely sell for less than $400,000, and existing homes start at $500,000). In addition, Whistler will share hosting duties with Vancouver for the 2010 Olympic Winter Games. Planned venues include the main ski resort and the Callaghan Valley, 16 kilometers (10 miles) south of the village. Check out the latest at www.vancouver2010.com.

The best place to learn the full story of development in the valley is the **Whistler Museum** (4329 Main St., 604/932-2019; summer daily 10 A.M.–4 P.M., the rest of the year Fri.–Sun. 10 A.M.–4 P.M.; adult $2, child $1).

SUMMER RECREATION
Whistler Gondola

During the few months that they aren't covered in snow, the slopes of the ski resort come alive with locals and tourists alike enjoying hiking, guided naturalist walks, mountain biking, and horseback riding, or just marveling at the mountainscape from the comfort of the lifts. Die-hard skiers will even find glacier skiing here early in the summer (see sidebar, *Summer Skiing*). Over 50 kilometers (31 miles) of hiking trails wind around the mountains, including trails through the high alpine to destinations such as beautiful Harmony Lake (two kilometers/1.2 miles from the top of the gondola; Whistler Mountain) or to the toe of a small glacier (2.5 kilometers/1.6 miles) from the top of the gondola; Whistler Mountain. It's also possible to rent snowshoes for $6 per hour to walk across areas of year-round snowpack. Or for an adrenaline rush, take the gondola up then bicycle down the mountain with **Backroads Whistler** (604/932-3111, www.backroadswhistler.com).

Even if it's a beautiful day down in the valley, expect the unexpected and take a warm wind- or waterproof coat in anticipation of a change in the weather. Also, some of the hiking trails can be rough, so wear good hiking boots if you plan to explore away from the main trails.

Rates for the sightseeing lifts are adult $25, senior $20, child $7. A two-day pass is adult $29, senior $24, child $7. Summer lift hours are mid-June to September daily 10 A.M.–5 P.M., during the first couple of weekends of June and October 11 A.M.–4 P.M. These dates vary between the mountains and are totally dependent on snow cover, or the lack of it. Dining facilities are available on both mountains, or grab a picnic basket lunch from any of the delis down in the village. The best source of information is the **Whistler Activity Centre** (4010 Whistler Way, 604/938-2769 or 877/991-9988; daily 8:30 A.M.–5 P.M.).

Hiking

The easiest way to access the area's most spectacular hiking country is to take a sightseeing lift up Whistler or Blackcomb Mountain. But many other options exist. Walking around Whistler Valley you'll notice signposted trails all over the place. **Valley Trail** is a paved walkway/bikeway in summer, a cross-country ski trail in winter. It makes an almost complete tour of the valley, from Whistler Village to **Lost** and **Green Lakes,** along the **River of Golden Dreams,** and past three golf courses to **Alta, Nita,** and **Alpha Lakes,** and finally to Highway 99 in the Whistler Creekside area. If you'd rather do a short walk, head for Lost Lake via the two-

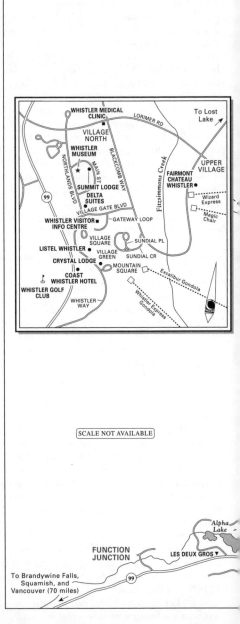

SCALE NOT AVAILABLE

Southwestern B.C.

WHISTLER

To Big Sky Golf and Country Club, Heliport,
Pemberton, Lillooet, and Nairn Falls Provincial Park

EMERALD
ESTATES

99

Green Lake

ALPINE
MEADOWS

RAINBOW DR

NICKLAUS
NORTH GOLF
COURSE

RIVERSIDE
RV RESORT

Fitzsimmons Creek

Valley Trail

River of Golden Dreams

Lost Lake

SHOESTRING LODGE

Lost Lake Park

CHATEAU
WHISTLER
GOLF COURSE

VILLAGE
NORTH

LORIMER RD

LOST LAKE RD

HI WHISTLER

BLACKCOMB WAY

UPPER
VILLAGE

ALTA LAKE RD

Alta Lake

WHISTLER
VILLAGE

Wizard Express

WHISTLER
GOLF CLUB

Excalibur

SEE DETAIL

Gondola

Lakeside Park

Blackcomb Mountain

Wayside Park

Valley
Trail

Nita
Lake

HOZ'S PUB/
EL TIPO'S

Whistler Express Gondola

Whistler Mountain

Quicksilver

WHISTLER
CREEKSIDE

To Singing Pass

kilometer (1.2-mile) trail from Parking Lot East at the back of Whistler Village, or via the WAVE transit bus from the middle of the village. Once at the beautiful lake, saunter along the shore, picnic, swim, or, in winter, cross-country ski.

Between Whistler and Blackcomb Mountains, a gravel road leads five kilometers (3.1 miles) to the trailhead for the **Singing Pass Trail.** From the parking lot, this trail follows the Fitzsimmons Creek watershed for 7.5 kilometers (4.7 miles) to Singing Pass, gaining 600 meters (2,000 feet) in elevation; allow 2.5 hours each way. From the pass, it's another two kilometers (1.2 miles) to beautiful **Russet Lake,** where you'll find a back-country campground.

On the opposite side of the valley, an eight-kilometer (five-mile) trail (three hours each way) leads from Alta Lake Road just north of the Whistler hostel up Twenty One Mile Creek to **Rainbow Lake.** The elevation gain is a strenuous 850 meters (2,800 feet).

Mountain Biking

The Whistler Valley is a perfect place to take a mountain bike—you'd need months to ride all the trails here. Many of the locals have abandoned their cars for bikes, which in some cases are worth much more than their cars! You can see them scooting along **Valley Trail,** a paved walk/bikeway that links the entire valley and is the resident bicyclists' freeway. Another popular place for mountain bikers is beautiful **Lost Lake,** two kilometers (1.2 miles) northeast of Whistler Village.

On the mountain slopes is **Whistler Bike Park,** perfect for adventurous riders to strut their stuff. Using the lifts to access a vertical drop of 1,200 meters (3,900 feet), it features three "Skill Centres," filled with obstacles for varying levels of skill; a Bikercross Course; and trails to the valley floor. Run the courses by yourself or join a group in a guided descent for $70 including bike rental.

If you didn't bring a bike, not to worry—they're for rent. Rental rates start at around $15 per hour, $30–95 per day. Or perhaps a guided bicycle tour of the local area sounds appealing—it's not a bad idea to have a guide at first. **Backroads Whistler** (604/932-3111, www.backroadswhistler.com)

runs a variety of tours, ranging from an easy ride along the valley floor to a hard-core downhill clinic ($80 per person). Backroads Whistler and the following companies rent bikes: **Can-ski Cycles** (Crystal Lodge, 4253 Village Square, 604/938-7755), **Spicy** (Rainbow Building, Gateway Loop, 604/905-2777), **Sportstop** (4112 Golfers Approach, 604/932-5495), **Whistler Bike Co.** (4050 Whistler Way, 604/938-9511), **Whistler Outdoor Experience** (Edgewater Outdoor center, Green Lake, Hwy. 99, 604/932-3389), and **Wild Willies** (4240 Gateway Loop, 604/938-8036).

Water Sports

Sunbathers head for the public beaches along the shores of **Alta Lake**—watching all the windsurfers whipping across the water or beginners repeatedly taking a plunge is a good source of summer entertainment. Wayside Park at the south end of the lake has a beach, a canoe launch, an offshore pontoon, a grassy area with picnic tables, and hiking/biking trails. At Lakeside Park, also on Alta Lake, **Whistler Outdoor Experience** (604/932-3389, www.whistleroutdoor.com) rents canoes for $20 an hour or $60 per half day, and kayaks for $16 an hour. You can also travel by canoe along the smooth-flowing River of Golden Dreams for $49 ($79 guided) or experience the way early explorers traveled by taking a voyageur canoe tour ($30 per person).

For a little white-water excitement, try river rafting with **Whistler River Adventures** (604/932-3532 or 888/932-3532, www.whistler-river.com), which provides guided scenic and white-water tours between the end of May and early September. Outings range from an easy float down the Green River for $69 per person to the white-water thrills of a full-day trip on the Elaho River for $150.

Golfing

Whistler boasts four world-class championship golf courses, each with its own character and charm. The entire valley has gained a reputation as a golfing destination, with many accommodations offering package deals that include greens fees. Still, golfing at Whistler is as expensive as

White-water rafting is a popular summertime pursuit in the Whistler Valley.

anywhere in the country. All the courses below hold a golf shop with club rentals ($40–50) and golfing apparel, and a clubhouse with dining facilities. The golfing season runs mid-May to October, so in late spring you can ski in the morning and golf in the afternoon.

Designed by Arnold Palmer, **Whistler Golf Club** (between Whistler Village and Alta Lake, 604/932-3280 or 800/376-1777) offers large greens and narrow wooded fairways over a challenging 6,676-yard par-72 layout. Greens fees are $159 (the twilight rate of $99 is offered after 4 P.M.), cart rental is $35, and club rental costs from $35.

On the other side of the village is **Chateau Whistler Golf Club** (Blackcomb Way, 604/938-2092 or 888/938-2092). Designed by renowned golf-course architect Robert Trent Jones Jr., this 6,635-yard course takes advantage of the rugged terrain of Blackcomb Mountain's lower slopes through holes that rise and fall with the lay of the land. Greens fees are $225, which includes the use of a cart equipped with a computerized yardage meter. After 3 P.M., rates drop to $145.

The Jack Nicklaus–designed **Nicklaus North** course (just north of Whistler Village, 604/938-9898) is an open layout holding numerous water hazards, It boasts 360-degree mountain vistas and plays to a challenging 6,900 yards from the back markers. Weekend greens fees are $210, discounted to $165 midweek.

Farther up the valley is **Big Sky Golf and Country Club** (604/894-6106 or 800/668-7900), a lengthy par-72 course of over 7,000 yards; $157 per round with cart rental an additional $35.

Flightseeing

Nothing beats the spectacular sight of the Coast Mountains' majestic peaks, glaciers, icy-blue lakes, and lush mountain meadows from an unforgettable vantage point high in the sky. **Whistler Air** (604/932-6615 or 888/806-2299) will take you aloft in a floatplane from Green Lake, three kilometers (1.9 miles) north of Whistler Village. A 30-minute flight over the glaciers of Garibaldi Provincial Park costs $99; a 40-minute flight over the Pemberton Ice Cap goes for $129; and an 80-minute flight landing on a high alpine lake runs $169. You can also charter the whole plane (minimum four people) for a remote backcountry adventure.

SKIING AND SNOWBOARDING

No matter what your ability, the skiing at **Whistler/Blackcomb,** consistently rated as North America's number one ski destination, makes for a winter holiday you won't forget in a hurry. Until the 1997–98 season, the ski area comprised two different resorts which in themselves boasted impressive statistics. Combined, they now overshadow all other North American resorts in terms of size and stature. The two lift-served mountains, Whistler and Blackcomb, are separated by a steep-sided valley through which Fitzsimmons Creek flows, with lifts converging at Whistler Village. Skiing is over almost 3,000 hectares (7,400 acres), comprising more than 200 groomed runs, hundreds of unmarked trails through forested areas, three glaciers, and 12 bowls. Blackcomb and Whistler Mountains are 2,284 meters (7,500 feet) and 2,182 meters (7,160 feet) high respectively. The lift-served vertical rise of Blackcomb is 1,609

meters (5,280 feet), the highest in North America, but Whistler is only slightly lower at 1,530 meters (5,020 feet). (When Blackcomb and Whistler operated as separate entities, they boasted North America's highest and second-highest vertical rises.) In total, the resort has 34 lifts, including three gondolas, 12 high-speed quad chairlifts, five triples, one double, and 12 surface lifts. The terrain is rated Intermediate over 55 percent of the resort, with the remaining 45 percent split evenly between Beginner and Expert. Snowboarders are well catered to with four terrain parks and numerous half pipes. The length of season is also impressive, running from November to early May with the Horstman Glacier open for skiing for a few weeks of summer (see sidebar, *Summer Skiing*).

The two mountains are similar not only in height but also size. Whistler offers 1,480 hectares (3,660 acres) of skiing, Blackcomb slightly less. From Whistler Village, a five-kilometer-long (3.1-mile-long) gondola lifts skiers more than a vertical kilometer up Whistler Mountain (the one on the right as you look up at the resort from the valley floor) above the valley to east-facing slopes served by eight chairlifts

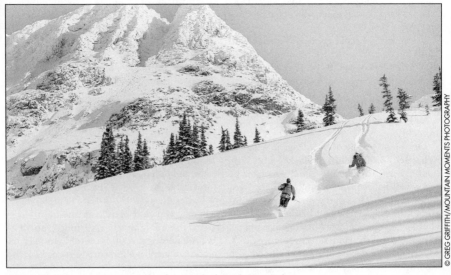

downhill skiers enjoying a powder day on Blackcomb Mountain

and a T-bar. Over the back of the main mountain, the Harmony Express quad chairlift serves 400 hectares (1,000 acres) of bowl skiing. Much of Blackcomb Mountain is out of sight from the valley; over half the skiing is above the tree line, and over the back are two massive powder-filled bowls.

For many, the resort can be overwhelming. Trail maps detail all marked runs but can't convey the vast size of the area. A great way to get to know the mountain is on an orientation tour; these leave throughout the day from various meeting points (ask when and where as you buy your ticket) and are free. **Whistler/Blackcomb Ski and Snowboard School** (604/932-3434 or 800/766-0449) is the country's largest ski school and offers various lesson packages and programs, such as the Esprit, a three-day, women's-only "camp" that provides instruction in a variety of disciplines.

Lift tickets are adult $73, senior and youth $64, child $39, and those under seven ski for free. The resort's website (www.whistlerblackcomb.com) contains everything you'll need to know about the resort and booking winter accommodation packages, or call the general inquiries desk (604/932-3434 or 800/766-0449). For accommodation information call Whistler Central Reservations (604/904-7060 or 888/403-4727).

Cross-Country Skiing

Many kilometers of trails wind through snow-covered terrain in the valley. Starting at Whistler Village and running in a long loop past Lost Lake and Green Lake is the **Valley Trail,** a paved walk/bikeway in summer that becomes a popular cross-country ski trail in winter. The biggest concentration of trails lies near Lost Lake and on the adjacent Chateau Whistler Golf Course. Most trails are groomed, while some are track set, and a five-kilometer stretch is illuminated for night skiing. The trail system is operated by the **Whistler Nordic Cross-country Ski Club** (604/932-6436), which collects a fee of $15 for a day pass from a ticket booth near Lost Lake, where you'll also find a cozy warming hut.

Heli-Skiing

Heli-skiing is offered by **Whistler Heli-skiing** (Crystal Lodge, 604/932-4105), which takes strong intermediate and expert adventurers high into the Coast Mountains to ski fields of untracked powder. Rates of $670 include a day's skiing, transportation to and from the heliport north of Whistler Village, a gourmet lunch, and the guide.

INDOOR RECREATION

Great Wall, under the Westbrook Hotel (4340 Sundial Cres., 604/905-7625; daily 10 A.M.–10 P.M.), is an indoor climbing wall with varying degrees of slope and an overhang. It costs $16 for a day pass with instruction and equipment rental ($8) extra.

Pamper Yourself

Whistler Body Wrap (4433 Sundial Place, Whistler Village, 604/932-4710) offers a wide variety of spa treatments, including massages, facials, body wraps, and salon services. A standard 25-minute massage costs $75, or a full day of treatments—including an herbal body wrap—and lunch costs from $360. **Vida Wellness Spa** (Fairmont Chateau Whistler, 4599 Chateau Blvd., 604/938-2086) is a more luxurious facility styled on Romanesque surroundings. It offers all the same services but at a higher cost.

ENTERTAINMENT AND EVENTS
Drinking and Dancing

Throughout the year you can usually find live evening entertainment in Whistler Village. The **Garibaldi Lift Co. Bar & Grill** (2320 London Lane, 604/905-2220) features live entertainment most nights—often blues and jazz—and good food at reasonable prices. At **Buffalo Bill's** (Timberline Lodge, 4122 Village Green, 604/932-6613) expect anything from reggae to rock. For over a decade, **Tommy Africa's** (4216 Gateway Dr., 604/932-6090) has been one of the village's hottest nightspots. It's popular with the younger crowd, pumping out high-volume reggae across the valley's most crowded dance floor. Head to

Savage Beagle (4222 Village Square, 604/938-3337), nightly between 8 P.M. and 2 A.M. for dance, house, and alternative music.

The Boot Pub, in the Shoestring Lodge (Nancy Greene Way, 604/932-3338), offers some of the cheapest drinks in the valley and live music three nights a week.

Black's Pub (Westbrook Hotel, Mountain Square, 604/932-6945) offers more than 90 international beers and a quiet atmosphere in a small upstairs English-style bar. Another more refined watering hole is the Crystal Lounge (Crystal Lodge, 4154 Village Square, 604/932-2221).

Events

The winter season is packed with ski and snowboard races, but the biggest is the World Ski & Snowboard Festival, through mid-April (604/938-3399, www.wssf.com). This innovative event brings together the very best winter athletes for the World Skiing Invitational and the World Snowboarding Championship. These are only the flagships of this 10-day extravaganza, which also includes demo days, exhibitions, and a film festival.

Each weekend in May and June and daily through summer, the streets of Whistler come alive with street entertainment such as musicians, jugglers, and comedians. The last weekend of May is the official end of the ski season up on Blackcomb Mountain, with a Slush Cup and live music.

Canada Day, July 1, is celebrated with a parade through Whistler Village. Whistler Arts Music Festival, the first full weekend of July, includes lots of free entertainment, including outdoor film screenings and street music.

During Oktoberfest, many restaurants and businesses dress themselves up in a Bavarian theme. The festival also features dancing in the streets and, of course, a beer hall.

ACCOMMODATIONS AND CAMPING

Whistler's accommodations range from a hostel and inexpensive dorm beds to luxury resort hotels. It's just a matter of selecting one to suit your budget and location preference. Skiers may want to be right in Whistler Village or by the gondola base in Whistler Creekside so they can stroll out their door, strap on skis, and jump on a lift. (The term "slopeside" describes accommodations within a five-minute walk of the lifts.)

Accommodation pricing in Whistler is very complex. The best advice is to shop around using the phone or Internet. Contact the lodgings themselves, then the booking agencies listed below to get a comparison.

Winter is most definitely high season, with the week after Christmas and all of February and March a high season within a high season, especially for lodgings within walking distance of the lifts or that are self-contained and capable of sleeping more than two people. These are also the accommodations that discount most heavily outside of winter. For example, at the Delta Whistler Village Suites website (www.deltahotels.com), type in a February date and then a July date under reservations—a bargain in July and over the top in winter.

Although winter is peak season, rates quoted below are for summertime.

Reservation Services

If you plan on skiing or golfing, a package deal is the way to go. These can be booked directly through many accommodations, but the following agencies offer a wider scope of choices. Tourism Whistler (604/664-5625 or 800/944-7853, www.tourismwhistler.com) is one option, as are the following: Allure Direct (604/707-6700, www.alluradirect.com/whistler), Champagne Chalets of Whistler (604/938-1184 or 800/465-3754, www.sportpak.com), Powder Resort Properties (604/684-9378 or 800/777-0185, www.powderresorts.com), Rainbow Retreats Accommodations (604/932-2343, website www.rainbowretreats.com), Resort Quest (604/932-6699 or 877/588-5800, website www.resortquest.com), and Whistler Central Reservations (604/905-4607 or 866/905-4607, www.whistler-resort.com).

Under $50

HI–Whistler (5678 Alta Lake Rd., 604/932-

5492, www.hihostels.ca) is on the western shore of Alta Lake, boasting magnificent views across the lake to the resort. It's relatively small (just 32 beds), with facilities including a communal kitchen, dining area, and big, cozy living area. Bike and canoe rentals are available. It's understandably popular year-round; members pay $20 per night, nonmembers $24 ($24 and $28 in winter). Check-in is 8–11 A.M. and 4–10 P.M. To get there from the south, take Alta Lake Road to the left off Highway 99 and watch for the small sign on the lake side of the road. WAVE transit buses depart Whistler Village and run right past the hostel door ($1.50).

The **Shoestring Lodge** (7124 Nancy Greene Dr., White Gold Estates, 604/932-3338 or 877/551-4954, www.shoestringlodge.com) started life in the 1960s as the Ski Boot Motel, one of the first lodgings in the valley. It has morphed into a popular hangout for budget travelers, mostly for its rowdy pub but also for its inexpensive dorm beds ($21 per night, $105 per week). Or go upscale and stay in a private room ($80 s or d). It's north of Whistler Village on the right side of the highway,

$50–100

There's not to much on offer in Whistler in this price bracket—it's either a dorm bed or an expensive hotel room. The exception is the **Shoestring Lodge** (7124 Nancy Greene Dr., 604/932-3338 or 877/551-4954, www.shoestringlodge.com), detailed above for its dormitories. It also has small double rooms (which can get noisy) with en suite bathrooms, TV, and daily housekeeping. Summer rates are $80 per night or $280 for a full week. It's out of the village, but the downstairs pub and bistro both serve meals.

$100–150

Ⓜ Crystal Lodge (4154 Village Green, 604/932-2221 or 800/667-3363, www.crystal-lodge.com) stands out as excellent value in the heart of the action of Whistler Village. Rooms in the original wing are spacious and have a homely feel. Summer rates ($125) are excellent. The North Wing, which opened in early 2005, holds larger suites that have balconies and mod-

ern amenities such as Internet access. Summer rates for these are a still-reasonable $269 s or d. All guests have the use of an outdoor hot tub and heated pool.

$150–200

The modern log cabins at the **Ⓜ Riverside RV Resort** (8018 Mons Rd., 604/905-5533 or 877/905-5533, www.whistlercamping.com) aren't very spacious, but you're in Whistler, so you'll be spending most of your time hiking, biking, and generally being outdoors anyway. The cabins ooze mountain charm and come complete with a small kitchen and TV/VCR combo for $150 ($175–205 in winter). An on-site grocery store and café save heading into town.

On the edge of the village and adjacent to one of the valley's best golf courses is **Coast Whistler Hotel** (4005 Whistler Way, 604/932-2522 or 800/663-5644, www.coastwhistlerhotel.com). Each of the 194 rooms is simply but stylishly decorated in pastel colors. Facilities include a heated outdoor pool, exercise room, hot tub, restaurant, and bar. Summer rates start at a rea-

Delta Whistler Village Suites

© ANDREW HEMPSTEAD

sonable $159 (from $109 in spring and fall), but the winter rate of $295 s or d is a little steep considering you're away from the ski lifts.

Centrally located **Delta Whistler Village Suites** (4308 Main St., 604/905-3987 or 888/299-3987, www.deltahotels.com) combines the conveniences of a full-service hotel with more than 200 kitchen-equipped units—the only such property in Whistler. Advertised rack rates are $180 s or d (summer), but check the website for promotional deals.

$200–250

In the heart of the action, **M Listel Whistler** (4121 Village Green, 604/932-1133 or 800/663-5472, www.listelhotel.com) is a self-contained resort complete with a year-round outdoor pool, outdoor hot tub, and laundry. The in-house Bearfoot Bistro means you don't need to leave for dinner. The contemporary styled rooms are $249 s or d through much of year, rising to $349 in February and March. Check the Listel website for specials.

Over $250

Summit Lodge (4359 Main St., 604/932-2778 or 888/913-8811, www.summitlodge.com) is a luxurious European Alps–style boutique hotel. Each of the 81 units features comfortable furnishings, a slate floor, a fireplace, a balcony, and a small kitchen. Off-season rates start at $300 s or d, rising to $450 in winter.

Fairmont Chateau Whistler, at the base of Blackcomb Mountain in Upper Village (604/938-8000 or 866/540-4424, www.fairmont.com), is Whistler's most luxurious lodging, with its own championship golf course, the Vida Wellness Spa, a health club with the best equipment money can buy, tennis courts, and all the facilities expected of one of the world's best accommodations. The massive lobby is decorated in the style of a rustic lodge, but the rooms couldn't be more different. Each is elegantly furnished and offers great mountain views. In the low season (late spring and fall) rooms start at $300 s or d; peak summer rates start at $380 s or d, winter rates at $460 s or d.

Camping

Enjoying a pleasant location just over two kilometers (1.2 miles) north of the village, **Riverside RV Resort** (8018 Mons Rd., 604/905-5533 or 877/905-5533, www.whistlercamping.com) is the only campground within town boundaries. It offers a modern bathroom complex (with in-floor heating), putting course, playground, hot tub, laundry, small general store, and a café (daily from 7 A.M.). Sites range $30–45, with a small wooded area set aside for walk-in tent campers. Cabins are $150 ($175–205 in winter).

Out of town, the closest campgrounds are in **Brandywine Falls Provincial Park,** 11 kilometers (6.8 miles) south, and **Nairn Falls Provincial Park,** 28 kilometers (17.4 miles) north. Both are open April–November and charge $14 per night. For more facilities, **Dryden Creek Resorts** (50 km/31 miles south, 604/898-9726 or 800/903-4690) is a good option.

FOOD

Like the town itself, the dining scene in Whistler is hip, ever-changing, and not particularly cheap. Many small cafés dot the cobbled walkways of Whistler Village, while most bars have reasonably priced pub-fare menus.

For a caffeine fix, **Moguls Coffee House** (4204 Village Square, 604/932-4845; daily from 6:30 A.M.) is as good as any place—it's popular with both locals and visitors, and the outdoor seating catches the morning sun.

Breakfast on the Mountain

Through the ski season, Whistler/Blackcomb offers breakfast on the mountain, as well as the chance to hit the slopes before the lifts officially open. On Blackcomb, it's coffee and cakes in the **Rendezvous Restaurant** for $9.50, while over on Whistler, a full buffet breakfast in **Pika's Restaurant** is $16. These breakfast deals must be paid for in conjunction with a lift pass, and lifts open at 7:30 A.M. for diners.

Cool and Casual

The rustic decor and great Canadian food at **Garibaldi Lift Co. Bar & Grill** (at the base of the Whistler Village gondola, 604/905-2220) have been a big hit since it opened in 1995. The bar and sundeck are popular après-ski hangouts, and by around 8 P.M. everyone's back for dinner. For western-style atmosphere with mountain views, head to the **Longhorn Saloon and Grill** (4290 Mountain Square, 604/932-5999; daily from 11 A.M.) and share a platter of finger food or order your own cut of prime Alberta beef, complete with trimmings for $18–27.

Ⓜ **Citta's Bistro** (4217 Village Stroll, Whistler Village, 604/932-4177; daily for lunch and dinner) has been around since Whistler first became a hip destination—and it's as popular today as it ever was. If it's a warm evening, try for a table on the patio and order a gourmet pizza for one ($14–17) to go with a locally brewed beer.

On the south side of Whistler Village, **Hoz's Pub** (2129 Lake Placid Rd., 604/932-5940; daily from 11:30 A.M.) is popular among locals for its well-priced food and untouristy atmosphere. Look for typical pub fare, as well as a few West Coast–inspired choices (battered salmon and chips, $11). If you feel like heading south of the border for dinner, have a beer at Hoz's, then move next door to **El Tipo's** (604/932-4424) to feast on the valley's best Mexican food. The chicken enchilada ($14) was a real treat. Children will enjoy the funky atmosphere and their own menu.

Steak

For steaks, seafood, a salad bar, fresh hot bread, and plenty of food at a reasonable price, the **Keg at the Mountain** (Whistler Village Inn, 4429 Sundial Pl., 604/932-5151; daily from 5:30 P.M.) is a sure thing. The atmosphere is casual, yet the service is slick and refreshingly attentive. Expect to pay from $14 for an entrée.

At Ⓜ **Hy's** (Delta Whistler Village Suites, 4308 Main St., 604/905-5555), you don't need to ask if the steak is good—everything on offer is top-notch AAA Alberta beef, including a signature, not-for-the-faint-hearted porterhouse. The scene is upmarket, with elegant tables set within richly colored wood walls. Starters range $8–12 with steaks starting at $28.

European

For great Greek food at reasonable prices, **Zeuski's Taverna** (4314 Main St., Town Plaza, Village North, 604/932-6009) is an excellent choice for lunch or dinner. For something different, sample the souvlaki cooked on the barbecue.

Restaurant entrepreneur Umberto Menghi operates numerous eateries in Vancouver and two restaurants in Whistler Village. Both are reasonably priced with menus influenced by the cuisine of Tuscany. Check out **Il Caminetto di Umberto** (4242 Village Stroll, 604/932-4442) and **Trattoria di Umberto** (4417 Sundial Place, 604/932-5858). The former, named for a fireplace that has been replaced by more tables, has a warm, welcoming atmosphere and a long menu of pastas from $18. The latter is less expensive and attracts a more casual crowd. Both are open daily for dinner.

Ⓜ **Araxi** (4222 Village Square, Whistler Village, 604/932-4540; daily from 5 P.M.) consistently wins awards for its traditional Italian menu, which takes advantage of produce from around the Lower Mainland. It also boasts an extensive wine list.

Les Deux Gros (one km/.6 mile west of Whistler Creekside, Alta Lake Rd., 604/932-4611; Tues.–Sun. 5:30–10:30 P.M.) does a memorable job of combining classic French cooking with mountain ambience. Mains such as oven-roasted Cornish hen and beef béarnaise range $16–36.

Asian

Reasonably priced Mongolian fare is on the menu at **Mongolie Grill** (4295 Whistler Way, Whistler Village, 604/938-9416; daily from 11:30 A.M.). This is one of the better places to take children. They'll love choosing their own ingredients—meats, vegetables, etc.—with matching sauces, and then watch the speedy chefs fry up the personalized dish in front of them.

INFORMATION AND SERVICES

The **Whistler Visitor Info Centre** is centrally located (4230 Gateway Dr., 604/932-5922; daily 9 A.M.–6 P.M.). Also in the village is the **Whistler**

2010 Info Centre (604/932-2010; Thurs.–Sun. 11 A.M.–5 P.M.), where you can learn all about the Olympic Winter Games and the planning and development that goes along with hosting the world's premier sporting event.

Good sources of pretrip planning information are **Tourism Whistler** (www.tourismwhistler .com) and the **Whistler Chamber of Commerce** website (www.whistlerchamber.com).

Three newspapers are good sources of local information: the daily *Question* (www.whistlerquestion .com); the tourist-oriented *Whistler this Week* (www.whistlerthisweek.com); and the weekly *Pique* (www.piquenewsmagazine.com).

In Whistler Village you'll find a post office, banks, a currency exchange, laundry, supermarket, and liquor store. **Whistler Medical Centre** is at 4380 Lorimer (604/932-3977).

Whistler Public Library (4329 Main St., 604/932-5564; Mon.–Tues. and Thurs. 10 A.M.–8 P.M., Fri.–Sun. 10 A.M.–5 P.M.) has an international selection of newspapers and magazines, plus free public Internet access.

TRANSPORTATION

Getting There

Whistler has no airport; instead, you can fly in with **Whistler Air** (604/932-6615 or 888/806-2299, www.whistler.com), which operates scheduled floatplane flights between downtown Vancouver and Green Lake (just north of Whistler Village) for $149 one-way, $249 round-trip. The flight takes around 30 minutes and the baggage limit is 25 pounds plus $1 for every extra pound.

Vancouver International Airport, 130 kilometers (81 miles) to the south, is the main gateway to Whistler. **Perimeter** (604/266-5386 or 877/317-7788) provides bus service between the two up to 11 times daily; adult $65, child $45. Buses make stops at some Vancouver hotels and a short rest stop at pretty Shannon Falls. **Greyhound** (800/667-0882, www.whistlerbus.com) runs six buses daily between Vancouver's Pacific Central Station (1150 Station St.) and Whistler Village; $30 one-way, $54 round-trip, with connections from the airport.

Getting Around

Once you're in Whistler, getting around is pretty easy—if you're staying in Whistler Village, everything you need is within easy walking distance. **WAVE** (Whistler and Valley Express; 604/932-4020) operates extensive bus routes throughout the valley daily 6 A.M.–midnight. Routes radiate from Village Exchange in Whistler Village south to Whistler Creekside and as far north as Emerald Estates on the shore of Green Lake. Fare is $1.50, senior and child $1.25 (exact change only). A 10-ride WAVE Card is adult $13, senior and child $11.

For a cab call **Sea to Sky Taxi** (604/932-3333) or **Whistler Taxi** (604/938-3333).

Rental car-agencies in Whistler include **Budget** (604/932-1236) and **Thrifty** (604/938-0302).

The Gold Nugget Route

The route north between Whistler and Lillooet is best traveled in good weather—the scenery is so spectacular you don't want to miss *anything*. See white-topped peaks all around you and big glacier-colored rivers. If you have the time, stop at provincial parks along the way for always-good scenery and outdoor activities.

Make your first stop north of Whistler at **Nairn Falls Provincial Park,** on the banks of Green River, where a wooded trail leads to a waterfall. Stay overnight at the campground (Apr.–Nov., $14).

Pemberton

This small logging community is growing rapidly as a cheaper housing alternative for Whistler workers, who commute the 32 kilometers (20 miles) south. Surrounded by mountains, trees, lakes, and rivers, Pemberton sits in a fertile valley known for its potatoes. It's only a short distance south of the Lillooet River, a main transportation route to the Cariboo during the 1860s' gold-rush days. Today's visitors mostly leave their gold pans at home, coming mainly to fish or to hike in the beautiful valleys around Pemberton.

The summer-only **Pemberton Visitor Info Centre** (604/894-6175, www.pembertonchamber.com) is back out of town on Highway 99.

North to Lillooet

From Pemberton you can take one of three routes to Lillooet. Whichever route you decide on, it's important to note that the weather can change rapidly, and even in summer you might find yourself traveling through a sudden snowstorm at higher elevations. However, the scenery makes the effort worthwhile. You'll see beautiful lakes, fast rivers, summer wildflowers, deep-blue mountains, steep ravines, never-ending forests, and vistas in every shade of green imaginable. Campgrounds and picnic areas mark all the best locations.

The most direct way—the route once taken by fortune seekers heading toward the Cariboo goldfields—is paved Highway 99. A few minutes' drive out of Mount Currie, the highway begins switchbacking, as it climbs abruptly into the Coast Mountains and crests at a 1,300-meter-high (4,260-foot-high) pass. Just before the pass is 1,460-hectare (3,600-acre) **Joffre Lakes Provincial Park,** where a short trail (allow 20 minutes round-trip) leads to Lower Joffre Lake. The trail continues beyond the first lake, making an elevation gain of 400 meters (1,300 feet) before reaching the main body of water, 10 kilometers (6.2 miles) from the highway.

From the pass, Highway 99 loses over 1,000 meters (3,300 feet) of elevation in its descent to Lillooet. Along the way is narrow **Duffey Lake** (the highway itself is referred to locally as the "Duffey Lake Road"), backed by the steep-sided Cayoosh Range. At the north end of the lake is a provincial park with camping ($14 per night).

The second route (summer only) spurs north through Mount Currie following the Birkenhead River, passing the turnoff to 9,755-hectare (24,100-acre) **Birkenhead Lake Provincial Park,** then descending to **D'Arcy.** Beyond this point, the road can get extremely rough, so check conditions in town before setting out.

The third, northernmost, and longest route, over 200 kilometers (124 miles) of mostly unpaved road (also summer only), climbs north along the Lillooet River through Pemberton Meadows, over Hurley Pass, and to the historic mining communities of **Gold Bridge** and **Bralorne** before closely following the shore of Carpenter Lake in an easterly direction back to Lillooet.

For information on **Lillooet,** the confluence of the three above routes, see the *Cariboo Country* section of the *Central British Columbia* chapter.

East from Vancouver

FRASER VALLEY

When you leave Vancouver and head due east, you travel through the most built-up and heavily populated area of British Columbia, skirting modern cities, residential suburbs, and zones of heavy industry. However, it's not an unattractive area—the main roads follow the mighty Fraser River through a fertile valley of rolling farmland dotted with historic villages, and beautiful mountains line the horizon in just about any direction.

You have a choice of two major routes. The TransCanada Highway, on the south side of the Fraser River, speeds you out of southeast Vancouver through Abbotsford and scenic Chilliwack to Hope. Slower, more picturesque Highway 7 meanders along the north side of the Fraser River through **Mission,** named after a Roman Catholic mission school built in 1861. The town is now known for its Benedictine monastery, which offers a retreat center open to the public. The highway then passes the access road to **Harrison Hot Springs** and crosses over the Fraser River to Hope. In summer you can pick and choose from an endless number of roadside stands selling fresh fruit at bargain prices—the raspberries in July are delectable.

Fort Langley National Historic Site

In 1827, the Hudson's Bay Company established a settlement 48 kilometers (30 miles) upstream from the mouth of the Fraser River as part of a network of trading posts, provision depots, and administrative centers that stretched across Western Canada. The original site was abandoned in 1838 in favor of another, farther upstream, where today the settlement has been re-created. It was the abundance of fur-bearing mammals that led to the region's settlement originally, but within a decade salmon had become its mainstay. Through its formative years, the fort played a major role in the development of British Columbia. Out of its gates have poured native fur and salmon traders, adventurous explorers who opened up

the interior, company traders, and fortune seekers heading for the goldfields of the upper Fraser River. When British Columbia became a crown colony on November 19, 1858, the official proclamation was uttered here in the "big house." In the process, Fort Langley was declared capital of the colony, but one year later, the entire colonial government moved to the more central New Westminster.

Today, the restored riverside trading post (23433 Mavis St., Fort Langley, 604/513-4777; Mar.–Oct. 10 A.M.–5 P.M.; adult $5.75, senior $5, child $3) springs to life as park interpreters in period costumes animate the fort's history. The park is within walking distance of Fort Langley village, where many businesses are built in a heritage style and you'll find dozens of antique shops,

Bridal Veil Falls, east of Chilliwack, makes a pleasant stop on the journey through the Fraser Valley.

boutiques, restaurants, and cafés along its main tree-lined street.

To get there, follow Highway 1 for 50 kilometers (31 miles) east from downtown and head north toward the Fraser River from Exit 66 on 232nd Street then Glover Road. From the highway it's five kilometers (3.1 miles) to downtown Fort Langley; the fort itself lies a few blocks east of the main street. It's well posted from Highway 1.

East Toward Hope

If you've visited Fort Langley, backtrack south to continue east along the valley. Instead of continuing along Highway 1, cross the transcontinental highway on Glover Road to Langley city center, then head east on Old Yale Road and into an area laced with lazy country roads. If you decide to cross from Highway 1 to Highway 7 at Abbotsford, make the detour to delightful **Clayburn Village,** originally a company town for a local brickworks. As you'd expect, most of the neat houses are built of brick, providing a local atmosphere a world away from the surrounding modern subdivisions. Along the main street, **Clayburn Village Store** (Wright St., Tues.–Sat. 9 A.M.–5 P.M., Sun. noon A.M.–5 P.M.) is a general store that has changed little in appearance since opening almost 100 years ago. The highlight is the delicious Devonshire tea, although children will say it's the candy sold from big glass jars. Reach the store by taking Exit 92 north from Highway 1, follow Highway 11 north for six kilometers (3.7 miles), and then head east along Clayburn Road.

It is possible to continue east through Clayburn to **Sumas Mountain Provincial Park** (ask directions at the local general store), or take Exit 95 from Highway 1 to Sumas Mountain Road, then take Batts Road, which climbs steadily up the mountain's southern slopes. From the end of this service road, it's a short climb to the 900-meter (2,950-foot) summit of Sumas Mountain, from which views extend north across the Fraser River and south across a patchwork of farmland to Washington's snowcapped Mount Baker. From the pullout one kilometer (.6 mile) from the end of road, a hiking trail descends for 1.6 kilometers

(one mile) to forest-encircled Chadsey Lake and a lakeside picnic area.

If you're heading east of out of city, plan on gassing up at one of the stations beside Exit 95—they are generally cheaper than those closer to downtown and definitely less expensive than those farther east.

Farther east along the TransCanada Highway, **Cultus Lake Provincial Park,** 11 kilometers (6.8 miles) south of Chilliwack, holds a warm-water lake surrounded by mountains—a good spot for swimming, picnicking, or camping. A day pass is $5 per vehicle and camping is $22 per night.

Kilby Historic Store and Farm

Off the beaten track and often missed by those unfamiliar with the area, this historic site (604/796-9576; Mar.–mid-May Sat.–Sun. 11 A.M.–4 P.M., late May–early Sept. daily 11 A.M.–5 P.M.) lies on the north side of the Fraser River, near the turnoff to Harrison Hot Springs, 40 kilometers (25 miles) east of Mission and six kilometers (3.7 miles) west of Agassiz (look for the inconspicuous sign close to Harrison Mills). The fascinating museum/country store, which operated until the early 1970s, is fully stocked with all the old brands and types of goods that were commonplace in the 1920s and '30s. The two-hectare (five-acre) riverside grounds contain farm equipment, farm animals, a gift shop, and a café serving delicious home-style cooking.

Around the corner, you can picnic, swim, and fish at **Harrison Bay.**

Harrison Hot Springs

Of British Columbia's 60 natural hot springs, the closest to Vancouver is Harrison Hot Springs, on the north side of the Fraser Valley, 125 kilometers (78 miles) east of downtown. Known as the "Spa of Canada," the springs lie on the sandy southern shores of the Lower Mainland's largest body of water, **Harrison Lake.** Since the opening of the province's first resort in 1886, the springs have spurred much surrounding development. Coast Salish were the first to take advantage of the soothing water. Then in the late 1850s, gold miners stumbled upon the springs. Due to a historical agreement, only the Harrison Hot Springs Resort has water rights, but the hotel operates **Harrison Public Pool** (corner of Harrison Hot Springs Rd. and Esplanade Ave., 604/796-2244; summer daily 8 A.M.–9 P.M., the rest of the year daily 9 A.M.–9 P.M.; adult $8, senior and child $5.75). Scalding 74°C (165°F) mineral water is pumped from its source, cooled to a soothing 38°C (100°F), then pumped into the pool. The lake itself provides many recreation opportunities, with good swimming, sailing, canoeing, and fishing for rainbow trout. Through town to the north is 1,220-hectare (3,010-acre) **Sasquatch Provincial Park,** named for a tall, hairy, unshaven beast that supposedly inhabits the area. The park extends from a day-use area on the bank of Harrison Lake to picturesque tree-encircled lakes, each with road access, short hiking trails, and picnic areas.

Lakeside **Harrison Hot Springs Resort** (100 Esplanade, 604/796-2244 or 800/663-2266, www.harrisonresort.com) is the town's most elegant accommodation, and it offers guests use of a large indoor and outdoor complex of mineral pools, complete with grassed areas, lots of outdoor furniture, and a café. Other facilities include boat and canoe rentals, sailing lessons, and a restaurant and lounge bar. Most of the 323 rooms have private balconies, many with spectacular views across the lake. Summer rates range $160–240 s or d, but check the website for specials. Within walking distance of the public hot pool and lake is **Glencoe Motel** (259 Hot Springs Rd., 604/796-2574, www.glencoemotel.com; $68 s, $78 d). The least expensive overnight option is to camp at one of three campgrounds along the road into town or through town in lakeside **Sasquatch Provincial Park.**

Harrison Hot Springs Visitor Info Centre is beside the main road into town (604/796-3425; summer daily 8 A.M.–6 P.M.).

HOPE AND VICINITY

Locals say "all roads lead to Hope"—and they're right. On a finger of land at the confluence of the Fraser and Coquihalla Rivers, 158 kilometers (98 miles) east of Vancouver, Hope (pop. 7,000)

the Othello-Quintette Tunnels

really is a hub. The TransCanada Highway and Highway 7 from Vancouver, the Coquihalla Highway to Kamloops, and Highway 3 from the Okanagan all meet at Hope. Don't be put off by first impressions of the town itself. Surrounded by magnificent mountains and rivers, with a couple of great wilderness areas only a short drive away and an abundance of recreational opportunities, Hope is a great place to spend some time.

Simon Fraser, after whom the Fraser River was named, stopped in this area in 1808 after leading the first expedition south down Fraser River Canyon. By 1848 Fort Hope had been set up by the Hudson's Bay Company as a fur-trading post. With the discovery of gold in the canyon in 1858, Hope became a busy stopping point and meeting spot for adventurers and fortune seekers. How did Hope get its name? No one really knows, but most theories revolve around various explorers or settlers feeling some kind of hope at reaching the river junction at which the town lies.

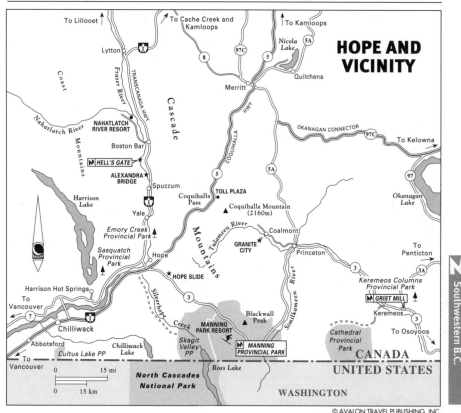

© AVALON TRAVEL PUBLISHING, INC.

Town Sights

To find out more about the history of Hope, visit **Hope Museum** (919 Water Ave., 604/869-7322; May–June daily 9 A.M.–5 P.M., July–Aug. daily 8 A.M.–8 P.M.), in the same building as the information center. The museum's comprehensive collection of pioneer artifacts is displayed in several re-created settings, including a kitchen, bedroom, parlor, schoolroom, and blacksmith shop. Other exhibits focus on local native crafts and on artifacts from the original Fort Hope and goldrush days. Outside, climb on the Hope Gold Mill, a restored gold-ore concentrator from the Coquihalla area.

While you're discovering the downtown area, check out the authentic **Japanese garden** in Memorial Park beside the town hall. The garden was constructed to commemorate Tashme, a World War II internment camp for Japanese-Canadians that was east of Hope. Also don't miss the tree-stump art in Memorial Park. The eagle holding a salmon in its claws (in front of the district office) was carved from a tree with root rot, and it was one of the original tree-stump works of art. As the years go by, more and more carvings (28 at last count) are added by chainsaw artist Pete Ryan. During summer look for him in the park, working on his latest creation.

Othello-Quintette Tunnels

These five huge tunnels through a steep gorge of **Coquihalla Canyon** were carved out of solid granite by the Kettle Valley Railway, completing a route for the company's steam locomotives between Vancouver and Nelson. The tunnels opened in 1916, but the line was plagued by snow, rock slides, and washouts, and closed for repairs more often than it was open. It was eventually abandoned in 1959. By 1962 the tracks and four steel bridges over the awesome Coquihalla River gorge had been removed. Today a short, tree-shaded walk takes you from the **Coquihalla Canyon Provincial Park** parking lot to the massive, dark tunnels, now a popular tourist attraction. Stroll through them and over the sturdy wooden bridges to admire the gorge and the power and the roar of the Coquihalla River below. If you'd visited the tunnels back in 1981 you would have seen Sylvester Stallone swinging through the canyons during the filming of the first Rambo movie, *First Blood.* To get to the tunnels from downtown, take Wallace Street to 6th Avenue and turn right. Turn left on Kawkawa Lake Road, crossing the Coquihalla River Bridge and railway tracks. At the first intersection take the right branch, Othello Road, and continue until you see a sign to the right (over a rise and easy to miss) pointing to the recreation area. The tunnels are closed November–April.

On the way up to the tunnels, **Kawkawa Lake** is a pleasant body of water with a high concentration of kokanee and a lakeside picnic area.

Skagit Valley Provincial Park

This remote wilderness of 32,577 hectares (80,500 acres) southeast of Hope is bordered to the east by Manning Provincial Park and to the south by the U.S.–Canada border. Access is along the Silver-Skagit Road, which branches south off Flood Hope Road four kilometers (2.5 miles) southwest of Hope. This rough gravel road climbs steadily for 39 kilometers (24 miles) to the park entrance, then continues 22 kilometers (14 miles) farther to the international border and road's end at **Ross Lake Reservoir.**

Through the park, the road follows the Skagit River, which flows northward from Ross Lake Reservoir through a magnificent valley cloaked in spruce, pine, aspen, and maple. Black bears, cougars, wolves, coyotes, deer, beavers, and over 200 species of birds are all present within the park.

Outdoor enthusiasts can hike trails suited mainly to overnight excursions. Skagit River Trail begins just east of where the park access road crosses the river, following the river downstream for 15 kilometers (9.3 miles) to a day-use area beside Highway 3. Fishing in the Skagit River is good for Dolly Varden and rainbow trout. The access road is dotted with day-use areas, including Shawatum, six kilometers (3.7 miles) from the park entrance, which was the site of a bustling town with saloons, restaurants, a sawmill, and a daily newspaper—until it was discovered that the only gold found in the area had been planted.

Within the park are two campgrounds; **Silvertip** is three kilometers from the park entrance, while **Ross Lake** is near the end of the road. Over the border, within the boundary of Ross Lake National Recreation Area, is **Hozomeen Campground.** All sites are $13. Another option for camping is **Silver Lake Provincial Park,** six kilometers (3.7 miles) along the park access road from Hope; $14.

Hope Slide

On Highway 3, about 18 kilometers (11 miles) southeast of Hope, the effects of one of nature's amazing forces can be seen. On January 9, 1965, a minor earthquake caused a huge section of mountain to come crashing down, filling the bottom of the Nicolum Creek Valley, destroying about three kilometers (1.9 miles) of the Hope–Princeton Highway, and killing four motorists. The highway, viewpoint, and parking area are built over the Hope Slide, but you can still see the slide's treeless boundaries along the south side of the valley.

Accommodations and Camping

Hope doesn't offer much hope if you're looking for upscale lodging. Instead you'll find a motley collection of roadside motels in town and across the TransCanada Highway on Old Hope–Princeton Way. Best value of the downtown options is the **Best Continental Motel** (860 Fraser Ave., 604/869-9726; $59–80 s or d), which also has a restaurant.

Out on Old Hope–Princeton Way, **Royal Lodge Motel** (604/869-5358 or 877/500-6620) has rooms for $65 s, $70 d, with kitchens an extra $5. The much newer **Alpine Motel** (Old Hope–Princeton Way, 604/869-9931 or 877/869-9931) offers large, comfortably furnished rooms, a pool, and a pleasant setting; from $70 s, $76 d. In a beautiful spot four kilometers (2.5 miles) north of Hope, **Beautiful Lake of the Woods Resort** (TransCanada Hwy., 604/869-9211 or 888/508-2211) sits on a lake with views of the surrounding mountainscape. The property is a resort in name only, but facilities include a restaurant and canoe rentals ($5 per hour). Uninspiring motel rooms are $65 s, $75 d; cabins are $75–95 d.

Along the road up to the tunnels, **Coquihalla Campground** (Kawkawa Lake Rd., 604/869-7119 or 888/869-7118; Apr.–Oct.) sits right beside the river. Trees surround most sites, and facilities include hot showers, a barbecue area, laundry, and game room. Unserviced sites are $18, hookups $22–26.

Food

Chinese **Kan-Yon Restaurant** (800 3rd Ave., 604/869-2212; daily 8 A.M.–11 P.M.) looks unremarkable from the outside, but dishes are well-prepared and portions are generous. Combination dinners run $9–13, and most entrées are under $12. The **Home Restaurant,** in a stylish two-story building at 665 Old Hope–Princeton Way (604/869-5241), is recommended for family-style dining (expect to pay around $25 per person for a three-course meal).

Information

Right downtown, the friendly staff at **Hope Visitor Info Centre** (919 Water Ave., 604/869-2021; daily 9 A.M.–5 P.M., with extended summer hours of 8 A.M.–8 P.M.) can help you decide which of the routes to take out of Hope but might also convince you to stay in town a little longer.

FRASER RIVER CANYON

From Hope, the old TransCanada Highway runs north along the west bank of the fast-flowing Fraser River. Although the new Coquihalla Highway is a much shorter option for those heading for Kamloops and beyond, the old highway offers many interesting stops and is by far the preferred route for those not in a hurry. Head north through downtown Hope, cross the Fraser River, take the first right and you're on your way.

The first worthwhile stop is tiny **Emory Creek Provincial Park,** 15 kilometers (9.3 miles) from Hope. Stopping at this quiet riverside park, it's hard to believe that a little over

Southwestern B.C.

WHITE-WATER RAFTING

The Thompson and Fraser Rivers offer some of Canada's most exciting white-water rafting, and both are run commercially by a number of companies. The town of **Lytton,** at the confluence of the two rivers, is home to a couple of companies, with others spread south along the TransCanada Highway.

Whichever operator you go with, and whichever river you choose to run, you'll be in for the trip of a lifetime. The Thompson is known for its high water, the mighty Fraser for its spectacular canyon and obstacles such as Hell's Gate. Those looking for an extra thrill also run the Nahatlatch, a tributary of the Fraser.

All companies include a great lunch (such as a salmon barbecue) and all transfers, charging around $100–120 for a full day. Other options are overnight trips (from $250) and weeklong floats from deep in the interior (from $1,300). From south to north, companies include: **Fraser River Raft Expeditions** (Yale, 604/863-2336 or 800/363-7238, www.fraserraft.com), **REO Rafting** (Boston Bar, 604/461-7238 or 800/736-7238, www.reorafting.com), **Kumsheen Raft Adventures** (Lytton, 604/455-2296 or 800/663-6667, www.kumsheen.com), and **Hyak Wilderness Adventures** (Lytton, 604/734-8622 or 800/663-7238, www.hyak.com).

100 years ago it was the site of Emory City, complete with saloons, a brewery, a large sawmill, and all the other businesses of a bustling frontier gold town. The city had virtually disappeared by the 1890s, and today no hint of its short-lived presence remains. Wander along riverside trails, try some fishing, or stay at one of the wooded campsites ($14).

Yale

This small town of 200 has quite a history. It started off as one of the many Hudson's Bay Company posts, then became a transportation center at the head of the navigable lower section of the Fraser River—the terminus of one of the largest sternwheeler operations on the west coast. Enormous Lady Franklin Rock blocked the upriver section to steamer traffic, so all goods heading for the interior had to be carried from this point by wagon train along the famous Cariboo Wagon Road.

In 1858 Yale was a flourishing gold-rush town of 20,000, filled with tents, shacks, bars, gambling joints, and shops. But when the gold ran out so did most of the population, and Yale dwindled to the small forestry and service center it has been for 100 years. If you want to find out more about Yale's historic past, the gold rush, the Cariboo Wagon Road, and railway construction, visit the **Yale Museum** (Douglas St., 604/863-2324; summer Wed.–Sat. 9:30 A.M.–5:30 P.M.) and the adjacent historic 1863 **St. John's Church.**

If you're looking for a place to spend the night, choose between the downtown, 12-room **Fort Yale Motel** (604/863-2216; $45 s or d) or head back down the highway 12 kilometers (7.5 miles) to the campground at **Emory Creek Provincial Park** ($14). Along the TransCanada Highway through town is a small **information booth** (604/863-2324; summer daily 9 A.M.–6 P.M.).

Alexandra Bridge

The treacherous Fraser Canyon posed a major transportation obstacle between the trails from the south and the interior. Several routes across the river were attempted, including a canoe cross-

ing, a cable ferry, and the 1848 Anderson Bridge trail from Fort Yale to Spuzzum.

The gold rush of the 1850s and the onslaught of gold miners and mule trains on the route increased the need for a safe river crossing. In 1863, Alexandra Bridge, 22 kilometers (14 miles) north of Yale, was completed. However, with the successful completion of the Canadian Pacific Railway line through the canyon, the bridge and the Cariboo Wagon Road fell into disrepair.

The popularity of the automobile forced engineers to construct a new suspension bridge in 1926. The new bridge used the original abutments and lasted right up to 1962, when it was replaced by today's bridge on Highway 1. **Alexandra Bridge Provincial Park** now protects a section of the old Cariboo Wagon Road, including the old bridge. The trail down to the bridge makes a good place to get out and stretch your legs.

Hell's Gate

At well-known Hell's Gate, the Fraser River powers its way through a narrow, glacially carved, 34-meter-high gorge. When Simon Fraser saw this section of the gorge in 1808 he wrote "we had to travel where no human being should venture—for surely we have encountered the gates of hell," and the name stuck. In 1914 a massive rockslide rocketed down into the gorge, blocking it even further and resulting in the almost total obliteration of the sockeye salmon population that spawned farther upstream. In 1944 giant concrete fishways were built to slow the waters and allow the spawning salmon to jump upstream—the river soon swarmed with salmon once again. Today you can cross the canyon aboard the 25-passenger **Hell's Gate Airtram** (604/867-9277), which runs mid-April to mid-October daily 10 A.M.–4 P.M., with extended hours of 9:30 A.M.–4:30 P.M. in July and August. Across the river you can browse through landscaped gardens, learn more about the fishway and salmon, or even try your hand at gold panning. Part of the complex (accessible by tram only) is the **Salmon House Restaurant** (same hours as the tram). I'm always wary of dining rooms associated with commercial attractions, but this place will pleasantly surprise you with a richly delicious salmon chowder ($5–8) and a variety of salmon mains under $18.

North Toward Cache Creek

Another small town with a gold-rush history, **Boston Bar** is today a popular white-water rafting mecca for those brave enough to float the Fraser River's roaring rapids. A bridge crossing at Boston Bar accesses the **Nahatlatch River,** renowned for white-water kayaking. Along quieter stretches of this river are some great fishing spots, three lakes, and numerous primitive campgrounds. **REO Rafting Adventure Resort** (16 km/10 miles west from Boston Bar, 604/461-7238 or 800/736-7238, www.reorafting.com) offers a few campsites for $16 and tent cabins from $50, or stay in a log cabin, and take a raft trip, with all meals included, for $180 per person for one night. As the name suggests, the resort is the base for REO Rafting, but horseback riding, rock climbing, and guided hiking are also offered.

Continuing up the canyon, the narrow highway winds northward for 34 kilometers (21 miles) to **Lytton,** a historic village at the confluence of the Fraser and Thompson Rivers, before spurring eastward and following the Thompson River. This route eventually reaches Cache Creek, the gateway to Cariboo Country (see the *Central British Columbia* chapter), and continues on to the major interior city of Kamloops.

COQUIHALLA HIGHWAY

Opened in late spring 1986, the Coquihalla Highway is the most direct link between Hope and the interior of British Columbia. It saves at least 90 minutes by cutting 72 kilometers (45 miles) from the trip between Hope and Kamloops and bypassing the TransCanada Highway's narrow, winding stretch along the Fraser River Canyon. Along the 190-kilometer (118-mile) route are many worthwhile stops, but only one that's compulsory—a toll plaza at Coquihalla Pass, 115 kilometers (71 miles) from Hope, where $10 is collected from each vehicle.

The highway ascends and descends through magnificent mountain and river scenery to dry semiarid grasslands. You'll cruise through the valleys of the Lower Coquihalla River and Boston Bar Creek, climb to the 1,240-meter (4,070-foot) summit of Coquihalla Pass near Coquihalla Lake, descend along the Coldwater River, then climb the Coldwater's eastern valley slope to Merritt. From Merritt the highway climbs the valleys of the Nicola River and Clapperton Creek to join the TransCanada Highway eight kilometers (five miles) west of Kamloops.

Merritt

This town of 8,000 in the Nicola Valley, 115 kilometers (71 miles) north of Hope, provides the only services along the Coquihalla Highway. It's also the exit point for those heading east to the Okanagan on the Okanagan Connector.

Make your first stop off the highway at **Merritt Visitor Info Centre,** on a high point east of the highway (250/378-5634; daily 9 A.M.–5 P.M.). Upstairs in this large log building is an intriguing forestry exhibition, and behind the building is the **Godey Creek Hiking Trail,** which takes you 1.4 kilometers (.9 mile) each way to a lookout cabin; allow one hour for the round-trip.

Each July, **Merritt Mountain Music Festival** (604/860-1470, www.mountainfest.com) attracts tens of thousands of country-music lovers for a weekend of concerts featuring the biggest names in country music.

Since the Coquihalla Highway opened, many motels have been built around Merritt, but by far the best choice is one of the originals, the **Ⓜ Quilchena Hotel** (250/378-2611, www.quilchena.com), on Nicola Lake, 20 kilometers (12 miles) east of town on Highway 5A (take Exit 290). Built in 1908 and still part of a working ranch, the property is a destination in itself, with golfing ($18 for nine holes, $23 for 18), horseback riding ($25 for a one-hour trail ride), swimming, biking (rentals available), canoeing, and fishing. The hotel itself is a stately old building surrounded by well-tended gardens and oozing Victorian charm. A grand staircase leads up to guest rooms decorated with period antiques, lace curtains, and solid wooden beds. Rates for rooms with shared bathrooms are $71–87, while en suite rooms are $109–125. Downstairs is a saloon (complete with bullet holes in the bar) and a restaurant serving up beef raised on the hotel ranch.

⋈ MANNING PROVINCIAL PARK

This spectacular 70,844-hectare (175,100-acre) park in the Cascade Mountains, 64 kilometers (40 miles) east of Hope along Highway 3, stretches down to the Canada–U.S. border. Highway 3 makes a U through the park—from the northwest to south to northeast corners. But to really appreciate the park, you need to get off the highway—take in the beautiful bodies of water, drive up to a wonderful stretch of high alpine meadows, or hike on the numerous trails. Within the park are two major watersheds; the Skagit River flows west to the Fraser River, and the Similkameen River flows east into the Columbia River. The many tributaries of these two rivers flow down from the highest peaks of the rain-drenched Cascade Mountains, through dense subalpine forests of Engelmann spruce, Douglas fir, western red cedar, and hemlock to the valley through which Highway 3 runs. Wildlife is abundant, including populations of black bear, moose, elk, coyote, and beaver.

Summer Recreation

A highlight of the park is the paved road immediately across Highway 3 from Manning Park Resort; it climbs steadily to **Cascade Lookout**, a viewpoint offering a magnificent 180-degree panoramic view. Beyond the lookout, the road turns to gravel and continues climbing for nine kilometers, ending at a parking lot beneath 2,063-meter (6,700-foot) Blackwall Peak. From this area of flower-filled alpine meadows, views extend over the park's remote northern boundary. Take time to soak up the color by taking one of the short trails originating from the parking lot. Or hike **Heather Trail** (10 kilometers/6.2 miles each way; allow three hours) to Three Brothers Mountain. If you're there between late July and mid-August, you won't believe what you'll see—

a rich yellow, orange, and white carpet of wildflowers as far as you can see.

Along Highway 3 are some short self-guided nature trails, including a 700-meter (.4-mile) walk (20 minutes) through a stand of ancient western red cedars. The trailhead is Sumallo Grove day-use area, 10 kilometers (6.2 miles) east of where Highway 3 enters the park from the west. Just east of the Visitor Information Centre, on the south side of the road, is the 500-meter (.3-mile) **Beaver Pond Trail.** If you notice people arriving on foot in this parking lot with worn soles, bent backs, and great big smiles on their faces, give them a pat on the back—they may have just completed one of the world's greatest long-distance hikes. The **Pacific Crest Trail** runs 3,860 kilometers/2,400 miles from the U.S.–Mexico border to this small and undistinguished trailhead.

During the summer months you can fish in rivers, streams, and lakes for Dolly Varden and rainbow trout (get a license first) or explore **Lightning Lake** in a canoe; lakeside rentals cost $14 per hour. At **Manning Park Corral** (next to Manning Park Resort, 250/840-8844), you can go on a one-hour trail ride for $25, or spend all day on horseback with a hearty trailside lunch thrown in for $118.

Skiing

The park gets plenty of dry snow for good downhill and cross-country skiing. At **Manning Park Resort** (250/840-8822 or 800/330-3321, www.manningpark.com), 11 kilometers (6.8 miles) west of Manning Park Resort along Gibson Pass Road, downhill enthusiasts can take advantage of a 437-meter (1,430-foot) vertical rise served by two chairlifts, a T-bar, and a rope tow. Most runs are for intermediate skiers, but novices and experts will also find suitable terrain. Lift tickets are adult $34, senior $22, child $20, under six free. The resort is geared toward families, with other activities including a skating rink, terrain park, and tubing park, keeping all ages happy. On-hill facilities include a cafeteria, ski school, and ski rentals (from $25 for a full day). A free shuttle bus transfers guests to the ski area from Manning Park Resort, which offers winter packages from $130 for two nights' midweek high season accommodations and two days' skiing.

Along with 190 kilometers (118 miles) of wilderness trails, cross-country skiers can enjoy 30 kilometers (19 miles) of groomed trails for $15 per day. Cross-country skis rent for $15 per day.

Accommodations

In the heart of the park on Highway 3, **Manning Park Resort** (250/840-8822 or 800/330-3321, www.manningpark.com) is a full-service lodging providing comfortable hotel rooms, cabins, and triplexes, as well as a dining room, self-serve cafeteria, small grocery store, and an open fireside lounge. Other facilities include saunas, an indoor pool, a TV room, a fitness center, tennis courts, a coin-operated laundry, and a gift shop. Through summer, rooms in the main lodge are $124–134 s or d, and chalets with kitchens range $155–279. The rest of the year rates are reduced, with rooms from $69 and cabins from $119.

Camping

The park's four campgrounds hold 355 sites; in summer, get in early to be assured of snagging one. Each campground provides drinking water and toilets. Firewood is available for a fee. The most popular campground is **Lightning Lake,** two kilometers (1.2 miles) west of Manning Park Resort on Gibson Pass Road, which has showers; $22 per night. Others include **Coldspring Campground,** on Highway 3 two kilometers (1.2 miles) west of the resort; **Hampton Campground,** on Highway 3 four kilometers (2.5 miles) east of the resort; and **Mule Deer Campground,** four kilometers (2.5 miles) farther east. These three charge $14 per night.

Information

The park's **Visitor Information Centre** (250/840-8836; summer daily 8:30 A.M.–4:30 P.M., weekdays only the rest of the year) is one kilometer (.6 mile) east of Manning Park Resort. Inside, you'll find displays on recreation opportunities and on the area's natural and cultural history, as well as maps and detailed information about park facilities. In July and August park interpreters offer guided walks, interesting slide shows,

and evening talks at the amphitheater on Gibson Pass Road; scan information boards around the park or inquire at the Visitor Information Centre to see what's on.

CONTINUING TOWARD THE OKANAGAN VALLEY

From the eastern boundary of Manning Provincial Park, Highway 3 follows the Similkameen River north to Princeton, then turns sharply southeast to Osoyoos, at the southern end of the Okanagan Valley, a total distance of 158 kilometers (98 miles).

Princeton

At the confluence of the Similkameen and Tulameen Rivers, surrounded by low tree-covered hills, lies the small friendly ranching town of Princeton (pop. 3,000). **Princeton and District**

The crumbling remains of Princeton Castle are the centerpiece of a unique resort on the outskirts of Princeton.

Pioneer Museum (167 Vermilion Ave., 250/295-7588; Mon.–Fri. 1–5 P.M.) features pioneer artifacts from Granite City, Chinese and Interior Salish artifacts, and a good fossil display.

On the northeast side of Princeton, the stone-and-concrete ruins of a 1910 cement plant have been incorporated in a unique resort complex, **Princeton Castle** (Hwy. 5A, 250/295-7988 or 888/228-8881, www.castleresort.com). The cement works was built at a cost of $1 million, yet operated for only one year. In the ensuing decades, the buildings have been reclaimed by nature. Around, through, and over the crumbling ruins grow trees, wild roses, lilacs, and lupines. (Take a look at the concrete paths and steps leading down from the back of the administrative building to the ruins—the concrete is loaded with fossilized shells.) Surrounding the ruins are cabins and chalets of varying configurations, with the larger chalets taking pride of place along a ridge overlooking a sparkling creek. One-bed cabins with no linen and shared bathrooms are $75 s or d, while chalets complete with bathrooms, kitchens, and TV cost from $165. Beyond the ruins, a road leads up to the resort campground, where sites are $20–25 and tepees (no linen) are rented for $45 per night. Aside from admiring the ruins, children will love the large playground, while all ages can enjoy horseback riding or canoeing on the small lake. To get there from Princeton, cross the bridge at the north end of Bridge Street, turn right on Old Hedley Road, cross Highway 5, turn left on Five Mile Road, then continue until the sign to the park leads you right.

Just a short stroll from downtown, **Riverside Motel** (307 Thomas Ave. at the north end of Bridge St., 250/295-6232) was built in 1934 as a hunting and fishing lodge. The aptly named motel is right beside the river, and in the height of summer the water level drops to expose a small beach and shallow swimming hole. Ask the owner to show you a photo of the place taken in 1937—the cabins still look exactly the same. Each basic cabin has a toilet, a shower, and a kitchen with a fridge, stove, cooking utensils, crockery, and cutlery. Rates are a very reasonable $38–70 s or d.

For a meal, head downtown to the **Princeton Hotel** (258 Bridge St., 250/295-3355); order bistro-style at the small window across from the bar.

At the east entrance to town, **Princeton Visitor Info Centre** (Hwy. 3, 250/295-3103) is open year-round 9 A.M.–5 P.M., daily in summer but Monday–Friday only the rest of the year.

Coalmont and Beyond

If you want to see some impressive canyon scenery off the main tourist drag, cross the river at the north end of Princeton's Bridge Street and turn left, heading west toward Coalmont for 18 kilometers (11 miles). Coalmont came to the forefront when gold-rush activity moved from Granite City (see sidebar) to this village in 1911. Today, you can't help but notice that the town's residents have a sense of humor. The welcoming sign states that Coalmont has no industry but plenty of activity in the form of sleeping and daydreaming. It also claims Coalmont has a hot, cold, wet, and dry climate, warns traveling salesmen to stay away, and advises single women that

GRANITE CITY

After the discovery of a gold nugget in Granite Creek back in 1885, a 13-saloon gold-rush city sprang to life on this spot. Soon it was the third-largest city in the province, supporting a population of over 2,000. But the boom was short-lived, and the town was quickly abandoned. What remains of Granite City lies two kilometers (1.2 miles) from Coalmont. To get there, head straight through Coalmont to Granite Creek, turn left on Hope Street, right over the creek, and then follow the road to a fork. Straight ahead is the site of the boomtown, marked by a riverside cairn and the broken-down remains of a few log buildings among wild lilac bushes—it's really up to your imagination to re-create the good ol' days. On the bluff to the north of Granite City (take the right fork and then the first right) is a small graveyard with headstones showing dates from the boom years.

their safety is not guaranteed due to the predominance of bachelors. The attractive 1911 **Coalmont Hotel** (250/295-6066) still serves up beer to thirsty travelers, while quite a number of homes—some with backyards crammed with eclectic collections of rusting mine machinery—line the streets.

The main road through Coalmont winds its way north to Merritt, providing a handy shortcut, if that's the direction you're heading. The only town en route is the hamlet of **Tulameen** (pop. 250). Along the main street, the museum in a one-room log schoolhouse may or may not be open, while at the north end of town, you'll probably have the beach at **Otter Bay Provincial Park** to yourself.

Hedley and Vicinity

From Princeton, Highway 3 takes you on a scenic route through the beautiful **Similkameen River Valley,** which holds lots of places to camp, in either provincial parks or private campgrounds. Between Princeton and Keremeos the road follows the Dewdney Trail, a 468-kilometer (290-mile) track used in the 1860s to connect Hope with the Wildhorse Creek goldfields. This stretch itself has also been a major mining area, supplying a fortune in gold, silver, nickel, and copper over the years.

One of the richest mines was the Mascot Mine, unique in that the mine entrance was perched 850 vertical meters (2,800 feet) above the mining town of Hedley. To immerse yourself in the history of the mining era wander around the tree-lined streets of Hedley or consider staying at **Colonial Inn B&B** (Colonial Rd., 250/292-8131; Apr.–Oct.), a historic guest house surrounded by mature gardens. Three of the five guest rooms have private bathrooms, and a cooked breakfast is included in the rates of $77 s, $88–99 d. Camping out back is $20.

The landscape east of Princeton is different from that to the west, but the change is most pronounced east of Hedley—from ragged, tree-covered mountains through rolling hills covered in sagebrush and lush irrigated orchards around Keremeos to desert (complete with lizards, cactus,

and rattlesnakes) around Osoyoos on the Canada–U.S. border.

Cathedral Provincial Park

Wilderness hikers and mountaineers should not miss the turnoff to this spectacular 33,272-hectare (82,200-acre) park just west of Keremeos. Access along the 21-kilometer (13-mile) road leading into the park is restricted to guests of **M Cathedral Lakes Lodge** (250/226-7560 or 888/255-4453, www.cathedral-lakes-lodge.com) or those willing to walk. For this reason, most park visitors stay at the resort, which provides accommodations, meals, use of canoes, a recreation room and hot tub, and transportation to and from the base camp. The minimum stay is a two-day package: original cabins and bungalow rooms start at $335 per person, while rooms in the main lodge sell for $386. Rates include all meals and the shuttle ride. The lodge also offers the option of a day trip for $75 per person, which includes the shuttle and lunch.

About 60 kilometers (37 miles) of wilderness trails lead from the resort to a variety of striking and enticingly named rock formations, including Stone City, Giant Cleft, Devil's Woodpile, Macabre Tower, Grimface Mountain, Denture Ridge, and Smokey the Bear. Wander through meadows waving with dainty alpine flowers, climb peaks for tremendous views, fish for trout in sparkling turquoise lakes, capture on film immense glacier-topped mountains.

KEREMEOS

As you approach mountain-surrounded Keremeos from the west, the road is lined with lush irrigated orchards and fruit stands, one after another, which is probably what inspired the town's claim to fame as the "Fruit Stand Capital of Canada." Keremeos has one of the longest growing seasons in the province. Try a tastebud-tingling fruit-juice shake in summer; recommended is the second-to-last stand as you head east out of town. Harvest dates are mid-June to mid-July for cherries; mid-July to early August for apricots; mid-July to early September for peaches; mid-August to mid-September for pears; early

© ANDREW HEMPSTEAD

Southwestern B.C.

Grist Mill, Keremeos

August to mid-October for apples; early to mid-September for plums; early September to early October for grapes.

Grist Mill

The town's main historic attraction is the Grist Mill (250/499-2888; adult $5, child $2.50), a restored water-powered mill built in 1877. This is where pioneer Similkameen Valley settlers used to grind locally produced wheat into flour. Costumed interpreters lead tours of the property

daily late May–early October, then invite you to try your hand at the many informative and entertaining hands-on displays in the museum and visitor center. A pleasant tearoom overlooks garden plots carefully planted to reflect various eras (the pancake breakfast on summer weekends is a treat). Outside of summer, the grounds are open for inspection. To get there, go through town on the main highway, turn north on Highway 3A toward Penticton, then right at the Historic Site sign on Upper Bench Road.

Flour ground at the Grist Mill is used in breads available on-site, as well as at the brightly painted **Hanna's Bakery** (614 7th Ave., 250/499-2522; Mon.–Sat. 2 A.M.–5 P.M.), which is difficult to miss driving down Keremeos's main street. Sit inside and check your email or sit out front and watch the world of Keremeos go by as you tuck into a meat pie or sweet treat.

Keremeos Columns

Another local highlight, although it takes some effort to reach, is **Keremeos Columns Provincial Park.** The park is named for a 90-meter (300-foot) cliff of remarkable hexagonal basalt columns rising from a lava base just outside the park boundary (the columns were supposed to be in the park but because of a surveying accident actually stand on private land). Access the viewpoint by taking a steep eight-kilometer (five-mile) logging road off Highway 3 about four kilometers (2.5 miles) north of town (turn right at the Keremeos cemetery), then take another steep six-kilometer (3.7-mile) hike (allow at least three hours one-way) across private property; ask for permission and trail details at the house at the end of the paved road.

Okanagan Valley

This warm, sunny valley 400 kilometers (250 miles) east of Vancouver extends 180 kilometers (112 miles) between the U.S.–Canada border in the south and the TransCanada Highway in the north. Lush orchards and vineyards, fertile irrigated croplands, low rolling hills, and a string of beautiful lakes line the valley floor, where you'll also find 40 golf courses, dozens of commercial attractions, and lots and lots of people—especially in summer.

The Okanagan Valley's three main cities—**Penticton, Kelowna,** and **Vernon**—are spread around long, narrow **Okanagan Lake** and collectively hold the bulk of interior British Columbia's population. Numerous smaller communities also ring the lakeshore, doubling or tripling in size in July and August when hordes of vacationers turn the valley into one big resort. Most of these summer pilgrims are Canadians from cooler climes, who come in search of guaranteed sunshine, lazy days on a beach, and a take-away tan. In winter, the valley draws pilgrims of another sort—skiers and snowboarders on their way to the world-class slopes flanking the valley.

Must-Sees

Look for **M** to find the sights and activities you can't miss and **N** for the best dining and lodging.

M Desert Centre: You'll forget everything you've heard about Canada, the cold, and igloos when you visit the Desert Centre at Osoyoos (page 260).

M Summerland: On a map of the Okanagan, Summerland is just a small dot with an enticing name. But this lakeside hamlet is home to one of the valley's finest wineries (Sumac Ridge) and the departure point for train rides along the Kettle River Railway (page 268).

M Wineries: Spring and fall are particularly good times for touring valley wineries, such as the grand Mission Hill Family Estate (page 273).

M Davison Orchards: Children will love these orchards near Vernon, where they can explore a working farm on a wagon tour (page 283).

M Kalamalka Lake: Choosing a favorite Okanagan lake is difficult, but my nod goes to Kalamalka Lake, between Kelowna and Vernon, for its beautiful hue, sandy beaches, and warm clear water (page 283).

M Silver Star Mountain Resort: This resort has more than just great skiing and boarding; its gold-rush-style buildings and a packed summer activity program make it a worthwhile destination at any time of year (page 285).

Orchards dominate the valley north and south of Penticton.

OKANAGAN VALLEY

All the credit for developing the Okanagan into Canada's fruit basket goes to the original planter, Father Charles Pandosy, a French oblate priest who established a mission in the Kelowna area in 1859. Within a couple of years he had successfully introduced apple trees to the district. The trees positively blossomed under his care, thanks to the valley's long five-and-a-half-month growing season, over 2,000 hours of sunshine a year, relatively mild winters, and the ready availability of water. Soon fruit orchards of all types were springing up everywhere, and today the Okanagan Valley region produces 30 percent of Canada's apples, 60 percent of its cherries, 20 percent of its peaches, half of its pears and plums, and all the apricots in the country.

PLANNING YOUR TIME

Regardless of your approach to the Okanagan Valley, you'll spend time driving **Highway 97,** which is the main north–south thoroughfare. This highway passes through the four largest towns—from south to north **Osoyoos, Penticton, Kelowna,** and **Vernon**—closely parallels Okanagan Lake, and is rarely out of sight of an orchard or vineyard. It's a truly spectacular drive, but don't plan on doing it in one day. You could plan to spend at least one day in and around each population center, mixing traditional sights such as the **Desert Centre** at Osoyoos with **winery tours,** golf, and time out on the beaches. Younger children will revel in the many outdoor activities—take a wagon ride around **Davison Orchards,** schedule a half-day at a fun park, or get back to nature in one of the many provincial parks.

If you have a beach-loving family in tow on your British Columbia vacation, the Okanagan Valley is the place to plan a break from the rigors of sightseeing. Use my accommodation recommendations scattered through this chapter to choose a lodging that suits your needs and budget, and make reservations as far in advance as possible. Even if you haven't set your itinerary for the rest of your travels, having a few days' downtime to look forward to will make your vacation more enjoyable.

As in the rest of British Columbia, July through August is by far the busiest time of year in the Okanagan. This is when temperatures are at their hottest and the waterways at their busiest. If you're planning on camping, reserve a spot as far in advance as possible, especially at commercial lakeside campgrounds. As a general rule, the summer weather will be hot and windy along the valley floor, with temperatures cooling off as you climb into the surrounding mountains. Take this into consideration if you don't like the heat, and plan on staying somewhere like Beaver Lake Resort, in the mountains in Kelowna, or **Silver Star Mountain Resort,** near Vernon.

The winter resorts of the Okanagan Valley are not as well known as Whistler and their counterparts in the Canadian Rockies, but each of the three biggest has undergone massive expansion projects within the last decade. This has created a world-class destination for winter visitors, especially families looking for a variety of slopes and amenities at reasonable prices. If you do decide to visit during the cooler months, you'll find the major attractions open, but with shorter hours. Many wineries close completely during winter.

OSOYOOS

This town of 4,500 is nestled on the west shore of **Osoyoos Lake,** Canada's warmest freshwater lake (up to 24°C, 75°F in summer). The town also boasts Canada's highest year-round average temperature. The older main street leads down to the lakefront and **Gyro Community Park,** where a floating swimming pool provides the perfect spot for families to cool off.

Desert Centre

Away from the valley floor and its many orchards, the landscape is surprisingly arid. In one particular area, a 100-hectare (250-acre) "pocket desert" has the distinction of being Canada's driest spot, receiving less than 300 millimeters (11 inches) of precipitation annually. It is a desert in the truest sense, complete with sand, cacti, prickly pear, sagebrush, lizards, scorpions, rattlesnakes, and other desert dwellers, including 23 invertebrates

OSOYOOS

© AVALON TRAVEL PUBLISHING, INC.

Okanagan Valley

found nowhere else in the world. Learn more about this unique landscape at the Desert Centre (250/495-2470 or 877/899-0897; daily 10 A.M.–3 P.M.; adult $6, senior $5, child $3), a research and interpretive facility, where a boardwalk leads through this very un-Canadian environment. To get there follow Highway 97 north from Osoyoos and take 146th Avenue west.

Scenic Drive

For a bird's-eye view of the lake, take Highway 3 west from town 12 kilometers (7.5 miles), then follow a 20-kilometer (12-mile) gravel road to the 1,874-meter (6,150-foot) summit of **Mount Kobau.** Short trails there lead to viewpoints of the Similkameen and Okanagan Valleys. Along the section of Highway 3 before the turnoff, watch for **Spotted Lake,** a bizarre natural phenomenon on the south side of the road. As sum-

mer progresses and the lake's water evaporates, high concentrations of magnesium, calcium, and sodium crystallize, forming colorful circles.

Accommodations

In summer, Osoyoos Lake attracts hordes of water lovers and sun worshippers, so getting accommodations can be difficult—especially along the prime stretch of lakefront east of downtown along Highway 3. You'll need to book well in advance to get a room during summer at the **Sandy Beach Motel** (6706 Ponderosa Dr., 250/495-6931 or 866/495-6931, www.sandy-beachmotel.com), but you'll be glad you did. Set on a private stretch of sandy beach, the 25-kitchen-equipped units face a grassy courtyard, landscaped with crushed gravel pathways and cacti. Summer rates range $110–220 s or d, dropping as low as $80 in winter.

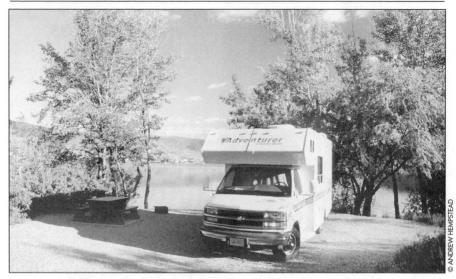

lakeside camping at Haynes Point Provincial Park

Along the same stretch, but larger and less personal, is **Holiday Inn Sunspree Resort** (Hwy. 3, 250/495-7223 or 877/786-7773, www.holidayinnosoyoos). It offers 85 rooms, many overlooking the resort's private beach, as well as a rooftop garden, fitness center, boat rentals, and a restaurant. Rates start at $169 s or d (although the least expensive rooms are fairly small).

Camping
Haynes Point Provincial Park protects an extremely narrow low-lying spit that juts into Osoyoos Lake south of downtown. At the far end of the spit is a beautiful campground, with many sites enjoying lakefront settings ($22 per night). Like most other provincial parks, Haynes Point has no showers or hookups, so if you need more amenities, consider **Walton's Mountain Resort** (3207 Lakeshore Dr., 250/495-7033, www.waltonsmountainresort.com; Apr.–mid-Oct.; $28–36). This campground (almost directly opposite Haynes Point)

has sites set around a working orchard and offers its own private beach, along with facilities such as showers.

Food
Walk down Main Street and take your pick from various cafés and the usual smattering of Italian and Chinese restaurants. **The Coffee Bar** (8523 Main St.; daily from 7:30 A.M.) features a good range of coffee concoctions in a modern setting. At the same corner is the **Wildfire Grill** (8523 Main St., 250/495-2215; daily for lunch and dinner), which has a quiet patio out back. Expect contemporary takes on traditional dishes, with most dinner mains in the $16–24 range.

Information
In a parking lot at the corner of Highways 3 and 97 is **Osoyoos Visitor Info Centre** (250/495-7142 or 888/676-9667, www.destinationosoyoos.com; summer daily 8:30 A.M.–4:30 P.M., rest of the year Mon.–Fri.).

Okanagan Valley

Penticton

One of the Okanagan's three major population centers, Penticton (pop. 33,000) lies between the north end of Skaha Lake and the south end of Okanagan Lake. The city gets its name from the nomadic Salish natives, in whose tongue Penticton means "Place to Stay Forever."

Approaching from the south, you'll see a roadside plaque honoring pioneer Thomas Ellis, who arrived in the valley in 1886, built a great cattle empire, and planted the area's first orchard. Today fruit orchards are everywhere. Penticton's nickname is Peach City; the annual **Peach Festival** celebrates the harvest in mid-August with a week of sailboat races, parades, games, and entertainment. Penticton also participates in the **Okanagan Wine Festival,** the first weekend of October, another fruitful event.

SIGHTS AND RECREATION

Along Okanagan Lake

Wander west along the tree-shaded shores of Lake Okanagan to see the **SS *Sicamous*** (1099 Lakeshore Dr. W, 250/492-0403; daily 10 A.M.–4 P.M. extended to 7 A.M.–7 P.M. in summer; adult $5, senior $4, child $1). This Canadian Pacific Railway sternwheeler operated on Okanagan Lake 1914–1936. Now it rests on the lakeshore, and it's easy to spend an hour wandering through the ship, peeking into the purser's office, admiring the furnishings in the grand dining room, and clambering up to the observation deck.

The adjacent **rose garden** (free) is worth a stroll to see perfect blooms and manicured lawns, and to read all the stats on the **Okanagan Lake Dam** and flood-control system. Next to the rose garden is **Loco Landing** (250/770-1896), an ambitious mini-golf complex with an Okanagan theme.

At the opposite end of Lakeshore Drive (to the east) is the **Art Gallery of the South Okanagan** (199 Front St., 250/493-2928; Tues.–Fri. 10 A.M.–5 P.M., Sat.–Sun. 1–5 P.M.). The craft shop is a good place to pick up creative treasures and handmade souvenirs. Continue east from

the gallery to the local **marina**—another enjoyable spot for a lakeside stroll.

Penticton Museum

This museum (785 Main St., 250/490-2451; Mon.–Sat. 10 A.M.–5 P.M.; $2) houses an excellent collection of western Canadiana, covering natural history, local native peoples, the fur-trading days, the gold rush, railways, early Chinese residents, and sternwheelers. It also features an enormous taxidermy section; mining, ranching, and ghost-town artifacts and treasures; and assorted military miscellany.

To Naramata

A 14-kilometer (8.7-mile) secondary road runs northeast out of Penticton, skirting the east side of Okanagan Lake and passing through the small community of Naramata. The first of many well-respected wineries along the way is the **Red Rooster Winery** (891 Naramat Rd., 250/496-5674; Apr.–Oct. 10 A.M.–6 P.M.), easily recognized by the mission-style tasting room beside the highway. No tours—instead enjoy a tasting session of the winery's acclaimed Pinot Gris and Chardonnay wines, then soak up the lake views over a cheese platter or slice of quiche on the veranda. Next up is the aptly named **Hillside Estate** (1350 Naramata Rd., 250/493-6294), with an impressive three-story wooden building holding the main winery. Hillside is known for its Pinot Noir, but it also produces an unusually dry but fruity Riesling. It's open for tours daily 10 A.M.–6 P.M. and for lunch daily from 11 A.M.

Naramata itself is a charming lakeside village, far removed from the commercialism of Penticton. Access to the lake is somewhat limited, although the public beach at Manitou Park is good for swimming.

Continue through Naramata and up into the mountains, where the road fizzles out near the south border of undeveloped Okanagan Mountain Provincial Park. The only way to get into this piece of untouched wilderness is to walk or boat over. Hike in for the day for a picnic, some

Okanagan Valley

fishing, or to explore the 24 kilometers (15 miles) of trails. The park was devastated by wildfires in 2003, so check the status of trails at the information center in Penticton.

Skiing and Snowboarding

Sunniest of the Okanagan resorts is **Apex Mountain Resort** (250/292-8222 or 877/777-2739, www.apexresort.com), 31 kilometers (19 miles) west of Penticton, which provides 605 vertical meters (1,990 feet) and 56 runs over 450 hectares (1,100 acres). The slopes are served by a T-bar and two chairlifts, one of which—the Quickdraw Express—zips skiers and boarders to the summit of Beaconsfield Mountain and opens up most of the expert terrain. Boarders are catered to with a terrain park and half pipe, or you can slide downhill on an inflatable tube in the tube park. The epicenter of the western-style base village is Mountainside Lodge, a day-use facility with eateries, a lounge, a ski and snowboard school, and a rental outlet. The resort is open daily December to mid-April, with one run open for night skiing on Wednesday, Friday, and Saturday. Lift tickets are adult $48, senior $39, child $29, kids under seven free.

Events

Penticton seems to have festivals, parades, events, or competitions going on throughout the year. The biggest event is the annual **Penticton Peach Festival** (250/492-9830 or 800/663-5052, www.peachfest.com), held on the first weekend of August; it's a tradition going back more than 50 years. Events include peach tasting, the crowning of Miss Penticton, Kiddies Day (the Sunday), a sandcastle competition, fireworks, and nightly entertainment in Gyro Park.

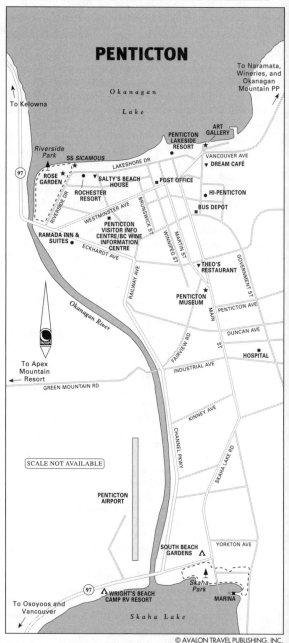

Other annual happenings include **Mid-Winter Break-Out** (250/490-3078) in mid-February, which includes everything from ice carving to a Polar Bear Dip; the **Spring Wine Festival** (250/861-6654, www.owfs.com), hosted by many local wineries in late April; the **Penticton Highland Games** (250/492-7073), the first Sunday of July in Kings Park; the **Ironman Canada** (250/493-5922) triathlon the last Sunday in August; and the **Pentastic Jazz Festival** (800/663-100, www.pentasticjazz.com) the second weekend of September. Two major wine festivals are a valley highlight; for details see the *Kelowna* section or check the website www.owfs.com.

ACCOMMODATIONS AND CAMPING

Under $50

As you'd expect in a resort town, the only accommodation under $50 is in a dormitory. **HI–Penticton** (464 Ellis St., 250/492-3992, www.hihostels.ca) occupies a 1950s white stucco residence close to the heart of downtown. Facilities include a kitchen, laundry, bike rentals, and an outdoor barbecue area; $17 per night for members of Hostelling International, $21 for nonmembers, and private rooms for $42 s or d. Check-in is 8 A.M.–noon and 5–10 P.M.

OKANAGAN WINES

Okanagan wines receive acclaim worldwide, although this success is only recent. In fact, it was doubted that quality grapes could be grown north of the 49th parallel until the late 1980s, when NAFTA forced local vintners to revisit their quality control. As a result, most of the original hybrid vines were ripped out and replaced with classic European varietals.

The valley's climate—long summer days and cool nights—produces small grapes with a higher-than-usual sugar content, creating intensely flavored and aromatic wines. A wide variety of red and white wine grapes are planted, with the reds thriving in the warmer south end of the valley, where Merlot, Cabernet Franc, and Pinot Noir grapes produce the best local wines. The entire wine-making process in the Okanagan has been one of experimentation, and along the way more unusual varietals such as Ehrenfelser and Auxerrois have been grown with success, make tasting local wines all the more interesting.

Okanagan Valley winery

The best introduction to the valley's vino offerings is the **British Columbia Wine Information Centre** (888 Westminster Ave., Penticton, 250/490-2006; summer daily 9 A.M.–5:30 P.M., the rest of the year weekdays only). As much a wine shop as anything else, it offers plenty of information along with wine tour maps and knowledgeable staff to set you off in the right direction.

Okanagan Valley

© ANDREW HEMPSTEAD

$50–100

The **Village Motel** (244 Robinson Dr., Naramata, 250/496-5535, www.villagemotel.com) will bring back memories of a bygone era. Located in the village of Naramata, 14 kilometers (8.7 miles) north of Penticton, the nine guest rooms are nicely decorated and open to landscaped gardens and a communal barbecue area. Regular rooms are $68 s or d, or pay $114 for a kitchen unit. The motel is within walking distance of the lake.

$100–150

The least expensive of several lodgings on Lakeshore Drive, close to both the lake and downtown, is the 36-room **Rochester Resort** (970 Lakeshore Dr., 250/493-1128 or 800/567-4904; from $109 s or d). All units have a kitchen and there's a communal barbecue area for guest use. Rooms here in the winter sell for as low as $60.

When the snow has melted at Apex Mountain Resort, 31 kilometers (19 miles) west of Penticton, the on-hill lodgings provide steeply discounted rooms for visitors looking to escape the busy valley floor. Check the resort's website (www.apexresort.com) for packages, or book a room at my favorite lodging, **M Sheeprock Lodge** (250/292-8558 or 877/677-1555, www.sheeprocklodge.com; closed spring and fall), which features distinctive alpine architecture and smallish but comfortable rooms with a distinctive western theme. Summer rates are $109 s or d, and in winter rooms start at $149. The lodge is also home to a restaurant that specializes in stone-grill steaks, cooked to order at your table.

Over $150

For the atmosphere of an old-fashioned resort, it's difficult to go past the **M Naramata Heritage Inn & Spa** (3625 1st St., Naramata, 250/496-6808 or 866/617-1188, www.naramatainn.com; from $185 s or d), north of Penticton along the east side of the lake. Dating to 1908, the hotel has been completely renovated, yet none of its historic appeal has been lost. The guest rooms have mission-style beds covered with plush duvets, bathrooms with heated floors and claw-foot tubs,

and either a balcony or patio. Other amenities include spa services, a wine bar with live jazz on Friday evenings, and a fine-dining restaurant.

Away from the water, **Ramada Inn & Suites** (1050 Eckhardt Ave. W, 250/492-8926 or 800/665-4966, www.pentictonramada.com) is a family-friendly, self-contained resort adjacent to an 18-hole golf course. Amenities include an outdoor pool, sprawling courtyard, playground, fitness center, restaurant, and poolside bar. The rooms are decorated in smart color schemes and are air-conditioned. Rates start at $159 s or d, but in the off-season you'll pay around the same for a Jacuzzi suite.

The six-story **Penticton Lakeside Resort** (21 Lakeshore Dr. W, 250/493-8221 or 800/663-9400, www.rpbhotels.com) is an upscale, downtown property right on the lake. It has over 200 rooms, an indoor pool overlooking the lake, a whirlpool, saunas, two tennis courts, a bar with a lakeside deck, and a restaurant. In July and August rooms start at $249, rising to $280 for a hot tub suite. Prices go down from there, to as low as $100 in the depths of winter.

Camping

All Penticton's commercial campgrounds are south of downtown around the north end of Skaha Lake. They're very popular in summer, so make reservations in advance if possible. The least-crowded seems to be **Wright's Beach Camp RV Park** (4071 Skaha Lake Rd., 250/492-7120, www.wrightsbeachcamp.com; Apr.–mid-Oct.), which is a little bit surprising because it's right on the lake and has a huge playground and an outdoor pool. Sites are $25–40 per night.

Across from Sudbury Beach and adjacent to Highway 97 is **South Beach Gardens** (3815 Skaha Lake Rd., 250/492-0628; May–Sept.), which charges $25 for an unserviced site and $30–35 for hookups.

If being by the lake isn't important, choose to stay at **Twin Lakes Golf & RV Resort** (Hwy. 3A, 250/497-8379, www.twinlakesgolfresort.com; Apr.–mid-Oct.), 19 kilometers (12 miles) southwest of Penticton. The campground is in the middle of a full-length golf course (greens fee $45, but discounted for campers), which is surrounded by barren cliffs. Amenities include modern washrooms, free firewood, a restaurant, and a lounge. Tent sites are $16, full hookups $25. A five-minute drive west of the campground, you can fish from the banks of Yellow Lake for brook trout and perch. To get to Twin Lakes, head south from Penticton and turn west off Highway 97 at Kaleden. If you're traveling east from Princeton, turn off Highway 3 at Keremeos.

OTHER PRACTICALITIES

Food

Penticton has a wide variety of restaurants spread along the beach and through downtown. My favorite is the **M Dream Café** (74 Front St., 250/490-9012; Mon.–Fri. 11 A.M.–8 P.M., Sat.–Sun. 10 A.M.–8 P.M.), away from the water but with a dreamy ambience (think eclectic furniture, colorful kites hanging from the ceiling, and soothing background music), friendly staff, and innovative cuisine. The menu takes inspiration from throughout Asia and steers clear of red meat: poached lime chicken panini, salmon spinach pie, rice noodle wraps, and tandoori chicken.

Across the road from the beach along the busy downtown tourist strip is **Salty's Beach House** (1000 Lakeshore Dr., 250/493-5001; daily from 11 A.M.), with tables inside and out. The menu blends conventional pub fare with Thai and Caribbean cuisine such as pad Thai ($9) and a mango chicken sandwich ($7). The fruity drink menu befits the location.

On Main Street between Okanagan and Skaha Lakes are several decent eateries. At **Theo's Restaurant** (687 Main St., 250/492-4019) you can tuck into European favorites such as lamb mousakka ($14) and herbed tiger prawns ($23) in a large open-plan eatery with lots of greenery.

In Kaleden, south of Penticton, the **Historic 1912 Restaurant** (250/497-6888; daily for dinner) provides the opportunity to enjoy some of the valley's best food in a historic lakefront location. The menu takes advantage of fresh local produce wherever possible, changing as different fruits and vegetables become avail-

able. It was the latter, a huge platter of sautéed seasonal vegetables for $19, that caught my eye when eating here. The house specialties are gourmet dinners for two or four, such as chateaubriand tenderloin carved at your table for $95 (serves two), complete with a starter and dessert.

Information and Services

Penticton Visitor Info Centre (888 Westminster Ave. W, 250/493-4055 or 800/663-5052, www.penticton.org; summer daily 8 A.M.–8 P.M., the rest of the year Mon.–Fri. 9 A.M.–6 P.M., Sat.–Sun. 10 A.M.–5 P.M.) is not particularly well signed, but it's worth stopping at nevertheless. Inside the adobe-style structure is free Internet access, a wine information center, and lots of local literature. From the south, follow the signs north to Kelowna and take Westminster Avenue right off Eckhardt Avenue (Highway 97); it's off to the right after a few blocks. Coming into town from the north, cross the canal and take the second turn on the left (Westminster Avenue).

Okanagan Books (233 Main St., 250/493-1941) stocks a wide range of local reading and all the current bestsellers. Across the road, **Books 'n Things** is the city's premier used bookstore. Both are closed Sunday.

Penticton Regional Hospital is on Carmi Avenue (250/492-4000). The **post office** is on the corner of Winnipeg Street and Nanaimo Avenue.

Transportation

Visitors flying into the Okanagan use Kelowna Airport, to the north, where they pick up rental cars. The **Greyhound Bus Depot** (307 Ellis St., 250/493-4101) is busy with services heading south to Osoyoos and north through the Okanagan Valley to Salmon Arm on the TransCanada Highway.

Getting around town is easy on **Penticton Transit System** (250/492-5602).

NORTH OF PENTICTON

Highway 97 links Penticton and Kelowna, running along the west side of Okanagan Lake for the entire 60 kilometers (37 miles). The first worthwhile stop is tiny **Sun-Oka Beach Provincial Park,** a sun-drenched, south-facing park with a sandy beach, paddle boat rentals, and a concession.

Summerland

As you enter picturesque Summerland, nestled between Giants Head Mountain and the lake 16 kilometers (10 miles) north of Penticton, turn west (away from the lake) at either of the stoplights and follow the signs to Prairie Valley Station, the departure point for **Kettle River Railway** (250/494-8422 or 877/494-8424). This steam train, dating to the early 1900s, runs along a historic 10-kilometer (6.2-mile) stretch of track, through orchards and vineyards, and over a 75-meter-high trestle bridge. Departures are late May to mid-October Saturday–Monday at 10:30 A.M. and 1:30 P.M., with additional trips in July and August on Thursday and Friday. The fare for the 90-minute round-trip is adult $18, senior $15, child $10.

Another interesting stop is **Summerland Sweets** factory (Canyon View Rd., 250/494-0377) to see syrups, jams, and candy being made from fresh and frozen fruit; from Highway 97 take the Dunn Street or Arkell Road exit west, turn right on Gartrell Road, left on Happy Valley Road, right on Hillborn Street, then left on Canyon View Road.

Sumac Ridge Estate (one km/.6 mile north of Summerland on the lake side of the highway, 250/494-0451) was British Columbia's first estate winery. Today, this well-recognized name appears on a wide variety of red and white wines, including an award-winning Cabernet Franc and one of the Okanagan's few sparkling wines. Tours and tastings are offered May–October daily 10 A.M.–4 P.M. on the hour, and a bistro is open daily for lunch.

Continuing Toward Kelowna

On the way to Kelowna you pass two entrances to **Okanagan Lake Provincial Park,** a grassy, beach-fringed park popular for boating and swimming. Ponderosa pines line the shore while exotic trees such as maple and oak shade dozens of picnic tables. Camping is $18.50 a night April–October.

Farther along is the community of **Peachland.** Crammed between a rocky bluff and Okanagan Lake, Peachland was founded in 1808 by Manitoba entrepreneur and newspaperman John Robinson, who came to the Okanagan in search of mining prospects but turned his talents to developing the delicious locally grown dessert peaches. The drive through downtown is a pleasant diversion from Highway 97. On one side is the lake and a long pebbly beach dotted with grassed areas of parkland and supervised swimming areas. On the other is a collection of shops and cafés.

Kelowna

British Columbia's largest city outside the Lower Mainland and Victoria, Kelowna (pop. 104,000) lies on the shores of 170-kilometer-long (106-mile-long) Okanagan Lake, approximately halfway between Penticton in the south and Vernon in the north. The city combines a scenic location among semiarid mountains with an unbeatable climate of long, sunny summers and short, mild winters. The low rolling hills around the city hold lush terraced orchards, and the numerous local vineyards produce some excellent wines. Visitors flock here in summer to enjoy the area's sparkling lakes, sandy beaches, numerous provincial parks, and golfing; in winter they come for great skiing and boarding at nearby Big White Ski Resort.

History

For thousands of years before the arrival of the first Europeans, the nomadic Salish people inhabited the Okanagan Valley, hunting (*kelowna* is a Salish word for grizzly bear), gathering, and fishing. The first European to settle in the valley was an oblate missionary, Father Pandosy, who established a mission on the southern outskirts of present-day downtown Kelowna in 1859. Since the first apple trees were planted at the mission, Kelowna has thrived as the center of the Okanagan fruit, vegetable, and vineyard industry (the valley is Canada's largest fruit-growing region).

In 1960, Kelowna's population stood at 24,000 and began expanding soon after as wide-scale forestry, agriculture, and tourism took hold. As local services have improved, the region has become more attractive to Canadians looking for a relaxing lifestyle in warmer climes. Since the opening of the Okanagan Connector in 1986, traveling time between Vancouver and Kelowna has been cut from around six hours to under four hours, and the population has exploded, with the number of wineries doubling since the mid-1980s, luxurious resorts being built along the lake, new golf courses opening every year, and subdivisions carving away land in the surrounding hills. Along the way, Kelowna has managed to retain its charm and small-town values. This was evident in 2003 when everyone came together to help out as wildfires swept down into the city from Okanagan Mountain, forcing the evacuation of 30,000 residents and destroying 200 homes.

SIGHTS
Along the Waterfront

Right downtown, beautiful **City Park** is the largest of Kelowna's many parks. Its 14 hectares (35 acres) hold lots of flowers and large shady trees, expansive lawns, and a long sandy beach. You can rent a boat, houseboat, and fishing equipment at one of several marinas. Water-skiing and parasailing are also popular activities. Near the entrance to the park is the large, sparkling-white, attention-grabbing Dow Reid sculpture *Sails,* as well as a replica of the famed lake-dwelling serpent, Ogopogo (see sidebar).

At the south end of the park is one end of the **Okanagan Lake Bridge.** Built in 1958, this 1,400-meter-long floating bridge, anchored to the lakebed in 24 spots, is the only such structure in Canada.

A promenade leads north from the Ogopogo statue past a large marina and a prime waterfront site undergoing redevelopment. Beyond the construction is the **Grand Okanagan,** the Okanagan's most luxurious accommodation. Even if you can't afford a lakefront suite, the resort holds a bar and restaurant with water views, and full spa services. Beyond the resort, the promenade crosses a small lock, which allows boaters to travel between the higher water level of an artificial lagoon and the lake itself.

Other Downtown Sights

Kelowna Museum (470 Queensway Ave., 250/763-2417; summer Mon.–Sat. 10 A.M.–5 P.M., the rest of the year Tues.–Sat. 10 A.M.–5 P.M.; donation) is opposite the post office; look for the brightly painted totem pole marking the entrance. The museum holds a mishmash of fas-

Okanagan Valley

cinating displays, including horse-drawn carriages; fossils found in the Princeton area; indigenous arts, crafts, clothing, jewelry, beads, and furs; children's books and games; radio equipment; pioneer artifacts; re-creations of an 1861 Kelowna trading post and a Chinese store; and a display of the interior of a Salish winter dwelling.

Behind the museum is **Kasugai Gardens.** Built with the cooperation of Kelowna's Japanese sister city, Kasugai, the gardens are a quiet retreat from the downtown business district; admission is free and the gates are locked at dusk. **Kelowna Art Gallery** (1315 Water St., 250/762-2226; Tues.–Sat. 10 A.M.–5 P.M., Sun. 1–5 P.M.; donation) is a modern facility hosting touring exhibitions and maintaining a permanent collection of contemporary and historical works by artists from throughout the province.

In an old downtown packing house, complete with exposed red-brick walls and hand-hewn wooden beams, the **Orchard Museum** (1304 Ellis St., 250/763-0433; Tues.–Sat. 10 A.M.–5 P.M.) tells the story of the local orchard industry through rare photographs, displays, and a hands-on discovery corner. In the same building, the **Wine Museum** (250/868-0441; Mon.–Sat. 10 A.M.–5 P.M., Sun. noon–5 P.M.) has information on local wineries and tours, and sells the finished product.

Benvoulin Heritage Park

This park (east of downtown at 2279 Benvoulin Rd.) surrounds the Gothic revival Benvoulin Church, which dates to 1892. The church and a historic residence also within the grounds are closed to the public, but the garden holds the most interest. It is a "xeriscape" garden, which are designed to take advantage of the local climate and environment. In this case, plants grown here require little moisture, reflective of problems encountered by professional and amateur gardeners along the entire valley.

Pandosy Mission Provincial Heritage Site

Farther south along Benvoulin Road is the site of the mission established by Father Pandosy in 1859. The route meanders through lush irri-

Okanagan Valley

KELOWNA

Knox Mountain Park

KNOX MOUNTAIN DR

GLENMORE RD

CROWLEY AVE

TRAIN STATION

Waterfront Park

RICHTER ST

ETHEL ST

GORDON DR

HIGH RD

GLENMORE DR

★ SUN-RYPE PRODUCTS

ELLIS ST

BERNARD AVE

City Park

HARVEY AVE

ABBOTT ST

● COAST CAPRI HOTEL

SEE "DOWNTOWN KELOWNA" MAP

SUTHERLAND AVE

CADDER AVE

SPRINGFIELD RD

HOSPITAL ■

PANDOSY ST

SPORTS RENT ■

SIESTA MOTOR INN

KLO RD

LANFRANCO

Gyro Beach

Rotary Beach

HIAWATHA RV PARK

● MANTEO RESORT

● HOTEL ELDORADO

To Cedar Creek Estate Winery and Okanagan Mountain Provincial Park

★ PANDOSY MISSION PROVINCIAL HISTORIC SITE

BENVOULIN RD

Mission Creek

Benvoulin Heritage Park

Mission Creek Regional Park

KELOWNA LAND & ORCHARD COMPANY ★

DUNSTER RD

EAST KELOWNA RD

EAST KELOWNA RD

THE HARVEST GOLF CLUB

McCULLOCH RD

To Winfield, Okanagan Golf Club, Airport, and Vernon

SCANDIA GOLF & GAMES ■

LEATHEED RD

● DAYS INN

33

BEST WESTERN INN KELOWNA ■

To Big White Ski Resort and Grand Forks

BUS DEPOT ■

97

▼ CARMELLE'S RESTAURANT

WENRICK CRES

SCALE NOT AVAILABLE

To Kettle Valley Railway and Gallagher's Canyon Golf & Country Club

Okanagan Valley

© AVALON TRAVEL PUBLISHING, INC.

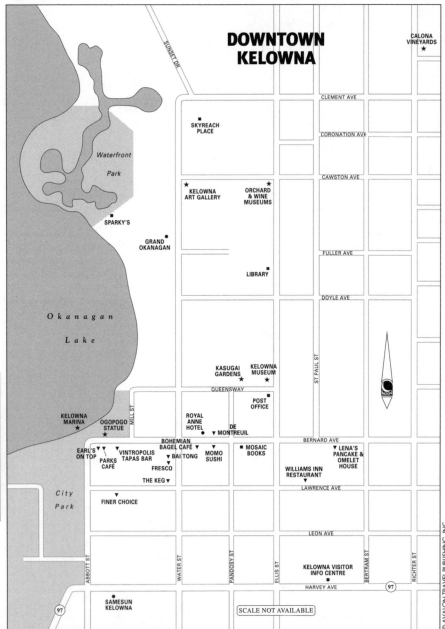

DOWNTOWN KELOWNA

CALONA VINEYARDS ★

CLEMENT AVE

CORONATION AVE

CAWSTON AVE

FULLER AVE

DOYLE AVE

SUNSET DR

SKYREACH PLACE ■

Waterfront Park

KELOWNA ART GALLERY ★

ORCHARD & WINE MUSEUMS ★

LIBRARY ■

SPARKY'S ■

GRAND OKANAGAN ●

Okanagan Lake

KASUGAI GARDENS ★

KELOWNA MUSEUM ★

ST PAUL ST

QUEENSWAY

POST OFFICE ■

KELOWNA MARINA ★

OGOPOGO STATUE ★

MILL ST

ROYAL ANNE HOTEL ●

DE MONTREUIL ▼

BERNARD AVE

EARL'S ON TOP ▼▼

PARKS CAFÉ ▼

VINTROPOLIS TAPAS BAR ▼

BOHEMIAN BAGEL CAFÉ ▼

BAI TONG ▼

FRESCO ▼

MOMO SUSHI ●

MOSAIC BOOKS ■

WILLIAMS INN RESTAURANT ▼

LENA'S PANCAKE & OMELET HOUSE ▼

THE KEG ▼

LAWRENCE AVE

City Park

FINER CHOICE ▼

LEON AVE

ABBOTT ST

WATER ST

PANDOSY ST

ELLIS ST

KELOWNA VISITOR INFO CENTRE ■

BERTRAM ST

RICHTER ST

97

SAMESUN KELOWNA ■

HARVEY AVE

97

SCALE NOT AVAILABLE

Okanagan Valley

© ANDREW HEMPSTEAD

one of the original buildings at Pandosy Mission

gated farmlands and orchards, past nurseries, fields of grass-munching horses, and large country homes with picture-perfect flower and vegetable gardens. Father Pandosy, an oblate priest, operated a church, school, and farm here, ministering to natives and whites until his death in 1891. His mission claimed a lot of "firsts"—first white settlement in the Okanagan Valley, first school in the valley, first fruit and vine crops in the valley, and first Roman Catholic mission in the B.C. interior. Not much has changed within the broken-down wooden fences that hold the mission—four of the eight buildings on-site date to Pandosy's era, including a chapel and barn. The mission is open daily from 8 A.M. to dark, and the $2 donation includes an informative tour of the buildings, grounds, and antique farming equipment.

Wineries

Viticulture has been a mainstay of the Okanagan's economy for almost a century, but it has really taken off in the last decade, with local wines exported and winning awards worldwide. Most of the local wineries welcome visitors with tours and free tastings year-round (but call ahead outside of summer to check hours). Due to the popularity of visiting the wineries, most now charge a small fee for tasting. **Okanagan Wine Country Tours** (250/868-4463 or 866/689-9463) has a variety of tours, including a full-day of touring and tasting for $110 per person.

One of the province's oldest wineries, in operation since 1932, is **Calona Vineyards** (downtown at 1125 Richter St., 250/762-9144; daily 9 A.M.–6 P.M.). There's no actual vineyard, just a large winery that uses grapes grown throughout the valley. Calona offers tours throughout the year at 2 P.M. (more frequently in summer), with tastings and sales in a room set up as a cellar.

Across Okanagan Lake from Kelowna is **Mission Hill Family Estate** (1730 Mission Hill Rd., Westbank, 250/768-7611), high atop a ridge and surrounded by vineyards with stunning lake views. Mission Hill, British Columbia's most successful winery, completed massive expansions in 2001, including a 45-meter-high bell tower, open for the public to climb. Tours depart three times daily, each ending with an informal tasting session at the Wine and Food Interpretation Centre (daily 10 A.M.–7 P.M.). At nearby **Quail's Gate Estate Winery** (3303 Boucherie Rd., 250/769-4451) the Reserve Pinot Noir is a signature wine—enjoy a glass or two alfresco at the winery bistro (May–Oct. 11 A.M.–4 P.M. and 5 P.M.–dusk). Winery tours are conducted May–October up to six times daily.

Back on the main highway, farther south is **Hainle Vineyards Estate Winery** (5355 Trepanier Bench Rd., Peachland, 250/767-2525; Tues.–Sun. 10 A.M.–5 P.M.). Walter Hainle was a pioneer in the development of ice wines, and while this is the style that the vineyard is best known for, limited quantities of red and white wines are also produced. Lunch and light snacks are offered noon–3 P.M.

Across the lake from the above wineries is the much-heralded **Cedar Creek Estate Winery** (5445 Lakeshore Dr., 250/764-8866), where the vineyards and extensive gardens overlook Lake

Okanagan Valley

OGOPOGO

Ogopogo is the friendly Loch Ness–style sea serpent that allegedly lives on the bottom of "bottomless" Lake Okanagan. Local natives told the first white settlers who came to live in the Okanagan Valley that a fast-swimming monster called N'ha-a-tik, meaning "Devil of the Lake," lived in a deep part of the lake near present-day Kelowna. Whenever they had to canoe near that particular point, they unceremoniously threw an animal overboard as a sacrifice.

© ANDREW HEMPSTEAD

Since 1942, when the mysterious monster became known as Ogopogo, thousands of sightings have allegedly been made, and the creature has been the subject of feature stories on the television shows *Unsolved Mysteries* and *Inside Edition*. Consensus is that Ogopogo is a snakelike creature with small humps, green skin, and a nice big smile, the latter feature confirmed by enterprising locals who print his image on T-shirts, posters, and postcards.

Although many times a prize has been put up for anyone providing definitive proof of Ogopogo's existence—the most recent is $2 million—no one has yet claimed the reward. Anyway, keep your eyes open and your camera at hand; you just never know, you may be one of the few (sober) ones to spot him.

Okanagan. Tours are offered in summer daily 11 A.M.–4 P.M.

Gray Monk Estate Winery (22 km/13.7 miles north of Kelowna on Camp Rd., Winfield, 250/766-3168) is a family affair most recognized for its German-style wines, including Gewürztraminer and a Pinot Gris. Tours are offered April–October on the hour 11 A.M.–4 P.M., the rest of the year on Sunday at 2 P.M.

Other Agricultural and Industrial Tours

You could probably spend a couple of weeks taking one tour a day around Kelowna—orchard tours, vineyard tours, fruit-factory tours, forestry tours, and industrial tours. One that all tour-lovers will enjoy is the free 30-minute tour of **Sun-Rype Products** (1165 Ethel St., 250/860-7973; June–Sept. Mon.–Fri. 9 A.M.–3 P.M.), which shows you how apple juice, applesauce, and pie fillings are created. **Kelowna Land and Orchard Co.** (3002 Dunster Rd., 250/763-1091), for which K.L.O. Road is named, is a 60-hectare apple orchard that was established in 1904. Tours of the orchard aboard a tractor-drawn wagon depart daily at 11 A.M., 1 P.M., and 3 P.M. A store and teahouse are on-site.

If you have your own transportation, take the self-guided **McCulloch Forest Tour** along a short forest route southeast of Kelowna; pick up a brochure with a map to various points of interest at the information center.

RECREATION

On the Lake

During the warm and sunny months of summer, Okanagan Lake comes alive with a colorful array of watercraft, fishermen, and swimmers out on the water, and sunbathers dot the surrounding sandy beaches. The busiest spot is the stretch of sand fronting City Park, right downtown. Beyond the beach's northern end, you can rent watercraft from **Sparky's** (250/862-2469), in front of the Grand Okanagan; rent small power boats at **Kelowna Marina**

(250/861-8001); or go parachuting behind a boat with **Kelowna Parasail Adventures** (250/868-4838) for $48 per person.

Gyro Beach and adjacent **Rotary Beach** are beautiful stretches of sand south of downtown along Lakeshore Drive. Less crowded are the beaches in **Okanagan Mountain Provincial Park,** farther south.

Sports Rent (3000 Pandosy St., 250/861-5699) rents kayaks from $25 per day, canoes for $35 per day, and wetsuits.

Hiking and Biking

The **Kettle Valley Railway** bed, which winds around the back of Kelowna, may be protected as a national historic site, but unfortunately nothing could protect its 18 trestle bridges from 2003 wildfires. Plans are in place to have them rebuilt, but until then, opportunities for extended trips along the rail bed are somewhat limited. It's still an interesting spot, well worth the effort to reach. To get there take K.L.O. Road to McCulloch Road, turn south (right) and then south (right) again, following Myra Forest Service Road for 8.5 kilometers (5.3 miles). From the parking lot at this point, it's under one kilometer (.6 mile) to the first of the burnt trestles.

The cacti-covered top of **Knox Mountain** offers great lake and city views. A hiking trail and a paved road popular with bicyclists both lead to the summit. To get there head north out of town along the lakeshore, passing pretty, lakeside Sutherland Park (good views of Crown Forest Mill and log rafts), then take Knox Mountain Drive up to Knox Mountain Park, stopping at Crown Viewpoint on the way to the top. Trails lead off the summit in all directions, and in May the mountain swarms with activity as cars and motorcycles race up the mountain during the **Knox Mountain Hill Climb.**

Golfing

Many of Canada's best resort-style golf courses lie in and around Kelowna. These courses, combined with a mild climate and relatively well-priced greens fees, make the Okanagan one of the country's finest golfing destinations. All the courses listed offer club rentals, power carts (gen-

erally around $30), and on-course dining facilities. **Okanagan Reservations** (250/493-3200 or 800/663-1900, www.okres.bc.ca) offers golf packages from $100 per person per night.

The **Harvest Golf Club** (250/862-3103 or 800/257-8577), sitting on terraced land southeast of downtown, offers golfers views back across the city and lake. This 7,109-yard course features fairways lined with fruit trees, large greens, lots of water hazards, and a magnificent clubhouse. Greens fees are $100; the twilight rate is $54. Get there by taking K.L.O. Road east from Pandosy Street. Adjacent to Harvest is **Orchard Greens** (2777 K.L.O. Rd., 250/868-3844; $16), a fun little nine-hole layout that winds its way through a working apple orchard.

Continue east from the Harvest Golf Club and you'll eventually reach **Gallagher's Canyon Golf & Country Club** (250/861-4240), one of Canada's finest golf courses. Not particularly long, this immaculately manicured course snakes through a canyon and opens up to fairways lined with mature pine trees. It is a par-72 course that plays to 6,800 yards. Greens fees are $105 a round, or pay $55 after 4 P.M.

North of town and opposite the airport is **Okanagan Golf Club** (250/765-5955), a residential and resort complex featuring 36 of the valley's finest holes. Designed by Jack Nicklaus's company, **The Bear** opened for the 1999 season while **The Quail,** featuring multitiered fairways and large elevations, has been a long-time local favorite. Both courses play to a par of 72 and are just under 7,000 yards from the back tees. Greens fees are $95, with a discounted twilight rate of $55 for each course.

Okanagan Valley Wine Train

This touristy venture (250/712-9888 or 800/674-8725) runs north from Kelowna through the heart of orchard country then through some of the province's finest ranching land to Armstrong. Passengers can travel in regular rail carriages, but most opt for the themed carriages, such as "Hollywood," "Country and Western," or "Rock 'n' Roll." The fare is $80, which includes a meal and a Las Vegas–style show in Armstrong. To ride the train costs only

$30. The trip departs July–mid-October every Saturday at 5:30 P.M.

Fun Parks

North of downtown, **Scandia Golf & Games** (2898 Hwy. 97 N, 250/765-2355) is a sprawling complex of indoor and outdoor mini-golf courses, with one of the indoor layouts lit only by fluorescent lights and glowing golf balls. Head south across the floating bridge to access the following three attractions. Immediately after crossing the lake, turn left to access **19 Greens** (2050 Campbell Rd., 250/769-0213; Apr.–Oct. 11 A.M.–midnight), a mini-putt golf course that uses real grass to create fun for all ages. **Mariner's Reef Waterpark & Slides** (Westbank, 250/768-5141; adult $22, children 4–6 $15). Also in Westbank is **Old MacDonald's Farm** (Hwy. 97, 250/768-5167; adult $9, senior or child $7.50), with farm animals and exotic animals, as well as mini-golf and pony rides. Both these places are open May–September.

Skiing and Snowboarding

Big White Ski Resort (250/765-3101 or 800/663-2772, www.bigwhite.com), 57 kilometers (35 miles) east of Kelowna on Highway 33, is one of the Okanagan's three major winter resorts and B.C.'s second largest. Its network of modern lifts, including a gondola and four high-speed quads, opens up over 850 hectares (2,100 acres) of terrain. Lifts operate December through mid-April daily 8:30 A.M.–3:30 P.M., and for night skiing and boarding Tuesday–Saturday 5–9 P.M. Lift tickets are adult $60, senior $52, child $30, 70 and over and under five free. Adjacent to the main lift-served area is Happy Valley Adventure Centre, a tube park with its own lift. Big White is also home to a terrain park, half pipe, cross-country trails, and an ice-skating rink. On-mountain facilities in the 9,000-bed base village include rental shops, a ski and snowboard school, accommodations, restaurants and cafés, and a large mall.

Nightlife

Enjoy a drink overlooking Okanagan Lake in the stylish lounge at the **Hotel Eldorado** (500 Cook Rd., 250/763-7500; daily from 11 A.M.). Right downtown, **Sgt. O'Flaherty's,** in the Royal Anne Hotel (348 Bernard Ave., 250/860-6409), is a friendly pub with bands churning out a variety of music styles nightly from 9 P.M.

At **Lake City Casino** (Grand Okanagan, 1310 Water St., 250/860-9467), don't expect the ritz and glitz of Las Vegas—this is gambling Canadian style, with the action restricted to slot machines, blackjack, roulette, Caribbean stud poker, and mini baccarat, and everyone's ushered out the front door at 2 A.M.

Sunshine Theatre (250/763-4025) puts on 3–4 plays throughout the summer; pick up a schedule at the information center. The **Uptown Cinema Centre** (1521 Water St., 250/762-0099) screens films.

Festivals and Events

The **Spring Wine Festival** (250/861-6654, www.owfs.com) is somewhat less pretentious than the fall equivalent, with many wineries not normally open to the public offering tours and tasting sessions through late April. On the first weekend of May, the **Apple Blossom Festival** coincides with the beginning of the apple-picking season. The event features fun family events out at the Kelowna Land and Orchard Company on Dunster Road. The **Knox Mountain Hill Climb,** North America's longest paved motor-vehicle hill climb, has been contested annually since 1957; it's on in late May.

Throughout July, the mobile **Mozart Festival** (250/762-3747, www.okanaganmozartfestival.com) takes place, with classical performances at venues throughout the city, including at local churches and museums. Each of the 10 concerts costs $15 per person. The second weekend of July, wander down to the marina at the Hotel Eldorado to admire watercraft displayed at the **Antique and Classic Boat Show** (250/763-8603). On the first weekend of August, the Sunshine Theatre Co. presents the **Kelowna Comedy Festival** (250/763-4025, www.kelownacomedyfestival.com) at various indoor and outdoor venues. Held on streets, in parks, and at venues through the city, the **Kelowna Fringe**

Festival (250/763-1661) brings eclectic modern theater productions late in August.

The valley's biggest event is the **Fall Wine Festival** (250/861-6654, www.owfs.com), held annually over 10 days from the last full weekend of September to celebrate the end of the grape harvest. Thousands of visitors participate in food and wine tastings, releases of new wines, cooking classes, and art displays with all sections of the industry participating. The **apple harvest** is celebrated during the same period at the Orchard Museum (1304 Ellis St., 250/763-0433), with apple tastings and displays.

ACCOMMODATIONS AND CAMPING

Under $50

Samesun Kelowna (245 Harvey St., 250/763-5013 or 888/562-2783, www.samesun.com) is a centrally located, purpose-built backpacker lodge. Inside the distinctive three-story building are 120 beds, many in private rooms (with shared bathrooms), with communal kitchens, bathrooms, a large lounge area, and public Internet access. Out back is a pleasant grassed barbecue area and a beach volleyball court. Rates are $26 for a dorm bed, $63 s or d in a private room. Pickups from the bus depot are free, drop-offs a reasonable $2. The owners of the Samesun operate a winter-only backpacker lodge up at Big White Ski Resort, 57 kilometers (35 miles) east of town (250/765-2100 or 888/595-6411). Dorms cost $27.40, private rooms $63.

$50–100

High in the highlands northeast of Kelowna, **M Beaver Lake Resort** (250/762-2225, www.beaverlakeresort.com, May–Oct.) is very different from the beachy resort complexes down on the valley floor. Set in a forest on the edge of a lake famed for rainbow trout fishing, the resort comprises a restaurant, a horseback-riding operation (with afternoon pony rides for kids), and a fishing shop. Boat rentals are well priced at $45 per 24 hours, inclusive of gas. Canoes, kayaks, and belly boats are $30 per day. Cabins range from tiny "camping cabins" that share

© ANDREW HEMPSTEAD

Beaver Lake Resort

bathrooms ($35 s or d) to peeled log chalets with full kitchens ($125). Cabin 9 is typical—it's rustic but enjoys an absolute lakefront setting, a private floating dock, big deck, full kitchen, log fireplace, one bedroom, and a loft, all for under $100 per night. Make cabin reservations well in advance—locals know a bargain when they see one and book their favorite cabin up to a year in advance. Camping is $18 (no hookups). To get there, head north to Winfield, then 16 kilometers (10 miles) east on Beaver Lake Road.

South of downtown, the **Siesta Motor Inn** (3152 Lakeshore Rd., 250/763-5013 or 800/663-4347, www.siestamotorinn.com) offers a beachside atmosphere one block from the water. Rooms open onto a wide balcony overlooking a courtyard and pool. Rooms range $99–148 s or d; many rooms have kitchenettes.

$100–150

Built in 1926 and moved to its present location in 1989, the **Hotel Eldorado** (500 Cook Rd.,

Okanagan Valley

south of downtown along Pandosy St., 250/763-7500, www.eldoradokelowna.com) is a delightful lakeside accommodation offering just 19 rooms, each furnished with antiques and many offering a lake view and private balcony. Hotel facilities include a lakefront café, a restaurant, a lounge, and a marina with boat rentals. Summer rates range $169–239 s or d, with only the more expensive rooms having water views. Off-season rates start at $89.

Highway 97 (also known as Harvey Avenue) north of downtown holds many motels tucked between shopping malls, gas stations, and fast-food restaurants. Along this strip is **Days Inn Kelowna** (2469 Hwy. 97 N, 250/868-3297 or 800/337-7177, www.daysinn.com), with large, modern rooms decorated in Santa Fe style, as well as an outdoor pool and hot tub; the smallest rooms cost $119 s or d, but it's worth an extra $20 for a much-larger suite. As at all Days Inns, rates include a light breakfast.

$150–200

North of downtown, **Best Western Inn Kelowna** (2402 Hwy. 97 N, 250/860-1212 or 888/860-1212, www.bestwesterninnkelowna.com) is a good choice for those who want the amenities of a full resort but don't want to pay for a waterfront location. Rooms are set around a grassed courtyard, complete with putting greens and an outdoor hot tub. Other facilities include an indoor pool, spa services, fitness room, and a restaurant and pub. The rooms are spacious and modern and come filled with niceties such as air-conditioning, bathrobes, hair dryers, Internet access, and free local calls. Rates start at $174 s or d, which includes continental breakfast, but as always, check the hotel website for deals and packages.

Over $200

Overlooking the same stretch of lake as the Hotel Eldorado is the colorful and modern **M Manteo Resort** (3766 Lakeshore Rd., 250/860-1031 or 888/462-6836, www.manteo.com). This self-contained complex includes a 78-room hotel and guest and resident facilities such as a private beach, marina with boat rentals, pool complex with a water slide, tennis courts, a small movie theater, a lounge with billiard table, and a barbecue area. Rates start at $235 s or d for a contemporary-styled hotel room ($265 with a water view), but villas that sleep six can be rented for $535 per night. Outside of summer, bed and breakfast is around $150 per couple.

The grandest of Kelowna's accommodations is **The Grand Okanagan** (1310 Water St., 250/763-4500 or 800/465-4651, www.grandokanagan.com), a sprawling lakeside development right downtown and integrated with local walking paths. Along the lake side of the resort is a convoluted lagoon, with its own private lock and watercraft rentals, while farther along are eateries and a bar with outdoor seating. Inside, once past the cavernous lobby, you'll find a fitness center, spa services, restaurants, a lounge bar, and 205 luxuriously appointed rooms. In summer, standard rooms are $259 s or d, with suites from $325. The best deals are the packages, which include, for example, breakfast, dinner, and a room upgrade for an additional $70. Off-season rates start at $159 room only.

Lake Okanagan Resort (on the west side of Okanagan Lake 17 km/10.6 miles north along Westside Rd., 250/769-3511 or 800/663-3273, www.lakeokanagan.com) sprawls over 100 hectares (250 acres) of absolute waterfront property. It offers tennis courts, a par-3 golf course, swimming pools, a full-service marina, and horseback riding. In the main lodge is a restaurant open daily for dinner, a more casual café where dining alfresco is the order of the day, a poolside bar, and an upstairs lounge. The spacious units are each kitchen-equipped and have private balconies but are in need of an upgrade. Between mid-June and mid-September, a two-night package including one dinner and one breakfast is $284 per person, discounted to $184 the rest of the year.

Camping

The closest campground to downtown is **Hiawatha RV Park** (3787 Lakeshore Rd., 250/861-4837 or 888/784-7275, www.hiawatharvpark.com). It has a tenting area, showers, a laundry, game room, and playground; tent sites $36, hookups $40–45.

Most of the other commercial campgrounds are on the west shore of Okanagan Lake at West-bank. If you've got a beach-loving family in tow, plan ahead by booking a site at **Happy Valley Resort** (4026 Pritchard Dr., 250/768-7703, www.happyvalleyresort.com; mid-Apr.–Oct.). This lakefront campground has a beautiful sandy stretch of beach and a large playground. Sites are $30–35.

Two provincial parks in the vicinity of Kelowna offer camping. The closest is **Bear Creek Provincial Park,** across the bridge from downtown and then nine kilometers (5.6 miles) north on Westside Road. The campground holds 122 sites nestled under cottonwood trees. This park is a world away from the busy nearby commercial campgrounds, but arrive early in the day to ensure a site; $22 per night includes showers. Campers also enjoy a short beach and trails that cross back over Westside Road and into desert-like terrain above the lake. **Fintry Provincial Park** lies a further 23 kilometers (14.3 miles) north along Westside Road in the same beachside setting as Bear Creek, although the campground is less developed; $22 per night. A trail leads from the campground to a deep canyon along Shorts Creek.

FOOD

Downtown Kelowna has a great number of dining choices, for everything from a quick coffee to a full meal, but many of the city's finer restaurants are away from the business core, along quiet country roads or at the many golf clubs.

Downtown Cafés

The business of breakfast doesn't get going until around 8 A.M. in the downtown area, but one exception is **Lena's Pancake & Omelet House** (553 Bernard St.), which opens its doors at 6:30 A.M.—the perfect place for a meal after an early morning walk along the lakefront; cooked breakfasts start at $3.99. Toward the lake, the **Bohemian Bagel Cafe** (363 Bernard Ave., 250/862-3517; Mon.–Fri. 7:30 A.M.–4:30 P.M., Sat. 9 A.M.–3 P.M.) has a loyal local following for gourmet coffee and bagels baked in-house. One block farther west is **Parks Café** (227 Bernard Ave., 250/979-0222; daily from 8 A.M.), most notable for inexpensive breakfasts such as a broccoli omelet—as well as more traditional eggs-and-bacon dishes. Lunch is also worthwhile, highlighted by healthy sandwiches made to order with chicken roasted in-house, homemade quiche, and the like.

If you're browsing for a book at Mosaic Books, follow the aroma of freshly brewed coffee through to the adjacent **Mosaic Coffee Shop** (411 Bernard Ave., 250/763-4418; Mon.–Fri. 7:30 A.M.–4 P.M., Sat. 9 A.M.–4:30 P.M., Sun. 11 A.M.–4:30 P.M.).

Family-Style Dining

Opposite City Park, **Earl's on Top** (upstairs at 211 Bernard Ave., 250/763-2777; Sun.–Mon. 11:30 A.M.–11 P.M., Tues.–Sat. 11:30 A.M.–midnight) does a booming business with a younger crowd. The atmosphere features a shiny, black-and-white decor with flashy neon lighting (nothing beats a neon palm tree) and a mass of plants. Grab a table on the rooftop garden patio and absorb the lake view, or just pretend you're outside (not hard to do with all the plants). The menu offers a wide variety of soups, salads, burgers, chicken, seafood, steak, and pasta dishes—even tapas. Lunch ranges $5–12, dinner $6–20. The **Keg Restaurant** (1580 Water St., 250/763-5435; daily 4–11 P.M.) has a 60-item salad bar, steaks, seafood, prime rib, and steak or chicken fajitas. Expect to pay $8–19 for a main course.

Canadian

Fresco (1560 Water St., 250/868-8805; daily from 5:30 P.M.) is the latest addition to Kelowna's dining scene. In the surrounds of a heritage commercial building are elegant table settings, a martini bar, and comfortable sofas. The menu is typically West Coast, but more adventurous than you'd expect this far from Vancouver. Mains range $21–32 while Signature Collection dishes such as oat-crusted arctic char are $42.

Also downtown, **de Montreuil Restaurant** (368 Bernard St., 250/860-5508) is a starkly decorated yet stylish restaurant. The menu offers many mouthwatering choices, such as an Australian rack of lamb basted in fresh rosemary and garlic. The table d'hôte menus offer the best value—two courses for $30, three for $36, and four for $41. It's open weekdays for lunch, daily for dinner, and also for Sunday brunch.

The delicious small-plate dishes at **M Vintropolis Tapas Bar** (231 Bernard Ave., 250/762-7682; daily 5–11 P.M.) provide the perfect accompaniment to Okanagan wines served by the glass. The dining room is a long, narrow space, simply decorated so nothing is taken away from menu choices, such as salmon sashimi, coconut curry tiger prawns, and wonderful bruschetta.

European

A longtime favorite with well-dressed locals is **Finer Choice** (237 Lawrence Ave., 250/763-0422; Mon.–Fri. for lunch, daily from 5 P.M. for dinner), an elegant dining room decorated with antiques and oozing old-world charm. The waitpersons are attentive and the food well prepared; expect to pay $16–25 for the mostly European-inspired dinner entrées.

Farther east along the same street is **Williams Inn** (526 Lawrence Ave., 250/763-5136; daily for lunch and dinner), with table settings spread over two stories of a restored heritage house. The menu features lots of B.C. seafood and game, but the European training of the chefs is reflected in the style of dishes such as pheasant flambéed at your table. Dinner mains range $18–28.

Asian

Bai Tong (upstairs at 1530 Water St., 250/763-8638; Mon.–Fri. 11:30 A.M.–2:30 P.M. and 5–10 P.M.) is a step above your average small-town Asian restaurant. Feast on chicken cooked in a black bean sauce then wrapped in lettuce leaves, or stir-fry combos of vegetables and noodles with your choice of meat.

You'll find Kelowna's best Japanese food at **Momo Sushi** (377 Bernard Ave., 250/763-1030; Tues.–Sat. for lunch and dinner, Sun. dinner only).

INFORMATION AND SERVICES

Kelowna Visitor Info Centre (544 Harvey Ave., 250/861-1515 or 800/663-4345, www.tourismkelowna.org; summer daily 9 A.M.–7 P.M., the rest of the year daily 9 A.M.–5 P.M.) is beside Highway 97 as it passes through the center of the city—watch for the signs. Coming into town from the south on Highway 97, turn left on Richter Street at the traffic lights and go back one block. A good map for immediate orientation is posted outside the center; it also incorporates a legend of motels and attractions.

Mosaic Books (411 Bernard Ave., 250/763-4418 or 800/663-1225; Mon.–Wed. 8 A.M.–6 P.M., Thurs.–Fri. 8 A.M.–9 P.M., Sat. 9 A.M.–6 P.M., Sun. 11 A.M.–5 P.M.) is an independent bookseller that has been serving the valley for over 30 years. Besides an excellent collection of western Canadian titles, it has a wide selection of magazines and an in-house coffee bar. The eye-catching, semicircular building on Ellis Street is **Kelowna Library** (1380 Ellis St., 250/762-2800; Mon. 10 A.M.–5:30 P.M., Tues.–Thurs. 10 A.M.–9 P.M., Fri.–Sat. 10 A.M.–5:30 P.M.).

The **post office** is right downtown on Queensway Avenue. **Kelowna General Hospital** is on the corner of Strathcona Avenue and Pandosy Street (250/862-4000).

TRANSPORTATION
Getting There

Modern **Kelowna Airport,** the province's third busiest, is 15 kilometers (9.3 miles) north of downtown along Highway 97. It's served by **Air Canada** (250/542-3302) and **WestJet** (800/538-5696), both of which offer daily flights to and from Vancouver, Calgary, and Edmonton. At the airport are car-rental outlets, a lounge bar, and a casual café.

Greyhound (2366 Leckie Rd., 250/860-3835 or 800/661-8747) provides bus service throughout the Okanagan and beyond. Local buses are run by **Kelowna Regional Transit System.** Get schedule and route information from the downtown terminal (Bernard Ave. at Ellis St., 250/860-8121).

Getting Around

For a taxi, call **Kelowna Cabs** (250/762-2222) or **Checkmate Cabs** (250/861-1111). Another taxi service is offered by **Okanagan Shuttle** (250/766-4280, www.okanaganshuttle.com), which schedules personalized drop-offs at local wineries, golf courses, and the airport.

Rental-car agencies include: **Avis** (250/491-9500), **Budget** (250/491-7368), **Hertz** (250/765-3822), **National** (250/762-0622), **Rent-a-wreck** (250/763-6632), and **Thrifty** (250/868-2151). All these companies have vehicles out at the airport, but call in advance to ensure availability, especially in midsummer and during the ski season.

Sports Rent (3000 Pandosy St., 250/861-5699) rents mountain bikes for $7–10 per hour and $21–30 per day.

Vernon and Vicinity

The city of Vernon (pop. 35,000) lies between Okanagan, Kalamalka, and Swan Lakes, at the north end of the Okanagan Valley 50 kilometers (31 miles) from Kelowna. The city itself holds little of interest; the surrounding area boasts the main attractions. Among the area highlights: many sandy public beaches; local provincial parks; Silver Star Mountain Resort, a year-round recreation paradise east of the city; and fishing in more than 100 lakes within an hour's drive of the city.

History

When gold was discovered at Cherry Creek (now Monashee Creek), east of Vernon, a small gold rush resulted. But some of the miners noticed the agricultural potential of the Vernon area and decided to plant instead of pan. Forbes George Vernon, after whom the town was named in 1887, was one of these early settlers. Another, Cornelius O'Keefe, was bound for gold in the Cariboo when he noticed the area's lush growth of bunchgrass—prime feed for cattle and horses—and decided to stay put and establish a ranch. Between the 1860s and 1870s, a number of large ranches sprang up. By 1890 over 4,000 head of cattle were mowing the bunchgrass on the rangelands around Vernon.

When construction began on the Shuswap and Okanagan Railroad connecting Vernon with the Canadian Pacific Railway mainline at Sicamous, Vernon began to grow. By 1891, the year the first passenger train puffed into town, Vernon had evolved from a sleepy little cattle community into a thriving town of 500 residents. That same year, Lord Aberdeen bought the Coldstream Ranch from Forbes George Vernon, subdivided it, and sold the parcels at affordable prices, thereby encouraging settlement. He also promoted the idea of growing trees in the area. Vernon became a city in 1892, which makes it the oldest city in the B.C. interior and fifth-oldest in the province.

SIGHTS AND RECREATION

In Town

Greater Vernon Museum and Archives (3009 32nd Ave., 250/542-3142; summer Mon.–Sat. 10 A.M.–5 P.M., the rest of the year Tues.–Sat. 10 A.M.–5 P.M.) holds photos from the early 1900s and a large collection of pioneer and native artifacts. Displays cover natural history, recreation, period clothing, and steamships. In the same vicinity is **Vernon Public Art Gallery** (3228 31st Ave., 250/545-3173; Mon.–Fri. 10 A.M.–5 P.M., Sat. noon–4 P.M.), featuring works by local artists as well as touring exhibitions.

Polson Park (off Hwy. 97 at 25th Ave.) has a Chinese teahouse, a small Japanese garden, and paths along a willow-lined creek, but most people go to stare at the spectacular floral clock—nine meters (30 feet) wide, made up of more than 3,500 plants, and the only one of its kind in western Canada.

Historic O'Keefe Ranch

Established in 1867, the O'Keefe Ranch (250/542-7868; May–Sept. daily 9 A.M.–5 P.M., until 6 P.M. in July and Aug.; adult $7, senior

To Kamloops

To Armstrong and Sicamous

HISTORIC
O'KEEFE
RANCH ★

97A

SILVER STAR
MOUNTAIN
RESORT

WESTSIDE

97

Swan Lake

Goose Lake

GRIZZLY DEN

VISITOR INFO CENTRE (SEASONAL)

Okanagan Lake

DAVISON
ORCHARDS

OLD KAMLOOPS RD

48TH
AVE

SILVER STAR RD

VERNON AND
VICINITY

BELLA VISTA RD

SEE DETAIL

OKANAGAN LANDING RD

VISITOR INFO CENTRE

DUTCH'S TENT &
TRAILER COURT

BLUE HERON

Kal Beach

KALAMALKA RD

6

PREDATOR RIDGE
GOLF RESORT

KAL LAKE LOOKOUT ★

Kekuli Bay
Provincial Park

Kalamalka Lake
Provincial Park

To Coldstream Valley
and The Kootenays

Ellison
Provincial
Park

97

KALAMALKA
LAKE

MOON

SCALE NOT AVAILABLE

To Kelowna

BEST WESTERN
VERNON LODGE

97

BEAN TO CUP

39TH AVE

SILVER STAR MOTEL

INTERMEZZO

POST OFFICE

MUSEUM

32ND AVE

GREYHOUND BUS DEPOT

KELLY O'BRYAN'S RESTAURANT

ART GALLERY ★

30TH AVE

35TH ST

27TH ST

15TH ST

25TH AVE

POLSON
PARK MOTEL

97

Polson
Park

6

Kal Beach is a wonderful spot to cool off on a summer day.

$5.50, child $4.50), 13 kilometers (eight miles) north of Vernon toward Kamloops on Highway 97, was one of the Okanagan's first cattle ranches. Today you can tour the opulent, fully furnished O'Keefe Mansion and other noteworthy outbuildings, including a furnished old log house that was the O'Keefes' original home; a working blacksmith's shop; the still-in-use St. Ann's Church, where services have been held since 1889; a fully stocked general store where you can buy postcards and old-fashioned candy; and the Chinese cook's bunkhouse. If you worked up an appetite in your explorations, visit the **Homestead Restaurant** (daily for lunch and weekends for dinner).

Davison Orchards

Dozens of farms surround Vernon, but one in particular, Davison Orchards (west of downtown off Bella Vista Rd., 250/549-3266; mid-May–early Nov. daily 8 A.M.–8 P.M.) is worth a visit. Set on a sloping hill with views extending across Kalamalka Lake and up the Coldstream Valley, this family-operated business is a hive of tourist activity throughout the warmer months. A self-guided walk leads through a garden where everything from cucumbers to cantaloupe is grown, a wagon tour traverses the entire 20-hectare (50-acre) property, and there's a Critter Corral, a café with outside dining, an ice cream stand, and, of course, a fruit and vegetable market.

Ellison Provincial Park

Follow Okanagan Landing Road (from 25th Avenue off Highway 97) west to access the northern reaches of Okanagan Lake and this 200-hectare (494-acre) lakefront park, 16 kilometers (10 miles) from downtown. Most of the park is on a bench, with trails leading to and along the rocky shore. Ellison is best known by divers as B.C.'s first freshwater marine park. Enjoy shallow-water snorkeling and diving, weed beds full of life, underwater rock formations, a plastic bubble "Dive Dome," a deep-water wreck, and beach showers. Camping is $17.

Kalamalka Lake

If you've driven up to Vernon from Kelowna, this was the beautiful lake that Highway 97

Okanagan Valley

paralleled for much of the way. It's known as a "marl" lake, because as summer warms the water, the limestone bedrock forms crystals that reflect the sunlight, creating a distinctive aquamarine color that is all the more stunning with surrounding parched hills as a backdrop. The continuously changing emerald and turquoise water and surrounding mountain panorama is best appreciated from **Kal Lake Lookout,** five kilometers (3.1 miles) back toward Kelowna along Highway 97. Just south of the information center, a steep road winds down to the lakeshore and fine **Kal Beach,** fringed by trees. Parking is across the railway line from the beach (access is under the rail bridge). Also on the beach is a concession and, at the east end, a pub with a huge deck.

Continue beyond the beach for eight kilometers (five miles) to **Kalamalka Lake Provincial Park.** Within this 978-hectare (2,420-acre) park, a 1.5-kilometer (.9-mile) trail winds down through bunchgrass and ponderosa pines to Turtle Head Point, while other trails lead to a lowlying wetland and lofty viewpoint.

Golfing

South of Vernon off Highway 97 is 27-hole **Predator Ridge Golf Resort** (250/542-3436 or 888/578-6688), one of Canada's best resort-style courses. Set on a high plateau, this links-style course takes advantage of natural hazards and undulates with the lay of the land. From the back markers, it plays 7,114 yards and to a par of 73 but is rated at 75.4, an indication of its challenging nature. Through the day rates are $105 for 18 holes, while the twilight rate is $58.

Festivals and Events

In early February, Vernon and nearby Silver Star spring to life to celebrate **Vernon Winter Carnival** with parades, sleigh rides, ice sculptures, hot air balloon rides, and the "Over the Hill Downhill" team ski race at Silver Star. Get all the event information and dates at the information center.

Two local attractions host events through the year. The highlights are an **Old Time Fair** at Historic O'Keefe Ranch in mid-July and the **Apple Harvest Hoedown** and **Pumpkin Festival** in mid-September and mid-October, respectively, at Davison Orchards. Local rodeos are held at Falkland on the third weekend of August and in Armstrong on the weekend closest to September 1.

ACCOMMODATIONS AND CAMPING

Downtown and around the outskirts of Vernon is the usual collection of hotels and motels of greatly varying standards. These are handy for a simple overnight stay, but to make the most of your time in the area, book a room at the Grizzly Den or up at Silver Star Mountain Resort.

$50–100

Polson Park Motel (3201 24th Ave., 250/549-2231 or 800/480-2231, www.polsonparkmotel.com; $55 s, $65 d) is the least expensive of Vernon's 20-odd motels. Across from Polson Park, the three-story motel has an outdoor pool and basic rooms. Continuing north along Highway 97 (32nd Street) through the center of Vernon are more roadside-style motels, including **Silver Star Motel** (3700 32nd St., 250/545-0501), which charges from $45 s, $50 d, $65 for a kitchenette.

$100–150

You could stay at one of the downtown, mid-priced choices like the **Best Western Vernon Lodge** (3914 32nd St. 250/545-3385 or 800/663-4422, www.rpbhotels.com; $109 s, $119 d), where stylishly decorated rooms overlook an enclosed three-story tropical atrium. But don't. Instead make reservations at the **Ⅵ Grizzly Den** (7981 Silver Star Rd., 250/549-7181, www.thegrizzlyden.com), a big, beautiful log home nine kilometers (5.6 miles) along the road to Silver Star. The Great Room, a communal lounge area anchored by a stone fireplace, is a natural evening gathering place. The four guest rooms are configured differently, ranging from the Kodiak Room ($100 s or d) to the Turret Suite ($290 s or d), which comes with a handcrafted log bed, big-screen TV, and luxurious bathroom.

Camping

Dutch's Tent and Trailer Court, three kilometers (1.9 miles) south of downtown (Kalamalka Rd., 250/545-1023), is a five-minute walk from Kal Beach and Kalamalka Lake. The park has hot showers, a laundry, and a snack bar. Tent sites are $19, hookups $21–26.

Two provincial parks within a 15-minute drive of downtown provide campsites. Sixteen kilometers (10 miles) southwest of town on Okanagan Landing Road is **Ellison Provincial Park,** on the east shore of Okanagan Lake ($17 per night), while south along Highway 97 toward Kelowna, **Kekuli Bay Provincial Park** slopes down to a boat launch and pebbly beach on Kalamalka Lake, but it's open to the elements ($22).

OTHER PRACTICALITIES

Food

The dining choices in Vernon have improved vastly in recent years, as has the coffee scene. The best coffee joint is **Bean to Cup** (3903 27th St., 250/503-2222; daily 6 A.M.–midnight), in a converted residential house. It offers a wide range of hot drinks and light meals, best enjoyed on the heated patio.

At **Kelly O'Bryan's Restaurant** (2933 30th Ave., 250/549-2112; open daily 11 A.M.–midnight), tuck in to burgers, steak, seafood, salads, and pasta. **Intermezzo** (3206 34th Ave., 250/542-3853) has a casual yet somewhat romantic setting and is a locals' favorite for its wide choice of pastas. Daily specials are the best value—usually around $18 for two courses. For more of a dinnertime splurge try the **Garden Grill** at the Best Western Vernon Lodge (3914 32nd St., 250/545-3385). The dining room is set in a lush tropical garden with a stream flowing through the middle, and the menu features Continental cuisine with nightly specials. Open daily, for lunch from 11 A.M. and dinner from 5 P.M.

The **Blue Heron** (7673 Okanagan Landing Rd., 250/542-5550; daily from 11 A.M.) is a few kilometers west of downtown but well worth the drive. It sits right on Okanagan Lake, and a large deck right on the water is the most popular of the pub's three dining areas. The menu is fairly standard, with lots of dishes to share, but as it's off the tourist path, prices are reasonable.

Services and Information

The **Greyhound** bus depot is on the corner of 30th Street and 31st Avenue (250/545-0527). For local bus information and schedules, contact **Vernon Regional Transit System** (250/545-7221).

The **post office** is on the corner of 31st Street and 32nd Avenue. **Vernon Visitor Info Centre** (250/542-3256 or 800/665-0795, www.vernontourism.com; daily 8:30 A.M.–6 P.M., till 6:30 P.M. in summer) is in a spruced-up heritage house on Highway 97 at the south end of town, If you're driving in from the north, make a stop at the seasonal info center (6326 Hwy. 97 N).

◪ SILVER STAR MOUNTAIN RESORT

For summer or winter recreation, head up to Silver Star Mountain Resort (250/542-0224 or 800/663-4431, www.silverstarmtn.com), a colorful gold-rush-era-style, fully self-contained resort town 22 kilometers (13.6 miles) northeast of Vernon (take 48th Avenue off Highway 97). The views of Vernon as you climb the mountain are worth the fairly long, steep drive, and the resort at the top offers great skiing and snowboarding, plus summer recreation to suit all ages.

Summer Activities

Silver Star offers the biggest range of summer recreation of any alpine resort in the interior. Starting at the end of June, a chairlift runs from the village to the top of Silver Star Mountain (1,915 meters/6,280 feet) for terrific views of Vernon and surrounding lakes. Much of the alpine area around the summit is protected by 8,714-hectare (21,500-acre) **Silver Star Provincial Park;** pick up a hiking guide in the village. The summer lift operates June–September daily 10 A.M.–4 P.M.; $12 for one ride, or buy an all-day pass for $29 (the day pass includes access to hiking and biking trails). To learn more about the mountain's natural history, take the naturalist-led three-hour wildflower tour Thursday–Sunday at 1 P.M.; $25 per person, which includes a chair-lift ride. Mountain-bike rentals are $14 for one hour, $25 for two hours, and $36 for a full day.

Skiing and Snowboarding

November–April, skiers and boarders mob Silver Star, coming for great terrain and the facilities of an outstanding on-hill village. The two main faces—Vance Creek, good for beginners, and Putnam Creek, for intermediates and experts—are served by five chairlifts and a couple of T-bars. The resort's 80 runs cover 1,135 hectares (2,800 acres) with a vertical rise of 760 meters (2,490 feet). Lift tickets are adult $52, senior $38, child $28; those over 70 and under six ski free. For snow reports call 250/542-1745. Through winter a shuttle bus operates between Kelowna Airport and the mountain; book through central reservations (800/663-4431).

Silver Star Cross-country Centre features 35 kilometers (22 miles) of groomed and set tracks, while beyond these are 50 kilometers (31 miles) of backcountry trails. A day pass is $15 per person; rentals are available for an additional $18.

Accommodations

The base village contains numerous types of accommodations; book year-round through central reservations (800/663-4431, www.silver-starmtn.com) or contact each accommodation directly. The rates quoted are for summer, which is low season. Through winter, expect to pay double (except at the Samesun property).

Least expensive is **Samesun Silver Star** (250/861-3001 or 888/562-2783, www.samesun.com), one of Canada's only ski-in, ski-out backpacker lodges. Facilities include a modern communal kitchen, plenty of table space for dining, and 140 beds in dorms and private rooms. Dorm beds are $24.50, private rooms $63.

The **Kickwillie Inn** (250/542-4548 or 800/551-7466, www.pinnacles.com) is part of the adjacent and much larger Pinnacles Suite Hotel but has the better value rooms; from $119 s or d with a kitchen. The **Lord Aberdeen Hotel** (250/542-1992 or 800/553-5885, www.lordaberdeen.com) also offers self-contained suites and is similarly priced. The most luxurious on-mountain lodging is **Silver Star Club Resort** (250/549-5191 or 800/610-0805, www.silverstarclubresort.com), which offers standard hotel rooms and self-contained suites spread through three buildings. Guests enjoy use of all facilities at the nearby National Altitude Training Centre. Summer rates start at $105 s or d, rising to $145 for a suite.

The Kootenays

The wild and rugged Kootenays region of British Columbia lies east of the Okanagan Valley and south of the TransCanada Highway. It is bordered by the United States to the south and Alberta to the east. Three north-to-south-trending mountain ranges—the **Monashees, Selkirks,** and **Purcells**—run parallel to each other across the region, separated by lush green valleys and narrow lakes up to 150 kilometers (93 miles) long. The snowcapped mountains and forested valleys abound with wildlife, including large populations of deer, elk, moose, black bears, and grizzly bears.

Europeans first entered the Kootenays in the late 1800s, searching for precious metals such as gold, silver, lead, and zinc, all of which were found in large quantities. While many of the boomtowns from this era have slipped into oblivion, others live on: Sandon is a ghost town, Fort Steele survives as a heritage theme park, and the grand old city of Nelson is today a heritage masterpiece, its streets lined with restored buildings.

Recreational opportunities abound throughout the Kootenays in all seasons. In summer, anglers flock to the lakes and rivers for trout, kokanee, and bass. Other visitors enjoy canoeing, swimming, or sunbathing on the beaches, or take to the mountains for hiking and wildlife viewing. Much of the region's higher elevations are protected in rugged and remote parks, including the spectacular **Valhalla, Kokanee Glacier, Top of the World,** and **Purcell Wilderness Conservancy Provincial Parks.** While these natural preserves offer plenty of opportunities for

© ANDREW HEMPSTEAD

Must-Sees

Look for **M** to find the sights and activities you can't miss and **M** for the best dining and lodging.

M Red Mountain: Rossland is a beautiful town to visit at any time of year, but in wintertime, the steep slopes of nearby Red Mountain draw experienced skiers and boarders from across the land (page 293).

M Sandon: In the late 1800s, Sandon was home to over 5,000 miners. Today, you could fit the entire population in the back of a pickup truck—not that they'd want to leave western Canada's most authentic ghost town (page 297).

M Kokanee Glacier Provincial Park: This remote park takes some effort to reach, but the rewards are many, including alpine lakes, ancient glaciers, and abundant wildlife (page 305).

M Crawford Bay: Even if the crafty shops don't appeal to you, the price of visiting will—the village is accessed by the world's longest free ferry ride (page 307).

M Creston Valley Wildlife Management Area: Protecting vital resting grounds along the Pacific

© ANDREW HEMPSTEAD

The streets of downtown Rossland are lined with restored buildings from the gold rush era.

Flyway, this site provides a haven for more than 250 species of birds, including osprey, the rare Forester's tern, and a nesting colony of western grebe. (page 308).

M Fort Steele Heritage Town: The gold rush era comes to life through costumed interpreters and musical theater. You can even try your hand at panning for gold (page 316).

The Kootenays

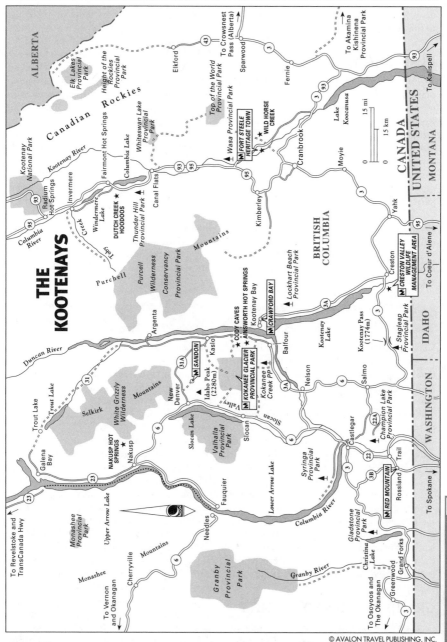

© AVALON TRAVEL PUBLISHING, INC.

day-trippers, it takes extended backcountry trips to fully experience their beauty.

PLANNING YOUR TIME

The most important thing to remember when planning a driving tour through the Kootenays is that the region is very mountainous. Roads are generally narrow and winding, with mountain passes and ferry crossings slowing down travel time considerably. The main east–west thoroughfare is Highway 3, which runs through the southern extent of the region, traversing no less than five mountain passes between Osoyoos in the west and Cranbrook in the east. Even without detours north, allow a couple of days to travel this route from one end to the other. Besides official "attractions" like **Creston Valley Wildlife Management Area,** you might be tempted to linger at the many roadside parks and mountain look-

outs. Two main roads lead north from Highway 3, both eventually making their way north to the TransCanada Highway (Central British Columbia). Highway 6 is the westernmost of the two, passing the historic town of **Nelson** and the ghost town of **Sandon.** In the East Kootenays, Highway 3 continues its eastward course to southern Alberta while Highway 93/95 jogs north through the Columbia Valley, where historic parks such as **Fort Steele Heritage Town** and natural highlights like Fairmont Hot Springs are the main attractions.

In colder months the mountains of the Kootenays catch a phenomenal amount of snow, turning the whole region into a winter wonderland. You won't find any major resorts here; however, three small but legendary ski areas—**Red Mountain, Whitewater,** and **Fernie**—attract adventurous powderhounds with some of North America's highest snowfalls and steepest lift-served slopes.

West Kootenays

Clustered on the edge of the Monashee Range in the western Kootenays are several communities that seem a world away from the hustle and the bustle of the nearby Okanagan Valley. Grand Forks, Rossland, Trail, and Castlegar all boomed at the turn of the 20th century, when thousands of gold-hungry prospectors descended on the slopes of Red Mountain. Today Red Mountain draws more powderhounds than prospectors, and lakes, rivers, parks, and peaks are the area's main attractions.

In addition to mining history, the West Kootenays are also known as the home of the Doukhobors, a religious sect of Russian immigrants who arrived in the early 1900s to till the land and practice their faith in peace. Aspects of their unique culture and lifestyle can be seen today in Grand Forks and elsewhere in the region.

GRAND FORKS AND VICINITY

Perched at the confluence of the Granby and Kettle Rivers, Grand Forks (pop. 4,200) started

out as a Hudson's Bay Company trading post and later became a mining town, home to the largest nonferrous smelter in the British Empire. At the turn of the 20th century, the rough-and-ready town was full of miners, ranchers, and land speculators. But then a very different group arrived in the valley.

The Doukhobors, a religious sect practicing pacifism and vegetarianism, fled persecution in their Russian homeland and set up communes in British Columbia in the early 1900s. They kept a low profile—farming, making everything they needed, and operating many successful communal enterprises. The sect added a contrasting element to the area's social mix until Doukhobor leader Peter Verigin died in 1924. After his death, the sect's way of life deteriorated, and the communes dispersed. Today many Doukhobor descendants live in Grand Forks. Although they no longer live in communal villages, they still follow their beliefs and speak Russian, which is taught in local schools. To find out more about the intriguing Doukhobor lifestyle, visit **Moun-**

tain View Doukhobor Museum (Hardy Mountain Rd., 250/442-8855), a 1912 Doukhobor communal farmhouse, or Doukhobor Heritage Centre (6110 Reservoir Rd., 250/442-3523), with similar displays.

Grand Forks also features a mix of historic early-20th-century homes and restored civic buildings. Downtown's Boundary Museum (7370 5th St., 250/442-3737; June–Oct. daily 10:30 A.M.– 4:30 P.M.) displays mining artifacts, historic photos, and pioneer memorabilia.

Grand Forks is the gateway to remote Granby Provincial Park. This 40,845-hectare park protects the upper reaches of the Granby River along with an old-growth forest of red cedar. The park is well off the beaten path, and access is recommended only in a four-wheel-drive vehicle. To get there, head north out of Grand Forks; take the left fork 40 kilometers (25 miles) from town, then another left fork at the 59-kilometer (37-mile) mark and again at the 60-kilometer (37-mile) mark. The road ends at the park boundary, five kilometers (3.1 miles) farther north. Get more information from the Forest Service office in Grand Forks (250/442-5411).

Practicalities

In a pleasant setting on the west edge of town, Pinegrove Motel (209 Central Ave., 250/442-8203; May–Oct.) offers rooms from $80 s, $90 d (with a huge discount for travelers aged 50 or older). Campers gravitate to the riverside municipal campground (mid-May–mid-Oct.; $12–18) at the end of 5th Street. Showers and hookups are offered.

At first glance, Omega II Restaurant (7400 Hwy. 3, 250/442-3124; daily 8 A.M.–9 P.M.), on the east side of town, looks no different from any other small-town restaurant, but on closer inspection you'll see the roots of Grand Forks show themselves with Russian dishes such as borscht and *galooptsi* (meat-filled cabbage rolls). Try a little of everything by ordering a platter of Russian specialties for $18 per person.

Adjacent to the museum on 5th Street is Grand Forks Visitor Info Centre (7362 5th St., 250/442-2833, www.grandforkschamber.com; Mon.–Fri. 9:30 A.M.–4:30 P.M.).

Christina Lake

This 19-kilometer-long (12-mile-long) lake, 25 kilometers (16 miles) east of Grand Forks along Highway 3, is a summer favorite for folks from throughout the West Kootenays, who come for the lake's warm waters and fishing for rainbow trout, bass, and kokanee. On the western edge of town is Christina Lake Golf Club, a pleasant 18-hole layout; greens fees are $45, or play after 4 P.M. for $32.

The town of Christina Lake is spread around the southern end of the lake, where the best beach is protected from development by a small day-use area. The best-value motel is the New Horizon Motel (250/447-9312 or 888/859-0159, www.newhorizonmotel.com), along the highway at the eastern edge of town. Rooms are spacious and comfortable, and although the summer rate is $76 s, $86 d, at any other time of the year rooms are under $60.

The best of many commercial campgrounds at Christina Lake is Cascade Cove RV Park (1290 River Rd., 250/447-6662; Apr.–Oct.), which offers tent sites for $18 and serviced sites for $21–24. To the north, you sacrifice amenities like hookups and showers for much quieter forested setting at Texas Creek Campground, which is within Gladstone Provincial Park. Sites are $14 and no reservations are taken.

Along Highway 3 is a good grocery store, gas, a seasonal information center, and a bunch of eateries. At Moon Beans (Johnson Rd., 250/447-9591; daily 8 A.M.–4:30 P.M.), you can sip coffee while checking your email on the public computers—or forget about the outside world and blend in with vacationers by ordering lunch to stay.

ROSSLAND

Clinging to the slopes of an extinct volcanic crater deep in the tree-covered Monashee Mountains, Rossland (pop. 4,000) was once a gold-rush boomtown known as "The Golden City." The precious yellow metal was discovered on 1,580-meter (5,180-foot) Red Mountain by Joe Moris in 1890. Moris, like thousands of other prospectors unaware of the nearby wealth, had

OLAUS JELDNESS

In the late 1890s, after the first frantic summer of gold mining on Red Mountain, a group of prospectors put on a winter carnival, including a ski race down the slopes of Red Mountain. The organizer was Olaus Jeldness, a legendary Norwegian who had prospected all over the western United States before moving north of the border. Jeldness admitted that the mountain was "far too steep and the snow conditions too extreme" for a proper race. But it went ahead nevertheless. First the competitors hiked all the way to the summit. Then Jeldness gave the signal to go before strapping on his own skis and schussing off after the rest of the field. Despite their head start, Jeldness easily passed the other racers to become Canada's first national champion. His wooden skis and trophies are housed in the Western Canada Ski Hall of Fame in the Rossland Museum.

Jeldness was the first of many heroes to have skied the legendary slopes of "Red"—the mountain has been a breeding ground for more members of the Canadian National Ski Team than any other resort, not bad considering the adjacent town has just 4,000 residents.

been traveling eastward on the Dewdney Trail to goldfields farther away. He nevertheless staked five claims on Red Mountain, the richest of which, Le Roi, later sold for $3 million. When word got out, thousands of diggers rushed in, and the township of Rossland was born. The town's population peaked at 7,000 in 1897. At that time, the city boasted four newspapers, 40 saloons, and daily rail service south to Spokane. By 1929, the mountain had yielded six million tons of ore worth $165 million. Today, tourism supplies the bulk of Rossland's gold; the town serves as a mecca for mountain-bike enthusiasts and adventurous skiers and boarders.

Sights

Downtown Rossland is a picturesque place full of historic buildings and old-fashioned street lamps. Pick up a *How to find your way around the twisting, hilly, scenic, tree-lined, and sometimes confusing (because it's situated on the side of a mountain—which is really what makes this place so great) streets and trails of Rossland* pamphlet from the museum, library, or downtown shops, and hit the streets.

On the west side of downtown is the **Rossland Museum** (Hwy. 3B and Columbia Ave., 250/362-7722, summer daily 9 A.M.–5 P.M., adult $5, senior $4, child $2). At the entrance of the Le Roi mine, the museum catalogs the

area's lustrous geological and human history. The museum also holds the Western Canada Ski Hall of Fame, which honors such luminaries as Olaus Jeldness—instigator of the local ski craze—and champion skier Nancy Greene, a local heroine who won a gold medal in the 1968 Olympics.

To experience the day-to-day life of the early hardrock miners, tour **Le Roi Gold Mine,** next to the museum complex. Outside the mine sits a gigantic compressor, a simulated mine shaft, and large pieces of mining machinery. The gold mine itself, just up the path, provides an introductory course in local geology with its displays of mineral veins, dikes, faults, and old and new mining equipment. The 45-minute tour includes detailed explanations of how ore is mined, trammed, drilled, and blasted, and tells you how to differentiate igneous, metamorphic, and sedimentary rocks. Museum admission is included in the tour cost of adult $10, senior $7, child $4.

Mountain Biking

Each spring, Rossland comes alive with pedal power as mountain-bike enthusiasts take advantage of the maze of old logging and mining trails surrounding the city. Now known as the "Mountain Bike Capital of Canada," Rossland has hosted both the Canadian and North American championships. Rent bikes from

The Powderhound (2040 Columbia Ave., 250/362-5311).

![M] Red Mountain

The site of what was once one of the world's richest gold mines is now part of an alpine resort offering some of North America's most challenging lift-served runs. Facilities on the mountain have certainly improved since the days of Olaus Jeldness, but Red Mountain (250/362-7384 or 800/663-0105, www.redresort.com) is no megaresort. Nevertheless, the skiing and boarding are still world-class. While two mountains provide opportunities for all ability levels, the resort holds most appeal for experts—and as any local will tell you, the advertised 640 hectares (1,580 acres) of terrain doesn't do justice to the opportunities for skiing in the backcountry. The heart-stopping face of Red Mountain is the star of the show. But adjacent Granite Mountain offers a vertical rise of 880 meters (2,890 feet) and almost unlimited intermediate, expert, and extreme skiing and boarding, mostly on unmarked trails through powder-filled glades. Beginners are catered to with a magic carpet while shredders will gravitate to the terrain park. Lift tickets are adult $48, senior $30, child under 12 $25, and those six and under ski for free.

A groomed cross-country ski trail leads five kilometers (3.1 miles) into town, and a short snowshoe loop creates a diversion from the slopes above. Across the road from the resort, **Blackjack** Nordic area offers 40 kilometers (25 miles) of groomed tracks. Cross-country skiers can also explore the many old logging roads in the area.

Accommodations

The ![M] **Ram's Head Inn** (250/362-9577 or 877/267-4323, www.ramshead.bc.ca), one of Canada's premier small lodges, lies in the woods at the base of Red Mountain. Primarily designed for wintertime, the inn offers 14 ultra-comfy guest rooms that ooze mountain magnetism. Factor in a congenial dining room (only breakfast in summer), a game room, sauna, outdoor hot tub, and a spacious communal lounge with luxurious chairs and a large fireplace, and you have the perfect place to spend a couple of nights. Summer rates are very reasonable at $70 s or d for a queen room and $92 for a king. The bed-and-gourmet breakfast option is $88 s or d and $110 respectively. Winter packages average around $100–120 per person per night, including lift tickets.

Also up at the resort is the **Red Shutter Inn** (250/362-5131, www.redshutter.ca), a cozy little bed-and-breakfast with shared bathrooms, a lounge area, and hot tub; summer rates are $55 s, $65 d. Rates double in winter.

Food

Each morning, locals converge on the **Sunshine Café** (2116 Columbia Ave., 250/362-5099; Mon.–Sat. 7 A.M.–7 P.M.) for hearty cooked breakfasts from $6. The rest of the day, the café offers a diverse menu including Mexican and Indian dishes. **Goldrush Books and Espresso** (2063 Washington St., 250/362-5333; Mon.–Sat. 7 A.M.–3:30 P.M., Sun. 7 A.M.–1 P.M.) sets a few tables around bookshelves full of local and Canadian literature.

For more substantial fare, head up the hill to **Idgie's** (1999 2nd Ave., 250/362-0078; daily 5–9:30 P.M.), a small restaurant with a surprisingly global menu that features dishes like blackened red snapper and Thai chicken curry in the $15–20 range. In the same building is **Misty Mountain Pizza** (1999 2nd Ave., 250/362-5266; daily 4:30–10 P.M.), with good take-out pizza under $18.

On the road up to Red Mountain, **Rock Cut Neighbourhood Pub** (250/362-5814; daily from 11 A.M.) is busiest in winter but opens year-round. It offers typical pub fare, smartly presented and well priced. Enjoy the mountain surroundings by eating on the heated deck.

Information

Rossland Visitor Info Centre (250/362-7722 or 888/448-7444, www.rossland.com; summer daily 9 A.M.–5 P.M.) is in the museum complex south of downtown at the corner of Highway 3B and Columbia Avenue.

TRAIL AND VICINITY

Sprawling along both sides of the mighty Columbia River, Trail (pop. 8,000) lies 10 kilometers (6.2 miles) and 600 vertical meters (2,000 feet) below Rossland. It's probable that neither your first nor your subsequent impression of Trail will be positive. The world's largest lead and zinc smelter dominates the downtown area, its 120-meter smokestacks belching thick plumes of smoke into the atmosphere 24 hours a day. The smelter is the foundation of Consolidated Mining and Smelting Co. (Cominco), one of the world's largest mining companies, and poor Trail is often described as "Cominco with a town built around it." Head to the **Cominco Interpretive Centre** (1199 Bay Ave.) to learn about the smelting process. Free tours of the **Cominco complex** show you the area where ores are melted and separated and tell you about the byproducts, such as fertilizers, converted from the waste. The tours depart from the interpretive center, but to book a tour call the information center (250/368-3144).

Trail Visitor Info Centre (1199 Bay Ave., 250/368-3144 or 877/636-9569) is open 9 A.M.–5 P.M. daily in summer, weekdays only the rest of the year.

Champion Lakes Provincial Park

Escape the smokestacks in this 1,426-hectare (3,520-acre) park, 23 kilometers (14.3 miles) east along Highway 3B toward Nelson, then a few kilometers farther along the access road. The park encompasses a chain of three small lakes nestled in the Bonnington Range. Hiking trails connect the lakes; First Lake, accessed from a trail at road's end, is the least busy. Camping is $17.

Salmo Toward Creston

East of Trail on Highway 3, the small village of Salmo (pop. 1,100) features old-fashioned wooden buildings, a small museum (open in summer daily 1–5 P.M.), and streets decorated in summer with huge hanging flower baskets bursting with brilliant color. The promise of quick fortune brought prospectors to gold diggings in the Salmo River watershed through the 1860s, but as in so many other boomtowns in the Kootenays, the riches were short-lived. Those who stayed in the area turned to logging cedar and pine from the surrounding Selkirk Mountains as a source of income.

About 35 kilometers (21.7 miles) east of Salmo, at 1,133-hectare (2,800-acre) **Stagleap Provincial Park,** travelers can pause to picnic by Bridal Lake or go for a short hike.

Continuing east from there, you'll crest 1,774-meter (5,820-foot) **Kootenay Pass,** where a beautiful alpine lake makes a pleasant stop. The parking lots at either end of the lake are linked by a short trail that showcases stunted trees of this high alpine environment. From the pass, Highway 3 descends to Creston (see *Kootenay Lake and Creston*).

CASTLEGAR

Though endowed with the rich history of the Doukhobors, Castlegar (pop. 7,400) is not a particularly attractive place. Spread out along the barren Columbia River Valley, it's a real crossroads town. Here the Kootenay River drains into the much larger Columbia River, Highway 3 passes through east to west, Highway 3A leads north to Nelson, and Highway 22 leads south to Rossland and Trail. The town is also the major air gateway for the Kootenays.

The area's first nonnative residents, the Doukhobors, arrived in 1908. These pacifist Russian immigrants planted orchards, built sawmills, and even operated a jam factory while living in segregated villages along the valley floor. Many of their descendants still live in the area. Today, mining, transportation, and hydroelectric-power production sustain the local economy.

Doukhobor Sights

Castlegar's major attraction is the **Doukhobor Village Museum** (east side of the river along Hwy. 3A, 250/365-6622; daily 9 A.M.–6 P.M.; adult $5, child $2.50). The village allows a glimpse of the traditional lifestyle of these intriguing Russian immigrants. Admission includes

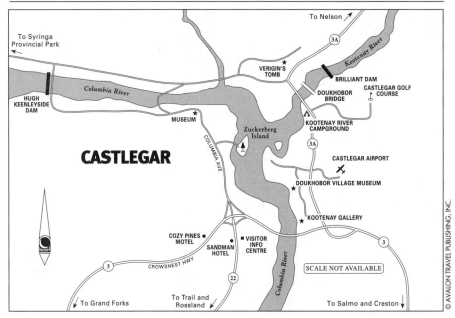

a guided tour, led by Doukhobor descendants, through the main building and the simply furnished brick dwellings and outbuildings. Along the way you'll see some of the sect's artifacts, including hand-woven clothing, crocheted bedspreads and shawls, a barn full of antique farming implements, and carved wooden spoons and ladles. Also featured is a historic photo collection of the original Doukhobor settlements in Saskatchewan and British Columbia.

Zuckerberg Island, at the confluence of the Kootenay and Columbia Rivers, was the home of Russian immigrant Alexander Zuckerberg, who came to Castlegar to teach Doukhobor children in 1931. Connected to the mainland by a 150-meter suspension bridge, the tree-covered two-hectare (five-acre) island is interesting to explore. A one-kilometer (.6-mile) trail passes a full-scale model of a *ckukuli* (native winter pit house), as well as a Hiroshima memorial, Russian orthodox chapel house, cemetery, log house, and many other Zuckerberg creations. To get there, turn off Highway 22 at 9th Street, turn left on 7th Avenue, then immediately turn right.

While you're in a Russian frame of mind, visit the old **Doukhobor Bridge,** which crosses the Kootenay River along Highway 3A. It was built by the Doukhobors in the 1910s as a link from their community to Nelson; none of them had any bridge-building experience, but the 100-meter-long, hand-poured concrete suspension bridge was used until 1968, and the remains can still be seen today. On the north side of the river just west of the bridge lies **Verigin's Tomb,** the final resting place of Peter Verigin, the spiritual leader who led the Doukhobors to the Kootenays. To get there from the north side of the Kootenay River, head west toward Robson and take Terrace Road to the right. The tomb sits on a high bluff, surrounded by manicured gardens.

Other Sights

Along the same road as the Doukhobor Village Museum is West Kootenay National Exhibition Centre, housing the **Kootenay Gallery** (250/365-3337; year-round Mon.–Fri. 10:30 A.M.–4:30 P.M. as well as summer weekends noon–4:30 P.M.; donation). The gallery displays a good variety of artworks, often including elaborate exhibits from larger national galleries.

North of town off Highway 3A, the enormous **Hugh Keenleyside Dam** spans the Columbia River to form Lower Arrow Lake. The structure features a lock system that allows boats to pass from one side of the dam to the other, despite the differing water levels.

Practicalities

The comfortable and reasonably priced **Cozy Pines Motel** (2100 Crestview Cres., 250/365-5613, $55 s, $60 d) offers spotless rooms with kitchenettes. Immediately south of the Highway 3 and Highway 22 intersection is the **Sandman Hotel** (1944 Columbia Ave., 250/365-8444 or 800/726-3626, www.sandman.ca; $110 s, $120 d), with an indoor pool and a 24-hour restaurant. Campers looking for hookups should head to **Kootenay River Kampground** (651 Rosedale Rd., 250/365-5604; $16–22), beside the river north of the airport. The setting at **Syringa Provincial Park** ($17), on the banks of Lower Arrow Lake north out of town toward Nelson, then west off Highway 3A, is much nicer, but facilities are limited.

Services and Information

Castlegar Airport, along Highway 3A, is the Kootenays' air transportation hub. It's served by **Air Canada** (888/247-2262) with direct flights from Vancouver. **Budget** has a rental desk out at the airport (250/365-5733).

Castlegar Visitor Info Centre (off Columbia Ave. at 1995 6th Ave., 250/365-6313) is open in summer daily 8 A.M.–7 P.M., the rest of the year Monday–Friday 9 A.M.–5 P.M.

THE SLOCAN VALLEY

The historically rich Slocan Valley, or "Silvery Slocan," nestles snugly between the Slocan and Valhalla Ranges of the Selkirk Mountains. In the 1890s the valley sprang into the limelight when silver was discovered at Sandon. It's much quieter today, offering many picturesque towns and an abundance of outdoor-recreation opportunities.

New Denver

Western gateway to "Silver Country," this picturesque town of 600 is on Slocan Lake, opposite Valhalla Provincial Park. Originally called Eldo-

Heritage buildings line the streets of New Denver.

© ANDREW HEMPSTEAD

The Kootenays

rado and renamed after Denver, Colorado, the town reached its mining peak in the 1890s.

Today the main street is lined with funky false-front stores and pioneer-style buildings left over from the prosperous silver days. Visit the **Silvery Slocan Museum** (6th Ave. and Bellevue Dr., 250/358-2201, July–early Sept.) to find out all about New Denver's heyday.

Down on the lake within easy walking distance of the main street, **Sweet Dreams Guesthouse** (702 Eldorado St., 250/358-2415, www.newdenverbc.com) offers five large guest rooms and a cooked breakfast for $60 s, $80–95 d. Out of New Denver to the south, **N Silverton Resort** (250/358-7157, www.silvertonresort.com; $110–260 s or d) takes advantage of its watery location with self-contained cottages that are as close to the water as any I've seen in British Columbia. Campers can head to a **municipal campground** (May–Sept.; $15–18), on the south side of the town and with full hookups, or **Rosebery Provincial Park,** on Wilson Creek six kilometers (3.7 miles) north of town ($14).

New Denver Visitor Info Centre (202 6th Ave., 250/358-2719, www.slocanlake.com; July–early Sept. daily 9 A.M.–5 P.M.) is a friendly little place with lots of ideas that will tempt you to linger longer in the area.

Valhalla Provincial Park

This 49,893-hectare (123,290-acre) park preserves the high peaks, deep valleys, and magnificent alpine lakes between the Valhalla Range of the Selkirk Mountains on the west and the west shores of Slocan Lake on the east. The most imposing peaks are in the south of the park, where spectacular spires rise above alpine meadows to a height of 2,800 meters (9,190 feet).

Roads come to an abrupt end at the north and south ends of the park, so the most popular access is by boat from New Denver or Slocan, across the lake. An eight-kilometer (five-mile) lakeshore trail also connects Slocan with the west shore. There, hiking trails lead into the heart of the park. The most rewarding and popular is the **Beatrice Lake Trail,** 12.5 kilometers (7.8 miles) each way. As with all trails starting from the lake, elevation gain is steady; you'll climb just under

VALHALLA WILDERNESS SOCIETY

O riginally founded in the 1970s to lobby for the establishment of Valhalla Provincial Park, the Valhalla Wilderness Society was instrumental in convincing the B.C. government to designate the Khutzeymateen Valley, north of Prince Rupert, as Canada's first grizzly bear sanctuary. Closer to home, the organization also successfully campaigned for the creation of the White Grizzly Wilderness. Its latest crusade is for the protection for the habitat of the Kermode bear in the north of the province and more generalized wilderness protection, such as saving the world's boreal forests.

The society is still headquartered in New Denver. The office (307 6th St., under the Valhalla Trading Post sign) holds a small retail outlet selling books, posters, calendars, and shirts. For more information contact the Valhalla Wilderness Society directly (250/358-2333, www.vws.org).

1,000 vertical meters (3,280 feet) as you pass Little Cahill and Cahill Lakes and enter the massive cirque in which Beatrice Lake lies. From the backcountry campground at the lake, a vast wilderness is yours to explore. Another trail, one of the park's steepest, begins across Slocan Lake from New Denver and climbs **Sharp Creek.** Elevation gain is a scary 1,400 meters (4,600 feet), most of it made in the final push to a point overlooking **New Denver Glacier.**

The best source of trail and transportation information is **Valhalla Wilderness Society** (307 6th Ave., New Denver, 250/358-2333), a group of local environmentalists who were instrumental in the establishment of the park. At the society's office you can pick up a copy of the detailed *Trail Guide to Valhalla Provincial Park.*

N Sandon

The original Slocan Valley boomtown, Sandon once was a thriving town of 5,000 people. After the discovery of silver on the slopes of Idaho Peak, Sandon grew quickly and at one time boasted 24 hotels, 23 saloons, banks, general stores, mining brokers' offices, and a newspaper. Its main link to the outside world was the Kaslo & Slocan Railway, built in 1895 to connect Sandon with sternwheeler transportation on Kootenay Lake.

Sandon was destroyed by fire in 1902 but quickly rebuilt and incorporated as a city in 1908. The Great Depression of 1929 put an end to the heyday, but the town remained the "soul of the Silvery Slocan" until the spring of 1955. That year the creek running through town flooded, sweeping away most of the city and leaving a ghost town. Today you can count the population on two hands.

The best place to start a visit to Sandon is the 1900 city hall, where the *Sandon Walking Tour Guide* is sold ($1). The brochure details all the original structures—only a fraction of which remain—with a map that makes exploring on foot more enjoyable. Up the creek from city hall is **Sandon Museum,** where exhibits bring the old town back to life, and **Silversmith Mine Powerhouse,** which still supplies power to the few remaining residents and retains its title as western Canada's oldest operating hydroelectric plant. Also on this side of the creek is the road to 2,280-meter (7,480-foot) **Idaho Peak.** The road is very rough, passable only in July and August. From the end of the 12-kilometer (7.5-mile) road, a steep one-kilometer (.6-mile) trail leads to the summit and spectacular 360-degree views of the Kootenays.

Along the north side of Carpenter Creek, buildings in various states of disrepair line a road leading to the mining area of Cody. On the same side of the creek, the **K&S Historic Trail** follows the route taken by the old wood-burning engines of the Kaslo & Slocan Railway as they carried rich silver ore from Sandon to Kaslo. The railway was destroyed by fire in 1910. The hiking trail, 5.6 kilometers (3.5 miles) each way, passes several mining sites and provides fabulous views of the **New Denver Glacier,** across Slocan Lake in Valhalla Provincial Park.

The only services in Sandon are a souvenir shop in the old city hall and the **Tin Cup Cafe,** which was built as a private home in 1895 and is now open for coffee and light snacks. It's on the north side of Carpenter Creek at the far end of town.

NAKUSP

Forty-eight kilometers (30 miles) northwest of New Denver, Nakusp (pop. 1,800) was established during the mining-boom years. Today the small town is best known for its hot springs and its stunning location on Upper Arrow Lake at the foot of the Selkirk Mountains.

Nakusp Museum (6th Ave.; July–Aug. daily 9 A.M.–5 P.M.; $1) features an odd but intriguing collection of items, including pre-dam photos of the towns now flooded beneath the Arrow Lakes.

Nakusp Hot Springs

To get to these hot springs (250/265-4528; summer daily 9:30 A.M.–10 P.M., the rest of the year daily 10 A.M.–9:30 P.M.; adult $9.25, senior and child $8.25), take Highway 23 north out of town for one kilometer (.6 mile), then follow the signposted road along Kuskanax Creek for 12 kilometers (7.5 miles).

To see the source of the springs, take the sandy 500-meter (.3-mile) trail that starts behind the pools. You'll cross the river and clamber through damp rainforest crammed with ferns and mosses, then come to an impressive waterfall where you can smell the sulfur from the springs.

Practicalities

A nearby resort, with its own private hot springs, is **Halcyon Hot Springs** (32 km/20 miles north of Nakusp, 250/265-3554 or 888/689-4699, www.halcyon-hotsprings.com). Accommodations are in cabins, cottages (my favorite), chalets, or a luxury family-oriented Lodge Suite, with rates ranging $76–248 s or d. Tent camping is $18, hookups $26.50, and tepees $58. **Nakusp Village Campground** (8th St., 250/265-4019; May–Oct.), within walking distance of the beach and the main street, has large shaded sites, coin-operated showers, and firewood; unserviced sites $16, powered sites $19.

The place to be seen in Nakusp is the **Broadway Deli Bistro** (408 Broadway St. W, 250/265-

3767; daily from 7 A.M.), where you'll find great coffee and a constant stream of muffins coming out of the oven.

Nakusp Visitor Info Centre (92 6th Ave., 250/265-4234 or 800/909-8819; summer daily 8 A.M.–4 P.M., the rest of the year weekdays only).

Cherryville and Vicinity

From Needles, Highway 6 ascends steeply to the high peaks of the Monashee Mountains and the village of Cherryville. Along the main street, the **Monashee Woolen Mill** (250/547-6040; Mon.–Fri. 8:30 A.M.–3 P.M.) opened in 1998 as a mill complex using antique machinery and old-time techniques. Materials come from locally raised sheep, as well as alpacas and musk oxen. The owners give tours, and you can try your hand at spinning. A small on-site store sells everything from raw materials to a variety of finished products. Cherryville is also the jumping-off point for remote 7,513-hectare (18,560-acre) **Monashee Provincial Park.** Access is north along 46-kilometer (28.6 miles) Sugar Lake Road then on foot along a rough 12-kilometer (7.5-mile) trail.

From Cherryville, Highway 6 descends to the **Coldstream Valley,** where you'll see field crops, orchards, and low, rolling hills; paddocks where horses frolic in fluorescent-green grass; rustic old barns in various degrees of disrepair; and well-loved old homes. At **Lumby** a road leads 37 kilometers (23 miles) northeast to **Mabel Lake Provincial Park,** with a tree-shaded picnic area and camping for $14 per night. You're now a short drive from Vernon (see the *Okanagan Valley* chapter).

Nelson

The elegant city of Nelson (pop. 9,700) lies in a picturesque setting on the West Arm of Kootenay Lake, 660 kilometers (410 miles) east of Vancouver. Its relaxed pace, hilly tree-lined streets, and late-19th-century architectural treasures have helped attract a mix of jaded big-city types, artists, and counterculture seekers. For visitors there is much to see and do around town, many good places to eat, and an eclectic atmosphere unlike anywhere else in the province. But while the city itself is uniquely charming, the surrounding wilderness of the Selkirk Mountains is Nelson's biggest draw. The area's many lakes provide excellent fishing, sailing, and canoeing, as well as some of British Columbia's best inland beaches. Trails suitable for hikers of all fitness levels lace Kokanee Glacier Provincial Park's alpine reaches. Old logging and mining trails attract happy hordes of mountain-bikers. And nearby hot springs provide a welcome relief at the end of a hard day's play. In addition, when the snow starts flying, powderhounds flock to Whitewater Winter Resort for some of North America's best lift-served powder skiing and boarding.

History

After the discovery of copper and silver deposits on Toad Mountain in 1886, Nelson sprang up as a small mining camp along the banks of Ward Creek. The early mines proved profitable, and the town expanded rapidly. Construction of a smelter began at the end of 1895, and wagon roads, railroads, and steamboat routes were developed to serve the local mining boom. Soon Nelson became the commercial and cultural center of the Kootenays, at its peak boasting 23 hotels and six saloons. Although mining operations waned by the turn of the century, silver had left a grand impact on Nelson. It was the first city in the province to operate an electric power plant (on Cottonwood Creek) and the smallest city in the country to have a streetcar system.

SIGHTS

Architecture

Nelson has 350 designated heritage buildings, more per capita than any other city in British Columbia, save Victoria. Most can be viewed by walking around the downtown core between Baker and Vernon Streets. Pick up the detailed

Heritage Walking Tour or *Heritage Motoring Tour* brochures from the information center. The walking-tour brochure details 26 downtown buildings, including the 1909 courthouse on Ward Street and the impressive stone-and-brick 1902 city hall on the corner of Ward and Vernon Streets.

Museums

Nelson's two museums are both worth visiting. **Nelson Museum** (402 Anderson St., 250/352-9813; in summer Mon.–Sat. 1–6 P.M., the rest of the year Mon.–Sat. 1–4 P.M.) concentrates on local history, with displays covering native peoples, explorers, miners, traders, early transportation, Nelson's contribution to World War I, and the Doukhobors (a Russian religious sect that

settled in the Kootenays). It also contains the *Ladybird,* a record-breaking speedboat designed prior to the advent of hydroplanes in the 1950s.

To absorb some of Nelson's mining history, visit the **Chamber of Mines Museum** (Hall St., 250/352-5242; Mon.–Fri. 10 A.M.–4 P.M.; donation), which smells exactly like you imagine a mining museum would. The walls are lined with mineral samples, mining artifacts, and historic photos, while in the center big tables are covered in claim maps and related literature.

Nelson Artwalk

Organized by the local arts council, Nelson's annual Artwalk highlights the work of up to 100 local artists. Throughout summer, works are dis-

© ANDREW HEMPSTEAD

Nelson's historic buildings today hold many cafés and restaurants.

played city-wide at various venues such as restaurants, hotels, the theater building, art galleries, and even the local pool hall. On the last Friday of every month, receptions are held at each of the venues. The receptions feature live entertainment, refreshments, and the artists themselves, on hand to discuss their work. A brochure available at the information center and motels and galleries around town contains biographies of each featured artist, tells where his or her work is displayed, and provides a map showing you the easiest way to get from one venue to the next. Drop by the information center or call 250/352-2402 for details.

PARKS AND RECREATION
City Parks

For a good view of the city and lake, head to **Gyro Park,** beyond the east end of Vernon Street. **Lakeside Park,** another pleasant green spot, is by Nelson Bridge and has a sandy beach, tennis courts, and a picnic area. **Cottonwood Falls** tumble from below a highway overpass off

Baker Street, but the surrounding area has been nicely landscaped and is well worth a visit, especially when spring run-off creates a massive flow of water.

Hiking and Biking

The best nearby hiking is in **Kokanee Glacier Provincial Park** (see *Kootenay Lake and Creston*), but the bed of the Burlington Northern Railway, built in 1893, provides an interesting nine-kilometer (5.5-mile) trek right on Nelson's back doorstep. Access the railway from the top end of South Cherry Street. The many old logging and mining roads surrounding the city are great for mountain biking; one favorite is the **Svoboda Bike Trail,** accessed along Elwyn Street beyond the college. For bike rentals and a trail map, head to **Gerick Cycle and Sports** (702 Baker St., 250/354-4622).

Fishing

Kootenay Lake holds kokanee, Dolly Varden, and rainbow trout, and the lake's feeder streams also provide good fishing opportunities. Contact

The Kootenays

the information center for registered fishing guides.

Those content to view fish rather than catch them can watch spawning kokanee at the mouth of **Kokanee Creek,** 20 kilometers (12 miles) northeast of town on Highway 3A, and at **Red-fish Creek,** five kilometers (3.1 miles) farther northeast, where an interpretive center offers displays describing the kokanee's life cycle. Kokanee are landlocked salmon. Instead of migrating in from the ocean like their anadromous cousins, kokanee spend their lives in the larger lakes of British Columbia's interior, spawning each summer in the rivers and streams draining into the lakes.

Skiing and Boarding

Legendary powder and an off-the-beaten-path location make **Whitewater Winter Resort** (250/354-4944 or 800/666-9420, www.ski-whitewater.com) a hidden gem. The small resort 20 kilometers (12 miles) south of Nelson sits beneath a string of 2,400-meter (7,900-foot) peaks that catch an amazing amount of snow. Three double chairlifts access 18 marked trails (the Summit Chair opens up the best powder-packed slopes). The area's abundant snowfall makes for a long season, but conditions are best in February and March. Whitewater has no on-mountain accommodations—just the lifts and a day lodge with a cafeteria, rental shop, and ski/snowboard school. Lift tickets are adult $45, senior and youth $34.

Up near the Whitewater base village is an 18-kilometer (11-mile) network of groomed cross-country ski trails through the Hummingbird Valley, or head to **Apex-Busk Cross-country Ski Area,** off Highway 6, 12 kilometers (7.5 miles) south of Nelson.

Entertainment

The **Heritage Inn** (422 Vernon St., 250/352-5331) is the center of Nelson's after-dark scene. This old hotel contains **Mike's Place,** a bar that comes alive with a disco Wednesday–Saturday from 10 P.M., as well as the elegant **Library,** with tapestried chairs by a fireplace, books to read, and an elaborate draped ceiling—the per-

fect place to head to for a quiet drink. Down on the water, the bar in the **Prestige Lakeside Resort** (701 Lakeside Dr., 250/352-7222) has an expansive deck that catches the afternoon sun. Another popular drinking hole is **Bogustown Neighbourhood Pub,** toward the Nelson Bridge (712 Nelson Ave., 250/354-1313), with a fireplace and outdoor patio. (The pub's intriguing name was coined by miners who were attracted to the city for its supposed wealth but were never paid).

ACCOMMODATIONS AND CAMPING

Under $50

Right downtown, the **M Dancing Bear Inn** (171 Baker St., 250/352-7573 or 877/352-7573, www.dancingbearinn.com) offers clean and comfortable accommodations at a very reasonable price. It features a cozy lounge area with a TV, reading material, information on local attractions and restaurants, and a cupboard full of board games. Other facilities include Internet access, a kitchen, a laundry, and lockers. The dorm-style rooms are spacious, with a maximum of six beds in each. A few doubles and a single room are also available. Members of Hostelling International pay $17 per night, nonmembers $20; private rooms are $40–46 d.

$50–100

The 1898 **Heritage Inn** (422 Vernon St., 250/352-5331, www.heritageinn.org) is a city landmark. It provides attractive, recently refurbished rooms, some with lake views, for $69–89 s, $79–99 d, including breakfast in the downstairs restaurant. The more expensive rooms are larger and generally have better views.

The following choices are out of the city to the north. **Villa Motel** (250/352-5515 or 888/352-5515, www.thevillamotel.com) and **North Shore Inn** (250/352-6606 or 800/593-6636, www.nshoreinn.com) are directly across Nelson Bridge from downtown. Both offer regular motel rooms of a respectable standard for $70 s, $80 d.

$100–150

The pick of Nelson's many guesthouses is the **M Kiwi Vine Guest House** (215 Houston St., 250/352-2297, www.kiwivine.com), named for fruit-filled vines running along the back fence. Accommodation is in two suites, one with two bedrooms and the other with three. Each is decorated with inspiring color schemes and comes with a full kitchen, lounge with TV/DVD combo, and outdoor space that comes together at a great little playground that young children won't want to leave. The nightly per suite rate is great value at $125 s or d, or stay a full week for $750.

The construction of the **Prestige Lakeside Resort** (701 Lakeside Dr., 250/352-7222, www.prestigeinn.com) is the first stage in the redevelopment of Nelson's waterfront. This resort features a spa facility, fitness center, swimming pool, private marina, restaurants, and lakeside rooms from $149 s or d and theme suites from $209.

Camping

Right downtown, **City Tourist Park** (corner High St. and Willow St., 250/352-9031; tents $15, hookups $21) isn't particularly impressive. It's surrounded by houses, its sites are closely spaced, and the washrooms could be cleaner. Reaching the campground is a little tricky, so take a careful look at the town map before trying to find it (from downtown, take the first left after the civic center along Vernon Street, then the right fork). A much better choice is lakeside **Kokanee Creek Provincial Park** (20 km/12.5 miles northeast of Nelson on Hwy. 3A, 250/825-4421). Although the large park offers more than 100 sites, it's often full; the beautiful location makes this one of the Kootenays' most popular campgrounds. Unserviced sites are $22. If the park is full, continue eight kilometers (five miles) farther northeast to Balfour, where you'll find two commercial campgrounds.

FOOD AND DRINK

Nelson's reputation as a center of good eating has come ahead in leaps and bounds during recent years, but a few old Chinese places hang on along Baker Street and remain open later than all the other restaurants listed.

The best place for breakfast is the **Heritage Inn** (422 Vernon St., 250/352-5331, daily 7:30 A.M.–8:30 P.M.). Cooked breakfasts are huge, especially the omelets (from $6.50), which come piled high with delicious hash browns.

Cafés

The counterculture of Nelson is evident at the **M Kootenay Co-op** (295 Baker St., 250/354-4077), where you can pick up goat's milk ice cream, organic apple juice, hemp toaster waffles, west coast salmon caught by Nisga'a natives, eco-sweet chocolate, and preservative-free bread. If you're looking for lunch on the run, pick up healthy snacks, such as sweet curry rolls and vegan carrot cake, from the deli counter.

Over the last few years, the **Vienna Cafe** (411 Kootenay St., 250/354-4646; Mon.–Fri. 9 A.M.–5:30 P.M., Sat. 9 A.M.–5 P.M.), in Packrat Annie's bookstore, has lost its counterculture vibe, but the food has gotten better. You can't go wrong with a chicken burger—free range of course—loaded with feta cheese and green pepper ($8). A generous serving of vegetarian five-bean chili will set you back $5, or order a bowl of butternut squash soup livened up by a dash of maple syrup for $6. Excellent!

Up from the main street, push past the spoiled city kids posing as hippies and duck in to **Oso Negro** (522 Victoria St., 250/352-7661; Mon.–Sat. 7 A.M.–6 P.M., Sun. 9 A.M.–4 P.M.) for rich coffee roasted in-house. The bagels and other baked goods are also recommended.

Restaurants

Outer Clove (536 Stanley St., 250/354-1667; Mon.–Sat. 11:30 A.M.–9 P.M.) is typical of Nelson's better restaurants, appealing to modern tastes but in a relaxed, low-key environment. The emphasis is on garlic (it's even an ingredient in a couple of the desserts), with tapas from $5 (you'd need three for a filling meal) and dinners $12–20. All lunch items are under $10.

The best pizza in town comes straight from the wood-fired oven at **Max & Irma's Kitchen** (515 Kootenay St., 250/352-2332; daily 11 A.M.–9 P.M.).

M The Kootenays

Order your favorite off the standard menu ($12–14) or pay $7 for a base and build your own from a large assortment of mouthwatering toppings.

Tucked into a back alley behind the main street is **M All Seasons Café** (620 Herridge Lane, 250/352-0101), a small yet stylish place with a delightful tree-shaded patio. Dishes such as proscuitto-wrapped beef tenderloin with a side of maple-roasted yams will have you raving, while desserts like chai crème brûlée will have you wishing you had more room. As a bonus, All Seasons has a small but well-thought-out selection of wines by the glass from $5.

OTHER PRACTICALITIES

Information

All the information you'll need on Nelson and the Kootenays is available at **Nelson Visitor Info Centre** (225 Hall St., 250/352-3433, www.discovernelson.com, summer daily 8:30 A.M.–6 P.M., the rest of the year Mon.–Fri. 8:30 A.M.–4:30 P.M.).

Otter Books (398 Baker St., 250/352-3434; Mon.–Sat. 9:30 A.M.–5:30 P.M., Sun. 11 A.M.–4 P.M.) has an excellent selection of books about the Kootenays ranging from ghost town guides to the history of the Kettle River Railway. **Packrat**

Annie's (411 Kootenay St., 250/354-4722) sells used books, tapes, and CDs, and offers good people-watching opportunities.

Services

Kootenay Hospital is east of downtown (3 View St., 250/352-3111). The **post office** is at 514 Vernon Street. Check your email at **Net Idea** (625 Front St., 250/352-3512; Mon.–Fri. 9 A.M.–5:30 P.M., Sat. 10 A.M.–4 P.M.).

Transportation

Although a prime chunk of lakeside real estate, right in town, is taken up by a small airstrip, no scheduled flights serve Nelson. The closest commercial airport is at Castlegar, 45 kilometers (28 miles) away. **Nelson Mountain Air** (250/354-1456) is a local flightseeing operation based at Nelson City Wharf; a flight to and around Kokanee Glacier costs $125 per person.

Long-distance bus transportation is provided by **Greyhound.** The depot is at the Chahko-Mika Mall (1112 Lakeside Dr., 250/352-3939). From Vancouver, buses come into Nelson via Castlegar, then continue east to Cranbrook via Salmo.

Local car-rental agencies include **Rent-a-wreck** (250/352-5122) and **Thrifty** (250/352-2811). For details of local bus transportation, call the **Nelson Transit System** (250/352-8201).

Kootenay Lake and Creston

Heading first north, then east from Nelson, Highway 3A follows a narrow arm of Kootenay Lake before coming to the main, 100-kilometer-long (62-mile-long) body of water at Balfour. From there, you have a choice of routes. You can cross Kootenay Lake by ferry and follow the east shore of the lake down to Creston, or you can continue north up the west shore of the lake, passing through Ainsworth Hot Springs and Kaslo before arcing back west to Slocan Valley and Arrow Lake.

Kokanee Creek Provincial Park

This 257-hectare (630-acre) park 20 kilometers (12.4 miles) northeast of Nelson features a great

beach and one of the Kootenays' most popular campgrounds. Short trails crisscross the park, and kokanee (freshwater salmon) can be viewed in Kokanee Creek at the end of summer (access is from the visitor center). Instead of migrating in from the ocean like their anadromous cousins, kokanee spend their lives in the larger lakes of British Columbia's interior, spawning each summer in the rivers and streams draining into the lakes. The super-popular day-use area runs the length of a one-kilometer (.6-mile) sandy beach. The large campground's sites have showers, but no hookups, and they fill fast through summer; $22 per night. A visitor center (250/825-4421, mid-June–mid-Sept. daily 9 A.M.–9 P.M.) holds displays on local ecosystems, trail reports for Kokanee Glacier Provincial Park, and other useful information.

⛰ Kokanee Glacier Provincial Park

Straddling the highest peaks of the Selkirk Mountains, this 32,035-hectare (79,160-acre) mountain wilderness park can be seen from downtown Nelson. The steep and narrow gravel roads into the park are often impassable until late June, and the hiking trails remain snow-covered even later; check road and trail conditions at the visitor center in the park before setting off. But don't let these things discourage you from visiting. This is one of B.C.'s premier provincial parks, filled with magnificent scenery and abundant wildlife and providing some unrivaled opportunities for backcountry travel.

The park is named for a massive glacier that, along with two other glaciers and 30 lakes, feeds dozens of creeks and rivers flowing west to Slocan Lake and east to Kootenay Lake. Almost entirely above 1,800 meters (5,900 feet), the park's environment is very different from the valley floor—dominated by barren peaks and, for a few short weeks in the middle of summer, meadows of lush subalpine wildflowers.

The heart of the park is too steep and rugged to be penetrated by roads, so all the best features must be reached on foot. The main access is via an unsealed road that spurs off Highway 3A 20 kilometers (12.4 miles) from Nelson and follows Kokanee Creek 16 kilometers (10 miles) to **Gibson Lake.** A 2.5-kilometer (1.6-mile) trail circles the lake, but the best hiking is farther afield. From Gibson Lake, it's four kilometers (2.5 miles) uphill to beautiful **Kokanee Lake.** There the trail flattens out, continuing three kilometers to Kaslo Lake and a further two kilometers (1.2 miles) to a backcountry campground ($5 per person) and **Slocan Chief Cabin,** a century-old structure that sleeps 12 ($15 per person). Total elevation gain along this trail is 600 meters (1,970 feet), but most of this is gained in the moderately steep ascent to Kokanee Lake. From the cabin, those experienced in alpine travel have many opportunities for exploring surrounding peaks and Kokanee Glacier.

The park can also be accessed from a rough, 24-kilometer (15-mile) unsealed road that begins six kilometers (3.7 miles) west of Kaslo and ends at the **Joker Millsite** trailhead. From here a steep five-kilometer (3.1-mile) trail leads to Slocan Chief Cabin and a trail of similar length (with an elevation gain of 450 meters/1,480 feet) goes to a backcountry campground at **Joker Lakes,** two beautiful bodies of water in a glacial cirque surrounded by towering peaks.

Because of the park's remote location, it's vital to pick up information on road and hiking-trail conditions (in years of high snowfall, some hiking trails are impassable until late July) at the **visitor center** in Kootenay Creek Provincial Park (250/825-4421; summer 9 A.M.–9 P.M.). The center can provide you with detailed directions to other park access points and give you up-to-the-minute information on which trails, if any, are closed due to bear activity.

Balfour

The picturesque village of Balfour lies at the junction of the north, south, and west arms of Kootenay Lake. Here you can easily while away the better part of a day, enjoying beautiful lake views from a waterfront café or watching the local community of partially tame Canada geese honking for handouts down on the beach.

Back in the 1890s, sternwheelers plied the lake, dropping off prospectors and supplies at isolated mining camps and settlements along its shores. But completion of the railway in the early 1900s quickly put most of the sternwheelers out of action. Today one public ferry remains, and it's "North America's longest free ferry ride." The 45-minute trip across Kootenay Lake from Balfour to Kootenay Bay offers majestic lake and mountain scenery and makes a good route to Creston and points east (see *Across Kootenay Lake to Creston*).

AINSWORTH HOT SPRINGS

Overlooking Kootenay Lake from a hillside 17 kilometers north of Balfour, these springs were discovered in the early 1800s by local natives who found that the hot, odorless water (high in mag-

The Kootenays

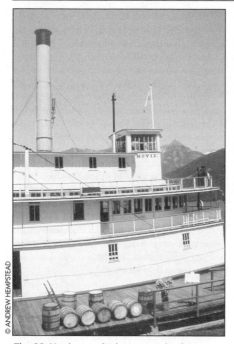

© ANDREW HEMPSTEAD

The SS *Moyie* was the last sternwheeler on Kootenay Lake.

discovered by prospector Henry Cody in the 1890s. Made up of several large chambers totaling 800 meters (2,600 feet) in length, the caves also hold an underground creek that drops over Cody Falls. Experienced spelunkers can explore the caves unguided, but others will want to join a tour with **Hiad Venture Corp.** (250/353-7364). Based at the caves' entrance, this company offer tours July through August daily from 10 A.M. The one-hour option is adult $15, child $10, but the three-hour tour (adult $50, child $40) is more adventurous and passes formations you won't see on the shorter trip. To get to the caves, turn off Highway 31 just north of Ainsworth Hot Springs, follow a narrow 15-kilometer (9.3-mile) gravel road to a trailhead, then hike 20 minutes.

KASLO AND VICINITY

Tree-lined streets graced by elegant late-19th-century architecture, lake and mountain views from almost every street, and the world's oldest passenger sternwheeler tied up at the wharf make Kaslo (pop. 1,100), 70 kilometers (44 miles) north of Nelson, a worthwhile stop.

Another of the Kootenays' great boomtowns, Kaslo began as a sawmill community in 1889. But nearby silver strikes in 1893 quickly turned the town into a bustling city of 3,000 and an important commercial hub; a railway brought silver down from Sandon to Kaslo, where it was loaded onto steamers and shipped out to Creston and the outside world. The town's 1898 city hall is one of only two wooden buildings in the country that are still the seats of local government.

Sights

Dry-docked by the lakefront stands the 50-meter-long **SS *Moyie*** (summer daily 9:30 A.M.–5 P.M.; adult $5, senior $4, child $3), the last Canadian Pacific Railway sternwheeler to splash up Kootenay Lake. Built in 1897 and launched the following year at Nelson, the grand old red-and-white vessel was used for transportation of passengers, freight, and mail right up until its retirement in 1957. Today the ship serves as a

nesium sulfate, calcium sulfate, and sodium carbonate) helped heal their wounds and ease their aches and pains. Today the springs have been commercialized and include a main outdoor pool, a hot tub, steam bath, and cold plunge pool. Rates are $7 for a single entry or $11 per day (discounts for seniors and children). The pools are open year-round, with summer hours 10 A.M.–9:30 P.M. (from 8:30 A.M. for resort guests).

If you want a bit more pampering, stay at **Ainsworth Hot Springs Resort** (250/229-4212 or 800/668-1171, www.hotnaturally.com), which features exercise and massage rooms, a lounge, and a licensed restaurant overlooking the main pool and beautiful Kootenay Lake. Room rates are $118 s or d, but you'll pay $128–158 for a lake view. Rates start at $100 in the off-season.

Cody Caves Provincial Park

High above the hot springs, this cave system was

museum containing a fine collection of photos, antiques, and artifacts of the region.

Practicalities

Right downtown, the **Kaslo Motel** (330 D Ave., 250/353-2431 or 877/353-2431, www.kaslomotel.com; $45–52 s or d) has clean and convenient but basic rooms, some with small kitchens. North of town, the **Lakewood Inn** (Kohle Rd., 250/353-2395, www.lakewoodinn.com) has been taking in guests since the 1920s. Lakefront cabins are $80–100, while campers pay from $17.50.

Kaslo Visitor Info Centre (324 Front St., 250/353-2525) is open mid-May to mid-October daily 9 A.M.–8 P.M.

North from Kaslo

Highway 31 leads north from Kaslo to **Galena Bay,** 50 kilometers (31 miles) south of Revelstoke. The road parallels Kootenay Lake before turning to gravel and climbing into the Selkirks. A turnoff to the east, 32 kilometers (20 miles) north of Kaslo, loops around the north end of Kootenay Lake to **Argenta.** Founded by two Quaker families from Argenta, California, in the early 1950s, this quaint hamlet has no tourist facilities but is worth the short detour from Highway 31.

The highlight of the road north from the Argenta turnoff is **Trout Lake,** a narrow body of water surrounded by 2,000-meter-high (6,560-foot-high) peaks. The lake's outlet, at its extreme southern end, is a spawning area for rainbow trout; you'll also find a small provincial park and camping. From this point the road gets pretty rough, climbing high above the lake and winding around steep gullies. At the north end of the lake is the remote community of Trout Lake, the center of a short-lived gold rush.

White Grizzly Wilderness

Straddling the Selkirk Mountains north of Highway 31A, this area protects 137,000 hectares (338,530 acres) of mountainous terrain that is prime territory for grizzly bears. Within the boundary of this wilderness zone, further protection to native habitat is provided by **Goat Range Provincial Park,** accessible along an old

logging road north from New Denver. The best way to visit the area is on a guided hike with the Valhalla Society in New Denver (307 6th Ave., 250/358-7789). The full-day trip begins with a one-hour slide show teaching species identification and safe travel in bear country. Then it's out into the field to visit an uninhabited black bear den and hike along the Whitewater Glacier Trail, from which grizzlies can often be seen at a safe distance across the valley. Tour cost is adult $50, children $25. For further information on the area, including a topographical map showing trails ($4), head to the Valhalla Society headquarters in New Denver.

ACROSS KOOTENAY LAKE TO CRESTON

From Balfour, the world's longest free ferry ride takes you across Kootenay Lake to **Kootenay Bay.** Launched in 2000, the *Osprey* offers lots of outside spots at which to sit and soak up the surrounding mountain panorama.

◪ Crawford Bay

From the ferry dock, Highway 3A traverses a low ridge before dropping into Crawford Bay, a small community sandwiched between the Purcell Mountains and the water. Artisan outlets have put this village of 200 on the map. On the left as you descend the hill is **North Woven Broom** (250/227-9245), western Canada's only traditional broom manufacturer. The raw materials (from California and Mexico) are handcrafted into brooms using 19th-century methods. Stop in anytime and you're likely to find craftspeople hard at work and eager to share their knowledge of this lost art. The workshop is crammed with brooms of all shapes and sizes, ranging in price $30–65. A little farther along is **Kootenay Forge** (250/227-9466; daily 9 A.M.–5 P.M.), a traditional blacksmith shop where you can watch artisans practicing this ancient trade.

Also at Crawford Bay is **Kokanee Springs Golf Resort** (250/227-9226 or 800/979-7999; late Apr.–early Oct.), one of the province's most picturesque courses. Featuring water views, forested fairways, huge greens, large elevation drops, and colorful flower beds around the tee boxes, it is not only a beautiful place to golf, it's also very challenging. Greens fees are a reasonable $67 (twilight rates from $39 on weekends).

The pick of local accommodations is **N Wedgwood Manor** (250/227-9233 or 800/862-0022, www.wedgewoodcountryinn .com; Apr.–mid-Oct.). Set on 20 beautiful hectares (50 acres) adjacent to the golf course and within walking distance of a beach, this 1910 home offers six heritage-style rooms, each with a private bathroom. Guests can relax in the library or in the extensive gardens. Rates are $85–140 s or d. Right on the golf course is **Kokanee Springs Lodge** (250/227-9226 or 800/979-7999, www.kokaneesprings.com). The 56 rooms and eight suites are decorated in a stylish deep blue color, offset by the natural colors of wooden trim and furniture. High-season rates start at $140–165 s or d, but most guests stay as part of a golfing package (from $130 per person per night).

South along Kootenay Lake

From Crawford Bay, it's 80 kilometers (50 miles) of lake-hugging road to Creston. Along the way you'll pass small clusters of houses and a number of resorts. **Mountain Shores Marina & Resort** (13 km/eight miles from Crawford Bay, 250/223-8258) is a lakefront resort with a pool and marina. Campsites are crowded, but the location is superb. Tent sites are $18, hookups $20–24. Continuing south, **Lockhart Beach Provincial Park** has a small campground with sites for $14 per night.

CRESTON

In a wide, fertile valley at the extreme southern end of Kootenay Lake lies Creston, a thriving agricultural center of 4,800. Although the town is south of the Kootenays' most spectacular mountains, the scenery is still impressive; the Selkirk Mountains flank the valley to the west, while the Purcell Mountains do the same to the east. No mineral riches have been found around Creston, but the lure of gold and silver farther

afield drew hopefuls through the valley, turning it into a prime transportation link across British Columbia's remote southern interior. As the town grew, agriculture became the mainstay of the local economy. Fruit stands lining Highway 3 on the east side of Creston from the west are a sign of the district's most obvious industry. Stop for locally grown asparagus (May–early June), strawberries (July), cherries (mid-July to mid-Aug.), peaches (late July–Sept.), and apples (Aug.–Oct.).

N Creston Valley Wildlife Management Area

This 7,000-hectare (17,300-acre) wildlife reserve lies 10 kilometers (6.2 miles) west of Creston (250/428-3259; May–Aug. daily 9 A.M.–5 P.M., Apr. and Oct. Wed.–Sun. 9 A.M.–4 P.M.). It extends from Kootenay Lake to the Canada–U.S. border. Protecting vital resting grounds along the Pacific Flyway, the site provides a haven for more than 250 species of birds, including a large population of osprey, a flock of the rare Forester's tern, and a nesting colony of western grebe. Start a visit at the park's wildlife center, where displays focus on the abundant birdlife, as well as on mammals and reptiles present in the reserve. From the center, hiking trails lead along dikes separating wetlands and ponds. Admission is $3, and you can take a guided canoe trip for just $7 per person. Even along the boardwalk leading into the center you may spy some local residents—turtles that sun themselves on half-submerged logs. Special events through the year coincide with various natural cycles, such as the spring **Osprey Festival.**

Other Sights

Creston & District Museum (219 Devon St., 403/428-9262; summer daily 10 A.M.–3:30 P.M.), on the west side of town and south across the railway tracks, is home to a Kutenai canoe, unlike any other in North America but similar to the style used by the Gilyaki people in Russia, leading ethnologists to speculate about the possible links. West of the museum is **Kootenay Candles** (1511 Northwest Blvd., 250/428-9785), where candles are handcrafted and sold at a factory retail outlet.

Creston is home to the **Columbia Brewery** (1220 Erickson St., 250/428-9344), producer of British Columbia's popular Kokanee beer. Tours are offered in summer Monday–Friday at 9:30 A.M., 11:30 A.M., 1 P.M., and 2:30 P.M. At the brewery entrance is Kokanee Beer Gear, a retail shop open weekdays 9 A.M.–4 P.M.

Lodging and Food

The best lodging options are north of town (see *South along Kootenay Lake*), but you could stay right downtown at the aptly named **Downtowner Motor Inn** (1218 Canyon St., 250/428-2238 or 800/665-9904; $50 s, $56 d), which sports an easily recognized blue-and-white exterior. **Scottie's RV Park** (1409 Erickson Rd.,

250/428-4256 or 800/982-4256) enjoys a pleasant treed setting across the road from the Columbia Brewery. Tent sites are $18, hookups $20–24.

The busiest place in town each morning is **Creston Valley Bakery** (113 10th Ave., 250/428-2661), where you'll find plenty of tables and a large selection of freshly baked cakes and pastries.

Information

Creston Visitor Info Centre is in a small log building at the top end of the main street (1711 Canyon St., 250/428-4342, summer daily 9 A.M.–6 P.M., the rest of the year weekdays 9 A.M.–5 P.M.).

East Kootenays

In the southeastern corner of the province, the East Kootenays encompass the Purcell Mountains and the upper reaches of the Columbia River, with the Rocky Mountains rising abruptly from the Columbia Valley to the Continental Divide and the British Columbia–Alberta border to the west. The crossroads of the region is the service center of **Cranbrook,** from where Highway 3 heads west to **Fernie** and the neighboring province of Alberta, and Highway 93/95 parallels the Columbia River northward through a region dotted with golf courses, hot springs, and many provincial parks.

EAST FROM CRESTON

From Creston, the Crowsnest Highway (Highway 3) crosses the **Purcell Mountains** and descends to Cranbrook, the region's largest town. The distance between the two towns is a little over 100 kilometers (62 miles).

Yahk

Yahk grew into a thriving lumber town in the 1920s but was abandoned by the 1930s. Today empty houses and a still-operating hotel are all that remains along the main street, but the pioneer **museum** keeps history alive with its dis-

plays of household artifacts and costumes from the past. Tiny **Yahk Provincial Park** lies beside the rushing Moyie River east of town. Fishing in the river is good for rainbow trout and Dolly Varden; camping is $14 per night (this campground has only 26 sites, so arrive in early afternoon to be assured of a spot).

South of Yahk is the **Kingsgate port of entry,** open daily 24 hours.

Moyie

North from Yahk, Highway 3/95 parallels the Moyie River to its source at **Moyie Lake,** a deep-blue body of water backed by cliffs. Halfway along the lake, Moyie, once boasting a population of 1,500, today holds nothing more than a few historic buildings, a pub, and a gas station; the 1904 church on Tavistock Street and the 1907 fire hall beside the highway are among the original survivors. Miners working the nearby St. Eugene Mine for lead and silver were the first settlers. The old mine is visible back up the hill by wandering down to the lakeshore.

Around 13 kilometers (eight miles) north of town is 91-hectare (220-acre) **Moyie Lake Provincial Park,** which has a sandy swimming beach, short interpretive trails, and the chance to view kokanee spawning on gravel river beds. The

The Kootenays

large campground has semiprivate sites, hot showers, and a weekend interpretive program; $22 per site.

CRANBROOK

Crossroads of the eastern Kootenays, Cranbrook (pop. 19,000) nestles at the base of the Purcell Mountains 106 kilometers east of Creston and provides spectacular views eastward to the Canadian Rockies. The city itself has few tourist attractions, but with all the surrounding wilderness and nearby Fort Steele Heritage Town, it's a good base for further exploration. Cranbrook also claims to be British Columbia's sunniest town, with 2,224 hours of sunshine annually.

History

Originally this area was a campsite for Kootenay natives; the first European landowners were the Galbraiths, who ran the ferry across the Kootenay River at Fort Steele. In the 1880s the family sold its holdings to Colonel James Baker, who met with little success in his initial attempts to establish a townsite here. But Baker's fortunes turned around quickly when the Canadian Pacific Railway ran its line right through the struggling settlement. The town rapidly grew, and in 1905 the city of Cranbrook was incorporated. Today

this service and transportation center is the region's major city and has an economy based on forestry, mining, ranching, and the new College of the Rockies.

Canadian Museum of Rail Travel

Cranbrook's main attraction, this museum is on a siding of the main CPR line directly opposite downtown (Van Horne St., 250/489-3918; Apr.–mid-Oct. daily 10 A.M.–6 P.M., mid-Oct.–Mar. Tues.–Sat. noon–5 P.M.). Most of the displays are outdoors, spread along three sets of track, including the only surviving set of railcars from the Trans-Canada Limited, a luxury train (also called "The Millionaires' Train") built for the Canadian Pacific Railway in 1929. The dining, sleeping, and solarium lounge cars sport inlaid mahogany and walnut paneling, plush upholstery, and brass fixtures. Restoration displays, a viewing corridor, a model railway display, a slide show, guided tours of the car interiors, and tea and scones in the Argyle Dining Car are included in the price of the two-hour Deluxe Tour (adult $12, senior $10, child $6.50). You can choose abbreviated tours (from adult $5.25, senior $4.50, child $2.25), but you'll miss the best of the museum. Even if you don't take the full tour, you can wander through the railway garden to enjoy a light snack in the dining car (11:30 A.M.–2 P.M.)

SAM STEELE

In uniform by age 16, Sam Steele was part of the famous march west by the North West Mounted Police in 1874. In 1887, Steele led 75 Mounties across the mountains to the Kootenays, establishing a post where miners had been crossing the Kootenay River on their way to the Wild Horse Creek goldfields. Steele and his men settled land-ownership disputes between local natives and new ranchers, easing friction and maintaining order. As more mineral discoveries were made through the region, Fort Steele, as the post had become known, grew into a bustling town. But when the railway bypassed the town in 1898, Fort Steele's population plummeted. Steele meanwhile had moved on, bringing law and order to the Klondike goldfields and leading a regiment that fought the Boers in South Africa. After a lifetime of serving his country, Steele passed away in 1919, aged 70.

Today, the memory of the man lives on at **Fort Steele Heritage Town** and during Cranbrook's **Sam Steele Days** (250/426-4161, www.samsteeledays.com), which take place over the third weekend in June. Expect a huge parade, the Sweetheart Pageant, loggers' sports, bicycle and wheelchair races, a truck rodeo, sporting events, live theater, and whatever else the Sam Steele Society comes up with each year.

To Airport and Kimberley

To St Eugene's
Mission Church

To Fort Steele, Fernie,
and Radium Hot
Springs

OLD AIRPORT RD

95A

3
95

CRANBROOK

VISITOR INFO
CENTRE

22ND ST N

THEATRE RD

CRANBROOK ST

GREYHOUND BUS DEPOT

MOON

SCALE NOT AVAILABLE

6TH ST NW

LAZY BEAR
LODGE

"THE STRIP"

KOOTENAY ST

6TH ST N

VICTORIA AVE

4TH ST N

VAN HORNE ST

2ND ST N

CANADIAN MUSEUM
OF RAIL TRAVEL

ROTARY
CLOCK TOWER

HOSPITAL

24TH AVE

BAKER ST MIDORAK

LIBRARY

VILLAGE BAKER

SWING STREET
COFFEEHOUSE

LOTUS BOOKS

1ST ST S

POST OFFICE

MT BAKER
RV PARK

2ND ST S

9TH AVE S

3RD ST S

3RD AVE S

14TH AVE S

VICTORIA AVE

HERITAGE
ESTATE MOTEL

11TH ST S

To Jimsmith
Lake PP

3
95

JIMSMITH LAKE RD

VISITOR INFO CENTRE
(SEASONAL)

Elizabeth Lake
Bird Sanctuary

To Creston and
Vancouver

The Kootenays

and to see, but not use, the railway's silver, china, and glassware collection.

Heritage Walking Tour

The locals are proud of their downtown heritage buildings, which you can view on a self-guided walking tour by picking up the handy *Cranbrook Heritage Tour* brochure from either information center or the railway museum (stop number one on the tour). Start at the Rotary Clock Tower in Cranbrook Square—the tower is an exact replica of the old post office tower that stood across Baker Street at the corner of 10th Avenue. The original tower was demolished in 1971, much to the dismay of Cranbrook preservationists, but the clock from the old tower was incorporated into the replica. You can still see the home of Colonel Baker—the original Cranbrook developer for whom downtown's main street is named—in Baker Park off 1st Street South (Mon.–Fri. 9 A.M.–5 P.M.). Many other heritage homes are found between 10th and 13th Avenues and 1st and 4th Streets South.

If you're still in a heritage mood and heading for Kimberley, take Old Airport Road (a continuation of Theatre Road) north to **St. Eu-** gene's Mission Church, between Cranbrook and Kimberley. Built in 1897, this is the finest Gothic-style mission church in the province; it features beautiful, hand-painted Italian stained-glass windows.

Elizabeth Lake Bird Sanctuary

Beside the highway at the southern city limits (park at the information center), this large area of wetlands is a haven for many species of waterfowl, including Canada geese and teal, ringneck, scaup, redhead, bufflehead, goldeneye, and ruddy ducks. You can also see coots, grebes, black terns, and songbirds. Mammals present include muskrats, white-tailed deer, and occasionally moose.

Accommodations and Camping

Most motels are along Highway 3 through town. The highway is known as Van Horne Street south of 4th Street North and Cranbrook Street to the north. On average, motel prices here are among the lowest in the province, making it a good spot to rest overnight.

The flower-basket-adorned **Heritage Estate Motel** (362 Van Horne St., 250/426-3862 or 800/670-1001) is definitely the best value-for-

Canadian Museum of Rail Travel

© ANDREW HEMPSTEAD

money choice. The rooms are spacious, and each contains complimentary tea and coffee. Rates are $50 s, $65 d in summer but drop as low as $45 s, $55 d the rest of the year. I'm not the only one who regards this place as a bargain, so book ahead in summer. Continuing north, in the heart of the commercial strip, **Lazy Bear Lodge** (621 Cranbrook St., 250/426-6086 or 888/808-6086, $60 s, $65 d) is an old roadside motel snazzed up with log trim, beds of bright flowers, and a colorful coat of paint. The rooms remain basic, but each has a coffeemaker, and some have a fridge and microwave. Out front is a small swimming pool for guest use.

Camping

One of the area's most attractive campgrounds is in **Jimsmith Lake Provincial Park,** four kilometers (2.5 miles) off the main highway at the southern outskirts of the city. The park's wooded campsites are $14 per night. Downtown, **Mt. Baker RV Park** (14th Ave. and 1st St. S, 250/489-0056) provides grassy tent sites for $18 and hookups for $20–24.

Food

The earliest opener of Cranbrook's many cafés is the **Village Baker** (821 Baker St., 250/489-2863; Mon.–Fri. 5 A.M.–5:30 P.M., Sat. 5 A.M.–4 P.M.), where you can relax in an adjacent café with a massive muffin and a coffee for just $4. Another local café is **Swing Street Coffeehouse** (16 11th Ave. S, 250/426-5358, Mon.–Fri. 8 A.M.–5 P.M., Sat. 9 A.M.–5 P.M.).

If you want a quick lunch but don't want to eat at a fast-food chain, make a stop at **Pita Wrapbit** (1517 Cranbrook St. N, 250/426-5626; daily 6 A.M.–8 P.M.), where wraps are made to order for $6–8.

Casual **Midorak** (1015 Baker St., 250/489-4808; Mon.–Sat. 11 A.M.–2:30 P.M., daily 5–9 P.M.) has a menu that suits all tastes—think Thai chicken curry ($17), feta herb-crusted rack of lamb ($26), and a creamy shellfish pescatore $18.

Information and Services

Cranbrook has two information centers, one at each end of the city. The main **Cranbrook Visi-**

tor Info Centre (2279 Cranbrook St. N, 250/426-5914 or 800/222-6174, www.cranbrookchamber.com) is open in summer daily 8:30 A.M.–7 P.M., the rest of the year Mon.–Fri. 8:30 A.M.–4:30 P.M. At the southern entrance to the city is a seasonal center (July–Aug. daily 9 A.M.–5 P.M.).

Lotus Books (33 10th Ave. S, 250/426-3415) is loaded with local reading material, including some interesting books on the gold rush era.

Cranbrook Regional Hospital is off 2nd Street on 24th Avenue North (250/426-5281). The **post office** is downtown (corner of 10th Ave. and 1st St. S).

Transportation

Cranbrook Airport, on the north side of town off Highway 95A, is served by **Air Canada** (888/247-2262) and **WestJet** (800/538-5696). Both offer daily flights between Cranbrook and Vancouver. From the **Greyhound** bus depot (1229 Cranbrook St., 250/426-3331 or 800/661-8747), bus service runs at least once daily east to Fernie, Sparwood, and into Alberta; west to Creston and Castlegar; and north to Kimberley, Radium Hot Springs, and through Kootenay National Park to Banff and on to Calgary.

Rental-car agencies based at the airport include: **Budget** (250/489-4371), **National** (250/489-0911), and **Rent-a-wreck** (250/426-3004). For a cab call **Star Taxi** (250/426-5511).

FERNIE AND VICINITY

Fernie (pop. 5,200) nestles in the Elk Valley 100 kilometers (62 miles) east of Cranbrook on Highway 3. The town itself is a coal-mining and forestry center offering little of visitor interest, but in winter one of British Columbia's great little alpine resorts comes alive nearby. Town center is a couple of blocks south of the highway, holding the usual array of historic buildings and small-town shops. Look for an impressive redbrick courthouse on 4th Avenue and a good bakery on 2nd Avenue. About 12 kilometers (7.5 miles) south of town is 259-hectare (850-acre) **Mount Fernie Provincial Park,** where hiking trails lead along a picturesque creek and to a waterfall.

The Kootenays

Fernie Alpine Resort

Fernie Alpine Resort (14 km/8.7 miles south of Fernie, 250/423-4655, www.skifernie.com) is another of British Columbia's legendary winter resorts, boasting massive annual snowfalls, challenging skiing and riding, and uncrowded slopes. Fernie has long held a reputation throughout the west as a hidden gem, and development was minimal until the late 1990s, when the resort was bought by the Resorts of the Canadian Rockies, which also owns resorts such as Lake Louise. New lifts opened soon after, and the base facilities were expanded. One thing that remains the same is the fantastic terrain, all 1,215 hectares (3,000 acres) of it. The lift-serviced area lies under a massive ridge that catches an incredible nine meters (30 feet) of snow each year, filling a wide open bowl with enough of the white fluffy stuff to please all powderhounds. A few runs are groomed, but the steeper stuff—down open bowls and through trees—is the main attraction. The resort's total vertical rise

is 857 meters (2,810 feet), with many of the challenging slopes at higher elevations and in Cedar and Timber Bowls. Lift tickets cost adult $56, senior $45, child $15; under six ski free. The resort is open mid-December through mid-April, but the best conditions are in January and February. In July and August, one chairlift operates, opening up hiking and mountain-biking terrain. Hikers pay $10 per ride or $24 for a day pass. Use the lift to take the hard work out of mountain biking for $30 for a full day. Bikes can be rented at the base village for $25–40. Other summer activities include horseback riding, dog carting (a summer version of mushing), guided hikes, tennis, and photography courses. Accommodations are available on the hill, and visitors with RVs are offered hookups and shower facilities.

Accommodations and Camping

Fernie's numerous budget-priced accommodations make the town a great base for budget-conscious travelers. Best of the bunch is **⚡ Samesun International Lodge** (Hwy. 3, 250/861-3001 or 877/562-2783, www.samesun.com). This converted motel has a game room, communal kitchen, loads of parking, a laundry, Internet access, and even an outdoor pool. Accommodations are in dorms ($21.40 per bed) and private rooms ($59–119 s or d). In between the high summer and winter seasons, regular motel rooms go for as low as $40—a great deal. **Park Place Lodge** (742 Hwy. 3, 250/423-6871 or 888/381-7275, www.parkplacelodge.com) is a modern three-story hotel along the main road. Amenities include spacious and elegant rooms opening to an atrium, the Red Rock Bistro, and a pub. Summer rates are from a reasonable $99 s, $109 d, with golf and ski packages starting from $85 per person.

Up at the alpine resort, **Griz Inn** (250/423-9221 or 800/661-0118, www.grizinn.com) offers 45 kitchen-equipped suites, an indoor pool, hot tub, and restaurant. Through summer, room rates start at a reasonable $85 s or d, while a condo unit is $130 for up to four people.

The best bet for campers is **Mount Fernie Provincial Park** (mid-May–Sept.; $14), 12 kilometers (7.5 miles) south of town and four kilometers (2.5 miles) north of the Akamina-Kishinena Provincial Park access road. Facilities are basic, but it's a pleasant setting, and a short trail leads along Lizard Creek to a waterfall.

Food

You will find a good selection of restaurants scattered through the downtown core, but my best picks are along the highway. **Jamochas Coffee House** (851 7th Ave., 250/423-6977) is the pick of many local caffeine joints (and it serves up some delicious homemade soups). Opposite the Samesun lodge, the **⚡ Curry Bowl** (932 7th Ave., 250/423-2695; Tues.–Sun. 5–10 P.M.) won't win any design awards, but with delicious dishes like mango shrimp curry ($14) and a Vietnamese chicken stir-fry ($11), it really doesn't matter. **⚡ Yamagoya** (741 7th Ave., 250/430-0080) is a stylish dining room that offers top-notch Japanese cuisine at equally reasonable prices.

Information

Beside the highway, through town to the north, is **Fernie Visitor Info Centre** (250/423-6868, www.ferniechamber.com), a good source of information for those interested in exploring the surrounding wilderness.

Akamina-Kishinena Provincial Park

Bordering Glacier National Park (Montana, U.S.) and Waterton Lakes National Park (Alberta), this remote tract of 10,921 hectares (27,000 acres) protects the extreme southeastern corner of British Columbia. The park is named for its two main waterways, which flow southward into Montana. This was the main reason for the park's recent creation; now, alongside Waterton Lakes National Park, entire watersheds of Glacier National Park are protected. The landscape has changed little in thousands of years, since the Kootenay rested in the open meadows beside Kishinena Creek before crossing the Continental Divide to hunt bison on the prairies. The only access is on foot from one of two trailheads. The longer option is from the end of an unsealed road that leaves Highway 3 at 16 kilometers (10 miles) south of Fernie. The road leads 110 kilometers (68 miles) into the Flathead River Valley, where trails climb along Kishinena then Akamina Creek into the park. The most popular and easiest access to the park is by hiking trail from the Akamina Parkway in Waterton Lakes National Park (Alberta). The signposted trailhead is 15 kilometers (nine miles) along this road from Waterton townsite. From the parkway, the trail gains 110 meters (360 feet) of elevation in 1.5 kilometers (.9 mile) before reaching the boundary of the park high atop the Continental Divide. After a further 700 meters (.4 mile), the trail divides. The closest of two subalpine bodies of water, **Forum Lake,** is 2.2 kilometers (1.4 miles) to the left up a tedious ascent of Forum Creek. Colorful meadows surround the lake's outlet, while a layered headwall provides a stunning backdrop. Allow 1.5 hours for this 4.4-kilometer (2.7-mile) hike. Nestled below Akamina Ridge, **Wall Lake** is straight ahead from the junction, 2.7 kilometers (1.7 miles). The best source of information is the Fernie information center.

The Kootenays

Sparwood

Thirty kilometers (18.6 miles) northeast of Fernie, Sparwood (pop. 3,800) began as three separate coal-mining towns: Michel, Middletown, and Natal. In the 1960s, a resurgence of civic pride saw the old towns demolished and replaced by the new center of Sparwood.

The coal seams and part of the mining operations can be seen on the ridge high above Sparwood, but a more eye-catching element of the local industry is the world's largest truck, which sits beside Highway 3 in the center of town. Beside the truck is **Sparwood Visitor Info Centre** (250/425-2423 or 877/485-8185, www.sparwoodchamber.bc.ca), where you can arrange a tour of the mines. Those looking for a roof over their head should plan on staying down the road in Fernie, while campers will enjoy **Mountain Shadows Campground** (Hwy. 3, 250/425-7815; May–Oct.), set among trees immediately south of town. Unserviced sites are $12, hookups $14–20, which includes the use of hot showers.

Elkford

Surrounded by towering peaks, this coal-mining community of 2,500 lies 35 kilometers (22 miles) north of Sparwood on Highway 43, which continues north to remote Elk Lakes Provincial Park, 67 kilometers (42 miles) farther north. Abundant recreation opportunities in the area include fishing in the Elk River, wildlife viewing, and hiking and mountain biking on hundreds of kilometers of logging and mining roads. In winter, these same roads are a mecca for snowmobilers. The community has few services, but there's a small **municipal campground** ($16) within walking distance of downtown. On Front Street is the **Elkford Visitor Info Centre** (250/865-4614 or 877/355-9453, www.tourismelkford.ca).

Elk Lakes Provincial Park

This park encompasses more than 17,000 hectares (42,000 acres) of rugged wilderness 67 kilometers (42 miles) north of the nearest town, Elkford. At the end of the road, a kiosk holds a park map and up-to-date trail conditions. From this point it's an easy one-kilometer (.6-mile)

walk to **Lower Elk Lake** and then another kilometer beyond the end of the lake to **Upper Elk Lake.** At the lower lake, a narrow trail climbs to a lookout. Aside from the long drive in, the ratio of effort to reward in reaching these lakes is unmatched in the Canadian Rockies. The stunningly beautiful upper lake is surrounded by steep snowcapped peaks, and several avalanche paths end right at water's edge. Fishing in the lower lake is productive for Dolly Varden and cutthroat trout.

NORTH FROM CRANBROOK

From Cranbrook, the highway north divides, with the western option passing through Kimberley and a more direct route following the Kootenay River through an area that was flooded with miners after gold was discovered on Wild Horse Creek in 1865.

Fort Steele Heritage Town

At Fort Steele Heritage Town (250/417-6000; mid-May–early Oct. daily 9:30 A.M.–6 P.M.; adult $10.50, senior $9, child $2), 16 kilometers (10 miles) north of Cranbrook, you'll see over 60 restored, reconstructed, fully furnished buildings, including log barracks, hotels, a courthouse, jail, museum, dentist's office, ferry office, printing office, and a general store crammed to the rafters with intriguing historical artifacts. In summer, the park staff brings Fort Steele back to life with appropriately costumed working blacksmiths, carpenters, quilters, weavers, bakers, ice-cream makers, and many others. Hop on a stagecoach or a steam train, heckle a street politician, witness a crime and testify at a trial, pan for gold, watch a silent movie, and view operatic performances in the Opera House. Some of the theatrical performances inside cost extra. One of the highlights is Fort Steele Follies, a professional 1880s'-style live-theater company performing a musical comedy at the Wild Horse Theatre. Showtimes are summer only daily at 2 P.M. (adult $6, senior $5, child $2).

A few commercial facilities surround the main entrance to Fort Steele. The largest is **Fort**

Steele Resort and RV Park (250/489-4268, www.fortsteele.com), which offers a heated pool, showers, laundry, and a barbecue and cooking facility. Unserviced sites are $20, serviced sites $24–32.

Wild Horse Creek

To get to the original Wild Horse Creek diggings, continue north from Fort Steele and take the logging road to Bull River and Kootenay Trout Hatchery (turn at the campground), then the first road on the left (before the creek crossing). Fisherville—the first township in the East Kootenays and once home to over 5,000 miners—was established at the diggings in 1864 but was relocated upstream when it was discovered that the richest seam of gold was right below the main street.

About five kilometers (three miles) from the highway is Wild Horse Graveyard. From this point you can hike a section of Wild Horse Creek to see a number of historic sites, including the Chinese burial ground, the site of the Wild Horse post office, the remains of Fisherville, and the diggings. It takes about two hours to do the trail, allowing for stops at all the plaques along the way. Hikers can also saunter down the last 2.5 kilometers (1.6 miles) of the Dewdney Trail, imagining all the men and packhorses, loaded to the hilt, that once struggled from the Fraser Valley to the East Kootenays in search of fortune.

KIMBERLEY

Kimberley (pop. 7,000), 31 kilometers (19 miles) north of Cranbrook on Highway 95A, is a charming little town, with no commercial strip or fast-food outlets, just streets of old stucco mining cottages with a downtown that's been "Bavarianized." In fact, Kimberley is also known as the "Bavarian City." Most of the local shops and businesses, and many of Kimberley's homes, have been decorated Bavarian-style with dark wood finish and flowery trim, steep triangular roofs, fancy balconies, brightly painted window shutters, and flower-filled window boxes. The Bavarianization occurred in the 1970s, when a group of local businesspeople devised the idea to attract tourists. They did such a good job of luring visitors that many Europeans found Kimberley appealing and joined the town's resident population—the European-style delis and restaurants you see downtown are mostly authentic.

Although named for a famous South African diamond mine, Kimberley boomed as a result of the silver and lead deposits unearthed on nearby North Star Mountain. The deposits were discovered in 1892, and by 1899 over 200 claims had been staked. As was so often the case, only operations run by larger companies proved profitable. The last of these, and one of the world's largest lead and zinc mines, Cominco's **Sullivan Mine,** closed in late 2001 as reserves became exhausted.

Bavarian Platzl

Strolling the Bavarian Platzl, you'll feel as though you've just driven into a village high in the Swiss Alps, with only bell-wearing cows and brightly dressed milkmaids missing. This is the focus of downtown—a cheerful, redbrick, pedestrian plaza complete with babbling brook, ornamental

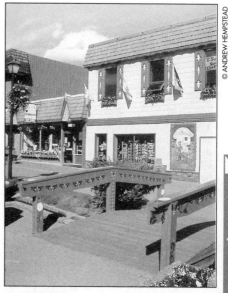

Bavarian Platzl

© ANDREW HEMPSTEAD

The Kootenays

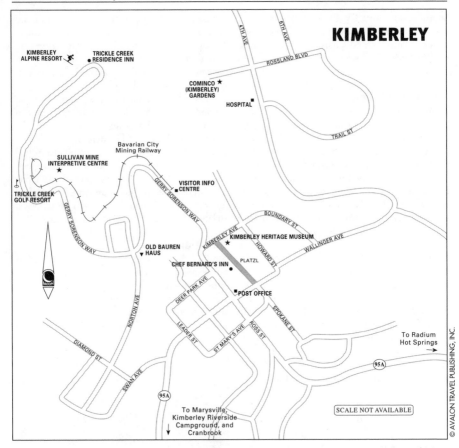

KIMBERLEY

KIMBERLEY ALPINE RESORT

TRICKLE CREEK RESIDENCE INN

4TH AVE

6TH AVE

ROSSLAND BLVD

COMINCO ★ (KIMBERLEY) GARDENS

HOSPITAL

TRAIL ST

Bavarian City Mining Railway

SULLIVAN MINE INTERPRETIVE CENTRE

TRICKLE CREEK GOLF RESORT

GERRY SORENSON WAY

VISITOR INFO CENTRE

GERRY SORENSON WAY

NORTON AVE

OLD BAUREN HAUS

CHEF BERNARD'S INN

KIMBERLEY AVE

BOUNDARY ST

KIMBERLEY HERITAGE MUSEUM

HOWARD ST

WALLINGER AVE

PLATZL

DEER PARK AVE

POST OFFICE

SPOKANE ST

LEADER ST

ST MARY'S AVE

ROSS ST

DIAMOND ST

SWAN AVE

95A

To Radium Hot Springs →

95A

95A

To Marysville, Kimberley Riverside Campground, and Cranbrook

SCALE NOT AVAILABLE

© AVALON TRAVEL PUBLISHING, INC.

bridges, and the "World's Largest Cuckoo Clock" ("Happy Hans" pops out and yodels on the hour). Shops, many German restaurants, and delis line the plaza, selling European specialties. At the far end of the Platzl, **Kimberley Heritage Museum** (250/427-7510, summer Mon.–Sat. 9 A.M.–4:30 P.M., the rest of the year Mon.–Sat. 1–4 P.M.) houses mining-history exhibits, a stuffed grizzly bear, a hodgepodge of artifacts, and displays relating to all the locally popular outdoor sports.

Other Sights

Cominco Gardens, also known as Kimberley Gardens, enjoys a hilltop location (4th Ave.,

250/427-2293; $3). Originally planted in 1927 to promote a fertilizer developed by Cominco, the one-hectare (2.5-acre) gardens now hold close to 50,000 flowers.

The **Bavarian City Mining Railway** (250/ 427-2929) was constructed from materials salvaged from mining towns around the province. The seven-kilometer track climbs a steep-sided valley, crosses a trestle bridge, and stops at particularly impressive mountain viewpoints and the original townsite before arriving at the **Sullivan Mine Interpretive Centre,** which stands on the site of a massive reclamation project. The train operates up to six times daily through summer; adult $7, child $3.

Golfing

The Columbia Valley is one of British Columbia's premier golfing destinations, and while most of the best courses are farther north, Kimberley is home to the par-72, 6,896-yard **Trickle Creek Golf Resort** (250/427-5171 or 877/282-1200), which lies along the lower slopes of North Star Mountain at the base of Kimberley Alpine Resort. The resort course–style layout is generally regarded as one of the best in the valley, featuring huge elevation changes (such as the par-3 11th hole, which drops over 20 meters/66 feet from tee to green) and stunning mountain scenery. Greens fees are $99, or play after 2 P.M. for $75. Dating to 1924, **Kimberley Golf Course** (in Marysville, 250/427-4161) is much shorter at just 6,000 yards, but fairways lined with mature ponderosa pines and small greens add to the challenge. Greens fees are $45.

Kimberley Alpine Resort

From early December to early April, this resort (250/427-4881 or 800/258-7669, www.skikimberley.com) provides great skiing and snowboarding on a wide variety of slopes four kilometers (2.5 miles) west of downtown. Currently there are 67 named runs covering 738 hectares (1,800 acres), with a maximum vertical rise of 750 meters (2,460 feet). Most beginners and intermediates will be content on the well-groomed main slopes, while more experienced skiers and boarders will want to head to the expert terrain served by the Easter Chair. Additional facilities at the resort include two snowboard parks, a cross-country ski area, an ice-skating rink, accommodations, and restaurants. Lift tickets are adult $49, senior $39, child $20.

Summer activities include chairlift rides, hiking, mountain biking, and luge rides; head to the Adventure Desk in the Marriott Hotel (250/427-6743) for details.

Accommodations and Camping

If you plan on a golfing or a winter vacation in Kimberley, contact **Kimberley Vacations** (250/427-4877 or 800/667-0871, www.kimberleyvacations.bc.ca) for the best package deals. Otherwise contact one of the following choices.

© ANDREW HEMPSTEAD

Kimberley's best accommodation, the Trickle Creek Residence Inn, is up at the alpine resort.

If you don't mind being a couple of kilometers out of town, **Travellaire Motel** (toward Marysville at 2660 Warren Ave., 250/427-2252 or 800/477-4499) provides excellent value. It's only a small place, but it is regularly revamped and decked out with new beds and furniture. There's also a barbecue area for guest use. Rates are $55 s, $65 d, or pay an extra $8 for a room with a small kitchenette. **Trickle Creek Residence Inn** is a Marriott affiliate at the base of Kimberley Alpine Resort (250/427-5175 or 877/282-1200, www.skikimberley.com). This stunning log and stone structure holds 80 spacious rooms, each with a kitchen, balcony, and fireplace. Guest facilities include a fitness center and a year-round outdoor heated pool. Summer rates are $149 s or d for a studio room and $169 for a one-bedroom suite. Check the website for golf and ski packages.

Kimberley Riverside Campground (250/427-2929 or 877/999-2929, www.kimberleycampground.com; May–mid-Oct.) is seven kilometers (4.3 miles) south of downtown on Highway 95A and then three kilometers (1.9

The Kootenays

miles) west along St. Mary's River Road. Tent sites are $18, hookups $22–26.

Food

European gourmet specialties, predominantly German, are available all around town. The **Gasthaus** (in the Platzl, 250/427-4851, daily except Tues. 11:30 A.M.–10 P.M.) features German lunches, such as goulash ($7), and German dinner specialties, such as bratwurst, rheinischer sauerbraten, wienerschnitzel, and kassler rippchen ($11–17.50). Away from the Platzl, **Old Bauren Haus** (280 Norton Ave., 250/427-5133, dinner only, closed Tues.) features Bavarian specialties and plenty of atmosphere. It's in a post-and-beam building originally constructed about 350 years ago in southern Bavaria. The building was taken apart, shipped to Canada, and painstakingly rebuilt.

Garden Treasures (Cominco Gardens, 250/427-0501, mid-June–early Sept. daily 10 A.M.–6 P.M.) serves a classic afternoon tea, accompanied by desserts and delectables such as fresh-baked scones with jam. Prices are reasonable and the atmosphere, inside a real greenhouse, is delightful; the stunning pink-and-green interior is complemented by hanging plants, flowery tablecloths, and views of the distant mountains and gardens.

Information

For more information on Kimberley and the surrounding area, drop by **Kimberley Visitor Info Centre** (115 Gerry Sorensen Way, 250/427-3666, summer daily 9 A.M.–7 P.M., the rest of year Mon.–Fri. 9 A.M.–5 P.M.).

CONTINUING NORTH TOWARD INVERMERE

This stretch of highway passes through a deep valley chock-full of commercial facilities like world-class golf courses, resorts, and hot springs. The low elevation makes for relatively mild winters and an early start to the summer season. And with the Purcell Mountains on one side and the Rockies on the other, the valley certainly doesn't lack for scenery.

Wasa Provincial Park

Unlike the several backcountry parks in the area, 144-hectare (360-acre) Wasa Provincial Park, 30 kilometers (19 miles) north of Kimberley, is easily accessible off the main highway. The lake is warm, making for good summer swimming; fishing is possible but only so-so. Facilities include picnic tables, a nature trail, and swimming and water-sports areas. The park is open year-round, but the $15 camp fee is collected only May–September.

Whiteswan Lake Provincial Park

Continuing north, the Rockies close in and the scenery becomes unbelievably beautiful. Twenty-eight kilometers (17 miles) north of Skookumchuck and five kilometers (3.1 miles) south of Canal Flats, an unsealed logging road takes off east into the mountains, leading to 1,994-hectare (4,930-acre) Whiteswan Lake Provincial Park. The road climbs steadily from the highway, entering Lussier Gorge after 11 kilometers (6.8 miles). Within the gorge, a steep trail leads down to **Lussier Hot Springs.** Two small pools have been constructed to contain the odorless hot (43°C/110°F) water as it bubbles out of the ground and flows into the Lussier River. Within the park itself, the road closely follows the southern shorelines of first **Alces Lake** then the larger **Whiteswan Lake.** The two lakes attract abundant birdlife; loons, grebes, and herons are all common. They also attract anglers, who come for great rainbow trout fishing. Both lakes are stocked and have a daily quota of two fish per person.

The park road passes four popular campgrounds. The sites are $14 per night and fill on a first-come, first-served basis. All sites come with a picnic table and fire grate. There are no hookups or showers and reservations aren't taken.

Top of the World Provincial Park

If you thought the scenery around Whiteswan Lake was wild and remote, wait till you see this 8,790-hectare (21,720-acre) wilderness a rough 52 kilometers (32 miles) from Highway 95 (turn off the Whiteswan Lake access road at Alces Lake). You can't drive into the park, but it's a fairly easy six-kilometer (3.7-mile) hike from the end of the road to picturesque **Fish Lake,** the park's largest body of water. The trail climbs alongside the pretty Lussier River to the lake, which is encircled with Engelmann spruce and surrounded by peaks up to 2,500 meters (8,200 feet) high. The hike to the lake gains just over 200 vertical meters (660 vertical feet) and makes a good day trip. Trails from the lake lead to other alpine lakes and to a viewpoint that allows a good overall perspective on the high plateau for which the park is named. Fish Lake is productive for cutthroat trout and Dolly Varden.

Bring everything you'll need because there are no services within the park. Camping is possible at one of four designated areas for $5 per person, or you can stay in the large cabin nestled in trees beside Fish Lake ($15 per person).

Height of the Rockies Provincial Park

This long and narrow, 68,000-hectare (134,000-acre) park protects a 50-kilometer-long section of the Canadian Rockies, including a 25-kilometer-long stretch bordering the Continental Divide. It is accessible only on foot and is not a destination for the casual day-tripper. Mountains dominate the landscape, with 26 peaks—some of which remained unnamed until recently—rising over the magical 10,000-foot (3,050-meter) mark. They lie in two distinct ranges: the **Royal Group** in the north, and the **Italian Group** in the south. The dominant peak is 3,460-meter (11,350-foot) **Mount King George,** in the Royal Group, which is flanked by massive hanging glaciers on its north- and east-facing slopes. Mountain goats thrive on all massifs, while the remote valleys are home to high concentrations of elk and grizzly bears.

The park can be reached from two directions. Neither is signposted, so before setting out for the park, pick up a good map of the area at a local information center or Forest Service office. The following directions are intended only as a guide.

Connor Lake is the most popular destination in the south of the park. It is reached by passing through Whiteswan Lake Provincial Park, then continuing along a rough logging road that parallels the White River to its upper reaches. (The most important intersection to watch for is 11 kilometers/6.8 miles from Whiteswan Lake; stay right, immediately crossing the river.) At the end of the road, a tortuous 72 kilometers (45 miles) from Highway 93/95, is a small area set aside for tents and horse corrals. From this trailhead, it's an easy walk up Maiyuk Creek and over a low ridge to Connor Lake, where you'll enjoy great views of the Italian Group to the north and Mount Forsyth to the southwest.

Small **Queen Mary Lake** lies in the western shadow of the impressive Royal Group. It is generally the destination only of those on horseback or mountaineers continuing into the Royal Group. To get there, turn off Highway 93/95 at Canal Flats and follow a logging road up the Kootenay River watershed. For the first 48 kilometers (30 miles), the road follows the Kootenay itself. Then it turns westward and climbs along the south side of the Palliser River a further 35 kilometers (22 miles) to road's end. From this point, it's a 12-kilometer (7.5-mile) hike up a forested valley, with numerous creek crossings, to the lake.

Canal Flats

The small lumber-mill town of Canal Flats lies between the Kootenay River and Columbia Lake. David Thompson, the first European explorer in this neck of the woods, crossed from the lake to the river in 1808, naming the flat McGillivray's Portage. In 1889 the two waterways were connected by a canal with a single lock, but the passage was so narrow and dangerous that only two steamboats ever got through.

North of Canal Flats, the highway passes tiny **Thunder Hill Provincial Park,** which overlooks turquoise-and-blue Columbia Lake. The highway then approaches and passes the weirdly shaped **Dutch Creek Hoodoos,** a set of photogenic rock formations carved over time by ice, water, and wind. On the north side of the bridge over Dutch Creek, take the unmarked road down to the left (or, for southbound travelers, the road to the right before the bridge) and scramble around the scree slopes below the hoodoos.

The Kootenays

It's impossible to miss the Dutch Creek Hoodoos driving north from Canal Flats.

Fairmont Hot Springs

Kootenay natives used these springs as a healing source for eons prior to the arrival of Europeans, but they wouldn't recognize the place today. Surrounding the site is **Fairmont Hot Springs Resort** (250/345-6311 or 800/663-4979, www .fairmontresort.com), comprising a four-star resort, golf courses, a ski resort, and an airstrip long enough to land a Boeing 737.

Despite all the commercialism, the hot springs are still the main attraction. Their appeal is simple; unlike most other springs, the hot water bubbling up from underground here contains calcium, not sulfur with its attendant smell. The pools are a magical experience, especially in the evening. Lazily swim or float around in the large warm pool, dive into the cool pool, or sit 'n' sizzle in the hot pool and watch the setting sun color the steep faces of the Canadian Rockies immediately behind the resort. Admission is adult $8, child $6.50. For an additional fee, spa treatments, herbal wraps, and massages are offered. The pools are open daily 8 A.M.–10 P.M.

Most scenic of the resort's two 18-hole golf courses is **Riverside.** The course is relatively short,

but multiple water hazards, including the Columbia River winding through the layout, create a challenge for all levels of golfer. The river, surrounding mountains, bunkers filled with pure-white silica, well-manicured fairways and greens, and an award-winning layout combine to make this one of Canada's best resort courses. Greens fees are $70 for 18 holes. The other course, **Mountainside,** meanders through the forest adjacent to the resort itself; greens fees are $65.

Behind the hot springs is **Fairmont Hot Springs Ski Area,** unique in western Canada in that access is restricted to resort guests. The terrain is limited to an area served by one chairlift and a platter, but the mountain vistas and the unique opportunity to soak in hot springs after a day on the slopes make a winter trip to Fairmont worthwhile. The resort also has a short half pipe for snowboarders as well as rentals and a ski/snowboard school. The resort is laced with cross-country ski trails, and horse-drawn sleigh rides are offered whenever there's snow on the ground.

A lodge with upscale accommodations and a campground make up the rest of the resort complex. Rooms in the lodge are $179–265 s or d, with the more expensive having a loft and kitchen. Discounted ski, golf, and spa packages are usually available; check the website. In the off-season, rooms go for less than $100. Campers have a choice of over 300 sites spread around tree-shaded grounds, all just a one-minute stroll from the hot pools and open year-round. Unserviced sites are $21 while hookups range $27–41 (no tents), discounted outside of summer.

South of the resort is **Spruce Grove Resort** (Hwy. 3, 250/345-6561 or 888/629-4004, www.sprucegroveresort.com), where campsites ($20–29) are spread through the forest and along a quiet eddy in the Columbia River.

INVERMERE AND VICINITY

The next area to lure travelers off Highway 93/95 is **Windermere Lake.** Overlooking the lake, the town of **Invermere** (pop. 3,800) is the commercial center of the Columbia Valley. The lake and surrounding wilderness is a recreational playground, especially popular among landlocked

Albertans. The area was the site of an 1807 post set up by David Thompson to trade with Kootenay natives (a small plaque along the road to Wilmer marks the exact spot), the first such trading post along the Columbia River. The first official town in the valley, known as Athalmer, was alongside the outlet of Lake Windermere, but continual flooding led to the town's expansion on higher ground. The original townsite is now a popular recreation area, where a pleasant grassy area dotted with picnic tables runs right down to a sandy beach and the warm, shallow waters of the lake. It's on the left as you travel along the Invermere access road. As you approach the town itself, consider a stop at **Windermere Valley Museum** (622 3rd St., 250/342-9769), where the entire history of the valley is contained in seven separate buildings. The main street itself (7th Avenue) is lined with restored heritage buildings and streetlights bedecked with hanging baskets overflowing with colorful flowers.

Panorama Mountain Village

Recent years have seen a big push at promoting Panorama, in the Purcell Mountains immediately west of Invermere, as a year-round destination by its owners, Intrawest. The resort has a long way to go before becoming the "next Whistler," also owned by Intrawest, but Panorama Mountain Village, comprising a redeveloped base area, a residential subdivision, an open-air gondola to move visitors between the two main villages, a year-round water park, and a resort-style golf course, is just the first step in future plans.

Greywolf Golf Course (250/341-4100) is a challenging 7,140 yards from the back tees, with water coming into play on 14 of the 18 holes, including the signature sixth hole, "the Cliffhanger," which requires an accurate tee shot across a narrow canyon to a green backed by towering cliffs. Greens fees are $119, dropping to $75 for twilight rates. During the warmer months, there are also chairlift rides (noon–5 P.M.), white-water-rafting and inflatable kayak trips down Toby Creek, and horseback riding, and in the village itself you'll find tennis, a climbing wall, and a swimming pool.

Skiing first put Panorama on the map, mainly because the resort boasts the fourth-highest vertical rise of all North American winter resorts (1,200 meters/3,940 feet), behind only Whistler/Blackcomb, also in British Columbia, and Big Sky, Montana. Despite the impressive relief, Panorama offers slopes suitable for all levels of expertise. Lift tickets are adult $59, senior $49, child $27.

The village is also home to **R.K. Heli-Ski** (250/342-3889 or 800/661-6060, www.rkheliski.com), which operates out of its own "heliplex," complete with a lounge and restaurant. The company is one of the few heli-ski operations that specialize in day trips.

Accommodations in Panorama Mountain Village are all relatively new and can be booked through the resort's main switchboard (250/342-6941 or 800/663-2929, www.panoramaresort.com), as can all summer activities. Outside of the resort's marketing department, summer is still thought of as the off-season, and there are some great summer deals to be had, such as two nights' accommodation and unlimited use of the chairlift for $99 per person.

Purcell Wilderness Conservancy Provincial Park

If you take the road west from Invermere beyond Panorama Resort, you'll end up nine kilometers from the boundary of Purcell Wilderness Conservancy, a 106,290-hectare (262,260-acre) wilderness straddling the heart of the rugged Purcell Mountains. No roads and few trails penetrate the preserve. The end of the road is the trailhead for a 61-kilometer (38-mile) hike—up Toby Creek, over 2,256-meter (7,400-foot) Earl Grey Pass, and along the Hamill Creek watershed. The trail ends on Kootenay Lake, six kilometers (3.7 miles) east of Highway 31, 40 kilometers (25 miles) north of Kaslo.

Accommodations

The motels in downtown Invermere are a bit overpriced; the best option is **N Delphine Lodge** (250/342-6851; $80–100), two kilometers (1.2 miles) north in the small village of Wilmer. Restored to its former glory, this

19th-century hotel has been converted to a boutique bed-and-breakfast. On warm afternoons, you can relax in the beautiful garden, then move inside to the comfy lounge. Rates include a cooked breakfast. Another option is to stay out of town at Panorama Mountain Village (250/342-6941 or 800/663-2929, www.panoramaresort.com).

Food

On a Saturday morning in downtown Invermere, you'll find all sorts of goodies at the outdoor market, which happens right on the main street. Farther down the hill, the Quality Bakery (888/681-9977) lives up to its name with a huge range of ultra-healthy sandwiches and not-so-healthy cakes and pastries. The town's most up-scale dining room is **Strand's** (up the hill from the main street at 818 12th St., 250/342-6344; daily 5–9 P.M.). It's contained in a restored 1912 heritage house set on landscaped gardens, with diners seated in small, intimate rooms and offered an immaculately presented seasonal menu that often includes delicacies such as trout, salmon, and venison that are served with a wide selection of vegetables. Dine before 6 P.M. to take advantage of a three-course special for $14.

Information

Along the main drag is the **Invermere Visitor Info Centre** (corner of 5th St. and 7th Ave., 250/342-2844, www.adventurevalley.com; July–Aug. daily 9 A.M.–5 P.M.).

Canadian Rockies

The highest peaks of the Canadian Rockies form British Columbia's eastern boundary, separating the province from neighboring Alberta. On the British Columbia side of the Canadian Rockies (often called the **B.C. Rockies**) are **Kootenay** and **Yoho National Parks** and their gateway towns of **Radium Hot Springs** and **Golden.** The two national parks may lack the bustling resort towns of their famous Albertan neighbors, Banff and Jasper, but they boast the same magnificent mountain vistas, glacially fed streams and rivers, unlimited hiking opportunities, and abundant wildlife.

Many factors combine to make the Canadian Rockies so beautiful. The peaks themselves ex-hibit drastically altered sedimentary layers visible from miles away, especially when accentuated by a particular angle of sunlight or a dusting of snow. Between the peaks lie numerous cirques—basins gouged into the mountains by glaciers. These cirques fill with glacial meltwater each spring, creating lakes that shimmer a trademark translucent green. And thanks to a climate that keeps the tree line low and the vegetation relatively sparse, fantastic views of the wide sweeping valleys are assured.

Encompassing close to 20,000 square kilometers (7,700 square miles) of Mother Nature's finest offerings, Kootenay and Yoho, along with neighboring Banff and Jasper National Parks (both of which lie across the Continental Divide in Alberta) have been declared a World Heritage Site by UNESCO. For detailed coverage of the entire mountain range north of the 49th parallel, see *Moon Handbooks Canadian Rockies*.

PLANNING YOUR TIME

Lay out a map of British Columbia, and it's obvious that visiting both Kootenay and Yoho National Parks as part of a loop through the Canadian Rockies is an obvious extension to a trip to the Kootenay region. What the map won't tell you is that nowhere in British Columbia is the scenery-to-distance traveled ratio as good as it is in this part of the province. For the traveler, this means you should schedule a little longer than you may think to see everything.

Just one road passes through **Kootenay National Park,** and you can travel from one end to the other in under two hours. But plan to spend at least a full day in the park, making stops at the **hot springs** and the **Paint Pots** and allowing time to hike the **Stanley Glacier Trail.** The town of **Radium Hot Springs** is an excellent base for exploring the British Columbia Rockies. Not only are lodgings relatively inexpensive, but the town's commercial campgrounds have more facilities than those in the parks (especially notable if you're traveling with children), there's good golfing, and bird-watchers will delight in exploring the Columbia River Wetlands.

Yoho National Park is a gem of a destination, well worth visiting even for just a day. If you make the loop through Kootenay via Lake Louise (Banff National Park), plan on overnighting in Yoho before continuing west along the TransCanada Highway to Golden. Scheduling a full day in the park allows enough time to drive to **Takakkaw Falls,** hike the loop trail around **Emerald Lake,** and enjoy lunch in between at one of the restaurants I recommend. The highlight of a visit to Yoho is **Lake O'Hara,** one of the most special places in the Canadian Rockies. Unlike at the region's other famous lakes, you can't simply drive up to O'Hara. Instead, you must make advance reservations for a shuttle bus that trundles up a restricted-access road to the lake.

The summer tourist season in the British Columbia Rockies is shorter than the rest of the province. Emerald Lake doesn't become ice-free until early June, and the road to Takakkaw Falls remains closed until mid-June. While July and August are the prime months to visit, September is also pleasant, both weather- and crowd-wise. Lake O'Hara doesn't become snow-free until early July, but the best time to visit is the last week of September, when the forests of larch have turned a brilliant gold color.

If you follow the loop this chapter takes, you'll end up in **Golden,** where a gondola ride at **Kicking Horse Mountain Resort** is the highlight.

Must-Sees

Look for **M** to find the sights and activities you can't miss and **M** for the best dining and lodging.

CANADIAN ROCKIES

Emerald
M Lake

M   **M**
Kicking Horse   Lake O'Hara
Mountain Resort

Stanley
M Glacier Trail
M   ALBERTA
The
Paint Pots

Radium Hot
M Springs

© ANDREW HEMPSTEAD

Emerald Lake, Yoho National Park

M **Stanley Glacier Trail:** Although it takes around 90 minutes to reach the end of the trail, the stunning views make it worth every step (page 341).

M **Emerald Lake:** At Emerald Lake, you can hike, canoe, fish, or simply soak up the mountain scenery (page 348).

M **Lake O'Hara:** Quite simply, this is a magical lake. Access is limited by a quota system, so take heed of the reservation information and be prepared for a day of hiking you will always remember (page 349).

M **Radium Hot Springs:** After a long day hiking the best recipe for soothing aching muscles is a soak in hot springs (page 338).

M **The Paint Pots:** Paint pots are a unique natural wonder that make for a colorful stop along Highway 93 (page 339).

M **Kicking Horse Mountain Resort:** I've ridden each of the four gondolas in the Canadian Rockies, and my favorite for unbeatable top-of-the-world views is at Kicking Horse Mountain Resort, near Golden (page 357).

© AVALON TRAVEL PUBLISHING, INC.

Radium Hot Springs and Vicinity

One of two main western gateways to the Canadian Rockies is the small town of Radium Hot Springs (pop. 900), which lies at the junction of Highways 93 and 95, 140 kilometers (87 miles) north of Cranbrook and a stunning two-hour drive through Kootenay National Park from the famous resort town of Banff. Its setting is spectacular; most of town lies on benchlands above the Columbia River, from where the panoramic views take in the Rockies to the east and the Purcell Mountains to the west. As well as providing accommodations and other services for mountain visitors and highway travelers, Radium is a destination in itself for many. Aside from the town's namesake (see *Kootenay National Park*), the area boasts a wildlife-rich wetland, two excellent golf courses, and many other recreational opportunities.

SIGHTS AND RECREATION

Columbia River Wetland

Radium sits in the Rocky Mountain Trench, which has been carved over millions of years by the Columbia River. From its headwaters south of Radium, the Columbia flows northward through a 180-kilometer-long (110-mile-long) wetland to Golden, continuing north for a similar distance before reversing course and flowing south into the United States. The wetland nearby Radium holds international significance, not only for its size (26,000 hectares/64,250 acres), but also for the sheer concentration of wildlife it supports. More than 100 species of birds live among the sedges, grasses, dogwoods, and black cottonwoods surrounding the convoluted banks of the Columbia. Of special interest are blue herons in large numbers and ospreys in one of the world's highest concentrations.

The wetland also lies along the Pacific Flyway, so particularly large numbers of ducks, Canada geese, and other migratory birds gather here in spring and autumn. The northbound spring migration is celebrated with the **Wings over the Rockies Bird Festival** (888/933-3311,

www.wingsovertherockies.org), which is held in the first week of May in conjunction with International Migratory Bird Day. The festival features ornithologist speakers, field trips on foot and by boat, workshops, and events tailored especially for children, all of which take place in Radium and throughout the valley. At any time of year, use the festival website to source the valley's best birding spots.

Golfing

The Columbia River Valley supports many golf courses and is marketed around western Canada as a golfing destination. Aside from the excellent resort-style courses and stunning Canadian Rockies scenery, golfers here enjoy the area's mild climate. Warm temperatures allow golfing as early as March and as late as October—a longer season than is typical at other mountain courses.

The 36-hole **Springs at Radium Golf Resort** is a highlight of golfing the Canadian Rockies, comprising two very different courses. One of them, the 6,767-yard, par-72 **Springs Course** (250/347-6200 or 800/667-6444), is generally regarded as one of British Columbia's top 10 resort courses. It lies between the town and steep cliffs that descend to the Columbia River far below. Immaculately groomed fairways following the land's natural contours, near-perfect greens, and more than 70 bunkers filled with imported sand do little to take away from the surrounding mountainscape. Greens fees are $80 for 18 holes (discounted to $54 after 4 P.M.). The resort's second course, the **Resort Course** (250/347-6266 or 800/667-6444) is much shorter (5,306 yards from the tips), but tighter and still challenging. It is nestled in the shadow of the Rockies to the south of Radium, circling the resort's other facilities, which include accommodations, tennis courts, and many other exercise facilities. Greens fees are $49, discounted to $34 after 4 P.M. Both courses have club and cart rentals, with the Springs Course also home to a driving range and teaching academy.

Other Recreation

While golfing is the big draw at Radium, the village is also a base for **Kootenay River Runners** (250/347-9210 or 800/599-4399), who offer white-water rafting trips for adult $64, child $49 for a half-day trip, adult $90, child $74 full-day. This company also offers a more relaxing evening float through the Columbia River Wetland in large and stable voyageur canoes. The floats depart daily at 5:30 P.M., and the cost is adult $49, child $35. Horse fanciers can rent a ride at **Longhorn Stables** (one km/.6 mile north of town, 250/347-9755).

ACCOMMODATIONS

Radium, with a population of just 900, has more than 30 motels, an indication of its importance as a highway stop for overnight travelers. Those along the access road to Kootenay National Park come alive with color through summer as each tries to outdo the others with floral landscaping. When booking any of these accommodations, ask about free passes to the hot pools.

Under $50

At the top end of the motel strip, closest to the

national park, **⋈ Misty River Lodge** (5036 Hwy. 93, 250/347-9912, www.radiumhostel .bc.ca) provides an excellent base for travelers on a budget. This converted motel has 11 beds in dormitories ($21 per person) and private rooms that include a $60 room with valley views and $79 room that combines valley views with a full kitchen. Amenities include a communal kitchen, a lounge, and a big deck with even bigger views to the distant Purcell Mountains. You can also rent bikes and canoes.

$50–100

Kootenay Motel is along Highway 93, up the hill from the junction of Highway 95 (250/347-9490 or 877/908-2020). The rooms are nothing special (but air-conditioned) and rent from $50 s, $58 d, $5 extra for a kitchenette. Also on-site is a barbecue area and pleasant gazebo.

Up the hill a little and across the road is **Black Bear's Inn** (250/347-9565 or 800/688-6138, www.blackbearsinn.com; Apr.–Oct.), with a pleasant outdoor barbecue area; basic sleeping rooms are $69 s or d, or pay $99 for a room with a private balcony overlooking the valley.

Back down toward town is the **Alpen Motel** (250/347-9823 or 888/788-3891, www.alpenmotel.com; Mar.–Oct.), which arguably has the best and brightest flowers out front. The air-conditioned rooms are the best along the strip, which is reflected in the price ($99–109 s or d), which includes passes to the hot springs.

Several older motels lie in the quiet residential streets west of highways 93/95. Least expensive is the **Ritz Motel** (4883 Stanley St., 250/347-9644 or 877/347-9644, www.ritzmotel.com; $60–90 s or d), which is an older motel, but the 13 pine-paneled rooms are large, with separate sleeping areas. Some have kitchens and are air-conditioned. Check-in starts at the earlier-than-usual time of 2 P.M.

Although it undergoes regular revamps, rates at the **Pinewood Motel** (4870 Stanley St., 250/347-9529 or 888/557-5567, www.pinewoodmotel .ca) start at a reasonable $70 s or d, or pay $80 for a kitchen-equipped unit with a separate bedroom.

The **Park Inn** (4873 Stanley St., 250/347-9582 or 800/858-1155, www.parkinn.bc.ca) has similar rates to the rest of the bunch, features an indoor pool, and has a covered barbecue area. Standard rooms are $70 s, $75 d, while those with kitchenettes are $80 s, $85 d.

Over $100

Three kilometers (1.9 miles) south of town, **Radium Resort** (250/347-9311 or 800/667-6444, www.radiumresort.com) is surrounded by an 18-hole golf course and holds a wide variety of facilities, including a health club, indoor pool, restaurant, and lounge. Guest rooms overlook the golf course and are linked to the main lodge building by a covered walkway. Regular motel rooms range $160–190 s or d, while kitchen-equipped condos sleeping up to six people start at $240 per night. Check the website or call for specials (rooms are often sold for around $100, even in the middle of summer). Additionally, golf, ski, and spa packages lower rates considerably, especially before and after summer's peak season.

Radium's newest accommodation, the **Prestige Inn** (7493 Main St. W, 250/347-2300 or 877/737-8443, www.prestigeinn.com) sits at the town's main intersection. Facilities include a fitness room, indoor pool, gift shop, spa services, an Italian restaurant, and a lounge bar. Summer rates are $180–230 s or d, but these rates are almost halved in winter.

Campgrounds

Within Kootenay National Park, but accessed from in town off Highway 93/95, is **Redstreak Campground** (see *Kootenay National Park*). The closest commercial camping is at **Canyon RV Resort,** nestled in its own private valley immediately north of the Highway 93/95 junction (250/347-9564, www.canyonrv.com; Apr.–Oct.; $22–25 per site). Treed sites are spread along a pleasant creek and all facilities are provided.

Spur Valley Golf Resort, 18 kilometers (11 miles) north of Radium along Highway 95 (250/347-9822, www.spurvalley.com) has 100 sites set around a large grassy area. Part of the resort is a full-length nine-hole golf course (across the road) and tennis courts. Sites range $20–24, with firewood an extra $5 per bundle.

Perfectly described by its name, **Dry Gulch Provincial Park** offers 26 sites four kilometers (2.5 miles) south of town. Typical of provincial park camping, each site has a picnic table and fire pit but no hookups, and reservations are not taken; $15 per night.

FOOD

The town of Radium Hot Springs holds several good choices for a food break. For breakfast, head to **M Springs Course** restaurant (Stanley St., 250/347-9311; Apr.–Oct. daily 7 A.M.–9 P.M.), at the golf course on the west side of the highway. The view from the deck, overlooking the Columbia River and Purcell Mountains, is nothing short of stunning. The food is good and remarkably inexpensive; in the morning, for example, an omelet with three fillings, hash browns, and toast is just $9. Lunch and dinner are also well priced, with a massive Caesar salad for $7 and main meals $10–18.50, including pastas for $11.

Back in town, **Back Country Jack's** (Main St. W., 250/347-0097; daily 11 A.M.–11 P.M.) is decorated with real antiques and real hard bench seats in private booths. There's a wide variety of platters to share, including Cowboy Caviar (nachos and baked beans) for $7.50 and a surprisingly good barbecued chicken soup ($5). For a main, the half-chicken, half-ribs, and all the extras for two ($24) is a good deal. Across the road, **Horsethief Creek Pub and Eatery** (Main St. E, 250/347-6400), serves up similar fare in more modern surroundings. Both places have a few outdoor tables.

Along the main drag is **Screamer's,** the place to hang out with an ice cream on a hot summer's afternoon. The ice cream here has been researched many times, most often when returning from camping trips in the Columbia Valley. Also along this strip is **Mountainside Market,** with an excellent choice of groceries and an in-house deli and butcher.

The restaurant at the **Radium Resort** (three km/1.9 miles south of town, 250/347-9311) caters mostly to golfers throughout the day and resort guests in the evening, but everybody is welcome. Enjoy lunch on the outdoor patio for around $10, or dine on sea bass smothered with a fruit-filled salsa for $24 in the evening. Buffets are offered on Wednesday and Friday nights from 6 P.M. ($22).

INFORMATION

On the east side of the highway, just south of the Highway 93/95 junction, is the **Radium Hot Springs Visitor Info Centre** (250/347-9331 or 800/347-9704, www.rhs.bc.ca). This building is also home to the national park information center. It's open weekdays year-round and in the busier summer months daily 9 A.M.–7 P.M.

NORTH FROM RADIUM ALONG HIGHWAY 95

From Radium, most travelers head into Kootenay National Park, but another option is to continue north for 105 kilometers (65 miles) to Golden, from where the TransCanada Highway heads east, through Yoho National Park and across the Continental Divide to Banff National Park, which is in the neighboring province of Alberta. From this point it is possible to continue south and link up with Highway 93, making a 350-kilometer loop through the three parks.

Between Radium and Golden several small, historic towns are worthy of a stop. The first is **Edgewater,** where a farmers' market is held each Saturday. Farther north is **Brisco.** Named for a member of the 1859 Palliser expedition, Brisco was founded on the mining industry and later grew as a regional center for surrounding farmland. Brisco General Store is a throwback to those earlier times, selling just about everything. Nearby **Spillimacheen,** meaning "White-water" to the natives, sits at the confluence of the Spillimacheen River and Bugaboo Creek.

Bugaboo Glacier Provincial Park

Inaccessible to all but the most experienced hikers and climbers, this vast tract of wilderness in the Purcell Mountains northwest of Radium Hot Springs is reached along a 45-kilometer (28-mile) gravel road west from Brisco. At road's end, a trail climbs steeply to a glaciated area that rivals the Canadian Rockies in beauty.

Aside from the icefields covering half the park, the most dominant features here are spectacular granite spires rising to elevations above 3,000 meters (9,840 feet). While the Purcell Mountains are an ancient range 1.5 billion years old, the spires formed as intrusions thrust skyward only about 70 million years ago. Since then, erosion has shaped them into today's granite needles towering over the surrounding icefields.

For nearly 100 years the Bugaboos have been a mecca for climbers, but first ascents have been made as recently as the 1970s. In 1972, the Alpine Club of Canada built the **Conrad Kain Hut** as a base for hikers and climbers wanting to explore the park. The hut, equipped with stoves and bunk beds for 50 people, is named for the first mountaineer to climb the highest spire. It's a strenuous five-kilometer (3.1-mile) hike from the end of the road, up a valley carved by the retreating Bugaboo Glacier. The trail gains around 700 meters (2,300 feet) in elevation; allow at least two hours. Camping is also possible near the hut. No set trails lead from the hut to the spires or icefields, and you'll need climbing and glacier-travel experience to continue deeper into the park.

The Bugaboos were the birthplace of heli-skiing. It was here in the mid-1960s that Hans Gmoser used a helicopter to transport skiers into normally inaccessible areas. **Canadian Mountain Holidays** (403/762-7100 or 800/661-0252, www.cmhski.com), the company Gmoser founded, now has a lodge deep in the Bugaboos.

MOUNT ASSINIBOINE PROVINCIAL PARK

Named for one of the Canadian Rockies' most spectacular peaks, this 39,050-hectare (96,500-acre), roughly triangular park lies northeast of Radium Hot Springs, sandwiched between Kootenay National Park to the west and Banff National Park to the east. It's inaccessible by road; access is on foot or by helicopter. A haven for experienced hikers, the park offers alpine meadows, lakes, glaciers, and many peaks higher than 3,050 meters (10,000 feet) to explore. The park's highest peak, 3,618-meter (11,870-foot) Mount Assiniboine (seventh-highest in the Canadian Rockies), is known as the Matterhorn of the Rockies for its resemblance to that famous Swiss landmark. The striking peak can be seen from many points well outside the boundaries of the park, including Buller Pond in Kananaskis Country and Sunshine Village winter resort in Banff National Park.

The peak is named for the Assiniboine people, who ventured into this section of the Canadian Rockies many thousands of years before European exploration. The name Assiniboine means "stone boilers"—a reference to these people's preferred cooking method. The mountain was sighted and named by a geological survey team in 1885, but the first ascent wasn't made until 1901.

Lake Magog is the destination of most park visitors. Here you'll find the park's only facilities and the trailheads for several interesting and varied day hikes. One of the most popular walks is along the Sunburst Valley/Nub Ridge trail. From Lake Magog, small Sunburst Lake is reached in about 20 minutes, then the trail continues northwest a short distance to Cerulean Lake. From this lake's outlet, the trail descends slowly along the Mitchell River to a junction four kilometers (2.5 miles) from Lake Magog. Take the right fork, which climbs through a dense subalpine forest to Elizabeth Lake, nestled in the southern shadow of Nub Peak. From this point, instead of descending back to Cerulean Lake, take the Nub Ridge trail, which climbs steadily for one kilometer (.6 mile) to a magnificent viewpoint high above Lake Magog. From the viewpoint, it's just less than four kilometers (2.5 miles), downhill all the way, to the valley floor. The total length of this outing is 11 kilometers (6.8 miles), and as elevation gained is only just over 400 meters (1,310 feet), the trail can comfortably be completed in four hours.

Approaching the Park on Foot

Three trails provide access to **Lake Magog,** the park's largest body of water. The most popular

comes in from the northeast, starting at Sunshine Village winter resort in Banff National
Park and leading 29 kilometers (18 miles) via
Citadel Pass to the lake. Not only is this trail
spectacular, but the high elevation of the trailhead (2,100 meters/6,890 feet) makes for a relatively easy approach. Another approach is from
the east, in Spray Valley Provincial Park
(Kananaskis Country). The trailhead is at the
southern end of Spray Lake; take the Mount
Shark staging area turnoff 40 kilometers (25
miles) south of Canmore. By the time the trail
has climbed the Bryant Creek drainage to
2,165-meter (7,100-foot) Assiniboine Pass, all
elevation gain (450 meters/1,480 feet) has been
made. At 27 kilometers (17 miles), this is the
shortest approach, but its elevation gain is
greater than the other two trails. The longest
and least-used access is from Highway 93 at
Simpson River in Kootenay National Park. This
trail climbs the Simpson River and Surprise
Creek drainages and crosses 2,270-meter
(7,450-foot) Ferro Pass to the lake for a total
length of 32 kilometers (20 miles).

The Easy Way In

If these long approaches put visiting the park
out of your reach, there's one more option:
you can fly in by helicopter from the Mount
Shark Helipad, at the southern end of Spray
Valley Provincial Park, 40 kilometers (25 miles)
southwest of Canmore. Flights depart at
11:30 A.M. Wednesday, Friday, and Sunday
and cost $128.40 per person each way, includ-
ing an 18-kilogram (40-pound) per-person
baggage limit. Although **Alpine Helicopters**
operates the flights, all bookings must be made
through the Mount Assiniboine Lodge (call
403/678-2883 Mon.–Fri. 8 A.M.–2 P.M., www
.mountassiniboine.com).

If you're planning on hiking into the park,
Alpine Helicopters will fly your gear in for $1.50
per pound (.45 kilogram). This same company,
which also operates from a base in Canmore,
charges $185 per person for a 30-minute flight-
seeing trip over the park. For more information,
call Alpine Helicopters (403/678-4802,
www.alpinehelicopter.com).

Mount Assiniboine Lodge

Getting to and staying at █ Mount Assiniboine
Lodge isn't cheap, but the number of repeat guests
is testament to an experience that you will never
forget. The mountain scenery may take most of
the kudos, but the lodge's congenial atmosphere,
overseen by longtime hosts the Renners, makes
the stay equally memorable. Built in 1928 by
the CPR, the delightfully rustic lodge is in a lakeside meadow below the distinctive peak. The
main building holds six double rooms that share
bathroom facilities and a dining area where hearty
meals (included in the rates) are served up com-
munal-style. Scattered in the surrounding trees
are six one-room cabins that sleep 2–5 people.
Each has running water and uses propane to heat
and light the space. Outhouses and showers are
shared. The rate for lodge rooms is $190 per per-
son; cabin accommodations range $190–240.
Children 12 and under are $120. You can reach
the lodge on foot (see *Approaching the Park on
Foot*) or fly in with Alpine Helicopters from a
helipad in Kananaskis Country (see *The Easy
Way In*). The fare and departure days are the
same as for campers; the only difference is that
guests depart at 1 P.M. If you decide to hike in (or
out), the charge for luggage transfers is $1.50
per pound (.45 kilogram).

The operating season is mid-June to the first
weekend of October and then mid-February to
mid-April for cross-country skiing. There is a
minimum stay of two nights and a weight limit of
18 kilograms (40 pounds) on luggage for the
flight. The lodge has no landline phone; for reservations or information you will need call 403/
678-2883 (Mon.–Fri. 8 A.M.–2 P.M.) or check
the website www.assiniboinelodge.com.

Between 4 and 5 P.M. each afternoon, the lodge
opens its doors to campers for a simple afternoon
tea of lemonade, fresh pastries, and tea ($7).

Campgrounds

Lake Magog is the park's main facility area, such
as it is. A designated camping area on a low ridge
above the lake's west shore provides a source of
drinking water, pit toilets, and bear-proof food
caches. Open fires are prohibited. Sites are $5
per person per night. No reservations are taken,

but even those who visit frequently have told me they've never seen it full. Also at the lake are the **Naiset Huts,** where bunk beds cost $20 per person per night (book through Mount Assiniboine Lodge at 403/678-2883 Mon.–Fri. 8 A.M.–2 P.M., www.mountassiniboine.com). The cabins contain nothing more than bunk beds with mattresses, so you'll need a stove, food, a sleeping bag, and your own source of light.

Information

In addition to contacting the government agency responsible for the park (Ministry of Water, Land, and Air Protection, www.bcparks.ca or www.gov.bc.ca/wlap), information and up-to-date trail conditions is available at park information centers located in Radium Hot Springs, Lake Louise, and Banff.

Kootenay National Park

Shaped like a lightning bolt, this narrow 140,600-hectare (347,400-acre) park lies northeast of Radium Hot Springs, bordered to the east by Banff National Park and Mount Assiniboine Provincial Park and to the north by Yoho National Park. Highway 93, extending for 94 km (58 miles) through the park, provides spectacular mountain vistas. Along the route you'll find many short and easy interpretive hikes, scenic viewpoints, hot springs, picnic areas, and roadside interpretive exhibits. The park isn't particularly noted for its day-hiking opportunities, but backpacker destinations such as Kaufmann Lake and the Rockwall rival almost any other area in the Canadian Rockies.

Even if you never leave the highway, the scarred hillsides from wildfires that swept through the park in 2001 and 2003 will be obvious. The fires jumped the highway in places, burnt bridges and information booths, and forced the closure of some trails due to the danger of falling trees; check at local information centers for the latest updates.

Day-use areas, a gas station and lodge, and three campgrounds are the only roadside services inside the park; Radium Hot Springs, at the junction of Highways 93 and 95 (see *Radium Hot Springs and Vicinity*), is the park's main service center. The park is open year-round, although you should check road conditions in winter, when avalanche-control work and snowstorms can close Highway 93 for short periods of time.

Flora

In the lowest areas of the park, in the Kootenay River Valley, Douglas fir and lodgepole pine find a home. Along the upper stretches of the Ver-

milion River Valley, where the elevation is higher, Engelmann spruce thrive, while immediately above lie forests of subalpine fir. The tree line in the park is at around 2,000 meters (6,560 feet) above sea level. This is the alpine, where low-growing species such as **willow** and **heather** predominate. For a short period each summer, these elevations come alive with color as forget-me-nots, avens, and avalanche lilies flower. Of special interest is the interpretive trail through Vermilion Pass Burn, where fire destroyed 2,400 hectares (5,930 acres) of forest in 1968. Lodgepole pine is the dominant species here. The area affected by the more recent wildfires is an excellent place to see the natural regeneration process at work.

Fauna

Large mammals tend to remain in the Kootenay and Vermilion river valleys. White-tailed deer, mule deer, moose, black bears, and elk live year-round at these lower elevations, as do bighorn sheep, which can be seen at mineral licks along Highway 93. The most common large mammal present in Kootenay is the mountain goat, but these flighty creatures stay at high elevations, feeding in alpine meadows throughout summer. Grizzlies number around 10 within the park; they range throughout the backcountry and occasionally are sighted in spring high on roadside avalanche slopes.

HISTORY

Although their traditional home was along the river valley to the south, the indigenous Kootenay

Canadian Rockies

KOOTENAY NATIONAL PARK

Mt Little
To Lake Louise
Quadra Mtn
Taylor Lake
Boom Lake
1A
Castle Mtn
CASTLE JUNCTION
ALBERTA

Tokumm Creek
Mt Whymper
Vermillion Pass
Storm Mtn
Mt Ishbel
1
BOW VALLEY PARKWAY

Mt Goodsir
Sharp Mtn
MARBLE CANYON
THE PAINT POTS
VERMILION PASS BURN
Twin Lakes
Redearth Cr
Pilot Mtn
River

Yoho National Park
MARBLE CANYON
STANLEY GLACIER TRAIL
Stanley Glacier
Stanley Peak
Shadow Lake
Banff National Park
To Banff

Mt Drysdale
93
Numa Falls
Isabelle Peak
Scarab Lake
Verdant
Bourgeau Lake
GONDOLA

Buttress Peak
The Rockwall
Vermillion
Sunshine Meadows
SUNSHINE VILLAGE

Mt Mollison
Beaverfoot River
Foster Peak
River
Quartz Hill

BRITISH COLUMBIA
Vermilion Range
Floe Lake
VERMILION CROSSING
Creek
Citadel Peak

To Golden
Kootenay
Mt Verendrye
Mt Shanks
River
Surprise

Spillimacheen
Mt Wardle
Simpson
Creek

Kootenay National Park
Mount Assiniboine Provincial Park

KOOTENAY CROSSING
Dolly
Creek
Mitchell River

Brisco
95
Mt Crook
Mt Selkirk

Columbia
Mt Kindersley
Dog Lake
Mt Harkin
Mt Docking

Frances Creek
Edgewater
MCLEOD MEADOWS
Kootenay

River
Kindersley Pass
VIEWPOINT
River
Cross River

Moon
Forster Creek
RADIUM HOT SPRINGS
Sinclair Pass
93
SETTLER'S RD

0   5 mi
0   5 km
Olive Lake
Radium Hot Springs
93
95
To Invermere and Panorama Mountain Village

© AVALON TRAVEL PUBLISHING, INC.

Canadian Rockies

NATIONAL PARK PASSES

Permits are required for entry into all national parks of the Canadian Rockies. A **National Parks Day Pass** is adult $7, senior $6, child $3.50 to a maximum of $14 per vehicle ($12 for seniors). It is interchangeable between parks and is valid until 4 P.M. the day following its purchase.

An annual **National Parks of Canada Pass,** good for entry into national parks across Canada, is adult $45, senior $38 to a maximum of $89 per vehicle. Both types of pass are available at the entrances to Kootenay and Yoho National Parks, at all park information centers, and at campground fee stations. For more information, check online at the Parks Canada website (www.pc.gc.ca).

people regularly came to this area to enjoy the hot springs—a meeting place for mountain and Plains bands. Natives called the springs Kootemik (Place of Hot Water). Early European visitors warped Kootemik into Kootenay and applied the name to the local residents. The natives traveled as far east as the Paint Pots area, to collect ocher for ceremonial painting purposes.

In 1905 Randolph Bruce, an Invermere businessman, persuaded the Canadian government and Canadian Pacific Railway (CPR) to build a road linking the Columbia River Valley to the prairie transportation hub of Calgary so that western produce could get out to eastern markets. Construction of the difficult **Banff–Windermere Road** began in 1911. But with three mountain ranges to negotiate and deep, fast-flowing rivers to cross, the money ran out after completion of only 22 kilometers (14 miles). In order to get the highway project going again, the provincial government agreed to hand over an eight-kilometer-wide (five-mile-wide) section of land along both sides of the proposed highway to the federal government. In return, the federal government agreed to finance completion of the highway. Originally called the Highway Park, the land became known as Kootenay National Park in 1920. The highway was finally com-

pleted in 1922, and the official ribbon-cutting ceremony was held at Kootenay Crossing in 1923; a plaque marks the spot.

DRIVING HIGHWAY 93

Climbing eastward from the town of Radium Hot Springs, Highway 93 (still known locally as the Banff–Windermere Highway) enters the boundary of Kootenay National Park at narrow **Sinclair Canyon,** a natural gateway to the wonders beyond. After squeezing through the canyon, the highway emerges at the actual springs that give the town of Radium Hot Springs its name.

Radium Hot Springs

This soothing attraction (250/347-9485; summer daily 9 A.M.–11 P.M., the rest of the year daily noon–9 P.M.) lies inside the park but just three kilometers (1.9 miles) northeast of the town of the same name, which is outside the park boundary. It was discovered many centuries ago by the Kootenay people, who, like today's visitors, came to enjoy the odorless mineral water that gushes out of the Redwall Fault at 44°C (111°F). Englishman Roland Stuart purchased the springs for $160 in 1890 and built rough concrete pools to contain the water. Development continued when a visiting millionaire—impressed by the improvement in his paralysis after soaking in the springs—contributed more money to the project. Originally known as Sinclair Hot Springs, after an early settler, the name was changed to Radium in 1915 for the high level of radioactivity in the water. With the declaration of Kootenay National Park in 1922, ownership reverted to the government.

Today the water is diverted from its natural course into the commercial pools, including one that is Canada's largest. Steep cliffs tower directly above the hot pool, whose waters are colored a milky blue by dissolved salts, which include calcium bicarbonate and sulfates of calcium, magnesium, and sodium. The hot pool (39°C, 97°F) is particularly stimulating in winter, when it's edged by snow and covered in steam—your head is almost cold in the chill air, but your submerged body melts into oblivion. Admission is adult $6.50 (or swim all day for $9.75), senior and child $5.50 (day pass $8.75). Towel and locker rentals are available, as are spa services. If you're camping at the park's Redstreak Campground, you can reach the complex on foot.

To Kootenay Valley

Leaving the hot springs, the road parallels Sinclair Creek, crests 1,486-meter (4,870-foot) Sinclair Pass, and passes small Olive Lake, which is ringed with bright yellow wildflowers in summer. At **Kootenay River Viewpoint** a splendid view overlooks the wild Kootenay River Valley below and the snowcapped mountains along the Continental Divide.

The highway then descends to the valley floor, passes two riverside picnic areas, and crosses the pretty Kootenay River at **Kootenay Crossing.** The official ribbon-cutting ceremony opening the Banff–Windermere Road took place here in 1923. Today you'll find a roadside historical exhibit, hiking trails, and a warden's station. As you cross the river and pass small, green Kootenay Pond, your eyes will revel in views of milky-green rivers, lush grassy meadows, tree-covered hills, and craggy, snowcapped peaks; keep your eyes peeled for mountain goats.

The highway then climbs over a low saddle and descends to the Vermilion River. On the descent, you'll pass a particularly nice picnic spot at Wardle Creek. Across the river, the mountainside is scarred black, the result of a wildfire that devastated over 4,000 hectares (9,900 acres) of forest in the summer of 2001. Left to take its natural course, the fire spread south along the Simpson River drainage and down to the Vermilion River, burning itself out as the first winter snow fell.

Paint Pots

A scenic one-kilometer (.6-mile) trail (20 minutes each way) leads over the Vermilion River to this unique natural wonder: three circular ponds stained red, orange, and mustard yellow by oxide-bearing springs. The natives, who believed that animal spirits resided in these springs, collected ocher from around the pools. They mixed it with animal fat or fish oil and then used it in cere-

monial body and rock painting. The ocher had a spiritual association and was used in important rituals. Europeans, seeing an opportunity to "add to the growing economy of the nation," mined the ocher in the early 1900s and shipped it to paint manufacturers in Calgary.

Several much longer hiking trails lead off the Paint Pots trail, including one of many routes to the Rockwall (see *Hiking*).

Marble Canyon

Be sure to stop and take the enjoyable self-guided trail, one kilometer (.6 mile) each way, that leads along this ice-carved, marble-streaked canyon. The walk takes only about 30 minutes or so, yet as one of several interpretive plaques says, it takes you back more than 500 million years.

From the parking lot, the trail follows a fault in the limestone and marble bedrock through Marble Canyon, which has been eroded to depths of 37 meters (130 feet) by fast-flowing Tokumm Creek. As the canyon narrows, water roars down

© ANDREW HEMPSTEAD

Marble Canyon

through it in a series of falls. The trail ends at a splendid viewpoint where a natural rock arch spans a gorge. Marble Canyon is also the trailhead for the Kaufmann Lake Trail.

East to the Continental Divide

Well before the Paint Pots, you'll see entire hillsides burnt by a devastating fire in 2003. As the highway climbs, the burnt areas become more apparent. Started by lightning, the blaze began as a number of fires, which came together to cross the highway, burn entire watersheds, and extend high up surrounding mountains to the extent of the tree line.

Continuing eastward from Marble Canyon, Highway 93 climbs steadily to the **Vermilion Pass Burn.** Lightning started the fire that roared through this area in 1968, destroying thousands of hectares of trees. Lodgepole pine, which requires the heat of a fire to release its seeds, and fireweed were the first plant species to sprout up through the charred ground. From the highway everything seems pretty dead, but along the .8-kilometer (half-mile) **Fireweed Trail** you'll see the growth of a new forest on the floor of the old.

The burn area is immediately west of the Continental Divide, which the highway crosses at an elevation of 1,640 meters (5,380 feet). The divide marks the border between Kootenay National Park to the west and Banff National Park in Alberta to the east. From the divide, it's 11 kilometers (6.8 miles) to Highway 1, from which point the Town of Banff lies 29 kilometers (18 miles) southeast and Lake Louise lies 27 kilometers (16.8 miles) northwest.

HIKING

Some 200 kilometers (124 miles) of trails lace Kootenay National Park. Hiking opportunities range from short interpretive walks to challenging treks through remote backcountry. All trails start from Highway 93 on the valley floor, so you'll be facing a strenuous climb to reach the park's high alpine areas, especially those in the south. For this reason, many hikes require an

overnight stay in the backcountry. The following hikes are listed from west to east.

Juniper Trail
- Length: 3.2 km/2 miles (one hour) round-trip
- Elevation gain: 90 meters/295 feet
- Rating: easy
- Trailhead: Highway 93, uphill from the west park gate

Named for the abundance of juniper along one section, this trail traverses a variety of terrain in a relatively short distance. You'll pass Sinclair Creek, an avalanche slope, and a lookout offering views of Windermere Valley and the Purcell Mountains. Beginning on the north side of the road just inside the park boundary, this trail rejoins the highway 1.5 kilometers (.9 mile) farther into the park. There you can retrace your steps back to the start or return along the highway via Sinclair Canyon.

Kindersley Summit
- Length: 10 km/6.2 miles (four hours) one-way
- Elevation gain: 1,050 meters/3,445 feet
- Rating: difficult
- Trailhead: Highway 93, two km (1.2 miles) west of Sinclair Pass

The elevation gain on this strenuous day hike will be a deterrent for many, but views from the summit will make up for the pain endured along the way. From Highway 93, the trail climbs through a valley for about three kilometers (1.9 miles), then switchbacks up across several avalanche paths and through more forest before emerging at an alpine meadow on Kindersley Pass. The final two-kilometer (1.2-mile) slog gets you higher, to an elevation of 2,400 meters (7,870 feet) at Kindersley Summit, a saddle between two slightly higher peaks. This is where the scenery makes the journey worthwhile. You'll enjoy views west to the Purcell Mountains, east to the Continental Divide, and, most spectacularly, north over the Kootenay River Valley. An alternate return route to the valley floor follows Sinclair Creek down from Kindersley Summit. This cuts two kilometers (1.2 miles) off the return distance.

Dog Lake
- Length: 2.6 km/1.6 miles (40 minutes) one-way
- Elevation gain: 80 meters (260 feet)
- Rating: easy
- Trailhead: McLeod Meadows Picnic Area, Highway 93

Dog Lake is no Mona Lisa, but it is a popular and easily reached destination, especially for those staying in McLeod Meadows Campground (if you're not camping, park at the picnic area 500 meters/.3 mile to the south). The trail first crosses the wide Kootenay River by footbridge. Then it hops a low ridge over to the shallow lake, which is fringed by marshes at the north end.

The Rockwall
- Length: 54 km/33.6 miles (three days) round-trip
- Elevation gain: 760 meters/2,490 feet
- Rating: moderate/difficult
- Trailhead: various points along Highway 93

This is one of the classic hikes in all of the Canadian Rockies. The Rockwall is a 30-kilometer-long (19-mile-long) east-facing escarpment that rises more than 1,000 meters (3,280 feet) from an alpine environment. Four different routes provide access to the spectacular feature; each begins along Highway 93 and traverses a steep valley to the Rockwall's base.

The most popular trail starts at the Paint Pots and follows Helmet Creek 12 kilometers (7.5 miles) to spectacular 365-meter (1,200-feet) Helmet Falls. A further 2.4 kilometers (1.5 miles) takes you to the beginning of the Rockwall trail and a campground, the first of five along the route. The trail then follows the Rockwall in a southeasterly direction for 30 kilometers (19 miles), passing magnificent glaciers, waterfalls, and lakes before ending at Floe Lake, 10.4 kilometers (6.5 miles) from the highway.

The Tumbling Creek and Numa Creek drainages provide alternative access routes to the Rockwall and require similar elevation gains. The elevation gain noted here is for the initial climb from the highway; along the route ascents are made to four additional passes, with elevation gains ranging 280–830 meters (920–2,720 feet).

Hikers will need to make arrangements for shuttle transportation between the beginning and end of this route—about 13 kilometers (eight miles) apart—or allow extra time to hike back. As elsewhere in the park, all hikers spending the night in the backcountry must register and pick up a permit ($8 per person per night) at either of the park information centers.

Kaufmann Lake
- Length: 15 km/9.3 miles (five hours) one-way
- Elevation gain: 570 meters
- Rating: moderate
- Trailhead: Highway 93, Marble Canyon parking lot

This is an overnight backpack trip to a beautiful lake in the extreme north end of the park. The trail follows Tokumm Creek the entire distance, passing through a forest of lodgepole pine before entering an open meadow and crossing many small waterways. Most elevation gain is made in the final two kilometers (1.2 miles), as the trail switchbacks up to the glacial cirque holding Kaufmann Lake. The exquisite lake is surrounded by peaks jutting as high as 3,400 meters (11,150 feet). Two campgrounds lie at the end of the trail.

Stanley Glacier Trail
- Length: 4.2 km/2.6 miles (90 minutes) one-way
- Elevation gain: 350 meters/1,150 feet
- Rating: moderate
- Trailhead: Highway 93, seven km (4.4 miles) west of the Continental Divide

Although this glacier is no more spectacular than those alongside the Icefields Parkway just a few minutes drive away, the sense of achievement of traveling on foot makes this trail well worth the effort. From Highway 93, the trail crosses the upper reaches of the Vermilion River, then begins a steady climb through an area burned by devastating fires in 1968. After two kilometers (1.3 miles), the trail levels off and begins winding through a massive U-shaped

The view from the end of the Stanley Glacier Trail is inspiring.

glacial valley, crossing Stanley Creek at the 2.4-kilometer (1.5-mile) mark. In open areas, fireweed, harebells, and yellow columbine carpet the ground. To the west, the sheer face of Mount Stanley rises 500 meters (1,640 feet) above the forest.

The trail officially ends atop the crest of a moraine after 4.2 kilometers (2.6 miles), with distant views to Stanley Glacier. It's possible (and worthwhile) to continue 1.3 kilometers (.8 mile) to the tree-topped plateau visible higher up the valley. After reaching the top of the first moraine beyond the official trail end, take the left fork, which switchbacks up and over another crest before making a steady ascent through slopes of loose scree to the plateau. Surprisingly, once on the plateau, you'll find a gurgling stream, a healthy population of marmots, and incredible views west to Stanley Glacier and north back down the valley. Be especially careful on the re-

turn trip—it's extremely easy to lose your footing on the loose rock.

ACCOMMODATIONS AND CAMPING

Accommodations within the park are limited, but the recommendations below are good ones. If you feel the need to be in town, see *Radium Hot Springs and Vicinity,* which has a dozen or so inexpensive motels.

$50–100

The only lodging in the heart of the park is **Kootenay Park Lodge** (403/762-9196, www.kootenayparklodge.com; mid-May–late Sept.), a cabin complex at Vermilion Crossing, 65 kilometers (40 miles) from Radium Hot Springs. Although no railway passes through the park, the 1923 lodge was one of many built by the Canadian Pacific Railway throughout the Canadian Rockies. It consists of a main lodge with restaurant, 10 cabins, a restaurant, and a gas station/grocery store. The most basic cabins ($90 s or d) have a bathroom, small fridge, and coffeemaker, with rates rising to $100–130 for a cabin with cooking facilities and a fireplace. Utensil and cooking kits are $10 per day.

$100–$150

The well-kept ⚑ **Cross River Cabins** (250/271-3296 or 877/659-7665; May–Sept.) have a real sense of privacy and of being away from the wellworn tourist path of Highway 93. And they are—tucked in a riverside setting 15 kilometers (9.3 miles) down Settler's Road, which branches off the highway 114 kilometers (71 miles) from Banff and 32 kilometers (20 miles) from Radium Hot Springs. The eight cabins are equipped with wood-burning fireplaces, log beds draped in down duvets, a toilet, and a sink. Showers are in the main building, along with the main lounge, cooking facilities, a dining area, and a deck. Guests bring their own food and cook in the full kitchen or out on the barbecue. As you can imagine, the atmosphere is convivial, with the cabins attracting outdoorsy types who want to enjoy the Canadian Rockies in their natural state—without room service and fine dining. The cost is $140 s or d, with a two-night minimum stay. Highly recommended.

Over $150

Ⓝ Nipika Mountain Resort (250/342-6516 or 877/647-4525, www.nipika.com) offers the same wilderness experience as the Cross River Cabins, and it's in the same vicinity—along Settler's Road, which branches off Highway 93 114 kilometers (71 miles) from Banff and 32 kilometers (20 miles) from Radium Hot Springs. Sleeping up to eight people, the cabins are larger than those at Cross River and have full en suite bathrooms and kitchens with wood-burning stoves ($140 s, $200 d). The cabins are modern but were constructed in a very traditional manner—the logs were milled on-site and construction is dovetail notching. Guests bring their own food and spend their days hiking, fishing, and wildlife watching. In winter, an extensive system of trails is groomed for cross-country skiing.

Campgrounds

The park's largest camping area is **Redstreak Campground** (mid-May–mid-Oct.), on a narrow plateau in the extreme southwest (vehicle access is from Highway 93/95 on the south side of Radium Hot Springs township), which holds 242 sites, showers, and kitchen shelters. In summer, free slide shows and talks are presented by park naturalists five nights a week and typically feature topics such as wolves, bears, the park's human history, or the effects of fire. Trails lead from the campground to the hot springs, town, and a couple of lookouts. Unserviced sites are $22, hookups $26–30. Fire permits cost $6 per site per night. A few sites can be reserved through the Parks Canada Campground Reservation Service (877/737-3783, www.pccamping.ca).

The park's two other campgrounds lie to the north of Radium Hot Springs along Highway 93. Both offer fewer facilities (no hookups or showers). The larger of the two is **McLeod Meadows Campground,** beside the Kootenay River 27 kilometers (16.8 miles) from Radium Hot Springs. Facilities include flush toilets, kitchen shelters, and a fire pit and picnic table at each of the 98 sites. **Marble Canyon,** across the highway from the natural attraction of the same name, offers 61 sites and similar facilities. Both are open mid-May to early September, and all sites cost $17. No reservations are taken in national park campgrounds, but for information, contact the park headquarters at 250/347-9615.

Hikers planning overnight trips in the backcountry must register at either of the park information centers and pick up a backcountry camping pass ($8 per person per night).

INFORMATION

Kootenay Park Information Centre (250/347-9615; summer daily 9 A.M.–7 P.M., the rest of the year weekdays only 9 A.M.–5 P.M.) is outside the park in the town of Radium Hot Springs, at the base of the access road to Redstreak Campground. Here you can collect a free map with hiking trail descriptions; find out about trail closures and campsite availability; get the weather forecast; browse through a gift shop; buy park passes and fishing licenses; and register for overnight backcountry trips.

The other source of park information is at **Kootenay Park Lodge,** at Vermilion Crossing (Apr.–May Fri.–Sun. 11 A.M.–6 P.M., June–Sept. daily 10 A.M.–7 P.M., and the early part of Oct. Fri.–Sun. 11 A.M.–6 P.M.). It's worth noting that this is the only privately operated official information center in any Canadian national park— a reflection on the folks running this lodge.

For further park information, contact the park superintendent (P.O. Box 220, Radium Hot Springs, BC V0A 1M0, 250/347-9615) or check the Parks Canada website (www.pc.gc.ca). For park road conditions, call 403/762-1450.

Canadian Rockies

Yoho National Park

Yoho, a Cree word of amazement, is a fitting name for this 131,300-hectare (324,450-acre) national park on the western slopes of the Canadian Rockies. East of Golden, the TransCanada Highway bisects the park. Kootenay National Park lies immediately to the south, while Banff National Park (Alberta) borders Yoho to the east.

Yoho is the smallest of the four contiguous Canadian Rockies national parks, but its wild and rugged landscape holds spectacular waterfalls, extensive icefields, a lake to rival those in Banff, and one of the world's most intriguing fossil beds. In addition, you'll find some of the finest hiking in all of Canada on the park's 300-kilometer (186-mile) trail system.

Within the park are four lodges, four campgrounds, and the small railway town of **Field,** offering basic services. The park is open year-round, although road conditions in winter can be treacherous, and occasional closures occur on Kicking Horse Pass. The road out to Takakkaw Falls is closed through winter, and it often doesn't reopen until mid-June.

THE LAND

The park extends west from the Continental Divide to the western main ranges of the Rocky Mountains. The jagged peaks along this section of the Continental Divide—including famous Mount Victoria, which forms the backdrop for Lake Louise—are some of the park's highest. But the award for Yoho's loftiest summit goes to 3,562-meter (11,686-foot) **Mount Goodsir,** southwest of the Continental Divide in the Ottertail Range.

The park's only watershed is that of the **Kicking Horse River,** which is fed by the Wapta and Waputik Icefields. The Kicking Horse, wide and braided for much of its course through the park, flows westward, joining the mighty Columbia River at Golden.

Flora

Elevations within the park cover a range of more than 2,500 meters (8,200 feet), making for distinct vegetation changes. Douglas fir is the climax

Elk are a common sight in Yoho National Park.

© ANDREW HEMPSTEAD

species at lower elevations, but lodgepole pine dominates areas affected by fire. Western red cedar, hemlock, and the delightful calypso orchid can be found in the damp valley around Emerald Lake. At higher elevations, where temperatures are lower and precipitation is higher, the familiar subalpine forests of Engelmann spruce and subalpine fir thrive. The northernmost extent of larch exists around Lake O'Hara. Larch is a conifer (evergreen), but its needles turn a stunning orange in fall—a photographer's delight. Above the tree line, where wind and rain have deposited soil, wildflowers such as heather, Indian paintbrush, and arnica create a carpet of color for a few short weeks midsummer.

Fauna

The animals for which Yoho is best known are fossilized in beds of shale and have been dead for over 500 million years. But they still create great interest for the role their remains have played in humanity's understanding of life on earth in prehistoric times. (See the sidebar, *Burgess Shale*.)

Large mammals are not as common in Yoho as in Kootenay National Park, simply because the

© AVALON TRAVEL PUBLISHING, INC.

Canadian Rockies

BURGESS SHALE

High on the rocky slopes above Mount Field is a layer of sedimentary rock known as the Burgess Shale, which contains what are considered to be the world's finest fossils from the Cambrian Period. The site is famous worldwide because it has unraveled the mysteries of a major stage of evolution.

In 1909, Smithsonian Institute paleontologist Charles Walcott was leading a pack train along the west slope of Mount Field, on the opposite side of the valley from the newly completed Spiral Tunnel, when he stumbled across these fossil beds. Encased in the shale, the fossils here are of marine invertebrates about 510 million years old. Generally, fossils are the remains of vertebrates, but at this site some freak event—probably a mudslide—suddenly buried thousands of soft-bodied animals (invertebrates), preserving them by keeping out the oxygen that would have decayed their delicate bodies. Walcott excavated an estimated 65,000 specimens from the site. Today paleontologists continue to uncover perfectly preserved fossils here—albeit in far fewer numbers than in Walcott's day. They've also uncovered additional fossil beds, similar in makeup and age, across the valley, on the north face of Mount Stephen.

Protected by UNESCO as a World Heritage Site, the two research areas are open only to those accompanied by a licensed guide. The **Burgess Shale Geoscience Foundation** (call 250/343-6006 or 800/343-3006 Mon.–Fri. 10 A.M.–3:30 P.M., www.burgess-shale.bc.ca) guides trips to both sites between July and mid-September. The access to **Walcott's Quarry** is along a strenuous 10-kilometer (6.2-mile) trail that gains 760 meters (2,500 feet) in elevation. Trips leave Friday–Monday at 8 A.M. from the trading post at the Field intersection, returning around 6:30 P.M.; $65 per person. Trips to the more easily reached **Mount Stephen Fossil Beds** depart Saturday and Sunday at 10 A.M., returning at around 4:30 P.M.; $45 per person. The trail to the Mount Stephen beds gains 520 meters (1,710 feet) of elevation in three kilometers (1.9 miles). The trails to both sites are unrelenting in their elevation gain—you must be fit to hike them. Reservations are a must.

terrain is so rugged. Valleys are inhabited by mule deer, elk, moose, and black bears, as well as a wide variety of smaller mammals. Porcupines are common along Yoho Valley Road. The park has a healthy population of grizzly bears, but sightings are relatively rare as the grizz tends to remain in remote valleys far from the busy TransCanada Highway corridor. Much of the park is above the tree line, where noisy marmots and pikas find a home, along with mountain goats. Around 200 bird species have been recorded within the park.

HISTORY

The Kootenay and Shuswap tribes of British Columbia were the first humans to travel through the rugged area that is now the national park. It's believed the men hid their families in the mountains before crossing over to the prairies to hunt buffalo and to trade with other tribes. On their return they set up seasonal camps along the Kicking Horse River to dry the buffalo meat and hides. They used a more northern route than that taken by travelers today, crossing the divide at Howse Pass and descending to the Kootenay Plains beyond the present-day junction of Highways 93 and 11.

The first Europeans to explore the valley of the Kicking Horse River were members of the 1858 Palliser Expedition, which set out to survey the west and report back to the British government on its suitability for settlement. The party approached from the south, climbing the Kootenay and Vermilion watersheds of present-day Kootenay National Park before descending to Wapta Falls. It was here that the unfortunate expedition geologist, Dr. James Hector, inadvertently gave the Kicking Horse River its name. While walking his horse over rough ground, he was kicked unconscious and took two hours to come to, by which time, so the story goes, other members of his party had begun digging his grave.

Guided by outfitter Tom Wilson, Major A. B. Rogers (for whom Rogers Pass to the west is named) surveyed Kicking Horse Pass in 1881. His favorable report to the Canadian Pacific Railway led to this route being chosen for the much-awaited transcontinental railway. The railbed was laid in 1884, and its grade was terribly steep; the first train to attempt the run suffered a brake failure and derailed, killing three workers. In 1909, after dozens more wrecks and derailments, the CPR rerouted the steepest section of the line through the Spiral Tunnels. The highway now follows the original rail grade.

The small township of Field started as a railway maintenance depot at the bottom of treacherous "Big Hill." In 1886 the Canadian Pacific Railway opened Mt. Stephen House in Field, as a dining stop for customers of the railway and to encourage visitors to this side of the mountains. The CPR then built lodges at several natural attractions in the area, including Emerald Lake Lodge in 1902, Lake O'Hara Lodge in 1913, and Wapta Lodge Bungalow Camp in 1921.

The coming of the railway was a prime catalyst in the formation of Yoho National Park. Upon the opening of the railway line in 1886, 2,600 hectares (6,425 acres) of land around the base of Mount Stephen were set aside as Mt. Stephen Park Reserve, Canada's second national park. In 1901 the reserve was expanded, and after three further boundary changes, the park of today came into being in 1930. Mining of lead, zinc, and silver continued until 1952, and today remnants of the Monarch and Kicking Horse mines can still be seen on the faces of Mount Stephen and Mount Field.

ROAD-ACCESSIBLE SIGHTS

As with all other parks of the Canadian Rockies, you don't need to travel deep into the backcountry to view the most spectacular features—many are visible from the roadside. The following sights are listed from east to west, starting at the park boundary (the Continental Divide).

Spiral Tunnel Viewpoint

The joy CPR president William Van Horne felt upon completion of his transcontinental rail line in 1886 was tempered by massive problems along a stretch of line west of Kicking Horse Pass. Big Hill was less than five kilometers (3.1 miles) long, but its gradient was so steep that runaway trains, crashes, and other disasters were common. A trail from Kicking Horse Campground takes you past the remains of one of those doomed trains.

Nearly 25 years after the line opened, railway engineers and builders finally solved the problem. By building two spiral tunnels down through two kilometers (1.2 miles) of solid rock to the valley floor, they lessened the grade dramatically and the terrors came to an end. Today the TransCanada Highway follows the original railbed. Along the way is a viewpoint with interpretive displays telling the fascinating story of Big Hill.

Yoho Valley

Fed by the Wapta Icefield in the far north of the park, the **Yoho River** flows through this spectacularly narrow valley, dropping more than 200 meters (660 feet) in the last kilometer before its confluence with the Kicking Horse River. The road leading up the valley passes the park's main campground, climbs a *very* tight series of switchbacks (watch for buses reversing through the middle section), and emerges at **Upper Spiral Tunnel Viewpoint,** which offers a different perspective on the aforementioned tunnel. A further 400 meters (.25 mile) along the road is a pullout for viewing the confluence of the Yoho and Kicking Horse Rivers—a particularly impressive sight as the former is glacier-fed and therefore silty, while the latter is lake-fed and clear.

Yoho Valley Road ends 14 kilometers (8.7 miles) from the main highway at **Takakkaw Falls,** the most impressive waterfall in the Canadian Rockies. The falls are fed by the Daly and Des Poilus Glaciers of the Waputik Icefield, which straddles the Continental Divide. Meaning "wonderful" in the language of the Cree, Takakkaw tumbles 254 meters (830 feet) over a

TAKAKKAW FALLS

The torrent, issuing from an icy cavern, rushes tempestuously down a deep, winding chasm till it gains the verge of the unbroken cliff, leaps forth in sudden wildness for a hundred and fifty feet, and then in a stupendous column of pure white sparkling water, broken by giant jets descending rocket-like and wreathed in volumed spray, dashes upon the rocks almost a thousand feet below, and, breaking into a milky series of cascading rushes for five hundred feet more, swirls into the swift current of the Yoho River.

—*Sir James Outram,* In the Heart of the Canadian Rockies

Much discussion is made of which is Canada's highest waterfall. Della Falls, on Vancouver Island, also in British Columbia, is 440 meters (1,440 feet), but this drop is broken by a ledge. Takakkaw Falls is considerably lower, at 254 meters (830 feet), but the drop is unbroken, which, officially, makes it Canada's highest. There is one thing of which there is no doubt: Takakkaw Falls will leave you breathless, much as it did famous alpinist Sir James Outram and everyone who has viewed the spectacle since.

Takakkaw Falls

© ANDREW HEMPSTEAD

sheer rock wall at the lip of the Yoho Valley, creating a spray bedecked by rainbows. It can be seen from the parking lot, but it's well worth the easy 10-minute stroll over the Yoho River to appreciate the sight in all its glory.

Natural Bridge

Three kilometers (1.9 miles) west of Field is the turnoff to famous Emerald Lake. On your way out to the lake, you pass another intriguing sight. At Natural Bridge, two kilometers (1.2 miles) down the road, the Kicking Horse River has worn a narrow hole through a limestone wall, creating a bridge. Over time, the bridge will collapse and, well, it won't be such an intriguing sight anymore. A trail leads to several view-

points—try to avoid the urge to join the idiots clambering over the top of the bridge.

Emerald Lake

Outfitter Tom Wilson stumbled on stunning Emerald Lake while guiding Major A. B. Rogers through the Kicking Horse River Valley in 1881. He was led to the lake by his horse, which had been purchased from natives. He later surmised that the horse had been accustomed to traveling up to the lake, meaning that the horse's former owners must have known about the lake before the white man arrived.

One of the jewels of the Canadian Rockies, the beautiful lake is surrounded by a forest of Engelmann spruce, as well as many peaks more than 3,000 meters (9,840 feet) high. It is covered in ice most of the year but comes alive with activity for a few short months in summer when hikers, canoeists, and horseback riders take advantage of the magnificent surroundings (see *Emerald Lake Hiking*). **Emerald Lake Lodge** is the grandest of Yoho's accommodations, offering a restaurant, café, lounge, and recreation facilities for both guests and nonguests (see *Accommodations and Camping*).

LAKE O'HARA

Nestled in a high bowl of lush alpine meadows, Lake O'Hara, 11 kilometers (6.8 miles) from the nearest public road, is surrounded by dozens of smaller alpine lakes and framed by spectacular peaks permanently mantled in snow. As if that weren't enough, the entire area is webbed by a network of hiking trails established over the last 90 years by luminaries such as Lawrence Grassi. Trails radiate from the lake in all directions; the longest is just 7.5 kilometers (4.7 miles), making Lake O'Hara an especially fine hub for day hiking. What makes this destination all the more special is that a quota system limits the number of visitors.

hiking through a high alpine meadow in Yoho National Park

© ANDREW HEMPSTEAD

Book the Bus

It's possible to walk to Lake O'Hara, but most visitors take the shuttle bus along a road closed to the public. The departure point is a signed parking lot 15 kilometers (9.3 miles) east of Field and three kilometers (1.9 miles) west of the Continental Divide. Buses for day visitors depart between mid-June and early October at 8:30 A.M. and 10:30 A.M., returning at 4:30 P.M. and 6:30 P.M. To book a seat, call the dedicated reservations line (250/343-6433). Reservations are taken up to three months in advance, but as numbers are limited, you will need to call *exactly* three months prior to get a seat; even then, call as early in the day as possible. Phone lines are open mid-March to April Monday–Thursday 8 A.M.–4 P.M., May Monday–Friday 8 A.M.–4 P.M., June–September daily 8 A.M.–4 P.M., and mid-September to early October Monday–Thursday 8 A.M.–4 P.M. The reservation fee is

$12 per booking and the bus fare is $15 per person round-trip. The procedure is simple enough, but to be assured a seat, it's important you get it right: for example, to visit on September 30 (when the larch are at their colorful peak), start dialing at 8 A.M. on June 30 (with a credit card ready). Six seats per day are set aside for those who haven't made advance reservations. They are allotted via the reservation number on a first-come, first-served basis. No-shows are filled on a standby basis by folks waiting around at the parking lot on the day of departure (generally, arrive around 7 A.M., head to the covered shelter, and you'll be the first in line). You have the best chance of snagging a seat on the 8:30 A.M. bus, especially if the weather is bad.

All times—bus departures and reservation center hours—are mountain standard time.

Other Considerations

After the 20-minute bus trip to the lake, day

hikers are dropped off at **Le Relais,** a homely log shelter where books and maps are sold, including the recommended Gem Trek *Lake Louise and Yoho* map. Hot drinks and light snacks are served—something to look forward to at the end of the day, as this is also the afternoon meeting place for the return trip (no reservations necessary).

Several overnight options are available at the lake—including a lodge, a campground, and a rustic hut—but each should be booked well in advance (see *Accommodations and Camping*).

Lake O'Hara Shoreline

• Length: 2.8 km/1.7 miles (40 minutes) one-way
• Elevation gain: minimal
• Rating: easy
• Trailhead: warden's cabin, across from Le Relais

Most people use sections of this easy loop around Lake O'Hara to access the trails, but it is an enjoyable walk in its own right, especially in the evening. Across from Le Relais, behind the warden's cabin, interpretive boards lay out the various options throughout the valley and explain local history. Heading in a clockwise direction from this point, the trail crosses Cataract Creek, the lake's outlet, then passes along the north shoreline, crossing gullies then reaching Seven Veil Falls at the 1.2-kilometer (.7-mile) mark. Traversing the cool, damp, southern shoreline, the trail passes branches to the Opabin Plateau and a short detour to Mary Lake. Lake O'Hara Lodge is passed at the 2.4-kilometer (1.5-mile) mark, from where it's a short stroll back along the road to Le Relais.

Lake Oesa

• Length: 3 km/1.9 miles (one hour) one-way
• Elevation gain: 240 meters/790 feet
• Rating: easy/moderate
• Trailhead: Shoreline Trail, 800 meters (.5 mile) beyond Cataract Creek

With the Continental Divide peaks of Mount Victoria (3,464 meters/11,365 feet) and Mount Lefroy (3,423 meters/11,230 feet) as a backdrop, this small aqua-colored lake surrounded by talus slopes is one of the area's gems. All the elevation gain is made in the first 2.4 km (1.6 miles), as the trail switchbacks to a ledge overlooking Lake O'Hara. The trail then levels out, passing three small bodies of water before climbing over a low rise and entering the cirque in which Lake Oesa lies.

Opabin Plateau Circuit

• Length: 5.9 km/3.7 miles (two hours) round-trip
• Elevation gain: 250 meters/820 feet
• Rating: easy/moderate
• Trailhead: Shoreline Trail

Separated from Lake Oesa by 2,848-meter (9,344-foot) Mount Yukness, this plateau high above the tree line dotted with small lakes is one of the most picturesque destinations in the Canadian Rockies. The time quoted is an absolute minimum because it's easy to spend an entire day exploring the alpine plateau and scrambling around the surrounding slopes. Two trails lead up to the plateau, which itself is laced with trails. The most direct route is the Opabin Plateau West Circuit, which branches right from the Shoreline Trail 300 meters (.2 mile) beyond Lake O'Hara Lodge. It then passes Mary Lake, climbs steeply, and reaches the plateau in a little less than two kilometers (1.2 miles). Opabin Prospect is an excellent lookout along the edge of the plateau. From this point, take the right forks to continue to the head of the Cirque and Opabin Lake. This section of trail passes through a lightly forested area of larch that comes alive with color the second week of September. From Opabin Lake, the East Circuit traverses the lower slopes of Yukness Mountain, passing Hungabee Lake then descending steeply to Lake O'Hara and ending back along the Shoreline Trail 600 meters (.4 mile) east of Lake O'Hara Lodge.

Lake McArthur

• Length: 3.5 km/2.2 miles (80 minutes) one-way
• Elevation gain: 300 meters (980 feet)
• Rating: easy/moderate
• Trailhead: Le Relais

A personal favorite, this trail leads to the largest

and (in my opinion) most stunning body of water in the Lake O'Hara area. Beginning from behind Le Relais, the trail passes through an open meadow and the Elizabeth Parker Hut; stay left to reach Schäffer Lake after 1.6 kilometers (one mile). At a junction beyond that lake, the left fork leads to Lake McArthur and the right fork to McArthur Pass. The lake option climbs steeply for 800 meters (.5 mile) then levels out and traverses a narrow ledge before entering the Lake McArthur Cirque. (Stay high, even if trails descending into the McArthur Valley look like they offer an easier approach.) After leveling off, the trail enters the alpine and quickly reaches its maximum elevation and the first views of Lake McArthur. Backed by Mount Biddle and the Biddle Glacier, the deep-blue lake and colorful alpine meadows are an unforgettable panorama.

Odaray Highline

- Length: 2.6 km/1.6 miles (one hour) one-way
- Elevation gain: 280 meters/920 feet
- Rating: easy/moderate
- Trailhead: Le Relais

For a panoramic overview of the Lake O'Hara area with a minimum of energy output, it's hard to beat this trail, which ends atop the Odaray Plateau west of the lake. This trail passes through an important wildlife corridor, and a voluntary program to limit use—and therefore human interference—is in place. Check with park staff for the latest access restrictions. From Le Relais, follow the Lake McArthur Trail to Schäffer Lake as detailed previously, then take the right fork, which climbs gently toward McArthur Pass. Just before the pass, take the right fork. From this point, it's a steep one kilometer (.6 mile) up to the lofty perch below Odaray Mountain.

Cathedral Basin

- Length: 7.5 km/4.7 miles (2.5 hours) one-way
- Elevation gain: 300 meters/980 feet
- Rating: moderate
- Trailhead: Lake O'Hara Campground

The trail out to Cathedral Basin is the longest in the Lake O'Hara area, yet it's still an easy day trip for most people. Reach the trailhead from Le Relais by walking the short distance back down the access road or by following Cataract Creek downstream from behind the warden's cabin. From the campground the trail heads northwest, crossing Morning Glory Creek at the 2.4-kilometer (1.5-mile) mark then passing Linda Lake. The final ascent to Cathedral Basin makes a wide loop through an area of ancient rock slides. From this point, the magnificent panorama of the Lake O'Hara area and the backdrop of the Continental Divide are laid out to the southeast.

EMERALD LAKE HIKING
Emerald Lake Loop

- Length: 5.2 km/3.2 miles (1.5 hours) round-trip
- Elevation gain: minimal
- Rating: easy
- Trailhead: Emerald Lake parking lot, nine km (5.6 miles) from Highway 1

One of the easiest yet most enjoyable walks in Yoho is around the park's most famous lake. The trail encircles the lake and can be hiked in either direction. The best views are from the western shoreline, where a massive avalanche has cleared away the forest of Engelmann spruce. Across the lake from this point, Mount Burgess can be seen rising an impressive 2,599 meters (8,530 feet). Traveling in a clockwise direction, beyond the avalanche slope, the trail to Emerald Basin veers off to the left, and at the 2.2-kilometer (1.4-mile) mark, a small bridge is crossed. Views from this point extend back across the lodge to the Ottertail Range. Beyond the lake's inlet, the vegetation changes dramatically. A lush forest of towering western red cedar creates a canopy, protecting moss-covered fallen trees, thimbleberry, and bunchberry extending to the water's edge. Just over one kilometer (.6 mile) from the bridge, the trail divides: the left fork leads back to the parking lot via a small forest-encircled pond, while the path straight ahead passes through the grounds of Emerald Lake Lodge. Park staff lead a guided hike around the lake every Saturday morning, departing at 10 A.M. from the parking lot trailhead.

Hamilton Falls

- Length: 800 meters/.5 mile (40 minutes) one-way
- Elevation gain: 60 meters/200 feet
- Rating: easy
- Trailhead: information kiosk, Emerald Lake parking lot

The trail to these falls begins from the Emerald Lake parking lot, down the hill from the bridge to the lodge. It's an easy walk through a forest of Engelmann spruce and subalpine fir to a viewpoint at the base of the falls. A little farther along, the trail begins switchbacking steeply and offers even better views of the cascade.

The trail continues beyond the waterfall to **Hamilton Lake,** which lies in a small glacial cirque a steep 880 vertical meters (2,890 feet) above Emerald Lake. Total distance from Emerald Lake to Hamilton Lake is 5.5 km/3.4 miles (2.5 hours) one-way.

Emerald Basin

- Length: 4.5 km/2.8 miles (1.5–2 hours) one-way
- Elevation gain: 280 meters/920 feet
- Rating: easy/moderate
- Trailhead: Emerald Lake Loop, 1.5 kilometers (.9 mile) from the parking lot

The trail to the delightful Emerald Basin begins from the west shore of Emerald Lake, from where it's a steady three-kilometer (1.9-mile) climb through a subalpine forest to the basin, which, chances are, you'll have to yourself. The most impressive sight awaiting you there is the south wall of the President Range, towering 800 vertical meters (2,625 feet) above.

YOHO VALLEY HIKING

The valley for which the park is named lies north of the TransCanada Highway. As well as the sights discussed previously, it provides many fine opportunities for serious day hikers to get off the beaten track. The following day hikes begin from different trailheads near the end of the road up Yoho Valley. In each case, leave your vehicle in the Takakkaw Falls parking lot.

Twin Falls

- Length: 8 km/5 miles (2.5 hours) one-way
- Elevation gain: 300 meters/980 feet
- Rating: moderate
- Trailhead: Takakkaw Falls parking lot, 14 km (8.7 miles) from Highway 1

This trail takes over where the road through the Yoho Valley ends, continuing in a northerly direction up the Yoho River to Twin Falls, passing many other waterfalls along the way. At spectacular Twin Falls, water from the Wapta Icefield divides in two before plunging off an 80-meter-high (262-foot-high) cliff. Mother Nature may work in amazing ways, but sometimes she needs a helping hand—or so the CPR thought. In the 1920s, the company dynamited one of the channels to make the falls more symmetrical. **Twin Falls Chalet** was built below the falls by the CPR in 1923 and today offers hikers light snacks through the middle of the day.

Iceline

- Length: 6.4 km/4 miles (2.5 hours) one-way
- Elevation gain: 690 meters/2,260 feet
- Rating: moderate/difficult
- Trailhead: Whiskey Jack Hostel

Constructed in 1987, this is one of the most spectacular day hikes in the Canadian Rockies. The length given is from Whiskey Jack Hostel to the highest point along the trail (2,250 meters/7,380 feet). (Day hikers are asked to leave their vehicles across the road from the hostel, in the Takakkaw Falls parking lot.) From the hostel, the trail begins a steep and steady one-kilometer (.6-mile) climb to a point where three options present themselves: the Iceline Trail is to the right, Yoho Pass is straight ahead, and Hidden Lakes is a 300-meter (.2-mile) detour to the left. The Iceline Trail option now enters its highlight—a four-kilometer (2.5-mile) traverse of a moraine below Emerald Glacier. Views across the valley improve as the trail climbs to its 2,220-meter (7,283-foot) crest. Many day hikers return from this point, although officially the trail continues into Little Yoho River Valley. Another option is to continue beyond Celeste Lake and loop back to Takakkaw Falls and the original trailhead, a total distance of 18 kilometers (11.2 miles).

Yoho Pass
• Length: 4.7 km/2.9 miles (two hours) one-way
• Elevation gain: 530 meters/1,740 feet
• Rating: moderate
• Trailhead: Whiskey Jack Hostel

The trail to Yoho Pass, which can be combined with the Iceline Trail, officially begins on the west side of Whiskey Jack Hostel, but hikers are asked to leave their vehicles across the road in the Takakkaw Falls parking lot. It leads 3.7 kilometers (2.3 miles) to picturesque, spruce-encircled Yoho Lake, then continues another easy one kilometer (.6 mile) to the pass. The pass is below the tree line, so views are limited, but from this point it's 5.5 kilometers (3.4 miles) and an elevation loss of 530 meters (1,740 feet) down to Emerald Lake; six kilometers (3.7 miles) and an elevation gain of 300 meters (985 feet) to spectacular Burgess Pass; or 2.4 kilometers (1.5 miles) north, with little elevation gain or loss, to an intersection with the Iceline Trail.

HIKES IN OTHER AREAS OF THE PARK

The hikes detailed as follows are along the Trans-Canada Highway. The hike to the world-famous Burgess Shale is detailed in the corresponding sidebar, *Burgess Shale.*

Paget Lookout
• Length: 3.5 km/2.2 miles (90 minutes) one-way
• Elevation gain: 520 meters/1,700 feet
• Rating: moderate
• Trailhead: Wapta Lake picnic area five km (3.1 miles) west of the Continental Divide

The trail to this viewpoint is moderately strenuous but worthwhile for the panorama of the Kicking Horse River Valley. The first section of trail traverses a forest of Engelmann spruce. Then the trail breaks out above the tree line just below the lookout, the site of an abandoned fire tower. As an alternative, branch right 1.4 kilometers (.9 mile) along the trail and continue two kilometers (1.2 miles) to **Sherbrooke Lake,** which is fed by the Waputik Icefield.

Hoodoo Trail
• Length: 3 km/1.9 miles (60–90 minutes) one-way
• Elevation gain: 460 meters/1,510 feet
• Rating: moderate
• Trailhead: Hoodoo Creek Campground, 23 km (14.3 miles) southwest of Field

Hoodoos are found in varying forms throughout the Canadian Rockies, but this outcrop, officially known as the Leanchoil Hoodoos, is among the most impressive. Hoodoos are formed by the erosion of relatively soft rock from beneath a cap of harder, more weather-resistant rock. Although these examples require some effort to reach, their intriguing appearance makes the trip worthwhile. The first half of the trail is relatively flat, leaving all the elevation gain to be made in the last, painful 1.5 kilometers (.9 mile).

Wapta Falls
• Length: 2.4 km/1.5 miles (45 minutes) one-way
• Elevation loss: minimal
• Rating: easy
• Trailhead: unmarked parking lot beside Highway 1, 25 km (15.5 miles) west of Field and five kilometers (3.1 miles) east of park boundary

In the park's extreme southwestern corner, this trail follows an old fire road for three kilometers (1.9 miles), then narrows for an easy stroll through thick forest to a viewpoint above these 30-meter-high (100-foot-high) falls on the Kicking Horse River. A steep, switchbacking descent leads 500 meters (.3 mile) to a viewpoint at the base of the falls.

OTHER RECREATION
Boating and Fishing
No river or stream is particularly well known for fishing, mainly because most of the water is glacially derived and therefore heavily silt-laden. Species present in the park's lakes and rivers include Dolly Varden, rainbow, lake, and cutthroat trout. A national park **fishing permit** costs $7 for seven days or $20 annually. **Emerald Lake Canoe Rentals** (250/343-6000; June–Sept.

9 A.M.–8 P.M.), in a small boatshed on the shore of Emerald Lake, rents canoes and small boats for $20 per hour, $35 for two hours, or $60 all day. Fishing in Emerald Lake isn't world-class, but there are some trout in the waters, and Emerald Lake Canoe Rentals offers a range of fishing tackle for rent or sale.

Horseback Riding
Emerald Lake Stables, at the lake of the same name (250/344-8982) rents, horses through the mid-June to early September season. A one-hour trip along the west shore of Emerald Lake costs $35. Two-hour rides are $70, three-hour rides $100, four-hour rides $130, and all-day rides with lunch go for $175.

Wintertime
The TransCanada Highway through the park is open year-round, but facilities are open only June through mid-September. Some of the trails at higher elevations are impassable until July. Wintertime attracts cross-country skiers who happily slide along the Yoho Valley to frozen Takakkaw Falls or follow the Lake O'Hara trails.

ACCOMMODATIONS AND CAMPING
The park provides a variety of options, all well-priced in comparison to Banff. Some travelers make Yoho a base for an entire Canadian Rockies vacation, traveling to Banff (just over an hour's drive east) or Golden (under an hour west) for supplies and civilized diversions.

Under $50
Hostelling International operates **HI–Whiskey Jack Wilderness Hostel** (403/760-7580 or 866/762-4122, www.hihostels.ca; mid-June–Sept.) in a meadow opposite Takakkaw Falls. Formerly cabins used by the CPR, then staff quarters for a privately run lodge that was destroyed by an avalanche, the hostel provides basic dormitory accommodations for up to 27 guests, who have use of a communal kitchen and showers. Members of Hostelling International pay $19 per night, nonmembers $23. Check-in is 5–11 P.M.

$100–150
The streets of Field are lined with private homes offering reasonably priced overnight accommodations in rooms of varying privacy and standard. One of the better choices is the **Alpine Guesthouse** (313 2nd Ave., 250/343-6878, www.alpineguesthouse.ca), with a two-bedroom suite—complete with a kitchen, cable TV, outdoor patio, and private entrance—for $130 per night. Like everywhere else in Field, it's within walking distance of the general store.

Also in Field is simple yet elegant **Kicking Horse Lodge** (100 Centre St., 250/343-6303 or 800/659-4944, www.kickinghorselodge.net), which offers 14 well-furnished motel-like rooms, a large comfortable lounge, and a restaurant (open in summer only). In July and August, rates are $145–160 s, $160–180 s or d with a kitchenette. The rest of the year, these same rooms are discounted as low as $80.

Over $150
N Emerald Lake Lodge (403/410-7417 or 800/663-6336, www.crmr.com) is a grand, luxury-class accommodation along the southern shore of one of the Canada's most magnificent lakes. Guests lap up the luxury of richly decorated duplex-style units and freestanding cabins. Each spacious unit is outfitted in an earthy heritage theme and has a wood-burning fireplace, private balcony, luxurious bathroom, comfortable bed topped by a plush duvet, and in-room coffee. Other lodge amenities include a hot tub and sauna, swimming pool, restaurant, lounge, and café. Guests can also go horseback riding or go boating and fishing on Emerald Lake. Rack rates start at $480 s or d, but book online for as low as $330 in summer and as low as $150 in November.

Comprising 29 cabins set around a main lodge alongside the Kicking Horse River, the **Cathedral Mountain Lodge** (250/343-6442, www.cathedralmountain.com; mid-May–Sept.; $365 s or d) complex lies one kilometer (.6 mile) along Yoho Valley Road from the TransCanada Highway. In recent years the original cabins have been replaced by fancy log chalets, with modern amenities and plenty of space to spread out. Each has a log bed, stone fireplace, bathroom with soaker tub, and private deck; A smallish restaurant (daily 7 A.M.–10 P.M.) and grocery store, both open to nonguests, are on the premises.

Spending a night at **Lake O'Hara Lodge** (250/343-6418, www.lakeohara.com) is a special experience, and one that draws familiar faces year and after year. On a practical level, it allows hikers not equipped for overnight camping the opportunity to explore one of the finest hiking destinations in all of the Canadian Rockies at their leisure. The 15 cabins, each with a private bathroom, are spread around the lakeshore, while within the main lodge are eight rooms, most of which are twins and share bathrooms. Rates of $420 d for a room in the main lodge (shared bathrooms) and $575–625 d for a lakeside cabin include all meals, taxes, gratuities, and transportation mid-June to September. Guests are transported to the lodge, which is 13 kilometers (eight miles) from Highway 1, by shuttle bus from a parking lot three kilometers (1.9 miles) west of the Continental Divide and 15 kilometers (nine miles) east of Field. Between February and April, the eight rooms in the main lodge are available for cross-country skiers for $240 per person, inclusive of meals and ski tours.

Campgrounds

As in other national parks, no reservations are taken for camping in Yoho's vehicle-accessible campgrounds. All sites have a picnic table and fire ring, with a fire permit costing $6 (includes firewood). When all campgrounds are filled, campers will be directed to overflow areas.

The park's main camping area is **Kicking Horse Campground** (mid-May–mid-Oct.; $22 per site), five kilometers (3.1 miles) northeast of Field along the road to Takakkaw Falls. Facilities include coin showers ($1), flush toilets, and kitchen shelters. Back toward the TransCanada Highway, **Monarch Campground** ($14 per site) offers more-limited facilities and less-private sites; **Hoodoo Creek Campground,** along the Trans-Canada Highway 23 kilometers (14 miles) southwest of Field, provides 106 private sites among the trees for $17 per vehicle. Facilities include

flush toilets, hot water, kitchen shelters, and an interpretive program.

At the end of the road up the Yoho Valley, **Takakkaw Falls Campground** (July–mid-Sept.; $14) is designed for tent campers only. Park at the end of the road and load up the carts with your gear for a pleasant 400-meter (.2-mile) walk along the valley floor. No showers are provided, and the only facilities are pit toilets and picnic tables.

Just below **Lake O'Hara,** alongside the access road, is a delightful little campground surrounded by some of the region's finest hiking. Each of 30 sites has a tent pad, fire pit, and picnic table, while other facilities include pit toilets, two kitchen shelters with woodstoves, and bearproof food caches. Reservations for sites are made in conjunction with the bus trip along the restricted-access road from Highway 1 to Lake O'Hara; for bus information see *Lake O'Hara.* Even though access is aboard a bus, you should treat the trip as one into the backcountry; passengers are limited to one large or two small bags, and no coolers or fold-up chairs are permitted on board the shuttle. Camping is $8 per person per night, the bus costs $15 per person round-trip, and the reservation fee is $12 per booking. Make reservations as far in advance as possible.

FOOD

Field

In downtown Field, **Truffle Pigs Café** (318 Stephen St., 250/343-6462) is one of those unexpected finds that make traveling such a joy. It's at the back of a general store, beyond racks of food basics and rental movies, with seating in a section off to the side or outside on a small patio. The best of the breakfast and lunch dishes are described on a massive blackboard, with freshly baked cookies and locally brewed coffee complementing sandwiches made to order from the glass-fronted deli. In the evening this place really shines, with dishes as adventurous as the spinach maple pecan salad ($11) and as simple as an Albertan-raised buffalo ribeye steak served with a port-based au jus and a baked potato ($25). It's open in summer daily 7:30 A.M.–10 P.M.; the rest of the year it's also open daily, but dinner is served only Friday and Saturday.

Across the road, the **Kicking Horse Lodge** (250/343-6303; daily 8 A.M.–11 A.M., noon–2:30 P.M., and 5–9 P.M.) has a small restaurant that has views over the valley floor. It offers a short but varied dinner menu featuring dishes of wide-ranging appeal (including a delicious herb-crusted pork tenderloin smothered in a mango apple chutney) as well as a daily special and a soup of the day, both of which actually are *special.*

Other Dining Options

Overlooking an arm of Emerald Lake, **Cilantro on the Lake** (250/343-6321; summer only) is a casual café featuring magnificent views from tables inside an open-fronted, log chalet-style building or out on the lakefront deck. The menu is varied—you can sit and sip a coffee or have a full lunch or dinner. Starters—such as thick and creamy corn and potato chowder—are all less than $10, while mains, such as an extravagantly rich beef tenderloin served with a lobster and mushroom cream sauce, range $22–33. The café is part of the **Emerald Lake Lodge** resort complex, which also includes a more formal but historically attractive dining room, where dinner dishes such as grilled caribou with huckleberry sauce ($32) are served daily from 6 P.M. This restaurant is also open year-round for breakfast and lunch, or choose the more casual lounge bar and sink into one of the comfy couches with an abbreviated but still appealing menu.

OTHER PRACTICALITIES

Information

The main source of information about the park is the **Field Visitor Centre** on the TransCanada Highway at Field (250/343-6783; summer daily 9 A.M.–7 p.m., the rest of year daily 9 A.M.–4 p.m.). Inside you'll find helpful staff, information boards, and interpretive panels. This is also the place to pick up backcountry camping permits, buy topographical maps, and find out schedules for campground interpretive programs. For more information, contact Yoho National Park (P.O. Box 99, Field, BC V0A 1G0, www.pc.gc.ca). For park road conditions, call 403/762-1450; for avalanche reports, call 403/762-1460.

Transportation

Transportation to and around the park is limited. **Greyhound** (403/762-6767) stops in Field daily on its route between Banff and Golden, from where it continues west to Vancouver. **Brewster** (403/762-6767) offers a 3.5-hour tour of the park, departing Lake Louise daily at 12:30 P.M. (summer only). This tour takes in the Yoho Valley and Emerald Lake. The cost is adult $53, child $26.50. Brewster's Mountain Lakes and Waterfalls Tour is an extended version of the previous tour, combining the best of Banff National Park with a trip over the divide into Yoho. It departs the Banff depot mid-June to early October daily at 8:10 A.M. The tour takes nine hours and costs $70 per person.

Golden

From the western boundary of Yoho National Park, the TransCanada Highway meanders down the beautiful Kicking Horse River Valley to the town of Golden (pop. 5,500), at the confluence of the Kicking Horse and Columbia Rivers. As well as being a destination in itself, Golden makes a good central base for exploring the region or as an overnight stop on a tour through the Canadian Rockies that takes in the national parks on the western side of the Continental Divide.

Although Golden is an industrial town through and through—with local mines and huge logging operations that include a lumber mill that opened in 1999—it's also gaining a reputation for local outdoor-recreation opportunities, most notably for its new four-season resort and white-water-rafting trips down the Kicking Horse River.

SIGHTS AND RECREATION

Take Highway 95 off the TransCanada Highway and you'll find yourself in the old section of town, a world away from the commercial strip along the main highway. There's not really much to see in town, although you may want to check out the small museum on 14th Street. The 8.8-kilometer (5.5-mile) **Rotary Loop** is a paved walking and biking trail that leads across the river from downtown via an impressive timber-frame pedestrian bridge then upstream across Highway 95 (10th Avenue South) to the campground.

The **Columbia River Wetland** (see *Radium Hot Springs and Vicinity*) extends as far north as Golden. One easily accessible point of the wetlands is **Reflection Lake,** on the southern outskirts of Golden. A small shelter provides a telescope for viewing the abundant birdlife.

Kicking Horse Mountain Resort

Kicking Horse Mountain Resort (250/439-5400 or 866/754-5425, www.kickinghorseresort.com) is a work in progress—a world-class, four-season destination resort that is being developed on the outskirts of Golden. The eight-person detachable Golden Eagle Express transports visitors high into the alpine late June through early September in just 18 minutes. The 360-degree panorama at the summit is equal to any other accessible point in the Canadian Rockies, with the Purcell Mountains immediately to the west and the Columbia Valley laid out below. Graded hiking trails lead from the upper terminal through a fragile, treeless environment, while mountain bikers revel in a challenging descent in excess of 1,000 meters (3,280 feet). The resort has also constructed a sanctuary for orphaned grizzly bears—an interesting diversion for visitors that is included in the price of a gondola ride. A single ride is adult $20, senior $17, child $11. A better deal are the lunchtime combo tickets for adult $29, senior $26, child $13. Mountain bikers pay $20 for a single ride or $32 to ride all day. A rent-and-ride package costs $63 for the full day, including a full-suspension bike. The gondola operates through summer Monday–Thursday 11 A.M.–8 P.M., Friday–Sunday 11 A.M.–10 P.M. For dining details, see *Food.*

With a vertical rise of 1,260 meters (4,130 feet), 50 percent of terrain designated for experts, lots of dry powder snow, and minimal crowds, Kicking Horse has developed a big reputation since opening for the 2000–2001 winter season. In addition to the 3.5-kilometer-long (2.2-mile-long) gondola ride, other chairlifts transport skiers and boarders to hidden bowls and, as of the 2002–2003 season, to a high point of 2,450 meters (8,040 feet), giving the resort North America's third-highest vertical rise (1,260 meters/4,135 feet). Lifts operate mid-December to early April and tickets are adult $56, senior and child $24. Facilities in the base lodge include rentals, a cafeteria, and a ski school, while the summit restaurant is also open daily for lunch and Friday and Saturday for dinner. To get to Kicking Horse, follow the signs from Highway 1 into town and take 7th Street North west from 10th Avenue North; it's over the Columbia River and 13 kilometers (eight miles) uphill from this intersection.

GOLDEN

To Blaeberry
Mountain Lodge
and Revelstoke

GREYHOUND BUS
DEPOT

14TH ST N

LEGENDZ
DINER

Hospital Creek

VISITOR INFO CENTRE (SEASONAL)

PONDEROSA
MOTOR INN

HUSKY GAS
STATION

COUNTRY GARDEN
RESTAURANT

To Golf Course
and Kicking
Horse Mountain
Resort

DYKE RD

9TH ST N

FISHER RD

95

7TH ST N

10TH AVE N

GOLDEN DONALD UPPER RD

To Kicking Horse
River Chalets and
Yoho National Park

GOLDEN VISITOR
INFO CENTRE

TRANSCANADA HWY

GOLDEN VIEW RD

BACCHUS
BOOKS

Columbia River

Kicking

GOLDEN BAKERY & DELI

5TH ST S

7TH ST S

6TH AVE S

7TH AVE S

8TH AVE S

Horse

River

KICKING HORSE GRILL

GOLDEN
MUNICIPAL
CAMPGROUND

9TH ST S

10TH ST S

11TH ST S

12TH ST S

13TH ST S

9TH AVE S

10TH AVE S

13TH AVE S

SPRUCE DR

95

VIEWING
SHELTER

Reflection
Lake

SCALE NOT AVAILABLE

To Cedar House
Café and Radium
Hot Springs

© AVALON TRAVEL PUBLISHING, INC.

White-Water Rafting

Anyone looking for white-water-rafting action will want to run the Kicking Horse River. The rafting season runs late May to mid-September, with river levels at their highest in late June. The Lower Canyon, immediately upstream of Golden, offers the biggest thrills, including a three-kilometer (1.9-mile) stretch of continuous rapids. Upstream of here the river is tamer but still makes for an exciting trip, while even farther upstream, near the western boundary of Yoho National Park, it's more of a float—a good adventure for the more timid visitor. The river is run by several companies, most of which offer the option of half-day ($60–80) or full-day ($100–150) trips. The cost varies with inclusions such as transportation from Banff and lunch.

Alpine Rafting (250/344-6778 or 888/599-5299) offers trips that range from a family-friendly float to the excitement of descending the Lower Canyon. Other local companies include **Wet 'n' Wild Adventures** (250/344-6546 or 800/668-9119), **Glacier Raft Company** (250/344-6521), **Kootenay River Runners** (250/347-9210 or 800/599-4399), and **Canadian Rockies Rafting** (403/678-6535 or 877/226-7625).

Other Summertime Recreation

Golden Golf and Country Club (250/344-2700 or 866/727-7222) is a challenging 18-hole course in a forested section of the valley through town and to the north. This course is generally in excellent condition, with water coming into play on many holes—including the signature 11th and 12th holes along Holt Creek—and numerous streams and lakes to catch wayward shots. Greens fees are $60, or there's a $46 twilight rate.

Check out the website of **Golden Mountain Adventures** (www.adventurerockies.com) for the full range of activities available in the valley. This company can also book packages using local operators and accommodations.

Adventurous souls are drawn to Golden for its thermals, perfect for hang-gliding and paragliding, and to the steep face of Jubilee Mountain, a renowned sport-climbing destina-tion. Cowboys descend on town the first weekend of August for **Golden Rodeo Days.**

ACCOMMODATIONS AND CAMPING

You can stay in one of the regular motels lining the highway, but don't. Instead, choose one of the unique mountain lodgings that surround the town.

$50–100

Blaeberry Mountain Lodge (250/344-5296, www.blaeberrymountainlodge.bc.ca) is on a 62-hectare (150-acre) property among total wilderness. Rooms are in the main lodge or self-contained cabins, with plenty of activities available to guests. Standard rooms with shared bathroom are $75 s or d, and the large cabins, which feature a separate bedroom and full kitchen, are $145. Breakfast and dinner are offered for $12 and $22, respectively. Blaeberry is nine kilometers (5.6 miles) north of Golden along Highway 1 then seven kilometers (4.3 miles) farther north along Moberly School Road.

If you must stay in a motel, and don't want to spend a fortune, choose the distinctive two-story, lime-green **Ponderosa Motor Inn** (on the Trans-Canada by 12th Ave., 250/344-2205 or 800/881-4233, www.ponderosamotorinn.bc.ca). It has 85 older rooms but offers impressive mountain views, a hot tub, a picnic area and gazebo, and a playground, making it a good value at just $78 s, $88 d ($52 s, $60 d outside of summer).

$100–150

The folks that operate the **Cedar House Café** (735 Hefti Rd., 250/344-4679, www.cedar-housecafe.com) have restored an adjacent cabin, infusing a modern feel without losing any of the property's original charm. Sleeping up to four people, the cabin is spacious and comes with a full kitchen, a wood-burning stove, a laundry, and TV/VCR. It costs just $150 per night.

Over $150

Along Highway 1, a 20-minute drive from Golden back toward Yoho National Park, **Kicking**

Horse River Chalets (2924 Kicking Horse Rd., 866/502-5171, www.kickinghorseriverchalets .com) comprises luxurious peeled-log cabins, each with full kitchen and dishwasher, wood-burning fireplace, balcony, and loft. The rate is $240 per night for up to four people.

Campgrounds

Continue south through the old part of town over the Kicking Horse River and take 9th Street South east at the traffic lights to reach **Golden Municipal Campground** (250/344-5412; mid-May–mid-Oct.). It's a quiet place, strung out along the river and two kilometers (1.2 miles) from downtown along a riverfront walkway. Facilities include picnic shelters, hot coin-operated showers, and 70 sites with fire pits. Adjacent is a recreation center with a swimming pool and fitness facility. Unpowered sites are $16, powered sites $18.

Golfers can stay out at the golf course in a specially developed area for $15 per night.

FOOD

Start your day with the locals at the **Golden Bakery & Deli** (419 9th Ave., 250/344-2928; Mon.–Sat. 6:30 A.M.–6 P.M.), where the coffee is always fresh and the faces friendly. Baked goodies include breads, pastries, cakes, and meat pies, with inexpensive daily specials displayed on a blackboard in a seating section off to the side of the main counter.

Constructed of rough-cut logs complete with bulging burls, the **Kicking Horse Grill** (1105 9th St. S, 250/344-2330; daily from 5:30 P.M.) is one of Golden's finest restaurants. The menu changes with the seasons but always offers distinctly international dishes ranging from paella to sushi. All but the beef dishes are less than $20, with generously portioned starter salads ranging $6.50–8.50.

At an elevation of 2,347 meters (7,700 feet), the **Eagle's Eye Restaurant** is the crowning glory of Kicking Horse Mountain Resort (250/439-5400 or 866/754-5425) and is Canada's highest restaurant. Access is by gondola from the resort's base village, 13 kilometers (eight miles)

west of downtown Golden. As you'd expect, the views are stunning and are set off by a stylish timber and stonework interior, including a floor-to-ceiling fireplace and a wide wraparound deck protected from the wind by glass paneling. It's open daily at 11 A.M. for a lunch costing adult $29, senior $26, child $13, which includes the gondola ride. Between 7 and 10 P.M. the setting becomes more romantic and the food more adventurous, but it remains distinctly Canadian. Dinner mains range $25–40 and include such delights as salmon baked in a saffron-vanilla cream and served with strawberry salsa ($28). All evening diners enjoy a complimentary gondola ride. Reservations required.

A five-minute drive south of Golden off Highway 95, the **Cedar House Café** (735 Hefti Rd., 250/344-4679; daily 5–10:30 P.M.) is an excellent choice for wonderfully-flavored food that takes advantage of seasonal Canadian produce. The nightly pasta specials are a good deal, or stick to menu choices such as oyster mushroom enchiladas ($18) and green Thai prawn curry ($16). The dining room is in a log building, but on warmer evenings you'll want to be outside on the deck.

OTHER PRACTICALITIES

Information and Services

The year-round **Golden Visitor Info Centre** is in the old railway station building (500 10th Avenue, 250/344-7125 or 800/622-4653, www .tourismgolden.com; weekdays 8:30 A.M.–4:30 P.M.). Back out on the highway is a seasonal information center (summer daily 9 A.M.–5 P.M.) in a converted gas station beside the Ponderosa Motor Inn. In addition to all the regular brochure racks, it has public Internet access and a handy map of local bike trails.

While accommodations, fast-food restaurants, and gas stations line the TransCanada Highway, downtown Golden holds other basic services, including the **post office** (502 9th Ave.). Ninth Avenue also has outdoor equipment shops and **Bacchus Books** (421 9th Ave., 250/344-5600; Mon.–Sat. 10 A.M.–6 P.M.), offering a wide selection of new and used books, with plenty of local reading and detailed maps of the Columbia Valley.

Transportation

Greyhound buses stop four times daily in Golden, utilizing an ATCO trailer tucked away beside the Esso gas station as a depot (250/344-6172). For a cab, call **Mount Seven Taxi** (250/344-5237).

Central British Columbia

Ranging from the western slopes of the Rocky Mountains to the Pacific Ocean, central British Columbia holds such varied natural features as the massive Fraser River, the lofty peaks of the Cariboo and Coast Mountains, and the deeply indented coastal fjords around Bella Coola.

The region's history is dominated by colorful sagas of Canada's biggest gold rush, when over 100,000 miners and fortune seekers passed through the area on their way to the goldfields. But the best remembered man in these parts was not a miner but an explorer. In 1793, Alexander Mackenzie left the Fraser River for the final leg of his epic transcontinental journey. Fourteen days later he reached the Pacific Ocean, becoming the first person to cross the continent.

Today the most heavily traveled route through central B.C. is the TransCanada Highway, which for the purposes of this book also forms the region's southern boundary. In the east of the province, the highway bisects **Glacier National Park,** a small but spectacular park of glaciers and towering peaks. Heading west from the park, the highway passes the heli-skiing hub of

© ANDREW HEMPSTEAD

Must-Sees

M Meadows in the Sky Parkway: From the TransCanada Highway, this road climbs to a magnificent alpine meadow high above the tree line (page 372).

M The Last Spike: Railway buffs, in particular, will enjoy seeing the spot where the final link was made in Canada's transcontinental railway (page 376).

M Wells Gray Provincial Park: Waterfalls and wildlife combine to make this a worthwhile detour between Kamloops and Jasper (page 385).

M Mount Robson Provincial Park: It's impossible not to be impressed on the drive into Mount Robson Provincial Park, unless of course clouds are covering the highest peak in the Canadian Rockies (page 390).

M Historic Hat Creek Ranch: Over 100 years since the Cariboo Wagon Road bustled with miners heading north in search of their fortune, it's still possible to experience the frontier feeling at this historic ranch (page 393).

Mount Robson

M Williams Lake Stampede: Rodeos take place across British Columbia, but none are bigger than the Williams Lake Stampede, on the first weekend of July (page 398).

M Bowron Lake Provincial Park: The main attraction in this park is the wilderness canoe circuit, but it's also worth visiting for its scenic locale—and hopefully you'll find time to go for a quick paddle (page 405).

© ANDREW HEMPSTEAD

Central British Columbia

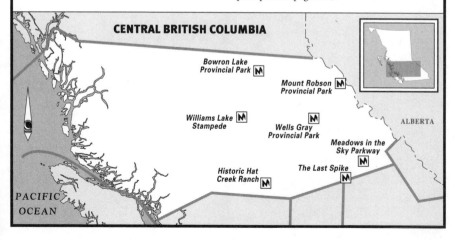

CENTRAL BRITISH COLUMBIA

Bowron Lake
Provincial Park **M**

Mount Robson **M**
Provincial Park

Williams Lake **M**
Stampede

M
Wells Gray
Provincial Park

ALBERTA

Meadows in the
Sky Parkway **M**

Historic Hat
Creek Ranch **M**

The Last Spike **M**

PACIFIC
OCEAN

Revelstoke and the watery playground of **Shuswap Lake** before coming to the large population center of **Kamloops.**

From Kamloops, two highways lead north. Highway 5 accesses **Wells Gray** and **Mount Robson Provincial Parks,** the former a vast forested wilderness and the latter named for one of the most spectacular mountain peaks in all of Canada. The other route, Highway 97, runs through **Cariboo Country,** best-known for the 1860s' gold-rush town of **Barkerville,** now completely restored and one of the highlights of a trip north.

PLANNING YOUR TIME

Planning how to spend your time in central British Columbia has as much to do with integrating the region with the rest of your itinerary as it does trying to work out how to hit all the highlights. The main route through the region is the east–west TransCanada Highway, which runs from Golden to Kamloops and on to Vancouver. This can easily be traveled in one day, but with two national parks and a string of interesting towns en route, the trip calls for at least one overnight stop (Revelstoke is a good choice). Even if you're in a hurry, detour along the **Meadows in the Sky Parkway** in Mount Revelstoke National Park. The region's biggest city is **Kamloops,** from where highways lead in four directions. Hands down, the most scenic is Highway 5 north to **Mount Robson Provincial Park,** from where the choices are to head northwest to Prince George (Northern British Columbia) or east to Jasper National Park and then south through to Banff. If you drive far enough north along Highway 97 from Kamloops, you'll reach

Prince George. A good way to kick off the long drive north is with a stop at **Historic Hat Creek** **Ranch,** where buildings from the Cariboo Gold Rush still stand.

Glacier National Park

Encompassing 135,000 hectares (333,600 acres) of the Selkirk Mountains west of the Rocky Mountain Trench, this park is a wonderland of jagged snowcapped peaks, extensive icefields, thundering waterfalls, steep-sided valleys, and fast-flowing rivers. The TransCanada Highway bisects the park, cresting at 1,327-meter (4,350-foot) **Rogers Pass.** From this lofty summit, Golden is 80 kilometers (50 miles) east and Revelstoke is 72 kilometers (45 miles) west.

Those from south of the 49th parallel probably associate the park's name with the American na-

tional park in Montana. The two parks share the same name and glaciated environment, but the similarities end there. In the "other" park, buses shuttle tourists here and there and the backcountry is crowded with hikers. Here in the Canadian version, commercialism is almost totally lacking and use of the backcountry is blissfully minimal.

The best place to start a visit to the park is **Rogers Pass Information Centre.** Looking south from the center, you can see the **Illecillewaet, Asulkan,** and **Swiss Glaciers.** As far as actual "sights" go, driving through the park you'll be surrounded by one of the most awe-inspiring

Central British Columbia

© AVALON TRAVEL PUBLISHING, INC.

panoramas visible from any Canadian highway. Each roadside viewpoint seems to outdo the last. You can also get out of the car and go hiking to get a better feeling for the park, but most of the trails entail strenuous climbs.

Through-traffic excepted, permits are required for entry into Glacier National Park; they're available from the information center. A one-day permit is $5 per person to a maximum of $12.50 per vehicle.

THE LAND

Regardless of whether you approach the park from the east or west, you'll be climbing from a valley only 600 meters (1,970 feet) above sea level to 1,327-meter (4,350-foot) Rogers Pass in under 15 kilometers (9.3 miles). The pass is not particularly high, but it's impressive. Surrounding peaks, many topping 3,050 meters (10,000 feet), rise dramatically from the pass and draw massive amounts of precipitation from eastward-moving clouds. The resulting heavy snows feed more than 400 glaciers and permanently cloak some 14 percent of the park's landscape in snow and ice. Most of the glaciers lie in the park's southern half. Notable among them are Deville Icefield, which surrounds 3,393-meter (11,130-foot) Mount Dawson, the park's highest peak, and Illecillewaet Icefield, whose glacial arms can be viewed up close from hiking trails starting at the Illecillewaet Campground.

Flora

Three distinct vegetation zones can be seen within the park—montane (600–1,300 meters/1,970–4,260 feet), subalpine (1,300–1,900 meters/4,260–6,230 feet), and alpine (1,900 meters/6,230 feet to over 3,050 meters/10,000 feet). The montane forest supports a lush variety of tree species, including mountain hemlock, subalpine fir, Engelmann spruce, western red cedar, western hemlock, lodgepole pine, whitebark pine, western white pine, black cottonwood, Douglas fir, aspen, and white birch.

Flower lovers will be impressed by the 600 species of flowering plants that have been identified within the park. The best time to see wildflowers in the high meadows and forests is early August, though an amazing profusion of color sweeps through the lower elevation forests starting in June, and in July the edge of the highway and avalanche paths turn bright yellow with wild lilies.

Fauna

The rugged terrain and long hard winters in Glacier National Park mean that resident mammals are a tough and hardy bunch. Healthy populations of both black and grizzly bears inhabit the park. The black bears often feed along the roadside in late spring. Grizzlies are less common and tend to remain in the backcountry, but early in the season, lingering snow can keep them at lower elevations; look for them on avalanche slopes. As is the case throughout the mountains, smaller mammals are most common. Columbia ground squirrels hang around campgrounds and picnic areas, and hoary marmots inhabit rocky areas at higher elevations. The only other common mammals in the park are moose, which live along Beaver Valley, and mountain goats, which live on and around all major peaks.

HISTORY

In a scenario familiar throughout western Canada, the proclamation of Glacier National Park was influenced by the Canadian Pacific Railway's desire to see tourists use its rail line. For CPR engineers, finding a passable train route through the Columbia Mountains proved a formidable challenge. The major obstacle was not the elevation, but the threat of avalanche; extremely high snowfalls in the area were coupled with narrow valleys and steep approaches from both east and west, all attributes spelling danger.

In 1881 Major A. B. Rogers, chief engineer of the CPR, scaled Rogers Pass from the west, along the Illecillewaet River. The following year he climbed the pass again, this time from the east. His success in reaching the pass from both directions led him to declare the route feasible for a railway. Through the next three summers rail workers toiled with picks and shovels, finally completing a railbed on November 7, 1885. The last spike was driven into the ground at Craigellachie, 100 kilometers (62 miles) to the west, and the transcontinental rail line was opened, with Rogers Pass an integral link in the vital transportation corridor.

To coincide with the opening, a national park was proclaimed, protecting the pass and surrounding wilderness and, much to the delight of the cash-strapped CPR, bringing visitors to the area—by rail of course. For the next three decades the CPR operated passenger and freight services over the pass, thrilling thousands of pioneer passengers. Unfortunately, despite railway engineering ingenuity, frequent and devastating avalanches took their toll, killing over 200 workers in the first 30 years of operation. Forced to stop the carnage, the CPR rerouted the line, tunneling under Mount Macdonald and the pass in 1916. The rerouted line bypassed the park's most spectacular scenery, and the number of visitors to the park dropped dramatically. To lessen the gradient still further, a new tunnel replaced the old in 1988. At 14.5 kilometers, it's North America's longest railway tunnel.

TransCanada Highway

In the early 1950s, a new team of engineers tackled the same problem—this time in an effort to build a highway across the pass. The tunnel approach that had worked for the railway was deemed impractical for a highway, so a new solution to the avalanche danger was required. In 1962 a route through the national park and over the pass was completed—this time with the addition of concrete snowsheds over sections of the highway. At the same time, the world's largest mobile avalanche-control program was created to stave off danger. Experts constantly monitor weather and snow conditions so they can accurately predict when and where avalanches will occur. Then they close the highway and dislodge potential slides with mobile howitzers, thereby stabilizing the slopes.

HIKING

The park's 21 hiking trails cover 140 kilometers (87 miles) and range from short interpretive

© ANDREW HEMPSTEAD

The snowcapped peaks of Glacier National Park can be seen from the highway.

walks to long, steep, difficult climbs. Aside from the interpretive trails, most gain a lot of elevation, rewarding the energetic hiker with outstanding views. Along flat ground, reasonably fit hikers can usually cover three kilometers (or more) in an hour, but on Glacier National Park's steep trails, up to double that time should be allowed. Opportunities for long-distance backcountry trips are limited to the far eastern end of the park. If you're planning an overnight trip into the backcountry you need to register and pick up a permit ($8 per person per night) from the information center. Remember, many of the park's high-elevation trails are covered in snow until well into July.

The two most popular interpretive trails are the **Abandoned Rails Interpretive Trail** (one kilometer/.6 mile; 20 minutes round-trip), which starts to the west of the information center, and the **Meeting of the Waters Trail** (one kilometer/.6 mile; 25 minutes round-trip), which starts behind Illecillewaet Campground, four kilometers (2.5 miles) south of the information center.

Avalanche Crest

- Length: 4.2 km/2.6 miles (2.5 hours) one-way
- Elevation gain: 800 meters/2,620 feet
- Rating: moderate/difficult
- Trailhead: Illecillewaet Campground

This trail begins behind the Illecillewaet Campground, four kilometers (2.5 miles) south of Rogers Pass Information Centre. As you face the large information board, the trail leads off to your left, climbing steeply through a subalpine forest for the first three kilometers (1.9 miles), then leveling out and providing stunning views below to Rogers Pass and south to Illecillewaet and Asulkan Glaciers.

Great Glacier

- Length: 4.8 km/3 miles (two hours) one-way
- Elevation gain: 320 meters/1,050 feet
- Rating: easy/moderate
- Trailhead: Illecillewaet Campground

Of the trails beginning from the campground, the Great Glacier Trail has the least elevation gain. But hard-core hikers will get the oppor-

tunity to scramble up rocky slopes to the toe of the Illecillewaet Glacier, 340 vertical meters (1,110 feet) higher.

Asulkan Valley

- Length: 6.5 km/4 miles (four hours) one-way
- Elevation gain: 930 meters/3,050 feet
- Rating: moderate/difficult
- Trailhead: Illecillewaet Campground

While elevation gain on this trail is similar to others in the steep-sided Illecillewaet River Valley, it is gained over a longer distance, meaning a less-strenuous outing. Nevertheless, a full day should be allowed round-trip. The trail follows Asulkan Brook through a valley of dense subalpine forest. Whereas other trails lead to panoramic overlooks, the highlight of this trail's final destination is a view of the immense icefield rising high above you.

Abbott Ridge

- Length: 5 km/3.1 miles (3.5 hours) one-way
- Elevation gain: 1,040 meters/3,410 feet
- Rating: difficult
- Trailhead: Illecillewaet Campground

Winding up the west slope of a steep valley, this trail is for the physically fit; the gradient averages 20 percent. For the first 2.5 kilometers (1.6 miles), wide switchbacks lead up to Marion Lake. The trail then continues upward to a high treeless ridge offering views extending eastward across the Illecillewaet Icefield and adjoining glaciers. The ridge itself rises a further 150 meters (490 feet) to the 2,454-meter (8,050-foot) summit of Mount Abbott.

Balu Pass

- Length: 5 kilometers/3.1 miles (3.5 hours) one-way
- Elevation gain: 1,020 meters/3,350 feet
- Rating: difficult
- Trailhead: information center parking lot

This trail climbs steeply and steadily between Mount Cheops to the south and a ridge of 2,700-meter (8,860-foot) peaks to the north. As elevation is gained, the valley closes in and the trail becomes steeper, finally ending at a pass 2,300 meters (7,450 feet) above sea level.

Hermit

- Length: 2.8 km/1.7 miles (two hours) one-way
- Elevation gain: 940 meters/3,080 feet
- Rating: difficult
- Trailhead: west side of the highway one km north of the information center

This trail climbs *very* steeply through a subalpine forest, breaking out above the tree line and ending at a view of glaciated peaks towering 1,000 meters (3,300 feet) above. Snow lingers on this trail well into July, so check conditions before heading out.

Copperstain

- Length: 16 km/10 miles (seven hours) one-way
- Elevation gain: 1,225 meters/4,020 feet
- Rating: difficult
- Trailhead: Beaver Gravel Pit, 12 km (7.5 miles) northeast of Rogers Pass Information Centre

Backcountry enthusiasts gravitate to the park's eastern flanks, where the Beaver Gravel Pit is the trailhead for two overnight hikes. The most popular of these is the Copperstain trail, leading to alpine meadows flanked by Bald Mountain and Copperstain Mountain. The climb is steady at first, ascending the Beaver River Valley for four kilometers (2.5 miles), then branching north along Grizzly and Copperstain Creeks for the final painful ascent to the meadows. Also from the gravel pit, a 42-kilometer (26-mile) trail leads up the Beaver River Valley to the park's extreme southeast corner. Backcountry camping is allowed anywhere along these two trails, but register first at the information center.

ACCOMMODATIONS AND CAMPING

Places to stay within Glacier are limited to one chain motel and two small campgrounds with no hookups. If you're looking for something more, plan on traveling 80 kilometers (50 miles) east to Golden or 72 kilometers (45 miles) west to Revelstoke.

Glacier Park Lodge

This Best Western affiliate motel (250/837-2126 or 800/528-1234, www.glacierparklodge.ca) lies beside the main information center atop Rogers Pass. It offers 50 midsize rooms with summer rates from $135 s, $150 d; off-season rates are under $100. The heated outdoor pool is usually empty. Hotel facilities include a 24-hour café, a restaurant offering reasonably priced buffets through all three meals, and a lounge.

Camping

At **Illecillewaet Campground** (3.5 km/2.2 miles south of Rogers Pass; late June–Sept.; $17), facilities include kitchen shelters, flush toilets, picnic tables, firewood, and an evening interpretive program. Sites are not particularly private, and the surrounding peaks and towering cedar trees mean little sunshine before noon, but the campground is the perfect base for exploring because it's the trailhead for the park's main concentration of hiking trails. When this campground fills, campers are directed to an overflow area in the nearby Sir Donald Picnic Area. Smaller **Loop Brook Campground** (three km/1.9 miles beyond the Illecillewaet Campground toward Revelstoke; July–Sept.; $17) holds just 20 sites.

With just 80 campsites in the entire park and no reservations taken, chances are good that both campgrounds will be full if you arrive late in the afternoon. If that's the case, head 40 kilometers (25 miles) west to **Canyon Hot Springs Resort** (250/837-2420, www.canyonhotsprings.com; May–Sept.), a family-style complex of accommodations and activities with something for everyone. Two massive swimming pools (open daily 9 A.M.–9 P.M.) filled with water pumped from nearby hot springs are the advertised highlight, while the short trail to historic Albert Canyon is a good way to escape the crowds. Aside from the solitude, you can explore the broken-down remains of log cabins dating to the days of highway construction. The resort offers showers, a laundry, and a restaurant. Unserviced sites are $20, serviced sites $29, basic sleeping cabins with no bathrooms $52, and self-contained chalets from $100.

TIME TRAVEL

Glacier National Park falls within two time zones. If you pass through the park westbound, turn your watch *back* one hour to **Pacific time.** If you're eastbound, turn it *forward* one hour to **Mountain time.**

INFORMATION

Rogers Pass Information Centre (250/837-7500, www.pc.gc.ca) is beside the highway 1.2 kilometers (.7 mile) north of the actual pass and resembles the old-fashioned snowsheds that once protected the railroad from avalanches. The center's fascinating displays focus on the park's natural and human history. Videos on various aspects of the park are shown on the TV (the viewing area by the fireplace is a great spot to while away time waiting for the clouds to lift), and the center's theater screens documentaries on mountain wildlife and avalanche protection. Staff members provide information on trail conditions and closures, operate a small bookstore, and conduct interpretive programs. The center is also the only place in the park to buy park passes, necessary for those planning any hiking or camping. If you already have a National Parks of Canada Pass, it must be presented for admission to the information center. Hours are April–mid-June 9 A.M.–5 P.M., mid-June–August 8 A.M.–7 P.M., September–November Thursday–Monday 9 A.M.–5 P.M., December–March daily 7 A.M.–5 P.M. For road conditions through the park call 250/837-6867.

Revelstoke

Revelstoke lies 72 kilometers (45 miles) west of Rogers Pass at the confluence of the Illecillewaet River and the mighty Columbia, surrounded by mountains—the Monashees to the west and the Selkirks to the east. The setting couldn't be more spectacular.

An 1850s' gold rush along the Columbia River brought the first Europeans to the area, but the town really began to grow with the coming of the railroad in the 1880s. In fact, the city is named for Lord Revelstoke, who provided funding for completion of the Canadian Pacific Railway's line through town. Finally, the TransCanada Highway came to town earlier this century, helping turn Revelstoke into today's midsize city of 8,500.

The town holds a couple of museums, but the main attractions are farther afield, including two massive dams, a national park on the back doorstep, and great skiing and snowboarding on Mount Mackenzie.

SIGHTS

The TransCanada Highway makes a lazy loop around the back of Revelstoke, missing downtown completely. It's well worth the detour to downtown, not just for the best dining, but to enjoy the laid-back atmosphere of a small city that has done an excellent job of preserving its heritage. The downtown core has been rejuvenated and centers around the appealing, all-brick Grizzly Plaza. Southwest from the plaza along Mackenzie Avenue are many frontier-style false fronted buildings and the art deco–style Roxy Theatre. Pick up the *Heritage Walking & Driving* brochure at the information center for routes that take in the highlights of downtown's many old buildings.

Museums

Railway buffs shouldn't miss **Revelstoke Railway Museum** (Victoria Rd., 250/837-6060; summer daily 9 A.M.–8 P.M., spring and fall daily 9 A.M.–5 P.M., winter Mon.–Fri. 1–5 P.M.; adult $6, senior $5, child $3), a re-creation of an early Canadian Pacific Railway station. Reflecting the importance of this mode of transportation in Revelstoke's history, the museum centers on a massive 1948 steam locomotive and Business Car No. 4, the ultimate in early rail-travel luxury.

© AVALON TRAVEL PUBLISHING, INC.

Revelstoke Museum (corner of Boyle Ave. and 1st St., 250/837-3067; summer Mon.–Sat. 10 A.M.–5 P.M., the rest of the year Mon.–Fri. 1–4 P.M.; donation) fills two stories of a historic downtown post office building. It preserves plenty of pioneer memorabilia and a great collection of historical black-and-white photos, and offers displays on local industries, early Chinese miners, and winter recreation.

Dams

The 1,900-kilometer (1,180-mile) Columbia River, North America's third-longest, is controlled by many dams. Four of these are in British Columbia and two are in the vicinity of Revelstoke. The dams also provide the necessary water for two massive hydroelectric operations. These two generating stations are each capable of producing 1,800 megawatts of electricity—or, combined, 30 percent of the province's needs.

Revelstoke Dam, eight kilometers (five miles) north of the city on Highway 23, was completed in 1985. It's 470 meters (1,540 feet) wide and 175 meters (590 feet) high. The massive reservoir behind the dam stretches over 130 kilometers (81 miles). Nestled in the valley downstream of the dam is the generating station. Exhibits at the two-story **Revelstoke Dam Visitor Centre** (250/814-6697; weekdays only, in summer 8 A.M.–7 P.M., the rest of the year 9 A.M.–5 P.M.; free), above the generating station, explain the valley's history and the operation and impact of the dams. From the center, a high-speed elevator whisks visitors to the top of the dam for an excellent view.

Upstream of Revelstoke Dam is **Mica Dam,** 140 kilometers (87 miles) via Highway 23 to the north. This dam is much larger—in fact, it's North America's highest earth-filled dam (240 meters/790 feet), stretching 792 meters (2,600 feet) at the crest across the Columbia River Valley. It backs up 200-kilometer-long (124-mile-long) **Kinbasket Lake,** extending north to Valemount and south to a point just north of Golden. **Mica Dam Visitor Centre** (summer daily 8 A.M.–8 P.M., late spring and early fall 9 A.M.–5 P.M.) is smaller than the one at Revelstoke Dam, but it has free powerhouse tours daily at 11 A.M. and 1:30 P.M.

MOUNT REVELSTOKE NATIONAL PARK

Visitors to this 26,000-hectare (64,250-acre) national park on the northern outskirts of Revelstoke can experience a high alpine environment from the enticingly named Meadows in the Sky Parkway, without any strenuous hiking.

The park protects the highest peaks of the **Clachnacudiann Range,** a northern arm of the Selkirk Mountains. The forested slopes of the range come to an icy apex around the Clachnacudiann Glacier and surrounding peaks, such as **Mount Coursier** and **Mount Inverness,** both 2,637 meters (8,650 feet) high. The park's diverse vegetation includes forests of ancient cedar along the Illecillewaet River, subalpine forests of Engelmann spruce and fir on higher slopes, and finally, above the tree line, meadows of low-growing shrubs that come alive with color for a few weeks in midsummer.

As with all Canadian national parks, a permit is required for entry; in this case it applies only for travel on the Meadows in the Sky Parkway. Permits are issued at the park gate, at the lower end of the parkway. A one-day permit is $5 per person to a maximum of $12.50 per vehicle.

Meadows in the Sky Parkway

This 26-kilometer (16-mile) road one kilometer (.6 mile) west of the downtown Revelstoke turnoff climbs from the TransCanada Highway to a magnificent alpine meadow high above the tree line. The road is very steep, gaining well over 1,000 meters (3,280 feet) of elevation as it climbs seemingly endless hairpin bends through a subalpine forest of Engelmann spruce, hemlock, and the odd towering cedar. The summit area is snowed in until mid- to late July, depending on how much snow has fallen the previous winter. The public road ends one kilometer (.6 mile) before the true summit. From this point, you have the option of taking a free shuttle bus (daily 10 A.M.–4:20 P.M., starting as soon as the snow melts off the road) or walking (20 minutes each way) to **Heather Lake.** From this point, the panoramic view takes in the Columbia River Valley and the distant Monashee Mountains, with hiking trails beckoning further exploration.

Heather Lake is the trailhead for the one-kilometer (round-trip) **Meadows in the Sky Trail,** which features signs explaining the flora of the fragile alpine environment. From the east side of Heather Lake, a nine-kilometer (5.6-mile) trail leads through alpine meadows to the **Jade Lakes.** Along the route, short side trails lead to **Miller** and **Eva Lakes.**

The park's main gate is closed 10 P.M.–7 A.M., prohibiting access.

More Hiking Opportunities

The park doesn't have an extensive network of hiking trails—just 10 marked trails totaling 65 kilometers (40 miles) in length. Most take under an hour and are posted with interpretive panels. Two of these start beside the TransCanada Highway east of Revelstoke, where the Illecillewaet River forms the park's southern boundary. The 500-meter (.3-mile) **Giant Cedars Boardwalk** (allow 10 minutes) traverses a meadow before disappearing into an ancient cedar forest and then along a sparkling creek. Farther west along the highway is the trailhead for **Skunk Cabbage Interpretive Trail,** which leads 1.2 kilometers (.7 mile) down to the Illecillewaet River; allow 40 minutes for the round-trip.

The park's most demanding trail is the 10-kilometer (6.2-mile) **Summit Trail,** which begins—or, more sensibly, ends—at the entrance to the Meadows in the Sky Parkway and runs to the Balsam Lake warden's cabin. The trail makes an elevation gain of 1,200 meters (3,940 feet), so allow at least 3.5 hours for this strenuous uphill slog. The eight-kilometer (five-mile) **Lindmark Trail** is equally strenuous, gaining 950 meters (3,120 feet) in elevation as it traverses up to Balsam Lake from the lookout eight kilometers (five miles) from the park gate.

Park Information
Services within the park are limited to picnic areas. Although backcountry camping is allowed in designated areas (permit required; $8 per person per night), no road-accessible campgrounds lie within the park.

Revelstoke is home to the park's **administration office** (300 3rd St., 250/837-7500; year-round Mon.–Fri. 8:30 A.M.–4:30 P.M.). Other sources of information are **Rogers Pass Information Centre,** in nearby Glacier National Park, and the Parks Canada website (www.pc.gc.ca).

RECREATION
In summer, recreation revolves around the national park, the local golf course, and the Columbia River. In winter, the local ski hill and a Sno-Cat operation draw the visitors. One of the most attractive things about Revelstoke in winter is the prices, with local accommodations combining with the resort to offer some of the best-priced packages to be found anywhere in Canada.

Skiing and Snowboarding
The local downhill resort is **Powder Springs** (250/837-5378 or 800/991-4455, www.cat-powder.com) on the lower slopes of Mount Mackenzie. The resort's two lifts serve a vertical rise of 300 meters (1,000 feet). Facilities include ski and snowboard rentals, a ski school, cafeteria, and bar. The season generally lasts from mid-December to late March, and adult lift tickets are adult $32. A massive expansion plan for this small resort has been on the drawing board for years, and eventually a gondola will whisk skiers from Revelstoke itself to the summit of Mount Mackenzie. In the meantime, it's possible to ski the mountain's higher slopes with **CAT Powder**

Skiing (250/837-5378 or 800/991-4455, www .catpowder.com). From the Powder Springs day lodge, a Sno-Cat takes skiers high above the lift-served slopes for up to 5,000 vertical meters (14,400 vertical feet) of powder skiing a day. Packages include skiing, accommodations, and all meals, and cost around $1,100 for two days, $1,640 for three days.

Nestled between the Selkirk and Monashee Mountains, Revelstoke is also the center of much heli-skiing. **Selkirk Tangiers Heli-skiing** (250/837-5378 or 800/663-7080, www.selkirk-tangiers .com) operates from town, offering all-inclusive packages—including seven days heli-skiing (over 30,000 meters/100,000 feet vertical), accommodations (at the Coast Hillcrest Resort Hotel), and meals. Prices range from $2,200 for three days in December to $6,500 for seven days in February. **Canadian Mountain Holidays** (403/762-7100 or 800/661-0252, www.cmh-ski.com) has heli-skiing lodges scattered throughout the remote backcountry of British Columbia, but in Revelstoke, the company's guests stay right downtown at the Regent Inn and are whisked off daily for the mountains.

Entertainment
In July and August, free entertainment takes place nightly at the **Grizzly Plaza bandshell,** at the bottom end of Mackenzie Avenue. Whether it be comedy or country, crowds of up to a couple of hundred gather, sitting in plastic chairs, snagging a table at a surrounding restaurant, or just standing in the background. For music and dancing of a more formal nature, the young crowd heads for **Big Eddy Inn** (2108 Big Eddy Rd., 250/837-9072). Downtown in the Regent Inn (112 1st St., 250/837-2107), you'll find live music or a DJ Wednesday–Saturday at the **River City Pub** and plenty of quiet corners at the more subdued **One Twelve Lounge.**

ACCOMMODATIONS AND CAMPING
Under $50
The best value of all accommodations in town is the **Ⅶ Samesun Revelstoke** (400 2nd St. W,

250/837-4050 or 877/562-2783, www.same-sun.com), within easy walking distance of downtown. Providing a true home away from home, this heritage house has been fully restored, complete with hardwood floors and comfortable beds with linen. Amenities include kitchen facilities, a laundry, free Internet access, bike rentals, and a game room. The 26 double and twin rooms share bathrooms, but beds are comfortable and linen is supplied. Rates are $21.40 per person for a dorm bed or $43 s or d in a private room.

$50–100

Downtown, the **Powder Springs Inn** (200 3rd St. W, 250/837-5151 or 800/991-4455, www.catpowder.com) is a renovated motel owned by the same company that operates the local ski hill and Sno-Cat operation, so it's busiest in winter. The rooms are great value year-round; $80 s or d in summer (and as low as $60 the rest of the year, with skiing packages equating to free skiing). A restaurant, spa services, and a hot tub are also on the premises.

Other motels are spread through downtown and out on the highway. The best is the **Revelstoke Lodge** (601 1st St. W, 250/837-2181 or 888/559-1979, www.revelstokelodge.com; $69 s, $79 d), with air-conditioned guest rooms set around a heated outdoor pool.

$100–150

To experience Revelstoke's most appealing accommodation, head 20 kilometers (12 miles) south of town on Highway 23 to **Mulvehill Creek Wilderness Inn** (250/837-3538 or 877/837-8649, www.mulvehillcreek.com). This well-designed property centers on a main cedar lodge trading on outdoor opportunities (canoeing, swimming, and fishing) and modern conveniences (heated pool, hot tub, en suite guest rooms). Rates of $125–145 s or d include a big breakfast buffet of egg dishes courtesy of the inn's chickens and homemade goodies such as breads and jams.

Camping

KOA Revelstoke (250/837-2085 or 800/562-3905, www.revelstokekoa.com; mid-April–mid-Oct.) is off the TransCanada Highway six kilometers (3.7 miles) east of downtown. The well-kept campground offers grassy sites, lots of trees, a swimming pool, propane-filling facilities, a well-stocked store, free hot showers, laundry facilities, and a main lodge that looks like a Swiss chalet. Tent sites are $21.50, RV sites range $23–32, tepees $34, and camping cabins (no bathrooms) $45. The fun stuff includes canoe rentals ($20 per day), inflatable rafts ($25 per day), two playgrounds, rock-climbing lessons, evening campfires, and pancake breakfasts.

Quiet **Williamson Lake Campground** (seven km/4.3 miles south of town on Airport Way, 250/837-5512 or 888/676-2267; mid-Apr.–Oct.) lies on the edge of a warm lake perfect for swimming. Shaded grassy sites, hot showers, a picnic shelter, and fire pits are all just above the shoreline. Sites are $16–20, or stay in a tepee for $25.

Finally, south along Highway 23 between Revelstoke and Shelter Bay there are three provincial parks offering sites for $14. No hookups are provided.

FOOD
Downtown

Near the downtown bandshell, **Conversations** (205 Mackenzie Ave., 250/837-4772) serves up gourmet coffees and light meals in a relaxed atmosphere. Across the road, the **Woolsey Creek Café** (212 Mackenzie St., 250/837-5500; daily from 8 A.M.) has a warm, friendly atmosphere but is always full and noisy with locals enjoying a wide range of well-prepared and remarkably inexpensive dishes. I had the Spanish seafood paella ($10), and it was as good as at city restaurants where you'd expect to pay double the price. Breakfasts and lunches are under $8, and dinners are all under $12.

Claudio's (204 Mackenzie Ave., 250/837-6743) is typical of small-town Italian restaurants across the continent, complete with widely spread tables with plenty of elbow room; red, white, and green paper tablecloths; and the local radio station playing in the background. The menu is also typical, with pizza, pasta, and meat dishes ranging $13–18 and daily specials somewhere in between. Claudio's also has a few tables on the sidewalk.

The stylish decor and relaxed atmosphere of **One Twelve Restaurant** (Regent Inn, 112 1st St., 250/837-2107; Mon.–Sat. from 5:30 P.M.) make it a popular place to go if you're in the mood for a bit of a splurge.

Out on the Highway

Despite the many good choices downtown, two options may appeal to hurried highway travelers because of their location. For breakfast, head to **Scotty's** (behind the Shell gas station, 250/837-4464). The service is fast and efficient, and seven bucks will get you the daily special or most any cooked meal on the menu. Across the road is the **Frontier Family Restaurant** (250/837-5119; 5 A.M.–10 P.M.), a typical roadside diner with nothing fancy that doesn't need to be. The wood interior is decorated with red-and-white checkered curtains, cowboy boots, hats, antlers, and cattle horns; the waitresses wear jeans; and a sign outside says "Y'all come back, y'hear!" On top of all that, the food is good. Huge breakfasts cost around $8 (try the "Hide-yer-plate-flapjacks"). Lunch is similarly priced, while dinner options include spaghetti with meatballs ($11) and a top sirloin steak ($16), both of which come with access to the soup and salad bar.

INFORMATION AND SERVICES

Revelstoke Visitor Info Centre (downtown at 204 Campbell Ave., 250/837-5345 or 800/487-1493, www.seerevelstoke.com) is open in summer daily 8 A.M.–7 P.M., the rest of the year Monday–Friday 8:30 A.M.–4:30 P.M. On the TransCanada Highway, in front of the Frontier Family Restaurant, is a seasonal information center (summer daily 7 A.M.–7 P.M. The **Revelstoke National Park administration office** is in the post office building (313 3rd St., 250/837-7500) and is open year-round (Mon.–Fri. 8:30 A.M.–4:30 P.M.).

Queen Victoria Hospital is on Newlands Road (off Airport Way), on the southeast side of town (250/837-2131). The **post office** is a couple of blocks from downtown at 307 3rd Street.

Greyhound buses come through Revelstoke 4–7 times daily in both directions along the TransCanada Highway. The depot is by the Sandman Inn (1899 Fraser Dr., 250/837-5874).

West Toward Kamloops

Continuing west along the TransCanada Highway from Revelstoke, it's 62 kilometers (39 miles) to the next town, Sicamous, then 42 kilometers (26 miles) farther to the much larger center of Salmon Arm. The first stop along the way should be intriguingly black **Summit Lake**, lying in a heavily forested ravine and fed by a waterfall that plunges over a cliff face high above. A few kilometers farther west is similarly black **Victor Lake**, also fed by a waterfall. Shoreside **Victor Lake Provincial Park** makes a good spot for a picnic.

Three Valley

Several attractions on the next stretch of road compete for your tourist dollar. On the shore of Three Valley Lake is the difficult-to-miss **Three Valley Gap** "ghost" town (250/837-2109; Apr.–mid-Oct. daily 8 A.M.–dusk; adult $8, child $4), a rebuilt pioneer community with more than 20 historic buildings moved to the site from around the province. Part of the same complex is **Three Valley Lake Chateau** (250/837-2109 or 888/667-2109, www.3valley.com; Apr.–mid-Oct.), a large motel (200 rooms) overlooking extensive gardens and the lake. Amenities include a café, restaurant, and indoor pool. Standard rooms are $115–150 s or d, while the Cave Honeymoon Suite—complete with stone walls, roof, fireplace, and bathroom—is $165 s or d.

The next commercial attraction, eight kilometers (five miles) west, is **Enchanted Forest** (250/837-9477; summer daily 8 A.M.–sunset; adult $6.50, child $5), where a trail through towering trees meanders past more than 250 handcrafted figurines to fairyland buildings and western Canada's biggest treehouse.

Farther west, **Beardale Castle Miniatureland** (250/836-2268; May–Sept. daily 9 A.M.–6 P.M.; adult $6, child $4) takes miniature appreciators through several European towns and a Haida fishing village, into the world of nursery rhymes and fairy tales, and on into the world of trains. Most of the displays are indoors, making Beardale a good rainy day diversion.

The Last Spike

At **Craigellachie,** signs point off the highway to the Last Spike. It was here on November 7, 1885, that a plain iron spike joined the last two sections of Canadian Pacific's transcontinental rail line, finally connecting Canada from sea to sea. A cairn with a plaque and a piece of railway line marks the spot. **Craigellachie Station** (May–Oct.) is home to a small information center/gift shop selling ice cream.

Sicamous

This town of 3,000, 62 kilometers (39 miles) west of Revelstoke, lies on the shore of **Shuswap** Lake and is known as the "Houseboat Capital of Canada." The lake itself is a convoluted body of water with four distinct arms, edged by secluded beaches, rocky coves, 25 marine parks, and more than 1,000 kilometers (620 miles) of shoreline. Houseboating is the number-one activity in these parts, and Sicamous is headquarters to major agencies, including: **Blue Water Houseboats** (250/836-2255 or 800/663-4024), **Three Buoys Houseboat Vacations** (250/836-2403 or 800/663-2333, www.threebouys.com), and **Twin Anchors Houseboat Vacations** (250/836-2450 or 800/663-4026, www.twinanchors.com). Rates vary greatly through the May–early October season. Expect to pay around $1,700 for four days' rental in July, with the same boat going for under $1,000 in September.

Sandwiched between the two natural features referenced in its name, **Hyde Mountain on Mara Lake Golf Course** (250/836-4653) is not particularly long, but golfers enjoy fantastic lake views from elevated greens. Rates, including cart rental, are $80. To get there, head three kilometers (1.9 miles) south of town on Old Spallumcheen Road, which branches off the TransCanada

A freight train passes by Craigellachie, famous as the spot where the final section of Canada's transcontinental rail line was completed in 1885.

Highway immediately west of the bridge. The clubhouse restaurant (daily 6:30 A.M.–midnight) combines good food with views to make it the best place in town to eat, even for non-golfers.

Highway 97A, south from Sicamous, is the main northern artery leading into the Okanagan Valley. Even if you're not planning on heading that far, it's worth taking this route a short way along the shoreline of Mara Lake. Aside from being particularly picturesque, the warm water tempts swimming. **Shoreline Resort** (two km/1.2 miles south along Hwy. 97A, 250/836-2855) is typical of the many summer getaways along this stretch of the lake. The sandy beach, watercraft rentals, outdoor games such as horseshoes and mini-golf, and nightly movies all add to the lively family atmosphere. Tent sites are $25 per night, hookups $30. Cabins are rented on a weekly basis for $600–750.

SALMON ARM

Known as the "Gem of the Shuswap," Salmon Arm (pop. 15,000) lies along the Salmon Arm of Shuswap Lake, surrounded by lush farmland and forested hills. Legend has it that the name was coined in the days when the rivers here were chockablock with salmon. Farmers used to spear the fish with pitchforks and use them for fertilizer.

Sights

From downtown, follow the Salmon Arm Wharf signs to lakeside **Marine Park,** where picnic tables dot the lawns and colorful flower boxes hang from the lampposts. The attractive **Salmon Arm Wharf,** the largest marina structure in British Columbia's interior, lures you out over the water, past a boat-launching area, a snack bar, and businesses renting motorboats and houseboats. A wide swath of lakefront on either side of the wharf is undeveloped, inviting exploration on foot. Immediately west of the wharf, you'll find a bird-watching hide tucked into the trees above a marshy area rich with birds.

Two kilometers (1.2 miles) east of Salmon Arm on Highway 97B, **R.J. Haney Heritage Park** (250/832-5243; June–early Sept. daily 10 A.M.– 5 P.M.; $4) holds the town's main historic attractions. Here you'll find the **Salmon Arm Museum,** which relates the town's earliest days through a slide show, photo albums, and the adjacent **Haney House,** an early-20th-century farmhouse on beautiful, parklike grounds. The park also holds a blacksmith's shop, an old fire hall, and a church.

For excellent views of Shuswap Lake, take **Fly Hills Scenic Drive,** which starts almost opposite the Salmon River Motel and RV Park on the TransCanada Highway west of town. From the highway, turn onto 40th Street and follow the scenic route signs: right on 10th Avenue, left on Salmon Valley Road, right on Christensen Road, left on 5th Avenue, left on 60th Street, right on 15th Avenue, then on up a Forest Service road into the Fly Hills. The road gets pretty rough in sections, but the higher you go, the better the views become.

Accommodations and Camping

Salmon River Motel and RV Park (one km/.6 mile west of Salmon Arm, 250/832-3065) offers 10 rooms of a reasonable standard for $59–79. Out back are a few tree-shaded campsites with hookups; $23. Closer to town is the Best Western–affiliated **Villager West Motor Inn** (61 10th St. SW, 250/832-9793), with an indoor pool; $70–90 s or d.

The landscaped **KOA Salmon Arm** (Hwy. 97B, 250/832-6489 or 800/562-9389, www .salmonarmkoa.com; mid-May–mid-Oct.) has hot showers, a laundry, a pleasant outdoor pool area, a convenience store, miniature golf, a playground, and a petting zoo. Tent sites are $35, full hookups $45, and rustic cabins $70. Highway 97B branches south toward Vernon just east of town.

Food

Head down through the center of town and over the rail line toward the main wharf to reach **Java Cabana** (680 Marine Dr., 250/832-2329; daily from 7:30 A.M.), a corner coffeehouse where patrons take full advantage of sunny outdoor table settings. With your coffee, try the Thai salad ($6), then check your email on the public terminals. Right on the lakefront here is the Prestige Inn, home to **Forster's** (251 Harbourfront Dr., 250/833-1154), specializing in prime rib ($16–20). The restaurant itself is as stylish as dining out gets in Salmon Arm, but if it's a warm evening, you'll want to be outside on the deck.

Near the Greyhound bus depot, the **Hideaway Pub** (995 Lakeshore Dr., 250/832-9442; daily 11 A.M.–11 P.M.) offers a long menu of pub grub, with a few surprises—such as Bavarian smokies with a side of pierogies ($9) and a shrimp and avocado sandwich ($9)—thrown in for good measure. **Mino's Greek House** (720 22nd St. NE, off the TransCanada Hwy. east of town, 250/832-2079) is where the locals splurge on southern European cuisine; mains start at $13.50.

Information and Services

Salmon Arm Visitor Info Centre (751 Marine Park Dr., 250/832-2230 or 877/725-6667) is open in summer daily 9 A.M.–6 P.M., the rest of the year Monday–Friday 9 A.M.–5 P.M. For information on the region before leaving home, contact **Tourism Shuswap** (800/661-4800, www.shuswap.bc.ca).

The **Greyhound** bus depot (10th St. W, 250/832-3962) is behind the Village West Mall on the TransCanada Highway.

CONTINUING WEST

Squilax

Squilax lies at the turnoff to Roderick Haig-Brown Provincial Park, 48 kilometers (30 miles) west of Salmon Arm. The town's one remaining building was originally a general store and is now the Hostelling International–affiliated **HI—Shuswap Lake** (250/675-2977, www.hihostels.ca). The hostel office and a store selling organic products are in the building, while the dorm beds and communal kitchen are in three railway cabooses (the living quarters for railway workers in days gone by). The carriages sit on a short stretch of rail line overlooking

the west end of Shuswap Lake. Rates are $16 for members and $20 for nonmembers. Check-in is 5–10 P.M. daily.

Adams River Sockeye Run

Turn off at the Squilax Bridge to get to 988-hectare (2,440-acre) **Roderick Haig-Brown Provincial Park,** named for noted British Columbian conservationist and writer Roderick Haig-Brown but best known for protecting in its entirety the Adams River sockeye salmon run, North America's biggest such run. The salmon runs occur annually, but every four years (2006, 2010, etc.) a dominant run brings up to two million fish congregating in the river. These salmon are near the end of their four-year life cycle, having hatched in the same section of the Adams River four years previously. Unlike other species, after hatching sockeye spend up to two years of their life in a "nursery" lake, which in the case of the Adams River run is Shuswap Lake. It is estimated that in conjunction with dominant runs 15 million Adams River sockeye enter the Pacific, with about 10 million running back toward their birthplace, of which just one in five make it past fishing nets to their birthplace. After an arduous 500-kilometer (310-mile) swim from the Pacific Ocean, the salmon spawn on shallow gravel bars here during the first three weeks of October (numbers generally peak in the second week).

Forested with Douglas fir, cottonwood, birch, hemlock, and cedar, the park flanks the Adams River between Adams Lake and Shuswap Lake, protecting the spawning grounds in their entirety. Undoubtedly, October 2006 is the best time to visit in the near future, but at other times, the park is still interesting and interpretive boards describe the salmon run you've missed. Large mammals are common, interesting canyons dot the riverbank, fishing is good, and hikers can traverse 40 kilometers (25 miles) of trails.

Kamloops

Kamloops (pop. 80,000), 110 kilometers (68 miles) west of Salmon Arm and 355 kilometers (220 miles) northeast of Vancouver, is the province's sixth-largest city and a main service center along the TransCanada Highway. The city holds a few interesting sights but is certainly no scenic gem—the surrounding landscape is dominated by barren parched rolling hills. The downtown area, however, lies along the south bank of the Thompson River and is set off by well-irrigated parkland.

Entering the city from the west, the TransCanada Highway descends the Aberdeen Hills, passing shopping malls, motels, and Kamloops Visitor Info Centre. The highway bypasses downtown; take Columbia Street West to get to the city center. From the east, the TransCanada Highway parallels the Thompson River through almost 20 kilometers (12.4 miles) of industrial and commercial sprawl.

History

The Secwepemc, whose descendents are now known as Shuswap, were the first people to live in this region, basing their lifestyle on hunting and salmon fishing. They knew the area as T'kumlups, meaning "Meeting of the Rivers." The first nonnative settlement occurred in 1812, when the North West Company established a fur-trading post at the confluence of the north and south branches of the Thompson River. Prospectors began arriving in 1858, followed by entrepreneurs who began setting up permanent businesses. Around the time of the town's founding, sternwheelers plied the Thompson River, dropping off passengers and collecting lumber. But the arrival of the railway in Kamloops contributed the most to the region's development; the Canadian Pacific Railway line was completed in 1885. Settlers flocked in on the trains; lumber and cattle were chugged out. The Canadian Northern Railway (now the Canadian National Railway) was completed in 1915, and Kamloops became a major transportation center. Today the local economy revolves around the forest-products industry, copper mining, cattle and sheep ranching, and tourism.

SIGHTS

Kamloops Museum and Art Gallery

Excellent displays at the three-story, gold-colored **Kamloops Museum** (207 Seymour St., 250/828-3576; summer Mon.–Fri. 9 A.M.–8 P.M., Sat. 10 A.M.–5 P.M., and Sun. 1–5 P.M., the rest of the year Tues.–Sat. 9:30 A.M.–4:30 P.M.; free) cover local native culture, the fur trade (peek in the reconstructed fur trader's cabin), pioneer days, natural history (many stuffed and mounted critters), industry, and transportation. You'll see a furnished late-19th-century living area, a stable complete with tack and carriage, a blacksmith shop, paddle wheels, old wall clocks and cameras, and a 15-minute slide presentation on the city's history.

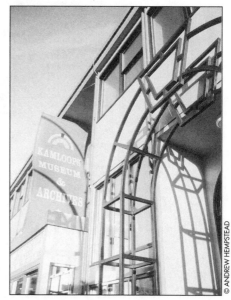

Kamloops Museum

Central British Columbia

KAMLOOPS

To Sun Peaks Resort, Wells Gray PP, and Mount Robson PP

PAUL LAKE RD

To Paul Lake PP and Harper Mountain Ski Area

HALSTON AVE

8TH ST

To Airport

N Thompson River

FORTUNE DR

TRANQUILLE DR

Thompson River

Riverside Park

RED BRIDGE

LORNE ST

MANDARIN RESTAURANT

D'AGOSTINO RESTAURANT

LANSDOWNE ST

RAILWAY STATION

MERLIN BOOKS   SANBIKE

POST OFFICE

HI-KAMLOOPS

SMORGASBORD

VICTORIA ST

ART GALLERY

SEYMOUR ST

PLAZA HERITAGE HOTEL

KAMLOOPS MUSEUM

BATTLE ST

1ST AVE   2ND AVE   3RD AVE

FOUNTAIN MOTEL

6TH AVE

NICOLA ST

COLUMBIA ST

5

OVERLANDER BRIDGE

LANSDOWNE ST

RED BRIDGE

ATHABASCA ST

MT PAUL WAY

S Thompson River

SECWEPEMC MUSEUM & HERITAGE PARK

SUMMIT DR

SEE DETAIL

LORNE ST

SEYMOUR ST

STORMS   RIVER ST

PAVILION THEATRE

BATTLE ST

1ST AVE   2ND AVE   3RD AVE   6TH AVE   NICOLA ST   9TH AVE   12TH AVE

COLUMBIA ST

To BC Wildlife Park, Campground, and Salmon Arm

SAGEBRUSH MOTEL

COLUMBIA ST W

DOUGLAS ST

HOSPITAL

SAGEBRUSH THEATRE

NOTRE DAME DR

GREYHOUND BUS DEPOT

ACCENT INN KAMLOOPS

TRANSCANADA HWY

SUMMIT DR

LAVAL CR

VISITOR INFO CENTRE

To Cache Creek, Coquihalla Hwy, and Vancouver

ALPINE MOTEL

5A

To Merritt

MOON

SCALE NOT AVAILABLE

© AVALON TRAVEL PUBLISHING, INC.

Kamloops Art Gallery (465 Victoria St., 250/828-3543; adult $5, child $3) features an impressive collection of more than 1,000 works by contemporary artists in all sorts of media— quite a contrast to the museum. The hours are Monday–Friday 10 A.M.–5 P.M., Saturday–Sunday noon–4 P.M. The gallery stays open until 9 P.M. on Thursday, when admission is by donation after 5 P.M.

Secwepemc Museum & Heritage Park

A living-history museum dedicated to the Shuswap tribe, this cultural attraction (250/828-9801; Mon.–Fri. 8:30 A.M.–4:30 P.M., until 8 P.M. in summer; adult $6, senior $4, child $4) offers numerous exhibits focusing on the Shuswaps' traditions and rich mythology. Highlights include an archaeological site dating back 2,000 years, a re-created Shuswap winter village, a salmon-fishing station, a garden filled with native plants for food and medicinal purposes, and a re-creation of a traditional summer shelter. To get to the park, follow Highway 5 north across the Thompson River and take the first right.

British Columbia Wildlife Park

This nonprofit park (TransCanada Hwy., 16 km/10 miles east of Kamloops, 250/573-3242; July–Aug. 8:30 A.M.–8 P.M., Sept.–June 8 A.M.–4 P.M.; adult $9, senior and child $8) is primarily a wildlife rehabilitation center, but among the more than 150 furry inhabitants are many species of mammals from western Canada, including a couple of grizzly bears, wolves, cougars, and lynx. Other attractions are a huge visitor center, a glass-walled beehive, and, for the kids, a petting zoo and miniature steam train.

RECREATION

Paul Lake Provincial Park

This small provincial park northeast of Kamloops is a relaxing, grassy, tree-shaded spot to take a picnic, go swimming in warm Paul Lake, or camp. And the drive out there, following Paul Creek past scrub-covered rolling hills and flower-filled meadows, is an enjoyable ramble through the countryside. At the park's day-use area you'll find the best beach, picnic tables, toilets, and changing rooms. Before settling down at the beach, take the 1.6-kilometer (one-mile) trail out to a bluff overlooking the valley. To get to the park, head north of Kamloops five kilometers (3.1 miles) on Highway 5, then 17 kilometers (10.5 miles) east on Paul Lake Road.

Sun Peaks Resort

In the last decade, this mountain village north of the city along Highway 5 (250/578-7222 or 800/807-3257, www.sunpeaksresort.com) has evolved from a medium-sized local ski hill to a year-round resort, with ongoing development both on the slopes and at the base village, where a golf course spreads out along the valley floor.

In summer, the Sunburst Express lift takes the hard work out of reaching the alpine for hikers and bikers. From the top of this lift, it's easy to descend back to the village on foot in less than an hour, but if the weather is good, consider exploring higher elevations, including the 2,152-meter (7,060-foot) summit of Mount Tod. Mountain-bike enthusiasts have many options, but the most popular destination is McGillivray Lake, accessed along a wide 6.2-kilometer (3.8-mile) trail from the village. Ride the lift all day for $14 ($28 with a mountain bike). Other activities include golfing a shortish resort-style 18-hole course, tennis, horseback riding, and fishing. The most popular events of a packed schedule are **Music in the Mountains** in late July, an **arts festival** the first weekend of August, and the **Canadian Mountain Bike Festival** in the middle of August.

High season for the resort is wintertime, when two high-speed lifts whisk skiers up the mountain. One of these—the Sunburst Express—links up with three more lifts that access intermediate and expert terrain above the tree line and an easy eight-kilometer (five-mile) cruising run back to the village. The total vertical rise is 882 meters (2,900 feet) over almost 1,000 hectares (3,300 acres) of terrain. Facilities at the resort include eateries, a rental shop, and the Snow Sports School. Lift tickets are adult $51, senior $36, child $29. On-mountain accommodations packages are good value—from $80 per person per night including a lift ticket.

Entertainment

Two River Junction (814 Lorne St., 250/314-1631) is a nightly dinner and musical revue presented for the entertainment of overnighting passengers on the Rocky Mountaineer, but anyone is welcome to attend. It tells the story of Billy Miner, a U.S. stagecoach robber who, it is claimed, coined the phrase "Hands Up!" and spent the last years of his life in the Kamloops region. The revue is $35 per person, $57 with the buffet-style dinner. The amateur and professional musicians of the **Kamloops Symphony Society** regularly present classical and pop performances at the **Sagebrush Theatre** (821 Munro St., 250/372-5000). The main season is October–April, but the first weekend of August the orchestra performs outdoors at Sun Peaks Resort. British Columbia's third-largest theater company, Kamloops-based **Western Canada Theatre,** presents live theatrical productions by top Canadian actors, producers, and designers. Performances take place in the **Pavilion Theatre** (1025 Lorne St., 250/372-3216).

ACCOMMODATIONS AND CAMPING

You won't find quaint or memorable here. Instead, expect reliable motels serving the needs of highway travelers spread throughout the city. On the western approach to the city many newer motels offer clean and comfortable rooms but no particular bargains. The top end of Columbia Street West has some unspectacular older motels for travelers on a budget.

Under $50

Built in 1909, the Old Courthouse is now home to **HI—Kamloops** (7 W. Seymour St., 250/828-7991 or 866/782-9526, www.hihostels.ca), one of the grandest hostels in Canada. The building has been renovated to make hostelers feel a little more comfortable than the original "guests," yet the historic charm remains in the vaulted ceilings, winding staircases, stained-glass windows, and Canadian flags. Upstairs in the main courtroom you can write letters in the witness stand, sit in the judge's seat to sign the guest register, or relax in the jury seats. The original jail cells now hold bathrooms. And if you try to do any ironing, you'll be sent to solitary confinement—where the ironing board is. Dorm beds are $16 for members, $20 for nonmembers, and private rooms are $35–45. Check-in is 8 A.M.–noon and 5 –10 P.M.

$50–100

It's nothing to write home about, but the **Fountain Motel** (506 Columbia St., 250/374-4451 or 800/253-1569, www.fountain.kamloops.com) offers a higher standard of rooms than the exterior may suggest; $56–68 s or d and kitchenettes an extra $10. The best of other similarly priced choices along a wide sweeping bend of Columbia Street West between the TransCanada Highway and downtown is the **Sagebrush Motel** (660 Columbia St. W, 250/372-3151, $45 s, $58 d). This place has air-conditioned rooms, each with a coffeemaker and biggish TV, as well as an adjacent restaurant open daily from 7 A.M. Across the TransCanada Highway, **Alpine Motel** (1393 Hugh Allan Dr., 250/374-0034 or 800/270-1260) offers standard rooms from $80, or suites with kitchen and hot tub for a few dollars more.

$100–150

Just off the highway near the west side access to downtown, **Accent Inn Kamloops** (1325 Columbia St. W, 250/374-8877 or 800/663-0298, www.accentinns.com) charges $119 s, $129 d for a modern and spacious room, with guests having use of an outdoor pool, hot tub, and fitness room. Free email in the lobby and a national paper delivered to your door are unexpected touches. Check the website of this small provincial chain for discounted rates.

Right downtown is the **Plaza Heritage Hotel** (405 Victoria St., 250/377-8075 or 877/977-5292, www.plazaheritagehotel.com), first opened in 1928 as one the interior's finest accommodations. Its restoration and opening as a boutique hotel is only recent. The 68 rooms feature rich woods, a heritage color scheme, and comfortable beds covered in plush duvets. The Heritage Restaurant and a stylish lounge bar are at street level. The smallest rooms are $139 s or d, but the king rooms are only $10 more.

Camping

Heading out of Kamloops to the east, 16 kilometers (10 miles) from downtown, **Kamloops RV Park** (9225 Dallas Dr., 250/573-3789) offers full hookups, coin-operated showers, a laundry, hot tub, and grocery store, and is next door to the wildlife park. Unserviced sites are $18, hookups $22–30.

The city's most scenic campground is at **Paul Lake Provincial Park,** north of Kamloops five km (3.1 miles) on Highway 5, then 17 kilometers (11 miles) east on Paul Lake Road. Facilities are basic (no hookups or showers), but the treed setting just a short walk to the beach makes up for it. All sites are $14.

FOOD

Kamloops has the usual family-style and fast-food restaurants along the highway, as well as some good dining choices in the downtown core.

Downtown

A good lunch spot slightly off the main downtown thoroughfare is the old-fashioned **Smorgasbord** (225 7th Ave., 250/377-0055; Mon.–Sat. 7 A.M.–5 P.M.), which is not a smorgasbord as the British know it, but a small café offering a wide range of soups, salads, and sandwiches, with a daily special offering the best value.

Superb sushi is the draw at **Sanbiki** (476 Victoria St., 250/377-8857; daily 11:30 A.M.–2:30 P.M. and 5:30–9:30 P.M.), in a distinctive orange building with a sun-splashed patio out front. The chefs do a great job of sourcing the freshest of ingredients, including—most importantly—seafood. A popular lunch combo dish is teriyaki chicken, tempura, California rolls, salad, and miso soup for $11. Other choices include asparagus Shira-ae, done in a creamy sesame sauce; hearty rice bowls; and crumbed panko prawns.

Although the simply decorated **Mandarin Restaurant** (256 Victoria St., 250/372-8398; Mon.–Sat. 11 A.M.–10 P.M., Sun. noon–8 P.M.) advertises the unusual combo of Chinese and Portuguese food, the menu is mostly the former. Give the buffet lunch a miss and instead plan on dinner. Among the offerings to start is lettuce wrapped with spiced minced beef ($7) and lots of seafood. Despite the long menu, there's no barbecued pork, so I opted for the chicken and almond stir-fry ($12) and a serving of fried rice ($3.50), which was delicious. Next door, **D'Agostino Restaurant** (258 Victoria St., 250/372-1111) is an informal, unpretentious Italian restaurant open daily for lunch and dinner.

East of downtown along the river is **Storms** (1502 River St., 250/372-1522; lunch and dinner daily), one of Kamloops's best restaurants. The elegant setting includes tables set on an outdoor deck overlooking the river. The menu features classic European and North American dishes, such as a succulent rack of lamb roasted in Dijon mustard and fresh rosemary for $23. Other mains start at $16, or just soak up the river atmosphere with a platter of appetizers for $19.

OTHER PRACTICALITIES

Information and Services

Kamloops Visitor Info Centre (250/374-3377 or 800/662-1994, www.adventurekamloops.com) is beside the TransCanada Highway on the western outskirts of town (at Hillside Rd. opposite the Aberdeen Mall). It's open in summer daily 8 A.M.–8 P.M., the rest of the year Monday–Friday 8:30 A.M.–4 P.M.

The biggest bookstore between Vancouver and Calgary is **Merlin Books** (448 Victoria St., 250/374-9553; Mon.–Fri. 8:30 A.M.–8 P.M., Sat. 8:30 A.M.–6 P.M., Sun. noon–8 P.M.). The selection is strong on local interest but offers plenty of everything else as well.

Royal Inland Hospital (311 Columbia St., 250/374-5111) is at the south end of 3rd Avenue. The **post office** is at 301 Seymour Street.

Transportation

Kamloops Airport is on Airport Road, seven kilometers northwest of city center; follow Tranquille Road through the North Shore until you come to Airport Road on the left. **Air Canada** (888/247-2262) has scheduled flights between Kamloops and Vancouver.

The railway station is right downtown at the

north end of 3rd Avenue. **VIA Rail** (800/561-8630) runs scheduled service three times weekly west to Vancouver and east to Jasper. Kamloops is also the overnight stop for the **Rocky Mountaineer Vacations** (800/665-7245), a summer-only luxurious rail trip between Vancouver, Jasper, and Banff (see *Getting There* in the *Know British Columbia* chapter for more details).

Greyhound provides daily service to most parts of the province from its Kamloops bus depot

(725 Notre Dame Dr., off Columbia St. W at the west end of town, 250/374-1212).

Local bus transportation (including out to the airport) is provided by **Kamloops Transit System** (250/376-1216); adult fare is $1.50, while a day pass is $5. Taxi companies include: **Kami Cabs** (250/374-5151) and **Yellow Cabs** (250/374-3333). For a rental car, call **Budget** (250/376-5423), **Hertz** (250/376-3022), or **National** (250/374-5737).

North to Mount Robson

From Kamloops, Highway 5 follows the North Thompson River to Tete Jaune Cache on Highway 16. This stretch of highway is part of the most direct route between Vancouver and Jasper National Park, and is also worthwhile for two excellent provincial parks—**Wells Gray,** a vast wilderness of rivers and mountains, and **Mount Robson,** protecting a spectacular peak that is the highest point in the Canadian Rockies.

Barriere

In the summer of 2003, Barriere, 66 kilometers (41 miles) north of Kamloops, was evacuated as wildfires surrounded the small town during a hot spell of weather that kept the surrounding mountains alight for six weeks. A sawmill, the town's main employer, and 70 homes were lost in the blaze. Driving through today, you will see scarred hillsides and open areas along the valley floor where burnt trees and buildings have been cleared.

Along the highway through town, the **Monte Carlo Motel** (Hwy. 5, 250/672-9676 or 888/660-5050; from $50 s, $60 d) is good value. The medium-sized rooms are air-conditioned, and if it's a hot day, take a dip in the outdoor pool.

CLEARWATER

The small town of Clearwater (pop. 1,600), 125 kilometers (78 miles) north of Kamloops, is the gateway to Wells Gray Provincial Park. A few motels, restaurants, gas stations, services, and an information center are on the highway;

the rest of the community is off the highway to the south.

Accommodations and Camping

A couple of good overnight options lie along the park access road, or stay in Clearwater at **Dutch Lake Resort & RV Park** (361 Ridge Rd., 250/674-3351 or 888/884-4424, www.dutch-lake.com; May–Oct.), where tent camping is $22 and hookups range $27–30. Cabins are $80–180, with the largest sleeping three couples and having full kitchens. Resort activities revolve around families and the water; the on-site restaurant (daily 8:30 A.M.–3 P.M. and 5–9 P.M.) has a wide patio overlooking the lake.

Food

Housed in a massive log building a few hundred meters along the park access road, the **N Flower Meadow Bakery** (444 Clearwater Valley Rd., 250/674-3654) is impossible to miss—and you won't want to either. The breakfast burritos ($5) are healthy and huge; the lemon meringues are also super-sized (but probably not as good for you), and the carrot cake will melt in your mouth. There's plenty of room for everyone, with the outdoor seating filling first. On your way out, buy an extra loaf of bread or a stacked sandwich to go for a picnic in the park. It's open in summer Monday–Friday 5 A.M.–8 P.M., Saturday 5 A.M.–6 P.M., and closes around 6 P.M. the rest of the year. On Thursday evenings (7 P.M. start) through summer, the friendly owners host a barbecue with live music—it's just that kind of place.

Information

At the turnoff to Wells Gray Provincial Park is **Clearwater Visitor Info Centre** (250/674-2646; summer daily 8 A.M.–6 P.M., the rest of the year weekdays 9 A.M.–5 P.M.). Look for the moose sculpture out front. It's a popular spot for tour buses (a handy restroom stop between Jasper and Kamloops, I was told by a coach driver), so if the center is crowded, bide your time with an ice cream from the adjacent log cabin.

WELLS GRAY PROVINCIAL PARK

Snow-clad peaks, extinct volcanoes, and ancient lava flows. Amazing waterfalls—so many the park is often referred to as the "Waterfall Park." Icy mineral springs, subalpine forest, and flower-filled meadows. Prolific wildlife (I counted six bears, five deer, and two moose on my last visit). An abundance of lakes and rivers where anglers can fish to their heart's content for rainbow trout and Dolly Varden.

The main access road into the 540,000-hectare (1,334,000-acre) park leads north from Clearwater for 37 kilometers (23 miles) to the park boundary. From there it continues 11 kilometers (6.8 miles) to one of the park's highlights, Helmcken Falls, where it turns to gravel and continues another 18 kilometers (11 miles) to its end at Clearwater Lake. Although this access road barely penetrates the park, driving its length is enough to get a taste of the rugged northern reaches. If it's not, you can take a canoe trip or boat tour from the end of the road.

Sights and Hikes

Make your first stop 10 kilometers (6.2 miles) from Clearwater, where a short trail leads through an old-growth forest of cedar and hemlock to a colorful lava canyon where 61-meter-high **Spahats Creek Falls** plummets over multicolored bedrock into the Clearwater River.

Continuing through the park, take a signposted gravel road to the west to **Green Viewing Tower** atop Green Mountain. The viewpoint provides panoramic views of a volcanic cone and many spectacular, rugged peaks, including snow-covered Garnet Peak, highest in the park.

Wells Gray is best known for its waterfalls, the two most spectacular of which are accessible by road. Southernmost is **Dawson Falls,** four kilometers (2.5 miles) into the park, where the **Murtle River** cascades over a 90-meter-wide ledge. A little farther along the main road is the **Mush Bowl** (or Devil's Punchbowl), where the river has carved huge holes in the riverbed. But save some film for incredible **Helmcken Falls,** British Columbia's fourth-highest falls, where the Murtle River cascades off the edge of Murtle Plateau in a sparkling, 137-meter-high torrent to join the Clearwater River. In winter, the frozen falls create an enormous ice cone as tall as a 20-story building.

For an enjoyable short walk from the road (20 minutes each way), hike the one-kilometer (.6-mile) trail out to **Ray Farm,** former home of one of the area's first settlers. John Bunyon Ray cleared his farm out of the wilderness in 1912, and he and his wife raised a family in this isolated spot. The picturesque abandoned farm buildings sit among rolling meadows full of wildflowers. From the farm, another short trail leads to a mineral spring.

Farther north up the road, a 500-meter (.3-mile) trail (10 minutes each way) winds through a stand of towering cedar trees to **Bailey's Chute,** a narrow rapids-filled passage. In fall, large numbers of chinook salmon battle the torrent, trying in vain to leap up the chute. After a number of valiant attempts, they're washed back downstream to the gravel beds where they spawn and die.

Clearwater Lake

The road ends at a boat ramp/canoe dock beside the southern end of Clearwater Lake, 66 kilometers (41 miles) from the town of Clearwater. To make the most of the lake, you really need to take to the water. Based just before where the road ends (take the Clearwater Campground turnoff), **Clearwater Lake Tours** (250/674-2121) offers a couple of options. A four-hour motorboat cruise to Rainbow Falls at the north end of the lake departs daily at 11 A.M. and costs adult $50, senior $38, child $30. Drinks are supplied, but bring lunch (preferably from Flower Meadow Bakery in Clearwater). The company has canoes for those who would rather propel themselves. A two-hour rental is $25, or pay $40 per day. The most popular overnight destination for paddlers is Azure Lake, 50 kilometers (31 miles) and a 500-meter (.3-mile) portage from the put-in point. Numerous wilderness campsites line the shores of both lakes.

Accommodations and Camping

Around halfway between Clearwater and Helmcken Falls, **M** **Wells Gray Guest Ranch** (250/674-2792 or 866/467-4346, www.wellsgrayranch.com; May–Oct.) is surrounded by grassy meadows full of wildflowers and grazing horses. Activities organized for guests include horseback riding ($35 for a 1.5-hour ride), canoeing, whitewater rafting, fishing, and western-style barbecues. Overnight options are: well-furnished, kitchen-equipped cabins ($120 s or d); ranch house rooms with shared bathrooms ($85 s or d); tepees ($15 per person); a bunkhouse ($10 per person); and a limited number of campsites ($14). The ranch also has a restaurant and saloon (daily 4 P.M.–midnight).

Continuing north, **Helmcken Falls Lodge** (250/674-3657, www.helmckenfalls.com) overlooks the golf course and seemingly endless forested hills. The main lodge was constructed as a fishing camp in the 1940s but has been revamped since, with motel-like rooms costing $124–155 s or d and the on-site restaurant cooking up simple, well-priced meals. Camping with hookups is $19–27.

Each of the three park campgrounds along the access road has drinking water, toilets, and picnic tables; none have hookups or showers. Sites cost $14 per night. Heading up the road from Clearwater, you'll pass, in order, **Spahats Creek Campground,** within walking distance of the falls; **Pyramid Campground,** just beyond Dawson Falls; **Falls Creek Campground,** with large riverside sites; and finally **Clearwater Lake Campground,** which is almost at the end of the road, right on the lake, and is the first to fill each night. Camping in the park is possible mid-May through October. Although

no reservations are taken, you can find out about campsite availability at the Clearwater Visitor Info Centre.

If you need a serviced site, stay at tranquil **Wells Gray Golf Resort & RV Park** (35 km/22 miles north of Clearwater, 250/674-0072; May–Oct.), which has 50 campsites set in the middle of a full-length nine-hole golf course (greens fee $18). Rates of $20–25 include full hookups, free firewood, and use of modern shower facilities.

Information

Park information is available at **Clearwater Visitor Info Centre** (250/674-2646; summer daily 8 A.M.–6 P.M., the rest of the year weekdays 9 A.M.–5 P.M.). The center sells two invaluable guidebooks to the park: *Exploring Wells Gray Park* and *Nature Wells Gray.*

BLUE RIVER

Although right on busy Highway 5, 215 kilometers (134 miles) north of Kamloops, this one-time railway division point has remained small, holding just a few hundred residents along with services for passing travelers. Lake Eleanor, in the middle of town, offers a good beach and swimming, but most visitors head into the surrounding wilderness—the Cariboo Mountains to the north, Wells Gray Provincial Park to the west, and the northern reaches of the North Thompson River just to the east. Access to the eastern reaches of Wells Gray Provincial Park is by a 24-kilometer (15-mile) gravel road heading west from the middle of Blue River. From the trailhead at the end of the road it's a 2.5-kilometer (1.5-mile) walk to **Murtle Lake,** the park's largest freshwater lake.

Accommodations and Camping

M **Mike Wiegele Resort** (250/673-8381 or 800/661-9170, www.wiegele.com) is designed for the wintertime heli-skiing crowd, but it's open year-round. Mike Wiegele was instrumental in the development of "fat boy" skis that helped revolutionize powder skiing by making it easier for everyone. His resort has grown from

TERRY FOX

Terry Fox is a name that is sure to come up at some point on your Canadian travels. In 1977, as a college-bound teenager, Fox lost his right leg to cancer. On April 12, 1980, after three years of training, with next to no sponsorship and little media coverage, he set off from Newfoundland on his **Marathon of Hope,** with the aim of raising money for cancer research. After running over 5,000 kilometers (3,100 miles) in 144 days, a recurrence of the cancer forced him to stop just outside Ontario's Thunder Bay. Cancer had begun spreading to his lungs, and on June 28, 1981, aged just 22, he died. As his run had progressed, the attention had grown, and, more importantly, the donations poured in. In total, his Marathon of Hope raised $24 million, far surpassing all goals.

The legacy of Terry Fox lives on in many ways, including 2,650-meter (8,700-foot) **Mount Terry Fox,** along the Yellowhead Highway; the **Terry Fox Run,** an annual fall event in many Canadian towns; Vancouver's **Terry Fox Plaza** and a tribute in the adjacent B.C. Sports Hall of Fame and Museum; and an annual $5 million scholarship fund.

humble beginnings to a world-class facility, featured in many ski movies and the host of the annual Powder 8 Championship. His latest venture is the development of lift-served skiing and boarding on remote Saddle Mountain, where the only access is by helicopter. Wintertime visitors enjoy some of the world's most famous powder skiing in the Cariboo and Monashee Mountains, then kick back each evening at the upscale resort in Blue River. Accommodation is in large two- to six-room log chalets in a private setting beside Lake Eleanor. Amenities include an ultramodern fitness center, game room, a restaurant overseen by European chefs, and a sports shop with bike rentals. In the off-season (April–November), if the resort hasn't been booked by a tour group, the rooms are one of British Columbia's best bargains—$110–195 s or d for a luxurious suite with a full kitchen, log fireplace, and comfortable lounge. The rates are somewhat flexible—if the dining room isn't open you may be charged less and be directed to another restaurant (also owned by the resort) across the highway.

Glacier Mountain Lodge (250/673-2393 or 877/452-2686, www.glaciermountainlodge.com) is another stylish Blue River accommodation, this one offering 33 well-appointed guest rooms. Summer rates of $89–130 s or d, including a continental breakfast buffet and use of a hot tub, make this place good value.

The least expensive place to stay in town is **Blue River Campground** (250/673-8203; May–mid-Oct.), where sites range $16–28 per night, or you can stay in a tepee for $35 s or d. The campground is within walking distance of Lake Eleanor.

VALEMOUNT AND BEYOND

North of Blue River, Highway 5 follows the North Thompson River through the Cariboo Mountains to Valemount, 20 kilometers (12 miles) south of the Yellowhead Highway.

Although most highway drivers hurry through town on their way to Jasper National Park, Valemount has plenty to offer those traveling at a slower pace. The town boasts two scenic golf courses, horseback riding with Borderline Guides (250/566-9161), lots of fishing holes (ask for a brochure at the information center), and mountain scenery all around. If you're passing through between mid-August and late September, be sure to visit Swift Creek, below the information center, where chinook salmon spawn after a 1,200-kilometer (745-mile) journey from the Pacific Ocean. At the south end of town is the spring-fed Cranberry Marsh, where you can expect to see Canada geese, teals, ducks, and red-winged blackbirds. Park at the Holiday Inn and follow the marked trail 500 meters (.3 mile) to a bird tower for the best viewing opportunities. The highway

Calumet Ridge

Calumet Peak

Mumm Peak

Mural Glacier

Mt Phillips

Suncurrent Glacier

Robson Pass

Upright Mtn

Toboggan Falls

Berg Lake

Moose

Reef Icefield

Whitehorn Mtn

Rearguard Mtn

Emperor Falls

River

Robson Cirque

Mt Robson

Resplendent Mtn

Rainbow Range

Kinney Lake

Mount Robson

Mt Kain

Robson

Provincial

EMPEROR RIDGE

MT ROBSON VISITOR CENTRE

ROBSON RIVER

Park

River

HWY

ROBSON MEADOWS

To Prince George

MOUNT ROBSON LODGE

MOUNTAIN RIVER LODGE

River

Moose Lake

16

Fraser

YELLOWHEAD

16

Tête Jaune Cache

Moose Marsh

Mt Terry Fox

McLennan

Mt Terry Fox Provincial Park

The Comb

River

Swift Creek

Sleeper Mountains

Valemount

Sleeper

5

Creek

MOON

0   5 mi

0   5 km

Creek

Yellowjacket

Kinbasket Lake

Canoe River

To Kamloops

MOUNT ROBSON
PROVINCIAL PARK

Mt Stornoway

Mt Sassenach

De Smet Range

Mt Strange

Jasper

National

Harvey Lake

Park

Snaring

Mt McCord

Mt Mahood

Mt McNaughton

Victoria Cross Ranges

BRITISH COLUMBIA

ALBERTA

Mt Bridgland

Deer

Creek

Miette

Portal Lake

16

Yellowhead Mtn

Yellowhead Lake

LUCERNE

Yellowhead Pass

To Jasper

Fitzwilliam Basin

Mt Fitzwilliam

Clairvaux Creek

Ghita

Fraser

Creek

Waddington Peak

River

The Ramparts

© AVALON TRAVEL PUBLISHING, INC.

bypasses the older section of town; turn east at 5th Avenue, cross the rail line, and head north to reach **Valemount Museum** (1090 Main St., 250/566-4177), set in a 1914 railway station.

Practicalities

 Mica Mountain Lodge (Old Tete Jaune Rd., 250/566-9816 or 888/440-6422, www.micamountainlodge.bc.ca) is in a wilderness setting on the northwest side of town. During summer, guests ride horses, canoe, fish, and mountain bike. Come winter, it's cross-country skiing, dog sledding, and snowmobiling that are the major draws. The cabins are charming and practical, with full kitchens, three-piece en suite bathrooms, decks, TVs, and pine log beds. Summer rates are quoted at $125 s or d, but many visitors stay as part of an activity package. **Irvin's Park and Campground** (one km/.6 mile north of town, 250/566-4781, www .irvins.ca) has a few tent sites along one side, but it's best suited mostly for RVs and trailers; $23–29 per rig.

Cariboo Grill (1002 5th Ave., 250/566-8244; daily from 4:30 P.M.) is in an oversized log building beyond the downtown core along 5th Avenue. It's a good place for enjoying simple, hearty food from a mostly steak-and-seafood menu (mains $14–20).

Tourism Valemount (250/566-4846, www .valemount.org) operates a **Visitor Info Centre** along Highway 5, across from the turnoff to downtown. It's open mid-May to mid-September.

Valemount to Mount Robson

From the Yellowhead Highway junction 20 kilometers (12 miles) north of Valemount, Prince George is 270 kilometers (168 miles) to the west, and the British Columbia–Alberta border is 76 kilometers (47 miles) east. Although most of the distance to the border is through Mount Robson Provincial Park, two worthwhile stops lie between the highway junction and the park. The first of these is **Rearguard Falls,** a one-kilometer (.6-mile) hike (20 minutes each way) from the highway. Eight kilometers (five miles) downstream from the falls—some 1,200 kilometers (745 miles) up the Fraser River from the Pacific

Central British Columbia

Ocean—is a spawning grounds for Pacific salmon; many of the hardy fish make it all the way to the falls. Farther east along the highway is a viewpoint for **Mount Terry Fox** (see sidebar, *Terry Fox*).

MOUNT ROBSON PROVINCIAL PARK

Spectacular Mount Robson Provincial Park was created in 1913 to protect 224,866 hectares (555,650 acres) of steep canyons and wide forested valleys; icy lakes, rivers, and streams; and rugged mountain peaks permanently blanketed in snow and ice. Towering over the park's western entrance is magnificent 3,954-meter (12,970-foot) **Mount Robson,** highest peak in the Canadian Rockies. The park lies along the Continental Divide, in British Columbia, adjacent to Jasper National Park. The main watershed is the Fraser River, one of British Columbia's most important waterways. From within the

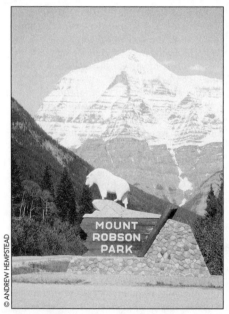

The approach to Mount Robson Provincial Park is stunning.

park it flows northwest to Prince George then southward through the heart of the province to drain into the Pacific Ocean at Vancouver. Highway 16, from where many roadside sights present themselves, splits the park in two, but for many visitors it is the famous Berg Lake Trail to which they are attracted.

Flora and Fauna

The elevation differences within the park are as great as anywhere else in the Canadian Rockies, giving rise to a great variety of flora and fauna. The main service center lies in a forested valley at an elevation of just 840 meters (2,770 feet), right in the heart of the montane. The oft-photographed view of Mount Robson from the visitor center is framed by a stand of trembling aspen across a cleared meadow, but the most common tree at this elevation, and one that covers the valley floor, is Douglas fir. Western red cedar and hemlock thrive in damp sections of the park. As with the rest of the Canadian Rockies, the subalpine is dominated by Engelmann spruce and, at higher elevations, subalpine fir. The alpine zone in the park begins at around 2,300 meters (7,550 feet).

In spring black bears are often seen feasting on dandelions by the roadside, but their larger relative, the grizzly, rarely makes an appearance in the busy valley through which Highway 16 winds. Elk, moose, and mountain goats are also present, as are many smaller critters. Over 170 bird species have been identified, with the rare harlequin duck a special joy to watch as it passes though the park each spring.

History

Local Shuswap natives called Mount Robson Yuh-hai-has-hun ("Mountain of the Spiral Road") for its layered appearance. Historians guess that the peak's European name honors a member of the Hudson's Bay Company, though details of the christening have been lost to history.

Mountaineers were attracted to the challenge of climbing Mount Robson at the very beginning of this century, but the first official ascent took place in 1913, the same year the park as we know it today was created. Led by Swiss guide

© ANDREW HEMPSTEAD

Conrad Kain, the first ascent party was made up of members of the Alpine Club of Canada. Although this was the first official summit climb, the summit had been attempted four years earlier by the Reverend George Kinney and friends. Kinney thought he'd made the summit, but he was climbing the summit ridge in a heavy fog; a cairn and a message recording the names of the members of Kinney's climbing team were later found on the ridge about 100 vertical meters from the top.

Roadside Sights

If you're approaching the park from the west along Highway 16, you'll see **Mount Robson** long before you reach the park boundary, provided the weather is cooperating. It's impossible to confuse this distinctive peak with those that surround it—no wonder it's known as the "Monarch of the Canadian Rockies." Once inside the park boundary, the highway climbs gradually to the main facility area, where you'll find a visitor center, campgrounds, a gas station, and a restaurant. On a clear day the panorama from this lump of commercialism is equal to any sight in British Columbia. The sheer west face of Mount Robson slices skyward just seven kilometers away across a flower-filled meadow. This is as close as you can get to the peak in your car.

From the park's only service area, the highway climbs steeply then parallels photogenic **Moose Lake.** Waterfalls on the far side of the lake create a scenic backdrop. The Moose River drains into the Fraser River at **Moose Marsh,** a good spot for wildlife watching at the southeast end of the lake. Moose often feed here at dawn and dusk, and waterfowl are present throughout the day. Continuing westward, the highway crosses the upper reaches of the Fraser River before passing long and narrow Yellowhead Lake at the foot of 2,458-meter (8,060-foot) **Yellowhead Mountain.**

Finally, Highway 16 exits the park at the 1,066-meter (3,500-foot) **Yellowhead Pass,** on the British Columbia–Alberta border 60 kilometers (37.2 miles) east of the visitor center. It's the lowest highway pass over the Continental Divide. Right before the pass is picturesque **Portal Lake,** with a small lakeside picnic area.

Berg Lake Trail

- Length: 19.5 km/12 miles (eight hours) one-way
- Elevation gain: 725 meters/2,380 feet
- Rating: moderate/difficult
- Trailhead: two km (1.2 miles) north of the visitor center along a narrow access road

This is the most popular overnight hike in the Canadian Rockies, but don't let the crowds put you off—the hike is well worth it. Beautiful aqua-colored Berg Lake lies below the north face of Mount Robson, which rises 2,400 meters (7,880 feet) directly behind the lake. Glaciers on the mountain's shoulder regularly calve off into the lake, resulting in the icebergs that give the lake its name. It's possible to traverse the trail's first section and return the same day, but to get all the way to Berg Lake and back you need to stay in the backcountry overnight. Along the route are seven primitive campgrounds, including three along the lakeshore. Overnight hikers must register at the visitor center and pay a camping fee of $6 per person per night. Only 75 campsites lie along the trail. Bookings for these sites are taken at the visitor center or through BC Parks (604/689-9025 or 800/689-9025). Book early as the quota fills quickly.

From the trailhead, the trail follows the Robson River 4.5 kilometers (2.8 miles) through dense subalpine forest to glacially fed **Kinney Lake.** There the trail narrows, crossing the fast-flowing river at the eight-kilometer (five-mile) mark and climbing alongside it. The next four kilometers (2.5 miles), through the steep-sided Valley of a Thousand Falls, are the most demanding, but views of four spectacular waterfalls ease the pain of the 500-vertical-meter (1,640-vertical-foot) climb. The first glimpses of Mount Robson come soon after reaching the head of the valley, from where it's another kilometer to the outlet of Berg Lake, 17.5 kilometers (10.9 miles) from the trailhead. The first of three lakeside campgrounds is two kilometers (1.2 miles) from this point.

While the panorama from the lake is stunning, most hikers who have come this far want to spend some time exploring the area. From the north end of the lake, trails lead to Toboggan Falls and more mountain views, to the head of Robson Glacier, and to Robson Pass, which opens up the remote northern reaches of Jasper National Park.

If the walk in seems too ambitious, **Robson Helimagic** (250/566-4700 or 877/454-4700) makes drop-offs at Robson Pass from Valemount every Monday and Friday; $185 per person (minimum four). This company also offers regular flightseeing from $145 per person for a 36-minute flight.

Other Hikes in the Park

Aside from the busy trail to Berg Lake, the park holds only two other established trails. The shortest of the two ascends the slopes of **Yellowhead Mountain.** From the trailhead across the rail line at Yellowhead Lake it's a steady climb through subalpine forest to the first viewpoint at the one-kilometer mark. Another three kilometers (1.9 miles) and a total elevation gain of 720 meters (2,060 feet) brings you to flower-filled meadows and panoramic views extending east to the Continental Divide and west to the Selwyn Range. Allow two hours each way for this hike.

The other option is the 13-kilometer (eight-mile) one-way **Fitzwilliam Basin Trail,** which requires an overnight stay in the backcountry. Elevation gain is 950 meters (3,120 feet), so it's a fairly demanding trail. From the trailhead on the south side of Highway 16, three kilometers (1.9 miles) east of Lucerne Campground, the trail climbs steadily for six kilometers to the confluence of Rockingham and Fitzwilliam Creeks. Although easy to follow, the remaining seven kilometers (4.3 miles) along the northern slopes of 2,911-meter (9,550-foot) Mount Fitzwilliam are rough going. After ascending a steep ridge the trail all but dissipates, but many camping spots can be found in the wide lake-filled basin.

Accommodations and Camping

Mountain River Lodge (four km/2.5 miles west of the visitor center, 250/566-9899 or 888/566-9899, www.mtrobson.com) is in a delightful setting right alongside the Fraser River. The main lodge holds four guest rooms, each with a different character, a balcony, and private bathroom. The smallest of the rooms (with twin beds and a private bathroom down the hall) is $85 s or d, while the other three are $105; rates include a cooked breakfast. Self-contained cabins cost $125 per night, with breakfast available at an extra charge. One kilometer (.6 mile) west of Mountain River Lodge is **Mount Robson Lodge** (250/566-4821 or 888/566-4821, www.mountrobsonlodge.com; May–Oct.), with 18 free-standing cabins ($70–125 s or d); the more expensive ones have kitchens, or eat at the small coffee shop.

Within the park are four auto-accessible campgrounds, with another just outside the park boundary. Three of these are park operated. Closest to the visitor center (and my favorite) is **Robson River Campground,** where numerous trails lead down to the river for the classic upstream view of Mount Robson. It's also only a short walk to the visitor center and a café. Across the highway is the larger **Robson Meadows Campground,** with 125 sites set on a spiral road system that centers on an outdoor theater that hosts evening interpretive programs through summer. A number of sites at Robson Meadows can be reserved through www.discovercamping.ca. Both campgrounds have flush toilets and showers but no hookups; $17 per site. Beside the east end of Yellowhead Lake (swimming for the brave), 50 kilometers (31 miles) from the visitor center, is the more rustic **Lucerne Campground,** where sites are $14. Facilities include drinking water, pit toilets, and picnic tables. All facilities are open May to mid-September. **Emperor Ridge Campground** (250/566-8438; mid-May–late Sept.) is a small commercial facility right behind the visitor center; $14.50 per site including hot showers but no hookups. **Robson Shadows Campground** is part of Mount Robson Lodge (250/566-4821 or 888/566-4821, www.mountrobsonlodge.com; May–Oct.), outside of the park and five kilometers (3.1 miles) west of visitor center. It also has showers but no hookups. Sites are $15 per night.

Information

At the park's western entrance, **Mount Robson Visitor Centre** (250/566-9174, www.bcparks.ca) features informative natural-history slide shows, an evening interpretive program, and trail reports updated daily. The center stocks the brochure *Mount Robson Provincial Park,* which provides sufficient information if you're only driving through the park. Hikers and climbers can pick up more detailed trail descriptions and topographical maps ($11) at the center. Hours are mid-June to mid-September daily 8 A.M.–8 P.M., mid-May to mid-June and mid-September to mid-October daily 8 A.M.–5 P.M., closed the rest of the year.

Cariboo Country

The wild, sparsely populated Cariboo region extends from Kamloops north to Prince George and west to the Pacific Ocean. Its most dramatic natural features are the mountain ranges rising like bookends to either side. In the west, the **Coast Mountains** run parallel to the coast and rise to a height of 4,016 meters (13,200 feet) at **Mount Waddington.** In the east, the **Cariboo Mountains** harbor numerous alpine lakes, high peaks, and several provincial parks.

Between the two ranges flows the **Fraser River,** which is flanked to the west by expansive plateaus home to British Columbia's biggest ranches. This is cowboy country, where horseback holidays and the famous Williams Lake Stampede are the main visitor drawcards. This was once gold-rush country—most of the region's towns began as stopping places along the Gold Rush Trail. Those such as **100 Mile House** owe their names to the trail but have remained small, while others, such as **Williams Lake** and **Quesnel,** have continued to grow and are service centers for the ranching and forestry industries. The only coastal access in Cariboo Country is via Highway 20, which runs through **Tweedsmuir Provincial Park** to **Bella Coola,** at the head of a long fjord.

CACHE CREEK

A town born with the fur trade at a spot where traders cached furs and food supplies, Cache Creek was once the largest town between Vancouver, 337 kilometers (200 miles) to the south, and Kamloops, 80 kilometers (50 miles) to the east. But since the new Coquihalla Highway opened, the town is but a shadow of its former self. It still lies on the most direct route between the south and north ends of the province, and travelers not willing to pay the $10 toll on the Coquihalla Highway still pass through, even though it costs them at least an extra $5 in gas.

The surrounding desertlike climate is intriguing; sagebrush and cacti grow on the relatively barren volcanic landscape, and tumbleweeds blow through town. Due to the town's former highway prominence, the main drag is lined with motels, roadside diners, and gas stations.

▶ Historic Hat Creek Ranch

Between 1885 and 1905, the Cariboo Wagon Road bustled with stagecoaches and freight wagons. One of the few sections of the original road still open to the public is at Hat Creek Ranch, 11 kilometers north of Cache Creek on Highway 97 (250/457-9722 or 800/782-0922, www.hatcreekranch.com; mid-May–mid-Oct. daily 10 A.M.–6 P.M.). Many of the original buildings—some dating as far back as 1861—still stand, and visitors can watch the blacksmith at his forge, appreciate a collection of antique farm machinery, enjoy a picnic lunch in the orchard, or take a guided tour of the ranch house. Admission to the ranch is free, but a donation is requested after touring the house.

Accommodations

The **Sage Hills Motel** (1390 Hwy. 97, 250/457-6451 or 888/649-9494) is one of many local motels that would have filled every night before the highway was rerouted. Today, it's seen better days, but the owners try their best, keeping the place clean and planting a colorful bed of flowers out front each spring.

Central British Columbia

ECHO VALLEY RANCH RESORT

Echo Valley Ranch Resort

© ANDREW HEMPSTEAD

You can choose between several guest ranches in Cariboo Country, but none comes close to the luxury offered at Echo Valley Ranch Resort (northwest of Clinton, 800/253-8831, www.evranch.com). Deep in the heart of ranching country, the resort provides the opportunity to immerse yourself in western culture while indulging in the amenities of an upmarket lodge. The emphasis is on horseback riding, with lessons and guided rides scheduled each day, but there are plenty of other things to do, such as taking a four-wheel-drive excursion into the nearby Fraser River Canyon, watching a falcon trainer at work, and learning about native culture. The centerpiece of the sprawling property is an impressive main lodge, built entirely of glistening spruce logs. Inside is a comfortable lounge area, the communal dining room overlooking an open kitchen, and a downstairs billiards and TV room. Adjacent is an impressive Baan Thai structure, with full spa services, and the Pavilion, for quiet contemplation.

Rooms in the main lodge are beautifully furnished, and each has a private balcony, while the Honeymoon Cabin sits high above a deep ravine and has a wraparound deck complete with hot tub. Dining is ranch style, at a couple of long tables with plenty of interaction between guests. But the food is anything but chili and beans from a one-time chef to European royalty.

As you'd expect, staying at Echo Valley isn't cheap (from $400 per person per night in high season), but it's a very special place that my wife and I hold dear memories of from our own honeymoon.

Rates are $45 s or d, while units with kitchens are $55. At **Hat Creek Ranch** (250/457-9722 or 800/782-0922, www.hatcreekranch.com) a lack of creature comforts is a trade-off for experiencing the western atmosphere of this historic property. The cabins ($65 for up to four people) have bunk beds with no linen (bring your own sleeping bags), but do have a bathroom and coffeemaker; tepees are $35 s or d; pitch a tent ($10); or hook up to a powered site ($15). Other amenities include modern bathrooms, native sweat lodges (similar to a sauna), and a restaurant. Summer temperatures around Cache Creek can get very high, so the outdoor pool at **Brookside Campsite** (Trans-Canada Hwy., east of town, 250/457-6633; Apr.–Oct.; $15–21) is a good enough reason to choose this commercial campground with all facilities.

LILLOOET

This historic town of 2,500 was founded as Mile 0 of the 1858 Cariboo Wagon Road—also known as the Gold Rush Trail—which led north to the Barkerville and Wells goldfields. Several towns along the Gold Rush Trail—70 Mile House, 100 Mile House, and 150 Mile House, among them—were named for their distance up the wagon road from Lillooet.

With thousands of prospectors passing through in the mid-1800s, Lillooet was the scene of its own gold rush. Originally known as Cayoosh Flat, the town was renamed in the mid-1860s. (The new name was a misspelling of Leel-wat, the name of a tribe of natives who lived to the north.) By this time the city held some 16,000 residents, making it the second-largest population center north of San Francisco and west of Chicago. But as with all other boomtowns, the population explosion was short-lived. As all the most productive local goldfields were worked dry, prospectors continued north on the Cariboo Wagon Road or east on the Dewdney Trail.

A row of rusty farming relics out front marks **Lillooet Museum** (790 Main St., 250/256-4308; mid-May–Oct. Tues.–Sat. 11 A.M.–3 P.M., extended to daily 9 A.M.–5 P.M. in July and Aug.). Inside are ore samples and details about the one-time boomtown's mining history and growth. Within the museum is the local visitor info center. After visiting here, saunter along wide Main Street and pretend you're back in the gold-rush era—which won't be hard if you happen to be here in June during **Only in Lillooet Days.** During this weeklong celebration, the town recreates the Old West with all sorts of entertaining events. Lillooet is also home to the unique **Sheep Pasture Golf Course** (five km/3.1 miles southwest of town, 250/256-4484; Apr.–Oct.; $10), a nine-hole layout on a working sheep farm.

Accommodations and Camping

One block up the hill from the museum, **4 Pines Motel** (108 8th Ave., 250/256-4247 or 800/753-2576, www.4pinesmotel.com) has older rooms ($60 s or d) and a newer wing ($80 s or d). **Cayoosh Creek Campground** is a treed spot near the south end of town, where Cayoosh Creek drains into the much larger Fraser River. Facilities include hot showers and hookups. Unserviced sites are $16, powered sites $21.

CLINTON TO 100 MILE HOUSE

Clinton

Originally called 47 Mile House, the old-fashioned town of Clinton lies 40 kilometers (25 miles) north of Cache Creek on Highway 97. The original roadhouse, opened in 1861 at the junction of the original Cariboo Wagon Road and the new route north from Yale, burned down in 1958. Until the fire, the roadhouse was the site of the annual **Clinton Ball,** a fancy-dress wingding that attracted people from all over the area each May. The ball continues to this day but in other locations.

South Cariboo Historical Museum (Hwy. 97, 250/459-2442; summer Mon.–Fri. 10 A.M.–6 P.M.) occupies an old schoolhouse made of handmade bricks fired locally in the 1890s. The museum contains pioneer belongings, guns, historical photos, native and Chinese artifacts, freight wagons, and all sorts of items from the gold-rush days.

A nearby natural attraction worth seeing is Painted Chasm, in **Chasm Provincial Park,** 16 kilometers (10 miles) north of town then four kilometers (2.5 miles) east. During the last ice age, glacial meltwater carved a 300-meter-deep box canyon out of mineral-laden volcanic bedrock. It's quite a spectacle when the sunlight brings out the sparkling reds, yellows, and purples of the minerals.

The huge log structure on the main street is **Cariboo Lodge Resort** (250/459-7992 or 877/459-7992, www.caribolodgebc.com). Although the rooms are motel-like, rates are reasonable ($70 s, $80 d) and a downstairs restaurant and western-style pub mean you don't have to leave the building after checking in.

Big Bar Guest Ranch

If experiencing ranch life sounds appealing, it's worth spending at least a couple of days at 🅼 Big Bar Guest Ranch (250/459-2333, www.bigbar-ranch.com), which offers accommodations in comfortable lodge rooms ($135 per person per day including meals served ranch-style) or tepees ($75 per person including meals), or you can camp for $25. You're free to enjoy the days as you please—try your hand at gold panning, saddle up for a trail ride, herd cattle with the cowboys, cast a line in a local lake, or go for a hike. In the evening, visitors congregate around the campfire or retreat to a large billiards room. To get to the ranch, turn off the highway nine kilometers (5.6 miles) north of Clinton and head west for 45 kilometers (28 miles).

Around six kilometers (3.7 miles) before the ranch is **Big Bar Lake Provincial Park,** which offers fishing for rainbow trout and swimming in both the lake and the adjacent river; campsites $14. Also in the vicinity is the enormous **Gang Ranch.** Started in the 1860s, the ranch was at one time North America's largest and today spreads over 400,000 hectares (990,000 acres).

North to 100 Mile House

Back on the main highway, between 70 Mile House and 100 Mile House, are several turnoffs leading to hundreds of lakes, big and small. All information centers in Cariboo Country stock the invaluable *Cariboo-Chilcotin Fishing Guide.* Updated annually, the booklet features essential fishing information (where, when, and with what) for many of the lakes, plus maps, camping spots, and even recipes for the ones that didn't get away.

The most accessible provincial park between Clinton and 100 Mile House is at **Green Lake,** 14 kilometers (8.7 miles) east of Highway 97 (turn off Highway 97 16 kilometers/10 miles northeast of 70 Mile House). This large, emerald-colored shallow lake lies along an old Hudson's Bay Company fur-brigade trail; you can see traces of the trail along the lake's shoreline. The park has a shaded lakeside picnic area, a playground, horseshoe pits, relatively warm water for swimming, and a campground ($14 per night; mid-May–Sept.).

Passing through 100 Mile House, it's difficult to miss the **South Cariboo Visitor Info Centre**—just look for the world's largest cross-country skis out front (250/395-5353 or 877/511-5353, www.southcaribootourism.com; year-round Mon.–Fri. 8:30 A.M.–4:30 P.M., longer hours in summer). At the north end of town, one of the original Cariboo stagecoaches is on display. And bird-watchers might want to detour a couple of kilometers west of town to a wetlands reserve where waterfowl are prolific. A smaller wetland lies directly behind the information center, with signage depicting the many species that are often present.

Toward Williams Lake

Three kilometers (1.9 miles) north of 100 Mile House, a road heads east off the highway, leading 30 kilometers (18.6 miles) to **Ruth Lake,** which is stocked with rainbow trout; 44 kilometers (27 miles) to **Canim Beach Provincial Park,** with campsites for $14; 70 kilometers (43.4 miles) to

Canim River Falls, between Canim and Mahood Lakes; and 86 kilometers (53 miles) to the western border of **Wells Gray Provincial Park** (see *North to Mount Robson*), where you'll find a primitive campground.

Back out on the highway and continuing north, you'll come to 19-kilometer-long (12-mile-long) **Lac La Hache,** named for a trader who dropped his axe in the water. This is one of the most picturesque bodies of water in Cariboo Country, known by boat anglers for its populations of kokanee and lake trout. At the lake's south end is the small community of Lac La Hache, with a small museum and information center on the east side of the highway. At the lake's north end, a provincial park offers campsites for $14.

The next main turnoff, at **150 Mile House,** takes you on a 65-kilometer (40-mile) scenic drive (the last 10 kilometers/6.2 miles are unpaved) northeast to **Horsefly Lake Provincial Park,** protecting a forest of old-growth western red cedar and Douglas fir. You can swim, rent a canoe, or just relax on the pebbly beach. The small campground has sites for $14.

WILLIAMS LAKE

Originally bypassed by the builders of the Cariboo Wagon Road because of protests from a stubborn landowner, Williams Lake (pop. 11,000), 95 kilometers (59 miles) north of 100 Mile House, has ironically become the Cariboo region's largest city. No one knows for sure how the city got its name, but the most popular theory is that it was named after Shuswap chief Willyum, who kept the peace as best he could between the valley's indigenous people and early white settlers. Today the ranching and forestry center is best known for the Williams Lake Stampede, one of Canada's biggest rodeos.

History

When gold seekers poured into the Cariboo in 1860, Williams Lake became a regional postal center and headquarters for the gold commissioner. It was destined for boomtown status until the Cariboo Wagon Road bypassed the town in

WILLIAMS LAKE

To Lac La Hache and Kamloops

LAUGHING LOON
NEIGHBOURHOOD PUB

BIL-NOR RESTAURANT

DRUMMOND
LODGE MOTEL

Scout
Island

To Airport, Quesnel, and
Prince George

BROADWAY

VISITOR INFO
CENTRE

LAKEVIEW CRES

BORLAND DR

DONALD RD

FRASER
INN
HOTEL

GREYHOUND BUS
DEPOT

CARSON DR

SCOUT ISLAND
NATURE CENTRE

Williams Lake

5TH AVE N

HOSPITAL

8TH AVE N

STAMPEDE
GROUNDS

BORLAND ST

PROCTOR ST

3RD AVE N

OLIVER ST

7TH AVE S

5TH AVE S

BARNARD ST

20

MUSEUM ★

COMER ST

1ST AVE N

PRIMAL SONG GALLERY

MACKENZIE AVE

S LAKESIDE DR

POST OFFICE

4TH AVE S

BC RAIL STATION

3RD AVE S

2ND AVE S

CHILCOTIN HWY

HODGSON RD

STATION HOUSE
GALLERY

SCALE NOT AVAILABLE

CARIBOO
COLLEGE

To Bella Coola

© AVALON TRAVEL PUBLISHING, INC.

Central British Columbia

1863, thus terminating the small community's reason for being.

Despite the town's uncertain future, William Pinchbeck decided to stay in the valley. He and fellow settler William Lyne started a large farm that supplied the gold camps with bacon, ham, fresh vegetables, and flour, as well as whiskey from their own distillery. In addition to being a farmer, Pinchbeck acted as the local judge, lawyer, and doctor.

In September 1919 the Pacific Great Eastern Railway (now BC Rail) ran tracks around the lake, and Williams Lake came back to life. To celebrate the event, the town held a large picnic and rodeo—the first Williams Lake Stampede. By 1920 the town had hotels, stores, and homes, and ranchers were thrilled to be able to put their cattle on the train instead of herding them south on cattle drives.

Sights

The highlight of the large **Museum of the Cariboo Chilcotin** (113 4th Ave. N, 250/392-7404, summer Mon.–Sat. 10 A.M.–4 P.M., the rest of the year Tues.–Sat. 11 A.M.–4 P.M.; $2) is the BC Cowboy Hall of Fame and associated rodeo, ranching, and Stampede displays. Other exhibits include historical photos, remains of the Chinese settlement at Quesnel Forks, and all kinds of picks, pans, and axes from the gold-mining days.

Many stores in town sell the painting, pottery, weaving, photography, and jewelry of local artisans. These include: **Station House Gallery,** in the original railway station (1 Mackenzie Ave. N, 250/392-6113) and **Primal Song Gallery** (369 Oliver St., 250/392-7171), holding the distinctive works of local artist Andrew Kiss.

On the eastern outskirts of the city, **Scout Island Nature Centre** (250/398-8532, May–mid-Sept. Mon.–Fri. 9 A.M.–4 P.M., Sun. 1–4 P.M.; free) is surrounded by wetlands that serve as a staging area for migratory waterfowl. Colorful displays inside the center catalog the surrounding ecosystem, but the idea is to get out into the wetlands. Wander along one of the short hiking trails or climb the observation tower for a bird's-eye view of the wild landscape.

Outdoor Recreation

Opportunities for outdoor recreation abound in the area. One of many ranches offering horseback riding is **Springhouse Trails Ranch** (Dog Creek Rd., 250/392-4780; May–Sept.). Horse rental is $18 an hour or $75 per day, and you can stay out on the ranch overnight (see *Accommodations and Camping*). The ranch is 20 kilometers (12 miles) southwest of town off Highway 20.

The region's diverse waterways provide plenty of opportunities for boating. Numerous gently flowing streams and serene lakes make perfect spots for canoe and kayak discovery trips, while the Fraser River provides opportunities for exciting rafting trips down steep-walled canyons, through semi-arid hill country, and past abandoned boom towns. **Chilko River Expeditions** (250/398-6711 or 800/967-7238), offers a full-day trip in rafts and inflatable kayaks for $120 per person. Fishing in local waters is rewarding, yielding a variety of trout, steelhead, Dolly Varden, and kokanee (although the fishing in Williams Lake itself is poor). The booklet *Cariboo-Chilcotin Fishing Guide,* available at the information center, details the region's most productive lakes.

Williams Lake Stampede

On the first weekend of July, the town comes alive as the best cowboys in the land compete in the Williams Lake Stampede (250/398-8388 or 800/717-6336, www.williamslakestampede.com), one of Canada's largest rodeos with $100,000 up for grabs. The whole town dresses up for the occasion; the locals put on Western garb, and the shopfronts are decorated accordingly. The highlight of each day's action is the rodeo, when cowboys compete for big bucks in bareback riding, saddle-bronc riding, calf-roping, steer-wrestling, chuckwagon racing, and the crowd favorite, bull riding. Scheduled around these traditional rodeo events are cow-milking contests, barrel racing, tractor pulls, cattle penning, chariot races, raft races, a parade, barn dances, all-you-can-eat breakfasts and steak-outs, and a host of other decidedly Western-flavored activities.

Stampede headquarters is below the main grandstand. This is where you can purchase tickets and Stampede memorabilia; many of the event posters have become collectors' items.

Accommodations and Camping

If you're after somewhere to simply rest your head, stay on the east side of town at the **Drummond Lodge Motel** (Hwy. 97 one km/.6 mile east of downtown, 250/392-5334 or 800/667-4555, www.drummondlodge.com; $75–85 s or d including a light breakfast), set on extensive grounds overlooking the lake.

For a more memorable overnight experience—longer if you can afford it—plan on spending time at **Tyee Lake Resort** (Tyee Lake Rd., 250/989-9850 or 866/989-9850, www.tyeelakeresort.com). Set on a perfect little lake, the main lodge holds 18 guest rooms, each decked out with handcrafted wooden furniture and a small balcony. The rates top out at very reasonable $139 in July and August, including breakfast. You can also camp; tents $12, RVs $18 (no hookups). Fishing is the most popular outdoor activity—troll for rainbow trout for best results—with canoes, motorboats, and fishing tackle for rent. The resort restaurant is also worth mentioning. It's open daily for lunch and dinner, and offerings include Indonesian beef satay at lunch ($7.25) and New York steak pan-fried with a mustard glaze ($22) in the evening. Tyee Lake requires some effort to reach, so you should plan on spending at least two nights at the resort. The turn-off is 47 km (29 miles) north of Williams Lake toward Quesnel; turn east at McLeese Lake, following Beaver Lake Rd. for 10 km (6.2 miles), then following the resort signs for 12 km (7.4 miles) south.

If a ranching vacation is more your style, consider **Springhouse Trails Ranch,** 20 kilometers (12 miles) southwest of town (on Dog Lake Rd., 250/392-4780, www.springhousetrails.com), where horseback riding is $18 an hour. The basic but comfortable rooms are $61 s, $69 d, and all-inclusive package deals are available from $130 per person per day, including accommodations, meals taken in a communal dining room, and riding. You can also camp here for $24 a night, with full hookups. Children especially will love this place.

Food

Williams Lake lacks outstanding eateries but has no shortage of typical family-style restaurants. One of these is the **Great Cariboo Steak Company,** in the Fraser Inn Hotel (285 Donald Rd., 250/398-7055), open on weekdays from 6 A.M., Saturday from 7 A.M., Sunday from 8 A.M. Breakfast ranges $5–10; all-you-can-eat lunch buffets are $10; sandwiches, croissants, and burgers run $6.50–9; and dinner prices range from $8.50 for the all-you-can-eat salad bar to $14–21 for steak, prime rib, chicken, seafood, and pasta dishes. On the northern edge of town, the **Laughing Loon Neighbourhood Pub** (1730 S. Broadway, 250/398-5666) offers a wide-ranging menu of beef, chicken, and pork dishes in a welcoming atmosphere. The building itself is new, but decor is heritage-style.

Information

Beside the highway on the east side of town is **Williams Lake Visitor Info Centre** (1148 Broadway, 250/392-5025, www.williamslakechamber .com), open in summer daily 8 A.M.–6 P.M., the rest of the year Monday–Friday 9 A.M.–5 P.M.

Transportation

Williams Lake Airport, 13 kilometers (eight miles) northwest of downtown, is served by **Air Canada** (888/247-2262), offering flights to and from Prince George, Vancouver, and Kamloops. The **Greyhound** bus depot is just off Highway 97 (215 Donald Rd., 250/398-7733). Daily services run north to Prince George and south to Vancouver. The local outlet of **National** can be reached by calling 250/392-2976.

HIGHWAY 20

Highway 20 west of Williams Lake leads 485 kilometers (301 miles) to Bella Coola, the only road-accessible town along the 500 kilometers (310 miles) of coastline between Powell River and Prince Rupert. The highway is paved less than half its length; the rest of the way it's mostly all-weather gravel and can be slow going in spots. But experiencing the vast and varied wilderness of the **Chilcotin Coast** is worthy of as much time as

you can afford. And with a ferry at the end of the road providing a link to Port Hardy, on Vancouver Island, you'll only need to make the trip one-way.

Services along Highway 20 are spaced at regular intervals, but don't take the trip too lightly; make sure your vehicle is in good condition, and carry tools and spare tires to alleviate the necessity of an expensive tow-truck ride.

West from Williams Lake

The road west from Williams Lake meanders through the Fraser River Valley before beginning a steady climb to the **Chilcotin Plateau,** the heart of British Columbia's ranching country. The landscape is open—most of the land has been cleared by generations of ranchers.

The first worthwhile detour is **Junction Sheep Range Provincial Park,** which lies at the end of a 20-kilometer (12-mile) unpaved road that branches south off Highway 20 at Riske Creek, 47 kilometers (29 miles) west of Williams Lake. The triangular park protects 4,573 hectares (11,300 acres) of mostly semi-arid grasslands between the Fraser and Chilcotin Rivers, home to around 600 bighorn sheep. The confluence of these two major rivers forms the southern tip of the park and can be reached on foot in well under one hour from the end of the access road. The park has no day-use facility or camping.

Back on Highway 20, the first community with services is **Alexis Creek,** 114 kilometers (71 miles) west of Williams Lake. Beside the Chilcotin River, 10 kilometers (6.2 miles) west of Alexis Creek, is **Bull Canyon Provincial Park** at a bend in the Chilcotin River. The park campground ($14) is open mid-May through September.

Continuing west, the highway follows the Chilcotin River for 60 kilometers (37 miles) to Chilanko Forks; here a spur road leads 10 kilometers (6.2 miles) north to **Puntzi Lake.** This picturesque body of water is home to a number of low-key fishing resorts, including **Poplar Grove Resort** (250/481-1186 or 800/578-6804, www.poplargroveresort.com). Small lakeside cabins come with basic cooking facilities and shared washrooms ($42–85 s or d), or choose the en suite lodge units ($65–90 s or d). Camping with hookups is $16–20). If you plan on rising early to fish for kokanee, make arrangements to rent a motorboat the night before.

Chilko Lake

Continuing toward the coast, Highway 20 narrows and turns to gravel at the small community of Tatla Lake, which is also the turnoff to remote **Ts'il-os Provincial Park.** Pronounced "SIGH-loss," Ts'il-os is the native Chilcotin name for the park's highest peak, 3,066-meter (10,060-foot) Mount Tatlow, but its most magnificent feature is 84-kilometer-long (52-mile-long), glacially fed Chilko Lake, which is ringed by the highest peaks of the Coast Mountains. The park is home to a wide variety of wildlife, including grizzly and black bears, bighorn sheep, and, at higher elevations, mountain goats. Fishing in the lake is legendary for rainbow trout (to 2.7 kilograms/six pounds). The park access road parallels the lake's northeast shore and holds a number of accommodations. The best of these, 60 kilometers (37 miles) south of Highway 20, is **M Chilko Lake Resort** (250/481-3333, www.chilkolake.com). If you stay here, you can go canoeing, fish on the lake river, take a dip in the pool, play tennis, saddle up for a horseback ride, or kick back and do absolutely nothing at all. Rooms in the main lodge are $160 s or d, and the much larger bungalows are $220. Call or visit the lodge's website for information on packages.

Toward the Coast

From Tatla Lake, Highway 20 continues westward, climbing steadily to **Nimpo Lake,** where more self-contained resorts put the emphasis on fishing. **Stewart's Lodge** (250/742-3388 or 800/668-4335, www.stewartslodge.com) is one of the larger operations, with cabins on Nimpo Lake ($85–195 s or d) and six "outpost" cabins at remote lakes throughout the Chilcotin region.

From this point, it's 10 kilometers (6.2 miles) west to **Anahim Lake,** where anglers will be tempted to linger at **Anahim Lake Resort** (250/742-3242 or 800/667-7212, www.anahim-lakeresort.com; May–Oct.), where rainbow trout fishing is consistently good throughout summer.

All but one cabin share a communal bathroom facility, but they all have a woodstove, fridge, running water, and screened-in veranda. A restaurant is open for all meals and you can rent boats from the resort marina. Cabins are $65–110 s or d, and camping is $20–24.

From Anahim Lake, it's a steady climb of another 30 kilometers (19 miles) to 1,524-meter (5,000-foot) **Heckman Pass** over the Coast Mountains. West across the pass, you face **"The Hill."** This infamous descent from Heckman Pass to the Bella Coola Valley drops nearly the full 1,524 meters (5,000 feet) in less than 10 kilometers (6.2 miles). Be prepared for numerous switchbacks and a gradient as steep as 18 percent.

Tweedsmuir Provincial Park

At nearly a million hectares (2.5 million acres), this is British Columbia's largest provincial park. Roughly triangular, the park is bounded by Ootsa Lake on the north, the high peaks of the Coast Mountains on the west, and the Rainbow Range—so named for its colorful volcanic formations—on the east. Within these boundaries lies an untouched landscape, wild and remote, holding numerous river systems, forested valleys, alpine meadows, waterfalls, and glaciers. Most of those park highlights are accessible only on foot.

Although the park's resident populations of large mammals are high, viewing opportunities are limited. Black and grizzly bears, mountain goats, caribou, wolves, and moose are all present, but they tend to remain well away from the highway. In early fall, grizzlies can occasionally be seen feeding on spawned-out salmon along the Atnarko River. Highway 20 meanders through the southern section of the park, but aside from two campgrounds and a handful of picnic areas along this route, the park is devoid of facilities.

The park's trail system is not extensive, and most established routes require an overnight stay in the backcountry. One exception is a trail to a series of kettle ponds formed by a receding glacier that stalled many thousands of years ago. This trail is four kilometers (2.5 miles) each way, beginning from a picnic area 16 kilometers (10 miles) west of Atnarko River Campground.

Campgrounds are on the north bank of the Atnarko River (at the base of The Hill) and 30 kilometers (18.6 miles) west at Fisheries Pool. Facilities at both include pit toilets, drinking water, and picnic tables; $14 a night. The best source of park information is the **BC Parks office** in Williams Lake (281 1st Ave. N, 250/398-4530, www.bcparks.ca). **Williams Lake Visitor Info Centre** also offers park information.

(For more details about the north end of the park, see *West from Prince George* in the *Northern British Columbia* chapter.)

BELLA COOLA

The urge to see what's at the end of the road brings many travelers over The Hill and down to Bella Coola (pop. 800), 485 kilometers (301 miles) west of Williams Lake. Here the Bella Coola River drains into North Bentinck Arm, a gateway to the Inside Passage and the Pacific Ocean. The town lies in a coastal valley that was originally the home of the Nuxalk tribe. On July 22, 1793, Alexander Mackenzie reached the coast here, simultaneously becoming the first nonnative to see the area and the first person to cross continental North America. That latter feat earned him a place in history as one of the world's greatest explorers.

Although the Hudson's Bay Company established a post at Bella Coola in 1869, it wasn't until 1894 that permanent settlement of Bella Coola Valley began in earnest. That year a group of Norwegians arrived and, seeing the fjords and snowcapped peaks, were reminded of home. They settled 15 kilometers (nine miles) inland at a spot on the river they named Hagensborg.

Sights and Recreation

Housed in a historic schoolhouse, the **Bella Coola Museum** Mon.–Sat. 10 A.M.–5 P.M.; $2) features artifacts of early Norwegian settlers and the Hudson's Bay Company. Over in Hagensborg, the many hand-hewn timber buildings still standing are testament to the construction skills of the early settlers.

Aside from the historic sites, there's plenty of outdoor recreation to keep visitors busy. Unfor-

tunately, most of the action is out on the water and requires the services of a boat charter company (not cheap). Fishing is the most popular activity; expect to pay from $100 per hour for four persons. Those with a sense of history will want to visit **Mackenzie Rock,** in the Dean Channel, where Alexander Mackenzie, in his own words, "mixed up some vermillion and melted grease and inscribed in large characters on the face of the rock on which we slept last night, this brief memorial: Alexander Mackenzie, from Canada, by Land, the Twenty Second of July, One Thousand Seven Hundred and Ninety Three." For charter information, contact **Bella Coola Outfitting** (604/946-0640, www.bcoutfitting.com).

Accommodations and Camping

Right on the river is **Bella Coola Motel** (Clayton St., 250/799-5323), with clean and comfortable rooms each with a full kitchen and TV for $80 s, $85 d. Camping here costs $20 per night. Between Bella Coola and Hagensborg, the friendly hosts at **Eagle Lodge** (250/799-5587 or 866/799-5587; June–Oct.) will make you feel welcome the moment you step through the front door. Each of eight rooms is configured differently, with the smallest having a twin bed ($60 s) and the largest a two-bedroom suite complete with a kitchen and fireplace ($120 s or d). A cooked breakfast is included and guests have use of an outdoor hot tub positioned to take full advantage of the rural setting. **Gnome's Home Campground and RV Park** (Hagensborg, 250/982-2504; Apr.–Oct.; $15–18), has showers, a cook shelter, a laundry, and is the starting point for a short trail leading through the temperate rainforest.

DISCOVERY COAST PASSAGE

BC Ferries (250/386-3431 or 888/223-3779, www.bcferries.com) sailings from Bella Coola open a remote section of the British Columbia coastline that would otherwise be inaccessible. The main route is between Bella Coola and Port Hardy (Vancouver Island). The direct sailing takes 13 hours, or 31 hours with all stops. Study the timetable (on the BC Ferries website) to see which sailing suits your needs. When the ferry does make a stop, it's only for around two hours each time, so if you want to get off, plan on overnighting until the next ferry comes by. Peak one-way fares for the entire trip are adult $110, child 5–11 $55, vehicle $215.

Shearwater

The most accessible and interesting stop along the Discovery Coast Passage is Shearwater, on Denny Island. Shearwater is an old cannery village that has also been a logging camp, a base for flying boats patrolling the coast during World War II, and a stop for major shipping lines. The community was sold off to a private enterprise and today operates as **Shearwater Marine Resort** (604/270-6204 or 800/663-2370, www.shearwater.ca), catering to up to 50 guests at a time. The accommodations are fairly basic, and aimed toward anglers chasing salmon and halibut, but the resort does have a marina with boat rentals and fishing charters, kayak rentals, a general

store, and the waterfront Fisherman's Bar & Grill. Rates are $65 s, $75–90 d, with the least expensive rooms sharing bathrooms.

QUESNEL

Back inland, Highway 97 north from Williams Lake takes you to Quesnel. The town (pop. 8,500) began during the Barkerville gold rush of the 1860s. Prospectors traveling north on the Fraser River disembarked at the confluence of the Fraser and Quesnel Rivers, and a town sprang up on the site. Today the town's economy continues to thrive, with an asphalt plant that opened in 1998 adding to the local ranching, mining, and, especially, forestry industries; Two Mile Flat, east of downtown, is North America's most concentrated wood-products manufacturing area. The town has a museum worth visiting, but the region's major attractions, Barkerville Historic Town and Bowron Lakes Provincial Park (see *East from Quesnel*), are out of town to the east along Highway 26.

© AVALON TRAVEL PUBLISHING, INC.

Sights

At **Heritage Corner** (Carson Ave. and Front St.) you can see the Old Fraser Bridge, the remains of the steamer *Enterprise,* a Cornish waterwheel used by gold miners, and the original Hudson's Bay Store. To learn all about Alexander Mackenzie or the gold-rush days, head to **Quesnel and District Museum** (Hwy. 97 at Carson Ave., 250/992-9580; May–Aug. daily 8:30 A.M.–4:30 P.M., Sept.–Apr. Tues.–Sat. 8:30 A.M.–4:30 P.M.; $3) which holds almost 30,000 artifacts. The scenic four-kilometer/2.5-mile (allow 75 minutes) **Riverfront Walking Trail** loops around the downtown core, with plaques honoring early residents; start at any point along the river.

Eight kilometers (five miles) west of Quesnel on Baker Drive are the geologically intriguing, glacially eroded hoodoos at **Pinnacles Provincial Park.** The viewpoint is one kilometer (.6 mile) from the day-use area; allow 40 minutes for the round-trip. Another local provincial park is **Ten Mile Lake,** 11 kilometers (6.8 miles) north of town. Fishing is regarded as good for rainbow trout, and there's a large beaver dam near the day-use area.

Billy Barker Days

The main event in Quesnel is the Billy Barker Days celebration, named for the prospector who made the first gold strike in the Cariboo. Over the third weekend of July, downtown streets are closed to traffic in favor of an outdoor crafts fair, parade, and dancing. Residents casually stroll around town in period costumes from the gold-mining days—men in cowboy hats, women in slinky long dresses with brightly feathered hats. The Quesnel Rodeo is one of some 150 events staged during the festival; a detailed schedule is available at the information center or by calling the organizing committee at 250/992-1234.

Accommodations and Camping

Right downtown is the **Cariboo Hotel** (254 Front St., 250/992-2333 or 800/665-3200). Built in 1896, this historic inn has nine restored guest rooms with TVs and phones; rates of $60

s, $65 d include a continental breakfast. Three blocks north, the **Travelodge Quesnel** (524 Front St., 250/992-7071 or 800/665-6995, www.quesneltravelodge.com; $60–100) is an older-style place, but the rooms are spacious and it has a small indoor pool. Farther north and across Highway 97 is the **Talisman Inn** (753 Front St., 250/992-7247 or 800/663-8090, www.talismaninn.bc.ca). Most of the 85 rooms are slightly dated ($65 s, $75 d), although the larger rooms, with more modern furnishings and particularly spacious bathrooms, along with microwaves and toasters, are best value ($90 s, $100 d). A light breakfast is included in all rates.

For campers who don't need services, the best bet is to head north 11 kilometers (6.8 miles) to **Ten Mile Lake Provincial Park.** Of the park's two campgrounds, Lakeside is best (sites 4–9 are closest to the water) and has hot showers and flush toilets ($17 per night). During the week, snagging a spot isn't usually a problem, but on weekends the campground fills with Quesnel locals who come for the swimming, fishing, and canoeing. Closer to town is **Robert's Roost Campground** (3121 Gook Rd., 250/747-2015 or 888/227-8877; Apr.–Oct.) on the west side of Dragon Lake. To get there, take Highway 97 south, turn east on Gook Road, and go to the end. Amenities include coin showers, a laundry, boat rentals, and a beach with swimming. Unserviced sites are $17, serviced sites $20–26.

Food

A popular coffeehouse is **Granville's** (383 Reid St., 250/992-3667), open daily from 8 A.M. **Savala's Steak House** (240 Reid St., 250/992-9453) is a solid, small-town Greek restaurant. With entrées such as steak, spareribs, pizza, and other Italian dishes you can have unlimited trips to the salad bar for $11–16. **Ulysses Restaurant** (122 Barlow Ave., 250/992-6606) specializes in southern European cuisine. A hearty plate of pasta or souvlaki is around $11–16.

Information

Quesnel Visitor Info Centre is beside Lebourdais Park (703 Carson Ave., 250/992-8716 or

800/992-4922, www.northcariboo.com; summer daily 8 A.M.–8 P.M., the rest of the year Mon.–Fri. 8:30 A.M.–4:30 P.M.).

EAST FROM QUESNEL

Cottonwood House Provincial Historic Park

About 28 kilometers (17.4 miles) east of Quesnel on Highway 26, this park (250/992-2071; adult $5, senior and child $2) preserves a roadhouse built in 1864 to serve Barkerville-bound gold-seekers. In addition to the old guesthouse, structures at the site include a barn, stable, and other outbuildings. You'll also find an interpretive center and displays of old farming equipment. In summer, carriage rides are a main attraction, while the handmade wood products make good souvenirs. Camping beside the Cottonwood River is $12–15, and cabins with shared bathrooms are $35 s or d, which includes site admission. The park is open mid-May to August daily 10 A.M.–5 P.M., September weekends only 10 A.M.–5 P.M.

Wells

A few kilometers before reaching Barkerville Historic Town, Highway 26 passes the village of Wells. Most local businesses hand out historic walking tour brochures of the town, which includes points of interest such as a one-time illegal gambling hall below a barber shop. In the center of the village is the 1933 **N Wells Hotel** (2341 Pooley St., 250/994-3427 or 800/860-2299, www.wellshotel.com), which has been wonderfully restored without losing its historic charm. Lounging in front of the log fireplace, surrounded by historic photos and with polished hardwood floors underfoot, is the perfect way to end a day of sightseeing. Or relax over dinner at a sidewalk table and watch the world of Wells go by. Rooms are in the original hotel or in a new wing, but all are well-furnished and good value at $75–120 s, $85–130 d including a continental breakfast. If it's bright lights you're after, head to **Jack O'-Clubs** (866/994-3222; June–early Sept. 2–10 P.M.), an old-style art deco gambling hall filled with slot machines.

Barkerville Historic Town

In 1862 Billy Barker struck gold on Williams Creek, in the north of Cariboo Country, 88 kilometers (55 miles) east of Quesnel. One of Canada's major gold rushes followed, as thousands of prospectors streamed in to what soon became known as Barkerville. The area turned out to be the richest of the Cariboo mining districts, yielding over $40 million in gold. By the mid-1860s Barkerville's population had peaked at over 10,000. But fortunes began to fade after the turn of the 20th century. In 1916 Barkerville was destroyed by fire. Although the town was quickly rebuilt, the gold played out soon thereafter, and many of the miners lost interest and moved on.

A hundred years after the first strike, the provincial government decided to make the town a heritage site and re-create its boomtown atmosphere. Today, Barkerville, 85 kilometers (53 miles) east of Quesnel, holds over 120 authentically restored buildings. Historic reenactments take place throughout summer, when the town's shops, stores, and restaurants all operate in a century-old time warp. Highlights include the town bakery, which sells some of the most mouthwatering baked goods in the province; stagecoach rides ($8); the chance to try your hand at gold-panning ($6); and the musical comedy performances at the Theatre Royal, presented 2–3 times daily ($12).

The grounds of Barkerville Historic Town are open year-round 8 A.M.–8 P.M., although many of the attractions and rides operate June–September and for shorter hours. An admission fee is charged only in summer; adult $12.50, senior $11.25, child $7.25, which allows entry for two days. For more information call 250/994-3332 or click through the links at www.heritage.gov.bc.ca.

You can spend the night in one of two historic buildings within the town. Inside and out, **Kelly House** (250/994-3328, www.kelly-house.ca) fits the heritage theme of Barkerville. The three guest rooms share bathrooms, but rates are reasonable at $85 s, $100 d, which includes a cooked breakfast that may include delightful apple pancakes topped with real cream. More upscale, the 1898 **St. George Hotel** (250/

994-0008 or 888/246-7690) has been fully restored and offers seven rooms, some of which share bathrooms; all are tastefully furnished with comfortable beds and authentic antiques. Rates are $160–180 s or d, which also includes a cooked breakfast.

The pick of three BC Parks-operated campgrounds (mid-June–Sept.) along the access road to the historic town is **Lowhee Campground** ($17), with showers and a playground. **Forest Rose** ($17) also has shower facilities. **Government Hill Campground** ($14) is closest to the historic site, but as all three campgrounds are within walking distance, this is of little consequence. It's also the most rustic, with pit toilets and no showers.

Bowron Lake Provincial Park

Best known for the **Bowron Lake Canoe Circuit,** Bowron Lake Provincial Park encompasses 149,207 hectares (386,700 acres) of magnificent forests, lakes, and rivers in the Cariboo Mountains. To get there, take Highway 26 east of Quesnel toward Barkerville, but just past Wells take a signposted gravel road to the north.

The park boundary follows a chain of six major lakes—Indianpoint, Isaac, Lanezi, Sandy, Spectacle, and Bowron—and some smaller lakes and waterways that, roughly, form a diamond-shaped circuit. Campsites, cabins, and cooking shelters are strategically spaced along the way. To circumnavigate the entire 116-kilometer (72-mile) route takes 6–10 days of paddling and requires seven portages, the most difficult being a 2.5-kilometer (1.5-mile) uphill hike at the very start. As well as being proficient in the use of canoes, those attempting the route should be well prepared for backcountry travel and wet weather. July and August are the most popular months; try to avoid departing on a weekend if you like solitude. September is one of the most colorful months, with lakeside trees in their fall colors.

Before setting out on the circuit, paddlers must obtain a permit from the BC Parks Registration Centre (May 15–Sept. 30 daily 7 A.M.–8 P.M.) at the end of the park access road. Permits cost $60 per person to a maximum of $120 per canoe. Because a limited number of persons are permitted on the circuit at any given time, you should reserve a spot as far in advance as possible (lines open January 2 for the following season) by calling 250/387-1642 or 800/435-5622. The reservation fee is $19.26 per canoe. A few spots are set aside each day for "drop-ins," but the sensible course of action is to reserve as far ahead as possible. For general park information, contact the local BC Parks district office (281 1st Ave. N, Williams Lake, 250/398-4350, www.bcparks.ca).

Two privately owned lodges near the end of the park access road provide meals and accommodations, and are as popular with those attempting the canoe circuit as with travelers who drive out simply to take in the wilderness setting. Both are right on Bowron Lake and offer canoe rentals ($10 per hour, $40 per day) and full outfitting services for those doing the lake circuit. Taking in guests since the 1930s, **Bowron Lake Lodge** (250/992-2733 or 800/519-3399, www.bowronlakelodge.com) has both lake and river frontage, including its own private sandy beach. Motel-style rooms are $70–90 s or d. Campers pay $20 per site and have access to a cook shelter and coin showers. **Beckers Lodge** (250/992-8864 or 800/808-4761, www.beckers.ca; May–early Oct.) has a choice of cabins ranging $80–200 s or d. The Trapper Cabins with shared bathrooms are the most basic, but I like the family-friendly Betty Wendle Cabin ($160 s or d), with an upstairs loft that has water views, a full kitchen, a practical bathroom, separate bedrooms, and solid wooden furnishings throughout. Camping is $20–25. The restaurant, in the original lodge building, sits on a high bluff and oozes historic charm. It's open June through mid-September for breakfast and dinner. At the very end of the access road is a provincial park campground with 25 sites but no hookups (mid-May–Sept.; $14).

Northern British Columbia

Wild, remote northern British Columbia extends from the Yellowhead Highway (Highway 16) north to the 60th parallel. Its mostly forested landscape is broken by two major mountain ranges—the Rockies and the Coast Mountains—and literally thousands of lakes, rivers, and streams. Wildlife is abundant here; the land is home to moose, deer, black and grizzly bears, elk, Dall's sheep, and mountain goats.

The region's largest city is **Prince George,** a forestry and service center 780 kilometers (484 miles) north of Vancouver in the heart of

Must-Sees

M Fort St. James National Historic Site: It's a little out of the way, but the detour to Canada's largest collection of buildings from the fur-trade era is well worthwhile (page 417).

M 'Ksan Historical Village: Learn about native culture at this village, where totem poles, longhouses, and Gitxsan arts and crafts are on display (page 425).

M North Pacific Historic Fishing Village: Step back in time to experience the sights and sounds of the west coast's oldest cannery village (page 435).

M Gwaii Haanas National Park Reserve: Traveling to the Queen Charlotte Islands is an adventure in itself, but to *really* get off the beaten track, schedule a trip to the Gwaii Haanas National Park Reserve (page 452).

M Hyder: Defining the tiny hamlet of Hyder is difficult. It's scenic, it's eccentric, and it's unforgettable—especially in late summer when bears

© ANDREW HEMPSTEAD

Grizzly bears are recognized by a distinctive hump behind the neck.

are as common as visitors along the main street (page 456).

M Liard River Hot Springs: This is more of a must-soak than a must-see (page 473).

M Atlin: British Columbia's most remote town, Atlin is also one of the most scenic. Take a trip out on to Atlin Lake to fully appreciate the surrounding wilderness (page 475).

Northern British Columbia

NORTHERN BRITISH COLUMBIA

ALBERTA

To Edmonton

64

49

2

Dawson Creek

Fort St John

Chetwynd

Monkman Provincial Park

To Quesnel and Williams Lake

Tumbler Ridge

Hudson's Hope

29

97

Mackenzie

97

Prince George

Fort Nelson

ALASKA HWY

McLeod Lake

16

To Fort Liard (NWT)

77

Fort St James
M FORT ST JAMES NATIONAL HISTORIC SITE

Vanderhoof

Stone Mountain Provincial Park

Wokkpash Recreation Area

Williston Lake

Trembleur Lake

Stuart Lake

M LIARD RIVER HOT SPRINGS

Mucho Lake Provincial Park

97

Mountains

Takla Lake

Burns Lake

Contact Creek

Liard River

Rocky

Babine Lake

Houston

M KSAN HISTORICAL VILLAGE

ALASKA HWY

Watson Lake

River

Stikine

Spatsizi Plateau Wilderness Provincial Park

Tatlatui Park

New Hazelton

Smithers

16

37

Terrace

37

Kitimat

37

Dease Lake

Meziadin Junction

Cranberry Junction

CASSIAR HWY

Mount Edziza Provincial Park

37

37A
M HYDER

Stewart

KHUTZEYMATEEN

16

YUKON

Telegraph Creek

Coast

Mountains

Prince Rupert

Port Edward
M NORTH PACIFIC HISTORIC FISHING VILLAGE

UNITED STATES

ALASKA

Queen Charlotte Islands

M ATLIN

100 mi

100 km

0

0

a recreational paradise. From Prince George, the Yellowhead Highway runs west to the towns of **Vanderhoof, Burns Lake, Smithers,** and **Terrace,** all jumping-off points for fishing and boating adventures on surrounding lakes and rivers.

The western terminus of the Yellowhead Highway is **Prince Rupert,** a busy coastal city at the north end of the BC Ferries network and a stop on the Alaska Marine Highway. It's northern B.C.'s sole coastal city; north of here the coastline is part of Alaska.

Off the coast from "Rupert" are the **Queen Charlotte Islands,** part of British Columbia yet entirely unique. The islands beckon adventure, with legendary fishing, great beachcombing, ancient Haida villages, and a typical laid-back island atmosphere.

Two routes head north off the Yellowhead Highway. The **Stewart-Cassiar Highway** begins west of Prince George and parallels the Coast Mountains, passing the turnoff to the twin towns of **Stewart** and **Hyder** and some remote provincial parks. It ends at its junction with the other route north—the famous **Alaska Highway.** Mile Zero of the Alaska Highway is at **Dawson Creek,** northeast of Prince George. From there the highway winds through kilometer after kilometer of boreal forest, past lakes and mountains to the great northland of Alaska.

PLANNING YOUR TIME

The most important thing to remember when planning your time in northern British Columbia is that this part of the province is vast. It is as big as all the other regions combined, so plan accordingly. Though you can loop up through Williams Lake to **Prince George** and then head south again, you'll be missing all the highlights. If you want to see the best of the region, schedule at least three days to drive the length of Highway 16 west to Prince Rupert. To drive the Alaska/Cassiar Highway loop will take at least another four days, including a stop at **Liard Hot Springs** and detours to **Hyder** and **Atlin.** Add another three days in the **Queen Charlotte Islands** for good measure. One good way to visit northern British Columbia without retracing your steps is to take the ferry between Prince Rupert and Vancouver Island in one direction. If you do make ferry connections in Prince Rupert, allow at least one full day in town and be sure to visit the **North Pacific Historic Fishing Village.**

The summer season in northern British Columbia is shorter than elsewhere in the province. For general interest travel, plan a trip during the peak July through August period. June and September are also good for traveling—it's still warm enough to camp out, and as a bonus, you'll miss the worst of the high-summer bug season. Those keen to see grizzly bears in their natural habitat will want to schedule a visit to the **Khutzeymateen** in June or to Hyder August–September.

Northern British Columbia

Prince George

British Columbia's seventh-largest city, Prince George (pop. 74,000) lies roughly at the geographical center of the province, at the confluence of the historically important Fraser and Nechako Rivers. The 1,360-kilometer-long (845-mile-long) Fraser is the province's longest river, while the Nechako is the Fraser's third-largest tributary. Together the two rivers flow for 50 kilometers (31 miles) within the city limits.

History

Early trappers and explorers used the rivers as transportation routes into the northern reaches of the province. When they discovered the region's wealth of wolf, fox, lynx, mink, wolverine, otter, and muskrat, they quickly established forts and trading posts by rivers and lakes so that furs could be sent out and supplies could be brought in. In 1807, Simon Fraser of the North West Company began construction of Fort George—named after then-reigning King George III of England—near the confluence of the Fraser and Nechako Rivers. The North West Company merged with the Hudson's Bay Company in 1821, and Fort George was operated as a Hudson's Bay Company post until 1915.

The railroad reached the area in 1908, and in 1915 the Grand Trunk Pacific Railway platted the

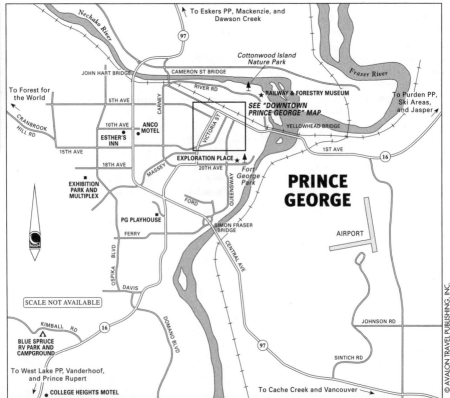

townsite of Prince George a few kilometers south of the original Fort George. The new town went on to become a major logging, sawmill, and pulp-mill town, the center of the white spruce industry in British Columbia's central interior. Hundreds of sawmills started cutting local timber, and Prince George became the self-proclaimed "Spruce Capital of the World." The city has continued from strength to strength and has grown to become northern British Columbia's economic, social, and cultural center.

SIGHTS

Connaught Hill Park

The best place to start a Prince George sightseeing trip is the top of Connaught Hill, which affords a panoramic view of the city. To get there from downtown, take Queensway Street south, turn right on Connaught Drive, then right again on Caine Drive. At the summit are grassy tree-shaded lawns, picnic spots, and several well-kept gardens bursting with color in summer.

Fort George Park

The site where Simon Fraser established Fort George in 1807 is today preserved as 36-hectare (90-acre) riverside Fort George Park. Trails lead through the park along the Fraser River and to the Indian Burial Grounds. Park highlights include the Exploration Place and the original **Fort George Railway Station,** just across from the museum, where on summer weekends and holidays noon–4 P.M., weather permitting, a miniature steam train provides rides along a kilometer or so of track; $2 per person. Next to the rail station is an old schoolhouse—if it's locked, peek in through the window at row after row of old-fashioned desks.

Exploration Place

This museum in Fort George Park (333 Becott Pl., 250/562-1612; July–Aug. Sun.–Tues. 10 A.M.–5 P.M. and Wed.–Sat. 10 A.M.–8 P.M., the rest of the year Wed.–Sun. 10 A.M.–5 P.M.) is an excellent place to discover the fascinating natural and human history of Prince George and the lifestyle and culture of the indigenous

Carrier tribe. The facility is filled with modern exhibits that go beyond the meaning of a museum in the usual sense. You'll find a technological dinosaur display, a small IMAX-style theater, high-speed Internet terminals, and many hands-on exhibits. Among the items on display in the History Hall are many stuffed and mounted specimens of wild animals and birds native to British Columbia—including two towering grizzly bears in the foyer—fine crafts of the local Carrier people, an impressive sternwheeler anchor, snowshoes, guns, horrific animal traps and other relics of the fur trade, artifacts from early sawmilling days, an old buggy, mockups of early business establishments, and a hands-on Science Centre. Admission is a worthwhile adult $8.95, senior $6.95, child $5.95, and for an extra $2 per person entry to the SimEX theater is included.

Prince George Railway and Forestry Museum

This outdoor museum (250/563-7351; daily 10 A.M.–6 P.M.; adult $6, senior $5, child $3) catalogs Prince George's industrial history. Take a self-guided tour through some of the antiquated railway cars and buildings, clamber on retired railway equipment, and chug back in time via the black-and-white photo displays and assorted memorabilia. To get there from downtown, take Highway 16 east to the River Road exit (just before the Yellowhead Bridge over the Fraser River) and continue north down River Road one kilometer to the museum.

Cottonwood Island Nature Park

Just down River Road from the railroad museum is the entrance to beautiful 33-hectare (81-acre) Cottonwood Island Nature Park—one of Prince George's 16 city parks and a beautiful spot for a quiet stroll or picnic. The park lies beside the Nechako River, which overflows each spring; over time, sediment from the overflow has built up an island. The park's dominant feature is an extensive forest of northern black cottonwood trees. In spring sticky buds cover the cottonwoods, and in summer the air is thick and the ground white with seed-bearing tufts of fluff.

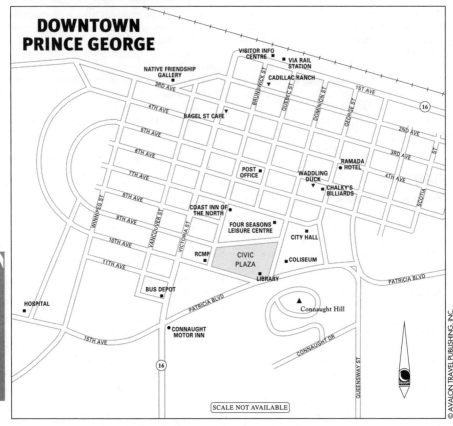

DOWNTOWN
PRINCE GEORGE

VISITOR INFO CENTRE
VIA RAIL STATION
NATIVE FRIENDSHIP GALLERY
3RD AVE
CADILLAC RANCH
4TH AVE
BAGEL ST CAFE
5TH AVE
6TH AVE
7TH AVE
POST OFFICE
WADDLING DUCK
RAMADA HOTEL
CHALKY'S BILLIARDS
8TH AVE
COAST INN OF THE NORTH
9TH AVE
FOUR SEASONS LEISURE CENTRE
CITY HALL
10TH AVE
RCMP
CIVIC PLAZA
COLISEUM
11TH AVE
LIBRARY
BUS DEPOT
PATRICIA BLVD
HOSPITAL
Connaught Hill
15TH AVE
CONNAUGHT MOTOR INN
CONNAUGHT DR
QUEENSWAY ST
BRUNSWICK ST
QUEBEC ST
DOMINION ST
GEORGE ST
1ST AVE
2ND AVE
3RD AVE
4TH AVE
SCOTIA ST
WINNIPEG ST
VANCOUVER ST
VICTORIA ST
16

SCALE NOT AVAILABLE

© AVALON TRAVEL PUBLISHING, INC.

You'll see all sorts of birds, and might spy the occasional beaver, fox, or moose. The park's trail system is extensive; the short walk between the main parking lot and the river is popular.

Eskers Provincial Park

This 3,979-hectare (9,830-acre) park 40 kilometers (25 miles) northwest of Prince George (access is off Highway 97 along Pine Marsh Rd.) is named for the park's main features. The eskers, or long gravel ridges, were deposited by a receding glacier at the end of the last ice age. Fifteen kilometers (9.3 miles) of hiking trails lead around Circle Lake to two viewing platforms and through forests of aspen, lodgepole pine, and Douglas fir.

Forestry Sights

Forestry is the heart and soul of Prince George's economy. In summer, **Canfor,** the largest Canadian-owned forest products company, offers tours of its operations. The four-hour tour takes in the climate-controlled seedlings nursery; the sawmill, where logs are processed into dimension lumber; and the pulp mill, where high-quality pulp is produced for paper manufacturers around the world. The tour is free, but visitors are required to wear long pants and closed-toe shoes for safety. Tours are very popular, so book ahead at 250/563-5493.

Forest for the World, a 106-hectare (262-acre) recreation area set aside for forest demonstrations, hiking, and cross-country skiing, was established in 1986 to commemorate Prince George's 75th anniversary. To get there, take 15th Avenue to the west end of the city, continue onto Foothills Boulevard, and turn left on Cranbrook Hill Road, which steeply climbs Cranbrook Hill. At the signs for Forest for the World, turn left on Kueng Road and continue to the end. From the parking lot, trails lead to Shane Lake (10 minutes one-way), where beavers and waterfowl are present, and to a hilltop viewpoint northwest of Shane Lake (15 minutes one-way).

Galleries

The architecturally stunning **Two Rivers Gallery** (Civic Plaza, corner of 10th Ave. and Dominion St., 250/614-7800; Tues.–Sat. 10 A.M.–5 P.M., Sun. noon–5 P.M.; adult $5, senior and child $4) is Prince George's major cultural attraction. The large permanent collection is the main drawcard, but temporary shows that change every four to five weeks are included in the admission fee. It's also a good place to buy high-quality local artwork at a reasonable price. Look for paintings, sculpture, pottery, beadwork, woven and painted silk items, and jewelry. On Thursday, admission is free after 3 P.M. and the gallery stays open until 9 P.M.

To see and buy all sorts of native arts and crafts, head for the **Native Art Gallery** in the Native Friendship Centre (600 3rd Ave., 250/614-7726; Tues.–Sat. 10 A.M.–4:30 P.M.). Throughout summer you can watch experienced carvers and painters teaching their students. Moccasins, jewelry, carvings, hand-printed cards, and sweatshirts with native designs are all for sale.

RECREATION
Summer Activities

Prince George is a convenient base for a wide range of outdoor pursuits. Anglers probe the area's lakes and rivers for trout, char, salmon, steelhead, Dolly Varden, whitefish, sturgeon, and grayling. The lakes also provide enjoyable canoeing and boating. Wildlife watchers will have a field day scanning the woods for black and grizzly bears, elk, mountain goats, bighorn sheep, woodland caribou, wolves, deer, and

moose. In spring, autumn, and winter, visit the unique **moose viewing area** near Tabor Mountain to see these enormous wild vegetarians in their natural habitat.

Hikers can follow the **Heritage River Trail** through the city, past interpretive signs detailing local natural history. The clearly marked gravel trail, open to hikers, joggers, cyclists, and cross-country skiers, runs between Cameron Street Bridge and Carrie Jane Gray Park. You can make an 11-kilometer (6.8-mile) loop of it if you complete the circuit by following Carney Street. Ask for the *Heritage River Trails* pamphlet at the information centers.

Those who prefer to get off the beaten track should instead request the *Prince George and Area Hiking Guide,* which describes seven trails in the area. One of the most popular of those listed in the guide is **Fort George Canyon Trail,** a 4.5-kilometer (2.8-mile) path through a canyon (striking in autumn) southeast of West Lake Provincial Park. To get there go west along Highway 16, turn south (left) on Blackwater Road, then east (left) on West Lake Road.

Indoor Activities

Four Seasons Leisure Pool (700 Dominion St., 250/561-7636; daily 6:30 A.M.–11 P.M.) charges $6 for use of the pools, saunas, hot tub, and water slide, as well as participation in several daily aqua-fitness classes. Children will love the indoor water slides at **Esther's Inn** (1151 Commercial Dr., 250/562-4131).

To shoot pool in a clean and bright setting, head to **Chalky's Billiards** (511 George St., 250/564-1283).

ENTERTAINMENT
Performing Arts

Studio 2880 (2880 15th Ave., 250/562-4526) is the local arts center, operated by the Community Arts Council. It hosts many cultural activities, acts as a ticket office for events, and organizes workshops, art classes, concerts, ballets, special events, and two major craft markets each year. In a similar vein, **Theatre North West** (556 North Nechako Rd., 250/563-6969) offers a five-play season running late September–May. The **Prince George Symphony Orchestra** (250/562-0800) combines professional and amateur musicians to produce a September–May performance season at Vanier Hall (2901 Griffiths, 250/562-6441).

Drinking and Dancing

Of the city's many pubs and nightclubs, one of the most popular is **Steamers** (2595 Queensway St., 250/562-6654), with typical pub meals and bands playing most weekends. For country music, it's impossible to go past the **Cadillac Ranch** (1380 2nd Ave., 250/563-7720), with a mixture of bands and DJ music, but it's always hard-core country and always busy. For a quiet drink in typical hotel surroundings, head for **Coaches Corner** (Ramada Hotel, 444 George St., 250/563-0055).

Festivals and Events

Prince George is certainly not short on year-round celebrations and goofy seasonal events; ask at the information centers for a free events calendar. In early January, the **Fete d'hiver** is a winter carnival featuring logging sports, scuba diving, dogsledding, and car races on the ice at nearby Tabor Lake. One month later the city goes berserk with a 10-day **Snow Daze,** featuring a snow ball and snow golf in bright crazy costumes, knurdling (jousting using padded poles), bed races on ice, and other hog-wild events. It's all finished off with a fireworks display. For details of these winter festivals call Prince George Festivals (250/564-3737).

In early June, the warmer half of the annual events calendar kicks off with the biennial (even years) **Forest Expo** (250/563-8833, www.forestexpo.bc.ca) held at Exhibition Park. The expo, North America's largest forestry exposition, is interesting even for those not involved in the industry, especially the displays of new technology.

On the middle weekend of August, the **Prince George Folkfest** (www.pgfolkfest.com) attracts a good range of performers from throughout Canada to Fort George Park. The following weekend, **Summerfest** (250/564-3737), the

largest of Prince George's festivals kicks off. A 10-block stretch of George Street is sealed off to vehicular traffic, as crowds converge for live entertainment, a food festival, arts and crafts, and a wide variety of free fun.

ACCOMMODATIONS AND CAMPING

Under $50

With no hostels, Prince George holds just one accommodation that falls into this price range. It's the **College Heights Motel** (five km/3.1 miles west of downtown along Highway 16, 250/964-4708) It has no toll-free number, no website, not even cable TV, but for $38 s, $45 d in high season, what do you expect? It's on the south side of the highway at the top of the rise.

$50–100

Most Prince George accommodations fall into the $50–100 range, and they are spread throughout the city. A few blocks south from downtown, where the Yellowhead Highway crosses Patricia Boulevard, is **Connaught Motor Inn** (1550 Victoria St., 250/562-4441 or 800/663-6620; $70 s, $75 d). It's a large place, with close to 100 air-conditioned rooms and a pool, sauna, and restaurant.

The most concentrated area of accommodations is along the Highway 97 bypass west of downtown. Least expensive of these is the **Anco Motel** (1630 Central St., 250/563-3671 or 800/663-3290), which charges from $55 s or d. The best value along this stretch, with comfortable rooms and a load of extras at a reasonable price, is **Esther's Inn** (1151 Commercial Crescent, 250/562-4131 or 800/663-6844, www.esthersinn.bc.ca; $60–90 s or d). Guest rooms surround a lush tropical atrium packed with palms and philodendrons, waterfalls, Polynesian artifacts, swimming pools, a water slide, and a thatched-roof restaurant.

$100–150

The **Ramada Hotel** (444 George St., 250/563-0055 or 800/830-8833, www.ramadaprincegeorge.com) is an unattractive but distinctive redbrick building in the heart of downtown. Amenities include a restaurant, lounge, pub, pool, sauna and whirlpool, casino, gift shop, and covered parking. Rack rates are $140–200 s or d, but you'd be crazy to pay this much; call or check the website, and you should be able to find a room for around $100, even in summer. In the same price category and also centrally located is the 193-room **Coast Inn of the North** (770 Brunswick St., 250/563-0121 or 800/663-1144, www.coasthotels.com). This full-service hotel has a smallish fitness room, an indoor pool, a sauna, and three in-house eateries (including a Japanese restaurant). Summer rates are $145 s, $155 d, but like the Ramada, check their website for perpetually discounted rooms.

Camping

Privately operated **Blue Spruce RV Park and Campground** (Kimball Rd., 250/964-7272 or 877/964-7272; Apr.–mid-Oct.) is five kilometers (3.1 miles) west on Highway 16 from the junction of Highway 97. It's a popular spot, filling up each night during the busy summer months. Each site has a picnic table and a barbecue grate, and the facilities include spotlessly clean heated bathrooms, a coin-operated laundry, a swimming pool, mini-golf, and a playground. Unserviced sites are $18, hookups $20–25. The closest provincial park to Prince George is at **Purden Lake,** 55 kilometers (34 miles) east of the city on Highway 16. The picturesque lake has a small stretch of sandy beach and offers fishing for rainbow trout and burbot. Sites are $14 a night.

FOOD

A few blocks from downtown is **Bagel Street Cafe** (1493 3rd Ave. at Victoria St., 250/960-1182). It's small—just one long row of stools—and gets crowded when workers from the government offices across the road are on a break, but it's inexpensive; coffee $1.80, hearty lunches from $5.50.

Restaurants

An excellent place for lunch is **Papaya Grove Restaurant** (Esther's Inn, 1151 Commercial Cres., 250/562-4131). You can choose from three different seating areas: under a thatched roof, around the pool, or in the bar. All are enclosed within a massive tropical indoor atrium. A set menu is offered, but the buffet is the most popular choice. The daily lunch buffet (11 A.M.–2 P.M.) is around $10, with a different theme each day. Sunday brunch is particularly good; for $15.95 you get all the usual breakfast choices, along with salmon, prawns, roast beef, and a staggering number of desserts. The dinner buffet is $16.95 Sunday–Thursday, $19.95 on Friday and Saturday when prime rib is served.

With its thoughtful menu and casually elegant setting, the @GB>Waddling Duck (1157 5th Ave., 250/561-5550, daily 11 A.M.–11 P.M.) stands out as the restaurant of choice for a nice night out in Prince George. The setting is a big old stone and brick building, with lots of exposed beams and polished wood throughout. The food blends western Canada produce with cooking styles from around the world: You find entrees ($11–28) like broiled bison with braised asparagus and grilled halibut in a lemon-thyme demi-glaze mixing it up with favorites like pasta primavera. I'm not usually a fan of tiramisu, but the Waddling Duck's version ($7) was delectable.

A popular spot for locals looking to splurge is the **M Log House Restaurant** (250/963-9577; Tues.–Sat. from 6 P.M.), overlooking Tabor Lake nine kilometers (5.6 miles) east of downtown. It's decorated in a typical northern style—the walls are crammed with antiques and trophy heads. Both the food and service are excellent. The menu is typically West Coast, with mains ranging $17.50–26.50.

INFORMATION AND SERVICES

Information and Books

Tourism Prince George operates an excellent information center right downtown (1300 1st Ave., 250/562-3700 or 800/668-7646, www .tourismpg.com; year-round Mon.–Fri. 8:30 A.M.– 5 P.M., with extended summer hours of daily 9 A.M.–8 P.M.). It also serves as a booking agent for ferries and VIA Rail.

Prince George Public Library (887 Dominion St., 250/563-9251; Mon.–Thurs. 10 A.M.–9 P.M., Fri.–Sat. 10 A.M.–5:30 P.M.) has newspapers and magazines from across North America, as well as a good display of native art and artifacts; **Mosquito Books** (Parkwood Mall, 1600 15th Ave., 250/563-6495; closed Sun.) features a great selection of local and northern British Columbia literature, plus major Canadian newspapers.

Services

The main **post office** is on the corner of 5th Avenue and Quebec Street. **Prince George Regional Hospital** is at 2000 15th Avenue, 250/565-2000 (routine calls) or 250/565-2444 (emergencies). A private health clinic deals with walk-in problems; turn off 15th Avenue on Edmonton by the hospital. The RCMP is on the corner of Brunswick and 10th Avenue, behind the library (250/562-3371).

TRANSPORTATION

Air

The airport is about 18 kilometers (11 miles) east of town and is served by connectors for **Air Canada** (888/247-2262) and **WestJet** (800/538-5696). Both these airlines fly daily to Vancouver and other regional centers, as well as to Calgary. The **Airporter** bus (250/563-2220) provides shuttle service between the airport and downtown.

Train

VIA Rail operates transcontinental service from Prince George west to Prince Rupert and east through Jasper and Edmonton to Toronto and beyond. The VIA Rail station is on 1st Avenue between Brunswick and Quebec Streets (250/564-5233).

Bus

Greyhound (1566 12th Ave., 250/564-5454 or 800/661-1145) runs regularly scheduled services from Prince George south to Kamloops and Vancouver (via Williams Lake and Quesnel); west along the Yellowhead Highway to Terrace and Prince Rupert; north to Dawson Creek via Chetwynd; and east along the Yellowhead Highway to Jasper and Edmonton.

Getting Around

The **Prince George Transit System** operates buses throughout the city daily except Sunday. Pick up a current *Prince George Rider's Guide* from the information centers or call 250/563-0011 for an automated timetable. Prince George **handyDART** (250/562-1394) provides door-to-door transportation for disabled passengers unable to use the regular bus service.

For a cab call **Prince George Taxi** (250/564-4444). Car-rental agencies with desks out at the airport are: **Budget** (250/563-2662), **National** (250/564-4847), and **Thrifty** (250/564-3499).

West from Prince George

VANDERHOOF

The first town west of Prince George (65 km/40 miles) is Vanderhoof (pop. 4,400), a service center for the Nechako Valley and British Columbia's geographical center (the exact spot is marked by a cairn five kilometers east of town). Vanderhoof grew as a stop on the Grand Trunk Pacific Railway. Today it's a prosperous farming and logging town.

Sights

The 1914 building at the corner of Highway 16 and Pine Avenue houses **Vanderhoof Community Museum** (250/567-2991; daily 10 A.M.–5 P.M.; $2). The museum displays mounted specimens of birds and animals, pioneer equipment, blacksmithing tools, a rock collection, and plenty of local history from gold-rush and pioneer days. The museum is on the grounds of a **Heritage Village,** which consists of 11 restored heritage buildings, among them a jail, 1922 schoolhouse, and a restored gambling room. Also in the village is the **OK Cafe,** where you can tuck in to hearty homemade soup and rolls, salads, and tasty pie and ice cream. It's inside a heritage-style building decorated with old-fashioned wallpaper and frilly curtains.

Vanderhoof's town symbol is the Canada goose. You can see these beautiful birds and other waterfowl in spring and fall at their transient home, **Nechako Bird Sanctuary,** along the banks of the Nechako River. Access it via the wooden bridge at the north end of Burrard Avenue, the town's main street.

If you want to get away from the main highway for a couple of hours, take a 100-kilometer (62-mile) detour south along a good gravel road (Nechako Avenue, then Kenney Dam Road) to **Kenney Dam,** once the world's largest earth-filled dam. From the far side of the dam, a 1.2-kilometer (.7-mile) trail (20 minutes each way) leads downriver to 18-meter-high (59-foot-high) **Cheslatta Falls** and a picnic area.

Practicalities

Inexpensive accommodations are available at the **Hillview Motel** (Hwy. 16, 250/567-4468 or 888/387-9788; $55 s, $65 d), at the east side of town. Similarly priced, but right downtown and home to Vanderhoof's best restaurant, is **North Country Inn** (2575 Burrard Ave., 250/567-3047; $59 s, $68 d).

Riverside Park Campground (250/567-4710; May–Sept.) enjoys a pleasant setting beside the Nechako River. Turn north off Highway 16 onto Burrard Avenue and continue through town; the campground is to the west side of Burrard Avenue. Showers and firewood are supplied. Tenters pay $15, those looking for hookups $17–21.

For delicious food at reasonable prices head to the comfortable **North Country Inn** (2575 Burrard Ave., 250/567-3047), where the restaurant is in a stunning alpine-style log building. Breakfasts are hearty and cost from $5; lunch is mostly burgers and sandwiches ranging $5–9. In the evening the soup and salad bar is $8, and steak, seafood, and pasta dinners run $10–29. Try the delicious chicken lasagna.

Vanderhoof Visitor Info Centre (2353 Burrard Ave., 250/567-2124 or 800/752-4094) is open year-round Monday–Friday 9 A.M.–5 P.M., with extended summer hours of daily 8:30 A.M.–6 P.M.

FORT ST. JAMES

A sealed road leads 60 kilometers (37 miles) north from Vanderhoof to Fort St. James (pop. 2,000), the earliest nonnative settlement in northern British Columbia. It's worth a detour up from the Yellowhead Highway to check out several sights of interest in the area.

Fort St. James National Historic Site

In the early 1800s, Fort St. James (250/996-7191; mid-May–Sept. daily 9 A.M.–5 P.M.; adult $6, senior $5, child $3) was the chief fur-trading post and capital of the large and prosperous district of New Caledonia—the name originally given to central B.C. by Simon Fraser.

When Fraser first arrived at Stuart Lake he was working for the North West Company, expanding the fur trade west of the Rockies and trying to find a water route to the Pacific. He established the fort among the cooperative local Carrier tribe in 1806. The natives did not fear the white people—they desired their iron, tools, weapons, and exotic jewelry. But establishment of the fort changed their lifestyle forever. In 1821, the fort became a Hudson's Bay Company outpost and continued to operate until the early 20th century.

Today the beautifully restored fort forms the centerpiece of a historic park that holds Canada's largest collection of original fur-trade buildings. Enter the fort through the Visitor Reception Centre, which holds displays on pioneer explorers, fur traders, and the indigenous Carrier people. An audio recording and a map trace the route of the early explorers, and a slide show fills you in on the restoration of the fort's original buildings. Free guided walking tours leave from the center May–September. In July and August, characters dressed in pioneer garb lurk in the log-constructed general store, the fish cache, the single men's bunkhouse, the main house, and the veggie garden. You're actively encouraged to get into the spirit of things and play along. Tell them you've just arrived by canoe, want to stay the night in the men's house, and need a good horse and some provisions . . . then see what happens!

Other Local Sights

Aside from the historic park, you can cruise west along the lakefront, first along Stuart Drive, then Lakeshore Drive. You'll pass Our Lady of Good Hope Catholic Church, built in 1873, and the **Russ Baker Memorial** (Baker was a local bush pilot who founded Pacific Western Airlines). Bush pilots played an important role during the early days of mining, fur trapping, and forestry in this area.

The area's natural attractions also make the side trip to Fort St. James worthwhile. Start with **Stuart Lake** itself, the province's seventh largest body of water. The lake is more than 90 kilometers (56 miles) long and up to 13 kilometers (eight miles) wide. It's known to produce rainbow trout up to seven kilograms (15 pounds) and lake char up to 13 kilograms (29 pounds), as well as lake trout, whitefish, and kokanee.

North of Fort St. James, Germanson Landing North Road (well-maintained but unpaved) leads to the **Takla-Nation Lakes** region—a favorite with campers in search of untouched wilderness and with anglers wanting to pull grayling, char, rainbow trout, and Dolly Varden from the region's dozens of fish-filled lakes.

The most popular of many local hiking trails is to summit of **Mount Pope,** where views extend across Stuart Lake; allow one hour each way for this three-kilometer (1.9-mile) walk. Get details on this and other trails at the local information center.

Practicalities

The best place to stay in the area is **Stuart Lodge** (Stones Bay Rd., 250/996-7917; $70–90 s or d), on the shore of Stuart Lake five kilometers (3.1 miles) west of Fort St. James. The complex's five cottages come with cooking facilities, decks, and TVs. If you'd prefer to be in town, stay at the **New Caledonia Motel** (167 Douglas Ave., 250/996-8051 or 866/996-8051), which charges $50 s, $55 d in the old wing and $59 s, $64 d for the newer rooms.

Paarens Beach Provincial Park and **Sowchea Bay Provincial Park,** west of Fort St. James, both offer lakeside tent and vehicle camping, swimming, fishing, picnic areas, and washrooms; open May–September with an $14 nightly fee for campers.

To get the scoop on the entire area, stop at **Fort St. James Visitor Info Centre** (115 Douglas Ave., 250/996-7023; July–Aug. daily 8 A.M.– 6 P.M. and May, June, and Sept. Mon.–Fri. 8:30 A.M.–4:30 P.M.).

FORT FRASER TO FRASER LAKE

Heading west from Vanderhoof, the Yellowhead Highway passes through low rolling terrain to Fort Fraser, one of the province's oldest communities; Simon Fraser established the former fur-trading post in 1806.

Continuing west, the highway crosses the wide Nechako River, passing the turnoff to **Beaumont Provincial Park.** The park offers boating on Fraser Lake, a short interpretive trail, and a campground (May–Oct.; $17 per site). The park also marks the eastern edge of an area known as the **Lakes District,** comprising more than 300 fish-filled lakes. Traveling this stretch of the highway in summer you'll notice all the vehicles hauling canoes, kayaks, or small fishing boats.

The town of Fraser Lake (pop. 1,400), 60 kilometers (37 miles) west of Vanderhoof, lies on a chunk of land sloping gently down to its namesake lake. In winter, trumpeter swans settle in at each end of the lake. In summer, a salmon run on the **Stellako River**—a short stretch of water between Fraser and Francois Lakes—draws scores of eager anglers. Overlooking Fraser Lake, **Piper's Glen Resort** (250/690-7565, www.pipersglenresort.com; May–Sept.) has a grassy lakeshore camping area with full hookups and showers; $15–18 per night for campers, $40 s or d in basic cabins. Guests can rent canoes and motorboats. **Fraser Lake Visitor Info Centre,** along the highway through town (250/699-8844; July–Aug. daily 8 A.M.–6 P.M.), offers tourism information and a small museum out back.

Just west of Fraser Lake, a turnoff leads south to **Francois Lake,** another popular fishing hole. **Glenannan Tourist Area,** at the lake's east end, boasts a handful of resorts providing everything an angler could possibly desire. **Francois Lake Resort** (250/699-6551; May–Oct.) rents motorboats and rustic cabins for $45–70 per night and campsites for $16–19 per night.

BURNS LAKE AND VICINITY

The first thing you see when you enter Burns Lake is an enormous chainsaw-carved trout with the inscription "Three Thousand Miles of Fishing!" That pretty much sums up what attracts visitors to the town and surrounding Lakes District.

Like other towns along the Yellowhead Highway, Burns Lake (pop. 1,900) grew after construction of the Grand Trunk Pacific Railway. Many buildings from those early railroad days remain, and **Deadman's Island** in Burns Lake got its name from an accident that killed two workers during the railway's construction. The one-hectare (2.5-acre) island is the province's smallest provincial park.

Sights

Continue west along the highway through town for about one kilometer until you come to the green-and-white **Heritage Centre** (daily 1–5 P.M.; $2), comprising a museum and the local information center. The museum is housed in a 1919 home whose furnished rooms contain an odd assortment of articles, including a collection of foreign currency, memorabilia from an old ship (viewed through a porthole), and typewriters that have seen better days.

Ask at the adjacent information center for a map showing all the heritage buildings around town. Of particular note is the **Bucket of Blood,** a historic fur-trading depot and gambling den where a murder occurred during a poker game. It's on the corner of Highway 16 and 5th Avenue. You'll also discover many gift shops where paintings and beadwork by the local Carrier bands are on display.

For a wonderful view of the area, follow 5th Avenue up the hill out of town, then take the turnoff to **Boer Mountain Forestry Lookout.** Rockhounds will prefer to head 6.5 kilometers (four miles) south of town to **Eagle Creek Agate Opal Site,** one of the province's few opal deposits. From the parking lot, a four-kilometer (2.5-mile) trail (70 minutes each way) leads to the creekside deposit and an intriguing outcrop of hoodoos.

Fish Fantasies

More than 300 lakes dot the high country between the Fraser and Skeena watersheds, and all are renowned fishing spots. To even mention all the lakes and their fishing possibilities would take a whole other book. Ask at the information center for the free *Burns Lake 3,000*

Miles of Fishing map and information sheet. The center also stocks brochures on local fishing resorts and guides, boat rentals, and floatplane adventures.

Burns Lake itself offers excellent fishing for rainbow, eastern brook, and cutthroat trout, as well as kokanee, chinook salmon, steelhead, lake char, and other species. The area between Burns Lake and Tweedsmuir Provincial Park is dotted with resorts and rustic lodges, most catering primarily to anglers.

Practicalities

On the east side of town before Highway 16 descends to the main street, **Wanakena Motel** (250/692-3151 or 888/413-3151; $50 s, $55–65 d) is an older place, but rooms are clean. For something a bit nicer, stay at the 45-room **Burns Lake Motor Inn** (Hwy. 16 W, 250/692-7545 or 800/663-2968; $65–70 s or d), where rates include tea and toast in the lobby.

KOA Burns Lake (Freeport Rd., 250/692-3105 or 800/562-0905; May–Sept.) is off Highway 16 about seven kilometers (4.3 miles) east of Burns Lake. Its picturesque tent sites lie up in a forested area, and each site has a picnic table. The large RV section below is out in the open and has full hookups, free showers, a laundry, store, and gift shop. Unserviced sites are $20, hookups $22–28. The nearest provincial park with a campground is along a gravel road north of Burns Lake. **Ethel F. Wilson Provincial Park** is on Pinkut Lake, 24 kilometers (15 miles) along this road; $14 a night.

A locally recommended eatery is the **Panhandle Restaurant** (710 Yellowhead Hwy., 250/692-3316; daily for dinner), serving reasonably priced Chinese dishes; open daily for dinner. Across the highway from Lakeview Mall, **Mulvaney's Pub** (250/692-3078) offers salads, burgers, and hearty pub-style meals at reasonable prices.

Burns Lake Visitor Info Centre is along the highway west of downtown (250/692-3773; summer Mon.–Fri. 8 A.M.–7 P.M., Sat.–Sun. 9 A.M.–5 P.M.). As well as town information, the staff provides hints on the best fishing spots and directions to Tweedsmuir Provincial Park.

TWEEDSMUIR PROVINCIAL PARK (NORTH)

The town of Burns Lake is not only near British Columbia's smallest provincial park (Deadman's Island in Burns Lake), it also happens to be the northern gateway to the largest: 981,000-hectare (2.42-million-acre) Tweedsmuir Provincial Park. The park extends over 200 kilometers (124 miles) from north to south. Its northern boundary, formed by **Ootsa** and **Whitesail Lakes,** is accessed along a network of gravel roads south from Burns Lake. The only road *within* the park is Highway 20 (see *Cariboo Country* in the *Central British Columbia* chapter).

Most of the park's northern section is made up of the **Quanchus Mountain Range,** holding many peaks topping 1,900 meters (6,230 feet), and the **Nechako Plateau,** which is riddled with lakes and streams. Wildlife abounds. If you're in the right place at the right time you can see caribou, mountain goats, moose, black and grizzly bears, mule deer, wolves, smaller mammals such as hoary marmots and wolverines, and many birds. The lakes are filled with fish, including rainbow trout, kokanee, mountain whitefish, and burbot.

Aside from fishing, the most popular activity in the park's northern reaches is boating, canoeing, or kayaking the circular route through Ootsa, Whitesail, Eutsuk, Tetachuck, and Natalkuz Lakes. Some portaging is required. Ootsa Lake is the main access to the park, but the shoreline has been described as a forest of drowned trees and floating hazards—very dangerous, with few places to land when frequent strong winds funnel across the lakes. Some channels have been cut through the dead trees to emergency landing areas; follow the large yellow diamond signs. Because of the strong winds, keep as close to the shoreline as possible. May is the windiest month.

Practicalities

Wilderness campsites sprinkle some of the lakes within the park. To get to Ootsa Lake, follow Highway 35 for 16 kilometers (10 miles) south from Burns Lake to Francois Lake, take the free vehicle ferry across Francois Lake, then continue south another 44 kilometers (27 miles) to the settlement of Ootsa Lake. To get *into* the park itself, you'll need a canoe, kayak, motorboat, or chartered floatplane. **Lakes District Air Services** (250/692-3229, www.lakesdistrictair.com) flies charters year-round from a base along Francois Lake Road—on floats in summer and skis in winter. Rates are $395 per hour for the three-passenger Cessna 185 and $510 per hour for the six-passenger Beaver. This company also owns fly-in cabins on Tesla and Coles Lakes. The cabins sleep four and come equipped with cooking facilities, hot showers, HF radios, and a couple of small motorboats. A four-day package deal, inclusive of charter flights, is $1,800 for two people or $2,700 for four; guests supply food, sleeping bags, and fishing gear.

TOPLEY TO TELKWA

Babine Lake

At Topley, 51 kilometers (32 miles) west of Burns Lake, a side road leads north to 177-kilometer-long (110-mile-long) Babine Lake, the province's largest natural lake and yet another spot known for producing trophy-size rainbow trout, Dolly Varden, kokanee, coho salmon, and whitefish. The rivers flowing in and out of the lake also splash with fish, including rainbow trout, steelhead, and salmon.

Topley Landing, 30 kilometers (19 miles) from the Yellowhead Highway, is a former trapping and trading center dating back to the 1700s. Beyond the landing, over the Fulton River, is **Red Bluff Provincial Park,** named for iron-impregnated cliffs nearby. The park's small campground enjoys a picturesque riverside location, but facilities are limited; $14 per night.

The road terminates at **Granisle,** formerly a company town where life revolved around a copper mine. In 1992 the mine closed, many residents moved out, and a developer moved in, attempting to attract retirees and holidaymakers. The preexisting mining-employee accommodations were refurbished to be sold as condominiums, and the former Granisle Village Inn was revamped and renamed the **Grande Isles Resort** (250/697-6322 or 800/671-4475, www.grandeislesresort.com). The latter is excellent value, with comfortable kitchenette units

© ANDREW HEMPSTEAD

Fishing draws many visitors to Babine Lake.

from $70 s or d. The sockeye salmon run in August and September, but other than that there's little reason to come out here. A free municipal campground is one kilometer (.6 mile) south of town. Firewood and pit toilets are provided.

Houston

Like Burns Lake, Houston's welcoming sign also proudly bears a carved fish—this time a steelhead. Houston calls itself "Steelhead Country," for the only species of trout that migrates to the ocean. The forestry town of 4,000 lies at the confluence of the Bulkley and Morice Rivers in the stunning Bulkley Valley, which enjoys the snowcapped Telkwa and Babine Ranges for a backdrop. As in the rest of this region, the local fishing is superb. At the information center pick up a copy of the local forestry district recreation map ($3), which shows all the area's rivers, lakes, logging roads, and campgrounds. The best steelhead fishing is in the Morice River—take the highway west toward Smithers, turn left at the Northwood Pulp Mill sign, and continue about 1.6 kilometers to the end. At the dirt road turn right (at the bridge). Both bait fishing and fly-fishing are popular here.

The pick of an ordinary bunch of motels lining the highway through town is the **Houston Motor Inn** (250/845-7112 or 800/994-8333; $58 s, $64 d). Camp at the Houston Motor Inn for $16–24.

The **Houston Visitor Info Centre** (Hwy. 16 at Benson Ave., 250/845-7640; summer daily 9 A.M.–5 P.M., weekdays only the rest of the year) is easy to spot—out front is world's largest fly-fishing rod.

Telkwa

As you continue west, the scenery just keeps getting better. You'll pass open fields and rolling, densely forested hills, all the while surrounded by snowcapped mountains peeking tantalizingly out of clouds. The neat little village of Telkwa lies at the confluence of the Bulkley and Telkwa Rivers, almost exactly halfway between Prince George and Prince Rupert. Several species of anadromous fish make spawning runs up the rivers here at various times of year—spring chinook salmon in late June, coho salmon in August, and steelhead between fall and freeze-up. The area also appeals to canoeists, offering stretches of water to suit novices through intermediates. Many of the buildings in the village were put up between 1908 and 1924. The Telkwa Museum Society puts out a *Walking Tour Through Historic Telkwa* brochure, which describes each of the buildings.

On the highway through town, the **M Douglas Resort Motel** (250/846-5679, www.douglasresortmotel.com) is one of the best places to stay between Prince George and the coast. It offers a beautiful riverside setting and is surrounded by gardens. Motel rooms are $75 s, $80 d, while self-contained log cabins, complete with fireplaces, are $90–125 s or d. Nearby **Tyhee Lake Provincial Park** has a good swimming beach, picnic facilities, and a campground with hot showers ($19 per site May–Sept., free the rest of the year).

SMITHERS AND VICINITY

The Coast Mountains surround the town of Smithers (pop. 5,400), while the splendid 2,560-meter (8,400-foot) Hudson Bay Mountain towers directly above. It's a vibrant community with some excellent accommodations, fine restaurants, and interesting arts-and-crafts shops. Hiking trails close to town lead to a magnificent glacier, intriguing fossil beds, and a remote recreation area.

Town Sights

With a backdrop of magnificent mountains, it's no surprise that Main Street is done up in a Bavarian theme. Visitors shop here for native crafts and tourist paraphernalia. The grand old 1925 courthouse, at the junction of the Yellowhead Highway and Main Street, is home to **Bulkley Valley Museum** (250/847-5322) and **Smithers Art Gallery** (250/847-3898). The museum has a predictable collection of historic artifacts, highlighted by an interesting collection of black-and-white photos. Both the museum and gallery are open in summer Monday–Saturday 11 A.M.–5 P.M.

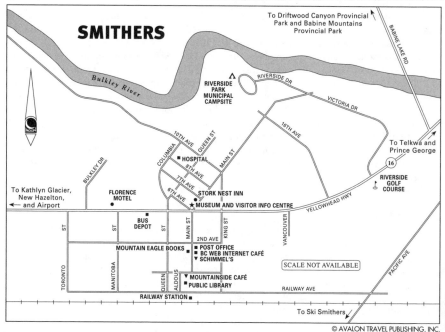

SMITHERS

To Driftwood Canyon Provincial
Park and Babine Mountains
Provincial Park

BABINE LAKE RD

Bulkley River

RIVERSIDE DR

RIVERSIDE
PARK
MUNICIPAL
CAMPSITE

VICTORIA DR

16TH AVE

10TH AVE

QUEEN ST

MAIN ST

COLUMBIA

HOSPITAL

8TH AVE

7TH AVE

6TH AVE

BULKLEY DR

To Kathlyn Glacier,
New Hazelton,
← and Airport

FLORENCE
MOTEL

STORK NEST INN

MUSEUM AND VISITOR INFO CENTRE

To Telkwa and
Prince George

16

RIVERSIDE
GOLF
COURSE

YELLOWHEAD HWY

BUS
DEPOT

ST

ST

ST

MAIN ST

KING ST

VANCOUVER

2ND AVE

MOUNTAIN EAGLE BOOKS

POST OFFICE
BC WEB INTERNET CAFÉ
SCHIMMEL'S

SCALE NOT AVAILABLE

PACIFIC AVE

TORONTO

MANITOBA

QUEEN

ALDOUS

MOUNTAINSIDE CAFÉ
PUBLIC LIBRARY

RAILWAY AVE

RAILWAY STATION

To Ski Smithers

© AVALON TRAVEL PUBLISHING, INC.

Northern British Columbia

Driftwood Canyon Provincial Park

Many millions of years ago, the Bulkley Valley had a subtropical climate. The area north of where Smithers now lies was a low wetland of swamps and shallow lakes. Over eons, deposited sediments covered and preserved the remains of the plants and animals that died in the water. Around a million years ago, a lava flow covered the entire region. But then during the last ice age, melting ice carved out a canyon that sliced right through the ancient wetlands, exposing the fossil beds.

Most of the fossils here are from plants, but insect and fish fossils have also been uncovered, including some of the world's oldest known trout fossils. A short walk from the road leads to a viewing platform over the east bank of Driftwood Creek, where interpretive panels describe the site's significance. Excavated specimens can be viewed in the Bulkley Valley Museum. The park is 17 kilometers (11 miles) northeast of town; take Highway 16 three kilometers (1.9 miles) east, head north on Old Babine Lake Road, turn left on Telkwa High Road, then right on Driftwood Road.

Babine Mountains Provincial Park

From Driftwood Canyon, Driftwood Road continues five kilometers (3.1 miles) to a parking lot—the trailhead for trails leading into Babine Mountains Provincial Park. The park protects 32,400 hectares (80,000 acres) of the Skeena Mountains, a remote wilderness dominated by rugged peaks, alpine plateaus, and glacier-fed lakes and rivers. The park is accessible only on foot, but you don't need to travel too far into the park to reach the best parts. From this trailhead, the **McCabe Trail** leads eight kilometers (five miles) one-way to the alpine meadows between Mounts Hyland and Harvey, while the **Silver King Basin Trail** climbs steadily through a subalpine forest for nine kilometers (5.6 miles) one-way to another alpine meadow. Allow three hours one way for either option.

Kathlyn Glacier and Vicinity

About eight kilometers (five miles) west of Smithers on the Yellowhead Highway, take the **Hudson Bay Mountain Lookout** turnout for magnificent views of the mountain and the quickly receding Kathlyn Glacier on its north face. In the same vicinity, turn south off the highway at Lake Kathlyn Road to the trailhead for **Glacier Gulch,** a strenuous 1,000 vertical meters (3,280 feet) above the parking lot. The trail is only six kilometers one-way, but allow at least three hours to reach the toe of Kathlyn Glacier. Just 500 meters (.3 mile) along the trail is dramatic **Twin Falls,** a worthy destination in itself. Beyond the Glacier Gulch trailhead, Lake Kathlyn Road ends, appropriately enough, at **Lake Kathlyn,** a photogenic body of water at the base of Hudson Bay Mountain.

Ski Smithers

This smallish winter resort (250/847-2058, www.skismithers.com) on Hudson Bay Mountain is mostly geared to beginners and intermediates, but a few of the 19 designated runs challenge more experienced skiers and boarders. Four lifts serve a vertical rise of 553 meters (1,750 feet) and 120 hectares (300 acres) of mostly intermediate terrain. Facilities include two day lodges, a rental shop, and a ski and snowboard school. A day pass is adults $35, senior $25, child $18; those under six and over 60 ski free. Cross-country skiers can choose from a 2.5-kilometer (1.6-mile) groomed trail on the mountain or the 10-kilometer (6.2-mile) **Pine Creek Loop** on the road to the resort. To get to the mountain take either Main Street or King Street south onto Railway Avenue and turn left; the base area is 23 kilometers (14 miles) from downtown Smithers.

Accommodations and Camping

Because skiers and snowboarders from throughout the north flock to the slopes of Hudson Bay Mountain when the snow falls, the local lodgings are apt to be as busy in winter as in summer. The 23-room **Stork Nest Inn** (1485 Main St., 250/847-3831, www.storknestinn.com; $65–78 s or d) is styled on a Bavarian lodge. It features comfortable rooms, a cooked breakfast, and airport transfers. Save a few bucks by staying at the **Florence Motel** (4160 Hwy. 16, 250/847-2678; $50 s, $65 d), but it's a bit rough around the edges.

The premier accommodation in this region is the **M Logpile Lodge** (3105 McCabe Rd., 250/847-5152, www.logpilelodge.com; Mar.–late Dec.; $85–135 s or d), north of town (call for directions) and surrounded by a magnificent mountain panorama. Guest rooms on the upper floor have vaulted ceilings, while exposed log walls dominate those on the lower floor. All seven rooms have solid log beds and private balconies. A big breakfast, cooked to order, will set you up for an activity-filled day (horseback riding, canoeing, fishing, and more) with local operators.

Riverside Park Municipal Campsite (May–Oct.; $11–14) is beside the Bulkley River, north of town. It provides shaded sites, a few electrical hookups, showers, and a cooking shelter. **Riverside Golf Course** (Hwy. 16 east of town, 250/847-3229; mid-Apr.–mid-Oct.) has better facilities and is within the bounds of a golf course; unserviced sites $17, serviced sites $19–22.

Food

Mountainside Café (3763 4th Ave., 250/847-3455; Mon.–Sat. 11 A.M.–8 P.M.) is a funky little space with a stylish yet uncomplicated decor. The varied menu includes everything from fish and chips to a Thai curry ($14). Expect live music on Thursday evening. At **Schimmel's** (1172 Main St., 250/847-9044, Tues.–Sat. 5:30 A.M.–5 P.M.), enjoy a range of delicious cakes and pastries, or enjoy a bowl of homemade soup ($3–5) with a sandwich ($4–7) made to order.

Information and Services

Tourism Smithers (250/847-5072 or 800/542-6673, www.tourismsmithers.com) operates the **Smithers Visitor Info Centre,** upstairs in the museum building (corner of Main St. and the Yellowhead Hwy.; summer daily 9 A.M.–6 P.M., the rest of the year Mon.–Fri. 8:30 A.M.–4:30 P.M.). A good source of northern literature is **Mountain Eagle Books** (1237 Main St., 250/847-5245). Check your email at **BC Web Internet Cafe** (1188 Main St., 250/877-6228; Mon.–Sat. 9 A.M.–6 P.M.).

Transportation

Smithers Airport, right beside Highway 16, four kilometers (2.5 miles) west of town, is served by **Air Canada** (888/247-2262). At the airport, **National** (250/847-2216) and **Thrifty** (250/847-3332) have a few rental cars. The **Greyhound** bus depot is on Highway 16, west of the information center (250/847-2204).

Continuing West from Smithers

The next place to stop and stretch your legs is the viewpoint at **Moricetown Canyon,** where the 500-meter-wide Bulkley River funnels and roars its way down through a 15-meter-wide canyon. Salmon desperately hurl themselves up these spectacular rapids in autumn. Below the canyon the river pours into a large pool, one of the best fishing spots in the area.

The canyon is part of **Moricetown Indian Reserve,** which recognizes an area that has been a Carrier village site for more than 5,000 years. Villagers still fish the canyon using traditional spears and nets; look for the locals congregated around the canyon in summer.

Continuing west, the scenery changes dramatically; suddenly pine trees line the Bulkley River and cover the hills and mountains. About 50 kilometers (31 miles) from Smithers, a four-kilometer (2.5-mile) unpaved road to the north leads to 307-hectare (760-acre) **Ross Lake Provincial Park,** named for a lake with crystal-clear waters full of trout and Dolly Varden. The backdrop is one of forested hills and spectacular snowcapped peaks. In the early mornings you can hear loons; in the evenings beavers slide into the water, slapping their tails. Facilities include a boat-launching area (no powerboats allowed), barbecue pits, picnic tables, and pit toilets. The park is a day-use area only, with no campsites.

NEW HAZELTON AND VICINITY

It's easy to be confused by the three Hazeltons—Hazelton, New Hazelton, and South Hazelton—situated at the most northerly point on the Yellowhead Highway. As usual, the arrival of the Grand Trunk Pacific Railway caused the confusion. The original Hazelton (called Old Town)

was established 50 years or so before the railway came. The other two Hazeltons were founded because each of their respective promoters thought he owned a better spot for a new railway town. Today the largest of the three small communities is New Hazelton (pop. 900), a service center watched over by spectacular Mount Rocher Deboule (French for "Mountain of the Rolling Rock").

Hazelton

From New Hazelton, Highway 62 leads about eight kilometers (five miles) northwest to Hazelton. Along the way it crosses the one-lane **Hagwilget Suspension Bridge,** 79 meters (260 feet) above the turbulent Bulkley River. Stop and read the plaque about the original footbridge—made from poles and cedar rope—that once spanned the gorge here; you'll be glad you live in modern times.

At the junction of the Bulkley and Skeena Rivers, Hazelton has retained its unique 1890s-style architecture and pioneer settlement atmosphere. Along the waterfront sits a museum (open daily 10 A.M.–5 P.M.), a landing with river views, and a café.

🅜 'Ksan Historical Village

'Ksan, which means "Between the Banks," is an authentically reconstructed Gitxsan village on the outskirts of Hazelton (250/842-5544 or 877/842-5518; Apr.–Sept. daily 9 A.M.–5 P.M.; adult $10, senior and child $8.50). In the main building a museum features cedar boxes and cedar-bark mats, woven and button blankets, masks, coppers (the most valuable single object a chief possessed), rattles used by shamans, and an art gallery with changing exhibitions. In the adjacent gift shop are the works of on-site artists. Beyond the museum is the main village, which can only be visited as part of a fascinating guided tour (included in admission). Tours leave every hour on the hour, visiting the burial house, food cache, smokehouse, community houses, and the 'Ksan artists' carving shop and studio. You'll see traditional Northwest Coast carved interiors, paintings and painted screens, totem poles, and fine examples of native artifacts, arts and crafts, tools and implements, and personal possessions. And you'll learn how the people lived and all about their beliefs and legends. On Friday nights from mid-July to mid-August, performances of traditional Gitxsan song and dance take place starting around 8 P.M.

Kispiox

The traditional Gitxsan village of Kispiox lies 16 kilometers (10 miles) north of Hazelton along Kispiox Valley Road (turn off on the Smithers side of Hazelton). Sights include a large group of red cedar **totem poles** near the confluence of the Skeena and Kispiox Rivers and the locally operated, log-constructed **Kispiox Salmon Hatchery** (daily 8 A.M.–5 P.M.). The hatchery can rear 500,000 salmon fry per year.

The Seven Sisters

These impressive peaks lie west of New Hazelton, immediately south of the junction of the Yellowhead Highway and Highway 37. From the highway you'll get only occasional glimpses of the range; for the best panorama take Highway 37 north across the Skeena River, turn west (left) toward Cedarvale, and stop after about 10 kilometers (6.2 miles) at the picnic area by Sedan Creek.

Several trails also lead to good views of the peaks. The one-kilometer (.6-mile) **Gull Creek Trail** climbs about 200 vertical meters (660 feet) from the trailhead at Gull Creek, which is signposted along Highway 16. Serious hikers can take any of a number of routes up into the heart of the range, but each is a strenuous slog. The easiest to follow is **Coyote Creek Trail,** an old mining road beginning from where Highway 16 crosses Coyote Creek. The nine-kilometer (5.6-mile) road ends at a few cabins often used by climbers. From there it's a six-kilometer (3.7-mile) climb along a rough trail that becomes increasingly difficult to follow. The trail ends on a high alpine ridge at the base of a large icefield.

Practicalities

Along the highway through New Hazelton is the **28 Inn** (250/842-6006 or 877/842-2828;

$55 s, $60 d), with slightly nicer rooms than the rates may suggest. It also has a restaurant and pub.

Between the highway and "Old" Hazelton is the log **M Hummingbird Restaurant** (250/842-5628; Mon.–Sat. 11 A.M.–2 P.M. and 5–9 P.M.), the best spot for a meal in all the Hazeltons. The wood interior is decorated with etched glass and hanging lamps, and you'll be dazzled by the million-dollar picture-window view of Mount Rocher Deboule. Tiny hummingbirds flit back and forth between the feeders outside the windows. At lunch, expect to pay around $6–9 for sandwiches, hamburgers, or a huge taco salad. At dinner choose from steaks, chicken, and pasta dishes, all for around $14–17.

At the intersection of Highways 16 and 62, **Hazelton Visitor Info Centre** (250/842-6071; mid-May–Sept. daily 8 A.M.–7 P.M.) has all the usual literature and holds a display detailing local history.

TERRACE AND VICINITY

Terrace (pop. 12,500) lies on the Yellowhead Highway, 580 kilometers (360 miles) west of Prince George and 146 kilometers (91 miles) east of Prince Rupert. The city is built on a series of steep terraces along the beautiful Skeena River, the province's second-largest river system, and is completely surrounded by the spectacular Hazelton and Coast Mountains. The town offers basic tourist services and little else. But the surrounding area makes up for it with a mix of intriguing sights, beautiful parks, and outstanding recreation opportunities.

Originally home of the Tsimshian, "Those Who Taste the Rain," the site that is now Terrace was founded by George Little in 1911. Little's sawmill operation got a boost with the arrival of the railway in 1914; his logs were used for railroad ties. Today the forestry industry still forms the basis for the city's economy.

Heritage Park

At this outdoor-indoor museum (4113 Sparks St., 250/635-4546; summer Wed.–Sun. 10 A.M.–6 P.M., the rest of the year Tues.–Sat. 10 A.M.–

© AVALON TRAVEL PUBLISHING, INC.

6 P.M.; adult $4, senior $3), a one-hour guided tour takes you through an old, beautifully furnished log hotel, a dance hall, a barn, and six authentic log cabins dating from between 1910 and 1955. Some of the cabins are furnished; others contain historical artifacts or collections of antique farming and mining equipment. The guide fills you in on the early history of Terrace—covering gold, copper, and lead mining; fur trading; construction of the telegraph line; logging; and the homesteaders of the late 1800s and early 1900s. To get there from downtown, head north up Skeenaview Street.

Nisga'a Memorial Lava Bed Provincial Park

Protecting Canada's youngest lava flow, the fascinating landscape of this 17,683-hectare (43,700-acre) park is unique within the province. The flow is about 18 kilometers (11 miles) long and three kilometers (1.9 miles) wide; experts think the molten rock spewed through the earth's crust between 1650 and 1750, killing an estimated 200 natives. You can see all different types of lava, as well as crevasses, spiky pinnacles, sinkholes, craters, and bright blue pools where underground rivers have risen to the surface. Explore

THE ELUSIVE KERMODE

Little known outside British Columbia is the Kermode (pronounced kerr-MO-dee), an elusive subspecies of black bear *(Ursus americanus kermodei)* inhabiting only the vast tract of wilderness north of Terrace and uninhabited Princess Royal Island south of Kitimat.

First studied by Francis Kermode, director of the provincial museum at the turn of the 20th century, the bear was originally thought to be a distinct species. It's slightly larger than other black bears, has a different jaw structure, and, although its color varies, some individuals are pure white. These white bears are not albinos, but instead contain a recessive gene that results in the light coloring.

The Tsimshian called the Kermode "Spirit Bear" and often rendered it in human form in their artwork. Once close to extinction, the Kermode is now fully protected.

the lava with caution—in some parts the surface may be unstable, and it's very hard on footgear. The only facilities are a day-use area and a couple of short hiking trails.

To get to the park, take Highway 16 west out of town for three kilometers (1.9 miles), then head north around the back of the sawmill on Kalum Lake Drive. The park is 78 kilometers (48.5 miles) along this road; watch for logging trucks during the week. The information center in Terrace has an interesting brochure on the lava beds.

Lakelse Lake Provincial Park

This 354-hectare (874-acre) park at the north end of beautiful Lakelse Lake offers good swimming beaches, boating, fishing, a large campground, a shaded picnic area, and a hiking trail through an old-growth forest of towering spruce, cedar, and hemlock. To get there, take Highway 37 south toward Kitimat for 26 kilometers (16 miles).

Hiking

Many trails in the area tempt hikers. For an easy stroll, take the three-kilometer (1.9-mile) path (50 minutes or less) around **Ferry Island,** in the middle of the Skeena River east of downtown (reached via Highway 16). More demanding is **Terrace Mountain Nature Trail,** a five-kilometer (3.1-mile) trail providing great views of the city and the surrounding area. It takes about two hours round-trip, because much of it is uphill. Start at the intersection of Halliwell Avenue and Anderson Street (by Heritage Park), climbing the lower slopes of Terrace Mountain to a cleared area where views are best, then descending to the end of Johnstone Street. Complete the circle by walking down Johnstone Street, turning right on Park Avenue, right again on Kalum Avenue, then continuing straight onto Skeenaview Avenue back to the trailhead.

Farther afield, consider scenic **Clearwater Lakes Trail,** which begins from Highway 37, 27 kilometers (16.8 miles) south of Terrace. The trail leads 1.8 kilometers (1.1 miles) to Little Clearwater Lake, then another 700 meters (.4 mile) to Big Clearwater Lake. The two lakes are linked by a shallow creek, along the banks of which are many good picnic spots and berries to pick in season. From the same parking lot, a trail leads 1.8 kilometers (1.1 miles) to a lookout with outstanding views of Lakelse Lake.

To get the rundown on all the best hikes in the area, ask for the handy *Terrace Hiking Trails* brochure at the information center.

Fishing

The Skeena River is chock-full of salmon and other fish. Steelhead can be caught April–May and August–November. Chinooks make their upstream migration in late May and again July through early August. Coho salmon run from August to early fall. Be sure to get a license and read up on the latest rules and regulations before hitting the rivers and lakes. Pick up a list of local guides and outfitters from the information center.

Skiing and Snowboarding

Shames Mountain (250/635-3773, www.shamesmountain.com) offers a vertical rise of

488 meters (1,600 feet) and virtually guaranteed good snow coverage. In the opening season (1990–1991) an amazing 2,400 centimeters (944 inches) of snow fell at the resort—nearly twice as much as at any other resort in North America. Current facilities include a day lodge, ski and snowboard school, chairlift, T-bar, and rope tow. Lift tickets are adult $35, senior $25, child $18. Lifts operate between Christmas and early April Wednesday–Sunday only.

Accommodations

The less expensive motels are strung out along Highway 16 on the eastern and western outskirts of the city. To the west, your best bet is **Cedars Motel** (4830 Hwy. 16, 250/635-2258 or 866/635-2258, www.cedarsmotel.net), which is nothing special but charges only $46 s, $48 d. On the other side of town is **Copper River Motel,** three kilometers (1.9 miles) east (4113 Hwy. 16, 250/635-6124 or 888/652-7222, www.copperrivermotel.com), set up for anglers, with fishing supplies and guides, 4WD rentals, and free ice. Rooms are clean and have coffee- and tea-making appliances. On the down side are the paper-thin walls. Summer rates are from $60 s, $65 d; a kitchen is available for an extra $10.

Right downtown is the moderately upscale **Coast Inn of the West** (4620 Lakelse Ave., 250/638-8141 or 800/663-1144, www.coasthotels.com), where each of the 60 air-conditioned rooms is decorated in stylish pastel colors. Facilities include a White Spot family restaurant and lounge, and a nearby aquatic center is open to guests. Rooms are $145 s, $155 d, but check the website for discounts.

Camping

On Ferry Island in the Skeena River, just over three kilometers east of downtown, **Ferry Island Campground** (250/635-4244; mid-Apr.–mid-Oct.) offers sheltered sites among birch and cottonwood trees, berry bushes, and wildflowers. A few sites have excellent views of the river and mountains, and a hiking trail runs through the woods and around the island. Facilities include picnic tables and shelters, fire grates, firewood, and pit toilets, but no showers. A few sites have electrical hookups. Unserviced sites are $13 per night; powered sites are $16.

A short drive from Terrace three provincial parks have campgrounds. **Kleanza Creek Provincial Park,** site of a short-lived gold rush, is 20 kilometers (12 miles) east of Terrace on Highway 16; $14 a night. In the opposite direction, 50 kilometers (31 miles) west of the city on Highway 16 is **Exchamsiks River Provincial Park;** $14 a night. **Lakelse Lake Provincial Park,** 16 kilometers (10 miles) south of Terrace along Highway 37, is the most developed of the three parks, offering a sandy beach, safe swimming, an interpretive amphitheater, hot showers, and flush toilets. Sites are $19 a night.

Food

One of the most popular places to go for breakfast is the **Northern Motor Inn,** near the Chevron gas station on Highway 16 just east of Terrace (250/635-6375). Large omelets, hash browns, toast, and coffee run around $7–8. Head to **Cafenara** (4716 Lazelle Ave., 250/638-1662; Mon.–Sat. 7 A.M.–9 P.M., Sun. 9 A.M.–4 P.M.) for your daily quota of caffeine in a big-city coffeehouse atmosphere.

For delicious Mexican food, head downtown to **Don Diego's** (3212 Kalum St., 250/635-2307; Mon.–Sat. 11 A.M.–9 P.M., Sun. 10 A.M.–2 P.M. and 5–9 P.M.), where many tables catch the evening sun. It's a small, bright restaurant with lots of plants and Mexican wall hangings. Lunch is $6–9 (the shrimp crepes are superb). Dinner entrées start at around $10. It's always busy, so you may have to wait for a table.

Information

Terrace Visitor Info Centre (4511 Keith Ave., 250/635-2063 or 800/499-1637, www.terrace-tourism.bc.ca; summer Mon.–Fri. 8:30 A.M.–8 P.M. and Sat.–Sun. 9 A.M.–8 P.M., the rest of the year Mon.–Fri. 9 A.M.–5 P.M.) is beside Highway 16 on the east side of town. The helpful staff will happily load you down with brochures and pamphlets and tell you everything there is to do in the area.

Books and Bookstores

In addition to a solid collection of northern literature, **Terrace Public Library** (4610 Park Ave., 250/638-8177; Tues.–Sat. noon–3 P.M. and 7–9 P.M., Sun. 1–4 P.M.) holds a community art gallery offering exhibitions that change monthly. For local reading and a good selection of Canadiana, head downtown to **Misty River Books** (4710 Lakelse Ave., 250/635-4428; Mon.–Thurs. and Sat. 9 A.M.–6 P.M., Fri. 9 A.M.–8 P.M.).

Transportation

Terrace and Kitimat Airport is on Highway 37 eight kilometers (five miles) south of Terrace. Both **Air Canada** (888/247-2262) and Terrace-based **Hawk Air** (250/635-4295) offer daily scheduled flights to Vancouver, with Hawk Air also serving Victoria and communities throughout the north. **VIA Rail** trains pass through town three times a week en route to Prince Rupert. The train station is just a small building on Railway Road that opens only when a train arrives or leaves. **Greyhound** (4620 Keith Ave., 250/635-4428) offers daily service west to Prince Rupert and east to Prince George. For a rental car, contact **Car To Go** (250/615-0101 or 866/227-8646, www.car-to-go.com), **Hertz** (250/635-6866), or **National** (250/635-6855).

KITIMAT

The planned industrial community of Kitimat (pop. 11,000), at the northern end of Douglas Channel 62 kilometers (39 miles) south of Terrace, was founded by the aluminum giant **Alcan** (Aluminum Company of Canada) in the 1950s. Described at the time by *National Geographic* as "the most expensive project ever attempted by private industry," the project included one of the world's largest aluminum smelters, a company town to serve the workers, and a massive hydroelectric scheme 75 kilometers (47 miles) south of Kitimat. The hydroelectric project intended to redirect the river's course to a power station at Kemano, then use the electricity generated there to run the Kitimat smelter. The government kicked in millions of dollars upgrading the region's infrastructure, but only the

first stages of the hydroelectric project were ever completed. Intense pressure from environmentalists and native organizations forced the provincial government to cancel the rest of the project in 1995.

Tours

The highlight of a visit to B.C.'s self-proclaimed "Aluminum City" is a guided industrial tour. The town's Alcan smelter, **Kitimat Works,** produces 270,000 tons of aluminum products worth $350 million annually. Tours, offered in summer Monday–Friday at 10:30 A.M. and 1:30 P.M., start with an audiovisual presentation, then it's into a bus for a drive around the works and down to the wharf. Tours are free, but book ahead (250/639-8259).

Methanex, Kitimat's newest industry and northern British Columbia's only **petrochemical plant,** offers tours June–August Monday and Wednesday at 3 P.M. Bearded men (or women) are not permitted on this tour. Book at 250/639-9292.

If all this industrial hooey gives you a headache, get back to nature at **Kitimat River Fish Hatchery** (250/639-9616), which releases 11 million trout and salmon annually. Tours are conducted three times daily through summer.

Other Sights

In **Radley Park,** along the Kitimat River, stands the province's largest living tree, a 50-meter-high (164-foot-high), 500-year-old Sitka spruce. It's behind the Riverlodge Recreation Centre. The **Centennial Museum** (293 City Centre, 250/632-7022; June–Aug. Mon.–Sat. 10 A.M.–5 P.M., the rest of the year Mon.–Fri. 10 A.M.–5 P.M. and Sat.–Sun. noon–5 P.M.) tells the story of the planned town and displays historic and native artifacts; a gallery features locally produced artwork.

Practicalities

Right downtown, **City Centre Motel** (480 City Centre, 250/632-4848 or 800/663-3391; $58 s, $62 d) features comfortable rooms, each with a fully equipped kitchen and tea- and coffee-making facilities. Kitimat's premier accommodation is **Minette Bay Lodge** (2255 Kitimat Village Rd., 250/632-2907 or 866/247-1513, www.minettebaylodge.com), a grand estate that looks like it has been transported from the English countryside to the Kitimat waterfront. Guests enjoy activities such as heli-hiking, jet boat tours, and fishing charters through the day, and then kick back in the lap of luxury. The guest rooms are spacious and feature a pinky pastel color scheme; most have water views. The rates of $250 per person include all meals. **Radley Park Campground** (May–Sept.; $18–20) has a riverside setting, showers, a few electrical hookups, and a kitchen shelter.

For the best breakfast in town, head to **The Chalet** (852 Tsimshian Blvd., 250/632-2662). **Pedro's Grill** (342 City Centre, 250/632-2199) also serves breakfast, although it doesn't open until 9 A.M. No surprises in this small-town restaurant: mains such as spaghetti and meatballs, pork cutlets, and Salisbury steak range $10–21, and the doors close at 9 P.M.

Kitimat Visitor Info Centre is at the north entrance to town (2109 Forest Ave., 250/632-6294 or 800/664-6554, www.visitkitimat.com).

WEST TOWARD PRINCE RUPERT

The 147-kilometer (91-mile) stretch of the Yellowhead Highway between Terrace and Prince Rupert rivals any stretch of road in the province for beauty. For almost the entire distance, the highway hugs the north bank of the beautiful Skeena River (Skeena is a Gitxsan word for "River of Mist"). On a fine day, views from the road are stunning—snow-dusted mountains, densely forested hillsides, ponds covered in yellow water lilies, and waterfalls like narrow ribbons of silver, snaking down vertical cliffs from the snow high above. In some sections the highway shrinks to two extremely narrow lanes neatly sandwiched between the railway tracks and the river—drive defensively.

Exchamsiks River Provincial Park, on the north side of the highway 50 kilometers (31 miles) west of Terrace, features a grassy picnic area where the deep green Exchamsiks River drains into the much larger Skeena River. Camping is $14 a night. As the highway continues westward, the Skeena widens, eventually becoming a tidal estuary. Sandbars and marshes, exposed at low tide, are a mass of colorful mosses, and wading birds feed in shallow pools. Keep an eye out for bald eagles on the sandbars or perched in the trees above the highway.

Just over 110 kilometers (68 miles) from Terrace, the highway leaves the river and meanders inland past high forested cliffs to **Prudhomme Lake,** on the north side of the highway. The lake holds a number of forested islands and is flanked by a small provincial park; campsites $14.

Northern British Columbia

Prince Rupert

Prince Rupert (pop. 16,000), on hilly Kaien Island 726 kilometers (451 miles) west of Prince George, is busy with travelers throughout the summer. The city itself holds an odd but intriguing mixture of cultural icons—totem poles, old English coats of arms and street names, high-rise hotels and civic buildings—all crammed together on the edge of the Pacific Ocean. Wildlife is varied and prolific. Prince Rupert is gateway to the Khutzeymateen Grizzly Bear Sanctuary, but even from town, you're likely to spot bald eagles, seals, and even black bears.

The city has always been a hub for travelers but has never been seen as a destination in itself. That began changing in the early 1990s, with the redevelopment of Cow Bay, and in 1999 the first cruise ship arrived at the newly constructed Atlin Dock. The area south along the waterfront from Cow Bay is still a wasteland of railyards and disused docks, but work has already begun on sprucing up this part of the city, and it will continue for many years to come. Plan to spend at least a day in the area, visiting the excellent museum, exploring an old cannery village, or maybe taking a harbor tour.

History

For at least 5,000 years, Kaien Island and the vicinity have been inhabited by the Coast Tsimshian, whose lives were traditionally dominated by fishing and food gathering. They followed the spring and summer salmon and oolichan runs, returning every season to the same village sites. Trade networks were established, artistic traditions emerged, and a class system evolved. Before 1790 the region was among the most heavily populated areas on British Columbia's coastline.

When Europeans arrived on the northwest coast, the local Tsimshian, eager to cash in on fur trading, moved to Fort Simpson, a Hudson's Bay Company post north of Prince Rupert. For a time, they continued to hold their traditional potlatches—days-long festivals filled with feasting, storytelling, and dancing in elaborate costumes and masks. But in 1884, the government, swayed by church lobbyists who claimed the practice was evil, banned potlatching, and this crucial, millennia-old element of the Tsimshians' economic, trade, and social structure effectively died out.

Prince Rupert was the brainchild of Charles M. Hays, general manager of the Grand Trunk Pacific Railway. In 1902, Hays devised a plan to build a rail line from North Bay, Ontario, to a new port on the central B.C. coast—a port he hoped would rival Vancouver and become *the* Pacific port for Canada. In 1914 the railway was completed, but unfortunately, Hays never saw it. He went down with the *Titanic* in 1912. The new city was named after pioneer English business magnate and adventurer Prince Rupert.

After World War I, fishing and fish processing became important parts of the city's economy, and during World War II Prince Rupert became a shipbuilding center and an American army base. Tourism started in the 1960s with the commencement of the B.C. and Alaska ferry services. Today, fishing is still the mainstay of the economy; up to 2,000 fishing vessels cruise the coast in search of salmon, herring, lingcod, sole, and halibut. Their total annual catch averages some 7,000 tons. Prince Rupert also boasts four fish-processing plants, extensive deepwater-port facilities, grain and coal terminals, and a thriving wood-products industry.

SIGHTS

Museum of Northern British Columbia

You can easily spend several hours at this fascinating museum, which occupies an imposing post-and-beam building overlooking the harbor (corner of 1st Ave. W and McBride St., 250/624-3207; early June–Aug. Mon.–Fri. 9 A.M.–8 P.M. and Sun. 9 A.M.–5 P.M., the rest of the year Mon.–Sat. 10 A.M.–5 P.M.; adult $5, child $1). Exhibits trace the history of Prince Rupert from 5,000-year-old Tsimshian settlements through

PRINCE RUPERT

SEE "DOWNTOWN PRINCE RUPERT" MAP

SCALE NOT AVAILABLE

Prince Rupert Harbour

Seal Cove

SEAL COVE RD

BELLIS RD

■ HARBOUR AIR
■ VANCOUVER ISLAND HELICOPTERS

8TH AVE E

11TH AVE E

FREDERICK ST

GEORGE HILLS WAY

PRINCE RUPERT BLVD

■ EARL MAH AQUATIC CENTRE

■ CIVIC CENTRE

★ OLDFIELD CREEK HATCHERY

Oldfield Creek

WANTAGE RD

Hays Creek

Cow Bay

5TH AVE

8TH AVE W

9TH AVE W

MCBRIDE

2ND AVE

SUMMIT AVE

■ HOSPITAL

PARK AVE

▲ Mt Hays (732 m)

11TH ST

Morse Creek

△ PARK AVE CAMPGROUND

■ BC FERRIES TERMINAL
■ ALASKA MARINE HWY

To Ketchikan

To Digby Island (Airport)

To Port Hardy

To Port Edward, Ridley Island, Prudhomme Lake PP., and Terrace

Butze Rapids

16

N Northern British Columbia

© AVALON TRAVEL PUBLISHING, INC.

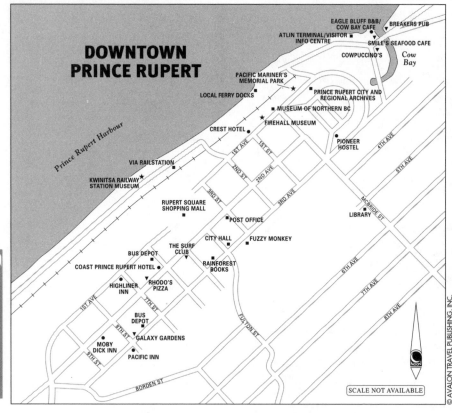

DOWNTOWN PRINCE RUPERT

EAGLE BLUFF B&B/ COW BAY CAFE
BREAKERS PUB
ATLIN TERMINAL/VISITOR INFO CENTRE
SMILE'S SEAFOOD CAFE
COWPUCCINO'S
Cow Bay
PACIFIC MARINER'S MEMORIAL PARK
PRINCE RUPERT CITY AND REGIONAL ARCHIVES
LOCAL FERRY DOCKS
MUSEUM OF NORTHERN BC
FIREHALL MUSEUM
CREST HOTEL
Prince Rupert Harbour
PIONEER HOSTEL
4TH AVE
VIA RAILSTATION
1ST AVE
1ST ST
5TH AVE
KWINITSA RAILWAY STATION MUSEUM
2ND ST
2ND AVE
3RD ST
3RD AVE
MCBRIDE ST
RUPERT SQUARE SHOPPING MALL
LIBRARY
POST OFFICE
CITY HALL
FUZZY MONKEY
THE SURF CLUB
BUS DEPOT
RAINFOREST BOOKS
6TH AVE
COAST PRINCE RUPERT HOTEL
7TH AVE
HIGHLINER INN
RHODO'S PIZZA
1ST AVE
7TH ST
BUS DEPOT
FULTON ST
8TH AVE
8TH ST
GALAXY GARDENS
MOBY DICK INN
9TH ST
PACIFIC INN
BORDEN ST
N
MOON
SCALE NOT AVAILABLE

© AVALON TRAVEL PUBLISHING, INC.

Northern British Columbia

fur-trading days to the founding of the city in 1914 as the western terminus of the Grand Trunk Pacific Railway. Many of the most fascinating displays spotlight the Coast Tsimshian natives—their history, culture, traditions, trade networks, and potlatches. Among the Tsimshian artifacts on display: totem poles, pots, masks, beautiful wooden boxes, blankets, baskets, shiny black argillite carvings, weapons, and petroglyphs. The Monumental Gallery—filled with contemporary art—is worth visiting for the sweeping harbor views alone.

Other Town Sights

Right by the Museum of Northern British Columbia is **Pacific Mariner's Memorial Park,** a grassed area with benches strategically placed for the best ocean views. A statue of a mariner staring out to sea is surrounded by plaques remembering those lost at sea. Also in the park is the *Kazu Maru,* a small fishing boat that drifted across the Pacific from Japan after its owner was lost. It washed up on the Queen Charlotte Islands in 1987, two years after it was reported missing. On the other side of the museum to the memorial park and beside the fire hall is the **Firehall Museum** (200 1st Ave. W, 250/627-4475), which features a 1925 REO Speedwagon along with various other firefighting memorabilia. It's open July and August daily 10 A.M.–4 P.M., but closes when there's a fire being fought in town. From this museum, continue south along 1st Avenue, then head to the foot of 2nd Street, which ends harborside. Here you'll find

PORT ESSINGTON

Port Essington, originally a Tsimshian village called Spokeshute, was established as a shipping settlement at the mouth of the Skeena River south of Prince Rupert. The settlement was serviced by sternwheelers and riverboats, and supplied Hudson's Bay Company brigades and ports. As the fur trade declined through the 1800s, the salmon industry here grew. The area soon had 12 canneries—mainly staffed by Chinese, Japanese, and native laborers.

The town flourished during fishing seasons and boasted hotels, restaurants, stores, and a red-light district. In the 1890s, miners stopped in on their way to northern Canadian goldfields, and the inevitable missionaries came to try to enforce Christianity. The port's boom days lasted until the arrival of the Grand Trunk Pacific Railway, when canneries were built near the railhead at Prince Rupert and Port Essington was abandoned. Today only charred fragments remain.

the **Kwinitsa Railway Station Museum** (250/624-3207; summer daily 9 A.M.–noon and 1–5 P.M.), housed in a small railway station—one of only four such remaining buildings that were once part of a chain of 400 identical stations along the Grand Trunk Railway. Displays tell the story of the railway and its implications for Prince Rupert.

If you find modern architecture interesting, you may want to walk around the **Civic Centre** (corner McBride St. and Wantage Rd.)—look for the three brightly painted totem poles out front. Adjacent to the Civic Centre is the ultra-modern **Prince Rupert Performing Arts Centre,** also worth a visit. In the same vicinity, along Wantage Road, is **Oldfield Creek Hatchery** (250/624-6733), where salmon smolt are raised and released into local rivers. On the same side of the city but a little farther out (just south of the industrial park) is **Butze Rapids.** The churning water of these reversing tidal rapids produces lots of floating foam, which local Tsimshian natives called *kaien*—hence the name Kaien Island, upon which the city of Prince Rupert stands. The rapids are reached along a 2.4-kilometer (1.5-mile) trail; allow 40 minutes each way.

North Pacific Historic Fishing Village

South of Prince Rupert in Port Edward, the North Pacific Historic Fishing Village (250/628-3538; mid-May–Sept. daily 9 A.M.–6 P.M.; adult $12, senior $10, under six free) is the oldest remaining cannery village from over 1,000 similar

facilities that were once operating along the west coast of North America. Dating to 1889 and now classified as a national historic site, this living museum is one of the highlights of a visit to Prince Rupert. You can find out everything you've ever wanted to know about fish, the fishing industry, canning—even which fish tastes the best (locals say it's red snapper every time). You're free to stroll at your own pace along the boardwalk through the riverside settlement with its many original buildings, including a church, schoolroom, general store, and living quarters. Guided tours are included in the entry fee, as is a seat at the *Skeena River Story,* a live performance and slide show presented through summer daily at 11:30 A.M., 1 P.M., 2:30 P.M., and 4 P.M. When you're done with the sightseeing, take lunch at the cannery café—ordering seafood of course.

To get to the village, head out of Prince Rupert on the Yellowhead Highway and take the first road to the right after leaving Kaien Island.

Touring Local Waterways

Once you're done with Prince Rupert's land-based attractions, plan on taking at least one water-based tour. There are no tour boats as such; instead, choose from scenic ferry rides, fishing charters, kayaking (see *Recreation*), or a grizzly bear viewing excursion into the Khutzeymateen (see sidebar).

Seashore Charters (Atlin Terminal, Cow Bay, 250/624-5645 or 800/667-4393, www.seashore charters.com) is a longtime booking agent representing local charter operators. Some of the options available include yacht trips; day-long cruises looking for eagles, waterfowl, seals, otters, porpoises, and killer whales; and fishing trips for salmon, halibut, or cod, with gear and bait supplied. Expect to pay from $100 per person for a fishing trip.

Ask at the Museum of Northern British Columbia or call 250/624-5645 about tours to **Laxspa'aws** (Pike Island), where shell middens, petroglyphs, and depressions from prehistoric houses point to human habitation up to 2,000 years ago. The website www.pikeisland.ca has more information.

Jump aboard the small ferries that run around the harbor to communities with no road connections for an inexpensive harbor cruise. Head down to the small docks at the bottom of McBride Street for route and schedule information, or call 250/624-3337. The shortest trip is a 15-minute run to **Dodge Cove** on Digby Island. There's not much to do on the island, but it's a nice cruise there and back, and it costs just $8 round-trip. The *Centurion IV* departs Prince Rupert Monday and Friday at 8:30 A.M. and makes a short stop before returning midafternoon; $15 one-way. For details call **BC Ferries** (250/624-5411).

RECREATION

Hiking

Hiking opportunities abound around the city. The Museum of North British Columbia (250/624-3207) offers daily historic walking tours and totem pole tours June–August. The cost of each is just $2 per person.

Walking trails lead from town to Cow Bay, Hays Creek, Morse Creek, the ferry terminals,

THE KHUTZEYMATEEN

Officially protected as a provincial park, the Khutzeymateen is a rugged and remote 44,300-hectare (109,500-acre) tract of wilderness 50 kilometers (31 miles) northeast of Prince Rupert that is Canada's only grizzly bear sanctuary. To the Tsimshian people, the area was known as the K'tzim-a-Deen, which translates to "The Long Inlet Surrounded by a Steep Valley." To Canadian conservationists the name Khutzeymateen is synonymous with one of their earliest victories—a 1984 decision to set aside an area where grizzly bears would be safe from hunters. In 1994, further protection was given with the proclamation of a provincial park where grizzly numbers were highest within the no-hunting zone. The park extends from the upper reaches of Khutzeymateen Inlet to the high peaks of the Kitimat Range, protecting the tidal zone at the head of the inlet where approximately 50 grizzly bears, fresh out of hibernation in May and June, come down to the water's edge to feed on sedges and grasses. Through summer, the bears remain in the area, feeding in the salmon-rich Khutzeymateen and Kateen Rivers.

Due to the inaccessibility of the region, most visitors arrive on a guided trip. **West Coast Launch** (250/624-3151 or 800/201-8377, www.westcoastlaunnch.com) runs visitors into the area by boat from Prince Rupert for $140 per person, but most of the six-hour trip is spent traveling. **Parkerville Adventures** (250/624-8243 or 888/580-2234) combines flights with a boat tour for maximum ground time; $350–500 per person for a six-hour trip. Overnight tours are run by **SunChaser Eco-Tours** (250/624-5472), which offers trips on a live-aboard motor cruiser. Departing from Prince Rupert and taking half a day to reach the sanctuary, the trips emphasize bear viewing, but time is also spent exploring other aspects of the area's natural and human history; from $1,600 for four days. **North Pacific Seaplanes** (250/627-1341 or 800/689-4254) has a one-hour flightseeing trip that takes in the Khutzeymateen. These tours depart Prince Rupert's Seal Cove floatplane base on demand and cost $265 per person.

and the low summit of Mount Oldfield. Pick up a map and descriptions for all the local trails at the information center. On one of my first visits to Prince Rupert, I blindly led a group of three others to the summit of 732-meter (2,400-foot) Mount Hays via an old gondola cut line. Halfway up we got tangled in head-high undergrowth, and then knee-deep snow. Therefore, I heartily recommend you take the more conventional route, a gravel road that leads off where Wantage Road ends. Once at the top, the views of Prince Rupert, the sound, southeastern Alaska, and bald eagles soaring through updrafts are second to none.

Sea Kayaking

The calm waters of Prince Rupert Harbour are perfect for kayaking. Even if you have had no experience in a kayak, **Eco-treks** (Cow Bay, 250/624-8311) will take you on an easy 1.5-hour paddle along the shoreline for $40 per person. A six-hour guided paddle to Tsimshian petroglyphs costs $100, including lunch. The company also rents kayaks; $50 per day for a single and $75 per day for a double, inclusive of spray skirts, paddles, and life jackets.

Arts and Entertainment

In the same complex as the recreation facilities listed above is the **Prince Rupert Performing Arts Centre** (corner McBride St. and Wantage Rd., 250/627-7529), where just about anything could be happening. Symphony concerts, plays, lectures, and operas are among the events scheduled.

The most popular spot in town for a beer is **Breakers Pub** (117 George Hills Way, Cow Bay, 250/624-5990; daily noon–midnight). This waterfront drinking hole boasts plenty of atmosphere, an outdoor deck with harbor views, and a bistro-style restaurant. Downtown and also with great water views, **Charley's Lounge** (Crest Hotel, 222 1st Ave. W, 250/624-6771) is more subdued than Breakers. It also has an impressive-for-this-far-north wine list and a semi-creative menu. Many rowdy bars can be found downtown—just follow your ears. For the dancing into the wee hours, try **Bogey's Cabaret** in the

Coast Prince Rupert Hotel (2nd Ave. between 6th and 7th Streets, 250/624-6711) or the **Surf Club** (200 5th St., 250/624-3050).

Shoot pool with the local kids at the **Fuzzy Monkey** (316 3rd St. W, 250/622-7665; 11:30 A.M.–midnight). It costs about $12 per table per hour.

Festivals and Events

The major annual celebration here is **Seafest,** on the second weekend of June. All sorts of wacky events involving the sea are scheduled—a canoe-dunking contest (the water's icy so no one wants to lose), bathtub races, and fish-filleting competitions. There's also a more serious side to the weekend—a memorial barbecue for those lost at sea followed by a ceremony to dedicate new bricks at the mariner's statue. Another event held in June (the 21st) is **National Aboriginal Day,** featuring a salmon feast and plenty of authentic native dancing and singing.

ACCOMMODATIONS AND CAMPING

Prince Rupert's 700 motel rooms fill fast every summer night (late June–early Sept.) with travelers waiting for ferries—so book well in advance (if you're traveling onward from Prince Rupert, you should have already made ferry reservations, so you know which nights you'll be in town). Accommodation choices are wide-ranging, and although no one property stands out as being good value, all are moderately priced. On the other hand, Prince Rupert has a great campground within easy walking distance of the ferry terminals.

Under $50

The distinctive blue and green **Pioneer Hostel** (167 3rd Ave. E, 250/624-2334 or 888/794-9998) has had the reputation of being a bit rough around the edges, but new owners and a new name are slowly turning things around. It's still mostly full of "steadies" in winter, but in summer daily and weekly accommodations are offered. Facilities include dorm rooms with shared bathrooms, an outside yard with a barbecue, a living room with TV, and a small but well-equipped kitchen. Dorm beds are $16–22, private rooms $43 s or d.

$50–100

My favorite Rupert accommodation is the **Eagle Bluff Bed and Breakfast** (201 Cow Bay Rd., 250/627-4955 or 800/833-1550). The house is built out over the water, overlooking the marina and harbor, and lies within easy walking distance of cafés and restaurants. Rates are $45 s, $65 d for a shared bath; $85 s, $95 d for a private bath; and $100 for a large suite sleeping five. A cooked breakfast—complete with freshly baked muffins—is included.

One of many reasonably priced motels is the **Moby Dick Inn** (935 2nd Ave. W, 250/624-6961 or 800/663-0822, www.mobydickinn.com; $79 s, $89 d), which is home to the best-priced breakfast restaurant in town. Also in the area is the **Pacific Inn** (909 3rd Ave. W, 250/627-1711 or 888/663-1999, www.pacificinn.bc.ca; $85 s or d), with larger rooms. A few blocks from downtown is **Inn on the Harbour** (720 1st Ave. W, 250/624-9107 or 800/663-8155), where you'll pay $75 s, $85 d, most of that for

the view. This place also has women-only rooms for the same price.

$100–150

The massive building right downtown is the 15-story **Highliner Inn** (815 1st Ave. W, 250/624-9060 or 888/561-7666, www.hojoprincerupert.com; from $120 s or d). This Howard Johnson affiliate is far from the best property in the chain, but most rooms have balconies and you can request a harbor view for a few bucks extra.

In a prime harborside location, the full-service **Crest Hotel** (222 1st Ave. W, 250/624-6771 or 800/663-8150, www.cresthotel.bc.ca) holds a glass-enclosed waterfront café, a dining room, and a lounge with water views. Rates for the stylishly decorated rooms start at $145 s or d. Upgrade to Crest Class for $165 s or d and enjoy water views and in-room amenities that include Internet access, a cordless phone, and coffee-making facilities.

The **Coast Prince Rupert Hotel** (118 6th St., 250/624-6711 or 800/663-1144, www.coasthotels.com) offers 92 reliable rooms, some with water views, and a downstairs restaurant and pub. Advertised rates are $155 s or d, but

Eagle Bluff Bed and Breakfast

© ANDREW HEMPSTEAD

show your AAA card, for example, and you'll get a room for under $100.

Camping

Like the rest of Rupert's accommodations, **Park Avenue Campground** (1750 Park Ave., 250/624-5861 or 800/667-1994) fills and empties on a daily basis with the arrival and departure of the ferries. If you know when you're arriving in the city, phone ahead to avoid any hassles. The campground is a one-kilometer hike from both the city center and ferry terminals. Facilities include hot showers, cooking shelters, a grassy tenting area, pay phones, a mail drop, and visitor information. Unserviced sites are $16, full hookups $26. The other alternative is **Prudhomme Lake Provincial Park,** along the Yellowhead Highway 16 kilometers (10 miles) east of downtown; $14 per night.

FOOD

Breakfast

Most of Rupert's larger motels have restaurants, but the place to head for substantial and inexpensive breakfasts is the **Moby Dick Inn** (935 2nd Ave. W, 250/624-6961). You can order anything from a bowl of fruit and a muffin ($4) to eggs, bacon, and toast ($5) or steak and eggs ($8). It's always crowded, and service can be slow. Just around the corner, the **Raffles Inn** (1080 3rd Ave. W, 250/624-9161) offers similar fare.

Cow Bay Cafés

East of downtown is Cow Bay, originally a fishy-smelling, rough-and-tumble part of town home to a large fishing fleet. The boats are still there, moored in a marina, and a few old buildings still stand. But for the most part, the bay is a changed place. Rowdy dives have been replaced by trendy art and crafts shops, restaurants, and two of the city's best cafés.

Cowpuccino's (25 Cow Bay Rd., 250/627-1395; daily 7:30 A.M.–10 P.M.) is a great little coffeehouse with freshly brewed coffee, magnificent muffins, delicious desserts, newspapers and magazines to read, and a laid-back atmosphere.

KING PACIFIC LODGE

King Pacific Lodge (604/987-5452 or 888/592-5464, www.kingpacificlodge.com; mid-May–mid-Sept.) provides an unforgettable wilderness experience, far removed from the casual highway traveler. The floating lodge is on remote Princess Royal Island, best known for its population of Kermode, the albino-like "Spirit Bear." Its three-story timber structure is built over the waters of a protected cove, the perfect base for searching out the abundant marine mammals, kayaking, and fishing. It is the latter that attracts most guests, with chinooks (kings) biting best May–July and peak season for other salmon August–September.

The minimum stay is three nights, with all packages including floatplane transportation from Prince Rupert, all meals and drinks, and all activities. The lodge itself holds 17 spacious guest rooms, each with ample amenities and luxurious furnishings. The Great Room is a sea-level lounge centered on a huge stone fireplace; a wraparound veranda faces the ocean out front. Gourmet meals are served in an elegant setting overlooking the water, with fresh seafood the order of the day.

Across the way and right on the harbor is **Cow Bay Cafe** (205 Cow Bay Rd., 250/627-1212; Tues.–Sun. 11 A.M.–8 P.M.), where you can sit at an outside table and take in the smells of the ocean, or stay inside and enjoy the greenery. Good home-cooked meals, including vegetarian dishes, and daily specials start at $7.

Seafood

Ask a local where to go for good seafood and the answer is invariably **N Smile's Seafood Cafe** (113 Cow Bay Rd., 250/624-3072; July–Aug. daily 9 A.M.–10 P.M., the rest of the year daily 11 A.M.–8 P.M.). This diner-style café, decorated with black-and-white fishing photos and colored-glass floats, has been serving seafood since 1934. It's always busy, mobbed by local fishermen, residents, and visitors no matter what time of day. The extensive menu includes seafood salads and sandwiches, burgers, fish and chips, shellfish, and seafood specialties. Prices range $6–25 per plate.

Another notable place for fresh seafood is the casual **M Boulet Seafood & Chowder House** (Pacific Inn, 909 3rd Ave. W, 250/624-9309; Mon.–Sat. 11 A.M.–9 P.M.). Especially good is the lunchtime clam chowder, served with a small loaf of bread, dessert, and tea or coffee for $9.

Other Restaurants

Galaxy Gardens (844 3rd Ave. W, 250/624-3122) boasts a once-flashy decor with lots of wicker and bamboo. On the menu are tasty chow meins, prawn and chicken dishes, and special combos. **Rhodos Pizza** (716 2nd Ave., 250/624-9797) serves up pizza, steak, and delicious Greek specialties from $9. On the walls are Greek plates and artifacts, and the background music is, naturally, Greek.

Combining water views, good food, and pleasant surroundings, the **Waterfront Restaurant** (Crest Hotel, 222 1st Ave. W, 250/624-6771) is as upscale as it gets in Prince Rupert. You could start with alder-smoked steelhead and then move on to oven-roasted salmon in a lemony Dijon crust. Or give seafood a break and choose beef tenderloin with a rosemary jus as a main. Either way, you'll pay $22–36 for a main.

INFORMATION AND SERVICES

Information

Prince Rupert Visitor Info Centre is in a converted fish plant along the Cow Bay waterfront (215 Cow Bay Rd., 250/624-5637 or 800/667-1994, www.tourismprincerupert.com; early June–early Sept. Mon.–Sat. 9 A.M.–8 P.M. and Sun. 9 A.M.–5 P.M., the rest of the year Mon.–Sat. 9 A.M.–5 P.M.). It's one of the best information centers around, with a knowledgeable staff and lots of printed material on Prince Rupert sights, walking tours, restaurants, services, and ferry schedules.

To search out local history, head to **Prince Rupert City & Regional Archives** (100 1st Ave. E, 250/624-3326; Mon.–Fri. 10 A.M.–3 P.M.), which holds 20,000 historical photographs, charts, and books.

Books

The **library** is just off McBride Avenue (101 6th Ave., 250/627-1345); an adjacent room provides public Internet access for a minimal charge. If you're looking for books, especially on B.C. native art or history, spend some time at **Rainforest Books** (515 3rd Ave. W, 250/624-9053; Mon.–Sat. 8:30 A.M.–6 P.M.). This bookstore also stocks a good selection of Queen Charlotte Islands material.

Services

Prince Rupert Regional Hospital is south of downtown (1305 Summit Ave., 250/624-2171). The **post office** is on 2nd Avenue at 3rd Street. **Laundries** are at 226 7th Street and 745 2nd Avenue West.

TRANSPORTATION

Air

Prince Rupert Airport is served by **Air Canada** (888/247-2262) and **Hawk Air** (800/487-1216), both with scheduled flights from Vancouver and the latter also from other provincial centers. The airport is west of town on Digby Island. It is linked to the city by a ferry that takes buses and foot passengers only—no vehicles. Airlines provide free bus transportation between the airport and downtown, via the ferry, but passengers must pay the ferry fare of $12 per person each way. The pickup point for Air Canada passengers is the information center; Hawk Air passengers are collected at the Highliner Inn.

Developed by the Royal Canadian Air Force in 1941, **Seal Cove Air Base** lies at the east end of town and serves as the seaplane base for Prince Rupert. To get there, take 5th Avenue east from McBride Street and follow the signs to Seal Cove. The largest operator is **North Pacific Seaplanes** (250/627-1341 or 800/689-4234), which makes scheduled flights to Kitkatla ($57), Kincolith ($85), Masset ($137), and Sandspit ($206). The company also offers flightseeing excursions, including a 20-minute flight over the city for $95 per person, an hour-long trip to the Khutzeymateen Valley grizzly bear sanctuary for $265 per person, and a three-hour trip to Ketchikan for $475 per person.

Rail

Prince Rupert is the western terminus of Canada's transcontinental rail system, which runs east from here to Prince George and Edmonton, across the prairies to Toronto, and on to the Atlantic provinces. The route through British Columbia is the highlight of the trip, especially the couple of hundred kilometers just outside Prince Rupert, where the line follows the Skeena River. To get to the **VIA Rail** station (250/627-7589) take 2nd Street north over the rail line. Trains arrive in Prince Rupert on Monday, Thursday, and Saturday at 8 P.M. and depart on Wednesday, Friday, and Sunday at 8 A.M. The station, which could do with a coat of paint, is only open a couple of hours either side of arrivals and departures.

Bus

From the local **Greyhound** bus depot (112 6th St., 250/624-5090), buses travel east along the Yellowhead Highway to Terrace and Prince George, then either north to the Alaska Highway, east to Jasper National Park and Edmonton, or south through Cariboo Country to Kamloops and on to Vancouver. The run between Prince George and Prince Rupert leaves twice daily. Reservations are not taken—just turn up and buy your ticket on the day you want to go.

BC Ferries

Prince Rupert is the northern terminus of the BC Ferries network (250/386-3431 or, toll-free in B.C., 888/223-3779, www.bcferries.com), which offers regular services south to Port Hardy on Vancouver Island and west to the Queen Charlotte Islands. The terminal is two kilometers (1.2 miles) from downtown, right alongside the Alaska Marine Highway terminal. Ferries serving Prince Rupert have both day rooms and sleeping cabins, shower facilities, food service, and plenty of room to sit back and relax. During the busy summer months it's imperative that you book well in advance, especially if you plan to transport a vehicle.

The 15-hour, 440-kilometer (273-mile) ferry trip between Prince Rupert and Port Hardy is a beautiful ride on the well-equipped *Queen of the North,* which departs in summer every second day at 7:30 A.M., arriving in Port Hardy that same night at 10:30 P.M. The rest of the year sailings are less frequent. The summer one-way fares are: adult $107, child 5–11 $53.50, vehicle $252. Discounts are available outside of summer and for B.C. seniors. Cabins ($50–60) and recliner chairs ($15) are available by reservation.

Alaska Marine Highway

The Alaska Marine Highway (907/465-3940 or 800/642-0066, www.Alaska.gov/ferry) operates an extensive network of ferries through southeastern Alaska and down to Prince Rupert. The first stop north from Prince Rupert is Ketchikan, six hours away. Walk-on passengers need not make reservations, but if you require a cabin or have a vehicle, make reservations as far in advance as possible (up to one year), especially for sailings between May and September.

Alaska Marine Highway ferries serving Prince Rupert include the *Taku, Matanuska,* and *Malaspina,* which together offer sailings 5–6 times weekly. Each of the comfortable boats offers cabins, a cafeteria, restaurant, bar, lounge areas, and showers. If you don't want to pay the extra for a cabin, sleep in one of the many lounge areas or out on the back of the boat. You can even pitch a tent in the solarium if you want.

Sample one-way fares (in US$) from Prince Rupert are as follows: to Ketchikan—adult $50, child 2–11 $20, vehicle up to 15 feet (4.5 meters) $88, cabin from $45; to Juneau—adult $132, child 2–11 $59, vehicle up to 15 feet $270, cabin from $98; to Haines—adult $150, child 2–11 $68, vehicle up to 15 feet $316, cabin from $122.

Check-in time is three hours ahead of sailing time—it takes up to two hours to go through Customs and one hour to load up. Foot passengers must be there one hour ahead of sailing.

For reservations or schedule information, contact the terminal and ticket office (250/627-1744 www.alaska.gov/ferry), which is open daily 9 A.M.–4 P.M. and for up to two hours before and after arrival and departure of vessels.

Getting Around

Local bus service along four routes is provided by **Prince Rupert Transit System** (2nd Ave. W, 250/624-3343). Adult fare starts at $2. All-day passes cost $3 and are available from the driver. Have exact fare ready—drivers don't carry change. The only car-rental agencies in town are **Budget** (250/627-7400) and **National** (250/624-5318). For a cab call **Skeena Taxis** (250/624-2185).

Queen Charlotte Islands

Wild. Quiet. Mysterious. Primordial. Inhabited by the proud and ferocious Haida people for over 10,000 years, the Queen Charlotte Islands spread like a large upside-down triangle approximately 100 kilometers (62 miles) off the northwest coast of mainland British Columbia, linked to the mainland by scheduled ferry and air services. Visitors have the opportunity to immerse themselves in native culture, view the abundant wildlife, explore the rugged coastline, and share a laid-back island camaraderie with the 4,600 permanent residents.

Of the chain's 150 mountainous and densely forested islands and islets, the main ones are **Graham Island** to the north and **Moresby Island** to the south, separated by narrow **Skidegate Channel.** The islands stretch 290 kilometers (180 miles) from north to south and up to 85 kilometers (53 miles) across. Running down the west side of the islands are the Queen Charlotte and San Christoval ranges, which effectively protect the east side from Pacific battering. Nevertheless, the east coast, where most of the population lives, still receives over 1,000 millimeters (39 inches) of rain annually.

Life on the islands is very different from elsewhere in the province. Visitors can expect a friendly reception and adequate services. Motel-style accommodations are available in each town, but bed-and-breakfasts provide a better glimpse of the island lifestyle. Other services are similar to any small town, though choices of fresh fruit and vegetables can be limited. Gasoline is only slightly more expensive than on the mainland, and raging nightlife is nonexistent.

Island Fauna

Known as the "Canadian Galapagos," the Queen Charlottes are home to an incredible array of fauna—both on land and in the water. The only land mammal indigenous to the islands is the Queen Charlotte otter, a subspecies of the mainland river otter. The world's largest black bears, estimated to number almost 10,000, call the islands home. Though they're a lot heftier than their mainland cousins, they're not a distinct subspecies. Their size comes from a short hibernation and a summer-long salmon feast. Black-tailed deer are common. They were introduced as a meat source and have multiplied many times over. Other land mammals include elk (also introduced), squirrels, beavers, and muskrats.

Stare out to sea to spot killer whales, dolphins, porpoises, harbor seals, sea lions, otters, and tufted puffins. If you visit between late April and June, you might spot gray whales feeding in Hecate Strait on their migration from Mexico to Alaska. The most accessible place to whale-watch is along Skidegate Inlet near the museum, where you don't even need to get out of your vehicle.

The antics of tufted puffins keep everyone amused, while serious birders search out cormorants, blue herons, bald eagles, oyster catchers, and guillemots.

The Haida

The Haida people have lived on the Queen Charlottes since time immemorial. Fearless warriors, expert hunters and fishermen, and skilled woodcarvers, they owned slaves and threw lavish potlatches. They had no written language, but they carved records of their tribal history, legends, and important events on totem poles rising up to 104 meters (340 feet) high. Living in villages scattered throughout the islands, they hunted sea otters for their luxuriant furs, fished for hal-

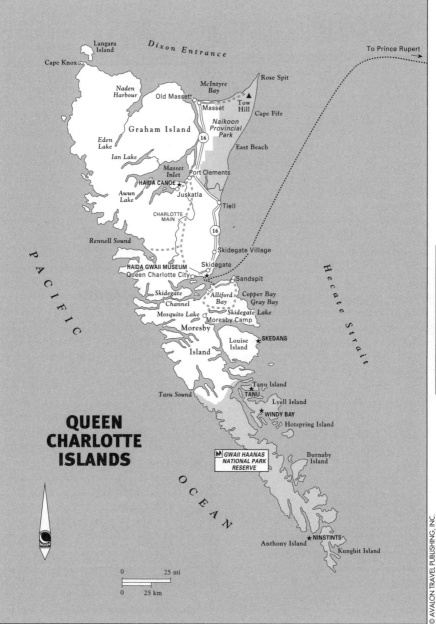

QUEEN CHARLOTTE ISLANDS

Langara Island
Cape Knox
Dixon Entrance
McIntyre Bay
Rose Spit
To Prince Rupert
Naden Harbour
Old Massett
Masset
Tow Hill
Cape Fife
Graham Island
Naikoon Provincial Park
Eden Lake
Ian Lake
East Beach
Masset Inlet
Port Clements
HAIDA CANOE
Awun Lake
Juskatla
Tlell
CHARLOTTE MAIN
Rennell Sound
Skidegate Village
HAIDA GWAII MUSEUM
Queen Charlotte City
Skidegate
Sandspit
Skidegate Channel
Alliford Bay
Copper Bay
Gray Bay
Mosquito Lake
Skidegate Lake
Moresby Camp
Moresby
Louise Island
SKEDANS
Island
Tasu Sound
Tanu Island
TANU
Lyell Island
WINDY BAY
Hotspring Island
GWAII HAANAS NATIONAL PARK RESERVE
Burnaby Island
Anthony Island
NINSTINTS
Kunghit Island

PACIFIC OCEAN

Hecate Strait

0   25 mi
0   25 km

© AVALON TRAVEL PUBLISHING, INC.

BEACHCOMBING ON THE CHARLOTTES

Beachcombing on the Queen Charlotte Islands is popular year-round, but it's especially good after heavy winter storms. You may find fishing floats from countries around the Pacific (glass balls from Japan are especially prized), bottles, rope, driftwood, shells, whale bones, semiprecious agate, or just about anything that floats. A few years back, a container of Nike runners broke apart somewhere in the Pacific; they were found scattered on beaches throughout the Charlottes and as far south as the Oregon coast. Before that, an abandoned fishing boat from Japan washed ashore and caused excitement; it's now on display in Prince Rupert.

ibut and Pacific salmon, and collected chitons, clams, and seaweed from tidepools.

The first contact the Haida had with Europeans occurred in 1774, when Spanish explorer Juan Perez discovered the Charlottes. The islands weren't given a European name until 1787, when British captain George Dixon arrived and began trading with the Haida. He named the islands after his queen, the wife of George III. The whites gave the Haida goods, liquor, tools, blankets, and firearms in exchange for sea otter furs; over a 40-year period the otters were hunted almost to extinction. In addition, the white traders brought European diseases that ravaged the Haida population.

At the turn of the 19th century, white settlers from the mainland began moving over to the Charlottes to live along the low-lying east coast and the protected shores of Masset Inlet. By the 1830s the traditional lifestyle of the Haida was coming to an end. The governments on the mainland prohibited the Haida from owning slaves and throwing potlatches—an important social and economic part of their culture—and forced all Haida children to attend missionary schools. The Haida abandoned their village sites and moved onto reserves at Skidegate and Masset on Graham Island.

Today totem poles are rising once again on the Queen Charlottes, as a renewed interest in Haida art and culture is compelling skilled elders to pass their knowledge on to younger generations. The first totem pole to be erected in 90 years was put up in 1969 in Masset, followed by one in 1978 at Skidegate. In 1986 a 15-meter (50-foot) dugout canoe, created out of a single huge cedar log, was commissioned for Vancouver's Expo86, and a second canoe was launched in Old Massett.

For many years the Haida struggled alongside the Island Protection Society to preserve their heritage. Their longtime efforts paid off in two major events: in 1981 the best-known of the abandoned Haida villages, **Ninstints,** was declared a UNESCO World Heritage Site, and in 1988 the southern section of the archipelago was proclaimed **Gwaii Haanas National Park Reserve.**

TRANSPORTATION

Air

The main gateway is Sandspit, where the small air terminal holds car-rental agencies (book ahead) and an information center, and across the road is the Sandspit Inn. **Air Canada** (888/247-2262) flies daily between Vancouver and Sandspit. **Hawk Air** (250/635-4295) offers daily service between Prince Rupert and Sandspit. The Airporter bus meets all Sandspit flights and transports passengers to Queen Charlotte City for $14.

From Prince Rupert's Seal Cove Air Base, **North Pacific Seaplanes** (250/627-1341 or 800/689-4234) has scheduled flights to Masset ($137) and Sandspit ($206).

Ferry

In summer, **BC Ferries** (250/386-3431 or, toll-free in B.C., 888/223-3779, www.bcferries.com) operates the *Queen of Prince Rupert* between Prince Rupert and Skidegate five or six times a week, less frequently the rest of the year. Departure times vary, but most often it's 11 A.M. from Prince Rupert (arriving Skidegate at 5:30 P.M.) and 11 P.M. from Skidegate (arriving Prince Rupert at 6 A.M. or 7:30 A.M.). Peak one-way fares:

adult $25, child $12.50, vehicle $93. B.C. seniors get a discount, as do all travelers outside the peak summer season. Cabins are available for $42–48.

The ferry terminal is five kilometers (3.1 miles) east of Queen Charlotte City at Skidegate. Taxis usually wait at the terminal when the ferry arrives; expect to pay around $12 to get into town.

Getting Around

A ferry connects Graham and Moresby Islands, departing hourly in each direction 7 A.M.–10 P.M.; peak round-trip fare is adult $5.25, child $2.75, vehicle $13. Apart from that, the islands have no public transportation. Handiest for vehicle-less ferry travelers is **Rustic Car Rentals,** based in Queen Charlotte City (250/559-4641). Both **Budget** (250/637-2330) and **Thrifty** (250/637-2299) have offices in Sandspit. All companies charge from $55 a day plus 20–35 cents a kilometer for the smallest vehicles, with no free daily allowance. Book well ahead.

To get around by floatplane, including to Gwaii Haanas National Park Reserve, call **South Moresby Air Charters** (250/559-4222).

QUEEN CHARLOTTE CITY

Known to the locals simply as "Charlotte," Queen Charlotte City is spread along the shores of Bearskin Bay, five kilometers (3.1 miles) west of the dock for the mainland ferry. It's not really a city at all—most places that include "city" in their name aren't—but instead a small laid-back fishing village of 1,100 people. Heritage buildings dating back to the early 1900s (most along the main road) are interspersed with all the services of small town, with a colorful array of private residences sprawl east and west, overlooking the water and backed by forested wilderness. The main street is 3rd Avenue, a continuation of the road from the ferry dock.

Accommodations and Camping

Queen Charlotte City is a good base for exploring the islands and has a wide variety of accommodations. Built in 1910, the old Premier Hotel has been totally renovated and now operates as **M Premier Creek Lodging** (3rd Ave., 250/559-8415 or 888/322-3388), offering beds to suit all budgets. In the main lodge, single "sleeping

© ANDREW HEMPSTEAD

Many island homes and businesses are decorated with colorful buoys, driftwood, and just about anything that floats.

rooms" with shared facilities cost $30 per person, but definitely worth the extra money are the rooms with private bathrooms, balconies, and harbor views (some with kitchens) for $65 s, $75 d. Behind the main lodge is the simple **Premier Creek Hostel** (same telephone numbers as the lodge). It has two four-bed dorms and one double room, a kitchen, living room, laundry, gas barbecue, and bike rentals ($30 per day); rates are $20 per person per night.

The least expensive rooms at **Dorothy and Mike's Guest House** (3127 2nd Ave., 250/559-8439) are $45–65 s or d and share baths, but my favorite is the en suite Kumdis Room ($80 s or d), where a sliding door opens to a private deck with fantastic views. Common areas include a kitchen, TV room, a large deck area, and a library overflowing with island literature. A hearty cooked breakfast will get you going each morning.

Moonglow Guest House (3611 Highway 33, 250/559-8845; $55 s, $65 d) has just one guest room, but it's a good one, with cooking facilities, a patio with views of Skidegate Inlet, and a private entrance. Behind the property, a trail leads along a creek to a waterfall. You can camp on the property for $10 per night.

Spruce Point Lodging (609 6th Ave., 250/559-8234; $60 s, $70 d) has a great downtown location with superb water views and offers bed-and-breakfast lodging in simple but comfortable rooms, each with a color TV.

Haydn Turner Park, through town to the west, has toilets, picnic tables, and fire rings for campers, but no showers or hookups; $8 per night.

Food and Drink

The place to go for breakfast is **Lam's** (3223 Wharf St., 250/559-4204; Mon.–Sat. 6:30 A.M.–3 P.M., Sun. 8 A.M.–3 P.M.). All the locals congregate here. In addition to water views, this place has plenty of atmosphere, and the food is good and plentiful for the price (cooked breakfasts from $6.50), but be prepared to wait for a table. For something more substantial, head to the Sea Raven Motel (3301 3rd Ave., 250/559-4423). Specializing in local seafood, the motel's no-frills dining room is open daily 7 A.M.–2 P.M. and 5–9 P.M. The seafood chowder ($5) is delicious. Howler's Pub and Bistro (3rd Ave., 250/559-8602; 11 A.M.–10 P.M.) has a downstairs pub and upstairs dining room. Menus in both are pub-like, but with a surprising number of vegetarian choices and a good selection of desserts. The **Oceana Restaurant** (3119 3rd Ave., 250/559-8633) specializes in Chinese dishes, with a typically large menu. Servings are big, but prices are a little higher than they should be. Closed Sunday.

Information

Down on the waterfront, **Queen Charlotte Visitor Info Centre** (3220 Wharf St., 250/559-8316; mid-May–mid-Sept. daily 10 A.M.–7 P.M.) offers natural history displays, a wide variety of brochures and information on everything that's going on around the islands, and current weather forecasts. The *Guide to the Queen Charlotte Islands,* which includes maps, details on all the villages, and more, is available at the center, or order a free copy online at www.qcinfo.com. This official tourism website and that of the local Internet service provider, www.qcislands.net, are loaded with pretrip planning information and links.

For island and North Coast literature, head to **Northwest Coast Books,** in a converted bunkhouse (720 Hwy. 33, 250/559-4681). The selection of new and used titles is incredible, with the bookstore wholesaling hard-to-find titles to galleries and museums across North America. **Rainbows Gallery** (3201 3rd Ave., 250/559-8420) also sells books, along with a good selection of locally crafted souvenirs.

Services

Emergency services in Queen Charlotte City include **Queen Charlotte Islands General Hospital** (3209 3rd Ave., 250/559-4300) and the **RCMP** (250/559-4421). The **post office** and a **laundry** are in the City Centre Building off 2nd Avenue.

NORTH TO PORT CLEMENTS

From Queen Charlotte City, Graham Island's main road follows the eastern coastline past the ferry terminal and Haida Gwaii Museum to the

Haida community of Skidegate Village, from where it's a pleasant 65-kilometer (40-mile) coastal drive to Port Clements.

Haida Gwaii Museum

While totem poles and other ancient Haida art can be seen in various places around the islands, this museum (250/559-4643) on the north side of the Skidegate Landing ferry terminal allows visitors the opportunity to see a variety of such art under one roof. Inside are striking Haida wood and argillite carvings, pioneer artifacts, a beautiful woven blanket, jewelry, historic black-and-white photos, stunning prints by Haida artist Robert Davidson, ancient totems from Tanu and Skedans dating to 1878, the skull of a humpback whale, shells galore, and a collection of stuffed birds. The imposing post-and-beam cedar building is open in summer Monday–Friday 10 A.M.–5 P.M., Saturday–Sunday 1–5 P.M.; closed Sunday and Tuesday the rest of the year. Admission is $4.

When you leave the museum, be sure to wander up the road and visit the longhouse-style **cedar carving shed,** where the fantastic 15-meter-long canoe *Loo Taas* (which means "Wave Eater") is housed. The striking red-and-black vessel was commissioned for Expo86 in Vancouver, after which it was paddled to the Queen Charlottes.

Between late April and early June, migrating **gray whales** rest and feed on shallow gravel bars of Skidegate Inlet in front of the museum on their annual 15,000-kilometer (9,300-mile) odyssey between Mexico and Alaska. Behind the museum a wooden deck overlooking the water is a great vantage point for watching these magnificent creatures, or continue a few hundred yards farther around the bay and search them out from the roadside.

Skidegate Village and Vicinity

Continuing north from the museum you'll soon come to Skidegate Village, a Haida reserve of 700 residents. A weathered totem pole, over 100 years old, still stands here, as well as six newer ones. Facing the beach is a traditional longhouse, home to the Skidegate Haida Band Council

House, where local artisans fashion miniature totem poles, argillite ornaments, and jewelry in traditional designs. Cross the road from the local rec center to the trailhead of a hiking trail to **Spirit Lake.** The trail passes through an old-growth forest of hemlock, Sitka spruce, and red cedar and passes two picturesque bodies of water, one with picnic tables. The round-trip is three kilometers (1.9 miles), an easy hour's walk.

From Skidegate, the road follows the shoreline of Hecate Strait, past driftwood-strewn beaches, an attractive old graveyard, and **Balance Rock,** one kilometer (.6 mile) north of Skidegate Village. A highway sign and turnout mark the start of a short trail down to the rock. Continuing north, the scenery becomes rural, as the road skirts land cleared by early settlers for cattle-grazing; watch for black-tailed deer in this area. Near **Lawn Hill** look for tree stumps that have been carved into the shapes of animals and birds.

Tlell

This small ranching community 48 kilometers (30 miles) north of Queen Charlotte City is the northernmost settlement on the east coast before the road swings inland toward Port Clements and Masset. Sandwiched between the Tlell River and the beach, Tlell is a haven for artisans; look for signs pointing the way to their outlets, which are concentrated on Richardson Road off Wiggins Road. The Tlell River is renowned for its freshwater fishing—cutthroat trout in summer, coho salmon in fall, and steelhead through winter.

Naikoon Provincial Park (Southern End)

Just north of Tlell is the southern tip of Naikoon Provincial Park. While the park's main entrance is farther north out of Masset, visitors exploring the Tlell area will find interesting things to see and do here in the park's south end as well. The main attraction down here is the wreck of the *Pesuta,* a wooden log barge that ran aground in 1928. To get there, park at the picnic area on the north side of the Tlell River and follow the river to its mouth, then walk north along the beach. It's about six kilometers (3.7 miles) each way. Keen hikers may want to attempt the **East**

Beach Hike, a 94-kilometer (58-mile) trail that leads all the way north from the Tlell River to Tow Hill via Rose Spit.

Misty Meadows Campground, immediately north of park headquarters, is uncrowded and costs only $14 per site for one of 30 scenic campsites. Facilities include a picnic area and pit toilets.

Port Clements

Weatherbeaten houses decorated with driftwood, shells, fishing floats, and other seawashed treasures line the streets of this logging and fishing village on the shore of Masset Inlet. **Port Clements Museum** (Bayview Dr., 250/557-4255) houses an intriguing selection of pioneer artifacts from the area, as well as black-and-white photos of logging camps and early village life. It's open through summer daily 1–5 P.M., weekends only the rest of the year.

Charlotte Main

This rough logging road links Port Clements to Queen Charlotte City via an inland route, a good alternative to returning via Tlell. To get to it, take Bayview Drive southwest out of Port Clements. Twelve kilometers (7.5 miles) from town, a short trail leads through the forest to an unfinished **Haida canoe,** estimated to have been abandoned around 100 years ago. Continuing south, the road passes through **Juskatla,** a logging camp established in the 1940s to supply spruce for World War II airplanes. Here you'll find the start of the Charlotte Main logging road, as well as the main office for the Weyerhaeuser logging company and, down on the waterfront, large log sorting machines. The company actively logs off Charlotte Main, so travel along the road is safest outside of operating hours (Mon.–Fri. 7 A.M.–6 P.M.). Check in at the office or call 250/559-4224 to check the status of the road before heading any farther.

From Juskatla, the logging road continues south to Queen Charlotte City. A turnoff to the west (signposted) leads to **Rennell Sound,** the only point on the remote west coast accessible by road. At the end of the road await great beachcombing opportunities and free primitive campsites. The final descent to the shore is a hair-raising 24 percent gradient, one of the steepest public roads in North America.

MASSET AND VICINITY

Originally named Graham City, Masset (pop. 900) is the oldest town on the Queen Charlottes. The Graham Steamship, Coal, and Lumber Company founded the settlement in 1909, just south of a Haida community named Massett. Over time, Massett became known as Old Massett or Haida, and Graham City was incorporated as Masset (with one "t"). The population has decreased since downsizing began on the local Canadian Armed Forces Station, where at one time half the local population lived. Today, Masset's economy revolves around the ocean, with most workers involved in the fishing industry—either as fisherfolk or as workers in the local fish canning and freezing plant.

As you enter town from the south, passing the information center and seaplane base, continue straight ahead to reach Naikoon Provincial Park, or cross Delkatla Inlet for downtown Masset and Old Massett.

Town Sights

Masset makes a good base from which to explore the beautiful surrounding area and Naikoon Provincial Park, but there's not much to do in town. Stroll around to see the **heritage buildings,** including the old schoolhouse and hospital, both on Collison Avenue, or head down to **government wharf,** where some interesting activity is almost always going on: boats coming and going, fishermen loading supplies or unloading their catch.

Delkatla Wildlife Sanctuary

Bordering Masset to the east is Delkatla Wildlife Sanctuary, where you can observe Canada geese, sandhill cranes, trumpeter swans, great blue herons, many varieties of ducks, and other waterfowl resting during migration. Several short walking trails wind through the preserve near town; follow Hodges Avenue west onto Trumpeter Drive and continue alongside the inlet to the trailhead. For better views, drive along Tow

Hill Road toward Naikoon Provincial Park, turning left at the sanctuary sign onto Masset Cemetery Road. Along this road, more signs mark trails or other points of interest. You first pass a turnout for the **Bird Walk Trail,** which winds along the edge of a marshy area. Then farther down the road, you come to **Simpson Viewing Tower.** The trail to the tower leads through a wide open meadow and marshes dotted with wildflowers, and the top of the lofty perch makes an excellent spot to watch the preserve's abundant waterfowl. You might also spy bald eagles, peregrine falcons, and other birds of prey, as well as four-legged marsh animals such as muskrats.

Back on Tow Hill Road, continue east to a parking lot and a trail to the beach. Just across from the parking lot is beautiful **Masset Cemetery,** where the graves are marked by large aboveground mounds of moss planted with flowering bulbs and surrounded by bushes and trees. It's a peaceful place to ponder the beauty of the Charlottes.

Old Massett

If you're in search of Haida treasures, head for the village of Old Massett, also known as Haida. It's just a five-minute drive from Masset, west down the coastal road. Go as far as the road takes you and you'll end up at the old blue schoolhouse, now **Ed Jones Haida Museum.** Inside, exhibits include a large collection of fascinating old photographs showing how the villages used to look, Haida art and prints, and some of the original totem poles from around the Queen Charlottes. Outside you'll find a partly completed canoe and a field sprinkled with more totems, these from a more recent era. The museum is open in summer Saturday and Sunday 9 A.M.–5 P.M.; admission by donation. Across from the museum is a carving shed where artists can be seen working throughout summer.

Continue up behind the museum to the impressive weathered building with the two totem poles out front; this is **Haida Arts and Jewellery** (250/626-5560, open Mon.–Sat. 11 A.M.–5 P.M., Sun. noon–5 P.M.), where you can buy custom argillite carvings, silk-screen prints, handcrafted silver and abalone jewelry, books on native culture, and greeting cards.

Langara Island

Langara Island, at the northwestern tip of the archipelago, is a rugged and remote place with wooded slopes ending at a rocky shoreline. A couple of small native villages, two lodges, and a beautifully restored 1913 lighthouse are the only human intrusions. The main attraction here is the salmon and halibut fishing; the provincial record-setting halibut, a 320-pounder, was pulled from local waters. Fishing is best April–September, when anglers book up the island's **Langara Fishing Lodge** and the newer **Langara Island Lodge.** Both lodges are operated by Langara Fishing Adventures (604/232-5532 or 800/668-7544, www.langara.com), flying clients in on charter flights directly from Vancouver; prices start at $3,500 for four days.

Accommodations and Camping

Several B&Bs in Masset provide lodgings and local flavor. Next to the pier, rustic **M Copper Beech House** (1590 Delkatla Rd., 250/626-5441) is a New England–style saltbox, decorated with sea treasures and with a beautiful flower garden. Rates of $75 s, $100 d ($125 for an en suite) include a delicious breakfast prepared by David Philips, whose enthusiasm for the islands is infectious. Philips does wonders with local produce—smoking his own seafood and making jams and preserves from locally harvested berries.

Alaska View Lodge (12 km/7.5 miles east of Masset on Tow Hill Rd., 250/626-3333 or 800/661-0019, www.alaskaviewlodge.com) is right on the beach and backed by dense temperate rainforest of Sitka spruce. Accommodations in the main building share bathrooms and range $50–60 s, $70–80 d, depending on the view. Closer to the beach, two rooms in the "Guesthouse" feature practical beach furniture and a joined deck; $70 s, $90 d. Continuing toward Tow Hill, **Rapid Ritchie's Rustic Rentals** (250/626-5472, www.beachcabins.com) is a similar setup, with cedar-shaked cabins spread through the forest. If you can do without modern conveniences, you'll love this place—and the rates ($40–75, cash only)—but be prepared for outhouses, no electricity, and no phones.

Village of Masset RV Site and Campground is on Tow Hill Road two kilometers north of Masset, opposite the Delkatla Wildlife Sanctuary. The campground features large, fairly private campsites with tables among the trees, and washrooms with coin-operated hot showers. Unserviced sites are $11, powered sites $17. Another option for campers is to continue 20 kilometers (12 miles) along the road into Naikoon Provincial Park.

Food

Even though Masset has a large fishing fleet, most of the catch ends up in mainland canneries. Your best choice for seafood is **Sandpiper Restaurant** (corner of Collison Ave. and Orr St., 250/626-3672; Mon.–Sat. 8:30 A.M.–9 P.M.), where the daily lunch specials are around $9 and dinner entrées range $14–24. **Pearl's** (corner of Main St. and Collison Ave., 250/626-3223; Mon.–Sat. for lunch and daily for dinner) features Chinese cuisine in an almost hospital-like atmosphere. For around $12 you can get an enor-

mous helping of chicken and vegetables in black bean sauce, along with a large bowl of steamed rice, tea, and the mandatory fortune cookie.

NAIKOON PROVINCIAL PARK

This spectacular park encompasses some 72,640 hectares (179,500 acres) along the northeast tip of Graham Island. Tlell marks the park's southern boundary, while access to the northern reaches is via the road out to Tow Hill, 26 kilometers (16 miles) east of Masset. The park's dominant features are its beaches, 97 kilometers (60 miles) of them, bordering Hecate Strait on the east and the turbulent Dixon Entrance on the north. Most of the rest of the park is lowlands, surrounded by stunted lodgepole pine, red and yellow cedar, western hemlock, and Sitka spruce. Wildlife is abundant; black-tailed deer, black bear, marten, river otter, raccoons, red squirrels, beaver, muskrat, small herds of wild cattle, and many species of birds inhabit the park. Dolphins, orcas, porpoises, and seals swim offshore year-round, and northern fur seals and California gray whales migrate north past the park in May and June.

© ANDREW HEMPSTEAD

a victim of the sea, Naikoon Provincial Park

Sights

The drive out to the park from Masset is superb, passing through seemingly endless moss-draped trees. Along the way you pass **Tow Hill Ecological Reserve,** a beautiful spruce forest where birds tweet from the treetops and the ground and most of the trees are completely cushioned by spongy yellow moss.

The road passes the base of Tow Hill and ends at the southern end of long, sandy **North Beach.** This strip of sand is a beachcomber's delight, as it is strewn with shells, driftwood, and shiny, sea-worn pebbles of every color under the sun. The beach is best known for semiprecious agate, ranging from light yellow in color to almost-translucent, which is found among piles of pebbles that become exposed at low tide starting about three kilometers (1.9 miles) along the beach. At the end of North Beach is **Rose Spit.** Known to the Haida as Naikoon, meaning "Long Nose," this narrow point of land separates the waters of Hecate Strait and Dixon Entrance. From the end of Tow Hill Rd., it's about 10 kilometers (6.2 miles) of easy beach walking to the end of the spit; if you allow six hours for the round-trip, you'll have enough time to enjoy a picnic lunch among the driftwood along the way.

Head back toward Masset, along the beach from the end of the road, and **Tow Hill** is impossible to miss. A one-kilometer (.6-mile) trail leads to the top of this 130-meter-high (430-foot-high) basalt monolith, or satisfy yourself with exploring the tidal pools at its base.

Cape Fife Trail

From near the end of the park access road, the Cape Fife Trail (three hours each way) heads in a southeasterly direction, passing boglands and stunted pine trees on its 10-kilometer (6.2-mile) route to **Fife Point,** overlooking Hecate Strait. The shore above the high-tide line is blanketed by a mass of driftwood logs, crushed together during the fierce storms that regularly lash this coast. A rough shelter at the end of the trail provides some protection from the elements. Backcountry camping is permitted; hide among the trees on especially windy days. From this point you can hike north along the beach to Rose Spit, described above, then continue back along North Beach to the parking lot at Hiellen River—a total of 34 kilometers (21 miles) and an easy two-day trip. Well-equipped adventurers can continue south from Fife Point along **East Beach** to finish at Tlell, a total distance of 72 kilometers (45 miles). This has become a popular hike—take your time (allow 4–5 days) and bring adequate food and water.

Practicalities

Agate Beach Campground is near Tow Hill, about 26 kilometers (16 miles) from Masset. The campsites lie along the back of the beach and offer outstanding views. A shelter and pit toilets are provided, but no showers. In summer you need to nab a spot early in the day—by late afternoon they're all taken. The campground is open year-round. Sites cost $14 per night May–September; the rest of the year they're free.

SANDSPIT AND VICINITY

Across Skidegate Channel from Queen Charlotte City, Sandspit (pop. 560) is the only community on Moresby Island. Home to the islands' main airport and linked to Graham Island by a short ferry trip, the town occupies a low-lying, windswept spit overlooking Shingle Bay. The northern half of Moresby Island is largely given over to logging, while the southern half and over 100 outlying islands fall within Gwaii Haanas National Park Reserve, which protects a high concentration of abandoned Haida villages.

Through town is **Willows Golf Course,** an exposed, nine-hole course on a coastal strip of land originally cleared for farming; greens fees are $16 and club rentals are available.

Into the Bush

Those determined to tour the forests in their own vehicle can make an enjoyable loop trip south out of Sandspit. Logging roads lace the forest, leading to beaches strewn with driftwood, streams alive with salmon and steelhead, and beautiful Skidegate and Mosquito Lakes (good trout fishing). Free campgrounds are available at Gray Bay and Mosquito Lake.

Accommodations and Camping

Sandspit lacks the appeal of communities on Graham Island, but services are available. **Seaport B&B** (371 Beach Rd., 250/637-5698) rents three basic rooms in a waterfront home. Rates of $35 s, $45 d include a self-serve breakfast and use of kitchen facilities. Friendly **Moresby Island Guest House** (385 Beach Rd., 250/637-5300; $30–75 d) is a popular kayakers' hangout across the road from Shingle Bay. Some of the 10 rooms share bathrooms, but everyone has use of a kitchen, laundry, and wide deck with water views. Bike rentals are also available.

Campgrounds are at **Gray Bay** and **Mosquito Lake** (named after the Mosquito airplane, not the pesky insects), both on the logging roads.

Information

Sandspit Visitor Info Centre is a small desk inside the airport terminal (250/637-5362; mid-May–mid-Sept. daily 9 A.M.–6 P.M.).

Transportation

Sandspit Airport, the main airport for the Queen Charlotte Islands, is on the east side of town beside Hecate Strait. It's served by **Air Canada** (888/247-2262) and **Hawk Air** (250/635-4295). The **Airporter** bus meets all flights, transporting passengers to Queen Charlotte City for $15 per person. **Budget** (250/637-2330) and **Thrifty** (250/637-2299) have car-rental agencies in Sandspit.

GWAII HAANAS NATIONAL PARK RESERVE

Renowned around the world for its ancient Haida villages dotted with totem poles, this park encompasses the southern half of Moresby Island as well as 137 smaller islands in the south of the archipelago—1,480 hectares (3,660 acres) of land and 1,600 kilometers (1,000 miles) of coastline. It's a remarkable place. Ancient brooding totems and remnants of mighty Haida longhouses stand against a backdrop of lush wilderness—dense trees, thick spongy moss, and rock-strewn beaches with incredibly clear water. Colonies of nesting seabirds and an abundance of marinelife—killer and minke whales, sea lions, tufted puffins—all add to the atmosphere.

Jointly managed by Parks Canada and the Haida nation, the park was established in 1988 after a long, bitter struggle between the Haida and forestry companies. The area now protected was home to seafaring Haida for almost 10,000 years, but by the early 1900s, less than 100 years after their first contact with whites, their communities were abandoned, the inhabitants having been wiped out by disease or having moved to Old Massett and Skidegate.

Nan Sdins (Ninstints) on tiny SGaang Gwaii (Anthony Island) near the south end of the park, was once home to around 300 Haida and had been occupied for thousands of years before the arrival of Europeans. Today, weathered totem poles stretch along the shoreline, with the nearby ruins of cedar longhouses slowly being consumed by the surrounding rainforest. Anthony Island was declared a UNESCO World Heritage Site in 1981, just 97 years after the last Haida families had abandoned their remote home. **Gandle K'in** (Hotspring Island), the site of another abandoned village, has the bonus of oceanfront hot pools that held special healing and spiritual qualities to the Haida. Other well-known villages include **Kuuna** (Skedans), closest to Sandspit; **T'aanuu** (Tanu); and **Hik'yah** (Windy Bay).

Park Practicalities

The only access to the park is by air or sea. If you aren't visiting the park as part of an organized tour, reserve a permit through Tourism BC (250/387-1642 or 800/435-5622; $15 per booking). A limited number of permits are issued for each day, in addition to six spots that are set aside on a standby basis. These can be claimed at the Queen Charlotte Visitor Info Centre (in Queen Charlotte City) at 8 A.M. on the day of departure. Either way, you must also purchase the permit itself ($10 per person per day) and participate in an orientation session; these are held at the Queen Charlotte Visitor Info Centre Monday–Friday at 8 A.M. and daily at 7:30 P.M. They run on demand at the Sandspit Visitor Info Centre. **Moresby Explorers** (250/637-2215 or 800/806-7633, www.moresbyexplorers.com)

provides drop-offs and pickups for those heading into the park unguided. Sample cost is $600 for two for kayak rental, use of a VHF radio, and boat transportation to the company's base camp in Crescent Inlet. **South Moresby Air Charters** is a floatplane operation based at the wharf in Queen Charlotte City (250/559-4222). Charter rates for four people (book in advance for the best chance of making up the numbers) are $480 to Skedans, $765 to Hotspring Island, and $1,800 to Nan Sdins. Rates include an hour's ground time at the destination, with the latter also including a short boat ride as the planes are unable to land right at Nan Sdins.

The above permit information is irrelevant if, like many visitors, you travel as part of a guided tour (although the operator will charge you the permit fee). **Archipelago Ventures** (604/255-9505 or 888/559-8317) combines the best of the park into a six-day tour that costs $1,800–1,900. The main mode of transportation is a stable 42-foot mother ship, with the focus on kayaking, hiking, and soaking up cul-ture in the abandoned Haida villages, including Nan Sdins. Along the way, freshly caught shrimp and halibut create enticing meals. The turnaround point for these tours is Rose Harbour; travel is by boat in one direction and floatplane in the other, which allows for a relaxed pace in one direction and a spectacular ride above the park in the other.

Ocean Light II Adventures (604/328-5339, www.oceanlight2.bc.ca) has been conducting sailing trips through the south end of the archipelago since well before the proclamation of a park. Board the company's 71-foot *Ocean Light II* for eight days of sailing, visiting all the best-known abandoned Haida villages, exploring the waterways, and searching out land and sea mammals. All meals and accommodations aboard the boat are included in the rate of $3,050 per person.

For general park information, click through the links on the Parks Canada website (www.pc.gc.ca). To contact the local park office, call 250/559-8818.

The Stewart-Cassiar Highway

An alternative to the Alaska Highway, this route—often referred to simply as "the Cassiar"—spurs north off the Yellowhead Highway 45 kilometers (28 miles) west of New Hazelton and leads north to the Yukon, joining the Alaska Highway just west of Watson Lake. The highway opens up a magnificent area of northern wilderness that in many ways rivals that along the more famous Alaska Highway.

The highlight of the Stewart-Cassiar Highway is definitely the side trip west to the twin coastal villages of **Stewart** and **Hyder.** But the route also passes the remote river town of **Telegraph Creek** and jumping-off points for various wilderness adventures.

From the Yellowhead Highway it's 155 kilometers (96 miles) north to Meziadin Junction, then 65 kilometers (40 miles) west to Stewart, official beginning of the Stewart-Cassiar Highway. Total length of the trip between the Yellowhead and Alaska Highways is 733 kilo-meters (455 miles), excluding the 130 kilometers (80 miles) round-trip for the jaunt out to Stewart.

Be Prepared

The highway is mainly paved, but improved gravel sections are found on the 80-kilometer (50-mile) stretch north of Meziadin Junction, the 40-kilometer (25-mile) stretch south of Kinaskan Lake, and for around 30 kilometers (19 miles) each side of Dease Lake. Be prepared for washboard conditions on these sections, especially after heavy rain. Dust and mud can also be problematic, and many narrow, one-lane bridges call for extra caution.

Gas stations and services can be found along the highway, but it's not a bad idea to fill up with gas wherever and whenever you get the opportunity. And to be on the safe side, take two spare tires, a basic tool kit, a gas can (filled!), and water. In summer, there's a regular flow of traffic, so if you do get stranded it shouldn't be too long before someone comes along.

FROM YELLOWHEAD HIGHWAY TO MEZIADIN JUNCTION

Tree-covered hills, dense patches of snow-white daisies, banks of pink-and-white clover and purple lupine, craggy mountains and distant peaks, beautiful lakes covered in yellow water lilies, and lots of logging trucks flying along the road—these are images of the 155 kilometers (96 miles) between the Yellowhead Highway and Meziadin Junction, the turnoff to Stewart.

Kitwanga

This small village just north of the Yellowhead Highway is home to **Kitwanga Fort National Historic Site,** the first national historic site commemorating native culture in western Canada. The site protects 13-meter (43-foot) high Battle Hill, where 200 years ago a native warrior named Nekt fought off attacks from hostile neighbors. A trail leads from the parking lot down to the flat area around the bottom of the hill, where you can read display panels describing the hill's history. The site is on Kitwanga Valley Road, overlooking the Kitwanga River, and is open year-round; admission free.

Gitanyow Totem Poles

Continuing north, you're paralleling what was commonly called the Grease Trail, the route coastal natives took to the interior to trade their oolichan (tiny oily fish) with other tribes. At the native village of Gitanyow (also called Kitwancool), 23 kilometers (14 miles) from Kitwanga, is the world's greatest remaining concentration of totem poles still in their original location. The oldest, "Hole in the Ice," is approximately 140 years old; some say it's the oldest standing totem pole in the world. It tells the story of a man preventing his people from starving by chopping a hole in the ice and doing a spot of ice fishing.

Meziadin Junction Toward Stewart

At the junction is a gas station and a small information center, open July–August only. Just

lakeside camping along the Stewart-Cassiar Highway

© ANDREW HEMPSTEAD

south of the junction is 335-hectare (830-acre) **Meziadin Lake Provincial Park,** along the northeast shore of Meziadin Lake, two kilometers from the highway. It's open mid-May to October and has good fishing for rainbow trout and Dolly Varden. Gravel campsites are set on tiers sloping downtown to the lakeshore—one of the most picturesque camping spots along the Cassiar. On the down side, facilities are limited to pit toilets, picnic tables, and fire pits; $14 per night.

From Meziadin Junction, Stewart is 65 kilometers (40 miles) west along a spectacular stretch of highway that crosses the glaciated Coast Mountains. The first 40 kilometers (25 miles) is all uphill, through thick subalpine forests and past lakes, waterfalls, and a string of glaciers sitting like thick icy slabs atop almost-vertical mountains. Suddenly, and quite unexpectedly, the highway rounds a corner and there in front of you is magnificent, intensely blue **Bear Glacier.** The glacier tumbles down into small Strohn Lake, where small icebergs float across the surface in the breeze. From Bear Glacier it's downhill all the way to Stewart. Keep an eye out for three mighty waterfalls on the north side of the highway, one after another. One plummets down into a large buildup of ice, complete with blue ice cave. This stretch of road is good for wildlife viewing; numerous mountain goats wander the hillsides, and black bears nose around the avalanche slopes in search of their next meal.

STEWART

The twin towns of Stewart, British Columbia, and Hyder, Alaska, straddle the international boundary at the headwaters of the **Portland Canal.** The road from Meziadin Junction is the tenuous sole link to the outside world—and when you arrive, you'll find both towns with the end-of-the-road feel you'd expect. The surrounding scenery alone is worthy of the drive. From Stewart, the Portland Canal, the world's fourth-longest fjord, extends 113 kilometers (70 miles) to the open ocean south of Ketchikan (Alaska), surrounded by mountains that rise to their highest point around Stewart.

Two brothers, Robert and John Stewart, were the first permanent settlers at the head of Portland Canal, arriving shortly after the turn of the 20th century. Prospecting through the surrounding mountains, they came across incredible wealth. Word got out, and by 1910 Stewart's population had boomed to 10,000. The main street was lined with busy shops, the city had four daily newspapers, and at least every second day a steamer loaded with new arrivals and supplies would dock at one of two long wharves. But the boom was short-lived, especially after the Grand Trunk Pacific Railway decided to build its western terminus at Prince Rupert. By the end of World War I the population had dwindled to 20. The Granduc copper mine, which operated between 1964 and the mid-1980s, revived the town's fortunes for a time, but today, what's left of the local economy revolves around the timber industry, which uses the Portland Canal to transport logs to southern markets.

To get the lowdown on the town's interesting past, head to **Stewart Historical Society Museum,** in the original city hall (Columbia St. between 6th and 7th Streets, 250/636-2568; mid-June–Aug. daily 9:30 A.M.–4:30 P.M.). Displays include a tool collection and exhibits on the town's boom-and-bust mining industry.

Practicalities

King Edward Hotel and Motel (5th Ave., 250/636-2244 or 800/663-3126, www.kingedwardmotel.com) spans both sides of the main drag. Rooms in the hotel section are $79 s, $89 d, while rooms with kitchens in the motel—which are slightly better than you may imagine from looking at the exterior—are $99 s, $109 d.

Nestled below the towering peaks of the Coast Mountains at the back of town is **Rainey Creek Campground** (on 8th Ave., 250/636-2537). Facilities are basic, and you need quarters for the showers; $13–18 a night. If this place is full, continue through town to Hyder, where you'll find two more campgrounds.

The small but ever-busy **Brothers Bakery** (5th Ave.) serves delicious cakes and breads at reasonable prices. Next door in an old three-story

STEWART AND HYDER: SOME QUICK FACTS

The twin towns of Stewart (Canada) and Hyder (United States) are separated by an international border, but you'd hardly know it. Crossing into Hyder comes without any of the formalities or checkpoints you'd expect at a border, and upon re-entering Canada, an ATCO trailer serves as the port of entry (until the mid-1990s there were no border checks at all), mostly in place to check for cheap U.S. booze purchased at the Hyder liquor store.

Residents of Both Towns . . .
- Send their kids to school in Canada.
- Are supplied power by B.C. Hydro.
- Use the Canadian phone system (area code 250).
- Are policed by the RCMP.
- Never have to wait for a drink—Hyder has one bar for every 30 residents.

Notes for the Traveler
- Buy your booze in Hyder—it's cheaper (but is only tax-free if you have been in town for more than 48 hours).
- Watch for bears—they often wander along the streets.
- Use Canadian currency in both towns.
- Post your mail on whichever side of the border saves the cost of international postage.
- Bring your passport—border checks are made when re-entering Canada.
- Don't miss the drive to Salmon Glacier.

building is **Bitter Creek Cafe** (250/636-2166), serving light meals at lunchtime. The only place open for dinner is the grandly named **King's Table Dining Room** (King Edward Hotel, 250/636-2244), but it's nothing special. Also in the hotel is a coffee shop, which is where the locals head for breakfast.

Stewart Visitor Info Centre overlooks the mudflats at the north end of 5th Avenue (250/636-9224 or 888/366-5999; mid-May–Sept. daily 8:30 A.M.–7 P.M.). The staff offers a wealth of local information, including directions out to Salmon Glacier, hiking-trail brochures, and history sheets. The main street (5th Avenue) also holds a grocery store, drugstore, post office, bank, and laundry.

Ⓜ HYDER

Continue through Stewart along the Portland Canal and, next thing you know, the road turns to gravel and you're in Hyder, Alaska, U.S.A.

(pop. 90)—without all the formalities and checkpoints you'd expect at an international border. Known as the "Friendliest little ghost town in Alaska," Hyder, where the emphasis is on soaking up the unique atmosphere rather than visiting traditional attractions, provides a glimpse of life at the end of the road. The main street is lined with a motley assortment of buildings, sandwiched between the water on one side and forested mountain slopes that rise dramatically over 2,000 meters (6,600 feet) on the other.

Settled by prospectors in the 1890s, Hyder once boasted a population of 10,000. The town thrived for many years, but today few of the original structures remain. Fires destroyed much of the old town, and no one ever bothered to rebuild. Head left at the end of the main road to reach the mudflats that once held the bulk of Hyder's early buildings. Continue along the dike and onto the long wharf for views back across town and to the snowcapped mountains beyond.

Glacier Inn

At one time Hyder boasted over 20 bars; today, amazingly, three remain, each licensed to be open 23 hours a day. They serve a population of 90 residents, as well as Stewart locals and travelers keen to reach the end of the road. Oldest and best known is the Glacier Inn, an almost windowless two-story wooden structure on the main drag. Join the tradition and tack a bill to the wall to ensure that you won't return broke, then toss back a shot of 190-proof, pure grain alcohol ($2.50) in one swallow to qualify for your "I've been Hyderized" card.

Fish Creek

Turn right at the end of Hyder's main street and follow the gravel road through town and along the Salmon River. Several kilometers beyond, at **Fish Creek Viewing Platform,** you can watch bears fishing and feasting at the all-you-can-eat chum salmon buffet. Generally, black bears arrive earliest, usually around the end of July. During August, brown bears (called grizzlies in the interior) move down from higher elevations to feed. This is a unique opportunity to watch a number of bears at once—one that costs many hundreds of dollars in southwestern Alaska—but keep your distance. Forest service staff are on hand to keep the crowds away from the bears, but they also love talking about "their" bears.

The Road to Salmon Glacier

From Fish Creek, the road continues to follow the Salmon River, passing an abandoned mining operation and then the ruins of a covered bridge that provided access to a remote mine up the Texas Creek watershed. From this point the road narrows considerably and becomes increasingly steep (travel is not recommended for RVs), crossing back into Canada and winding through former living quarters for the abandoned gold and mineral ore Premier Mine. The road makes a loop around tailing ponds and continues climbing steeply, with **Salmon Glacier** first coming into view 25 kilometers (16 miles) from Hyder. The road parallels the glacier and climbs to a high point after another 10 kilometers (6.2 miles), where the best lookout point is. This glacier, one of the largest in

Salmon Glacier

North America but also one of the most accessible, is one of British Columbia's most awesome sights, snaking for many kilometers through the highest peaks of the Coast Mountains.

Practicalities

Most services are back in Stewart, but Hyder does have accommodations and a couple of places to eat. Canadian money is used in all Hyder businesses except the post office, where only U.S. currency is accepted.

The **Sealaska Inn** (Premier Ave., 250/636-2486, www.sealaskainn.com) is an old two-story hotel with a row of very basic rooms on the top floor. Rooms with shared bathroom facilities are $36 s, $42 d, while those with private facilities are $64 s, $72 d. The hotel also operates two campgrounds as **Camp-run-a-muck.** Campers who don't require hookups pitch their tents or park beside the hotel ($16 per night), while toward Fish Creek is a small area set aside for RVs needing water and power hookups ($22). Both sections have bathrooms with showers, laundry facilities, fire pits, and free firewood.

Northern British Columbia

Also head to the Sealaska Inn if you're hungry; the kitchen serves up standard pub fare at reasonable prices.

NORTH OF MEZIADIN JUNCTION

For the first 200 kilometers (124 miles) north from Meziadin Junction, the highway follows the Bell-Irving River Valley, bordered by the Coast Mountains to the west and the Skeena Mountains to the east.

Around 100 kilometers (62 miles) from the junction, **Bell II Lodge** (604/881-8530 or 877/617-2288, www.bell2lodge.com) comes into view. It's the winter base for Last Frontier Heli-skiing but is a lot more than a spot to spend the night before heading north through the rest of the year. Fishing is the biggest attraction, especially through summer for chinook salmon and late September–early November for steelhead. Although many guests are serious anglers on week-long guided fishing packages, casual visitors are also welcomed. Rates for comfortable rooms in the main lodge are $94–128 s or d per night. Tent camping is $12 while RVs and trailers pay $19–28. Also here is a restaurant (open daily 7 A.M.–9 P.M.) and a bar. The lodge sells all the fishing tackle you'll need and offers daily guiding services, including heli-fishing.

Kinaskan Lake Provincial Park

At the 200-kilometer (124-mile) mark is 1,800-hectare (4,450-acre) Kinaskan Lake Provincial Park, known for its hungry rainbow trout. It's also the gateway for hikers heading west into much larger Mount Edziza Provincial Park. In the south of the park, a trail leads one kilometer (.6 mile) to great fishing at **Natadesleen Lake,** then a kilometer farther along an overgrown trail to beautiful, tiered **Cascade Falls.** Camping at the park is $14 a night.

Red Goat Lodge

Continuing north you'll come to Red Goat Lodge (250/234-3261 or 888/733-4628), a bed-and-breakfast and campground overlooking Eddontenajon Lake. The tenting area is up the hill

secluded among trees ($13), while larger pull-through sites with power hookups ($20) are closer to the water. Facilities for campers include coin showers and laundry facilities. The lodge building holds four tastefully decorated B&B rooms, each with private bath; rates of $75–105 s or d include a delicious home-cooked breakfast served in the "Breakfast Room," which boasts beautiful lake and mountain views.

Iskut and Vicinity

The small Tahltan town of Iskut has a post office, gas station, and grocery store (open daily 8 A.M.–9 P.M.). North of Iskut is **Bear Paw Ranch Resort** (250/234-3005), where you have the choice of staying in the main lodge building ($85 s or d) or northern-themed cabins ($70). The ranch offers horseback riding, fishing, canoe trips, and amenities including a restaurant, lounge, hot tub, and sauna.

Spatsizi Plateau Provincial Park

This park is British Columbia wilderness at its wildest—656,780 hectares (1.62 million acres) of broad plateaus, stunning glacier-capped peaks, roaring rivers, and fish-filled lakes. Wildlife abounds; grizzly bears, moose, wolves, wolverines, mountain goats, woodland caribou, and more than 100 species of birds are all present.

Access is on foot or by floatplane. Backcountry canoeing draws many, if not most, visitors to the park. The most popular trip begins with a floatplane flight to Tuaton Lake, at the headwaters of the Stikine River in the heart of the park. After putting in at the lake, you paddle the Stikine down to a pullout where the river crosses the Stewart-Cassiar Highway, a 250-kilometer (155-mile) journey with two short portages. Another popular trip begins with a five-kilometer (3.1-mile) portage from an old—and in some places rough—BC Rail grade that follows the park's southwestern boundary for 80 kilometers (50 miles). Reach the signposted trailhead via Eulue Lake Road, which spurs east from the Stewart-Cassiar Highway immediately north of Tatogga Lake. The portage takes you to the upper reaches of the Spatsizi River, a tributary of the Stikine. This route passes Cold Fish Lake, where you'll find eight cabins, a rustic sauna, and a cookhouse; $10 per person per night. At least seven days should be allowed for either trip.

For more information on canoe routes and the park, contact the BC Parks office in Dease Lake (250/771-4591).

Mount Edziza Provincial Park

This 230,000-hectare (568,300-acre) wilderness west of the Stewart-Cassiar Highway is one of the province's most inaccessible parks, but it's also one of the most magnificent and intriguing. The long and narrow park is bordered to the north by the road out to Telegraph Creek, to the west by Mess Creek, and to the east by Little Iskut River and a string of four lakes. Within these boundaries lies a moonlike volcanic landscape, above the tree line and dominated by 2,787-meter (9,140-foot) **Mount Edziza,** an extinct volcano whose glaciated crater is over two kilometers (1.2 miles) wide. Rather than blowing out in one massive and spectacular eruption, this volcano oozed periodically over the course of four million years, eventually covering an area 65 kilometers (40 miles) across with lava. Small eruptions in the vicinity of the central cone have created dozens of cinder cones, some perfectly symmetrical.

Access to the park is on foot, on horseback, or via a chartered floatplane from North Pacific Seaplanes (based at Tatogga Lake Resort, near Iskut; 250/234-3525). The easiest overland access is from Kinaskan Lake Provincial Park, 55 kilometers (34 miles) south of Iskut; from the west bank of the lake (accessed by boat), it's 24 kilometers (15 miles) by trail to Mowdade Lake, then another 25 kilometers (16 miles) to the first of the cinder cones, directly south of the main peak. This trail continues northward around Mount Edziza to Buckley Lake, ending across the Stikine River from Telegraph Creek. Charter-flight operators can drop hikers at any of the main lakes, but Mowdade is most popular for its vicinity to the park's most spectacular volcanic features.

Between Iskut and Dease Lake

On this stretch, the highway runs through the **Stikine River Provincial Park,** a long and narrow 217,000-hectare (536,200-acre) park straddling the Stikine River and linking Spatsizi Plateau Wilderness Park and Mount Edziza Provincial Park. The bridge over the Stikine River is used as a pull-out point for canoe trips that start in Spatsizi Plateau Provincial Park. Downstream from the bridge, the river flows in a torrent of white water through the **Grand Canyon of the Stikine,** an 85-kilometer (53-mile) long canyon with vertical rock walls towering more than 300 meters (1,000 feet). Only a few teams have successfully kayaked the canyon. In early September 1992, an unassuming 37-year-old man from Montana quietly slipped his kayak into the water at the Highway 37 bridge and became the first person to successfully descend the canyon solo.

Dease Lake

The small community of Dease Lake, on the shores of its namesake lake 65 kilometers (40 miles) north of Iskut, provides basic tourist services and a bit more.

Dease Lake's only accommodation is the **Northway Motor Inn** (250/771-5341), charging $70 s, $78 d for a basic room. The town has no campgrounds, but 10 kilometers (6.2 miles) south, where the highway crosses the **Tanzilla River,** is a rest area with picnic tables and pit toilets. The individual pull-through spots are large enough for most RVs.

The best place to eat is the **Boulder Cafe,** where an always-busy waitress will serve you breakfast ($5–9), lunch, or dinner (burgers $7, main dishes from $9) while you admire the old photographs lining the walls; open daily 8 A.M.–9 P.M. For takeout pizza and delicious soft-serve ice cream, head for the small ATCO trailer beside the gas station. Dease Lake also has a laundry and an intriguing gift shop.

Telegraph Creek

From Dease Lake an unsealed road leads 119 kilometers (74 miles) west along the Tanzilla River to Telegraph Creek (pop. 300), which lies on a terraced hill overlooking the Stikine River. Telegraph Creek, the farthest navigable point on the Stikine River, was on the first leg of the "Trail to the Interior" used during the Klondike Gold Rush. Gold-seekers started in Wrangell, Alaska, continued up the Stikine River by steamer to Telegraph Creek, then continued overland to Dease Lake and on to the Liard River. Later, Telegraph Creek grew as an important stopover point along the Yukon Telegraph Line, the main overland route between the Yukon and all points south before the construction of the Alaska Highway.

The town boasts friendly people, gorgeous scenery, and heritage buildings dating back to the 1860s. Jet-boat tours are popular—by the hour or day, upstream through Stikine Grand Canyon Provincial Park or down to Wrangell or Petersburg, Alaska (book through Stikine River-Song Lodge, 250/235-3196). A 20-kilometer (12-mile) road leads west from town to **Glenora,** which had 10,000 residents in its gold-rush heyday. Nowadays, only one or two of the original buildings remain.

Originally a Hudson's Bay Company store, the **Stikine RiverSong Lodge** (250/235-3196, www.stikineriversong.com) has eight guest rooms with shared baths for $60 s, $65 d. Use of a kitchen and Internet access incur a small extra charge. The lodge also has a café, general store, and gas station.

Continuing to the Alaska Highway

As you continue north from the turnoff to Telegraph Creek, the road parallels the east shore of Dease Lake. Good campsites are found by the lake, along with the occasional chunk of jade on the lakeshore—the area has been called the jade capital of the world. From Dease Lake to the Alaska Highway it's clear sailing for 235 kilometers (146 miles) along the northern slopes of the Cassiar Mountains.

Cassiar, 115 kilometers (71 miles) north of Dease Lake, was once a company town for Cassiar Asbestos Mine. The booming little burg held a thousand residents, a grocery store, liquor store, bank, supermarket, and a multimillion-dollar school. But in March 1992, the company pulled out and the residents followed suit. The following year the town was auctioned off right down to the last fence post. To get there head 16 kilometers (10 miles) along the Cassiar Spur road, passing a few old cabins and the back of a monstrous pile of green tailings. Don't expect any services.

The next worthwhile stop is 4,597-hectare (11,360-acre) **Boya Lake Provincial Park,** 150 kilometers (92 miles) north of Dease Lake and 85 kilometers (53 miles) from the Alaska Highway. White, claylike beaches ring the incredibly clear lake. Walking along the shoreline is worthwhile, or take the short hiking trail that leads to an active beaver pond. The park campground is open mid-May to September and costs $14 per site.

From Boya Lake, the highway continues north, paralleling the Dease River for around 20 kilometers (12 miles) and traversing the Liard Plain across the border and into the Yukon. From the border it's another four kilometers (2.5 miles) to the junction of the Alaska Highway, then 21 kilometers (13 miles) east to Watson Lake or 423 kilometers (263 miles) west to Whitehorse.

North from Prince George

The landscapes and lifestyles in the area northeast of Prince George are closely aligned with neighboring northwest Alberta. The region's dominant natural feature, the **Peace River,** flows east from B.C.'s northern Rockies across the border into Alberta, lacing the two provinces together both topographically and economically. Rich farmland flanks the river on both sides of the border, creating a common agricultural zone whose hub is Grande Prairie, Alberta. This region of B.C. also shares Alberta's mountain time zone.

Most travelers use the route north from Prince George to access Mile Zero of the Alaska Highway at Dawson Creek. But this direct route, a distance of 405 kilometers (252 miles), bypasses the region's highlight at **Hudson's Hope,** halfway between Chetwynd and Fort St. John. Whichever route you take, there's plenty to see and do, with interesting provincial parks and towns offering northern hospitality.

ALONG THE CROOKED RIVER

Heading north out of Prince George, Highway 97 climbs through low rolling hills to the Nechako Plateau before descending alongside the Crooked River to massive Williston Lake. Pastoral farmland lines much of the route, and in summer the roadside is ablaze with red-orange Indian paintbrush and purple lupine.

The first worthwhile stop is 970-hectare (2,300-acre) **Crooked River Provincial Park,** 80 kilometers (50 miles) north of Prince George. The park's centerpiece is Bear Lake, with a sandy beach, forested picnic area, and good canoeing. At the end of the park access road, a largish campground has well spaced sites (mid-May–Sept.; $14); easy access to a beach, pit toilets, drinking water, and a playground. From the entrance to the campground, a short trail leads to Squaw Lake, with good rainbow trout fishing (allow 15 minutes each way). Even if you're not an angler, the trail is worth taking, along with an alternative return route that follows the Crooked River to the starting point; allow 40 minutes for this two-kilometer (1.2-mile) loop.

Carp Lake Provincial Park

This 38,610-hectare (95,400-acre) park lies 140 kilometers (87 miles) north of Prince George on Highway 97, then 32 kilometers (20 miles) west (turn off at McLeod Lake) along a sometimes rough unsealed road. The park's epicenter is Carp Lake, a picturesque body of water dotted with islands and filled with fish, although you won't catch carp—the lake was named by explorer Simon Fraser, who noted Carrier Indians journeyed to the lake for fish "of the carp kind." Surrounded the lake are low hills and ridges, carved from the bedrock by receding glaciers at the end of the last ice age. Now thickly forested, aspen, spruce and lodgepole pine dominate, providing a home for larger mammals such as moose, deer, and black bear.

Carp Lake is renowned for its rainbow trout fishing (although you really need a canoe or motor boat to get out to the best fishing grounds), while the stretch of the McLeod River between the two campgrounds is popular for fly-fishing. A three-kilometer (1.9-mile) interpretive loop (allow 50 minutes round-trip) follows part of a route taken by early explorers and trappers, while from the main campground a one-kilometer (.6-mile) trail (20 minutes each way) leads to Rainbow Lake. Another equally short trail, along the access road in the park's northeast corner, leads to **War Falls.**

The park holds two campgrounds with facilities limited to pit toilets, picnic tables, and fire rings. Both are open mid-May–mid-September and cost $14 per night. The larger of the two, right on Carp Lake, is a 15-minute walk to a sandy beach inaccessible by road.

Mackenzie

The forestry town of Mackenzie (pop. 6,200) lies 180 kilometers (112 miles) north of Prince George on the southern arm of massive Williston Lake, North America's largest manmade reservoir. The town was founded in the 1960s as a base for the massive logging operation that cleared the way for construction of the dam.

Northern British Columbia

At the town's entrance is the world's largest tree crusher, used during that logging operation. Nearby **Morfee Lake** has swimming off a sandy beach. Take the logging road to the summit of Morfee Hill for lake views.

Tourist facilities in town are limited. The best-value accommodation is **Williston Lake Lodge** (Mackenzie Blvd., 250/997-3266 or 800/663-2964, www.willistonlakelodge.com; $58 s, $68 d). Each room has a coffeemaker and small fridge, with a guest laundry also available. On the town's southern outskirts, **Mackenzie Municipal RV Park** is little more than a gravel parking lot, but it holds a few grassy tent sites. Picnic tables, firewood, hot showers, and hookups are all supplied for $12–16 a night.

Out at the junction of Highways 97 and 39 is **Mackenzie Visitor Info Centre** (May–Aug. daily 9 A.M.–6 P.M.). For local information the rest of the year, head to the **Mackenzie Chamber of Commerce** (86 Centennial Dr., 250/997-5459 or 877/622-5360; Mon.–Fri. 8:30 A.M.–4:30 P.M.).

To Powder King Mountain Resort

Continuing east toward Chetwynd, the landscape becomes more dramatic as the highway climbs steadily up the western slopes of the Rocky Mountains. Look for signs to the west for **Bijoux Falls Provincial Park,** a small day-use area where the Misinchinka River plummets over a rocky outcrop.

Near **Pine Pass,** Powder King (250/964-0645, www.powderking.com) is a legendary destination, among the northernmost of any North American alpine resort, but best known for its incredible snowfall—over 12 meters (40 feet) annually. One triple chair and two surface lifts serve a vertical rise of 640 meters (2,100 feet) and 600 hectares (1,500 acres). The season lasts from December to early April and the lifts run Thursday–Sunday only. Privately owned cabins are spread around the base area, but the only guest beds are dorm-style in the main lodge. Rates are $45 per person, or $30 if you supply your own bedding. Also at the base village is a café and restaurant, a ski and board shop, and a rental shop, and lessons are available. Lift tickets are adult $40, senior $35, child $25.

From the resort, the highway meanders over one of its most scenic stretches—935-meter (3,070-foot) Pine Pass, atop the Continental Divide. From the pass, it's downhill all the way, following the Pine River to Chetwynd.

CHETWYND AND VICINITY

Chetwynd (pop. 2,800) lies at the relatively busy junction of Highways 97 and 29. The community was first established in 1912, when it was known as "Little Prairie," continuing today as an important center for resource-based industry such as oil and gas, and forestry. The highlight of town itself is the numerous log sculptures carved with chainsaws.

The one main road through town is lined with services. **Pinecone Motor Inn** (5224 53rd Ave., 250/788-3311 or 800/663-8082, $64 s, $68 d) has largish rooms with comfortable beds. On the east side of town, **Westwind RV Park** (Hwy. 97 N, 250/788-2190) has pull-through sites, a laundry, showers, and RV wash; sites range $14–22 per night. An option for campers who don't need services is the campground at **Moberly Lake Provincial Park,** 29 kilometers (18 miles) north of town; $14.

Chetwynd Visitor Info Centre (250/788-1943, www.gochetwynd.com; summer daily 8:30 A.M.–6 P.M.) is in a railway caboose beside the highway through town to the south.

Tumbler Ridge

Tumbler Ridge, 94 kilometers (58 miles) south of Chetwynd, is a modern boomtown that sprang up much the same way gold-rush towns did a hundred years ago. In the early 1980s, several Japanese coal companies agreed to develop mines and a town at the site of the rich Northeast Coal Deposits in return for the provincial government constructing a new railroad and coal-loading dock at Prince Rupert. Tumbler Ridge (pop. 4,300) was created virtually overnight to allow the employees of the Northeast Coal Project to settle in quickly and comfortably. From the start it held all the creature comforts, services, and recreational facilities you'd expect in a long-established town.

Although isolated and well off the main tourist trail, Tumbler Ridge does an excellent job of promoting itself as an outdoorsy destination for tourists. The region has been a hotbed of dinosaur discoveries in recent years. The main site of interest is along the Flatbed Creek, on the north side of town, where around 170 footprints estimated at 95 million years old have been discovered. On the far side of the river are *ankylosaur* footprints, left by ancient creatures known for their distinctive armoring. The town has developed an extensive system of hiking trails, complete with signage and a brochure detailing each (available at the information center). Kinuseo Falls, in Monkman Provincial Park, is one of many waterfalls close by town. Jet-boat tours leave Tumbler Ridge for Kinuseo and Bergeron Falls, which tumble off Bergeron Mountain in a narrow sliver. Upper Quality Falls is reached by foot (allow 15 minutes) from a parking lot 5.5 kilometers (3.4 miles) north of town. They have a classic "bridal veil" look, with a swimming hole at the base. Other local activities including golfing on a nine-hole course carved from the forest and canoeing on Moose Lake.

Give the regular motels a miss and consider **Golden Aspen B&B** (175 Kiskatinaw Cres., 250/242-4415 or 877/883-8835). The Aspen Suite, one of three guest rooms, has a private entrance, en suite bathroom with jetted tub, and a patio with mountain views for only $90 s, $95 d. All visitors have use of a TV room and Internet access, and enjoy a cooked breakfast. Downtown, the **Tumbler Ridge Inn** (275 Southgate St., 250/242-4277 or 800/663-3898) complex contains standard rooms ($58 s, $64 d), a coffee shop, pub, and restaurant. **Lions Flatbed Creek Campground** enjoys a pleasant riverside setting three kilometers (1.9 miles) north of town toward Chetwynd. Facilities include hot showers and a cooking shelter; sites are $10. The other option for campers is **Gwillim Lake Provincial Park,** halfway between Tumbler Ridge and Chetwynd; $14.

Tumbler Ridge Visitor Info Centre (Front St., 250/242-3123, www.tumblerridge.ca) is open June–early September Monday–Friday 8:30 A.M.–4:30 P.M.

Monkman Provincial Park

One of the most inspiring sights in the northern interior is **Kinuseo Falls,** where the Murray River drops 60 meters (200 feet) in a spectacular fan-shaped arc to the valley floor below. The falls are at the north end of 62,900-hectare (155,400-acre) Monkman Provincial Park, 60 kilometers (37 miles) southwest of Tumbler Ridge. This access road ends near the park entrance, where a short trail leads to a viewing platform for the falls. There's a picnic area and **Kinuseo Falls Campground,** where sites are spread alongside the Murray River; $14 a night.

Moberly Lake Provincial Park

North of Chetwynd, the 65-kilometer (40-mile) stretch of Highway 29 to Hudson's Hope passes Moberly Lake, a long and narrow body of water encircled by a typical boreal forest. Moberly Lake Provincial Park, at the lake's eastern end, has a day-use area, sandy beach, and information boards describing the region's natural history. Sites in the large campground are $14 a night.

HUDSON'S HOPE

Human habitation of the Peace River Valley predated Alexander Mackenzie's 1793 journey along the river by many thousands of years. But Mackenzie's detailed reports encouraged an influx of white settlers to the valley. In 1805, fur traders founded Hudson's Hope at a picturesque riverside site. Today the town's population is just over 1,000.

W.A.C. Bennett and Peace Canyon Dams

These two dams are the area's main attractions, their sheer size an awe-inspiring sight. Together the two facilities generate almost 40 percent of the hydroelectricity used in the province.

Larger of the two, the W.A.C. Bennett Dam, seven kilometers (4.3 miles) west of town, is one of the world's largest earth-filled structures. The 183-meter-high (600-foot-high) structure backs up **Williston Lake,** British Columbia's largest lake, which extends more than 300 kilometers (186 miles) along three flooded valleys. At the top

DINOSAURS IN THE PEACE RIVER VALLEY

During construction of Peace Canyon Dam, fossilized remains of the **plesiosaur,** a marine reptile, were discovered. This wasn't the first time evidence of prehistoric life had been discovered in the Peace River Valley. As early as 1922, dinosaur footprints over 100 million years old were found in the area where Hudson's Hope now lies. The footprints belonged to several species of dinosaurs, most common among them the **hadrosaur.** This plant-eater was around 10 meters (33 feet) long and weighed about four tons. It was amphibious but preferred the land, walking around on its hind legs ever-alert for the ancestors of the dreaded tyrannosaurus.

Footprints are as important as skeletons in unraveling the mysteries of dinosaurs. They provide clues about the ratios of various dinosaurs in a particular area, and information on herds and how they traveled. Most of the 1,500 dinosaur footprints discovered in the valley have been excavated and transported to museums throughout Canada (a couple are on display in the Hudson's Hope Museum). Plant and shell fossils can still be found. The best time for searching them out is after heavy rain—try looking downstream from the dam (a few short trails lead from the highway into the canyon, but it's a bit of a scramble). The best opportunity to learn more about local dinosaurs is in the **Peace Canyon Dam Visitor Centre** (250/783-9943, May–Oct. daily 8 A.M.–4 P.M., weekdays only the rest of the year).

of the dam's control building is **Bennett Dam Visitor Centre** (888/333-6667, May–Oct. daily 9 A.M.–6 P.M.), where displays catalog the construction tasks, a film celebrates the dam's opening, and the uses of electricity are detailed. Free guided bus tours of the dam are scheduled daily May–October 9:30 A.M.–4:30 P.M. and are available the rest of the year by appointment.

The much smaller Peace Canyon Dam is downstream from Bennett Dam, nine kilometers (5.6 miles) south of Hudson's Hope on Highway 29. **Peace Canyon Dam Visitor Centre** (250/783-9943, May–Oct. daily 8 A.M.–4 P.M., weekdays only the rest of the year), adjacent to the powerhouse, focuses on the fascinating natural history, exploration, and pioneers of the area, and the building of the Peace Canyon Project. You can also see the central control system, powerhouse, and switchgear station. Don't miss a trip up to the outside observation deck.

Hudson's Hope Museum

Across from Hudson's Hope Visitor Info Centre, a small park is dotted with historic buildings, such as a trapper's cabin and the log-walled St. Peter's Church, moved to the site from throughout the Peace River Valley. The site itself is of some historical significance—Simon Fraser spent the winter of 1805–1806 here. The main dis-

plays are housed in Hudson's Hope Museum (250/783-7535; mid-May–mid-Sept. daily 9:30 A.M.–5:30 P.M.; $4), which is crammed with geological specimens; dinosaur bones and casts of footprints discovered during dam construction; and historical artifacts that belonged to trappers, miners, and early homesteaders.

Practicalities

Neither of the town's accommodations is outstanding, but the **Sportsman Inn** (10501 Beattie Dr., 250/783-5523) has the biggest rooms (from $60 s or d) and an in-house pub and restaurant. The town's three municipal campgrounds each cost $12 per night. Closest to civilization is **King Gething Campground,** on the south end of town, which has flush toilets, coin-operated showers, and plenty of firewood. **Alwin Holland Park,** southeast of town, is more primitive (pit toilets) but is off the main highway and has some nice hiking trails. The third, **Dinosaur Lake Campground,** seven kilometers (4.3 miles) southeast, has pit toilets, firewood, and good fishing and swimming.

Hudson's Hope Visitor Info Centre (9555 Beattie Dr., 250/783-9154; summer daily 9 A.M.–6 P.M.) provides information on local attractions and offers brochures on nearby hiking opportunities.

Alaska Highway

When the Japanese threatened invasion of Canada and the United States during World War II, the Alaska Highway was quickly built to link Alaska with the Lower 48. It was the longest military road ever constructed in North America—an unsurpassed road-construction feat stretching 2,288 kilometers (1,422 miles) between Dawson Creek, B.C., and Delta Junction, Alaska.

Construction began March 9, 1942 and was completed, incredibly, on November 20 that same year. In less than nine months troops had bulldozed a rough trail snaking like a crooked finger through almost impenetrable muskeg and forest, making literally hundreds of detours around obstacles and constructing 133 bridges.

At a cost of more than $140 million, the highway was the major contributing factor to the growth of northern British Columbia in the 1940s. At the height of construction, the region's population boomed. Dawson Creek's population alone rose from 600 to over 10,000, and Whitehorse replaced Dawson City as a more convenient capital of the Yukon.

Driving the highway was notoriously difficult in its earliest days. Highway travelers returned with tales of endless mud holes and dust, washed-out bridges, flat tires, broken windshields and smashed headlights, wildlife in the road, mosquitoes the size of hummingbirds, and sparse facilities. But they also sported "I drove the Alaska Highway" bumper stickers as though they'd won a prize. Nowadays the route doesn't merit quite the bravado—it's paved most of the way, has roadside lodges fairly frequently, and can easily be driven in three days, or two at a pinch. What hasn't changed is the scenery. You'll still see kilometer after kilometer of unspoiled wilderness, including boreal forests of spruce and aspen, the majestic, snow-dusted peaks of the northern Canadian Rockies, and gorgeous rivers and streams (and you can still buy the stickers).

Although official signage along the Alaska Highway is in kilometers, many services are marked in miles, a legacy of imperial measurement. This only becomes confusing when you consider that highway improvements have shortened the original route. For example, Liard River Hot Springs is still marked as Mile 496, though it's now only 462 miles (754 kilometers) from Dawson Creek.

DAWSON CREEK

Although Dawson Creek (pop. 11,700) marks the southern end of the Alaska Highway, it's still a long way north—over 400 kilometers (250 miles) northeast of Prince George and 1,200 kilometers (746 miles) north of Vancouver. While the city thrives on its historic location at Mile Zero, it's also an important service center whose economy is more closely tied to neighboring Alberta, a few kilometers to the east, than to British Columbia.

Dawson Creek was named after Dr. George Mercer Dawson, a Canadian geologist who undertook numerous expeditions through the northwestern regions of Canada in the 1880s (Dawson City, in the Yukon, is also named in his honor). Dawson's glowing report on the region's fertility encouraged settlement—and led to the subsequent discovery of gas and oil fields. The 1931 arrival of the Northern Alberta Railway (N.A.R.) put Dawson Creek on the map, establishing the city as an agricultural service center. Agriculture is still the basis of Dawson Creek's economy; local products include wheat, oats, barley, canola, vegetables, specialty crops, cattle, dairy, hogs, sheep, poultry, and honey. Oil and gas rigs stand in the Elmsworth Basin south of the city, while pipelines and processing plants lie to the east.

Northern Alberta Railway (N.A.R.) Park

Upon entering town, make this park on the corner of Highway 2 and the Alaska Highway your first stop. Here you'll find Dawson Creek Visitor Info Centre, an art gallery, and the **Station Museum** (250/782-9595; May–early Sept. daily 8 A.M.–7 P.M., the rest of the year Tues.–Sat.

Northern British Columbia

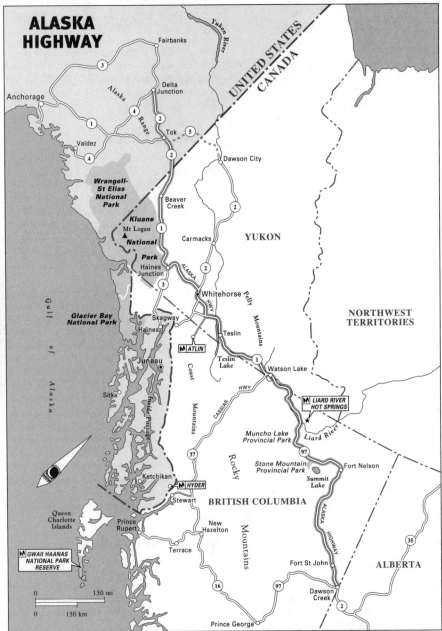

ALASKA HIGHWAY

Fairbanks

Yukon River

UNITED STATES
CANADA

3

Anchorage

Alaska

Delta
Junction

4

2

Tok

5

Valdez

2

4

Dawson City

Wrangell-
St Elias
National
Park

Beaver
Creek

2

Kluane

Mt Logan

1

Carmacks

YUKON

National

2

Range

ALASKA

Park

Haines
Junction

3

Whitehorse

**NORTHWEST
TERRITORIES**

Glacier Bay
National Park

Skagway

Pelly

Haines

Teslin

ATLIN

Mountains

Gulf

Coast

Teslin
Lake

1

Watson Lake

of

HWY

Alaska

Mountains

CASSIAR

LIARD RIVER
HOT SPRINGS

Juneau

Liard River

Sitka

Inside Passage

Muncho Lake
Provincial Park

37

Rocky

Stone Mountain
Provincial Park

97

Fort Nelson

Ketchikan

HYDER

Summit
Lake

Stewart

BRITISH COLUMBIA

Queen
Charlotte
Islands

Prince
Rupert

New
Hazelton

Mountains

ALASKA

35

GWAII HAANAS
NATIONAL PARK
RESERVE

Terrace

HIGHWAY

Fort St John

ALBERTA

16

97

Dawson
Creek

0   150 mi

0   150 km

2

Prince George

DAWSON CREEK

To Fort St John and
Delta Junction, Alaska

20TH ST

MILE ZERO RV
PARK AND
CAMPGROUND 97 ALASKA HWY

MILE ZERO CAFE

WALTER WRIGHT PIONEER VILLAGE

97 HART HWY

19TH ST

To Chetwynd
and Prince George

SUPER 8 MOTEL

ALASKA AVE

17TH ST 16TH ST GREYHOUND BUS DEPOT

CITY HALL

102ND AVE

15TH ST 14TH ST 13TH ST

7A ST 12TH ST

NAR PARK

MILE ZERO CAIRN

ALASKA
HOTEL/CAFE MILE ZERO
SIGNPOST

10TH ST

49

POST
OFFICE

11TH ST

To Peace River,
Alberta

SCALE NOT AVAILABLE

LIBRARY

106TH AVE

108TH AVE

8TH ST

110TH AVE

HOSPITAL

2

To The Granaries on Bear Mountain

To Airport and Grande Prairie, Alberta

NOON

Northern British Columbia

© AVALON TRAVEL PUBLISHING, INC.

10 A.M.–noon and 1–5 P.M.; $4). This marvelous and curious museum, housed in the original 1931 Northern Alberta Railway station, offers exhibits on a wide variety of topics, including construction of the Alaska Highway, the area's railroad history, pioneer life, and local flora and fauna. Among the unusual items on display: a rack of antlers estimated to be several thousand years old, a gas pump from the 1920s, a 1941 Massey-Harris cream separator, and the largest mammoth tusks found in western Canada.

In the annex of the towering grain elevator adjacent to the museum is the **Dawson Creek Art Gallery** (250/782-2601; June–Aug. daily 9 A.M.–5 P.M., the rest of the year Tues.–Fri.

10 A.M.–5 P.M.). The elevator itself is fascinating. It was saved from demolition and redesigned with a spiral walkway around the interior walls to make the most of the building's height.

Mile Zero

In front of N.A.R. Park is the **Mile Zero Cairn,** the Alaska Highway's official starting point. (The original marker was mowed down by a car in the 1940s.)

Despite the cairn's official status, the Mile Zero signpost in the center of 102nd Avenue at 10th Street is more often photographed. It reads "You are now entering the world famous Alaska Highway" and notes the following distances: Fort St.

John, 49 miles; Fort Nelson, 300 miles; White-horse, 918 miles; and Fairbanks, 1,523 miles.

Walter Wright Pioneer Village

One kilometer (.6 mile) west of N.A.R. Park at the Highway 97 split, this village of historical buildings holds two pioneer churches, a furnished log house, a general store, the Napoleon Loiselle Blacksmith Shop (containing many of his inventions), a trapper's cabin with handmade furniture, and two old schoolhouses. Scattered around are pieces of old farm machinery, tools, and equipment used by the area's first homesteaders. The village is named for the man responsible for finding and bringing all the buildings together. It's open June–September daily 10 A.M.–6 P.M.; admission is adult $5, senior or child $3.

Accommodations

In Dawson Creek, you can choose from regular motels spread along the Alaska Highway, such as the **Super 8 Motel** (1440 Alaska Ave., 250/782-8899 or 800/800-8000, www.super8.com; $99 s or d), or try one of following two options.

Dawson Creek's oldest and most colorful accommodation is the downtown **Alaska Hotel** (10209 10th St., 250/782-7998, www.alaska-hotel.com; $50–65 s, $55–75 d). Known as the Dew Drop Inn when it first opened in 1928, the hotel has been renovated in a colorful heritage style. Rooms remain basic, with no TVs or phones and shared bathroom facilities. A popular café and a pub are downstairs.

Located southwest of town, **ℕ The Granaries on Bear Mountain** (2106 Ski Hill Rd., 250/782-6304 or 888/782-6304, www.thegranaries.com; $160 s or d) is a wonderful surprise in a part of the province where roadside motels dominate. The guest rooms are ensconced in three circular granaries set around a manmade lake, with a profusion of colorful flowerbeds lining the shore-line. Each granary has been given a complete makeover—a snazzy new conical corrugated metal roof, sliding doors that open to a circular deck facing the lake, and a smart interior decor. Other features include cast-iron fireplaces, cooking facilities, jetted tubs, and a breakfast delivered to the door.

Campgrounds

Mile Zero RV Park and Campground (250/782-2590) isn't at Mile Zero of the famous highway—it's about one kilometer north from downtown—but it's the pick of Dawson Creek's numerous campgrounds. Sites sit around a large shaded grassy area, and each one has a picnic table. Facilities include hot showers and a laundry. Rates are $12–19 a night. Take Highway 97S west from town to reach **Northern Lights RV Park** (250/782-9433 or 888/414-9433; May–Oct.), which holds a mix of RV and tent sites ($17–23), an RV wash, free hot showers, and a laundry.

Food

The best-known eatery in town is the **ℕ Alaska Cafe,** in the Alaska Hotel (10209 10th St., 250/782-7040; daily from 11 A.M.). What originally opened as a candy store in the 1930s is today colorfully decorated in an old-fashioned style and serves tasty burgers, sandwiches, and croissants at lunch. The dinner menu is extensive and surprisingly adventurous, with choices such as asparagus crepes and bacon-wrapped scallops. I had the T-bone steak ($19), which was cooked exactly as I ordered it and came with a side of vegetables and a roasted potato piled high with fixings.

Mr. Mikes (1501 Alaska Ave., 250/782-1577; Sun.–Wed. 11 A.M.–11 P.M., Thurs.–Sat. 11 A.M.–midnight) is part of a small B.C. restaurant chain with a slickly presented format of healthy and modern food, well-versed waitpersons, and inviting decor. In Vancouver, it doesn't stand out; in Dawson Creek, it does. A burger and fries starts at $8, the vegetarian stir-fry is $11, or order a quality cut of Alberta beef for $19. British Columbian wines dominate the drink list.

Information

An almost obligatory stop for travelers heading north on the famous highway is **Dawson Creek Visitor Info Centre,** in the railway station at N.A.R. Park on Alaska Avenue (250/782-9595 or 866/645-3022, www.tourismdawsoncreek.com; May–Aug. daily 8 A.M.–7 P.M., Sept. Mon.–Sat.

9 A.M.–5 P.M., Oct.–Mar. Tues.–Sat. 10 A.M.–5 P.M., and Apr. Mon.–Sat. 9 A.M.–6 P.M.).

Transportation

Dawson Creek Municipal Airport is south of town on Highway 2. It's served by **Air Canada** (888/247-2262), which operates daily scheduled flights between Dawson Creek and southern B.C. cities, and **Hawk Air** (800/487-1216), with flights to Grande Prairie. From the **Greyhound** bus depot (1201 Alaska Ave. between 12th and 14th Streets, 250/782-3131) scheduled buses run between Dawson Creek and Prince George, Grande Prairie (Alberta), and north along the Alaska Highway to Whitehorse (Yukon).

North Toward Fort St. John

The initial 72 kilometers (45 miles) of the Alaska Highway between Dawson Creek and Fort St. John skirts nearly flat croplands and fields of wildflowers brilliantly abloom in summer. **Kiskatinaw Provincial Park,** 28 kilometers (17.4 miles) from Dawson Creek then four kilometers (2.5 miles) off the highway, straddles a short stretch of the original Alaska Highway, complete with a cambered trestle bridge over the Kiskatinaw River. The park is only 58 hectares (143 acres) but offers fishing and swimming in the Kiskatinaw River, plus camping (mid-May–Sept.; $14).

North of the park, the Alaska Highway descends through a steep ravine to the Peace River and the small township of **Taylor,** site of a huge oil refinery.

FORT ST. JOHN

As the second-largest community along the Alaska Highway (only Whitehorse, Yukon, is larger), Fort St. John (pop.15,100) is an important service center for local industries, including oil, gas, and coal extraction; forestry; and agriculture. It's one of the province's oldest nonnative settlements—the Beaver and Sekani tribes both occupied the area when white traders arrived in the 1790s—and served as a fur-trading post until 1823. But it wasn't until construction of the Alaska Highway began that Fort St. John really boomed.

DIGGING UP THE PAST

Overlooking Charlie Lake is **Charlie Lake Cave,** where buffalo bones and artifacts such as stone tools, a fluted basalt spear point, and a handmade stone bead have been discovered. Hunters may have hid there while chasing buffalo. Dated at 10,500 years old, this is the oldest such site discovered on the continent, leading archaeologists to postulate that this area was one of the earliest North American sites occupied by humans.

During the period of earliest occupation, Charlie Lake was a much larger body of water, an enormous ice-dammed lake where larger mammals were common. In the ensuing centuries, silt has built up on the floor of the cave, decreasing its original size.

The cave is on private property. Although access is not possible, a display in the Fort St. John–North Peace Museum tells the story of the cave dwellers and the archaeologists who excavated the site.

Fort St. John–North Peace Museum

You can't miss this museum complex (9323 100th St., 250/787-0430; summer daily 8 A.M.–8 P.M., the rest of the year Mon.–Sat. 11 A.M.–4 P.M.; adult $4, senior $3, child $2). Just look for the unique exhibits outside, including a skyscraping 40-meter-high **oil derrick** that came from Mile 143 of the Alaska Highway. In the museum local history springs to life with reconstructed historical interiors. A trapper's cabin recalls the original Rocky Mountain fort and fur-trading days, while the pioneer days are commemorated in fully furnished rooms, including a kitchen, bedroom, schoolroom, dentist's office, post office, outpost hospital, and blacksmith's shop. Don't miss the fur press, the birchbark canoe, and the grizzly bear with claws big enough to send shivers up your spine. Other exhibits detail the geological and mining ventures that the town thrives on today.

The museum also houses more than 6,000 restored and carefully cataloged artifacts; one display details the discovery in nearby Charlie Lake Cave of a bead and tools dating back some

10,500 years. Videos about the local area can be screened on request.

Peace River Canyon Lookout

This lookout provides splendid panoramic views taking in the wide, deep-green Peace River, its rocky canyon walls, and the lush fields along the canyon rim. From the museum/information center head south along 100th Street, crossing the Alaska Highway and continuing along the gravel road, which ends at the edge of the canyon. It's well worth the short drive.

Accommodations

Most motels in town are strung out along the Alaska Highway. One of the least expensive is **Blue Belle Motel** (9705 Alaska Hwy., 250/785-2613, $51 s, $57 d), where rooms have such amenities as microwaves and coffeemakers, while guests also have use of a barbecue and laundry facility.

The six-story **Quality Inn Northern Grand** (9830 100th Ave., 250/787-0521 or 800/663-8313, www.qualityinnnortherngrand.com; $109 s, $119 d) is a modern, full-service hotel with regularly revamped rooms that come with luxuries such as heated bathroom floors. There's also an indoor pool, a fitness room, a lounge, and a family-style restaurant. Book online for the best rates.

Campgrounds

Two small provincial parks with campgrounds lie along the shoreline of Charlie Lake, just over six kilometers (3.7 miles) north of town. **Charlie Lake Provincial Park,** at the junction of the Alaska Highway and Highway 29, is mainly a campground ($14 per site), while 312-hectare (770-acre) **Beatton Provincial Park,** on the lake's east shoreline, features beautiful aspen-lined hiking trails, a beach, boating, fishing, swimming, and camping ($14 per site). Both campgrounds are open mid-May to September and have facilities limited to pit toilets, picnic tables, fire rings, and drinking water.

For more facilities, check in to the **Rotary RV Park,** also beside Charlie Lake (Mile 52, Alaska Hwy., 250/785-1700). Amenities include hot showers and a laundry, and it's within walking distance of a general store and Jackfish Dundee's

restaurant. On the downside, there's not much shade. Sites are $12–18.

Food

Good coffee in Fort St. John is a relatively new phenomenon; try **Java on Main** (9905 100th Ave., 250/787-8424; Mon.–Sat. 7:30 A.M.–9 P.M., Sun. noon–6 P.M.) or, up the hill from the museum, **Cosmic Grounds** (10430 100th St., 250/261-6648; daily 7 A.M.–10 P.M.). For a substantial breakfast, head to **Fogg n' Suds,** in the Ramada Hotel (10103 98th Ave., 250/787-0779), which opens daily at 6 A.M.

My favorite place to eat in Fort St. John isn't in town, but 6.5 kilometers (four miles) north at Mile 52 of the Alaska Highway. **Jackfish Dundee's** (250/785-3233; daily 11 A.M.–10 P.M.) is in a big wooden building that has an inviting atmosphere and lake views. The food is delicious and well priced. Start with calamari with a tangy Thai sauce ($9) and choose from mains such as crab-stuffed sole ($15) and a juicy slab of Alberta beef ($18).

Information and Services

Fort St. John Visitor Info Centre (9523 100th St., 250/785-3033, www.cityfsj.com) is open May through mid-June daily 8 A.M.–6 P.M., mid-June through mid-September daily 8 A.M.–8 P.M., the rest of the year Monday–Friday 8 A.M.–5 P.M.

The **hospital** is on 100th Avenue, between 96th and 98th Streets (250/262-5200); the **post office** is on the corner of 101st Avenue and 102nd Street; and the **library** is on 100th Street between 106th and 107th Avenues.

The airport is about nine kilometers (5.6 miles) south of town and is serviced by **Air Canada** (888/247-2262) and **Central Mountain Air** (888/865-8585). The **Greyhound** bus depot is at 10355 101st Avenue (250/785-6695).

FORT ST. JOHN TO FORT NELSON

The 374-kilometer (232-mile) stretch of the Alaska Highway between Fort St. John and Fort Nelson passes through boreal forest and a landscape that becomes more and more mountainous.

It also provides one of your best chances of spotting wildlife, especially if you travel in the cool of the early morning. Species you may spy are moose, bear, deer, elk, and bison.

The first services north of Fort St. John are at Wonowon, 83 kilometers (52 miles) north of Fort St. John at Mile 102. The Husky gas station (250/772-3288) offers rooms from $60 and a few campsites for $18, as well as gas and a restaurant.

Pink Mountain

From Wonowon, the highway climbs steadily to Pink Mountain, at Mile 147. Numerous services perch on the low summit, where snow can fall year-round. On the west side of the highway, **Pink Mountain Campsite** (250/772-5133) provides tent and RV sites for $16 (power hookups). Showers are an extra $2.50. In typical northern fashion, it also has liquor, a laundry, and gas.

A few kilometers beyond the summit is **M Mae's Kitchen** (250/772-3215; year-round Mon.–Sat. 7 A.M.–10 P.M.), where breakfasts are huge and the pancakes ($6) and blueberry muffins ($3) are especially good. For lunch, try the house special buffalo burger, complete with fries and salad for $9.50.

Continuing northward, look for the "maintained" airstrip to the west—how would you like to land on that one? Not far north of Pink Mountain the highway passes into Pacific standard time—set your clock back one hour.

Sikanni Chief to Prophet River

The next services are 30 kilometers (19 miles) north of Pink Mountain at Sikanni Chief, where the highway passes through a low-lying area frequented by moose. The modern **Sikanni River RV Park** (250/772-5400) offers tent sites for $12, power/water hookups for $19, and small cabins with bathrooms and basic cooking facilities for $55 s, $65 d.

Twenty kilometers (12 miles) north from Sikanni Chief you'll pass the small **Buckinghorse River Wayside Provincial Park.** The river is alive with arctic grayling, providing the perfect meal for campers ($14 per site). From here north, a newer, scenic stretch of the highway runs through **Minaker River Valley** then parallels the **Prophet River,** passing a rustic campground (open May–Sept.; campsites $8) where a hiking trail leads down to the river. Farther along, at Mile 217, is the tiny community of **Prophet River,** with all visitor services.

North Toward Fort Nelson

The highway north to Fort Nelson was rerouted during 1991–1992, eliminating 132 bends and curves. The next place worth a detour, about 30 kilometers (19 miles) south of Fort Nelson and 12 kilometers (7.5 miles) south of the highway along a dirt road, is **Andy Bailey Provincial Park.** Adjacent to Jackfish Creek, the park has a sandy beach with good swimming, as well as fishing for northern pike and arctic grayling. Camping is $12 mid-May–mid-September.

FORT NELSON

At Mile 300 of the Alaska Highway, 454 kilometers (281 miles) north of Dawson Creek, Fort Nelson (pop. 4,300) is the largest town between Fort St. John and the Yukon. The **Muskwa, Prophet,** and **Sikanni Chief Rivers** all flow together here to create the large **Fort Nelson River,** which in turn flows into the even larger **Liard River** at Nelson Forks to the northwest. The earliest of many trading posts was built here in 1800. Over 200 years later, the town continues to be a supply center—now for the surrounding forestry, oil, and gas industries.

Sights

On the west side of the highway at the north end of town, **Fort Nelson Historical Museum** (250/774-3536; summer daily 8:30 A.M.–7:30 P.M.; adult $5, senior or child $3.25) contains a great collection of Alaska Highway construction items and native and pioneer artifacts. An interesting 30-minute movie, shown throughout the day, uses footage taken during the construction of the highway to effectively convey what a mammoth task the project was. The building is surrounded by machinery and vehicles used during the early days. Around back is a trapper's cabin crammed with antiques.

At the end of Mountain View Drive is the **Native Trail,** a four-kilometer (2.5-mile) self-guided interpretive trail that passes two native-style shelters and holds signs describing native foods, local wildlife, and trapping methods. Allow at least one hour round-trip.

Accommodations and Camping

Fort Nelson has many hotels and motels spread out along the Alaska Highway. The nicest is **Blue Bell Inn** (4103 50th Ave., 250/774-6961 or 800/663-5267; $64–99), next to the Petro-Canada gas station. The modern two-story lodging has air-conditioned rooms, a laundry, and an adjacent 24-hour restaurant.

Beside the museum is **Westend Campground** (250/774-2340; Apr.–Oct.), where you can choose from tent sites ($14) in an open area or hookups ($20–23) surrounded by trees. Facilities include coin-operated showers, a laundry, grocery store, RV service bays, and free firewood. On either side of town along the Alaska Highway, the closest camping is 30 kilometers (18.6 miles) south at **Andy Bailey Provincial Park** or 95 kilometers (59 miles) west at **Tetsa River Provincial Park.** Both facilities are open mid-May–mid-September and have no hookups. All sites are $14.

Food

As you enter town from the south, modern **Dan's Neighbourhood Pub** (4204 50th Ave. N, 250/774-3929; daily 11 A.M.–midnight) wouldn't look out of place in a big city—and it's always busy. All the usual fare is offered, with burgers $6–9, salads $4.50–8.50, and steak, chicken, and Mexican dishes from $11.

Information and Services

At Mile 300.5 of the Alaska Highway is **Fort Nelson Visitor Info Centre** (5319 50th Ave., 250/774-6868; mid-May–Sept. daily 8 A.M.–8 P.M., the rest of the year Mon.–Fri. 9:30 A.M.–4:30 P.M.). Here you can get information on road conditions and find out the current topics for the Welcome Visitor Program—a series of entertaining talks on local subjects, offered Monday–Thursday at 6:45 P.M.

The **post office** is on 51st Avenue. **Fort Nelson General Hospital** is at 5315 Liard Street (250/774-6916). The town also has plenty of gas stations, two banks, and a laundry.

From the **Greyhound** bus depot (5031 51st Ave., 250/774-6322) daily scheduled service runs south to Dawson Creek and northwest to Whitehorse.

CONTINUING TO WATSON LAKE

Awaiting the traveler on this 525-kilometer (326-mile) portion of the Alaska Highway are mountain peaks, glacial lakes, mountain streams, provincial parks with some great scenery, and the mighty Liard River.

Soon after leaving Fort Nelson you come to a junction with the gravel **Liard Highway,** which runs north 175 kilometers (109 miles) to Fort Liard in the Northwest Territories. From this junction, the Alaska Highway climbs the lower slopes of **Steamboat Mountain,** which, with a certain amount of imagination, resembles an upturned boat. Here you'll have tremendous views of the Rocky Mountains and the valley below. **Tetsa River Provincial Park,** 95 kilometers (59 miles) west of Fort Nelson and one kilometer (.6 mile) from the highway, offers grayling fishing in the river and short riverside hiking trails. A campground within the park has sites for $14 a night.

Summit Lake and Vicinity

This intensely blue lake, 140 kilometers (87 miles) west of Fort Nelson, is a popular stopping point for travelers. It lies at the north end of 25,691-hectare (63,480-acre) **Stone Mountain Provincial Park,** a vast wilderness at the northern reaches of the Rocky Mountains. Named for the predominantly stony nature of mountains that have been folded and faulted by massive forces deep below the Earth's surface, much of the park is above the tree line. For super-fit hikers, the best way to appreciate the landscape is by hiking the 2.6-kilometer (1.6-mile) **Summit Peak Trail,** which ends in a treeless alpine area a strenuous 1,000 vertical meters (3,300 feet) above the trailhead; allow at least two hours each way. The trailhead is on the north side of the highway, across from the campground. Much easier is the 2.5-kilometer (1.5-mile) trail to **Flower Springs Lake,** nestled in alpine peaks south of the highway. Allow one hour each way. The trailhead is three kilometers (1.9 miles) along Microwave Tower Road, which spurs south at the café.

At Summit Lake's eastern end is an exposed campground (expect snow any time of year) with pit toilets and picnic tables; $14 a night. Fishing in the lake is fair for rainbow trout and whitefish, although catch-and-release is encouraged. The **Summit Cafe** (daily 7 A.M.–10 P.M.) is a popular truck stop; hearty breakfasts are $4.50–10, and sandwiches and burgers start at $6.

Just beyond the lake, the highway crosses 1,295-meter (4,250-foot) **Summit Pass,** highest point along the Alaska Highway. From this lofty summit, the highway continues to **One-fifteen Creek Provincial Park,** where a short trail (allow 10 minutes round-trip) leads to huge beaver dams. Camping in the park is $14.

Toad River, 55 kilometers (34 miles) from Summit Lake and at Mile 422 of the Alaska Highway, is the next small service center. Here you'll find **Toad River Lodge** (250/232-5401, www.toadriverlodge.com), which has gas pumps and a restaurant (both open daily 6:30 A.M.–10 P.M.), old hotel-style rooms ($59 s, $64 d), simple cabins ($62 s, $67 d), tent sites ($15), and RV hookups ($22.50). Showers and firewood are free for campers and laundry costs $3 per load.

Muncho Lake Provincial Park

Lying among mountains and forested valleys at the north end of the Rocky Mountains, this 86,079-hectare (212,700-acre) park surrounds stunning **Muncho Lake,** one of the scenic highlights of the Alaska Highway.

As you enter the park from the east, **Folded Mountain** comes into view to the north. This easy-to-recognize peak is representative of the area's geology; it was created by extensive folding and faulting of limestone bedrock. But it's the park's namesake lake that will grab your attention. The magnificent, 12-kilometer-long (7.7-mile-

long) body of water is encircled by a dense spruce forest, which gives way to barren rocky slopes at higher elevations. Around three kilometers (1.9 miles) beyond the north end of the lake, natural mineral licks attract Stone sheep and woodland caribou to a roadside quarry. In the vicinity, a hiking trail leads to an escarpment above the Trout River; allow 20 minutes to walk the 1.5-kilometer (.9-mile) loop.

At around Mile 462 of the Alaska Highway, the small community of Muncho Lake spreads out along the eastern banks of the lake, providing services for park visitors. If you plan to overnight here, try to book ahead; motel rooms and campgrounds all fill up well in advance for July and August. **J & H Wilderness Motel & RV Resort** (250/776-3453) offers predictable motel rooms for $68 s or d as well as campsites with clean and modern facilities, including free hot showers, for $18–25. The resort's restaurant (daily 7 A.M.–10 P.M.) is particularly good, and portions are served with the trucker's appetite in mind; breakfasts from $4.50, dinners from $10, a burger with a huge portion of fries for $6.50. Spread along the lakeshore, ◼ **Northern Rockies Lodge** (250/776-3481 or 800/663-5269, www.northern-rockies-lodge.com) has a variety of accommodations, but a huge common room with a stone fireplace and towering cathedral ceiling brings it all together. Choose from older cabins and motel rooms ($69 s, $89 d), more comfortable rooms in the main lodge ($89 s, $99 d), or luxurious lakeside chalets ($160 s or d). RV sites by the lake are $22–35. Many guests visit as part of a fishing package, with services such as rentals and guides also available on a daily basis. The restaurant and a few lodge rooms are open year-round.

Campers who don't need serviced sites have the option of staying at two campgrounds in the provincial park itself, north of the town. Sites at these two campgrounds are all $14 a night, but with only 15 sites in each one, they fill up fast.

◼ Liard River Hot Springs

One of the most wonderful places to stop on the whole highway is this 1,082-hectare (2,670-acre) park, 40 kilometers (25 miles) north of

Muncho Lake. Most travelers understandably rush to soak their tired, dusty limbs in the hot pools. But the rest of the park is also worth exploring. Hot gases deep underground force heated ground water upward through a fault in the sedimentary rock. The water fills rock pools constructed by Alaska Highway workers in the 1940s, then overflows into a wide area of marshland. Even in the middle of winter, the water doesn't freeze, creating a microclimate of aquatic plants not normally associated with the northern latitude. Also inhabiting the swamp are many species of small fish plus mammals such as moose, woodland caribou, and black bear, as well as 100 species of birds.

A 500-meter (.3-mile) boardwalk leads from the main parking lot over warm-water swamps to **Alpha Pool,** where water bubbles up into a long, shallow concrete pool. The pool area, surrounded by decking, has pit toilets and changing rooms. A rough trail leads farther to undeveloped **Beta Pool,** which is cooler, much deeper, and not as busy.

At the entrance to the hot springs is a campground providing toilets and showers. Sites are $17 May–mid-October and $14 the rest of the year. In summer, a percentage of sites can be booked through www.discovercamping.ca. The rest (only 20 sites) are first-come, first-serve and are usually filled by noon each day. Gates to the hot springs and campground are locked between 11 P.M. and 6 A.M.

Opposite the park entrance, at Mile 497, is **Trapper Ray's Liard Hot Springs Lodge** (250/776-7349), which has rooms for $65 s or $70 d, campsites for $12–15, a small café, some grocery supplies, and gas. Back down the hill, at Mile 496, **Lower Liard River Lodge** (250/776-7341) offers rooms with shared facilities for $55 s, $60 d. This lodge has a great little café/restaurant and serves as the Greyhound bus stop.

To Watson Lake and Beyond

Anglers will find good fishing for grayling in the Liard River below **Smith River Falls,** 30 kilometers (19 miles) or so northwest of the hot springs. Canyon and river views dot the highway heading north and west, and visitor services are available at **Coal River** and **Fireside.** The highway crosses the 60th parallel and enters the Yukon just before Contact Creek Lodge (all services). It then meanders back and forth across the border

signpost forest at Watson Lake

© ANDREW HEMPSTEAD

six times before reaching the final crossing, 58 kilometers (36 miles) farther west.

Watson Lake (pop. 1,600), a major service center along the highway, lies just north of the British Columbia–Yukon border. The town is best known for the famous **Signpost Forest** started by Carl K. Lindley, a GI who was working on the Alaska Highway. Instructed to repair a directional sign, he added a mileage sign to his hometown of Danville, Illinois. Over the years others followed his lead, and today over 20,000 signs have been added. Behind the "forest" is the excellent **Visitor Reception Centre** (403/536-7469; summer daily 8 A.M.–8 P.M.). This facility provides visitors with historic information on the highway through extensive displays and an audiovisual presentation.

Twenty-one kilometers (13 miles) west of Watson Lake, the Alaska Highway meets the Stewart-Cassiar Highway, which leads south to the Yellowhead Highway between Prince George and Prince Rupert. The distance between Prince George and Watson Lake is almost identical via either the Alaska Highway or the Stewart-Cassiar Highway. The loop trip up one and back the other is around 2,450 kilometers (1,522 miles).

Continuing north on the Alaska Highway, it's 444 kilometers (276 miles) to Whitehorse, capital of the Yukon; 524 kilometers (326 miles) to Skagway, northernmost point of the Alaska Marine Highway; and 1,990 kilometers (1,237 miles) to Delta Junction, Alaska, the official end of the Alaska Highway. An excellent source of information for those continuing north is Don Pitcher's *Moon Handbooks Alaska.*

▶ ATLIN

The small community of Atlin is British Columbia's northernmost town and also the province's westernmost. It lies 370 kilometers (230 miles) west of Watson Lake along the Alaska Highway, then 100 kilometers (62 miles) south along a mostly unpaved road. Although isolated and a long way from the rest of the province, it's one of British Columbia's most picturesque and intriguing communities. The glaciated peaks of the Coast Mountains form a stunning backdrop for the town, which is on a gently sloping hill overlooking beautiful **Atlin Lake,** British Columbia's largest natural lake at over 135 kilometers (84 miles) long. The lake's southern end is within 301,140-hectare (744,120-acre) **Atlin Provincial Park,** which extends through the Coast Mountains, west to the Alaska border.

Atlin was a boomtown with more than 8,000 people during the 1898 Klondike gold rush, when gold was discovered in nearby Pine Creek. Today they're still finding some color hereabouts, but the town's population has dwindled to about 500.

Sights and Recreation

The highlight of Atlin is the surrounding scenery. The film adaptation of Farley Mowat's *Never Cry Wolf* was shot here, and it's easy to understand why. Wandering along the lakeshore you'll have outrageous views of sparkling peaks, glaciers, waterfalls, and mountain streams. Tied up on the lake in front of town is the **SS *Tarahme,*** a steamer built in 1916. The vessel plied the lake for 20 years, providing freight and transportation services. If you want to get out on the lake yourself, contact **Norseman Marine Adventures** (250/651-7535), which rents canoes ($20 per day), small motorboats ($20 per day), and houseboats (from $625 for four days).

Housed in a 1902 schoolhouse, **Atlin Historical Museum** (corner of 3rd St. and Trainor St., 250/651-7522; summer daily 9 A.M.–5:30 P.M.; $3) lets you relive the excitement of the gold rush and Atlin's early days and view a display of Tlingit artifacts. Scattered through town are many historic buildings and artifacts pretty much untouched from the gold-rush era. The **Pioneer Cemetery,** two kilometers (1.2 miles) east of town, reveals Atlin's pioneer history through stories and tales on weathered grave markers.

South of Atlin along Warm Springs Road are various lakes, camping areas, and, at the end of the road, **warm springs.** The springs bubble out of the ground at a pleasant 29°C (84°F) into shallow pools surrounded by flower-filled meadows.

Practicalities

The main accommodation in town is the **Atlin Inn** (1st St., 250/651-7546 or 800/682-8546). It's right in the center of town and has a café (open daily 7 A.M.–9 P.M.) and lounge with a lakeside patio. The rooms are as good as they get this far north, and at $105 s, $115 d they're still reasonable value. The inn also offers similarly priced kitchen-equipped cottages. An evening relaxing on a deck with sweeping lake-and-mountain views while freshly caught trout sizzle on the barbecue epitomizes the best of northern British Columbia—and **M Glacier View Cabins** (12 km/7.5 miles south of town along Warm Bay Rd., 250/651-7691, www.sidkatours.com; $80–110 s or d) is the place to do it. Each of the log cabins has a separate bedroom, bath-room, and cooking facilities (including the bar-becue on the deck). Hosts Peter and Edith Si-dler rent kayaks and canoes, as well as operate wilderness tours.

At the downtown marina, campsites with pow-ered hookups are $16. Book through **Norseman Marine Adventures** (250/651-7535). South of town, along the road to the warm springs, are four primitive **campgrounds.** The first of these, Pine Creek, has pit toilets and firewood but no drinking water; $5. The others at Palmer Lake, Atlin Lake, and the warm springs are free.

Atlin Visitor Info Centre is in the museum (250/651-7522; July–Aug. daily 9 A.M.–5:30 P.M., weekends only in June and Sept.). The local In-ternet service provider has links to town busi-nesses at www.atlin.net.

Know
British Columbia

The Land

British Columbia is Canada's third-largest province in area, behind Ontario and Quebec. Covering 948,596 square kilometers (366,252 square miles), it's four times larger than Great Britain, two and a half times as large as Japan, larger than all U.S. states except Alaska, and larger than California, Oregon, and Washington combined. The province is long north to south, relatively narrow east to west, and lies between the 49th and 60th parallels. Its largest city, Vancouver, is on the same latitude as Paris and the same longitude as San Francisco. To the south are the U.S. states of Washington, Idaho, and Montana; to the west the Pacific Ocean and the narrow panhandle of southeastern Alaska. To the north are Canada's Yukon Territory and Northwest Territories; to the east, across the Continental Divide, lies the Canadian province of Alberta. The land within those borders is dominated by mountain ranges, which trend northwest–southeast and are highest in the south.

Mountains

Mountains dominate British Columbia; half of the land area lies more than 1,000 meters (3,300 feet) above sea level. The province occupies part of the mountainous terrain that runs down the entire western margin of the Americas. It lies mainly in the Cordilleran Region, which is composed of Precambrian to Cenozoic rock formed into mountain ranges, deep intermountain troughs, and wide plateaus.

The landscape is defined by parallel north–south mountain ranges and a series of parallel valleys. The steep **Coast Mountains,** an unbroken chain extending for 1,500 kilometers (932 miles), rise abruptly from the Pacific Ocean. Their high point, and the highest peak completely in British Columbia, is 4,016-meter-high (13,180-foot-high) **Mount Waddington.** The province's highest point is shared with Alaska; 4,663-meter (15,300-foot) **Mount Fairweather** (sixth highest in Canada) is part of the **St. Elias Range,** a northern extension of the Coast Mountains that straddles the B.C.–Alaska border in the extreme northwest corner of the province. The province's eastern border is defined by the **Continental Divide** of the **Rocky Mountains,** which reach a high point north of the 49th parallel at 3,954-meter (13,000-foot) **Mount Robson.** In the south of the province between the Coast Mountains and the Rockies lie the **Columbia Mountains,** the collective name for the **Cariboo, Monashee, Selkirk,** and **Purcell Ranges.** These ranges rise to peak elevations of just over 3,000 meters (9,900 feet) and are separated by deep valleys and long, narrow lake systems. Only the highest of the Columbia Mountains—including some glaciated peaks in the Selkirks and Purcells—are snow-covered year-round. In the northern half of the province, the ranges are lower, wider, and less well-defined, rising to vast plateaus that extend hundreds of kilometers in all directions. The least obvious of the province's mountain ranges lies mostly underwater, off the west coast. The range rises above sea level at thousands of points, forming a string of islands, including Vancouver Island, whose high point is 2,200-meter (7,200-foot) **Mount Golden Hinde.**

Waterways

The province enjoys more than its share of waterways. Some 24,000 lakes, rivers, and streams contribute to British Columbia's two million hectares of freshwater surface area (approximately 2 percent of the province's landmass). The largest watershed is drained by the **Fraser River.** With its headwaters around Mt. Robson, this mighty river drains 233,000 square kilometers (90,000 square miles), almost 25 percent of the province, on its 1,368-kilometer (850-mile) journey to the Pacific Ocean at Vancouver. The Fraser is not the province's longest river, though. That title belongs to the 2,000-kilometer-long (1,240-mile-long) **Columbia River,** which follows a convoluted course through southeastern B.C.

before crossing the U.S. border and draining into the Pacific Ocean in Oregon.

The northern half of British Columbia comprises three major drainage basins: the 580-kilometer-long (360-mile-long) **Skeena River** flows westward through the heart of the province to the Pacific Ocean at Prince Rupert; the 1,900-kilometer-long (1,180-mile-long) **Peace River,** the only river system to cut across the Rocky Mountains, flows in a northeasterly direction into the Mackenzie River System, whose waters eventually flow into the Arctic Ocean; and in the far north, the **Liard River** drains a vast area of remote wilderness to also join the Mackenzie River.

Islands

British Columbia's deeply indented coastline comprises 6,500 islands. While most of these are uninhabited and many unexplored, the largest, 31,284-square-kilometer (12,100-square-mile) **Vancouver Island,** is home to over 500,000 people and holds the provincial capital (this island confusingly shares its name with the province's largest city, which lies on the mainland 50 kilometers/31 miles to the east). Between the mainland and Vancouver Island, 200 islands dot the Strait of Georgia, some of which are populated and all of which are protected from the wind- and wave-battering action of the Pacific Ocean by Vancouver Island. The other major island group is the **Queen Charlottes,** a remote archipelago linked geologically to Vancouver Island but with its own unique natural and human history.

CLIMATE

British Columbia's varied topography makes for radically varying **temperatures,** which rise or fall with changes in elevation, latitude, slope aspect, and distance from the ocean. The coastal region boasts the mildest climate of all Canada, but this comes with one drawback—it rains a lot. The two main cities, Vancouver and Victoria, lie within this zone. Most of the interior is influenced by both continental and maritime air, resulting in colder, relatively dry winters and hot, dry summers. And the northern latitudes are influenced by polar continental and arctic air masses, making for extremely cold, snowy winters and short, cool, wet summers.

Precipitation in British Columbia is strongly influenced by the lay of the land and the waft of the wind, resulting in an astonishing variation in rainfall from place to place. For example, Lillooet, in the sheltered Fraser River Valley, is Canada's driest community, whereas Port Renfrew on Vancouver Island's west coast averages 4,000 millimeters (157 inches) of precipitation annually. The amount of precipitation any given area receives is greatly determined by its location on the windward or lee side of the major mountain ranges—the windward side usually cops most of the downpour. Hence, the western side of the Coast Range is wet, the Interior Plateau on the east side of the Coast Range is relatively dry, and the western, windward side of the Rockies along the Alberta border is once again wet.

Flora and Fauna

FLORA

Two colors invariably jump to mind when you say "British Columbia": green and blue. Just about everywhere you travel in B.C. you see trees, trees, and more trees—around two-thirds of the province is forested. But the types of trees differ in each geographic and climatic region. Coastal regions are dominated by temperate rainforest, which requires at least 1,000 millimeters (40 inches) of rain annually and is predominantly evergreens. This biome is extremely rare: at the end of the last ice age it is estimated that .2 percent of the world's land area was temperate rainforest. Only 10 percent of these forests remain, 25 percent in British Columbia. This forest is mostly hemlock, western red cedar, and Sitka spruce. **Arbutus** (known as Pacific madrone in the United States) is an evergreen hardwood distinctive for its red bark and glossy oval-shaped leaves. It grows near saltwater at the southern end of Vancouver Island and on the Southern Gulf Islands. Forests of Douglas fir thrive in drier areas of the coast. Engelmann spruce is common throughout the interior at subalpine elevations. The interior also supports a mixture of Douglas fir and ponderosa pine in the south; interior western hemlock in the southeast; aspen and lodgepole pine in the central reaches; subboreal spruce, birch, and willow in the north; Sitka spruce in the west; and white spruce and black spruce in the northeast. The Queen Charlottes' rainforest is thickly covered in spongy pale green moss, which grows alongside coastal Douglas fir. In the region's subalpine areas you'll find mountain hemlock.

The official provincial floral emblem is the **Pacific dogwood,** a small tree sporting huge clusters of cream-colored flowers in spring and bright foliage and red berries in autumn. The tree is a protected plant in British Columbia; it's a punishable offense to pick from it or destroy it.

In summer, British Columbia turns on a really magnificent floral display. Wildflowers every color of the rainbow pop up on the roadsides—white and yellow daisies, purple lupines, pale pink and dark pink wild roses, bloodred Indian paintbrush, orange and black lilies, red and white clover, yellow buttercups, to name but a handful. And if you venture off the beaten track and up into the alpine meadows, the floral beauty is hard to believe. You can pick up a wildflower guide at most any local bookshop, and most of the national park visitor centers stock brochures on wildflower identification.

MAMMALS

British Columbia is one of the best provinces in Canada for wildlife watching. Thanks to a diverse topography that provides a wide variety of habitat, more species of mammals are found here than in any other province or territory in the country.

Bears

Two species of bears—black bears and grizzlies—are present in British Columbia. Both species are widespread and abundant across the province. The two can be differentiated by size and shape. Grizzlies are larger than black bears and have a flatter, dish-shaped face and a distinctive hump of muscle behind the neck. Color is not a reliable way to tell them apart. Black bears are not always black. They can be brown or cinnamon, causing them to be confused with the brown grizzly.

If you spot a bear feeding beside the road, chances are it's a **black bear.** These are the most common of all large mammals in British Columbia, estimated to number around 120,000, with the highest concentrations on Vancouver Island and the Queen Charlotte Islands. Their weight varies considerably (the larger ones are found in coastal areas), but males average 150 kilograms (330 pounds), females 100 kilograms (220 pounds). Their diet is omnivorous, consisting primarily of grasses and berries but supple-

© ANDREW HEMPSTEAD

Beavers are common in waterways across British Columbia.

mented by small mammals. They are not true hibernators, but in winter they can sleep for up to a month at a time before changing position. Young are born in late winter, while the mother is still asleep.

British Columbia's estimated 10,000 **grizzlies** are widespread in all mainland areas of the province but are only occasionally seen by casual observers. Most sightings occur along coastal areas (where they are generally called **brown bears**) during salmon runs (the Khutzeymateen, near Prince Rupert, is world-renowned as a grizzly viewing spot) and in spring and fall in alpine and subalpine zones. The bears' color ranges from light brown to almost black, with dark tan being the most common. On average, males weigh 250–350 kilograms (550–770 pounds). The bears eat small- and medium-sized mammals, and salmon and berries in fall. Like black bears, they sleep through most of the winter. When they emerge in early spring, the bears scavenge carcasses of animals that succumbed to the winter until the new spring vegetation becomes sufficiently plentiful.

The Deer Family

Mule deer and **white-tailed deer** are similar in size and appearance. Their color varies with the season but is generally light brown in summer, turning dirty gray in winter. While both species are considerably smaller than elk, the mule deer is a little stockier than the white-tailed deer. The mule deer has a white rump, a white tail with a dark tip, and large mule-like ears. It inhabits open forests along valley floors. The white-tailed deer's tail is dark on top, but when the animal runs, it holds its tail erect, revealing an all-white underside. White-tailed are common along valleys throughout British Columbia but especially prevalent on Vancouver Island. **Sitka** deer, a subspecies, inhabit the Queen Charlotte Islands.

The giant of the deer family, the **moose,** is an awkward-looking mammal that appears to have been designed by a cartoonist. It has the largest antlers of any animal in the world, stands up to 1.8 meters (5.9 feet) at the shoulder, and weighs up to 500 kilograms (1,100 pounds). Its body is dark brown, and it has a prominent nose, long spindly legs, small eyes, big ears, and an odd flap

Know British Columbia

WILDLIFE AND YOU

British Columbia's abundance of wildlife is one of its biggest drawcards. To help preserve this unique resource, obey fishing and hunting regulations and use common sense.

- **Do not feed the animals.** Many animals may seem tame, but feeding them endangers yourself, the animal, and other visitors. Animals become aggressive when looking for handouts.
- **Store food safely.** When camping, keep food in your vehicle or out of reach of animals. Just leaving it in a cooler isn't good enough.
- **Keep your distance.** Although it's tempting to get close to animals for a better look or a photograph, it disturbs the animal and, in many cases, can be dangerous.
- **Drive carefully.** The most common cause of premature death for larger mammals is being hit by cars.

Bears

Bears are dangerous, and while bear-human encounters happen regularly, their infamous reputation far exceeds the actual number of attacks that occur (in the last 20 years black bears have accounted for 12 fatalities and grizzly bears for five within British Columbia). That said, common sense is your best weapon against an attack. First and foremost, *keep a safe distance,* particularly if cubs are present—the protective mother will not be far away. *Never harass or attempt to feed a bear,* and resist the temptation to move in for an award-win-

ning close-up photo; they are wild animals and are totally unpredictable.

Before heading out on a hike, *ask local park or forest-service staff about the likelihood of encountering bears in the area,* and heed their advice. *Travel in groups,* never by yourself. Out on the trail, *watch for signs of recent bear activity,* such as fresh footprints or scat. *Make noise* when traveling through dense woods (take a noisemaker—a few rocks in a soft-drink can or a bell—or let out a loud yell every now and again to let wildlife know you're coming). *Bear spray* has become popular in recent years, but don't trust your life to it by taking unnecessary risks.

Bears will usually avoid you; however, you may come across the odd bruin. Bear talk is a favorite topic in the north, and everyone who has ever spent time in the wilderness has his or her own theory about the best course of action in the event of an encounter or an unlikely attack. On a few things, everyone agrees: *Stay in a group and back away slowly,* talking firmly the whole time; *do not run*—a bear can easily outrun a human. Black bears can climb trees but grizzlies can't. If an attack seems imminent and it's a black bear, the general consensus is to try to fight the animal off; if it's a grizzly, drop to the ground in a hunched-up position, covering your neck, and play dead.

Park staff can supply you with bear-aware literature, and many books have been written on the subject. One of the best is *Bear Attacks: Their Causes and Avoidance* (Lyons Press, 2002), by Canadian bear expert Stephen Herrero.

of skin called a bell dangling beneath its chin. Apart from all that, it's good-looking. Each spring the bull begins to grow palm-shaped antlers that by August will be fully grown. Moose are solitary animals, preferring marshy areas and weedy lakes, but they are known to wander to higher elevations searching out open spaces in summer. They forage in and around ponds on willows, aspen, birch, grasses, and all aquatic vegetation. They are most common in northern British Columbia.

The **elk** (also known as wapiti) has a tan body

with a dark-brown neck, dark-brown legs, and a white rump. This second-largest member of the deer family weighs 250–450 kilograms (550–990 pounds) and stands 1.5 meters (4.9 feet) at the shoulder. Pockets of elk inhabit valleys in the east of the province, but the animals are not particularly common.

Small populations of **woodland caribou** are restricted to the far north of the province. You may see them feeding in open areas at higher elevations along the Alaska Highway. Native people named the animal *caribou* (hoof scraper) for the way in which they feed in winter, scraping away snow with their hooves. Caribou are smaller than elk and have a dark-brown coat with creamy patches on the neck and rump.

Wild Dogs and Cats

Once inhabiting the region from Mexico to Alaska, the **wolf** was perceived as a threat by early European settlers and was the target of a relentless campaign to exterminate the species. Numbers have rebounded across the continent, including in British Columbia, where the vast wilderness is home to a widespread and stable population that numbers around 8,000 and is distributed across the province everywhere except the lower mainland and coastal islands. Wolves weigh up to 65 kilograms (145 pounds), stand a meter (3.3 feet) high at the shoulder, and resemble large huskies or German shepherds. Their color ranges from snow white to brown or black; those in British Columbia are most often shades of gray or brown. Unlike other predators they are not solitary but are intriguing animals that adhere to a complex social order, living in packs of 5–10 animals and roaming over hundreds of kilometers in search of prey.

The **coyote** is often confused for a wolf, when in fact it is much smaller, weighing up to only 15 kilograms (33 pounds). It has a pointed nose and long bushy tail. Its coloring is a mottled mix of brown and gray, with lighter-colored legs and belly. The coyote is a skillful and crafty hunter preying mainly on rodents. Coyotes have the remarkable ability to hear the movement of small mammals under the snow, allowing them to hunt these animals without actually seeing them. They are common and widespread at lower elevations throughout British Columbia (often patrolling the edges of highways and crossing open meadows in low-lying valleys).

Cougars (also called mountain lions, Mexican lions, pumas, and catamounts) are relatively plentiful in British Columbia, especially on Vancouver Island, where it is estimated the population numbers around 500. Adult males can grow to over two meters in length and weigh up to 90 kilograms (200 pounds). The fur generally ranges in color from light brown to a reddish-tinged gray, but occasionally black cougars are reported. Their athletic prowess puts Olympians to shame. They can spring forward more than eight meters from a standstill, leap four meters into the air, and safely jump from a height of 20 meters (66 feet). These solitary animals are versatile hunters whose acute vision takes in a peripheral span in excess of 200 degrees. They typically kill a large mammal such as a deer every two to three weeks, eating part of it and caching the rest. Their diet also includes coyotes, grouse, chipmunks, ground squirrels, and snowshoe hares.

The elusive **lynx** is identifiable by its pointy black ear tufts and an oversized tabby cat appearance. The animal has broad, padded paws that distribute its weight, allowing it to "float" on the surface of snow. It weighs up to 10 kilograms (22 pounds) but appears much larger because of its coat of long, thick fur. The lynx, uncommon but widespread throughout the interior, is a solitary creature that prefers the cover of subalpine forests, feeding mostly at night on snowshoe hares and other small mammals.

Sheep and Goats

Dall's sheep (also known as Rocky Mountain or bighorn sheep) are one of the most distinctive mammals of Canada. Easily recognized by their impressive horns, they are often seen grazing on grassy mountain slopes or at salt licks beside the road. The color of their coat varies with the season; in summer it's a brownish gray with a cream-colored belly and rump, turning lighter in winter. Bighorn sheep are particularly tolerant of humans and often approach parked vehicles; although they are not especially dangerous, you should not approach or feed them (as with all mammals).

The remarkable rock-climbing ability of nimble **mountain goats** allows them to live high in the mountains, retreating to rocky ledges or near-vertical slopes when threatened by predators.

Small Mammals

One of the animal kingdom's most industrious

WHALES OF BRITISH COLUMBIA

Whale-watching has gained great popularity off the B.C. coast in recent years. Most towns along the Vancouver Island coast offer trips out in various watercraft, many staying in sheltered waters where the whales are resting on migratory routes between Mexico and Alaska.

Once nearly extinct, today an estimated 20,000 **gray whales** swim the length of the British Columbia coast twice annually between Baja Mexico and the Bering Sea. The spring migration (March–April) is close to the shore, with whales stopping to rest and feed in places such as Clayoquot Sound and the Queen Charlotte Islands.

Orcas, best known as **killer whales,** are the largest member of the dolphin family. Adult males can reach 10 meters in length and up to 10 tons in weight, but their most distinctive feature is a dorsal fin that protrudes more than 1.5 meters from the back. Orcas are widespread in oceans around the world, but especially common along the B.C. coast, including Robson Bight, the world's only sanctuary established specially for the protection of the species. Three distinct populations live in B.C. waters: *resident* orcas feed primarily on salmon and travel in pods of up to 50; *transients* travel by themselves or in very small groups, feeding on marine mammals such as seals and whales; and *offshore* orcas live in the open ocean, traveling in pods and feeding only on fish. In total, they number around 500, with around 300 residents living in 15 pods.

Local waters are home to an abundance of other marine mammals. Porpoises, dolphins, and humpback whales frolic in coastal waters, and colonies of seals and sea lions can be viewed by boat or kayak.

mammals is the **beaver.** Growing to a length of 50 cm (20 inches) and tipping the scales at around 20 kilograms (44 pounds), it has a flat, rudderlike tail and webbed back feet that enable it to swim at speeds up to 10 kph (6.2 mph). The exploration of western Canada can be directly attributed to the beaver, whose pelt was in high demand in fashion-conscious Europe in the early 1800s. The beaver was never entirely wiped out from the mountains, and today the animals inhabit almost any forested valley with flowing water. Beavers build their dam walls and lodges of twigs, branches, sticks of felled trees, and mud. They eat the bark and smaller twigs of deciduous plants and store branches underwater, near the lodge, as a winter food supply.

Several species of **squirrel** are common in British Columbia, including the golden-mantled ground, Columbian, and red squirrels. **Marmots** are common and widespread, with various species living in different habitats. They are stocky creatures, weighing 4–9 kilograms (9–20 pounds). The **porcupine,** a small, squat animal, is easily recognized by its thick coat of quills. It eats roots and leaves but is also known for being destructive around wooden buildings and vehicle tires.

REPTILES

Reptiles don't like cold climates, and therefore they don't like Canada. British Columbia is home to just 17 of the world's 10,000-odd reptile species. All 17 inhabit dry, hot valleys of grassland, such as the Okanagan Valley. The breakdown includes nine species of snakes, five turtles, two lizards, and one species of skink. The province's only poisonous snake is the extremely rare **western rattlesnake,** which lives in the southern interior. Like other rattlers, it waits for prey rather than actively hunting and won't bite unless provoked.

BIRDS

Of the 454 bird species recorded in British Columbia, 300 breed within the province (the most of any province or territory), and of these, 35

Wander along the shoreline at low tide and you'll come across a wealth of marine life.

species nest nowhere else in Canada. The lower mainland is a migration stop for the million-odd birds that travel the Pacific Flyway each year. Huge populations of waterfowl winter at Boundary Bay near Vancouver, and large concentrations can also be seen around Fort St. James, Cranbrook, Prince George, and Lac La Hache. The province is home to half of the world's populations of both trumpeter swans and blue grouse, as well as a quarter of the world's bald eagles. You'll see beautiful Canada and snow geese, trumpeter and whistling swans, and all kinds of ducks.

British Columbia's official bird is the often-cheeky, vibrant blue-and-black **Steller's jay,** found throughout the province.

FISH

Of the 72 species of fish in British Columbia, 22 are considered sportfish. The two varieties most sought after by anglers are salmon, found in tidal waters along the coast, and trout, inhabiting the freshwater lakes and rivers of interior British Columbia. (For more information on fishing, please see *Recreation.*)

Salmon

Five species of salmon are native to the tidal waters of British Columbia. All are *anadromous;* that is, they spend their time in both freshwater and saltwater. The life cycle of these creatures is truly amazing. Hatching from small red eggs often hundreds of miles upriver from the ocean, the fry find their way to the ocean, undergoing massive internal changes along the way that allow them to survive in saltwater. Depending on the species, they then spend 2–6 years in the open water, traveling as far as the Bering Sea. After reaching maturity, they begin the epic journey back to their birthplace, to the exact patch of gravel on the same river from where they emerged. Their navigation system has evolved over a million years, using, it is believed, a sensory system that uses measurements of sunlight, the earth's magnetic field, and atmospheric pressure to find their home river. Once the salmon are in range of their home river, scent takes over, returning them to the exact spot where they were born. Once the salmon reach freshwater they stop eating. Unlike other species of fish (including Atlantic salmon), Pacific salmon die immediately after spawning; hence the importance of returning to their birthplace, a spot the salmon instinctively know gives them the best opportunity for their one chance to reproduce successfully.

Largest of the five salmon species is the **chinook,** which grows to 30 kilograms (66 pounds) in B.C. waters. Known as king salmon in the United States, chinooks are a prized sportfish most recognizable by their size but also by black gums and silver-spotted tails.

Averaging 2–3 kilograms (4.4–6.6 pounds), **sockeye** (red salmon) are the most streamlined of the Pacific salmon. They are distinguished from other species by a silvery-blue skin and prominent eyes. While other species swim into the ocean after hatching, the sockeye remain inland, in freshwater lakes and rivers, for at least a year before migrating into the Pacific. When it's ready to spawn, the body of the sockeye turns bright red and the head a dark green.

Chum (dog) salmon are very similar in appearance to sockeye, and the bodies also change dramatically when spawning; a white tip on the anal fin is the best form of identification. Bright, silver-colored **coho** (silver) average 1.5–3 kilograms (3.3–6.6 pounds). This species can be recognized by white gums and spots on the upper portion of the tail.

Smallest of the Pacific salmon are the **pinks,** which rarely weigh over four kilograms (nine pounds) and usually average around two. Their most dominant feature is a tail covered in large oval spots. They are most abundant in northern waters in even-numbered years and in southern waters in odd-numbered years.

Freshwater Fish

Trout are part of the same fish family as salmon, but, with one or two exceptions, they live in freshwater their entire lives. Interestingly, the trout of British Columbia are more closely related to Atlantic salmon than to any of the species of Pacific salmon detailed above. The predominant species is the **rainbow trout,** common in lakes and rivers throughout the province. It has an olive-green back and a red strip running along the center of its body. Many subspecies exist, such as the large Gerrard rainbow trout of the southern interior; the steelhead, an ocean-going rainbow, inhabits rivers flowing into the Pacific Ocean.

Other trout species present include the **bull trout,** which struggles to survive through high levels of fishing and a low reproductive cycle. **Cutthroat trout,** found in high-elevation lakes, are named for a bright red dash of color that runs from below the mouth almost to the gills. Colorful **brook trout** can be identified by their dark-green backs with pale splotches and purple-sheened sides. **Brown trout** are the only trout with both black and red spots.

The **lake trout,** which grows to 20 kilograms (44 pounds), is native to large, deep lakes throughout the province, but it is technically a member of the char family. The **kokanee** is a freshwater salmon native to major lakes and rivers of the southern interior. They are directly related to sockeye salmon and look similar in all aspects but size (kokanee rarely grow to over 30 cm/12 inches in length), spawning in the same freshwater range as sockeye.

The **whitefish,** a light gray fish, is native to lower elevation lakes and rivers across the province. **Arctic grayling** and **Dolly Varden trout** (named for a colorful character in a Charles Dickens story) inhabit northern waters. **Walleye** (also called pickerel) grow to 4.5 kilograms (10 pounds) and are common in sandy-bottomed areas of lakes in northeastern British Columbia. The monster freshwater fish of British Columbia is the **sturgeon,** growing to over 100 kilograms (220 pounds) in size and living for upwards of 100 years.

History

THE EARLIEST INHABITANTS

Human habitation of what is now British Columbia began around 15,000 years ago, when *Homo sapiens* migrated from northeast Asia across a land bridge spanning the Bering Strait. During this time, the northern latitudes of North America were covered by an ice cap, forcing these people to travel south down the west coast before fanning out across the ice-free southern latitudes. As the ice cap receded northward, the people drifted north also, perhaps only a few kilometers in an entire generation, and began crossing the 49th parallel about 12,000 years ago. By the time the ice cap had receded from all but the far north and the highest mountain peaks, two distinct cultures had formed—one along the coast and one in the interior. Within these two broad groups, many tribes formed, developing distinct cultures and languages.

The Northwest Coast

Around 12,000 years ago, Canada's west coast had become ice-free, and humans had begun settling along its entire length. Over time they had broken into distinct linguistic groups, including the **Coast Salish, Kwagiulth, Tsimshian, Gitksan, Nisga'a, Haida,** and **Tlingit,** but all had two things in common: their reliance on cedar and on salmon. They lived a very different lifestyle from the stereotypical "Indian"—they had no bison to depend on, they didn't ride horses, nor did they live in tepees, but instead developed a unique and intriguing culture that remains in place in small pockets along the west coast. These coastal bands lived comfortably off the land and the sea, hunting deer, beaver, bear, and sea otters; fishing for salmon, cod, and halibut; and harvesting edible kelp. They built huge 90-meter-long cedar houses and 20-meter-long dugout cedar canoes, and developed a distinctive and highly decorative arts style featuring animals, mythical creatures, and oddly shaped human forms believed to be supernatural ancestors.

West coast native society emphasized the material wealth of each chief and his tribe, displayed to others during special events called potlatches. The potlatch ceremonies marked important moments in tribal society, such as marriages, puberty celebrations, deaths, or totem-pole raisings. The wealth of a tribe became obvious when the chief gave away enormous quantities of gifts to his guests—the nobler the guest, the better the gift. The potlatch exchange was accompanied by much feasting, speech-making, dancing, and entertainment, all of which could last many days. Stories performed by hosts garbed in elaborate costumes and masks educated, entertained, and affirmed each clan's historical continuity.

The Interior Salish

Moving north with the receding ice cap around 10,000 years ago, the Salish fanned out across most of southwestern and interior British Columbia. After spending summers in the mountains hunting and gathering, they would move to lower elevations to harvest their most precious natural resource—salmon. At narrow canyons along the Fraser River and its tributaries, the Salish put their fishing skills to the test, netting, trapping, and spearing salmon as the fish traveled upstream to spawn. Much of the catch was preserved by drying or roasting, then pounded into a powder known as "pemmican" for later use or to be traded. The Salish wintered in earth-covered log structures known as pit houses. Depressions left by these ancient structures can still be seen in places such as Keatley Creek, alongside the Fraser River. Within the Salish Nation, four distinct tribes have been identified: the Lillooet, the Thompson (Nlaka'pamux), the Okanagan, and the Shuswap. The Shuswap occupied the largest area, with a territory that extended from the Fraser River to the Rocky Mountains; they were the only Salish who crossed the Rockies to hunt buffalo on the plains.

TOTEM POLES

Traveling through British Columbia you can't help but notice all the totem poles decorating the landscape. Totem poles are made of red (or occasionally yellow) cedar painted black, red, blue, yellow, and white, with colored pigment derived from minerals, plants, and salmon roe. They are erected as validation of a public record or documentation of an important event. Six types of poles are believed to have evolved in the following order: house post (an integral part of the house structure), mortuary (erected as a chief's or shaman's grave post, often with the bones or ashes in a box at the top of the pole), memorial (commemorating special events), frontal (a memorial or heraldic pole), welcome, and shame poles. None is an object of worship; each tells a story or history of a person's clan or family. The figures on the pole represent family lineage, animals, or a mythical character.

Since 1951, when a government ban on potlatch ceremonies (of which the raising of totem poles is an integral part) was lifted, the art form has been revived. Over the years, many totem poles have been moved from their original locations. Both historic and more modern poles can be viewed in British Columbia. The Haida, of the Queen Charlotte Islands, were renowned for their totem poles; many totem villages, long since abandoned, remain on the remote southern tip of the archipelago. Of these, **Ninstints** is regarded as the world's best example of an ancient Haida totem village. More modern totems can be found at **Stanley Park,** Vancouver; **Thunderbird Park,** Victoria; **Alert Bay,** Cormorant Island; and **Kitwancool,** at the south end of the Stewart–Cassiar Highway. The **Museum of Anthropology** in Vancouver also has an excellent collection.

You'll see totem poles in coastal communities throughout British Columbia.

The Kootenay

The Kootenay (other common spellings include Kootenai, Kootenae, and Kutenai) were once hunters of buffalo on the great American plains, but they were pushed westward by fierce enemies. Like the Salish did farther west, they then moved north with the receding ice cap. They crossed the 49th parallel around 10,000 years ago, settling in the Columbia River Valley, along the western edge of the Canadian Rockies. Like the Salish, they were hunters and gathers and came to rely on salmon. The Kootenay were generally friendly, mixing freely with the Salish and treating the earliest explorers, such as David Thompson, with respect. They regularly traveled east over the Rockies to hunt—to the wildlife-rich Kootenay Plains or farther south to the Great Plains in search of bison.

The Athabascans

Athabascan (often spelled Athapaskan) is the most widely spread of all North American linguistic groups, extending from the Rio Grande to Alaska. In 1793, when Alexander Mackenzie made his historic journey across the continent, he spent the last summer before reaching the west coast in Athabascan territory, which at that time included most of what is now northern British Columbia. The largest division of the Athabascans within this area was the **Carrier** group, so named for their custom requiring a woman to carry the ashes of her husband with her for a least a year. Aside from the fact that they cremated their dead, the Carrier had similar traits to those found throughout the Athabascan peoples—they lived simply and were generally friendly toward each other and neighboring tribes. They lived throughout the northern reaches of the Fraser River basin and along the Skeena River watershed. The Carrier, along with Athabascan tribes that lived farther north (including the Chilcotin, Tahltan, and Inland Tlingit) adopted many traits of their coastal neighbors, such as potlatch ceremonies and raising totem poles. Another Athabascan group inhabiting British Columbia was the **Beaver,** who were forced westward, up the Peace River watershed, by the warlike Cree (the name Peace River originated after the two groups eventually made peace). With no access to salmon-rich waters west of the Rocky Mountains, the Beaver hunted bison, moose, and caribou and were strongly influenced by the fur trade. Over the subcontinental divide to the north is the upper watershed of the mighty Mackenzie River; extending into the northeast corner of the province, this area was the traditional home of the **Slavey,** one of seven groups of the Dene (DEN-ay) people. Like the Beaver, they were nomadic hunters and gatherers but also relied heavily on fishing.

EUROPEAN EXPLORATION AND COLONIZATION

It was only a little more than 200 years ago that the first European explorers began to chart the northwest corner of North America. The area's geography presented formidable natural barriers to the east (the lofty Rocky Mountains) and the west (long stretches of ocean away from other landmasses).

By Sea

In the second half of the 18th century, curiosity about a western approach to the fabled Northwest Passage and a common desire to discover rich natural resources lured Russian, Spanish, British, and American explorers and fur traders along the coastline that is now British Columbia. In 1774, the ship of Mexican **Juan Perez** was the first vessel to explore the coastline and trade with the natives. He was quickly followed by Spaniard **Don Juan Francisco de la Bodega y Quadra,** who took possession of the coast of Alaska for Spain. England's **Captain James Cook** arrived in 1778 to spend some time at Nootka, becoming the first nonnative to actually come ashore, trading with the natives while he overhauled his ship. Cook received a number of luxuriantly soft sea otter furs, which he later sold at a huge profit in China. This news spawned a fur-trading rush that began in 1785 and continued for 25 years. Ship after loaded ship called in along the coast, trading iron, brass, copper, muskets, cloth, jewelry, and rum to the natives in exchange for furs. The indigenous people were eager to obtain the foreign goods, but they were also known for driving a hard bargain. The traders took the furs directly to China to trade for silk, tea, spices, ginger, and other luxuries. In 1789, Bodega y Quadra established a settlement at Nootka, but after ongoing problems with the British (who also claimed the area), he gave it up. In 1792, **Captain George Vancouver,** who had been the navigator on Cook's 1778 expedition, returned to the area and sailed into Burrard Inlet, claiming the land for Great Britain.

By Land

In the meantime, adventurous North West Company fur traders were crossing the Rockies in search of waterways to the coast. The first European to reach the coast was **Alexander Mackenzie,** who traveled via the Peace, Fraser, and West Road Rivers—you can still see the rock in the Dean Channel (off Bella Coola) where he inscribed "Alexander Mackenzie from Canada by land 22nd July 1793." Not far behind came other explorers, including **Simon Fraser,** who followed the Fraser River to the sea in 1808, and **David Thompson,** who followed the Columbia River to its mouth in 1811. Today the names of these men grace everything from rivers to motels. In the early 19th century, the North West Company established trading posts in **New Caledonia** (the name Simon Fraser gave to the northern interior). These posts were taken over by Hudson's Bay Company after amalgamation of the two companies in 1821.

The Native Response

The fur trade brought prosperity to the indigenous society, which was organized around wealth, possessions, and potlatches. The Hudson's Bay Company had no interest in interfering with the natives and, in general, treated them fairly. This early contact with Europeans resulted in expanded trade patterns and increased commerce between coastal and interior tribes. It also spurred the production of indigenous arts and crafts to new heights, as chiefs required more carved headgear, masks, costumes, feast dishes, and the like for the increasingly frequent ceremonial occasions that came with increased wealth.

However, commerce between the Europeans and locals also caused the indigenous tribes to abandon their traditional homesites and instead to cluster around the forts for trading and protection. In addition, the Europeans introduced muskets, alcohol, and disease (most significantly smallpox), all of which took their toll on the native population, which stood at around 60,000 in 1850. Christian missionaries soon arrived and tried to ban the natives' traditional potlatches. But not until land-grabbing white colonists showed up did major conflicts arise between native peoples and whites. Those land-ownership conflicts proved tenacious, continuing to this day.

Vancouver Island

The British government decided in 1849 that Vancouver Island should be colonized to confirm British sovereignty in the area and forestall any American expansion. Though mostly content to leave the island in the hands of the Hudson's Bay Company, the Brits nevertheless sent

Richard Blanshard out from England to become the island colony's first governor. Blanshard soon resigned and was replaced in 1851 by **James Douglas,** chief factor of the Hudson's Bay Company. Douglas had long been in control of the island, and his main concerns were to maintain law and order and to purchase land from the natives. He made treaties with the tribes in which the land became the "entire property of the white people forever." In return, tribes retained use of their village sites and enclosed fields, and could hunt and fish on unoccupied lands. Each indigenous family was paid a pitiful compensation.

In 1852, coal was discovered near Nanaimo, and English miners were imported to develop the deposits. Around the same time, loggers began felling the enormous timber stands along the Alberni Canal, and the Puget Sound Agricultural Association (a subsidiary of Hudson's Bay Company) developed several large farms in the Victoria region. By the 1850s, the town of Victoria, with its moderate climate and fertile soil, had developed into an agreeable settlement.

LAW, ORDER, AND GOLD

Firsts

In 1856 the first parliament west of the Great Lakes was elected, and Dr. J. S. Helmcken became speaker. (Today you can still see his house in Victoria.) Only two years later this still relatively unexplored and quiet part of the world was turned upside down with the first whispers of "gold" on the mainland, along the banks of the Fraser River. As the news spread, miners—mostly Americans—arrived by the shipload at Victoria, increasing the town's population from several hundred to more than 5,000. Fur trading faded as gold mining jumped to the forefront. Realizing that enormous wealth could be buried on the mainland, the British government quickly responded by creating a mainland colony that at first was named New Caledonia. Because France possessed a colony of the same name in the South Pacific, Queen Victoria was asked to change the name, which she did, using "Columbia," which appeared on local maps, and adding "British," making the name distinct from the Columbia River district across the border. In 1858, Governor James Douglas of Vancouver Island also became governor of B.C., giving up his Hudson's Bay Company position to serve both colonies. In 1866 the two colonies were combined into one.

Cariboo Gold

The lucrative Cariboo gold rush resulted in construction of the Cariboo Wagon Road (also called the Gold Rush Trail), an amazing engineering feat that opened up British Columbia's interior. Completed in 1865, the road connected Yale with Barkerville, one of the richest and wildest gold towns in North America. Mule trains and stagecoaches plied the route, and roadhouses and boomtowns dotted its entire length. Among the colorful characters of this era was Judge Matthew Baillie Begbie, an effective chief of law and order during a time when law and order might as easily have been nonexistent.

In addition to the gold miners, groups of settlers soon began arriving in the Cariboo. One such group, a horde known as the **Overlanders,** left Ontario and Quebec with carts, horses, and oxen in summer 1862, intent on crossing the vast plains and the Rockies to British Columbia. One detachment rafted down the Fraser River, the other down the North Thompson. Both arrived in Kamloops in autumn that same year. Some continued north up the Cariboo Gold Rush Trail, but others headed for the coast, having had more than their fill of adventure on the trip across.

Rapid Development

In addition to the Cariboo Wagon Road, other trails opened up more of the province in the early 1860s. The Hope-Princeton and Dewdney Trails into the Kootenays led to settlement in B.C.'s eastern regions. Salmon canning was also developed in the 1860s, and several canneries on both the lower Fraser and Skeena Rivers had the world market in their pockets. (You can still see one of the old canneries near Prince Rupert today.)

It wasn't until 1862 that Burrard Inlet—site of today's city of Vancouver—sprang onto the map with the building of a small lumber mill on the north shore. The region's tall, straight trees became much in demand. More lumber mills started up, and a healthy export market developed in only a few years. Farmers began to move into the area, and by the end of the 1860s a small town had been established. "Gassy Jack" Deighton started a very popular saloon on the south shore of Burrard Inlet near a lumber camp, and for some time the settlement was locally called Gastown. After the townsite was surveyed in 1870, the name was changed to Granville. Then in 1886, the town was officially renamed Vancouver, in honor of Captain George Vancouver. At this time, New Westminster was the official capital of the colony of British Columbia, much to the concern and disbelief of Vancouver Islanders, who strongly believed Victoria should have retained the position. Two years later, with the mainland gold rushes over, the capital reverted to Victoria, where it has remained ever since.

Confederation and Beyond

The next big issue to concern British Columbia was confederation. The eastern colonies had become one large dominion, and B.C. residents were invited to join. London and Ottawa both wanted B.C. to join to assist in counterbalancing the mighty U.S. power to the south. After much public debate, the southwesternmost colony entered the Confederation as the Province of British Columbia in July 1871—on the condition that the west coast be connected to the east by railway. Many roads were built during the 1870s, but it was the completion of the transcontinental railway in 1885 that really opened up B.C. to the rest of the country. Other railways followed, steamships plied the lakes and rivers, more roads were built, and industries—including logging, mining, farming, fishing, and tourism—started to develop.

During the 20th century, B.C. moved from roads to major multilane highways, from horses to ferries, and from gold mining to sportfishing.

Yet it still attracts explorers—backcountry hikers and mountain climbers in search of untrammeled wilderness, plenty of which remains.

THE PEOPLE

When British Columbia joined the confederation to become a Canadian province in 1871, its population was only 36,000, and 27,000 of the residents were natives. With the completion of the Canadian Pacific Railway in 1885, immigration during the early 20th century, and the rapid industrial development after World War II, the provincial population burgeoned. Between 1951 and 1971 it doubled. Today 3.7 million people live in British Columbia (12 percent of Canada's total). The population is concentrated in the southwest, namely in Vancouver, on the south end of Vancouver Island, and in the Okanagan Valley. These three areas make up less than 1 percent of the province but account for 80 percent of the population. The overall population density is just 3.5 people per square kilometer.

British Columbia is second only to Alberta as Canada's fastest growing province. Annual population growth through the 1990s averaged 2.5 percent, against a national average of 1.1 percent. Around 60 percent of this population growth can be attributed to westward migration across the country. Retirees make up a large percentage of these new arrivals, as to a lesser extent do young professionals.

Around 40 percent of British Columbians are of British origin, followed by 30 percent of other European lineage, mostly French and German. To really get the British feeling, just spend some time in Victoria—a city that has retained its original English customs and traditions from days gone by. First Nations make up 3.7 percent of the population. While the native peoples of British Columbia have adopted the technology and the ways of the European, they still remain a distinct group, contributing to and enriching the culture of the province. Asians have made up a significant percentage of the population since the mid-1800s, when they came in search of gold. More recently, the province saw an influx of settlers from Hong Kong prior to the 1997 transfer of control of that city from Britain to China.

Language

The main language spoken throughout the province is English, though almost 6 percent of the population also speaks French, Canada's second official language. All government information is written in both English and French throughout Canada.

The natives of British Columbia fall into 10 major ethnic groups by language: Nootka (west Vancouver Island), Coast Salish (southwest B.C.), Interior Salish (southern interior), Kootenay (in the Kootenay region), Athabascan (in the central and northeastern regions), Bella Coola and Northern Kwakiutl (along the central west coast), Tsimshian (in the northwest), Haida (on the Queen Charlotte Islands), and Inland Tlingit (in the far northwest corner of the province). However, most natives still speak English more than their mother tongue.

Economy and Government

ECONOMY

British Columbia's economy has always relied on resource-based activities. The first indigenous people hunted the region's abundant wildlife and fished in its trout- and salmon-filled rivers. Then Europeans arrived on the scene, reaping a bounty by cutting down forests for timber and slaughtering the wildlife for its fur. Luckily, the province is blessed with a wealth of natural resources. In addition to timber and wildlife, B.C. holds rich reserves of minerals, petroleum, natural gas, and coal, and water for hydroelectric power is plentiful.

As rising population numbers have put ever-increasing demands on these resources, conservation measures have become necessary. The province has imposed fishing and hunting seasons and limits, a freeze on rezoning agricultural land, and mandatory reforestation regulations, and has restrained hydroelectric development to protect salmon runs. By preserving its superb physical environment, the province will continue to attract outdoor enthusiasts and visitors from around the world, ensuring a steady stream of tourism revenues. But the ongoing battle between concerned conservationists and profit-motivated developers continues.

Forestry

Almost two-thirds of British Columbia—some 60 million hectares (148 million acres)—is forested, primarily in coniferous softwood (fir, hemlock, spruce, and pine). These forests provide about half the country's marketable wood and about 25 percent of the North American inventory. Along the coast the hemlock species is dominant; in the interior are forests of spruce and lodgepole pine. Douglas fir, balsam, and western red cedar are the other most valuable commercial trees. The provincial government owns 94 percent of the forestland, private companies own 5 percent, and the national government owns the remaining 1 percent. Private companies log much

of the provincially owned forest under license from the government. Around 75 million cubic meters of lumber are harvested annually, directly employing 85,000 workers. The forestry industry generates $10 billion annually in exports, more than all other industries combined.

Forestry has been the mainstay of the economy in this century. But pressures on the industry are steadily increasing as the demand grows to preserve the forests for wildlife, recreation, and as a resource for following generations.

Tourism

Tourism has rapidly ascended in economic importance; it's now the second-largest industry and the province's largest employer (more than 200,000 are directly employed in the industry). This segment continues to grow, as more and more people become aware of B.C.'s outstanding scenery; its numerous national, provincial, historic, and regional parks; and the bountiful outdoor recreation activities available year-round. **Tourism BC** promotes British Columbia to the world; latest figures record 26 million annual "visitor nights" (the number of visitors multiplied by the number of nights they stayed within British Columbia). Official visitor numbers are broken down to show that four million visitors were Canadians from outside British Columbia, four million were from the United States, while one million visitors originated from outside North America (Japan, Great Britain, and Germany provided most of these).

Mining

British Columbia is a mineral-rich province, and historically mining has been an important part of the economy. Since the first Cariboo gold rush in the late 1850s, the face of the industry has changed dramatically. Until the mid-1900s, most mining was underground, but today open-pit mining is the preferred method of mineral extraction. The province is home to 26 major mines and three mineral processing plants that produce $3.6 billion worth of exports. Coal is the most valuable sector of the mining industry, accounting for $800 million of exports (most to Japan and other Asian markets). Other mining is for metals (such as copper, gold, zinc, silver, molybdenum, and lead), industrial minerals (sulfur, asbestos, limestone, gypsum, and others), and structural materials (sand, gravel, dimension stone, and cement). In northeastern B.C., drilling for petroleum and natural gas also helps fuel the economy.

Agriculture

Cultivated land is sparse in mountainous B.C.—only 4 percent of the province is arable, with just 25 percent of this land regarded as prime for agriculture. Nevertheless, agriculture is an important part of the provincial economy; 19,000 farms growing 200 different crops contribute $1.4 billion annually. The most valuable sector of the industry is dairy farming, which is worth $260 million (that works out to an output of 510 million liters of milk a year). The best land for dairy cattle is found in the lower Fraser Valley, on southeast Vancouver Island, and in the north Okanagan-Shuswap areas. Almost all of British Columbia's fruit crops are grown in the Okanagan Valley; apples are the best-known produce, but a burgeoning viticulture industry relies on grapes from 50 vineyards. The province holds around 600,000 beef cattle, with these farms mainly found in the Cariboo, Chilcotin, Kamloops, Okanagan, and Kootenay regions. Although neighboring Alberta is renowned for its beef, Canada's largest ranch is operated by the Douglas Lake Cattle Co. near Merritt; 20,000 cattle are run on 200,000 hectares (494,000 acres). Poultry farms, vegetables, bulbs, and ornamental shrubs are found mostly in the Fraser River Valley and the southern end of Vancouver Island, while the northern Peace River region is the provincial grain basket, supporting a mixture of cereal crops. Agriculture provides an estimated 55–60 percent of the food required for British Columbia's needs.

Fishing

Commercial fishing, one of B.C.'s principal industries, is worth $1 billion annually and comes

commercial halibut fishermen at work

© ANDREW HEMPSTEAD

almost entirely from species that inhabit tidal waters. The province has 6,000 registered fishing boats and 600 fish farms. The industry concentrates on salmon (60 percent of total fishing revenues come from six species of salmon), with boats harvesting the five species indigenous to the Pacific Ocean and the aquaculture industry revolving around Atlantic salmon, which is more suited to farming. Other species harvested include herring, halibut, cod, sole, and shellfish, such as crabs. Canned and fresh fish are exported to markets all over the world—the province is considered the most productive fishing region in Canada. Japan is the largest export market, followed by Europe and the United States.

Recreational salt- and freshwater sportfishing for salmon, steelhead, and trout is also very popular. More than 600 licensed fishing guides, sportfishing lodges, and charter operators scattered throughout the province eagerly offer their services and expertise to both resident and nonresident fishing enthusiasts.

Film Industry

The film industry is the fastest-growing sector of the provincial economic pie; its value has quadrupled since 1997 to be worth $1.4 billion annually and to directly employ 35,000 locals. The province is ideal both as a location for shooting and as a production center (Vancouver ranks third behind only Los Angeles and New York as a production center, with 70 post-production facilities). Since the late 1970s more and more Hollywood production companies have discovered the beauty of B.C., its studio facilities, on-site production crews, and support services, as well as more recently a favorable exchange rate. The industry is overseen by the **BC Film Commission** (604/660-2732, www.bcfilmcommission.com).

Shipping and Maritime Commerce

The province boasts year-round ports, deep-sea international shipping lanes, log-towing vessels, specialized freight and passenger steamers, and all the requisite marine facilities. The United States and Japan are B.C.'s main export and import trading partners.

GOVERNMENT

Canada is a constitutional monarchy. Its system of government is based on England's, and the British monarch is also king or queen of Canada. However, because Canada is an independent nation, the British monarchy and government have no control over the political affairs of Canada. An appointed **governor general** based in Ottawa represents the Crown, as does a **lieutenant governor** in each province. Both roles are mainly ceremonial, but their "royal assent" is required to make any bill passed by Cabinet into law.

Elected representatives debate and enact laws affecting their constituents. The head of the federal government is the **prime minister,** and the head of each provincial government is its **premier.** The **speaker** is elected at the first session of each parliament to make sure parliamentary rules are followed. A bill goes through three grueling sessions in the legislature—a reading, a debate, and a second reading. When all the fine print

Parliament buildings in Victoria

has been given the royal nod, the bill then becomes a law.

In the B.C. legislature, the lieutenant governor is at the top of the ladder. Under him are the members of the **Legislative Assembly** (MLAs). Assembly members are elected for a period of up to five years, though an election for a new assembly can be called at any time by the lieutenant governor or on the advice of the premier. In the Legislative Assembly are the premier, the cabinet ministers and backbenchers, the leader of the official opposition, other parties, and independent members. All Canadian citizens and B.C. residents 19 years old and over can vote, providing they've lived in the province for at least six months.

The current ruling party is Gordon Campbell's **Liberal Party,** which swept to power in April 2001. Provincial politics in British Columbia have traditionally been a two-party struggle. In the most recent election, the Liberals defeated the New Democrats (NDP), who came to be reviled by the business community for tax burdens that stalled the local economy. The NDP first came to prominence in the late 1960s as the official opposition to the **Social Credit Party** (Socreds), advocating free enterprise and government restraint, who had ruled the province for two decades. After a 1972 NDP election win, the support of these two parties seesawed back and forth until 1991, when the Social Credit Party was almost totally destroyed by a string of scandals that went as high as the premier, Bill Vander Zalm.

The laws of B.C. are administered by the cabinet, premier, and lieutenant governor; they are interpreted by a **judiciary** made up of the Supreme Court of B.C., Court of Appeal, and County or Provincial Courts.

For information on the provincial government, its ministries, and current issues, surf the web to www.gov.bc.ca.

Recreation

The great outdoors: British Columbia certainly has plenty of it. The province encompasses some 948,600 square kilometers (366,250 square miles) of land area and a convoluted coastline totaling 25,000 kilometers (15,500 miles). With spectacular scenery around every bend, millions of hectares of parkland, and an abundance of wildlife, the province is an outdoorsperson's fantasy come true. Hiking, mountain climbing, fishing, hunting, boating, canoeing, whitewater rafting, scuba diving, downhill and cross-country skiing—it's all here. For specific recreation information, contact **Tourism British Columbia** (250/387-1642 or 800/435-5622, www.hellobc.com).

HIKING

Just about everywhere you go in British Columbia you'll find good hiking opportunities, from short, easy walks in city and regional parks to long, strenuous hikes in wilderness parks.

The mountains are great places to hike. Short trails lead to waterfalls, lakes, rock formations, and viewpoints, and longer trails wander high into alpine meadows tangled with wildflowers, past turquoise lakes, and up to snow-dusted peaks providing breathtaking views. Rustic huts are provided at regular intervals along wilderness trails. Perhaps the best known of British Columbia's hikes lies not in the Rockies but along the wild and remote west shore of Vancouver Island; backpackers return time and again to the **West Coast Trail,** an unforgettable 77-kilometer (48-mile) trek through Pacific Rim National Park.

To get the most out of a hiking trip, peruse the hiking section of any major bookstore—many books have been written on British Columbian hiking trails. Before setting off on a longer hike, study the trail guides and a topographical map of the area. Leave details of your intended route and itinerary with a relative or friend. And try to travel in groups of at least two in the backcountry.

NATIONAL PARK PASSES

Permits are required for entry into all Canadian national parks. A **National Parks Day Pass** is adult $7, senior $6, child $3.50 up to a maximum of $14 ($12 for two or more seniors) per vehicle. It is interchangeable among parks and is valid until 4 P.M. the day following its purchase. An annual **National Parks of Canada Pass,** good for entry into all of Canada's national parks for one year from the date of purchase, is adult $45, senior $38, child $22 up to a maximum of $89. The **Heritage Package Pass** (adult $59, senior $49 to a maximum of $119 per vehicle) is a good choice for history buffs. It allows unlimited entry into both national parks and national historic sites (six of which are in British Columbia) for a full year from purchase.

Annual and day passes are available at park gates, at all park information centers, and at campground fee stations. Day passes are also available from automated ticket machines at popular stopping points in Pacific Rim National Park. For more information, check the Parks Canada website (www.pc.gc.ca).

CYCLING AND MOUNTAIN BIKING

Cycling is a great way to explore British Columbia. The casual pace allows riders time to stop and appreciate the scenery, wildlife, and flowers that can easily be overlooked at high speeds. Some of the most popular areas for cycling trips are the **Southern Gulf Islands** between Vancouver Island and the mainland (quiet, laid-back, loads of sunshine, rural scenery, and lots of artists), the **east coast of Vancouver Island** (following the Strait of Georgia past lazy beaches and bustling towns), the **Kootenays** (forest-clad mountains, deep lakes, curious old gold- and silver-mining communities, and ghost towns—good mountain-bike country), and the **Rockies** (outstanding mountain scenery second to none, abundant wildlife often right beside the highways, hot springs, and hiking trails). Rocky Mountain routes suit the intermediate to advanced cyclist.

For information on touring, tour operators, bicycle routes, and local clubs, contact **Cycling B.C.** (Suite 332, 1367 W. Broadway, Vancouver, 604/737-3034) or, in the same building, the **Outdoor Recreation Foundation of B.C.** (604/737-3058). The Outdoor Recreation Foundation also publishes a series of maps covering much of British Columbia. These maps can by purchased directly from the council or at many sporting goods stores

and bookstores. A good source of online information is the **British Columbia Mountain Bike Guide** (www.bcmbg.com).

Biking Tours

Several companies offer cycling tours, among them **Benno's Adventure Tours** (604/738-5105), which offers eight-day trips through B.C. and the Canadian Rockies; **Backroads Whistler** (604/923-3111, www.backroadswhistler.com), through the Whistler Valley and beyond; **Backroads** (510/527-1555 or 800/462-2848, www.backroads.com), with a wide variety of trips through the region; and **VBT** (800/245-3868, www.vbt.com), which offers a seven-day ride through the national parks of the Canadian Rockies.

ON THE WATER
Canoeing and Kayaking

Canoes are a traditional form of transportation along British Columbia's numerous lakes and rivers. You can rent one at many of the more popular lakes, but if you bring your own you can slip into any body of water whenever you please, taking in the scenery and viewing wildlife from water level. One of the most popular canoe routes is in **Bowron Lake Provincial Park,** where a 117-kilometer (73-mile) circuit leads through a chain of lakes in the Cariboo Mountains.

PARKS AND PROTECTED AREAS

In response to a United Nations report on land use, the provincial government initiated a Protected Areas Strategy in 1992, which had at its core the aim of protecting 12 percent of land area at a time when just 6 percent was protected. As well as preserving the environment, the land use planning process involved creating recreational opportunities while also continuing sustainable economic development in areas that had relied on natural resources. To do this successfully the strategy included not only government and environmentalists, but also industry, the First Nations, and local communities. It was a huge undertaking, but in 2001 British Columbia surpassed the 12 percent goal, making it one of the first jurisdictions worldwide to do so. In just eight years the province managed to double its area of parks and protected areas—an increase of 4.8 million hectares.

Today visitors and locals alike enjoy over 800 protected areas totaling 11.7 million hectares (29 million acres) throughout British Columbia. From old-growth coastal rainforests to glaciated peaks and ranging in size from less than one hectare to over a million hectares (2.5 million acres), these parks provide almost unlimited recreation opportunities.

National Parks

British Columbia holds seven of Canada's 40 national parks. The most accessible is also the newest, **Southern Gulf Islands National Park,** which was created in 2003 by piecing together existing provincial and marine parks scattered throughout the archipelago. **Pacific Rim National Park** protects a stretch of Vancouver Island's rugged west coast, offering long beaches, remote islands, and the famous West Coast Trail to explore. In the east of the province, **Kootenay** and **Yoho National Parks** form a part of the UNESCO Rocky Mountains World Heritage Site; the two spectacular mountain parks lie just across the Continental Divide from the more famous Banff and Jasper National Parks in neighboring Alberta. Also protecting a mountainous landscape are **Glacier** and **Mount Revelstoke National Parks** along the TransCanada Highway. The most remote of B.C.'s national parks is **Gwaii Haanas** on the Queen Charlotte Islands. No roads access this park, which encompasses the southern half of an archipelago renowned the world over for ancient Haida villages. For general national park information, contact **Parks Canada** (www.pc.gc.ca).

Shorter but no less challenging is the **Powell Forest Canoe Route,** on the Sunshine Coast. Other, less-traveled destinations include **Slocan Lake, Wells Gray Provincial Park,** and the **Stikine River.** For information on canoe routes, courses, and clubs, contact the **Outdoor Recreation Council of B.C.** (604/737-3058, www.arcbc.ca).

Anywhere suitable for canoeing is also prime kayaking territory, although most keen kayakers look for white-water excitement. The best wilderness kayaking experiences are in the north, where access can be difficult but crowds are minimal. The **Stikine River** is challenging, with one stretch—the Grand Canyon of the Stikine—successfully run only a handful of times.

The province's long coastline is great for sea kayaking, and rentals are available in most coastal communities. The **Gulf Islands** are ideal for kayakers of all experience levels, while destinations such as **Desolation Sound,** the **Broken Group Islands,** and the **Queen Charlotte Islands** are the domain of experienced paddlers. Most outfits offering kayak rentals also provide lessons and often tours. One such Vancouver operation is the **Ecomarine Ocean Kayak Centre** (604/689-7520, www.ecomarine.com) based on Granville Island. Tofino, on Vancouver Island's west coast, is a mecca for sea kayakers. **Tofino Sea Kayaking Company** (250/725-4222 or 800/863-4664, www.tofino-kayaking .com) rents kayaks and leads tours through local waterways. **Northern Lights Expeditions** (360/734-6334 or 800/754-7402, www.sea kayaking.com) specializes in overnight expeditions along the B.C. coast. Each Northern Lights

Provincial Parks

BC Parks manages more than 800 protected areas, including almost 500 provincial parks. Many are day-use areas, others have campgrounds, but all have one thing in common—they protect a particularly scenic area, a unique natural feature, a wildlife habitat, or maybe a fish-filled lake.

Among these are: **Cypress Provincial Park,** on Vancouver's city limits and offering great views; **Carmanah Walbran Provincial Park,** protecting a magnificent old-growth forest on Vancouver Island; **Manning Provincial Park,** a high alpine area of snowcapped peaks and colorful flower-filled meadows; **Kokanee Glacier Provincial Park,** named for its spectacular icefield; **Mount Assiniboine Provincial Park,** a rugged Rocky Mountain wilderness perfect for extending hiking trips; **Mount Robson Provincial Park,** protecting the Canadian Rockies' highest peak; **Bowron Lake Provincial Park,** famous for its wilderness canoe route; and **Naikoon Provincial Park,** on the Queen Charlotte Islands.

Major new parks added in the last decade include **Valhalla Provincial Park,** a remote wilderness area in the heart of the Kootenays; **Khutzeyma-teen Provincial Park,** an important coastal grizzly bear habitat; the 6.5-million-hectare (16-million-acre) **Muskwa-Kechika Wilderness Area** of the northern Canadian Rockies; and, in the province's extreme northwest corner, **Tatshenshini-Alsek Provincial Park,** part of the world's largest UNESCO World Heritage Site.

For information on provincial parks, contact **BC Parks** (www.bcparks.ca), a division of the **Ministry of Water, Land, and Air Protection** (www.gov.bc.ca/wlap).

Forest Service Lands

Over half of British Columbia (59 million hectares/146 million acres) is forested and under the control of the Ministry of Forests, which manages the land for timber harvesting, recreational activities, and just as plain wilderness. Many recreation areas have been provided on forest land, but facilities are often limited. Get more information on recreation areas, forest roads, safety, and possible fire closures from the **Ministry of Forests** (www.gov.bc.ca/for), regional offices, or information centers throughout the province.

---

trip features three knowledgeable guides, all necessary equipment, and an emphasis on gourmet meals, such as shoreline salmon bakes, complete with wine and freshly baked breads. The six-day trip through the Strait of Georgia is US$1,395, but Northern Lights also offers other trips, including the luxury of a lodge-based trip for US$1,895.

White-Water Rafting

The best and easiest way to experience a white-water rafting trip is on a half- or full-day trip with a qualified guide. Close to Vancouver, the **Green, Fraser, Nahatlatch,** and **Thompson Rivers** are run commercially. In the Rockies, the **Kicking Horse River** provides the thrills. Expect to pay $90–120 for a full day's excitement, transfers, and lunch.

No experience is needed for most extended river trips. Close to Vancouver, the classic of these runs the Chilko, Chilcotin, then Fraser Rivers and lasts up to two weeks. In the far north of the province, the Tatshenshini and Alsek Rivers are a popular destination. **Canadian River Expeditions** (604/392-9195 or 800/898-7238, www.canriver.com), Canada's oldest rafting company, offers trips to both destinations for just over $4,000.

Boating

British Columbia's 25,000 kilometers (15,500 miles) of coastline, in particular the sheltered, island-dotted Strait of Georgia between Vancouver Island and the mainland, is a boater's paradise. Along it are sheltered coves, sandy beaches, beautiful marine parks, and facilities specifically designed for boaters—many accessible only by water. One of the most beautiful marine parks is **Desolation Sound,** north of Powell River; locals claim it's one of the world's best cruising grounds. Many of the enormous freshwater lakes inland are also excellent places for boating.

Yachties and yachties-to-be should head for **Cooper Boating** (1620 Duranleau St., Granville Island, 604/687-4110 or 888/999-6419, www.cooperboating.com), which boasts Canada's largest sailing school and also holds the country's biggest fleet for charters. For those with experience, Cooper's rents yachts (from $370 per day for a Catalina 32) for a day's local sailing, or take to the waters of the Strait of Georgia on a bareboat charter (from $1,451 per week for a Catalina 27).

Scuba Diving

Some of the world's most varied and spectacular cold-water diving lies off the coast of British Columbia. Diving is best in winter, when you can expect up to 40 meters of visibility. The diverse marinelife includes sponges, anemones, soft corals, rockfish (china, vermilion, and canary), rock scallops, and cukes. Plenty of shipwrecks also dot the underwater terrain. The most popular dive sites are off the Southern Gulf Islands, Ogden Point in Victoria, Nanaimo (for wreck diving), Telegraph Cove, Port Hardy, and Powell River (the scuba diving capital of Canada). Many of the coastal communities along Vancouver Island and the Sunshine Coast have dive shops with gear rentals and air tanks, and many can put you in touch with charter dive boats and guides.

A quick flip through the Vancouver Yellow Pages lets you know that scuba diving is alive and well north of the 49th parallel. The city's many scuba shops have everything you need, and they're excellent sources of information on all the best local spots. Coming highly recommended is **Rowand's Reef Scuba Shop** (1512 Duranleau St., Granville Island, 604/669-3483, www.rowandsreef.com; daily 10 A.M.–6 P.M.), a full-service dive shop offering rentals, sales, organized diving trips, and PADI dive-certification courses throughout the year. Available here and in most local bookstores are the diver's bibles *101 Dives from the Mainland of Washington and British Columbia* and *99 Dives from the San Juan Islands in Washington to the Gulf Islands,* both by Betty Pratt-Johnson. The local *Diver* magazine (www.divermag.com) is another good source of information; its scuba directory lists retail stores, resorts, charter boats, and other services.

FISHING
Freshwater

The province's freshwater anglers fish primarily for trout—mostly rainbow trout, but also Dolly Varden, lake, brook, brown, and cutthroat trout. One particular type of rainbow trout, the large anadromous **steelhead,** is renowned as a fighting fish and considered by locals to be the ultimate fishing challenge. Salmon are also abundant in the province; several seagoing species come up B.C.'s rivers to spawn. **Kokanee** rarely grow over one kilogram (2.2 pounds), but this freshwater salmon is an excellent sport fish inhabiting lakes of the southern interior. Feeding near the surface and caught on wet or dry artificial flies, they taste great, especially when smoked.

Fishing guides, tours, lodges (from rustic to luxurious), and packages are available throughout the province; one is sure to suit you. Expect to pay $200–400 a day for a guide, and up to several thousand dollars for several days at a luxury lodge with all meals and guided fishing included.

Fishing licenses are required, and prices vary according to your age and place of residence. Canadian residents pay $36 for a freshwater adult license, good for one year. All other Canadians pay $20 for a one-day license, $36 for an eight-day license, or $55 for a one-year. Nonresidents pay $20, $50, and $80, respectively. For more information contact the **Ministry of Water, Land, and Air Protection** (250/387-4573, www.gov.bc.ca/wlap) and request the *British Columbia Freshwater Fishing Regulations Synopsis.*

Tidal

The tidal waters of the Pacific Northwest offer some of the world's best fishing, with remote lodges scattered along the coast catering to all budgets. And although most keen anglers will want to head farther afield for the best fishing opportunities, many top fishing spots can be accessed on a day trip from Vancouver. The five species of Pacific salmon are most highly prized by anglers. The chinook (king) salmon in particular is the trophy fish of choice. They commonly weigh over 10 kilograms (22 pounds) and are occasionally caught at over 20 kilograms (44 pounds); those weighing over 12 kilograms (26.5 pounds) are often known as "tyee." Other salmon present are coho (silver), pink (humpback), sockeye (red), and chum (dog). Other species sought by local recreational anglers include halibut, lingcod, rockfish, cod, perch, and snapper.

A tidal-water sportfishing license for residents of British Columbia, good for one year from March 31, costs $22.47 ($11.77 for those 65 and over); for nonresidents, the same license costs $108.07, or $7.49 for a single-day license, $20.33 for three days, and $34.17 for five days. A **salmon conservation stamp** is an additional $6.42. Licenses are available from sporting stores, gas stations, marinas, and charter operators. When fish-tagging programs are on, you may be required to make a note of the date, location, and method of capture, or to record on the back of your license statistical information on the fish you catch. Read the current rules and regulations. For further information contact **Fisheries and Oceans Canada** (604/664-9250, www.pac.dfo-mpo.gc.ca).

The **Sport Fishing Institute of British Columbia** (604/270-3439, www.sportfishing.bc.ca) produces an annual magazine (free), *Sport Fishing,* that lists charter operators and fishing lodges and details license requirements.

GOLFING

Relative to the rest of Canada, British Columbia's climate is ideal for golfing, especially on Vancouver Island, where the sport can be enjoyed year-round. Many of the province's 280 courses are in spectacular mountain, ocean, or lake settings. Municipal courses offer the lowest greens

fees, generally $10–25, but the semiprivate, private, and resort courses usually boast the most spectacular locations. At these courses, greens fees can be as high as $225. At all but the smallest municipal courses, club rentals, power carts, and lessons are available, and at all but the most exclusive city courses, nonmembers are welcomed with open arms. The mild climate and abundance of water create ideal conditions for the upkeep of golf courses in the south of the province—you'll be surprised at how immaculately manicured most are. (In the north, many courses have oil-soaked or artificial-grass greens to make upkeep easier.)

SKIING AND SNOWBOARDING

Most of the developed winter recreation areas are in the southern third of the province. Whether you're a total beginner or an advanced daredevil, British Columbian resorts have a slope to suit you. The price of lift tickets is generally reasonable, and at the smaller, lesser-known resorts, you don't have to spend half your day lining up for the lifts.

The best known of all Canadian winter resorts is **Whistler/Blackcomb,** north of Vancouver, but others scattered through the southern interior provide world-class skiing and boarding on just-as-challenging slopes. The best of these include: **Big White Ski Resort** and **Silver Star Mountain Resort** in the Okanagan Valley; **Red Mountain** and **Whitewater** near Nelson; **Fernie Alpine Resort** near Fernie; **Panorama Resort** near Invermere; and **Sun Peaks Resort** north of Kamloops. In the north, **Powder King Mountain Resort,** north of Prince George, lives up to its name with an average annual snowfall around 12 meters/39 feet (among the highest of any North American resort). You can even go skiing and boarding out on Vancouver Island at **Mt. Washington Alpine Resort.**

Heli- and Sno-Cat Skiing and Boarding

Alternatives to resorts are also available. If you're an intermediate or advanced skier or snowboarder,

© DEAN THOMPSON/SOLSTICE PHOTOGRAPHY

snowboarding at Whistler

you can go heli-skiing and heli-boarding in the mind-boggling scenery and deep, untracked powder of the Coast and Chilcotin Ranges, the central Cariboo Mountains, the Bugaboos, and the British Columbia Rockies. The world's largest heli-ski operation is **CMH Heli-skiing** (403/762-7100 or 800/661-0252, www .cmhski.com), founded by Austrian mountain guide Hans Gmoser in the Bugaboos in 1965. Today the operation has grown to include almost limitless terrain over five mountain ranges accessed from 11 lodges. **Mike Wiegele Helicopter Skiing** (250/673-8381 or 800/661-9170, www.wiegele.com) offers heli-skiing and heli-boarding in the Monashee and Cariboo Mountains from a luxurious lodge at Blue River. From Panorama Resort, near Invermere, **R.K. Heliski** (250/342-3889 or 800/661-6060, www.rkheliski.com) offers heli-skiing day trips, one of the only operators to do so.

Another, less-expensive alternative is to hook up with one of the many Sno-Cat operations in the province. Sno-Cats are tracked, all-terrain vehicles that can transport skiers and boarders up through the snow to virgin slopes in high-country wilderness (similar to snow groomers but capable of carrying passengers). British Columbia has been a world leader in this type of skiing, and many operators are scattered through the province. Revelstoke is the Sno-Cat capital of the province. In this central B.C. town, **CAT Powder Skiing** (250/837-5151 or 800/991-4455, www.catpowder.com) offers day trips or overnight packages from its Revelstoke base. Through its location amid some of the continent's most consistent powder snow and because of its luxurious lodgings, **Island Lake Lodge** near Fernie (250/423-3700 or 888/422-8754, www.islandlakelodge.com) has gained a reputation for both its Sno-Cat skiing and its luxurious lodgings.

SHOPPING FOR NATIVE ARTS AND CRAFTS

Indigenous artistry tends to fall into one of two categories: "arts," such as woodcarving and painting, argillite carving, jade- and silverwork, and totem restoration (all generally attended to by the men), and "handicrafts," such as basketry, weaving, beadwork, skinwork, sewing, and knitting (generally created by the women). Today, all of these arts and crafts contribute significant income to First Nations communities.

Painting and woodcarving are probably the most recognized art forms of the northern west coast tribes. Throughout B.C.—in museums and people's homes, outdoors, and of course in all the shops—you can see brightly colored carved totems, canoes, paddles, fantastic masks, and ceremonial rattles, feast dishes, bowls, and spoons. Fabulous designs, many featuring animals or mythical legends, are also painstakingly painted in bright primary colors on paper. You can buy limited-edition, high-quality prints of these paintings at many Indian craft outlets. They are more reasonable in cost than carvings, yet just as stunning when effectively framed.

Basketry comes in a variety of styles and materials. Watch for decorative cedar-root (fairly rare) and cedar-bark baskets, still made on the west coast of Vancouver Island; spruce-root baskets from the Queen Charlotte Islands; and beautiful, functional, birch-bark baskets from the Hazelton area, between Prince George and Prince Rupert.

Beaded and fringed moccasins, jackets, vests, and gloves are available at most craft outlets. And all outdoorspersons should consider forking out for a heavy, water-resistant, raw-sheep-wool sweater; they're generally white or gray with a black design, much in demand because they're warm, good in the rain, rugged, and last longer than one lifetime. One of the best places to get your hands on one is the Cowichan Valley on Vancouver Island, although you can also find them in the Fraser Valley from Vancouver to Lytton and in native craft outlets. Expect to pay around $90–160 for the real thing, more in tourist shops.

Carved argillite (black slate) miniature totem poles, brooches, ashtrays, and other small items, highly decorated with geometric and animal designs, are created exclusively by the Haida on the Queen Charlotte Islands; the argillite comes from a quarry near Skidegate and can only be used by the Skidegate band. You can find argillite carvings in Skidegate and in craft shops in Prince Rupert, Victoria, and Vancouver. Silverwork is also popular, and some of the best is created by the Haida. Particularly notable is the work of Bill Reid, a Haida artist living in Vancouver. Jade jewelry can be seen in the Lillooet and Lytton areas.

Shops throughout British Columbia are generally open Monday–Friday 9 A.M.–5 P.M. and Saturday 9 A.M.–1 P.M. Major malls stay open all weekend.

Getting There

AIR

Vancouver International Airport (YVR) is British Columbia's main gateway and Canada's second-busiest airport. Regularly scheduled service to and from Vancouver is offered by major airlines throughout the world. Victoria may be the capital, but it comes in a distant second when it comes to international flights; the only destinations served from its international airport are major Canadian cities and Seattle.

Air Canada

After merging with Canadian Airlines in 2000, Air Canada (604/688-5515 or 888/247-2262, www.aircanada.ca or aircanada.com in the U.S.) became one of the world's largest airlines, serving five continents. It offers direct flights to Vancouver from the following North American cities: Calgary, Chicago, Edmonton, Halifax, Honolulu, Las Vegas, Los Angeles, Miami, Montreal, Ottawa, Phoenix, San Francisco, Seattle, Toronto,

Whitehorse, and Winnipeg. Air Canada also flies into Victoria directly from most western Canadian cities as well as Seattle.

From Europe, Air Canada flies directly from London to Vancouver, and from other major cities via Toronto. From the South Pacific, Air Canada operates flights via Honolulu from Sydney and in alliance with Air New Zealand from Auckland and other South Pacific islands to Honolulu, where passengers change to an Air Canada plane for the flight to Vancouver. Asian cities served by direct Air Canada flights from Vancouver include Beijing, Hong Kong, Nagoya, Osaka, Seoul, Shanghai, Taipei, and Tokyo. Air Canada's flights originating in the South American cities of Buenos Aires and Sao Paulo are routed through Toronto.

Other Canadian Airlines

WestJet (604/606-5525 or 800/538-5696, www.westjet.com) is a budget-priced airline, with specials advertised year-round. Based in Calgary, its western hub is the airport at Abbotsford, 72 kilometers (45 miles) east of downtown Vancouver. Flights also terminate at Vancouver's main airport and in Victoria. In addition to flights from regional centers throughout British Columbia, these three airports receive flights originating in Calgary, Edmonton, Hamilton, Ottawa, Regina, Saskatoon, Thunder Bay, and from as far east as St. John's, Newfoundland.

U.S. Airlines

Air Canada offers the most flights into Vancouver from the United States, but the city is also served by the following U.S. carriers: **Alaska Airlines** (800/252-7522, www.alaskaair.com) from Anchorage, Las Vegas, Los Angeles, Palm Springs, Phoenix, San Francisco, and Seattle; **American Airlines** (800/433-7300, www.aa.com), from Chicago and Dallas; **Continental Airlines** (800/231-0856, www.continental.com), from its Houston hub and New York (Newark); **Delta** (800/221-1212, www.delta.com) with summer-

---

AIR TAXES

The federal government imposes a tax of 7 percent of the ticket price plus $6 to a maximum of $55 on all flights departing Canada for the United States. For all other international destinations, the departure tax is set at $55. These taxes are generally included in the ticket purchase price, but it pays to ask when booking. Also built into the ticket price is Canada's **Air Travellers Security Charge;** $12 each sector for domestic flights, $20 for international flights.

Additionally, all passengers departing Vancouver must pay an **Airport Improvement Fee.** The "fee" on flights destined for all points within British Columbia and the Yukon is $5; elsewhere in North America it's $10, and on all other international flights it's $15. This fee is also included in your ticket price.

only flights from Atlanta; **Harmony Airways** (866/868-6789, www.harmonyairways.com), from Honolulu, Kahului, and Los Angeles; **Horizon Air** (800/547-9308, www.horizonair.com), from nearby Portland and Seattle; **Northwest Airlines** (800/225-2525, www.nwa.com), from Detroit, Memphis, and Minneapolis; **Skywest** (800/221-1212, www.skywest.com), from Salt Lake City; and finally **United Airlines** (800/241-6522, www.ual.com), from Chicago, Denver, San Francisco, and Seattle.

International Airlines

In addition to Air Canada's daily London–Vancouver flight, **British Airways** (800/247-9297, www.british-airways.com) also flies this route daily. Air Canada flights between Vancouver and continental Europe are routed through Toronto, but **KLM** (800/447-4747, www.klm.nl) has a daily nonstop flight to Vancouver from Amsterdam, and **Lufthansa** (800/563-5954, www.lufthansa.de) flies from Frankfurt and Munich.

Since the demise of Canadian Airlines, **Qantas** (604/279-6611, www.qantas.com.au) has begun flying between Brisbane, Melbourne, and Sydney to Vancouver via Honolulu. **Air New Zealand** (800/663-5494, www.airnz.com) operates in alliance with Air Canada, with a

---

CUTTING FLIGHT COSTS

Ticket structuring for air travel is so complex that finding the best deal requires some time and patience (or a good travel agent). In the first place, to get an idea of what you will be paying, call the airlines or check their websites and compare fares. Also look in the travel sections of major newspapers—particularly in weekend editions—where budget fares and package deals are frequently advertised. Although the Internet has changed the way many people shop for tickets, having a travel agent that you are comfortable in dealing with—who takes the time to call around, does some research to get you the best fare, and helps you take advantage of any available special offers or promotional deals—is an invaluable asset in starting your travels off on the right foot.

Within Canada, **Travel Cuts** (888/359-2887, www.travelcuts.com) and **Flight Centre** (888/967-5355, www.flightcentre.ca), both with offices in all major cities, including Vancouver and Victoria, consistently offer the lowest airfares available, with the latter guaranteeing the lowest. Flight Centre offers a similar guarantee from its U.S. offices (877/967-5351, www.flightcentre.us), as well as those in Great Britain (tel. 0870/499-0040, www.flightcentre.co.uk), Australia (tel. 13-31-33, www.flightcentre.com.au), and New Zealand (tel. 0800/24-35-44, www.flightcentre.co.nz). All Flight Centre toll-free numbers will put you through to the closest office from where you are calling. In London, **Trailfinders** (215 Kensington High St., Kensington, tel. 020/7937-5400, www.trailfinders.com) always has good deals to Canada and other North American destinations. Reservations can be made directly through airline or travel agency websites, or use the services of an Internet-only company such as **Travelocity** (www.travelocity.com) or **Expedia** (www.expedia.com).

Many cheaper tickets have strict restrictions regarding changes of flight dates, lengths of stay, and cancellations. A general rule: the cheaper the ticket, the more restrictions. Most travelers today fly on APEX (advance-purchase excursion) fares. These are usually the best value, though some (and, occasionally, many) restrictions apply. These might include minimum and maximum stays, and nonchangeable itineraries (or hefty penalties for changes); tickets may also be nonrefundable once purchased.

When you have found the best fare, open a **frequent flyer** membership with the airline—**Air Canada** (www.aeroplan.com) has a very popular reward program that makes rewards easily obtainable.

change of airline in Honolulu or Los Angeles. This airline makes stops throughout the South Pacific, including Nadi. **Air Pacific** (800/227-4446, www.airpacific.com) flies from points throughout the Pacific to Honolulu and then on to Vancouver.

Vancouver is the closest West Coast gateway from Asia, being more than 1,200 kilometers closer to Tokyo than Los Angeles. This and the city's large Asian population mean that it is well served by carriers from across the Pacific. In addition to Air Canada's eight Asian destinations, Vancouver is served by: **Air China** (800/685-0921, www.airchina.com), from Beijing; **All Nippon Airways** (888/422-7533, www.ana.co.jp), from Osaka and Tokyo in affiliation with Air Canada; **Cathay Pacific** (604/606-8888, www.cathaypacific.com), twice daily from Hong Kong; **Eva Air** (800/695-1188, www.evaair.com.tw), from Taipei; **Japan Airlines** (800/525-3663, www.jal.co.jp), from Tokyo; **Korean Air** (800/438-5000, www.koreanair.com), from Seoul; **Philippine Airlines** (800/435-9725, www.philippineair.com), from Manila; and **Singapore Airlines** (604/689-1223, www.singaporeair.com), from Singapore via Seoul.

Mexicana (800/531-7921, www.mexicana.com) flies between Mexico City and Vancouver.

RAIL

Rail travel opened up the province to the rest of the country in 1885, but it had lost much of its appeal by the beginning of the 1990s thanks to drastically reduced airfares. Today, however, improved service, a refitting of carriages, a competitive pricing structure, and the luxurious privately operated Rocky Mountaineer have helped trains regain popularity in western Canada.

VIA Rail

Government-run VIA Rail provides passenger-train service right across Canada. The **Canadian** is a thrice-weekly service between Toronto and Vancouver via Winnipeg, Saskatoon, Edmonton, Jasper, and Kamloops. Service is provided in two classes of travel: Economy features lots of legroom, reading lights, pillows and blankets, and a Skyline Car complete with bar service, while Silver and Blue class is more luxurious, featuring sleeping rooms, daytime seating, all meals, a lounge and dining car, and shower kits for all passengers. At Jasper (Alberta) the westbound transcontinental line divides, with one set of tracks continuing slightly north to Prince Rupert. Along this route, the **Skeena** makes three trips a week. It is a daytime-only service, with passengers transferred to Prince George accommodations for an overnight stay. It also offers first-class travel, in Totem class.

If you're traveling to British Columbia from any eastern province, the least expensive way to travel is on a **Canrailpass,** which allows unlimited travel anywhere on the VIA Rail system for 12 days within any given 30-day period. During high season (June 1–Oct. 15) the pass is adult $741, senior (over 60) and child $667, with extra days (up to three are allowed) $63 and $57 respectively. The rest of the year adult fares are $461, seniors and students $405, with extra days $40 and $36. VIA Rail has cooperated with Amtrak (800/872-7245) to offer a **North American Rail Pass,** with all the same seasonal dates and discounts as the Canrailpass. The cost for unlimited travel over 30 days is adult $1,004, senior and child $904; low-season passes are $711 and $640.

On regular fares, discounts of 25–40 percent apply to travel in all classes Oct.–June. Those over 60 and under 25 receive a 10 percent discount that can be combined with other seasonal fares. Check for advance-purchase restrictions on all discount tickets.

The VIA Rail website (www.viarail.ca) provides route, schedule, and fare information, takes reservations, and offers links to towns and sights en route. Or pick up a train schedule at any VIA Rail station.

Rocky Mountaineer

Rocky Mountaineer Vacations (604/606-7245 or 800/665-7245, www.rockymountaineer.com)

runs a luxurious rail trip to Vancouver from Banff or Calgary and Jasper, through the spectacular interior mountain ranges of British Columbia. Travel is during daylight hours only so you don't miss anything. Trains depart in either direction in the morning (every second or third day), overnighting at Kamloops. One-way travel in RedLeaf Service, which includes light meals, nonalcoholic drinks, and Kamloops accommodations, costs $699 per person d, $779 s from either Banff or Jasper and $769 per person d, $849 s from Calgary. GoldLeaf Service is the ultimate in luxury. Passengers ride in a two-story glass-domed car, eat in a separate dining area, and stay in Kamloops's most luxurious accommodations. GoldLeaf costs $1,379 per person d, $1,459 s from Banff or Jasper to Vancouver and $1,499 per person d, $1,579 s from Calgary. Outside of high season (mid-Apr.–May and the first two weeks of Oct.), fares are reduced around $150 per person in RedLeaf and $200 per person in GoldLeaf. Trains terminate in Vancouver off Terminal Avenue at 1755 Cottrell Street (behind Pacific Central Station).

BUS
Greyhound
Bus travel throughout Canada is easy with Greyhound (604/482-8747 or 800/661-8747, website www.greyhound.ca). The company offers Trans-Canada Highway service from Toronto, Winnipeg, Regina, and Calgary (Alberta) through Kamloops to Vancouver, as well as a more southerly route from Calgary through Cranbrook and the Kootenays to Vancouver. Among the northern routes: Edmonton and Jasper (Alberta) southwest to Vancouver or west to Prince Rupert; and Grande Prairie (Alberta) northwest through Dawson Creek to Whitehorse (Yukon). From the thousands of depots throughout North America, you can go just about anywhere you desire. Reservations are not necessary—just turn up when you want to go, buy your ticket, and kick back. As long as you use your ticket within 30 days, you can stop over wherever the bus stops and stay as long as you want.

When calling for information, ask about any special deals—sometimes excursion fares offered to certain destinations save you money if you buy a round-trip ticket; other times Greyhound offers good prices if you buy your ticket a month in advance. Other standard discounts apply to regular-fare tickets bought 7 or 14 days in advance; to travelers 65 and over; and for two people traveling together. At last report, Greyhound was offering a Go Anywhere Fare, on which you can travel between any two points in North America for one low fare; $129 one-way and $199 round-trip if bought 14 days in advance.

Greyhound's **Discovery Pass** comes in many forms, including passes valid only in Canada, in the western states and provinces, and in all of North America. The Canada Pass is sold in periods of 7 days ($249), 10 days ($319), 15 days ($379), 21 days ($419), 30 days ($449), 45 days ($535), and 60 days ($599) and allows unlimited travel west of Montreal. The Canada Pass Plus, which allows unlimited travel on all of Greyhound's Canadian routes, is sold in the same increments and ranges from $279 for 7 days to $685 for 60 days. Passes can be bought 14 or more days in advance online, 7 or more days in advance from any Canadian bus depot, or up to the day of departure from U.S. depots. The Domestic North America CanAm Pass, valid for Greyhound travel through North America, ranges from US$399 for a 15-day pass to US$639 for a 60-day pass. Outside of North America, the passes are the same, but they're sold as International Discovery Passes, with significant discounts; purchase them online more than 7 days in advance or at the Vancouver bus depot with proof of foreign residency.

Other Bus Lines
Quick Shuttle (604/940-4428 or 800/665-2122, www.quickcoach.com) operates a regular bus service to Pacific Central Station and major downtown Vancouver hotels from downtown Seattle (US$34 one-way) and SeaTac Airport (US$44 one-way).

Know British Columbia

FERRY

One of the most pleasurable ways to get your first view of British Columbia is from sea level. Many scheduled ferry services cross from Washington State to Victoria, on Vancouver Island, but no ferries run to Vancouver from south of the border.

From Washington State

From downtown Seattle (Pier 69), **Clipper Navigation** (800/888-2535, www.clippervacations .com) runs passenger-only ferries to Victoria's Inner Harbour. Full fare is adult US$81 one-way, US$133 round-trip. In summer, sailings are made five times daily, with the service running the rest of the year on a reduced schedule. Travel is discounted off-season, for seniors, and for children.

North of Seattle, Anacortes is the departure point for **Washington State Ferries** (206/464-6400, 250/381-1551, or 888/808-7977, www.wsdof.wa.gov/ferries) to Sidney (on Vancouver Island 32 kilometers/20 miles north of Victoria), with a stop made en route in the San Juan Islands. Sample fares are: adult US$13.80, senior US$6.90, vehicle and driver US$47. Make reservations at least 24 hours in advance.

The final option is to travel from Port Angeles to Victoria. Two companies offer service on this route. The **MV Coho** (250/386-2202 or 360/457-4491, www.cohoferry.com) runs year-round, with up to four crossings daily in summer; adult US$7.75, child US$3.90, vehicle US$29.75. The passenger-only **Victoria Express** (250/361-9144 or 800/663-1589, www.victoriaexpress.com) makes the crossing 2–4 times daily June–September; US$10 each way.

Getting Around

The best way to get around British Columbia is via your own vehicle—be it a car, RV, motorbike, or bicycle. It's easy to get around by bus and train, but you can't get off the beaten track and, let's face it, that's exactly where most of British Columbia is. It's also easy to get around by air—all the larger airports are served by scheduled intraprovincial flights, and charter services fly out of many of the smaller ones.

AIR

Air Canada Jazz (www.flyjazz.ca), a connector airline for Air Canada (604/688-5515 or 888/247-2262, www.aircanada.ca), serves most major B.C. cities from both Vancouver and Victoria international airports. The other major regional carrier is **WestJet** (604/606-5525 or 800/538-5696, www.westjet.com). **Pacific Coastal** (604/273-8666 or 800/663-2872, www.pacific-coastal.com) has flights to Vancouver's South Terminal (connected to the main terminals by shuttle) and Victoria International Airport from Campbell River, Comox, Cran-

brook, Port Hardy, Powell River, Williams Lake, and many remote coastal towns farther north. **Hawk Air** (250/635-4295 or 800/487-1216, www.hawkair.net) offers scheduled flights between the South Terminal and Terrace, Prince Rupert, and Sandspit. Also from the South Terminal, **KD Air** (604/688-9957 or 800/665-4244, www.kdair.com) flies daily to Qualicum (Vancouver Island), with a connecting ground shuttle to Port Alberni. **Sonicblue Airways** (604/278-1608 or 800/228-6608, www.sonicblueair.com) flies from the South Terminal and Victoria to Tofino/Ucluelet.

Seaplanes not only provide access to remote locations, but also fly scheduled routes between Vancouver, Victoria, and Nanaimo. From Coal Harbour (Vancouver), **Harbour Air** (604/688-1277 or 800/665-0212, www.harbour-air.com) and **West Coast Air** (604/606-6888 or 800/347-2222, www.westcoastair.com) have scheduled floatplane flights to Victoria's Inner Harbour. Expect to pay around $100 per person each way for any of these flights. **Baxter Aviation** (604/683-6525 or 800/661-5599, www.baxterair.com) has seaplane service between Vancouver and Nanaimo.

RAIL

The only intraprovincial rail service is VIA Rail's **Malahat** train (250/383-4324 or 800/561-8630, www.viarail.ca), which runs daily up the east coast of Vancouver Island between Victoria and Courtenay, making a pleasant day trip from the capital or a good alternative to scheduled buses. **Rocky Mountaineer Vacations** (604/606-7245 or 800/665-7245, www.rockymountaineer.com) will be offering scheduled passenger service from Vancouver to Whistler and beyond in 2006.

BUS

British Columbia by bus is a snap. Just about all the cities have local bus companies providing transportation in town and, in many cases, throughout their local region—check the transportation sections of each individual chapter for more details. **Greyhound** operates daily bus service to just about anywhere in the province. You don't need to make reservations—just buy your ticket and go. All scheduled services are nonsmoking. The bus depot in Vancouver is Pacific Central Station (1150 Station St., 604/482-8747 or 800/661-8747).

The one part of the province where Greyhound doesn't operate is Vancouver Island. There, **Island Coach Lines** (250/388-5248 or 800/663-8390, www.victoriatours.com) serves all of the island, running up the east coast to Port Hardy and out to the west coast at Tofino. Getting to the island itself is easy with **Pacific Coach Lines** (604/662-7575 or 800/661-1725, www.pacific-coach.com). Buses depart Vancouver every couple of hours 6 A.M.–9 P.M. Upon arrival at the ferry terminal, you board the ferry, then rejoin the bus across the other side for a final leg into downtown Vancouver or Victoria. The fare between Vancouver International Airport and downtown Victoria is $37.75 one-way, $73.50 round-trip; to Victoria from Pacific Central Station the cost is $32.25 one-way, $62.50 round-trip. The time

to either destination is around 3.5 hours, and the ferry fare is included in the price.

Backpacker Buses

For young travelers on a budget, the **Moose Travel Network** (604/777-9905 or 888/244-6673, www.moosenetwork.com) is an excellent way to travel around British Columbia. It runs along a number of different routes, including a 10-day loop originating in Vancouver and traveling to Jasper and Banff via Whistler ($449), a six-day trip between Vancouver and Banff via Jasper ($309), a two-day Banff–Jasper–Banff trip ($95), and a Banff–Vancouver shuttle that overnights in Kamloops ($107). On any of these trips, you can get on and off wherever you please (and jump aboard the next bus as it passes through) or bond with the crowd and stay on the fixed itinerary. Nights are spent at hostels en route. This cost isn't included in the tour, but your reservation is (so you don't need to worry about trying to find an empty bed at each stop). Food is also extra, but often all travelers pitch in a token amount to purchase dinner at a grocery store along the way. Buses run 3–7 times a week through a May to mid-October season.

FERRY

BC Ferries

Chances are, at some stage of your British Columbia adventure, you'll use the services of **BC Ferries** (250/386-3431 or, toll-free in B.C., 888/223-3779, www.bcferries.com), which serves 46 ports with a fleet of 40 vessels. All fares listed for "vehicles" in this book cover cars and trucks up to 6.1 meters (20 feet) long and under 2.1 meters (seven feet) high (or under two meters/six feet eight inches high on a few routes). Larger vehicles such as RVs pay more. Also note that prices listed for all types of vehicles are in addition to the passenger price; the vehicle's driver/rider/porter is not included in the vehicle fare.

Vancouver has two major ferry terminals. From **Tsawwassen,** south of downtown, ferries run regularly across the Strait of Georgia to the Vancouver Island centers of Swartz Bay (32 kilometers/20

© ANDREW HEMPSTEAD

soaking up the sun on the ferry crossing to Vancouver Island

miles north of Victoria) and Nanaimo. From **Horseshoe Bay,** west of downtown Vancouver, ferries ply the strait to Nanaimo. On weekends and holidays, the one-way fare on all routes between the mainland and Vancouver Island is adult $10.25, vehicle $35.75, motorcycle $18, bicycle $2.50; rates for motor vehicles are slightly lower on weekdays, and all fares are reduced mid-September–late June. B.C. seniors travel free Monday–Thursday (but must pay for their vehicles). In high season (late June–mid-Sept.), the ferries run about once an hour 7 A.M.–10 P.M. The rest of the year they run a little less frequently. Both crossings take around 90 minutes. Expect a wait in summer, particularly if you have an oversized vehicle (each ferry can accommodate far fewer large vehicles than standard-size cars and trucks). Limited vehicle reservations ($15 per booking) are accepted at 604/444-2890 or 888/724-5223, or online at www.bcferries.com.

Also from Horseshoe Bay, ferries run across Howe Sound to **Langdale,** gateway to the Sunshine Coast; round-trip fare is adult $8, vehicle $27.75, motorcycle $14, bicycle $2.50, canoe or kayak $4.

From **Powell River,** at the north end of the Sunshine Coast, ferries depart for **Comox** (Vancouver Island), making it possible to visit both the island and the Sunshine Coast without returning to Vancouver.

BC Ferries also provides regular services from Vancouver Island and the mainland to the **Southern Gulf Islands** of Salt Spring, North Pender, Mayne, Galiano, and Saturna. Other islands in the Strait of Georgia linked to Vancouver Island by ferry include: Thetis and Kuper (from Chemainus), Gabriola (from Nanaimo), Lasqueti (from Parksville), Denman and Hornby (from Buckley Bay), Quadra and Cortes (from Campbell River), Malcolm and Cormorant (from Port McNeil), and Texada (from Powell River). Fares for travel to these islands range adult $4.50–6.50, vehicles $11.50–22.50.

From **Port Hardy** at the northern tip of Vancouver Island, a ferry runs north up the coast to **Prince Rupert.** From the end of May through September the ferry goes every other day, from October through April once a week, and during May twice a week. Peak one-way fare is adult $106, child 5–11 $53, vehicle $241. Reservable cabins are available, as are discounts for B.C. seniors. The trip takes 15 hours and links up with the **Alaska Marine Highway** (see sidebar, *North to Alaska*). Also from Prince Rupert, ferries run out to the **Queen Charlotte Islands;** one-way fare is adult $25, child 5–11 $12.50, vehicle $93. These longer sailings require reservations, which should be made as far in advance as possible.

Inland Ferries

Many interior lakes and rivers are crossed by ferries owned and operated by the government. Of course, no service is available between freeze-up and breakup, but the rest of year, expect daily service from 6 A.M. until at least 10 P.M. Some of the ferries are small, capable of carrying just two vehicles, while others can transport up to 50. Passage is free on all these ferries, including the 45-minute sailing across Kootenay Lake between Balfour and Kootenay Bay—the world's longest free ferry trip.

DRIVING IN CANADA

United States and International Driver's Licenses are valid in Canada. All highway signs give distances in kilometers and speeds in kilometers per hour. Unless otherwise posted, the maximum speed limit on the highways is 100 kph (62 mph).

Use of safety belts is mandatory, and motorcyclists must wear helmets. Infants and toddlers weighing up to nine kilograms (20 pounds) must be strapped into an appropriate children's car seat. Use of a child car seat for larger children weighing 9–18 kilograms (20–40 pounds) is required of British Columbia residents and recommended to nonresidents. Before venturing north of the 49th parallel, U.S. residents should ask their vehicle insurance company for a Canadian Non-resident Inter-provincial Motor Vehicle Liability Insurance Card. You may also be asked to prove vehicle ownership, so carry your vehicle registration form. If you're involved in an accident with a B.C. vehicle, contact the near-est Insurance Corporation of British Columbia (ICBC) office (800/663-3051).

If you're a member in good standing of an automobile association, take your membership card—the Canadian AA provides members of related associations full services, including free maps, itineraries, excellent tour books, road- and weather-condition information, accommodations reservations, travel agency services, and emergency road services. For more information contact the **British Columbia Automobile Association** (604/268-5600 or 877/325-8888, www.bcaa.com).

Note: Drinking and driving (with a blood-alcohol level of .08 percent or higher) in B.C. can get you imprisoned for up to five years on a first offense and will cost you your license for at least 12 months.

Car Rental

All major car-rental companies have outlets at Vancouver International Airport, in downtown Vancouver, and in Victoria. Many companies also have cars available in towns and cities throughout the province. Try to book in advance, especially in summer. Expect to pay from $50 a day and $250 a week for a small economy car with unlimited kilometers.

Major rental companies with outlets in British Columbia include: **Alamo** (800/462-5266, www.alamo.com), **Avis** (800/974-0808, www.avis.ca), **Budget** (800/268-8900, www.budget.com), **Discount** (800/263-2355, www.discountcar.com), **Dollar** (800/800-4000, www.dollar.com), **Enterprise** (800/325-8007, www.enterprise.com), **Hertz** (800/263-0600, www.hertz.ca), **National** (800/227-7368, www.nationalcar.com), **Rent-a-wreck** (800/327-0116, www.rentawreck.ca), and **Thrifty** (800/847-4389, www.thrifty.com). Cheaper used cars are available from only $40 a day plus $.15 a kilometer from Vancouver-based **Lo-cost** (1105 Granville St., 604/689-9664 or 888/377-2277, www.locost.ca), which offers good deals for longer rentals. Lo-cost's office is handy to many mid-priced accommodations.

NORTH TO ALASKA

The **Alaska Marine Highway System** (907/465-3941 or 800/642-0066, www.dot .state.ak.us/amhs) is an extensive network of government-run ferries through Alaska's Inside Passage and along the British Columbia coast. Due to international border regulations, the only Canadian port of entry used by the ferry system is Prince Rupert in northern British Columbia. The system's southern terminus, though, is Bellingham, 70 kilometers (43 miles) south of Vancouver in Washington State. (If you're Alaska-bound and would like to include British Columbia in your itinerary, consider driving to Port Hardy, at the northern tip of Vancouver Island, and catching a BC Ferries vessel to Prince Rupert to link up with the Alaska Marine Highway). Make all reservations as far in advance as possible.

The **Alaska Pass** (206/463-6550 or 800/248-7598, website www.alaskapass.com) combines travel on the Alaska Marine Highway with other northern operators, including the White Pass & Yukon Railroad, Alaska Railroad, and Alaskon Express. Eight days' travel within any given 12-day period costs US$649, 12 days' travel within 21 days is US$799, or a straight 22-day pass is US$1,049. A booking fee of US$75 is added to all passes.

For tourist literature, contact the **Alaska Division of Tourism** (907/465-2010, www .travelalaska.com). The best guidebook for the state is Don Pitcher's *Moon Handbooks Alaska.*

RV and Camper Rental

You might consider renting a camper-van or other recreational vehicle for your trip. With one of these apartments-on-wheels, you won't need to worry about finding accommodations each night. Even the smallest units aren't cheap, but they can be a good deal for longer-term travel or for families or two couples traveling together. The smallest vans, capable of sleeping two people, start at $150 per day with 100 free kilometers (62 miles) per day. Standard extra charges include insurance, a preparation fee (usually around $50 per rental), a linen/cutlery charge (around $60 per person per trip), and taxes. Major agencies with rental outlets in Vancouver include **Cruise Canada** (800/327-7799, or, in the U.S., 800/327-7778, www.cruise-canada.com), **Canadream** (800/461-7368, www.canadream.com), and **Go West** (604/987-5288 or 800/661-8813, www.go-west.com). At the end of the summer season (early September), look for some great online bargains.

Visas and Officialdom

Entry for U.S. Citizens

United States citizens and permanent residents need only present some form of identification that proves citizenship and/or residency, such as a birth certificate, voter-registration card, driver's license with photo, or alien card (essential for nonresident aliens to reenter the United States). It never hurts to carry your passport as well.

Other Foreign Visitors

All other foreign visitors must have a valid passport and may need a visa or visitor permit depending on their country of residence and the vagaries of international politics. At present, visas are not required for citizens of the United States, British Commonwealth, or Western Europe. The standard entry permit is for six months, and you may be asked to show onward tickets or proof of sufficient funds to last you through your intended stay. Extensions are available from Citizenship and Immigration Canada offices in Vancouver and Victoria. This department's website (www.cic.gc.ca) is the best source of the latest entry requirements.

Entry by Private Aircraft or Boat

If you're going to enter Canada by private plane or boat, contact the **Canada Border Services Agency** (204/983-3500 or 800/461-9799, www.cbsa-asfc.gc.ca) in advance for a list of official ports of entry and their hours of operation.

Customs

You can take the following into Canada duty-free: reasonable quantities of clothes and personal effects, 50 cigars and 200 cigarettes, 200 grams of tobacco, 1.14 liters of spirits or wine, food for personal use, and gas (normal tank capacity). Pets from the United States can generally be brought into Canada, with certain caveats. Dogs and cats must be more than three months old and have a rabies certificate showing date of vaccination. Birds can be brought in only if they have not been mixing with other birds, and parrots need an export permit because they're on the endangered species list.

Handguns, automatic and semiautomatic weapons, and sawn-off rifles and shotguns are not allowed into Canada. Visitors with firearms must declare them at the border; restricted weapons will be held by Customs and can be picked up on exit from the country. Those not declared will be seized and charges may be laid. It is illegal to possess any firearm in a national park unless it is dismantled or carried in an enclosed case. Up to 5,000 rounds of ammunition may be imported but should be declared on entry.

On reentering the United States, if you've been in Canada more than 48 hours you can bring back up to US$400 worth of household and personal items, excluding alcohol and tobacco, duty-free. If you've been in Canada fewer than 48 hours, you may bring in only up to US$200 worth of such items duty-free.

For further information on all customs regulations contact **Canada Border Services Agency** (204/983-3500 or 800/461-9799, www.cbsa-asfc.gc.ca).

Know British Columbia

Accommodations and Food

HOTELS AND MOTELS

The best guide to hotels and motels is the free *Accommodations* book put out annually by Tourism BC. It's available at all information centers, from the website www.hellobc.com, or by calling 250/387-1642 or 800/435-5622. The book lists hotels, motels, lodges, resorts, bed-and-breakfasts, and campgrounds. It contains no ratings, simply listings with facilities and rates.

All rates quoted in this book are for a double room in the high season (summer, except in winter resort towns). Expect to pay less for downtown accommodations on weekends, and less outside of the busy July–August period.

Prices for a basic motel room in a small town start at $45 s, $50 d. In Vancouver and Victoria expect to pay at least double this amount for the least expensive rooms. The most luxurious lodgings in the province—Vancouver's Pan Pacific Hotel Vancouver, Victoria's grand old Fairmont Empress, or any one of Whistler's resort hotels, for example—charge over $300 per night for a basic room. Room rates outside the two major cities fluctuate greatly. For example, few lodgings on Vancouver Island charge less than $70, but along the TransCanada Highway, in places like Kamloops and Revelstoke, you can pay as little as $50 for a room. Try to plan ahead for summer travel and book as far in advance as possible, especially for accommodations in Vancouver and Prince Rupert, on Vancouver Island, and on the Queen Charlotte Islands.

Making Reservations

Rates quoted in this book are for a standard double room through the high season, which generally extends from June to early September (except in alpine resort towns such as Whistler). Almost all accommodations are less expensive outside of these busy months, some cutting their rates by as much as 50 percent. You'll enjoy the biggest seasonal discounts at properties that rely on summer tourists, such as those in Vancouver, on Vancouver Island, and in the Okanagan Valley. The same applies in Vancouver and to a lesser extent Victoria on weekends—many of big downtown hotels rely on business and convention travelers to fill the bulk of their rooms; when the end of the week rolls down, the hotels are left with rooms to fill at discounted rates Friday, Saturday, and Sunday nights.

While you have no influence over the seasonal and weekday/weekend pricing differences detailed above, *how* you reserve a room *can* make a difference in how much you pay. First and foremost, when it comes to searching out actual rates, the Internet is an invaluable tool. Tourism British Columbia offers discounted rates through its toll-free number (800/435-5622) and the website

© ANDREW HEMPSTEAD

For something a little different, plan to spend a night or two in a tepee—such as this one pictured at Princeton Castle Resort, east of Vancouver.

www.hellobc.com. All hotel websites listed in *Moon Handbooks British Columbia* show rates, and many have online reservation forms. Use these websites to search out specials, many of which are available only on the Internet.

Don't be afraid to negotiate during slower times. Even if the desk clerk has no control over rates, there's no harm in asking for a bigger room or one with a better view. Just look for a Vacancy sign hanging out front.

Most hotels offer auto association members an automatic 10 percent discount, and whereas senior discounts apply only to those over 60 or 65 on public transportation and at attractions, most hotels offer discounts to those over 50, with chains such as Best Western also allowing senior travelers a late checkout. "Corporate Rates" are a lot more flexible than in years gone past; some hotels require nothing more than the flash of a business card for a 10–20 percent discount.

When it comes to frequent flyer programs, you really do need to be a frequent flyer to achieve free flights, but the various loyalty programs offered by hotels often provide benefits simply for signing up.

BED-AND-BREAKFASTS

Bed-and-breakfast accommodations are found throughout British Columbia. Styles run the gamut from restored heritage homes to modern townhouses. They are usually private residences, with up to four guest rooms, and as the name suggests, breakfast is included. Rates fluctuate enormously. In Vancouver and Victoria, for example, they range $60–180 s, $70–210 d. Amenities also vary greatly—the "bed-and-breakfast" may be a single spare room in an otherwise regular family home or a full-time business in a purpose-built home (see sidebar, *Bed-and-Breakfasts and Bathrooms*). Regardless, guests can expect hearty home cooking, a peaceful atmosphere, personal service, knowledgeable hosts, and conversation with like-minded travelers.

Reservation Agencies

The **Western Canadian Bed & Breakfast**

ACCOMMODATION TAXES

Except for campgrounds and bed-and-breakfasts with fewer than four guest rooms, accommodations must add to their rates an 8 percent provincial hotel room tax and the Canada-wide 7 percent goods and services tax (the latter is refundable to visitors from outside the country). Additionally, a 2 percent hotel tax is administered in Vancouver only.

Innkeepers Association (P.O. Box 74534, 2803 W. 4th Ave., Vancouver, BC V6K 4P4, 604/255-9199, www.wcbbia.com) represents more than 140 bed-and-breakfasts across Western Canada. The association produces an informative brochure with simple descriptions and a color photo of each property, and manages an easily navigable website. This association doesn't take bookings—they must be made directly. **Bed and Breakfast Online** www.bbcanada.com) doesn't take bookings either, but links are provided and an ingenious search engine helps you find the accommodation that best fits your needs. If none of the recommendations in the Explore chapters of this book catches your eye, contact a local agency such as **Vancouver B&B Ltd.** (604/298-8815 or 800/488-1941, www.vancouverbandb.bc.ca) or **Old English B&B Registry** (604/986-5069, www.oldenglishbandb.com). Tell them what you're looking for and the price you're prepared to pay, and they'll find the right place for you.

BACKPACKER ACCOMMODATIONS

Budget travelers are enjoying more and more options in British Columbia, ranging from a converted downtown Vancouver hotel to a treehouse on Salt Spring Island, all for around $20 per person per night. Hostelling International (formerly the Youth Hostel Association) has undergone a radical change in direction and now appeals to all ages, and privately run "hostels" within the province fill the gaps. Either

Know British Columbia

BED-AND-BREAKFASTS AND BATHROOMS

In Europe, sharing a bathroom with fellow travelers at a bed-and-breakfast is both a common and accepted practice. In North America, bed-and-breakfast bathroom terminology is often confusing, more so since it can vary between operators. The Western Canadian Bed and Breakfast Innkeepers Association offers the following descriptions:

En Suite: Refers to a bathroom that is private, inside, and attached to the sleeping unit ("in suite").

Private: A bathroom that is for the sole use of a sleeping unit but may be outside of the room.

Shared or **Semiprivate:** Bathrooms that are used in common by more than one room. No more than two guest rooms should share a single bathroom.

If having a bathroom to yourself is important to you, clarify with the operator when reserving.

way, staying in what have universally become known as "backpackers' hostels" is an enjoyable and inexpensive way to travel through the province. Generally, you need to provide your own sleeping bag or linen, but most hostels supply extra bedding (if needed) at no charge. Accommodations are in dormitories (2–10 beds) or double rooms. Each also offers a communal kitchen, lounge area, and laundry facilities, while some have Internet access, bike rentals, and organized tours.

Hostelling International

The curfews and chores are long gone in this worldwide nonprofit organization of 4,200 hostels in 60 countries. Hostelling International–Canada operates 16 hostels in British Columbia, including three in Vancouver. For a dorm bed, members of Hostelling International pay $14–22 per night, nonmembers pay $20–32; single and double rooms are often available but are more expensive.

You don't *have* to be a member to stay in an affiliated hostel of Hostelling International, but membership pays for itself after only a few nights of discounted lodging. Aside from discounted rates, benefits of membership vary from country to country but often include discounted air, rail, and bus travel; discounts on car rental; and discounts on some attractions and commercial activities. For Canadians, the membership charge is $35 annually, or $175 for a lifetime membership. For more information contact **HI–Canada** (604/684-7111, www.hihostels.ca).

Joining the Hostelling International affiliate of your home country entitles you to reciprocal rights in Canada, as well as around the world. In the United States the contact address is **Hostelling International USA** (301/495-1240, www.hiusa.org); annual membership is adult US$28 and senior US$18, or become a lifetime member for US$250.

Other contact addresses include: **YHA England and Wales** (0870/770-8868, www.yha.org.uk), **YHA Australia** (based in all capital cities, including at 422 Kent St., Sydney, 02/9261-1111, www.yha.com.au), and **YHA New Zealand** (03/379-9970, www.yha.org.nz). Otherwise, click through the links on the Hostelling International website (www.hihostels.com) to your country of choice.

Other Backpacker Accommodations

Hostelling International isn't the only option when it comes to looking for budget accommodations in British Columbia. **Samesun Backpacker Lodges** (250/861-3001 or 877/562-2783, www.samesun.com) maintains excellent standards in seven lodges, while the **Pacific Hostelling Network** (www.pacifichostels.com) is a loosely affiliated organization that includes around 30 properties in British Columbia.

CAMPING

Almost every town in British Columbia has at least one campground, often with showers and water, electricity, and sewer hookups. Prices range

$8–22 in smaller towns, up to $45 in the cities and more popular tourist destinations. If you're planning a summer trip to Vancouver, Vancouver Island, the Sunshine Coast, Whistler, or the Okanagan Valley, try to book in advance. At other times and places, advance reservations aren't usually necessary.

National parks provide some of the nicest campgrounds in B.C. All have picnic tables, fire grates, toilets, and fresh drinking water, although only some provide showers. Prices range $12–20 depending on facilities and services. They are all open through summer, with each park having one area designated for winter camping. A percentage of sites can be reserved through the **Parks Canada Campground Reservation Service** (877/737-3783, www.pccamping.ca). Backcountry camping in a national park costs $8 per person per night.

Nearly 14,000 campsites lie scattered through 344 campgrounds in 275 provincial parks. Rates range $9–22 a night depending on facilities, most of which are basic. The fee is collected in different ways at different parks, but it's always *cash only.* Reserve a spot at the 60 most popular provincial parks by calling BC Parks' **Discover Camping** (604/689-9025 or 800/689-9025, www.discovercamping.ca). Reservations are taken between March 15 and September 15 for dates up to three months in advance. The reservation fee is $6.42 per night, to a maximum of $19.26, and is in addition to applicable camping fees.

Camping in the province's over 1,400 **Forest Service Campgrounds** costs $8–10 per site per night, which is collected on-site. For a list of site locations, pick up a Forest District recreation map from local information centers or surf the Internet to www.gov.bc.ca/for.

Commercial and provincial park campgrounds are listed in Tourism BC's invaluable *Accommodations* guide, available at all information centers, online at www.hellobc.com, or by calling 250/387-1642 or 800/435-5622.

FOOD AND DRINK

British Columbia is not world-renowned for its culinary delights, but the province does offer ex-

British Columbia is blessed with over 1,000 campgrounds, many enjoying prime lakefront locations.

cellent **West Coast** cuisine (also called fusion cooking), meaning an abundance of seafood and fresh produce prepared with an Asian influence. Otherwise, Canadian food is similar to American food—in general, bland and not very interesting. Burgers, hot dogs, chicken-in-a-box, and ready-made sandwiches are available across the province. In cities and large towns, some restaurants and fast-food outlets are open 24 hours.

Fine-dining restaurants and gourmet Continental cuisine are found in the large cities. Vancouver is the best place to eat; the city's 3,000-odd eateries serve a wide variety of ethnic foods and standard Canadiana at a complete range of prices. Victoria also enjoys its share of good restaurants, but it has the reputation of serving predominantly British food in as British an atmosphere as you could imagine outside of Britain.

Drink

British Columbian **wine** is highly regarded, having won awards throughout the world. The province is one of the few places in the world capable of producing **ice wines,** made by a process in which the grapes aren't harvested until *after* the first frost; the frost splits the skins and the fermentation process begins with the grapes still on the vine. These concentrated juices from classic varietals such as Riesling and Gewurztraminer create a super-sweet wine. Ice wine is generally marketed in a distinctively narrow 375-milliliter bottle and promoted as a dessert wine. The province holds four wine-growing regions. The largest concentration of B.C.'s 46 vineyards is in the Okanagan Valley, with more than 40 wineries ranging from large-scale commercial operations to small plots of grapes grown on hobby farms. Vancouver Island, the Fraser Valley, and the Similkameen Valley are also home to a number of wineries. Expect to pay $15–24 for a bottle of locally produced wine. For more information on the province's wine industry contact the **B.C. Wine Information Centre** (250/490-2006).

All the popular Canadian and American beers are available at bars and liquor stores. **Kokanee,** brewed in Creston and widely available throughout British Columbia, is a fine-tasting beer that should be taken on all camping trips.

The legal drinking age varies throughout Canada. In British Columbia it is 19.

Tips for Travelers

EMPLOYMENT AND STUDY

International visitors wishing to work or study in Canada must obtain authorization *before* entering the country. Authorization to work will only be granted if no qualified Canadians are available for the work in question. Applications for work and study are available from all Canadian embassies and must be submitted with a nonrefundable processing fee. The Canadian government has a reciprocal agreement with Australia for a limited number of **holiday work visas** to be issued each year. Australian citizens aged 30 and under are eligible; contact your nearest Canadian embassy or consulate. For general information on immigrating to Canada contact **Citizenship and Immigration Canada** (604/666-2171, www .cic.gc.ca).

VISITORS WITH DISABILITIES

A lack of mobility should not deter you from traveling to British Columbia, but definitely do some research before leaving home.

If you haven't traveled extensively, start by doing some research at the website of the **Access-Able Travel Source** (www.access-able.com), where you will find databases of specialist travel agencies and lodgings in western Canada that cater to travelers with disabilities. **Flying Wheels Travel** (507/451-5005, www.flyingwheelstravel .com) caters solely to the needs of travelers with disabilities. The **Society for Accessible Travel** and Hospitality (212/447-7284, www.sath.org) supplies information on tour operators, vehicle rentals, specific destinations, and companion services. For frequent travelers, the membership fee (US$45 per year) is well worthwhile. Emerging Horizons (www.emerginghorizons.com) is a U.S. quarterly magazine dedicated to travelers with special needs.

Access to Travel (800/465-7735, www.accesstotravel.gc.ca) is an initiative of the Canadian government that includes information on travel within and between Canadian cities. The website also has a lot of general travel information for those with disabilities. The **Canadian National Institute for the Blind** (www.cnib.ca) offers a wide range of services from its Vancouver office (604/431-2121). Finally, the **Canadian Paraplegic Association** (877/324-3611, www.canparaplegic.org), with a chapter office in Vancouver (604/324-3611), is another good source of information.

FAMILY TRAVEL

Whether you're traveling with toddlers or teens, family trips entail decisions affecting everything from where you stay to your choice of activities. Luckily for you, British Columbia is very family-friendly, with a variety of indoor and outdoor attractions aimed specifically at the younger generation, including a major children's festival in Vancouver the third weekend of May (www.childrensfestival.ca).

Admission prices for children are included throughout the Explore chapters of this book. As a general rule, these reduced prices are for kids 6–16 years old. For two adults and two or more children, always ask about family tickets. Children under 6 nearly always get in free. Most hotels and motels will happily accommodate children, but always try to reserve your room in advance and let the reservations desk know the ages of your brood. Often, children stay free in major hotels, and in the case of some major chains—such as Holiday Inn—eat free also. Generally, bed-and-breakfasts aren't suitable for children and in some cases don't accept kids at all. Ask ahead.

When it comes to traveling with children, let them help you plan the trip, looking at websites and reading up on British Columbia together. To make your vacation more enjoyable if you'll be spending a lot of time on the road, rent a minivan (all major rental agencies have a supply). Don't forget to bring along favorite toys and games from home—whatever you think will keep your kids entertained when the joys of sightseeing wear off.

The **Tourism British Columbia** website (www.hellobc.com) has sections devoted to children's activities within the two provinces. Another handy source of information is **Kid Friendly!** (604/541-6192, www.kidfriendly.org), a nonprofit organization that has compiled an online database of, you guessed it, kid-friendly attractions, lodgings, and restaurants throughout British Columbia. The website even has room for your children to write about their vacation. Another useful online tool is **Traveling Internationally with Your Kids** (www.travelwithyourkids.com).

Health and Safety

British Columbia is a healthy place. To visit, you don't need to get any vaccinations or booster shots. And when you arrive you can drink the water from the faucet and eat the food without worry.

If you need an ambulance, call 911 or the number listed on the inside front cover of local telephone directories. All the cities and most of the large towns have local hospitals—look in each Explore chapter of this book for locations and telephone numbers.

INSURANCE AND PRESCRIPTIONS

It's a good idea to get health insurance or some form of coverage before heading to Canada if you're going to be there for a while, but check that your plan covers foreign services. Hospital charges vary from place to place but can start at around $1,000 a day, and some facilities impose a surcharge for nonresidents. Some Canadian companies offer coverage specifically aimed at visitors.

If you're on medication take adequate supplies with you, and get a prescription from your doctor to cover the time you will be away. You may not be able to get a prescription filled at Canadian pharmacies without visiting a Canadian doctor, so don't wait till you've almost run out. If you wear glasses or contact lenses, ask your optometrist for a spare prescription in case you break or lose your lenses, and stock up on your usual cleaning supplies.

SEXUALLY TRANSMITTED DISEASES

AIDS and other venereal and needle-communicated diseases are as much of a concern here as anywhere in the world today. Take exactly the same precautions you would at home—use condoms, and don't share needles.

GIARDIA

Giardiasis, also known as beaver fever, is a real concern for those who drink water from backcountry water sources. It's caused by an intestinal parasite, *Giardia lamblia,* that lives in lakes, rivers, and streams. Once ingested, its effects, although not instantaneous, can be dramatic; severe diarrhea, cramps, and nausea are the most common. Preventive measures should always be taken and include boiling all water for at least 10 minutes, treating all water with iodine, or filtering all water using a filter with a small enough pore size to block the *Giardia* cysts.

WINTER TRAVEL CONSIDERATIONS

Travel through the province during winter months should not be undertaken lightly. Check antifreeze levels before setting out in a vehicle, and always carry a spare tire and blankets or sleeping bags.

Frostbite occurs in varying degrees. Most often it leaves a numbing, bruised sensation and the skin turns white. Exposed areas of skin such as the nose and ears are most susceptible, particularly when cold temperatures are accompanied by high winds.

Hypothermia occurs when the body fails to produce heat as fast as it loses it. Cold weather combined with hunger, fatigue, and dampness creates a recipe for disaster. Symptoms are not always apparent to the victim. The early signs are numbness, shivering, slurring of words, dizzy spells, and, in extreme cases, violent behavior, unconsciousness, and even death. The best treatment is to get the patient out of the cold, replace wet clothing with dry, slowly give hot liquids and sugary foods, and place the victim in a sleeping bag. Prevention is a better strategy; dress for cold in layers, including a waterproof outer layer, and wear a warm wool cap or other headgear.

Information and Services

MONEY

All prices quoted in this guidebook are in Canadian dollars and cents unless otherwise noted.

Canadian currency is based on dollars and cents, with 100 cents equal to 1 dollar. Coins come in denominations of 1, 5, 10, and 25 cents, and 1 and 2 dollars. The 11-sided, gold-colored, $1 coin is known as a "loonie" for the bird featured on it. The unique $2 coin is silver with a gold-colored insert. The most common notes are $5, $10, $20, and $50. A $100 bill does exist but is uncommon.

The safest way to carry money is in the form of traveler's checks from a reputable and well-known U.S. company such as American Express, Visa, or Bank of America; those are also the easiest checks to cash. Cash only the amount you need when you need it. Banks offer the best exchange rates, but other foreign-currency exchange outlets are available. It's also a good idea to start off with a couple of traveler's checks in Canadian dollars so you're never caught without *some* money if you don't make it to a bank on time.

Visa and MasterCard credit and debit cards are also readily accepted throughout British Columbia. By using these cards you eliminate the necessity of thinking about the exchange rate—the transaction and rate of exchange on the day of the transaction will automatically be reflected in the bill from your credit-card company. On the downside, you'll always get a better exchange rate when dealing directly with a bank. Most banks are open Monday–Friday 10 A.M.–3:30 P.M.

Costs

The cost of living in British Columbia is similar to that of all other Canadian provinces, but higher than in the United States. By planning ahead, having a tent or joining Hostelling International, and being prepared to cook your own meals it is possible to get by on well under $60 per person per day. If you will be staying in hotels or motels, accommodations will be your

CURRENCY EXCHANGE

The Canadian dollar lost value against the greenback through most of the last decade, dipping to record lows in 2002, when it was trading at US$1 per CDN$1.65.

Current exchange rates (into CDN$) for major currencies are:

US$1 = $1.30
AUS$1 = $.96
EURO = $1.60
HK$10 = $1.80
NZ$1 = $.85
UK£1 = $2.40
¥100 = $1.20

On the Internet, check current exchange rates at www.xe.com/ucc.

biggest expense. Gasoline is sold in liters (3.78 liters equals one U.S. gallon) and is generally 75–85 cents a liter for regular unleaded; surprisingly, Vancouver is one of the most expensive places to fill your gas tank.

Tipping charges are not usually added to your bill. You are expected to add a tip of 15 percent to the total amount for waiters and waitresses, barbers and hairdressers, taxi drivers, and other such service providers. Bellhops, doormen, and porters generally receive $1 per item of baggage.

Taxes

Canada imposes a 7 percent **goods and services tax (GST)** on most consumer purchases. The British Columbia government imposes its own 7.5 percent tax (PST) onto everything except groceries and books. So when you are looking at the price of anything, remember that the final cost you pay will include an additional 14.5 percent in taxes.

Nonresident visitors can get a rebate for the GST they pay on short-term accommodations and on most consumer goods bought in the country and taken home. Items not included in the Visitor Rebate Program include: gifts left in Canada, meals and restaurant charges, campground fees, services such as dry cleaning and shoe repair, alcoholic beverages, tobacco, automotive fuels, groceries, agricultural and fish products, prescription drugs and medical devices, and used goods that tend to increase in value, such as paintings, jewelry, rare books, and coins.

The rebate is available on services and retail purchases of at least $50 each, that total at least $200, or that were purchased within 60 days prior to your exit from the country. Rebates can be claimed any time within one year from the date of purchase. Include with your claim all receipts or vouchers that prove the GST was paid. Most visitors apply for the rebate at duty-free shops (also called Visitor Rebate Centres) when exiting the country. The duty-free shops can rebate up to $500 on the spot. For rebates over $500, mail your completed GST rebate form directly to Visitor Rebate Program, Summerside Tax Centre, Canada Revenue Agency, 275 Pope Rd., Suite 104, Summerside, PE C1N 6C6, Canada. You can also submit rebate forms for amounts less than $500 directly to the Canada Revenue Agency. If you've claimed by mail before, be aware that the rules have changed. Claims for goods (not accommodations) must be accompanied by a Proof of Export stamp, which you'll get at the border upon presentation of both the goods and corresponding receipts. Rebate checks from the government are issued in Canadian funds. For more info, contact the program directly (902/432-5608 or 800/668-4748, www.cra.arc.gc.ca/visitors).

MAPS AND INFORMATION

Maps

Driving maps are available at bookstores, gas stations, and gift shops throughout the province. In Vancouver, pick up maps at these specialty bookstores: **International Travel Maps and Books** (530 W. Broadway, 604/879-3621, www.itmb.com), **The Travel Bug** (3065 W. Broadway, 604/737-1122, www.travelbugbooks .ca), or **Wanderlust** (1929 W. 4th Ave., Kitsi-

lano, 604/739-2182). In Victoria, check out **Crown Publications** (521 Fort St., 250/386-4636). These stores stock many topographical maps and can order specific maps and marine charts for you.

If you're heading to the B.C. Rockies, look for **Gem Trek** maps (877/688-6277, www .gemtrek.com), which use computer-generated "3D Imagery" to clearly define changes in elevation and GPS to plot hiking trails. The backs of maps are filled with trail information and tidbits of history. Waterproofing is an added bonus.

Tourism Information

Begin planning your trip by contacting the government tourist office: **Tourism British Columbia** (250/387-1642 or 800/435-5622, www .hellobc.com). The literature and maps can be downloaded from the website or ordered by phone. As well as being a great source of tourist information, the agency produces the invaluable *Accommodations* guide and a road map. Other handy web addresses are www.canadatourism .com, the official site of the Canadian Tourism Commission, and www.tbc.gov.bc.ca, the site

TOURISM OFFICES

In addition to **Tourism BC** (250/387-1642 or 800/435-5622, www.hellobc.com) and the **Canadian Tourism Commission** (www.canadatourism .com), the following regional offices will assist in planning your trip to British Columbia:

Tourism Vancouver Island (250/754-3500, www.islands.bc.ca)

Tourism Victoria (250/953-2033 or 800/663-3883, www.tourismvictoria.com)

Thompson/Okanagan Tourism Association (250/860-5999 or 800/567-2275, www .thompsonokanagan.com)

Kootenay Rockies Tourism (250/427-4838 or 800/661-6603, www.bcrockies.com)

Cariboo Chilcotin Coast Tourism Association (Central British Columbia, 250/392-2226 or 800/663-5885, www.landwithout limits.com)

of the Ministry of Small Business, Tourism, and Culture.

Each town of any size in B.C. has a **Visitor Info Centre;** hours vary, but most are open June–August. (The Vancouver Visitor Info Centre is at 200 Burrard St., 604/683-2000.) When these are closed, head to the local chamber of commerce for information. Most chamber offices are open Monday–Friday year-round.

COMMUNICATIONS

Postal Services

Canada Post (www.canadapost.ca) issues postage stamps that must be used on all mail posted in Canada. First-class letters and postcards sent within Canada are $.50, to the United States $.85, to foreign destinations $1.45. Prices increase along with the weight of the mailing. You can buy stamps at post offices, automatic vending machines, most hotel lobbies, airports, many retail outlets, and some newsstands.

Telephone Services

The **area code** for Vancouver and the lower mainland, including the Sunshine Coast, as far north as Whistler, and east to Hope, is **604.** The are code for the rest of the province, including Victoria and all of Vancouver Island, is **250.** These prefixes must be dialed for all long-distance calls, including those made within the province.

The country code for Canada is 1, the same as the United States. Toll-free numbers have the 800, 888, or 877 prefix, and may be good within British Columbia, in Canada, throughout North America, or, in the case of major hotel chains and car-rental companies, worldwide.

To make an international call from Canada, dial the prefix 011 before the country code or dial 0 for operator assistance.

Public phones accept 5-, 10-, and 25-cent coins; local calls are $.35, and most long-distance calls cost at least $2.50 for the first minute. The least expensive way to make long-distance calls from a public phone is with a **phonecard.**

> ## HEADING FARTHER AFIELD?
>
> **Yukon Department of Tourism** (867/667-5036 or 800/661-0494, www.touryukon.com)
>
> **Alaska Division of Tourism** (907/465-2010, www.travelalaska.com)
>
> **Travel Alberta** (780/427-4321 or 800/252-3782, www.travelalberta.com)
>
> **NWT Arctic Tourism** (867/873-7200 or 800/661-0788, www.nwttravel.nt.ca)
>
> **Nunavut Tourism** (867/979-6551 or 866/686-2888, www.nunavuttourism.com)
>
> **Tourism Saskatchewan** (306/787-9600 or 800/667-7191, www.sasktourism.com)
>
> **Travel Manitoba** (204/945-3777 or 800/665-0040, www.travelmanitoba.com)

These are available from convenience stores, newsstands, and gas stations.

Public Internet Access

If your Internet provider doesn't allow you to access your email away from your home computer, open an email account with **Hotmail** (www.hotmail.com) or **Yahoo** (www.yahoo.com). Although there are restrictions to the size and number of emails you can store, and junk mail can be a problem, these services are handy and, best of all, free.

Public Internet access is available throughout British Columbia. Many larger hotels have high-speed access from guest rooms. Those that don't—usually mid- and lower-priced properties—often have an Internet booth in the lobby. Except for wilderness hostels, backpacker lodges provide inexpensive Internet access. You'll also find Internet booths in many cafés, in some McDonald's restaurants, and in public areas, such as Canada Place in Vancouver, where a credit card will get you as long as you need on the Net. Aside from a lack of privacy, the downside to these public access points is the lack of a mouse at most terminals—instead you must move around the screen using a touch pad.

WEIGHTS AND MEASURES

Canada officially adopted the **metric system** back in 1975, though you still hear grocers talking in ounces and pounds, golfers talking in yards, and seamen talking in nautical miles. Metric is the primary unit used in this book, but we've added imperial conversions for readers from the United States, Liberia, and Myanmar, the only three countries that have not adopted the metric system. You can also refer to the metric conversion chart in the back of this book.

Electrical voltage in British Columbia is 120 volts AC.

Time Zones

Most of British Columbia, including Vancouver and Victoria, is in the **Pacific time zone,** the same as Los Angeles and three hours before eastern time. The **mountain time zone** extends west into southern British Columbia, which includes Yoho and Kootenay National Parks as well as the towns of Golden and Radium Hot Springs.

Suggested Reading

NATURAL HISTORY

Baldwin, John. *Mountain Madness: Exploring British Columbia's Ultimate Wilderness*. Vancouver: Harbour Publishing, 1999. Filled with stunning photography, this coffee-table book is a worthwhile purchase for climbers or anyone interested in the natural landscapes of the Coast Mountains.

Cannings, Richard. *British Columbia: A Natural History*. Vancouver, Douglas & McIntyre, 1996. The natural history of the province divided into 10 chapters, from the earliest origins of the land to problems faced in the new millennium. It includes lots of color photos, diagrams, and maps.

Folkens, Peter. *Marine Mammals of British Columbia and the Pacific Northwest*. Vancouver: Harbour Publishing, 2001. In a waterproof, fold-away format, this booklet provides vital identification tips and habitat maps for 50 marine mammals, including all species of whales present in local waters.

Gadd, Ben. *Handbook of the Canadian Rockies*. Jasper: Corax Press, 1999. The latest edition of this classic guide is in color, and although bulky for backpackers, it's a must-read for anyone interested in the natural history of the Canadian Rockies.

Gill, Ian. *Haida Gwaii: Journeys through the Queen Charlotte Islands*. Vancouver: Raincoast Books, 1997. A personal and touching view of the Queen Charlottes complemented by the stunning color photography of David Nunuk.

Haig Brown, Roderick. *Return to the River.* Vancouver: Douglas & McIntyre, 1997. Although fictional, this story of the life of one salmon and its struggle through life is based on fact, and is a classic read for both anglers and naturalists. It was originally published in 1946 but has recently been reprinted and is available at most bookstores.

Hare, F. K., and M. K. Thomas. *Climate Canada*. Toronto: John Wiley & Sons, 1974. One of the most extensive works on Canada's climate ever written. Includes a chapter on how the climate is changing. Look for it in Vancouver's secondhand bookstores.

Herrero, Stephen. *Bear Attacks: Their Causes and Avoidances*. New York: Nick Lyons Books, 1995. Through a series of gruesome stories, this book catalogs the stormy relationship between people and bruins, provides hints on avoiding attacks, and tells what to do in case you're attacked.

Lyons, C. P. *Trees, Shrubs, and Flowers to Know in British Columbia.* Edmonton, Alberta: Lone Pine Publishing, 1995. This popular field guide makes the province's flora easy to identify through detailed descriptions and illustrations.

Osborne, Graham (photographer). *British Columbia: A Wild and Fragile Beauty.* Vancouver: Douglas & McIntyre, 1993. In my opinion this coffee-table book depicts the natural beauty of British Columbia better than any other edition currently in print. A short section of moving text accompanies each photograph.

Rezendes, Paul. *Tracking and the Art of Seeing.* Charlottesville, Virginia: Camden House Publishing, 1992. This is one of the best of many books dedicated to tracking North American mammals. It begins with a short essay on the relationship of humans with nature.

Whitaker, John. *National Audubon Society Field Guide to North American Mammals.* New York: Random House, 1997. One of a series of field guides produced by the National Audubon Society, this one details mammals through color plates and detailed descriptions of characteristics, habitat, and range.

HUMAN HISTORY

Coull, Cheryl. *A Traveller's Guide to Aboriginal B.C.* Vancouver: Whitecap Books, 1996. Although this book covers native sites throughout the province, the Lower Mainland (Vancouver) chapter is very comprehensive. Also included are details of annual festivals and events and hiking opportunities with a cultural slant.

Duff, Wilson. *The Indian History of British Columbia: The Impact of the White Man.* Victoria:

University of British Columbia Press, 1997. In this book Duff deals with the issues faced by natives in the last 150 years but also gives a good overview of their general history.

Jenness, Diamond. *The Indians of Canada.* Toronto: University of Toronto Press, 1977. Originally published in 1932, this is the classic study of natives in Canada, although Jenness's conclusion, that they were facing certain extinction by "the end of this century," is obviously outdated.

Johnson, Pauline. *Legends of Vancouver.* Vancouver: Douglas & McIntyre, 1998. First published in 1911, this book contains the writings of Pauline Johnson, a well-known writer and poet in the early part of the 1900s. She spent much of her time with native peoples, and this is her version of myths related to her by Joe Capilano, chief of the Squamish.

Lavallee, Omer. *Van Horne's Road.* Montreal: Railfare Enterprises, 1974. William C. Van Horne was instrumental in the construction of Canada's first transcontinental railway. This is the story of his dream and the boomtowns that sprang up along the route. Lavallee devotes the final chapter to Vancouver and how the arrival of the railway affected the young city and created a Canadian gateway to the Orient.

McMillan, Alan D. *Native Peoples and Cultures of Canada.* Vancouver: Douglas & McIntyre, 1997. A comprehensive look at the archaeology, anthropology, and ethnography of the native peoples of Canada. The last chapters delve into the problems facing these people today. The author is a professor at Vancouver's Simon Fraser University, so the chapters on the Pacific Northwest are particularly strong.

Reksten, Terry. *Rattenbury.* Victoria: Sono Nis Press, 1998. The biography of Francis Rattenbury, British Columbia's preeminent architect at the turn of the 20th century. The histories of his most famous Victoria and Vancouver buildings are given, and the final chapter looks at his infamous murder at the hands of his wife's young lover.

Scott, Chic. *Pushing the Limits.* Calgary: Rocky Mountain Books, 2000. A chronological history of mountaineering in Canada, with special emphasis on many largely unknown climbers and their feats, as well as the story of Swiss guides in Canada and a short section on ice climbing.

Smith, Cyndi. *Off the Beaten Track.* Jasper: Coyote Books, 1989. Accounts of women adventurers and mountaineers and their impact on the early history of western Canada.

Suttles, Wayne. *Northwest Coast. Vol. 7, Handbook of North American Indians.* Washington, D.C.: Smithsonian Institution, 1990. This volume is probably the most comprehensive piece ever written dedicated entirely to the natives of the Pacific Northwest.

ARTS, CRAFTS, AND GARDENS

Allen, D. *Totem Poles of the Northwest.* Surrey, B.C.: Hancock House Publishers Ltd., 1977. Describes the importance of totem poles to native culture and totem pole sites and their history.

Kew, Della, and P.E. Goddard. *Indian Art and Culture of the Northwest Coast.* Surrey, B.C.: Hancock House Publishers Ltd., 1997.

Twigg, Alan. *Vancouver and Its Writers.* Vancouver: Harbour Publishing, 1986. Vancouver has produced many fine writers, while other writers have moved to the city from elsewhere. This book gives short biographies on them all.

Varner, Collin, and Christine Allen. *Gardens of Vancouver.* Vancouver: Raincoast Books, 2000. Details public and private gardens through-

out the city using color photographs, planting plans, and descriptions of behind-the-scenes workings.

RECREATION GUIDES

Aitchison, Catherine J. *Birder Guide to Vancouver and the Lower Mainland.* Vancouver: Whitecap Books, 2001. This spiral-bound field guide details 350 species recorded in the region and gives detailed directions to the best viewing spots.

Hudson, Rick. *Field Guide to Gold, Gemstones, and Mineral Sites of British Columbia.* Victoria: Orca Books, 1999. This still-evolving series currently has two volumes in print. Volume 1 details sites on Vancouver Island, while Volume 2 covers sites around Vancouver and within a day's drive of the city. The history of each location, along with a map, what the site holds today, and interesting related facts make this a must-read for keen rockhounds.

Johnson, Leslie. *Basic Mountain Safety from A to Z.* Canmore: Altitude Books, 2000. Everything you need to know about safety in the mountains, including a large section on camping.

Kariel, Herbert G. *Alpine Huts in the Canadian Rockies, Selkirks, and Purcells.* Canmore, Alberta: Alpine Club of Canada, 1986. Covers the history of all huts in the above ranges, with current access routes and status and descriptions of nearby peaks to climb.

Lebrecht, Sue, and Judi Lees. *52 Weekend Activities around Vancouver.* Vancouver: Douglas & McIntyre, 1995. There's something for everyone in this popular book, whether it be nude beaches or skiing at Whistler.

Macaree, Mary, and David Macaree. *109 Walks in British Columbia's Lower Mainland.* Vancouver: Douglas & McIntyre, 1997. The fourth edition of this guide details over 100 easy walks throughout Vancouver, the Fraser River Valley, and as far north as Whistler. Two pages are devoted to each walk, including detailed text, a hand-drawn map, and a black-and-white photo.

Patton, Brian, and Bart Robinson. *The Canadian Rockies Trail Guide.* Banff: Summerthought, 2000. This regularly updated guide, first published in 1971, covers 230 hiking trails and 3,400 kilometers (2,100 miles) in the Canadian Rockies. A full page is devoted to each trail, making it the most comprehensive hiking book available.

Pratt-Johnson, Betty. *101 Dives from the Mainland of Washington and British Columbia.* Surrey, B.C.: Heritage House Publishing, 1999. This book is the best source for detailed information on diving around Vancouver and Georgia Strait. As well as precise directions, local diving-related services are listed. Its companion volume, *99 Dives from the San Juan Islands in Washington to the Gulf Islands,* encompasses the southern end of Georgia Strait.

Townsend, Chris. *The Backpacker's Handbook.* Camden, Maine: Ragged Mountain Press, 1998. Although some of the specifics on gear recommendations need updating, this is the best book for reading up your backcountry and hiking skills.

Woodsworth, Glenn. *Hot Springs of Western Canada.* West Vancouver: Gordon Soules Book Publishers, 1997. Details every known hot springs in western Canada, including both commercial and undeveloped sites. A short history, directions, and practicalities are given for each one.

OTHER GUIDEBOOKS

Canadian Automobile Association. *Tour Book: Western Canada and Alaska.* A free booklet available to members of the CAA and affiliated organizations.

Christie, Jack. *Inside Out British Columbia.* Vancouver: Raincoast Books, 1998. Although the organization of this book is sometimes difficult to follow, it is the most comprehensive guide available to all recreational opportunities the province has to offer, especially the provincial parks. Jack Christie is a prolific author who also writes *Day Trips from Vancouver* and *One-Day Getaways from Vancouver* (both published by Douglas & McIntyre, Vancouver).

Neering, Rosemary. *Eating Up Vancouver Island.* Vancouver: Whitecap Books, 2003. A guide to everything culinary on Vancouver Island, from the brewpubs of Victoria to the farms of the Cowichan Valley.

Pantel, Gerda. *The Canadian Bed and Breakfast Guide.* Toronto: Penguin Books Ltd., 2004. This guide lists all bed-and-breakfasts prepared to pay a fee, so the reviews aren't very objective. Prices included.

Tourism British Columbia. *Accommodations.* Updated annually, this free booklet is available at information centers throughout British Columbia by calling 250/387-1642 or 800/435-5622 or clicking to www.hellobc.com.

Western Canadian Bed & Breakfast Innkeepers Association. Contact this association (604/255-9199, www.wcbbia.com) for a free copy of its annual accommodations guide. It contains descriptions and prices of over 120 properties.

Wilson, Kasey. *Best Places Vancouver.* Seattle: Sasquatch Books, 2005. A review of Vancouver's best recreation pursuits, entertainment, shopping, accommodations, and restaurants. The star-rated restaurant section is particularly good.

ENCYCLOPEDIA

Francis, Daniel. *Encyclopedia of British Columbia.* Vancouver: Harbour Publishing, 2000.

This extraordinary compilation reputedly took 10 years of Francis's life to put together. It contains 4,000 entries over 824 pages in a coffee table–style format. The $99 book comes with an interactive CD-ROM, complete with hyperlinks. The book's website is www.knowbc.com.

MAGAZINES AND MAPS

British Columbia. Victoria. This quarterly magazine depicts the beauty of the province through stunning color photography and informative prose. It's available by subscription (604/713-0400 or 800/663-7611, www.bcmag.ca).

The Canadian Alpine Journal. Canmore, Alberta. Annual magazine of the Alpine Club of Canada (www.alpineclubofcanada.ca), with articles from its members and climbers from around the world.

Canadian Geographic. Ottawa: Royal Canadian Geographical Society (www.cangeo .com). Bimonthly publication pertaining to Canada's natural and human histories and resources.

Explore. Toronto. Bimonthly publication of adventure travel throughout Canada (www.explore-mag.com).

Gem Trek Publishing. This company (www .gemtrek.com) produces tearproof and waterproof maps for all regions of the Canadian Rockies. Relief shading clearly and concisely shows elevation, and all hiking trails have been plotted using a global positioning system. On the back of each map are descriptions of attractions and hikes, along with general, practical, and educational information.

MapArt. Driving maps for all of Canada, including provinces and cities. Maps are published as old-fashioned foldout versions, as well as laminated and in atlas form (www.mapart.com).

Nature Canada. Ottawa, Ontario. Quarterly magazine of the Canadian Nature Federation (www.cnf.ca).

Western Living. Vancouver, British Columbia. Lifestyle magazine for western Canada (www.westernliving.ca). Includes travel, history, homes, and cooking.

Internet Resources

ACCOMMODATIONS

Accent Inns: www.accentinns.com
Bed and Breakfast Online: www.bbcanada.com
Best Western: www.bestwestern.com
Days Inn: www.daysinn.com
Delta Hotels and Resorts: www.deltahotels.com
Fairmont Hotels and Resorts: www.fairmont.com
Holiday Inns: www.holiday-inn.com
Hostelling International: www.hihostels.com
Hostelling International–Canada: www.hihostels.ca
Howard Johnson: www.hojo.com

Radisson: www.radisson.com
Sandman Hotels: www.sandmanhotels.com
Super 8: www.super8.com
Western Canada Bed & Breakfast Innkeepers Association: www.wcbbia.com

AIRLINES

Air Canada: www.aircanada.ca
Air Canada Jazz: www.flyjazz.com
Air New Zealand: www.nzair.com
Air Pacific: www.airpacific.com
Alaska Airlines: www.alaksaair.com
All Nippon Airways: www.ana.co.jp
American Airlines: www.aa.com
British Airlines: www.britishairlines.com

Continental Airlines: www.continental.com
First Air: www.firstair.ca
Harbour Air: www.harbour-air.com
Hawk Air: www.hawkair.net
Japan Airlines: www.jal.co.jp
KLM: www.klm.nl
Lufthansa: www.lufthansa.de
North Pacific Seaplanes:
www.northpacificseaplanes.com
North Vancouver Air: www.northvanair.com
Northwest Airlines: www.nwa.com
Pacific Coastal: www.pacificcoastal.com
Qantas: www.qantas.com.au
Singapore Airlines: www.singaporeair.com
Tango: www.flytango.com
United Airlines: www.ual.com
WestJet: www.westjet.com

CAR AND RV RENTAL

Avis: www.avis.com
Budget: www.budget.com
Canadream: www.canadream.com
Cruise America: www.cruiseamerica.com
Cruise Canada: www.cruisecanada.com
Discount: www.discountcar.com
Dollar: www.dollar.com
Enterprise: www.enterprise.com
Go West: www.go-west.com
Hertz: www.hertz.com
Island Rent-A-Car: www.islandcar.ca
National: www.nationalcar.com
Rent-a-wreck: www.rentawreck.ca
Thrifty: www.thrifty.com

OTHER TRANSPORTATION AND TOURS

Alaska Marine Highway:
www.alaska.gov/ferry
BC Ferries: www.bcferries.com
Clipper Navigation: www.victoriaclipper.com
Greyhound: www.greyhound.ca
Gray Line Canada: www.grayline.ca

Moose Travel Network:
www.moosenetwork.com
MV *Coho:* www.cohoferry.com
Pacific Coach Lines: www.pacificcoach.com
Rocky Mountaineer Vacations:
www.rockymountaineer.com
Tofino Bus: www.tofinobus.com
VIA Rail: www.viarail.ca
Washington State Ferries:
www.wsdot.wa.gov/ferries
West Coast Trail Express: www.trailbus.com

TOURISM OFFICES

Canadian Tourism Commission:
www.canadatourism.com
Cariboo Chilcotin Coast Tourism Associa-
tion (Central British Columbia):
www.landwithoutlimits.com
Kootenay Rockies Tourism:
www.bcrockies.com
Northern BC Tourism Association:
www.nbctourism.com
Thompson/Okanagan Tourism Association:
www.thompsonokanagan.com
Tourism British Columbia:
www.hellobc.com
Tourism Vancouver:
www.tourismvancouver.com
Tourism Vancouver Island: www.islands.bc.ca
Tourism Victoria: www.tourismvictoria.com
Tourism Whistler: www.mywhistler.com

GOVERNMENT

Government of Canada: www.gc.ca
Citizenship and Immigration Canada:
www.cic.gc.ca
Canada Revenue Agency
(Visitor Rebate Program):
www.cra–arc.gc.ca
Government of British Columbia:
www.gov.bc.ca
Parks Canada: www.pc.gc.ca

Index

Canoeing/Kayaking

Fish/Fishing

Hiking

Museums

Skiing

Acknowledgments

A heartfelt thank you goes out to all the people who helped with the seventh edition of *Moon Handbooks British Columbia;* to the British Columbians who shared their knowledge of B.C. and their insight; to all the well-trained staff of Visitor Info Centres and national and provincial parks throughout British Columbia; and to all the travelers/readers who took the time to write to us offering suggestions to make each updated edition more comprehensive.

U.S.~Metric Conversion

To compute Celsius temperatures, subtract 32
from Fahrenheit and divide by 1.8. To go the
other way, multiply Celsius by 1.8 and add 32

1 inch	=	2.54 centimeters (cm)
1 foot	=	.304 meters (m)
1 yard	=	0.914 meters
1 mile	=	1.6093 kilometers (km)
1 km	=	.6214 miles
1 fathom	=	1.8288 m
1 chain	=	20.1168 m
1 furlong	=	201.168 m
1 acre	=	.4047 hectares
1 sq km	=	100 hectares
1 sq mile	=	2.59 square km
1 ounce	=	28.35 grams
1 pound	=	.4536 kilograms
1 short ton	=	.90718 metric ton
1 short ton	=	2000 pounds
1 long ton	=	1.016 metric tons
1 long ton	=	2240 pounds
1 metric ton	=	1000 kilograms
1 quart	=	.94635 liters
1 US gallon	=	3.7854 liters
1 Imperial gallon	=	4.5459 liters
1 nautical mile	=	1.852 km